CONTENTS

OF

VOLUME SECOND.

BOOK II.

CHAPTER XIII.

1562–1563.

HISTORY

OF THE

RISE OF THE HUGUENOTS

OF

FRANCE

BY

HENRY M. BAIRD

PROFESSOR IN THE UNIVERSITY OF THE CITY OF NEW YORK

VOL. II.

NEW YORK
CHARLES SCRIBNER'S SONS
1900

TROW DIRECTORY
PRINTING AND BOOKBINDING COMPANY
NEW YORK

CHAPTER XIV.

1563–1567.

CHAPTER XV.

1567–1568.

CONTENTS.

CHAPTER XVI.

1568–1570.

CHAPTER XVII.

1570–1572.

CHAPTER XIX.

1572.

CHAPTER XX.

1572–1574.

BOOK SECOND.

FROM THE EDICT OF JANUARY (1562) TO THE DEATH
OF CHARLES THE NINTH (1574).

BOOK SECOND.

FROM THE EDICT OF JANUARY (1562) TO THE DEATH OF CHARLES THE NINTH (1574).

CHAPTER XIII.

THE FIRST CIVIL WAR.

THE Edict of January was on its very face a compromise, and as such rested on no firm foundation. Inconsistent with itself,

Inconsisten-cies of the Edict of Jan-uary. it fully satisfied neither Huguenot nor Roman Catholic. The latter objected to the toleration which the edict extended; the former demanded the unrestricted freedom of worship which it denied. If the existence of two diverse religions was compatible with the welfare of the state, why ignominiously thrust the places of Protestant worship from the cities into the suburbs? If the two were irreconcilable, why suffer the Huguenots to assemble outside the walls?

Yet there was this difference between the attitude assumed by the rival parties with reference to the edict: while the

Huguenot leaders urge the observance of the edict. Roman Catholic leaders made no secret of their intention to insist upon its repeal,[1] the Huguenot leaders were urgent in their advice to the churches to conform strictly to its provisions, restraining the indis-

---

[1] The nuncio alone seems to have thought that the edict would work so well, that "in six months, or a year at farthest, there would not be a single Huguenot in France!" His ground of confidence was that many, if not most of the reformed, were influenced, not by zeal for religion, but by cupidity. Santa Croce to Card. Borromeo, Jan. 17, 1562, Aymon, i. 44; Cimber et Danjou, vi. 30.

creet zeal of their more impetuous members, and exhibiting due gratitude to Heaven for the amelioration of their lot. To the *people* it was, indeed, a bitter disappointment to be compelled to give up the church edifices, and to resort for public service to the outskirts of the town. Less keen was the regret experienced by others not less sincerely interested in the progress of the purer doctrines, who, on account of their appreciation of the violence of the opposition to be encountered, had not been so sanguine in their expectations. And so Beza and other prominent men of the Protestant Church, after obtaining from Chancellor L'Hospital some further explanations on doubtful points, addressed to their brethren in all parts of France a letter full of wholesome advice. "God," said they, "has deigned to employ new means of protecting His church in this kingdom, by placing those who profess the Gospel under the safeguard of the king, our natural prince, and of the magistrates and governors established by him. This should move us so much the more to praise the infinite goodness of our Heavenly Father, who has at length answered the cry of His children, and lovingly to obey the king, in order that he may be induced to aid our just cause." The provisional edict, they added, was not all that might yet be hoped for. As respected the surrender of the churches, those Huguenots who had seized them on their own individual authority ought rather to acknowledge their former indiscretion than deplore the necessity for restitution. In fine, annoyance at the loss of a few privileges ought to be forgotten in gratitude for the gain of many signal advantages. The letter produced a deep impression, and its salutary advice was followed scrupulously, if not cheerfully, even in southern France, where the Huguenots, in some places, outnumbered the adherents of the Romish Church.

The papal party was less ready to acquiesce. The Edict of January was, according to its representative writers, the most pernicious law for the kingdom that could have been devised. By forbidding the magistrates from interfering with the Protes-

---

[1] Hist. ecclés. des égl. réf., i. 428, 429. The letter is followed by an examination of the edict, article by article, as affecting the Protestants. Ib. i. 429-431.

tant conventicles held in the suburbs, by permitting the royal officers to attend, by conferring upon the ministers full liberty of officiating, a formal approval was, for the first time, given to the new sect under the authority of the royal seal.[1] The pulpits resounded with denunciations of the government. The King Seditious ser- of Navarre and the queen mother were assailed under mons. scriptural names, as favoring the false prophets of Baal. Scarcely a sermon was preached in which they did not figure as Ahab and Jezebel.[2] A single specimen of the spirited discourses in vogue will suffice. A Franciscan monk—one Barrier—the same from whose last Easter sermon an extract has already been given[3]—after reading the royal ordinance in his church of Sainte-Croix, in Provins, remarked: "Well now, gentlemen of Provins, what must I, and the other preachers of France, do? Must we obey this order? What shall we tell you? What shall we preach? 'The Gospel,' Sir Huguenot will say.

---

[1] Abbé Bruslart, Mém. de Condé, i. 70. Barbaro spoke the universal sentiment of the bigoted wing of the papal party when he described "the decree" as "full of concealed poison," as "the most powerful means of advancing the new religion," as "an edict so pestiferous and so poisonous, that it brought all the calamities that have since occurred." Tommaseo, Rel. des Amb. Vén., ii. 72.

[2] Claude Haton, 211. "Et longtemps depuis ne faisoient sermon qu'ilz Acab et Hiésabel et leurs persécutions ne fussent mis par eux en avant," etc. In fact, Catharine seemed fated to have her name linked to that of the infamous Queen of Israel. A Protestant poem, evidently of a date posterior to the massacre of Saint Bartholomew, is still extant in the National Library of Paris, in which the comparison of the two is drawn out at full length. The one was the ruin of Israel, the other of France. The one maintained idolatry, the other papacy. The one slew God's holy prophets, the other has slain a hundred thousand followers of the Gospel. Both have killed, in order to obtain the goods of their victims. But the unkindest verses are the last— even the very dogs will refuse to touch Catharine's "carrion."

> "En fin le jugement fut tel
> Que les chiens mengent Jhésabel
> Par une vangeance divine ;
> Mais la charongne de Catherine
> Sera différente en ce point,
> Car les chiens ne la vouldront point."

Appendix to Mém. de Claude Haton, ii. 1,110.
[3] Ante, i. 477.

And pray, stating that the errors of Calvin, of Martin Luther, of Beza, Malot, Peter Martyr, and other preachers, with their erroneous doctrine, condemned by the Church a thousand years ago, and since then by the holy œcumenical councils, are worthless and damnable—is not this preaching the Gospel? Bidding you beware of their teaching, bidding you refuse to listen to them, or read their books; telling you that they only seek to stir up sedition, murder, and robbery, as they have begun to do in Paris and numberless places in the realm—is not this preaching 'the Gospel?' But some one may say: 'Pray, friar, what are you saying? You are not obeying the king's edict; you are still talking of Calvin and his companions; you call them and those who hold their sentiments *heretics* and *Huguenots;* you will be denounced to the courts of justice, you will be thrown into prison—yes, you will be hung as a seditious person.' I answer, *that* is not unlikely, for Ahab and Jezebel put to death the prophets of God in their time, and gave all freedom to the false prophets of Baal. 'Stop, friar, you are saying too much, you will be hung.' Very well, then there will be a gray friar hung! Many others will therefore have to be hung, for God, by His Holy Spirit, will inspire the pillars of His church to uphold the edifice, which will never be overthrown until the end of the world, whatever blows may be struck at it." [1]

The parliaments exhibited scarcely less opposition to the edict than did the pulpits of the Roman Catholic churches. One—the Parliament of Dijon—never registered it at all; [2]

Opposition of the parliaments. while that of Paris instituted a long and decided resistance. " *Non possumus, nec debemus,*" " *non possumus, nec debemus pro conscientia,*" were the words in which it replied when repeatedly pressed to give formal sanction. [3] The counsellors were equally displeased with the contents of the edict, and with the irregularity committed in sending it first to the provincial parliaments. Even when the king, yielding to their importunity, by a supplementary "declaration," interpreted the provision of the edict relative to the attendance of royal officers

---

[1] Mém. de Claude Haton, 211, 212.

[2] Hist. ecclés. des égl. réf., i. 431.

[3] Abbé Bruslart, Mém. de Condé, i. 70, 71.

upon the reformed services, as applicable only to the bailiffs, seneschals, and other minor magistrates, and strictly prohibited the attendance of the members of parliament and other high judicatories,[1] the counsellors, instead of proceeding to the registry of the obnoxious law, returned a recommendation that the intolerant Edict of *July* be enforced![2] It was not possible until March to obtain a tardy assent to the reception of the January Edict into the legislation of the country, and then only a few of the judges vouchsafed to take part in the act.[3] The delay served to inflame yet more the passions of the people.

Scarcely had the edict which was to adjust the relations of the two religious parties been promulgated, when a new attempt was made to reconcile the antagonistic beliefs by the old, but New confer- ever unsuccessful method of a conference between ence. theologians. On the twenty-eighth of January a select company assembled in the large council-chamber of the royal palace of St. Germain, and commenced the discussion of the first topic submitted for their deliberation—the question of pictures or images and their worship. Catharine herself was present, with Antoine of Navarre and Jeanne d'Albret, Michel de l'Hospital, and other members of the council. On the papal side appeared the Cardinals of Bourbon, Tournon, and Ferrara, and a number of less elevated dignitaries. Beza and Marlorat were most prominent on the side of the reformed. The discussion was long and earnest, but it ended leaving all the disputants holding the same views that they had entertained at the outset. Beza condemned as idolatrous the practice of admitting statues or paintings into Christian churches, and urged their entire removal. The Inquisitor De Mouchy, Fra Giustiniano of Corfu, Maillard, dean of the Sorbonne, and others, attempted to refute his positions in a style of argument which

---

[1] Declaration of Feb. 14, 156½, Du Mont, Corps diplomatique, v. 91, 92.

[2] And, indeed, with modifications which were to render it still more severe. Letter of Beza to Calvin, Feb. 26, 1562, Baum, ii., App., 167.

[3] The registry took place on Friday, March 6th. Isambert, xiv. 124; La Fosse, 45, who says " Ledict édict fut publié en la salle du palais en ung vendredy, 5ᵉ [6ᵉ] de ce moys, *là où il y eut bien peu de conseillers et le président Baillet qui signèrent.*"

exhibited the extremes of profound learning and silly conceit. Bishop Montluc of Valence,[1] and four doctors of theology— Salignac, Bouteiller, D'Espense, and Picherel—not only admitted the flagrant abuses of image-worship, but drew up a paper in which they did not disguise their sentiments. They recommended the removal of representations of the Holy Trinity, and of pictures immodest in character, or of saints not recognized by the Church. They reprobated the custom of decking out the portraits of the saints with crowns and dresses, the celebration of processions in their honor, and the offering of gifts and vows. And they yielded so far to the demands of the Protestants as to desire that only the simple cross should be permitted to remain over the altar, while the pictures should be placed high upon the walls, where they could neither be kissed nor receive other objectionable marks of adoration.[2]   It was a futile task to reconcile views so discordant even among the Roman Catholic partisans. Two weeks were spent in profitless discussion, and, on the eleventh of February, the new colloquy was permitted to dissolve without having entered upon any of the more difficult questions that still remained upon the programme marked out for it.[3]   The cardinals had prevailed upon Catharine de' Medici to refer the settlement to the Council of Trent.[4]   The joy of De Mouchy, the inquisitor, and of his companions, knew no bounds when Chancellor L'Hospital declared the queen's pleasure, and requested the members to retire to their homes, and reduce their opinions to writing for future use.   They were ready to throw themselves on Beza's neck in

---

[1] The same prelate to whom Cardinal Lorraine doubtless referred in no complimentary terms, when, at the assembly of the clergy at Poissy, he said, " qu'il estoit contrainct de dire, *Duodecim sumus, sed unus ex nobis Diabolus est*, et passant plus outre, qu'il y avoit ung evesque de la compagnie . . . . qui avoit revelé ce qui se faisoit en laditte assemblée," etc.   Journal de Bruslart, Mém. de Condé, i. 50.

[2] See the document in Schlosser, Leben des Theodor de Beze, App., 359–361 ; Hist. ecclés. des égl. réf., i. 436, 437.

[3] Hist. ecclés. des égl. réf., i. 436–450 ; Baum, ii. 512–545.   In connection with Prof. Baum's long and thorough account of the colloquy, Beza's correspondence, printed in the appendix, is unusually interesting.

[4] " Cardinalium intercessione ac precibus mox soluta sunt omnia."   Beza to Bullinger, March 2, 1562.   Baum, ii., App., 169.

their delight at being relieved of the necessity of debating with him![1]

But, in truth, the time for the calm discussion of theological differences, the time for friendly salutation between the champions of the rival systems of faith, was rapidly drawing to a close. If some rays of sunshine still glanced athwart the landscape, conveying to the unpractised eye the impression of quiet serenity, there were also black and portentous clouds already rising far above the horizon. Those who could read the signs of the times had long watched their gathering, and they trembled before the coming of the storm. Although they were mercifully spared the full knowledge of the overwhelming ruin that would follow in the wake of that fearful war of the elements, they saw the angry commotion of the sky, and realized that the air was surcharged with material for the most destructive bolts of heaven. And yet it is the opinion of a contemporary, whose views are always worthy of careful consideration, that, had it not been for the final defection of the King of Navarre at this critical juncture, the great woes impending over France might still have been delayed or averted.[2] That unhappy prince seemed determined to earn the title of the "Julian Apostate" of the French Reformation. Plied by the arts of his own servants, D'Escars (of whom Mézeray pithily remarks that he was ready to sell himself for money to anybody, save his master) and the Bishop of Auxerre; flattered by the Triumvirate, tempted by the Spanish Ambassador, Cardinal Tournon, and the papal legate, he had long been playing a hypocritical part. He had been unwilling to break with the Huguenots before securing the golden fruit with which he was lured on, and so he was at the same time the agent and the

Defection of Antoine and its results.

---

[1] " Nihil hoc consilio gratius accidere potuit nostris adversariis quibus iste ludus minime placebat, adeo ut *ipse Demochares* . . . . *pene sui oblitus in meos amplexus rueret*, et ejus sodales honorifice me salutarent ! " Beza to Calvin, Feb. 26, 1562, ibid., 165. The Venetian Barbaro represents this second conference as an extremely efficient means of spreading heresy: " La qual [in San Germano] apportò un grandissimo scandalo e pregiudizio alla religion nostra, e diede alla loro, reputazione e fomento maggiore." Rel. des Amb. Vén., ii. 74.

[2] Hist. ecclés. des égl. réf., i. 432.

object of treachery. Even after he had sent in his submission to the Pope by the hands of D'Escars, he pretended, when remonstrated with by his Protestant friends, that "he would take care not to go so far that he could not easily extricate himself."[1] He did not even show displeasure when faithfully rebuked and warned.[2] Yet he had after long hesitation completely cast in his lot with the papal party. He was convinced at last that Philip was in earnest in his intention to give him the island of Sardinia, which was depicted to him as a terrestrial paradise, "worth four Navarres."[3] It was widely believed that he had received from the Holy See the promise of a divorce from his heretical consort, which, while permitting him to retain the possessions which she had justly forfeited by her spiritual rebellion, would enable him to marry the youthful Mary of Scots, and add a substantial crown to his titular claims.[4] But we would fain believe that even Antoine of Bourbon had not sunk to such a depth of infamy. Certain it is, however, that he now openly avowed his new devotion to the Romish Church, and that the authority of his name became a bulwark of strength to the refractory parliament in its endeavor to prevent the execution of the edict of toleration.[5] But he was unsuccessful in Constancy of dragging with him the wife whom he had been the Jeanne. instrument of inducing first to declare herself for the persecuted faith of the reformers. And when Catharine de' Medici, who cared nothing for religion, tried to persuade her to arrange matters with her husband, "Sooner," she said, "than ever go to mass, had I my kingdom and my son in my hand, I would cast them both into the depth of the sea, that they might

---

[1] "Qu'il ne s'y mettroit si avant qu'il ne s'en pust aisément tirer."   Hist. ecclés. des égl. réf., *ubi supra.*

[2] See the frank letter of Calvin, written to him about this time, in Bonnet, Lettres franç., ii. 441 ; Calvin's Letters, Amer. ed., iv. 247.

[3] "That pestilent yle of Sardigna!" exclaimed Sir Thomas Smith, a clever diplomatist and a nervous writer, "that the pore crowne of it should enter so farre into the pore Navarrian hed (which, I durst warraunt, shall never ware it), [as to] make him destroy his owen countrey, and to forsake the truth knowen!" Forbes, State Papers, ii. 164.

[4] Hist. ecclés. des égl. réf., *ubi supra;* De Thou, iii. (liv. xxviii.), 96–99.

[5] Letter of Beza to Calvin, Feb. 1, 1562, Baum, ii., App., 163.

not be a hinderance to me." [1] Brave mother of Henry the Fourth! Well would it have been, both for her son and for France, if that son had inherited more of Jeanne d'Albret's devotion to truth, and less of his father's lewdness and inconstancy!

As early as in February, Beza was of the opinion that the King of Navarre would not suffer him to remain longer in the realm to which he himself had invited him so earnestly only six months before. At all events, he would be publicly dismissed by the first of May, and with him many others. With this disquieting intelligence came also rumors of an alliance between the enemies of the Gospel and the Spaniard, which could not be treated with contempt as baseless fabrications. [2] But meanwhile the truth was making daily progress. At a

Immense crowds at Huguenot preaching.

single gathering for prayer and preaching, but a few days before, twenty-five thousand persons, it was computed, had been in attendance, representing all ranks of the population, among whom were many of the nobility. [3] In the city of Troyes, a few weeks later, eight or nine thousand persons assembled from the neighboring country to celebrate the Lord's Supper, and the number of communicants was so great that they could not all partake on a single day ; so the services were repeated on the morrow. [4] Elsewhere there

---

[1] Hist. ecclés. des égl. réf., i. 433.

[2] Letter to Calvin, Feb. 26, 1562, *apud* Baum, ii., App., 167, 168.

[3] Ibid., *ubi supra.*

[4] Recordon, Le protestantisme en Champagne (Paris, 1863), from MSS. of Nicholas Pithou, p. 105. This learned jurist, the equal of his more celebrated brothers in ability, and their superior in moral courage, has left his testimony respecting the beneficent influence of the reformed doctrines upon his fellow-citizens : " A la verité la ville de Troyes en général fit une perte incroyable en la rupture de cette Église. Car c'était une grande beauté et chose plus que émerveillable de la voir si bien fleurie. Il se voyoit en la jeunesse, touchée par la prédication de la parole de Dieu, qui auparavant était si dépravée que rien plus, un changement si subit et si étrange que les catholiques mêmes en étoient tout étonnés. Car, tels qui au précédent se laissaient aller du tout à leurs voluptez et s'étaient plongez en gourmandises, yvrogneries et jeux défendus, tellement qu'ils y passaient la plus grande et meilleure partie du temps, et faisaient un fort mauvais ménage, depuis qu'ils étaient entrés dans l'Église quittaient du tout leur vie passée et la détestaient,

was equal zeal and growth. Indeed, so rapid was the advance of Protestantism, so pressing the call for ministers, that the large and flourishing church of Orleans, in a letter written the last day of February, proclaimed their expectation of establishing a theological school to supply their own wants and those of the adjacent regions; and it is no insignificant mark of the power with which the reformatory movement still coursed on, that the canons of the great church of Sainte Croix had given notice of their intention to attend the lectures that were to be delivered![1] In such an encouraging strain did "the ministers, deacons, and elders" of the most Protestant city of northern France write on the day before that deplorable massacre of Vassy, which was to be the signal for an appeal from argument to arms, upon which the newly enkindled spirit of religious inquiry was to be quenched in partisan hatred and social confusion. Within less than two months the tread of an armed host was to be heard in the city which it had been hoped would be thronged by the pious students of the gospel of peace, and frenzied soldiers would be hurling upon the floors of Sainte Croix the statues of the saints that had long occupied their elevated niches.

The canons of Sainte Croix.

We must now turn to the events preceding the inauspicious occurrence the fruits of which proved so disastrous to the French church and state.

Having at length made sure of the co-operation of the King of Navarre in the contest upon which they had now resolved with the view of preventing the execution of the Edict of January, the Guises desired to strengthen themselves in the direction of Germany, and secure, if not the assistance, at least the neutrality of the Protestant princes. Could the Protestants on the other side of the Rhine be made indifferent spectators of the

---

se rangeant et se soumettant allègrement à la discipline ecclésiastique, ce qui était si agréable aux parents de tels personnages, que, quoiqu'ils fussent catholiques, ils en louaient Dieu." Ibid., pp. 107, 108.

[1] " Nous avons espérance que non seulement la jeunesse d'icy se façonnera par la main d'un si excellent ouvrier qui nous est venu ; mais que les chanoines mesmes de Sainte-Croix le viendront ouyr en ses leçons, ce qu'ils ont desja déclaré. De quoy sortiront des fruicts surmontant toute expectation." Gaberel, Hist. de l'égl. de Genève, i., Pièces justificatives, 168.

struggle, persuaded that their own creed resembled the faith of
the Roman Catholics much more than the creed of the Huguenots; could they be convinced that the Huguenots were
uneasy and rebellious radicals, whom it were better to crush
than to assist; could, consequently, the "reiters" and "lansquenets" be kept at home—it would, thought the Guises, be
easy, with the help of the German Catholics, perhaps of Spain
also, to render complete the papal supremacy in France, and
to crush Condé and the Châtillons to the earth. Accordingly,
the Guises extended to Duke Christopher of Würtemberg
an invitation to meet them in the little town of Saverne (or
Zabern, as it was called by the Germans), in Alsace, not far
from Strasbourg.[1] The duke came as he was requested, accompanied by his theologians, Brentius and Andreä; and the
interview, beginning on the fifteenth of February,[2] lasted four

The Guises
meet the
Duke of Wür-
temberg at
Saverne.
days. Four of the Guises were present; but the
conversations were chiefly with Francis, the Duke of
Guise, and Charles, the Cardinal of Lorraine; the
Cardinal of Guise and the Grand Prior of the Knights
of St. John taking little or no active part. Christopher and
Francis had been comrades in arms a score of years back, for
the former had served several years, and with no little distinction, in the French wars. This circumstance afforded an oppor-

---

[1] The archives of Stuttgart contain the instructive correspondence which
the Duke of Guise had, ever since the previous summer, maintained with the
Duke of Würtemberg. From the letters published in the Bulletin of the
French Protestant Historical Society (February and March, 1875), we see that
François endeavored to alienate Christopher from the Huguenots by representing the latter as bitter enemies of the Augsburg Confession, and as speaking of it with undisguised contempt. (Letter of July 2, 1561, Bull., xxiv.
72.) Christopher made no reply to these statements, but urged his correspondent to a candid examination of religious truth, irrespective of age or
prescription, reminding him (letter of Nov. 22, 1561) that our Lord Jesus
Christ "did not say 'I am the *ancient custom*,' but 'I am the *Truth*.'"
(Ibid., xxiv. 114.) And he added, sensibly enough, that, had the pagan
ancestors of both the French and the Germans followed the rule of blind
obedience to custom, they would certainly never have become Christians.
[2] Guise's original invitation was for Saturday, January 31st, but Christopher
pleaded engagements, and named, instead, Sunday, Feb. 15th. (Ibid., xxiv.
116, 117.)

tunity for the display of extraordinary friendship. And what did the brothers state, in this important consultation, respecting their own sentiments, the opinions of the Huguenots, and the condition of France? Happily, a minute account, in the form of a manuscript memorandum taken down at the time by Duke Christopher, is still extant in the archives of Stuttgart.[1] Little known, but authentic beyond the possibility of cavil, this document deserves more attention than it has received from historians; for it places in the clearest light the shameless mendacity of the Guises, and shows that the duke had nearly as good a claim as the cardinal, his brother, to the reputation which the Venetian ambassador tells us that Charles had earned "*of rarely telling the truth.*"

Duke Christopher made the acquaintance of Charles of Lorraine as a preacher on the morning after his arrival, when he heard him, in a sermon on the temptation in the wilderness, demonstrate that no other mediators or intercessors must be sought for but Jesus Christ, who is our only Saviour and the only propitiation for our sins. That day Christopher had a long conversation with Guise respecting the unhappy condition of France, which the latter ascribed in great part to the Huguenot ministers, whose unconciliatory conduct, he said, had rendered abortive the Colloquy of Poissy. Würtemberg corrected him by replying that the very accounts of the colloquy which Guise had sent him showed that the unsuccessful issue was owing to the prelates, who had evidently come determined to prevent any accommodation. He urged that the misfortunes that had befallen France were much rather to be ascribed to the cruel persecutions that had been inflicted on so many guiltless victims. " I cannot refrain from telling you," he added, " that you and your brother are strongly suspected in Germany of having contributed to cause the death, since the decease of Henry the Second—and even before, in his lifetime—of several thousands of persons who have been miserably executed on account of their faith. As a friend, and as a Christian, I must

---

[1] The relation was first noticed and printed by Sattler, in his Geschichte von Würtemberg unter den Herzögen. I have used the French translation by M. A. Muntz, in the Bulletin, iv. (1856) 184–196.

warn you. Beware, beware of innocent blood! Otherwise the
punishment of God will fall upon you in this life and in the
next." "He answered me," writes Würtemberg, "*with great
sighs:* 'I know that my brother and I are accused of that, and
Lying assur- of many other things also. But *we are wronged,*[1] as
ances. we shall both of us explain to you before we leave.'"

The cardinal entered more fully than his brother into the doc-
trinal conference, talking now with Würtemberg, now with his
theologian Brentius, and trying to persuade both that he was in
perfect accord with them. While pressing his German friends to
declare the Zwinglians and the Calvinists heretics—which they
carefully avoided doing—and urging them to state the punishment that ought to be inflicted on heretics, there seemed to be
no limit to the concessions which Lorraine was willing to make.
He *adored* and *invoked* only Christ in heaven. He merely *venerated* the wafer. He acknowledged that his party went too far in
calling the mass a sacrifice, and celebrating it for the living and
the dead. The mass was not a sacrifice, but a commemoration of
the sacrifice offered on the altar of the cross ("non sacrificium,
sed memoria sacrificii præstiti in ara crucis"). He believed
that the council assembled at Trent would do no good. When
the Romish hierarchy, with the Pope at its head, as the pretended vicar of God on earth, was objected to, he replied that
that matter could easily be adjusted. As for himself, "in the
absence of a red gown, he would willingly wear a black one."

He was asked whether, if Beza and his colleagues could be
brought to consent to sign the Augsburg confession, he also
would sign it. "You have heard it," he replied, "I take God
to witness that I believe as I have said, and that by God's
grace I shall live and die in these sentiments. I repeat it:
I have read the Confession of Augsburg, I have also read
Luther, Melanchthon, Brentius, and others; I entirely ap-

---

[1] In a letter of Würtemberg to Guise, written subsequently to the massacre
of Vassy, he reminds him of the advice he had given him, and of Guise's
assurances : "Vous savez aussi avec quelle asseurance vous m'avez respondu
que l'on vous faisoit grand tort de ce que l'on vous vouloit imposer estre cause
et autheur de la mort de tant de povres chrestiens qui ont espandu leur sang
par ci-devant," etc. Mémoires de Guise, 494.

prove their doctrines, and I might speedily agree with them in all that concerns the ecclesiastical hierarchy. *But I am compelled still to dissemble for a time*, that I may gain some that are yet weak in the faith." A little later he adverted to Würtemberg's remarks to Guise. " You informed my brother," he said, " that in Germany we are both of us suspected of having contributed to the execution of a large number of innocent Christians during the reigns of Henry and of Francis the Second. Well! I swear to you, in the name of God my Creator, and pledging the salvation of my soul, *that I am guilty of the death of no man condemned for religion's sake.* Those who were then privy to the deliberations of state can testify in my favor. On the contrary, whenever crimes of a religious character were under discussion, I used to say to King Henry or to King Francis the Second, that they did not belong to my department, that they had to do with the secular power, and I went away."[1] He even added that, although Du Bourg was in orders, he had begged the king to spare him as a learned man. "In like manner," says Würtemberg, "the Duke of Guise with great oaths affirmed that he was innocent of the death of those who had been condemned on account of their faith. 'The attempt,' he added, 'has frequently been made to kill us, both the cardinal and myself, with fire-arms, sword, and poison, and, although the culprits have been arrested, I never meddled with their punishment.'" And when the Duke of Würtemberg again " conjured them not to persecute the poor Christians of France, for God would not leave such a sin unpunished," both the

---

[1] There are some characters with whom mendacity has become so essential a part of their nature, that we cease to wonder at any possible extreme of lying. It was, however, no new thing with the cardinal to assume immaculate innocence. Over two years before this time, at the beginning of the reign of Francis II., when bloody persecution was at its height, Sir Nicholas Throkmorton wrote to Queen Elizabeth, Sept. 10, 1559 : " I am enformed that they here begin to persecute againe for religion more than ever they did ; and that at Paris there are three or four executed for the same, and diverse greate personages threatened shortly to be called to answer for their religion. Wherin the Cardinal of Lorraine having bene spoken unto, within these two daies, hathe said, *that it is not his faulte ; and that there is no man that more hateth extremités, then he dothe ;* and yet it is knowne that it is, notwithstanding, *alltogither by his occasion.*" Forbes, State Papers, i. 226, 227.

cardinal and the Duke of Guise gave him their right hands, promising on their princely faith, and by the salvation of their souls, that they would neither openly nor secretly persecute the partisans of the "new doctrines!" Such were the barefaced impostures which this "par nobile fratrum" desired Christopher of Würtemberg to publish for their vindication among the Lutherans of Germany. But the liars were not believed. The shrewd Landgrave of Hesse, on receiving Würtemberg's account, even before the news of the massacre of Vassy, came promptly to the conclusion that the whole thing was an attempt at deception. Christopher himself, in the light of later events, added to his manuscript these words: "Alas! It can now be seen how they have kept these promises! *Deus sit ultor doli et perjurii, cujus namque res agitur.*"[1]

The Guises deceive no one.

Meanwhile events of the greatest consequence were occurring at the capital. The very day after the Saverne conference began, Sir Nicholas Throkmorton wrote to Queen Elizabeth an account of "the strange issue" to which affairs had come at the French court since his last despatch, a little over a fortnight before. His letter gives a vivid and accurate view of the important crisis in the first half of February, 1562, which we present very nearly in the words of the ambassador himself. "The Cardinal of Ferrara," says Throkmorton, "has allured to his devotion the King of Navarre, the Constable, Marshal St. André, the Cardinal of Tournon, and others inclined to retain the Romish religion. All these are bent to repress the Protestant religion in France, and to find means either to range [bring over to their side] the Queen of Navarre, the Prince of Condé, the Admiral, and all others who favor that religion, or to expel them from the court, with all the ministers and preachers. The queen mother, fearing this conspiracy might be the means of losing her authority (which is as dear to her as one religion or the other), and mistrusting that the Constable was going about to reduce the man-

Throkmorton's account of the French court.

---

[1] Bulletin, iv. 196. De Thou's account of the Saverne conference (iii. (liv. xxix.) 127, 128) is pretty accurate so far as it goes, but has a more decidedly polemic tone than the Duke of Würtemberg's memorandum.

agement of the whole affair into the King of Navarre's hands, and so into his own, has caused the Constable to retire from the court, as it were in disgrace, and intended to do the like with the Cardinal of Tournon and the Marshal St. André. The King of Navarre being offended with these proceedings, and imputing part of her doings to the advice of the Admiral, the Cardinal Châtillon, and Monsieur D'Andelot, intended to compel those personages to retire also from the court. In these garboils [commotions] the Prince of Condé, being sick at Paris, was requested to repair to the court and stand her [Catharine] in stead. In this time there was great working on both sides to win the house of Guise. So the Queen Mother wrote to them—they being in the skirts of Almain—to come to the court with all speed. The like means were made [use of] by the King of Navarre, the Cardinal of Ferrara and the Constable, to ally them on their part. During these solicitations the Duke D'Aumale arrived at the court from them, who was requested to solicit the speedy repair to the court of the Duke of Guise and the Cardinal of Lorraine.

"The Prince of Condé went from hence in a horse litter to the court of St. Germain, where he found the Protestant preachers prohibited from preaching either in the King's house or in the town, and that the King of Navarre had solemnly vowed to retain and maintain the Romish religion, and had given order that his son should be instructed in the same. The Prince, finding the Queen of Navarre and the house of Châtillon ready to leave the court, fell again dangerously sick. Nevertheless his coming so revived them, as by the covert aid of the Queen Mother, they attempted to make the Protestant preachers preach again at the town's end of St. Germain, and were entreated to abide at the court, where there is an assembly which is like to last until Easter. The Cardinal of Ferrara assists daily at these disputes. The King of Navarre persists in the house of Châtillon retiring from the court, and it is believed the Queen of Navarre, and they, will not tarry long there."[1]

Such was the picture drawn by the skilful pencil of the Eng-

---

[1] Throkmorton to the Queen, Paris, Feb. 16, 1562. State Paper Office. I have followed closely the condensation in the Calendars.

lish envoy. It was certainly dark enough. Catharine and Navarre had sent Lansac to assure the Pope that they purposed to live in and defend the Roman Catholic religion. Sulpice had gone on a like mission to Spain. It was time, Throkmorton plainly told Queen Elizabeth, that she should show as great readiness in maintaining the Protestant religion as Ferrara and his associates showed in striving to overthrow it. And in a private despatch to Cecil, written the same day, he urged the secretary to dissuade her Majesty from longer retaining candles and cross on the altar of the royal chapel, at a time when even doctors of the Sorbonne consented to the removal of images of all sorts from over the altar in places of worship.[1]

From Saverne the Cardinal of Lorraine returned to his archbishopric of Rheims, while the duke, accompanied by the Cardinal of Guise, proceeded in the direction of the French capital. On his route he stopped at Joinville, one of the estates of the family, recently erected in their favor into a principality. Here he was joined by his wife, Anne d'Este ; here, too, he listened to fresh complaints made by his mother, Antoinette of Bourbon, against the insolence of the neighboring town of Vassy, where a considerable portion of the inhabitants had lately had the audacity to embrace the reformed faith.

Vassy, an important town of Champagne—though shorn of much of its influence by the removal of many of its dependen-
Vassy in Champagne.　cies to increase the dignity of Joinville—and one of the places assigned to Mary of Scots for her maintenance, had apparently for some time contained a few professors of the "new doctrines." It was, however, only in October, 1561, after the Colloquy of Poissy, that it was visited by a Protestant minister, who, during a brief sojourn, organized a church with elders and deacons. Notwithstanding
Origin of the Huguenot Church.　the disadvantage of having no pastor, and of having notoriously incurred the special hatred of the Guises, the reformed community grew with marvellous rapidity. For the Gospel was preached not merely in the printed sermons read from the pulpit, but by the lips of enthusiastic converts.

---

[1] Same to Cecil, of same date. State Paper Office.

When, after a short absence, the founder of the church of Vassy returned to the scene of his labors, he came into collision with the Bishop of Châlons, whose diocese included this town.   The bishop, unaccustomed to preach, set up a monk in opposition; but no one would come to hear him.   The prelate then went himself to the Protestant gathering, and sat through the "singing of the commandments" and a prayer.   But when he attempted to interrupt the services and asserted his episcopal authority, the minister firmly repelled the usurpation, taking his stand on the king's edict.   Then, waxing warm in the discussion, the dauntless Huguenot exposed the hypocrisy of the pretended shepherd, who, not entering the fold by canonical election, but intruding himself into it without consulting his charge, was more anxious to secure his own ease than to lead his sheep into green pastures.   The bishop soon retired from a field where he had found more than his match in argument : but the common people, who had come to witness his triumph over the Huguenot preacher, remained after his unexpected discomfiture, and the unequal contest resulted in fresh accessions to the ranks of the Protestants.   Equally unsuccessful was the Bishop of Châlons in the attempt to induce the king to issue a commission to the Duke of Guise against the unoffending inhabitants, and Vassy was spared the fate of Mérindol and Cabrières.   At Christmas nine hundred communicants, after profession of their faith, partook of the Lord's Supper according to the reformed rites ; and in January, 1562, after repeated solicitations, the church obtained the long-desired boon of a pastor, in the person of the able and pious Leonard Morel.   Thus far the history of Vassy differed little from that of hundreds of other towns in that age of wonderful awakening and growth, and would have attracted little attention had not its proximity to the Lorraine princes secured for it a tragic notoriety.[1]

---

[1] Discours entier de la persécution et cruauté exercée en la ville de Vassy, par le duc de Guise, le 1. de mars, 1562 ; reprinted in Mémoires de Condé, iii. 124-149, and Cimber et Danjou, iv. 123-156.   This lengthy Huguenot narrative enters into greater details respecting the early history of the church of Vassy than any of the other contemporary relations.   The account bears every mark of candor and accurate information.

On the twenty-eighth of February, Guise, with two hundred armed retainers, left Joinville. That night he slept at Dommartin-le-Franc. On Sunday morning, the first of March, he continued his journey. Whether by acci-

Approach of the Duke of Guise.

dent or from design, it is difficult to say, he drew near to Vassy about the time when the Huguenots were assembling for worship, and his ears caught the sound of their bell while he was still a quarter of a league distant. The ardor of Guise's followers was already at fever-heat. They had seen a poor artisan apprehended in a town that lay on their track, and summarily hung by their leader's order, for the simple offence of having had his child baptized after the reformed rites. When Guise heard the bell of the Vassy church, he turned to his suite to inquire what it meant. "It is the Huguenots' preaching," some one replied. "*Par la mort-Dieu*," broke in a second, "they will soon be huguenotted after another fashion!" Others began to make eager calculations respecting the extent of the plunder. A few minutes later an unlucky cobbler was espied, who, from his dress or manner, was mistaken for a Huguenot minister. It was well that he could answer the inquiries of the duke, before whom he was hurried, by assuring him that he was no clergyman and had never studied; otherwise, he was told, his case had been an extremely ugly one. [1]

On entering Vassy Guise repaired to the monastery chapel to hear mass said. He was followed by some of the gentlemen of his suite. Meantime, their valets found their way to the doors of the building in which the Protestants were worshipping, scarcely more than a stone's throw distant. This motley crowd was merely the vanguard of the Papists. Soon two or three gentlemen sent by Guise, according to his own account, to admonish the Huguenot assembly of their want of due obedience, entered the edifice, where they found twelve hundred persons quietly listening to the word of God. They were politely invited to sit down; but they replied by noisy interrup-

The massacre.

tion and threats. "*Mort-Dieu*, they must all be killed!" was their exclamation as they returned to report to Guise

---

[1] " Que son cas estoit bien sale s'il eust esté ministre."

what they had seen. The defenceless Huguenots were thrown into confusion by these significant menaces, and hastened to secure the entrance. It was too late. The duke himself was approaching, and a volley from the arquebuses of his troop speedily scattered the unarmed worshippers. It is unnecessary to describe in all its details of horror the scene that ensued. The door of the sheep-fold was open and the wolf was already upon his prey. All the pent-up hatred of a band of fanatical and savage soldiers was vented upon a crowd of men, women, and children, whose heterodoxy made them pleasing victims, and whose unarmed condition rendered victory easy. No age, no sex was respected. It was enough to be a Huguenot to be a fit object for the sword or the gun. To escape from the doomed building was only possible by running the gauntlet of the troops that lay in wait. Those who sought to climb from the roof to the adjacent houses were picked off by the arquebuses of the besieging party. Only after an hour and a half had elapsed were the soldiers of Guise called off by the trumpet sounding a joyful note of victory. The evidence of their prowess, however, remained on the field of contest, in fifty or sixty dead or dying men and women, and in nearly a hundred more or less dangerously wounded.[1]

In a few hours more Guise was resuming his journey toward Paris. He was told that the Huguenots of Vassy had forwarded their complaints to the king. "Let them go, let them go!" he exclaimed. "They will find there neither their Admiral nor their Chancellor."[2]

---

[1] The "Destruction du Saccagement" has preserved the names of forty-five persons who died by Tuesday, March 3d; the "Discours entier" has a complete list of forty-eight that died within a month, and refers to others besides. A contemporary engraving is extant depicting in quaint but lively style the murderous affair. Montfaucon reproduces it. So does also M. Horace Gourjon in a pamphlet entitled "Le Massacre de Vassy" (Paris, 1844). He gives, in addition, an exterior view of the barn in which the Huguenots were worshipping.

[2] Besides a brief Latin memoir of minor importance, there were published two detailed accounts of the massacre written by Huguenots. The one is entitled "Destruction du Saccagement, exercé cruellement par le Duc de Guise et sa cohorte, en la ville de Vassy, le premier jour de Mars, 1561. À Caens. M.D.LXII.," and having for its epigraph the second verse of the 79th psalm

Upon whose head rests the guilt of the massacre of Vassy? This was the question asked by every contemporary so soon as he realized the startling fact that the blow there struck was a signal that called every man to take the sword, and stand in defence of his own life. It is the question which history, more calm and dispassionate, because farther removed from the agitations of the day, now seeks to solve, as she looks back over the dreary torrents of blood that sprang from that disastrous source. The inquiry is not an idle one—for justice ought to find such a vindication in the records of past generations as may have been denied at the time of the commission of flagrant crimes.

The Huguenots declared Guise to be a murderer. Theodore Beza, in eloquent tones, demanded the punishment of the butcher

---

in Marot's poetical version, " The dead bodies of thy servants have they given to be meat unto the fowls of the heaven, the flesh of thy saints unto the beasts of the earth." (The year 1562, it will be remembered, did not commence in France until Easter Sunday, March 29th.) The account seems to have been composed on the spot and within a very few days of the occurrence. This may be inferred from the list of those who died being given only up to Tuesday, March 3d. The other narrative : " Discours entier de la persecution et cruauté exercée en la ville de Vassy," etc., enters into much greater detail, and is preceded by a full account of the early history of the Church. It was written and published a little later in the spring of 1562. Both memoirs are reprinted in the invaluable Archives curieuses of Messrs. Cimber et Danjou, iv. 103–110, and 123–156, as well as in the Mémoires de Condé, iii. 111–115, 124–149 (the former document with the title " Relation de l'occasion "), etc. Another contemporary account was written in Guise's interest, and contains a long extract of a letter of his to the Duke of Würtemberg : " Discours au vray et en abbregé de ce qui est dernièrement aduenu à Vassi, y passant Monseigneur le Duc de Guise. A Paris. M.D.LXII. . . . Par priuilege expres dudict Seigneur." (Cimber, iv. 111–122 ; Mém. de Condé, iii. 115–122). To these authorities must be added Guise's vindication in parliament (Cimber, iv. 157, etc., from Reg. of Parl. ; Mém. de Guise, 488, etc.), and his letter and that of the Cardinal of Lorraine to Christopher of Würtemberg, March 22 (Ib. 491, 492). Compare J. de Serres, De statu rel. et reip. (1571), ii. 13–17 ; De Thou, iii. 129, etc. ; Jehan de la Fosse, 45. Davila, bk. iii. in init., is more accurate than Castelnau, iii., c. 7. Claude Haton's account (Mémoires, i. 204–206) may be classed with the curiosities of literature. This veracious chronicler would have it that a crowd of Huguenots, with stones in their hands, and singing at the top of their voices, attempted to prevent the passage of the duke and his company through the outskirts of Vassy, where they were apparently worshipping in the open air ! Of course they were the aggressors.

of the human race. So imposing was the cry for retribution that the duke himself recognized the necessity of entering a formal aefence, which was disseminated by the press far and wide through France and Germany. He denied that the massacre was premeditated. He averred that it was merely an unfortunate incident brought about by the violence of the Protestants of Vassy, who had provided themselves with an abundant supply of stones and other missiles, and assailed those whom he had sent to remonstrate courteously with them. He stated the deaths at only twenty-five or thirty. Most of these had been occasioned by the indignant valets, who, on seeing their masters wounded, had rushed in to defend them. So much against his will had the affair occurred, that he had repeatedly but ineffectually commanded his men to desist. When he had himself received a slight wound from a stone thrown by the Huguenots, the sight of the blood flowing from it had infuriated his devoted followers.

The Duke's plea of want of premeditation we may, perhaps, accept as substantially true—so far, at least, as to suppose that he had formed no deliberate plan of slaughtering the inhabitants of Vassy who had adopted the reformed religion.[1] It is difficult, indeed, to accept the argument of Brantôme and Le Laboureur, who conceive that the fortuitous character of the event is proved by the circumstance that the deed was below the courage of Guise. Nor, perhaps, shall we give excessive credit to the asseverations of the duke, repeated, we are told, even on his death-bed. For why should these be more worthy of belief than the oaths with which the same nobleman had declared to Christopher of Würtemberg that he neither had persecuted, nor would persecute the Protestants of France? But the Duke of Guise admits that he knew that there was a growing community of Huguenots at Vassy—" scandalous, arrogant, extremely

---

[1] And yet there is great force in M. Sismondi's observation (Hist. des Français, xviii. 264) : "Malgré leur assertion, il est difficile de ne pas croire qu'au moment où ils se réunissoient en armes pour disputer aux protestans l'exercice public de leur culte que leur accordoit l'édit de janvier, c'étoit un coup prémédité que l'attaque du duc de Guise contre une congrégation de huguenots, composée, à ce qu'il assure, en partie de ses vassaux, et qui se trouvoit la première sur son passage à peu de distance de ses terres."

seditious persons," as he styles them. He tells us that he intended, as the representative of Mary Stuart, and as feudal lord of some of their number, to admonish them of their disobedience; and that for this purpose he sent Sieur de la Bresse (or Brosse) with others to interrupt their public worship. He accuses them, it is true, of having previously armed themselves with stones, and even of possessing weapons in an adjoining building; but what reason do the circumstances of the case give us for doubting that the report may have been based upon the fact that those who in this terror-stricken assembly attempted to save their lives resorted to whatever missiles they could lay their hands upon? If the presence of his wife, and of his brother the cardinal, is used by the duke as an argument to prove the absence of any sinister intentions on his part, how much stronger is the evidence afforded to the peaceable character of the Protestant gathering by the numbers of women and children found there? But the very fact that, as against the twenty-five or thirty Huguenots whom he concedes to have been slain in the encounter, he does not pretend to give the name of a single one of his own followers that was killed, shows clearly which side it was that came prepared for the fight. And yet who that knows the sanguinary spirit generally displayed by the Roman Catholic masses in the sixteenth century, could find much fault with the Huguenots of Vassy if they had really armed themselves to repel violence and protect their wives and children—if, in other words, they had used the common right of self-preservation?[1]

---

[1] It is extremely unfortunate that Mr. Froude should have based his account of French affairs at this important point upon so inaccurate and prejudiced a writer as Varillas. To be correct in his delineation of these transactions was almost as important for his object, as to be correct in the narration of purely English occurrences. If he desired to avoid the labor, from which he might well wish to be excused, of mastering the great accumulation of contemporary and original French authorities, he might have resorted with propriety, as he has done in the case of the massacre of St. Bartholomew's Day, to Henri Martin's noble history, or to the history of Sismondi, not to speak of Soldan, Von Polenz, and a host of others. Varillas wrote, about a century after the events he described, a number of works of slender literary, and still slighter historical value. His "Histoire de Charles IX." (Cologne, 1686)—the work which Mr. Froude has but too often followed—begins with an adulatory dedi-

The fact is that Guise was only witnessing the fruits of his instructions, enforced by his own example. He had given the first taste of blood, and now, perhaps without his actual command, the pack had taken the scent and hunted down the game. He was avowedly on a crusade to re-establish the supremacy of the Roman Catholic religion throughout France. If he had not hesitated to hang a poor pin-dealer for allowing his child to be baptized according to the forms of Calvin's liturgy; if he was on his way to Paris to restore the Edict of July by force of arms, it is idle to inquire whether he or his soldiers were responsible for the blood shed in peace. "He that sowed the seed is the author of the harvest."

The news quickly flew to Condé that the arch-enemy of the Protestants had begun the execution of the cruel projects he had so long been devising with his fanatical associates; that Guise was on his way toward seditious Paris, with hands yet dripping with the blood of the inhabitants of a quiet Champagnese town, surprised and murdered while engaged in the worship of their God. Indignant, and taking in the full measure of the responsibility imposed upon him as the most powerful member of the Protestant communion, the prince, who was Condé appeals with the court at the castle of Monceaux—built for to the king. herself by Catharine in a style of regal magnificence —laid before the king and his mother a full account of the tragic

---

cation to Louis XIV., the first sentence of which sufficiently reveals the author's prepossessions: "Sire, it is impossible to write the history of Charles IX. without beginning the panegyric of your Majesty." No wonder that Mr. Froude's account of the massacre of Vassy (History of England, vii. 401, 402), derived solely from this source (Hist. de Charles IX., i. 126, etc.), is as favorable to Guise as his most devoted partisan could have desired. But where in the world—even in Varillas—did the English historian ever find authority for the statement (vii. 402) that, in consequence of the necessity felt by Guise for temporizing, a little later "*the affair at Vassy was censured in a public decree*"? To have allowed *that* would have been for Guise to admit that he was guilty of murder, and that his enemies had not slandered him when they styled him a "butcher of the human race." The duke *never did* make such an acknowledgment; on the contrary, he asseverated his innocence in his last breath. What was really done on the occasion referred to was to try to shift the responsibility of the war from the shoulders of the papists to those of the Huguenots, by pretending to re-enact the edict of January with restrictions as to the capital.

occurrence. It was a pernicious example, he argued, and should be punished promptly and severely. Above all, the perpetrators ought not to be permitted to endanger the quiet of France by entering the capital. Catharine was alarmed and embarrassed by the intelligence; but, her fear of a conjunction between Guise and Navarre overcoming her reluctance to affront the Lorraine family, induced her to consent; and she wrote to the Duke, who had by this time reached his castle of Nanteuil, forbidding him to go to Paris, but inviting him to visit the court with a small escort. At the same time she gave orders to Saint André to repair at once to Lyons, of which he was the royal governor. But neither of the triumvirs showed any readiness to obey her orders. The duke curtly replied that he was too busy entertaining his friends to come to the king; the marshal promptly refused to leave the king while he was threatened by such perils.[1]

The King of Navarre now came from Paris to Monceaux, to guard the interests of the party he had espoused. He was closely followed by Theodore Beza and Francour, whom the Beza's remonstrance. Protestants of Paris had deputed, the former on behalf of the church, the latter of the nobility, to demand of the king the punishment of the authors of the massacre. The queen mother, as was her wont, gave a gracious audience, and promised that an investigation should be made. But Navarre, being present, seemed eager to display a neophyte's zeal, and retorted by blaming the Huguenots for going in arms to their places of worship. " True," said Beza, " but arms in the hands of the wise are instruments of peace, and the massacre of Vassy has shown the necessity under which the Protestants were laid." When Navarre exclaimed: "Whoever touches my brother of Guise with the tip of his finger, touches my whole body!" the reformer reminded him, as one whom Antoine had himself brought to France, that the way of justice is God's way, and that kings *owe* justice to their subjects. Finally, when he discovered, by Navarre's adoption of all the impotent excuses of Guise, that the former had sold himself to the

---

[1] Jean de Serres, ii. 17, 18; De Thou, iii. 132, 133.

enemies of the Gospel, Theodore Beza made that noble reply which has become classic as the motto of the French Reforma-

An anvil that has worn out many hammers. tion : "Sire, it is, in truth, the lot of the Church of God, in whose name I am speaking, to endure blows and not to strike them. *But also may it please you to remember that it is an anvil that has worn out many hammers.*" [1]

At Nanteuil, Guise had been visited by the constable, with two of his sons, by Saint André, and by other prominent leaders. Accompanied by them, he now took the decided step of going to Paris in spite of Catharine's prohibition. His entry resembled a triumphal procession.[2] In the midst of an escort estimated by eye-witnesses at two thousand horse, Francis of Guise avoided the more direct gate of St. Martin, and took that of St. Denis, through which the kings of France were accus-

Guise's entry into Paris. tomed to pass. Vast crowds turned out to meet him, and the cries of "*Vive Monsieur de Guise!*" sounding much like regal acclamations, were uttered without rebuke on all sides. The "prévost des marchands" and other members of the municipal government received him with great demonstrations of joy, as the defender of the faith. At the same hour the Prince of Condé, surrounded by a large number of Protestant noblemen, students, and citizens, was riding to one of the

---

[1] "Sire, c'est à la vérité à l'Église de Dieu, au nom de laquelle je parle, d'endurer les coups, et non pas d'en donner. Mais aussi vous plaira-t-il vous souvenir que *c'est une enclume qui a usé beaucoup de marteaux.*" Hist. ecclés. des égl. réf., ii. 1, 2 ; Pierre de Lestoile, Journal de Henri III. (ed. Petitot), i. 55 ; De Thou, iii. 132, 133.

[2] Journal de Jehan de la Fosse, 45, 46 ; Santa Croce to Borromeo, Aymon, i. 96, 97; Jean de Serres, ii. 18; Chantonnay, *ubi supra*, ii. 27; Hist. ecclés. des égl. réf., ii 2, 3 ; Throkmorton to the Queen, March 20th, State Paper Office ; De Thou, iii. 133 ; etc.   The date was the 15th of March, according to La Fosse; the 16th, according to Languet (ii. 212) and Throkmorton ; the 18th, according to Santa Croce; the 20th, according to J. de Serres.   I prefer to all the authority of a letter of one Chastaigner, written from Paris to a friend in Poitou on the very day of Guise's entry.   It is dated March 17th. "Quant aux nouvelles de Monsieur de Guyse, il est arrivé ce soir en ceste ville, Monsieur le connestable et Monsieur le maréchal de Saint-André avec luy, et en tout avoient bien deux mil chevaulx, les ungs disent plus." (Archives of Poitiers, and printed in Bulletin, xiii. (1864), 15, 16.)

preaching-places.[1] The two cavalcades met, but no collision ensued. The Huguenot and the papist courteously saluted each other, and then rode on. It is even reported that between the leaders themselves less sincere amenities were interchanged. Guise sent word to Condé that he and his company, whom he had assembled only on account of the malevolent, were at the prince's commands. Condé answered by saying that his own men were armed only to prevent the populace of Paris from making an attack upon the Protestants as they went to their place of worship.[2]

For weeks the position of the queen mother had been one of peculiar difficulty and anxiety. That she was "well inclined to advance the true religion," and "well affected for a general reformation in the Church," as Admiral Coligny at this time firmly believed,[3] is simply incredible. But, on the other hand, there can be little doubt that Catharine saw her interest in upholding the Huguenot party, of which Condé and the three Châtillon brothers were acknowledged leaders. Unfortunately, the King of Navarre, "hoping to compound with the King of Spain for his kingdom of Navarre," had become the tool of the opposite side—he was "*all Spanish now*"[4]—and Chantonnay, Philip's ambassador, was emboldened to make arrogant demands. The envoy declared that, "unless the house of Châtillon left the court, he was ordered to depart from France." Grave diplomatists shook their heads, and thought the menace very strange, "the rather that another prince should appoint what counsellors should remain at court;" and sage men inferred that "to such

Anxieties of Catharine de' Medici.

---

[1] This was not by accident. It had been planned by Condé, to show that the Huguenots were brave and determined, and it succeeded so well that it not only made an impression on the party of Guise, but also largely augmented the courage of his own men. Letter of Beza to Calvin, March 22, 1562, *apud* Baum, ii., App., 171. Condé had returned to Paris by the urgent request of the Protestants. Jean de Serres, ii. 19.

[2] Letter of Chastaigner, *ubi supra*.

[3] Throkmorton to the queen, March 6th, State Paper Office.

[4] "The King of Navarre was never so earnest on the Protestant side as he is now furious on the papists' part, insomuch as men suspect he will become a persecutor." Throkmorton to Cecil, March 9th, State Paper Office. Summary in Calendar.

princes as are afraid of shadows the King of Spain will enterprise far enough."[1]   None the less was Catharine deeply disturbed.   She felt distrust of the heads of the Roman Catholic party, but she feared to break entirely with them, and was forced to request the Protestant leaders to withdraw for a time from the vicinity of Paris.   That city itself presented to the eye a sufficiently strange and alarming aspect, "resembling more a frontier town or a place besieged than a court, a merchant city, or university."   Both sides were apprehensive of some sudden commotion, and the Protestant scholars, in great numbers, marched daily in arms to the "sermons," in spite of the opposition of the rector and his council.[2]   The capital was unquestionably no place for Catharine and her son, at the present moment.

At length, Catharine de' Medici, apprehensive of the growing power of the triumvirate, and dreading lest the king, falling into its hands, should become a mere puppet, her own influence being completely thrown into the shade, removed the court from Monceaux to Melun, a city on the upper Seine,

She removes the king to Melun.

about twenty-five miles south-east of Paris.[3]   She hoped apparently that, by placing herself nearer the strongly Huguenot banks of the Loire, she would be able at will to throw herself into the arms of either party, and, in making her own terms, secure future independence.   But she was not left undisturbed.   At Melun she received a deputation from Paris, consisting of the "prévost des marchands" and

---

[1] Throkmorton to the queen, March 6, 1562, State Paper Office.

[2] The same to Cecil, same date, State Paper Office.

[3] "Whilst these assemblies were in the town, the queen mother conceived great jealousy (the King of Navarre being allied to the said duke [Guise]), lest she should be put from the government and the king taken from her hands, to prevent which she left Monceaux, her own house, *for Orleans*, thinking they were secure there, because the Prince of Rochesurion (being governor of the king's person and also of Orleans) was not conjoined with the King of Navarre, the Duke of Guise, and the constable, in their purposes. The King of Navarre, perceiving this, would not consent to the king going to Orleans, and, after great disputes betwixt the queen mother and him, she, with the king, were constrained to reside all this Easter at Fontainebleau." Throkmorton to the queen, March 20, 1562, State Paper Office.   Summary in Calendar.

three " échevins," who came to entreat her, in the name of the
Roman Catholic people of the capital, to return and dissipate
by the king's arrival the dangers that were imminent on account
of Condé's presence, and to give the people the power to defend
themselves by restoring to them their arms.   Still hesitating,
still experiencing her old difficulty of forming any plans for
the distant future, and every moment balancing in her mind
what she should do the next, she nevertheless pushed
and thence to Fontainebleau. on ten miles farther southward, to the royal palace
of Fontainebleau, and found herself not far from
half the way to Orleans.   But change of place brought the
vacillating queen mother no nearer to a decision.   Soubise, the
last of the avowed Protestants to leave her, still dreamed he
Her painful indecision. might succeed in persuading her.   Day after day, in
company with Chancellor L'Hospital, the Huguenot
leader spent two or three hours alone with her in earnest argument.   " Sometimes," says a recently discovered contemporary
account, " they believed that they had gained everything, and
that she was ready to set off for Condé's camp ; then, all of a
sudden, so violent a fright seized her, that she lost all heart."
At last the time came when the triumvirs were expected to
appear at Fontainebleau on the morrow, to secure the prize of
the king's person.   Soubise and the indefatigable chancellor
made a last attempt.   Five or six times in one day they returned to the charge, although L'Hospital mournfully observed
that he had abandoned hope.   He knew Catharine well : she
could not be brought to a final resolution.[1]   It was even so.
Soubise himself was forced to admit it when, at the last moment—almost too late for his own safety—he hurriedly left,
Catharine still begging him to stand by her, and made his way
to his friends.

    It seems to have been during this time of painful anxiety
that Catharine wrote at least the last of those remarkable letters
to Condé which that prince afterward published in his own

---

[1] " Combien que le Chancelier luy dict, qu'il n'y espéroit plus rien, qu'elle
n'avoit point de résolution, qu'il la congnoissoit bien." Mémoires de la vie
de Jéhan l'Archevesque, Sieur de Soubise, printed from the hitherto unknown
MS. in the Bulletin, xxiii. (1874), 458, 459.

justification, and respecting the authenticity of which the queen
She implores would have been glad had she been able to make the
Condé's aid. world entertain doubts.   They breathed a spirit of
implicit confidence.   She called herself his " good cousin," that
was not less attached to him than a mother to a son.   She enjoined upon him to remember the protection which he was
bound to give to " the children, the mother, and the kingdom."
She called upon him not to desert her.   She declared that,
in the midst of so many adverse circumstances, she would be
driven almost to despair, " were it not for her trust in God,
and the assurance that Condé would assist her in preserving the
kingdom and service of the king, her son, in spite of those who
wished to ruin everything."   More than once she told him that
his kindness would not go unrequited ; and she declared that, if
she died before having an opportunity to testify her gratitude,
she would charge her children with the duty.[1]

In Paris events were rapidly succeeding each other.   Marshal
Montmorency, the constable's eldest son, was too upright a man
to serve the purposes of the triumvirs; and, with his father's
consent and by Navarre's authority, he was removed, and Cardinal
Bourbon installed in his place as governor of the city.[2]   A few
days after Antoine himself came to Paris and lodged in the
constable's house.   Here, with Guise, Saint André, and the other
chief statesmen who were of the same party, conferences were

---

[1] Four of the seven letters that constituted the whole correspondence are
printed in the Mém. de Condé, iii. 213–215.   Jean de Serres gives two of
them in his Comment. de statu rel. et reip., ii. 38, 39.   They were laid by
Condé's envoy before the princes of Germany, as evidence that he had not
taken up arms without the best warrant, and that he could not in any way be
regarded as a rebel.   They contain no allusion to any promise to lay down his
arms so soon as she sent him word—the pretext with which she strove at a
later time to palliate, in the eyes of the papal party at home and abroad, a
rather awkward step.   The curé of Mériot, while admitting the genuineness
of the letters, observes : " La cautelle et malice de la dame estoit si grande,
qu'elle se délectoit de mettre les princes en division et hayne les ungs contre
les aultres, affin qu'elle régnast et qu'elle demeurast gouvernante seulle de
son filz et du royaume."   Mém. de Cl. Haton, i. 269.   The queen mother's
exculpatory statements may be examined in Le Laboureur, Add. aux Mém.
de Castelnau, i. 763, 764.

[2] Bruslart, in Mém. de Condé, i. 75, 76 ; J. de Serres, ii. 20 ; La Fosse, 46 ;
De Thou, iii. 134.   The date is variously given—March 17th or 18th.

held to which Condé and his associates were not invited; and to these irregular gatherings, notwithstanding the absence of the king, the name of the *royal council* was given.[1]

There were nine or ten thousand horse—Papist and Huguenot—under arms in Paris.[2] It was evident that Condé and Guise could not longer remain in the city without involving it in the most bloody of civil contests. Under these circumstances the prince offered, through his brother, the Cardinal of Bourbon, to accede to the wish of Catharine, and leave Paris by one gate at the same moment that the triumvirs should leave by another. Indeed, without waiting to obtain their promise, he retired[3] with his body of Protestant noblesse to Meaux, where he had given a rendezvous to Admiral Coligny and others whom he had summoned from their homes. This step has generally been stigmatized as the first of Condé's egregious mistakes. Beza opposed it at the time, and likened the error to that of Pompey in abandoning Rome;[4] and the "History of the Reformed Churches" has perpetuated the comparison.[5] The same historical parallel was drawn by Étienne Pasquier.[6] But the judicious François de la Noue, surnamed *Bras-de-Fer*, thought very differently; and we must here, as in many other instances, prefer the opinion of the practical soldier to that of the eminent theologian or the learned jurist. Parliament, the clergy, the municipal government, the greater part of the university, and almost all the low populace, with the partisans and servants of the hostile princes and noblemen, were intensely Roman Catholic.[7] The three hundred resident Protestant gen-

Condé retires to Meaux.

---

[1] J. de Serres, ii. 21 ; De Thou, *ubi supra;* the Prince of Condé's declaration of the causes which have constrained him to undertake the defence of the royal authority, etc., *ap.* Mém. de Condé, iii. 222, etc. ; same in Latin in J. de Serres, ii. 46.

[2] Throkmorton to the queen, March 20, State Paper Office.

[3] March 23d. "Ce méme jour (lundi xxiii.) le Prince de Condé s'en partit de Paris pour s'en aller à une sienne maison, combien qu'il avoit dict qu'il ne bougeroit de Paris que M. de Guise ne s'en fut parti." Journal anonyme de l'an 1562, *ap.* Baum, iii. App., 175, note.

[4] Letter of March 28th, Baum, ii., App., 175, 176.

[5] Hist. ecclés. des égl. réf., ii. 3.

[6] Letter to Fonssomme, Œuvres choisies, ii. 248.

[7] One of the latest exploits of the populace was the disinterring of a Hugue-

tlemen, with as many more experienced soldiers, four hundred students, and a few untrained burgesses, were " but as a fly matched with an elephant." The novices of the convents and the priests' chambermaids, armed only with sticks, could have held them in check.[1] It were better to lose the advantages of the capital than to be overwhelmed within its walls by superior forces, being completely cut off from that part of France where the main strength of the Protestants lay.

From Meaux messengers were sent to the Protestant churches in all parts of France to request their aid, both in money and The Hugue- in men. " Since," said the letter they bore, " God not summons. has brought us to such a point that no one can disturb our repose without violating the protection it has pleased our king to accord us, and consequently without declaring himself an enemy of his Majesty and of this kingdom's peace, there is no law, divine or human, that does not permit us to take measures for defence, calling for help on those whom God has given the authority and the will to remedy these evils." [2]

Happily for the Huguenot cause, however, the nobles and gentry that favored it had not waited to receive this summons, but had, many of them, already set out to strengthen the forces of the prince. Among others, and by far more important than Admiral Co- all the rest, came Gaspard de Coligny, whose absence ligny's reluc- from court during the few previous weeks has been tance. regarded as one of the most untoward circumstances of the time. At his pleasant castle of Châtillon-sur-Loing, surrounded by his young family, he received intelligence, first, of the massacre, then of the ominous events that had occurred at the capital. Condé sent to solicit his support; his brothers and many friends urged him to rush at once to the rescue. But still, even after the threatening clouds had risen so high that they must soon burst over the devoted heads of the Huguenots,

not buried in the cemetery of the Holy Innocents, and throwing his body into a public sewer! March 15th, Journal de Jehan de la Fosse, 45.

[1] " Je cuide que si les novices des couvens et les chambrières des prestres seulement se fussent presentez à l'impourveue avec des bastons de cotterets (cotrets) ès mains, que cela leur eust fait tenir bride." Mém. de la Noue, c. ii.

[2] Circular letter dated Paris, March 25th, apud Baum, ii., App., 172.

the admiral continued to hesitate. Every instinct of his courageous nature prompted the skilful defender of St. Quentin to
place himself at once at the post of danger. But there was one
fear that seemed likely to overcome all his martial impulses.
It was the fear of initiating a civil war. He could not refer
to the subject without shuddering, for the horrors of such a
contest were so vividly impressed upon his mind that he regarded almost anything as preferable to the attempt to settle
domestic difficulties by an appeal to the sword. But the tears
and sighs of his wife, the noble Charlotte de Laval, at length
overmastered his reluctance. " To be prudent in men's esteem,"
she said, " is not to be wise in that of God, who has given you
the science of a general that you might use it for the good of
His children." When her husband rehearsed again the grounds
of his hesitation, and, calling upon her seriously to consider the
suffering, the privations, the anxiety, the bereavements, the
ignominy, the death which would await not only those dearest
to her, but herself, if the struggle should prove unsuccessful,
offered her three weeks to make her decision, with true womanly
magnanimity she replied : " The three weeks are already past ;
you will never be conquered by the strength of your enemies.
Make use of your resources, and bring not upon your head the
blood of those who may die within three weeks. I summon
you in God's name not to defraud us any more, or I shall be a
witness against you at His judgment." So deep was the impression which these words made upon Coligny, that, accepting his
wife's advice as the voice of heaven, he took horse without further delay, and joined Condé and the other Protestant leaders.[1]

It was unfortunate that the prince, for a week after leaving
Paris, should have felt too feeble to make any movement of
importance. Otherwise, by a rapid march, he might, according
to his plan,[2] have reached Fontainebleau in advance of his oppo-

---

[1] Agrippa d'Aubigné, i. 132, 133 (liv. iii., c. 2). This striking incident rests
on the sole authority of Agrippa d'Aubigné, who claims to have learned it
" de ceux qui estoient de la partie." Hotman, who wrote his *Gasparis Colinii Vita* (1575) at the earnest request of the admiral's *second* wife, makes no
allusion to a story throwing so much lustre upon the *first*.

[2] Throkmorton to the queen, April 10, 1562, State Paper Office.

nents, and, with the young king and his mother under his protection, have asserted his right as a prince of the blood to defend Charles against those who had unjustly usurped the functions of royalty. As it was, the unlucky delay was turned to profit by his enemies. These now took a step that put further deliberation on Catharine's part out of the question, and precluded any attempt to place the person of the king in Condé's hands. Leaving a small garrison in Paris, Guise proceeded with a strong body of troops to Fontainebleau, determined to bring the king and his mother back to Paris. Persuasion was first employed; but, that failing, the triumvirate were prepared to resort to force. Navarre, acting at Guise's suggestion, at length told Catharine distinctly that, as guardian of the minor king, he must see to it that he did not fall into his brother's hands; as

The king seized and brought to Paris.

for Catharine, she might remain or follow him, as she pleased.[1] Tears and remonstrances were of no avail.[2] Weeping and sad, Charles is said to have repeatedly exclaimed against being led away contrary to his will;[3] but the triumvirs would not be balked of their game, and so brought him with his mother first to Melun, then, after a few days, to the prison-like castle of Vincennes, and finally to the Louvre.[4]

---

[1] " Ou il faut que venez avec nous, ou nous emmenerons le Roy sans vous." Letter of Condé to the Emperor Ferdinand, April 20th, Mém. de Condé, iii. 305, etc.

[2] " Alors Leurs Majestez, ne pouvant mieux, eurent recours à quelques larmes." Mém. de Castelnau, liv. iii., c. 8.

[3] " Le Roy enfant de bonne nature et grande espérance, tesmoignoit non seulement par paroles, mais aussi avec abondance de larmes, extréme dueil et tristesse; et souventefois s'escriant, déploroit sa condition par telles paroles : ' Pourquoy ne me laissez-vous? Pour quelle raison me voy-je circuy et environné de gens armez? Pourquoy contre ma volonté me tirez-vous du lieu où je prenoye mon plaisir? Pourquoy deschirez-vous ainsi mon estat en ce mien aage?' " Letter of Condé, *ubi supra*, iii. 306.

[4] Charles the Ninth's entry into Paris was a sorry pageant compared with that of Guise only a few weeks earlier. " Only the merchants and a few counsellors of the city were present," says Jehan de la Fosse (p. 47). The king rode between the queen mother and the King of Navarre. According to Chamberlain, it was a *sober*, but not a *solemn* entry (C. to Chaloner, April 7, 1562, State Paper Office). Either when Guise returned to Paris from Fontainebleau, or on his previous entry into the city—it is difficult from Claude Haton's confused narrative to determine which was intended—the

The critical step had been taken to demonstrate that the reign of tolerance, according to the prescriptions of the Edict of The consta-   January, was at an end.   The constable, preceding the ble's exploits king to Paris, immediately upon his arrival instituted at the "tem- ples." a system of arbitrary arrests.   On the next morning (the fourth of April) he visited the "temple of Jerusalem,"[1] one of the two places which had been accorded to the Huguenots for their worship outside of the walls.   Under his direction the pulpit and the benches of the hearers were torn up, and a bonfire of wood and Bibles was speedily lighted, to the great delight of the populace of Paris.   In the afternoon the same exploits were repeated at the other Huguenot church, known from its situation, outside of the gate of St. Antoine, as "*Popincourt.*" Here, however, not only the benches, but the building itself was burned, and several adjacent houses were involved in the conflagration.   Having accomplished these outrages and encouraged the people to imitate his lawless example, the aged constable returned to the city.   He had well earned the contemptuous name which the Huguenots henceforth gave him of "Le Capitaine *Brûlebanc.*"[2]   If the triumvirate succeeded, it was plain that all liberty of worship was proscribed.   It was even believed that the Duchess of Guise had been sent to carry a message, in the king's name, to her mother, the aged Renée of France, to the effect that if she did not dismiss the Huguenot preachers from Montargis, and become a good Catholic, he would have her shut up for the rest of her life in a convent.[3]   Whatever truth there may have been in this story, one thing was certain : in Paris it would have been as much as any man's life was

---

people sang : " Blessed is he that cometh in the name of the Lord." Mémoires, i. 245.

[1] The singular name of this building is explained by the sign that hung before it.   " Apvril. En ung samedy. M. Anne de Montmorenssy, connétable de France, fut devant brasque *en la maison où pendoit pour enseigne la ville de Jérusalem*, où preschoient les huguenots, et fist mettre le feu dedans la maison." Journal de J. de la Fosse, 46.

[2] La Fosse, *ubi supra ;* J. de Serres, ii. 27 ; Hist. ecclés. des égl. ref., ii. 8 ; De Thou, iii. 136, 137 ; Bruslart, Mém. de Condé, i. 80 ; Santa Croce to Borromeo, April 5 (Aymon, i. 125) ; Throkmorton to the queen, *ubi supra.*

[3] Santa Croce to Borromeo, April 5th, Aymon, i. 126, and Cimber et Danjou, vi. 74.

worth to appear annoyed at the constable's exploit, or to oppose
the search made for arms in suspected houses.   Every good
Catholic had a piece of the Huguenots' benches or pulpit in his
house as a souvenir; "so odious," says a contemporary, "is the
new religion in this city."[1]   Meantime, on Easter Monday (the
thirtieth of March) Condé left Meaux at the head of fifteen
hundred horse, the flower of the French nobility, "better armed
with courage than with corselets"—says François de la Noue.
As they approached the capital, the whole city was thrown into
confusion, the gates were closed, and the chains stretched across
the streets.[2]   But the host passed by, and at St. Cloud crossed
the Seine without meeting any opposition.   Here the news of
the seizure of the person of Charles by the triumvirs first
reached the prince, and with it one great object of the expedition was frustrated.[3]   The Huguenots, however, did not delay,
but, instead of turning toward Fontainebleau, took a more
southerly route directly for the city of Orleans.   D'Andelot, to
whom the van had been confided, advanced by a rapid march,
and succeeded by a skilful movement in entering the city, of
which he took possession in the name of the Prince of Condé,
acting as lieutenant of the king unlawfully held in confinement.
Catharine de' Medici, who, having been forced into the party of
the triumvirs, had with her usual flexibility promptly decided
to make the most of her position, sent messengers to Condé
hoping to amuse him with negotiations while a powerful Roman
Catholic detachment should by another road reach Orleans un-

---

[1] Chantonnay, *ubi supra*, ii. 32.

[2] Journal de Jehan de la Fosse, 46.   The "Porte St. Honoré," before which
the Huguenots, after passing north of the city, presented themselves (Bruslart,
Mém. de Condé, i. 78), was in Francis I.'s time near the present "Palais
Royal," in the time of Louis XIII. near the "Madeleine."   See the map in
Dulaure, Histoire de Paris.

[3] Mém de la Noue, c. i.   The letter of Beza to Calvin from Meaux, March
28, 1562, shows, however, that even before the prince left that city it was
known that the triumvirs had set out for Fontainebleau.   Beza, not apparently without good reason, blamed the improvidence of Condé in not fore-
stalling the enemy.   "Hostes, relicto in urbe non magno præsidio, in aulam
abierunt quod difficile non erat et prospicere et impedire.   Sed aliter visum
est certis de causis, quas tamen nec satis intelligo nec probo."   Baum, ii.,
App., 176.

observed.[1] But the danger coming to Andelot's knowledge, he
succeeded in warning Condé; and the prince, with
D'Andelot the main body of the Protestant horse, after a break-
and Condé neck ride, threw himself, on the second of April, into
throw them-
selves into the city, which now became the headquarters of the re-
Orleans.
ligion in the kingdom.[2] The inhabitants came out to meet him
with every demonstration of joy, and received him between double lines of men, women, and children loudly singing the words of
the French psalms, so that the whole city resounded with them.[3]

No sooner had the Prince of Condé established himself upon
the banks of the Loire, than he took measures to explain to the
world the necessity and propriety of the step upon which he
had ventured. He wrote, and he induced the Protestant minis-
Condé's ters who were with him to write, to all the churches
justification. of France, urging them to send him reinforcements
of troops and to fill his empty treasury.[4] At the same time he

---

[1] Yet, if we may credit the unambiguous testimony of Jean de Tavannes,
Catharine did not cease to endeavor to favor the Huguenots. He assures us
that, a few months later, during the summer, his father, Gaspard de Tavannes, intercepted at Châlons a messenger whom Catharine had despatched to
her daughter the Duchess of Savoy ("qui agréoit ces nouvelles opinions")
ostensibly as a lute-player. Among his effects the prying governor of Burgundy found letters signed by the queen mother, containing some rather surprising suggestions. "La Royne luy escrivoit qu'elle estoit resolue de
favoriser les Huguenots, d'où elle esperoit son salut contre le gouvernement
du triumvirat . . . . qu'elle soupçonnoit vouloir oster la couronne à ses
enfans ; et prioit madame de Savoye d'aider lesdits Huguenots de Lyon, Dauphiné et Provence, et qu'elle persuadast son mary d'empescher les Suisses et
levée d'Italie des Catholiques." Mém. de Tavannes (Petitot ed.), ii. 341, 342.
Tavannes did not dare to detain the messenger, nor to take away his letters ;
and if, as his son asserts, the enmity of Catharine, which the discovery of her
secret gained for him, delayed his acquisition of the marshal's baton for ten
years, he certainly had some reason to remember and regret his ill-timed
curiosity.

[2] Mém. de la Noue, c. iii. ; De Thou, iii. 138; Letter of Beza, of April 5th,
Baum, ii., App., 177; Jean de Serres, ii. 24, 25 ; Bruslart, Mém. de Condé, i.
79. Chamberlain (to Chaloner, April 7, 1562), who on his way from Orleans
met the first detachment within a mile of that city—"a thousand handsome
gentlemen, well mounted, each having two or three daggs, galloping towards
him." State Paper Office.

[3] Hist. ecclés. des égl. réf., ii. 7.

[4] April 7th. Mém. de Condé, iii. 221; Hist. ecclés. des égl. réf., ii., 9 ; J.
de Serres, ii. 58, 59; De Thou, iii. 139. The historian of the reformed

published a " declaration " in justification of his resort to arms.
He recapitulated the successive steps that revealed the violent
purposes of the triumvirs—the retreat of the Guises and of the
constable from court, Nemours's attempt to carry the Duke of
Orleans out of the kingdom, the massacre at Vassy, Guise's refusal to visit the royal court and his defiant progress to the
capital, the insolent conduct of Montmorency and Saint-André,
the pretended *royal* council held away from the king, the detention of Charles and of his mother as prisoners.   And from all
these circumstances he showed the inevitable inference to be
that the triumvirs had for one of their chief objects the extirpation of the religion "which they call new," "either by open
violence or by the change of edicts, and the renewal of the most
cruel persecutions that have ever been exercised in the world."
It was not party interest that had induced him to take up arms,
he said, but loyalty to God, to his king, and to his native land,
a desire to free Charles from unlawful detention, and a purpose
to insist upon the execution of the royal edicts, especially that
of January, and to prevent new ministers of state from mis-
applying the sums raised for the payment of the national debts.
He warned all lovers of peace not to be astonished at any edicts
that might emanate from the royal seal so long as the king
remained a prisoner, and he begged Catharine to order the
triumvirs to lay down their arms.   If they did so, he declared
that he himself, although of a rank far different from theirs,
would consent to follow their example.[1]

The Huguenots had thrown off the shackles which a usurping
party about the king endeavored to fasten upon them ; but they
had not renounced the restraints of law.   And now,
Stringent ar-
ticles of asso-   at the very commencement of a great struggle for lib-
ciation.
erty, they entered into a solemn compact to banish licentious excesses from their army.   Protesting the purity of

churches, as well as Beza in his letter of March 28th (Baum, ii., App., 176),
complains bitterly of the slowness and parsimony of the Parisian Protestants,
who seemed to be unable to understand that war was actually upon them.

[1] April 8th.   Déclaration faicte par M. le prince de Condé, pour monstrer les
raisons qui l'ont contraint d'entreprendre la défence de l'authorité du Roy,"
etc.   Mém. de Condé, iii. 222–235 ; Jean de Serres, ii. 42–57 ; Hist. ecclés.
des égl. réf., ii. 9, 10 ; De Thou, iii. 139–141.

their motives, they swore to strive until the king's majority to attain the objects which had united them in a common struggle; but they promised with equal fervor to watch over the morals of their associates, and to suffer nothing that was contrary to God's honor or the king's edicts, to tolerate no idolatrous or superstitious practices, no blasphemy, no uncleanness or theft, no violation of churches by private authority. They declared their intention and desire to hear the Word of God preached by faithful ministers in the midst of the camps of war.[1]

The papal party was amazed at the opposition its extreme measures had created. In place of the timid weakling whom the triumvirate had expected, they saw a giant spring from the ground to confront them.[2] To Orleans flocked many of the highest nobles of the land. Besides Condé—after Navarre and Bourbon, the prince of the blood nearest to the crown—there were gathered to the Protestant standard the three Châtillons, Prince Porcien, Count de la Rochefoucauld, the Sieurs de Soubise, de Mouy, de Saint Fal, d'Esternay, Piennes, Rohan, Genlis, Grammont, Montgomery, and others of high station and of large influence and extensive landed possessions.[3] And, what was still more important, the capture of Orleans was but the signal for a general movement throughout France. In a few weeks the Huguenots, rising in their unsuspected strength, had rendered themselves masters of cities in almost every province. Along the Loire, Beaugency, Blois, Tours, and Angers declared for the Prince of Condé; in Normandy, Rouen, Havre, Dieppe, and Caen; in Berry and the neighboring provinces, Bourges, La Rochelle, Poitiers; along the Saône and Rhône, Châlons, Mâcon, Lyons, Vienne, Valence, Montélimart, Tournon, Orange; Gap and Grenoble in Dauphiny; almost the whole of the papal "Comtât Venaissin;" the Vivarais; the Cevennes; the greater part of Languedoc and

Huguenot nobles and cities.

---

[1] Traicté d'association, etc., April 11th. Mém. de Condé, iii. 258-262; J. Serres, ii. 31-37; De Thou, iii. 141.

[2] See Pasquier's letter to Fonssomme, already referred to, which contains a vivid picture of the confusion reigning in Paris, the surprise of the papal party, and the delight of the untrained populace at the prospect of war. Œuvres (ed. Feugère), ii. 246-250.

[3] Mém. de Castelnau, liv. iii., c. 8.

Gascony, with the important cities of Montauban, Castres, Castelnaudary, Beziers, Pézénas, Montpellier, Aiguesmortes, and Nismes.[1] In northern France alone, where the number of Protestants was small, the Huguenots obtained but a slight foothold.[2]

In the midst of this universal movement there was one point in the compact made by the confederates at Orleans, which it was found impossible to execute. How could the churches, with their altars, their statues, their pictures, their relics, their priestly vestments, be guaranteed from invasion?

Can iconoclasm be repressed?

To the Huguenot masses they were the temples and instruments of an idolatrous worship. Ought Christians to tolerate the existence of such abominations, even if sanctioned by the government? It was hard to draw a nice line of distinction between the overthrow of idolatry by public authority and by personal zeal. If there were any difference in the merit of the act, it was in favor of the man who vindicated the true religion at the risk of his own life. Nay, the Church itself had incontrovertibly given its sanction to this view by placing among the martyrs those primitive Christians who had upon their own responsibility entered heathen temples and overthrown the objects of the popular devotion. In those early centuries there had been manifested the same reckless exposure of life, the same supreme contempt for the claims of art in comparison with the demands of religion. The Minerva of Phidias or Praxiteles was no safer from the iconoclastic frenzy of the new convert from heathenism than the rude idol of a less cultivated age. The command, "Thou shalt not make unto thee any graven image," had not excepted from its prohibition the marvellous products of the Greek chisel.

It was here, therefore, that the chief insubordination of the

---

[1] Ibid., liv. iii., c. 9.

[2] Even so late as May 8, 1562, the English minister resident at the court, than whom probably no other person in France felt obliged to keep himself better informed, wrote to Cecil respecting the Prince of Condé's strength : " I can assur you att thys dyspatche *he ys the strongest partie*, and in suche state his matter standeth, that *these men* [the court] *wold fayne have a reasonable end, thoughe yt were with some dishonnour.*" MSS. State Paper Office, Duc d'Aumale, Princes de Condé, Pièces justif., i. 370.

Huguenot people manifested itself—not in licentious riot, not in bloodshed, not in pillage. Calvin, with his high sense of law and order, might in his letters reiterate the warnings against the irregularity which we have seen him uttering on a previous occasion;[1] the ministers might threaten the guilty with exclusion from the ordinances of the Church; Condé might denounce the penalty of death. The people could not restrain themselves or be restrained. They must remove what had been a stumbling-block to them and might become a snare to others. They felt no more compunction in breaking an image or tearing in pieces a picture, than a traveller, whom a highwayman has wounded, is aware of, when he destroys the weapons dropped by his assailant in his hurried flight. Indeed, they experienced a strange satisfaction in visiting upon the lifeless idol the punishment for the spiritual wrongs received at the hands of false teachers of religion.[2]

We have an illustration of the way in which the work of de-

---

[1] It is strange that a historian at once so conscientious and generally so well-informed as M. Rosseeuw Saint-Hilaire should, in his Histoire d'Espagne, ix. 60, 61, have made the grave mistake of holding Calvin responsible for the excesses of the iconoclasts. See the Bulletin, xiv. 127, etc., for a complete refutation.

[2] Like the undeceived dupe in the old Athenian comedy, who mournfully laments that he had been led to worship a bit of earthenware as a god :

Οἴμοι δείλαιος,
῾Οτε καὶ σὲ χυτρεοῦν ὄντα θεὸν ἡγησάμην.

(ARISTOPHANES, CLOUDS, 1473, 1474.)

On the other hand, the zealous Roman Catholic had his arguments for the preservation and worship of images, some of which may strike us as sufficiently whimsical. " I confess," says one, " that God has forbidden idols and idolatry, but He has not forbidden the images (or pictures) which we hold for the veneration of the saints. For if that were so, *He would not have left us the effigy of his holy face* painted in His likeness, on the cloth which that good lady Veronica presented Him, which yet to-day is looked upon with so much devotion in the church of St. Peter at Rome, nor the impression of His holy body represented in the ' saint suaire ' which is at Chambéry. Is it not found that Saint Luke thrice made with his own hand the portrait of Our Lady ? . . . . That holy evangelist ought certainly to have known the will of his Lord and Master better than you, my opponent, who wish to interpret the Scripture according to your sensuality." Discours des Guerres de Provence (Arch. curieuses, iv. 501, 502). Of course, the author never dreamed that his *facts* might possibly be disputed.

molition was accomplished in events occurring about this time
It bursts out at Caen. at Caen. Two or three inhabitants of this old Norman city were at Rouen when the churches were in-
vaded and sacked by an over-zealous crowd of sympathizers with
the "new doctrines." On their return to their native city, they
began at once to urge their friends to copy the example of the
provincial capital. The news reaching the ears of the magistrates of Caen, these endeavored—but to no purpose, as the sequel proved—to calm the feverish pulse of the people. On a
Friday night (May eighth), the storm broke out, and it raged
the whole of the next day. Church, chapel, and monastery could
testify to its violence. Quaint windows of stained glass and
rich old organs were dashed in pieces. Saints' effigies, to employ the quaint expression of a Roman Catholic eye-witness,
"were massacred." " So great was the damage inflicted, without any profit, that the loss was estimated at more than a hundred thousand crowns." Still less excusable were the acts of
vandalism which the rabble—ever ready to join in popular commotions and always throwing disgrace upon them—indulged.
The beautiful tombs of William, Duke of Normandy and
conqueror of England, and of the Duchess-queen Mathilda, the
pride of Caen, which had withstood the ravages of nearly five
hundred years, were ruthlessly destroyed. The monument of
Bishop Charles of Martigny, who had been ambassador under
Charles the Eighth and Louis the Twelfth, shared the same fate.
The zealous Roman Catholic who relates these occurrences
claims to have striven, although to no purpose, to rescue the
ashes of the conqueror from dispersion.[1]

The contagion spread even to Orleans. Here, as in other

---

[1] Les Recherches et Antiquitez de la ville de Caen, par Charles de Bourgue-
ville, sieur du lieu, de Bras, et de Brucourt. À Caen, 1588. Pt. ii. 170-172.
From page 76 onward the author gives us a record of notable events in
his own lifetime. So also at Cléry, it is to be regretted that, not content
with greatly injuring the famous church of Our Lady, the Huguenot populace,
inflamed by the indiscretion of the priests, desecrated the monuments of the
brave Dunois, and of Louis the Eleventh and his queen. Hist. ecclés. des
égl. réf., ii. 23. According to the author of the " Horribles cruautés des Huguenots en France " (Cimber et Danjou, vi. 304), they even burned the bones
of Louis ; nor did they respect those of the ancestors of the Prince of Condé.

places where the Huguenots had prevailed, there were but few
of the inhabitants that had not been drawn over to the reformed
faith, or at least pretended to embrace it. Yet Condé, in his
desire to convince the world that no partisan hatred moved him,
strictly prohibited the intrusion of Protestants into the churches,
and assured the ecclesiastics of protection so long as they chose
to remain in the city. For a time, consequently, their services
continued to be celebrated in the presence of the faithful few
and with closed doors; but soon, their fears getting the better
of their prudence, the priests and monks one by one made their
retreat from the Protestant capital. On the twenty-first of
April, word was brought to Condé that some of the churches
had been broken into during the preceding night, and that the
work of destruction was at that very moment going forward in
others. Hastening, in company with Coligny and other leaders,
to the spacious and imposing church of the Holy Rood (Sainte
Croix), he undertook, with blows and menaces, to check the furious onslaught. Seeing a Huguenot soldier who had climbed
aloft, and was preparing to hurl from its elevated niche one of
the saints that graced the wall of the church, the prince, in the
first ebullition of his anger, snatched an arquebuse from the
hands of one of his followers, and aimed it at the adventurous
iconoclast. The latter had seen the act, but was in no wise
daunted. Not desisting an instant from his pious enterprise, "Sir," he cried to Condé, "have patience
until I shall have overthrown this idol; and then let
me die, if that be your pleasure!"[1]

The "idol"
of Sainte
Croix.

The Huguenot soldier's fearless reply sounded the knell of
many a sacred painting and statue; for the destruction was accepted as God's work rather than man's.[2] Henceforth little
exertion was made to save these objects of mistaken devotion,
while the greatest care was taken to prevent the robbery of the
costly reliquaries and other precious possessions of the churches,

---

[1] "Monsieur, ayez patience que j'aie abattu cette idole, et puis que je meure,
s'il vous plait."

[2] "Comme étant ce fait plutôt œuvre de Dieu que des hommes." Hist.
ecclés. des égl. réf., ii. 20. "L'impétuosité des peuples était telle contre les
images, qu'il n'était possible aux hommes d'y résister." Ibid. ii. 23.

of which inventories were drawn up, and which were used only at the last extremity.[1]

Far different in character from the bloodless " massacres " of images and pictures in cities where the Huguenots gained the upper hand, were the massacres of living men wherever the papists retained their superiority. One of the most cruel and inexcusable was that which happened at Sens—a city sixty-five or seventy miles toward the southeast from Paris—where, on an ill-founded and malicious rumor that the reformed contemplated rising and destroying their Roman Catholic neighbors, the latter, at the instigation, it is said, of their archbishop, the Cardinal of Guise, and encouraged by the violent example of Constable Montmorency at Paris,[2] fell on the Protestants, murdered more than a hundred of both sexes and of every age, and threw their dead bodies into the waters of the Yonne.[3] While these victims of a blind bigotry were floating on under the windows of the Louvre toward the sea, Condé addressed to the queen mother a letter of warm remonstrance, and called upon her to avenge the causeless murder of so many innocent men and women ; expressing the fear that, if justice were denied by the king and by herself, the cry of innocent blood would reach high heaven, and God would be

Massacre of Huguenots at Sens.

---

[1] Hist. ecclés. des égl. réf., ii. 20–22.

[2] " Ledict moys," says Jehan de la Fosse in his journal (p. 47), "des citoyens de Sens tuèrent beaucoup de huguenots, voyant que monsieur le connétable avoict faict brûler Popincourt."

[3] Hist. ecclés. des égl. réf., ii. 242–245 ; Jean de Serres, ii. 40 ; De Thou, iii. 144. The massacre commenced on Sunday, April 12th (not 14th, as the Hist. ecclés. states), and was continued the next day or two. According to De Serres, the horrors of Sens seemed to efface those of Vassy itself. Read the really terrible paragraph on the subject in the contemporary " Remonstrance au Roy sur le faict des Idoles abbatues et déjettées hors des Temples " (Mém. de Condé, iii. 355–364), beginning " Où sont les meurtres, les boucheries des hommes passés au fil de l'espée, par l'espace de neuf jours en la ville de Sens? " The address to the Cardinal of Guise is not less severe than the address to his brother in the famous " Tigre " : " Te suffisoit-il pas, Cardinal, que le monde sceust que tu es Atheiste, Magicien, Nécromantien, sans le publier davantage, et faire ouvrir en pleine rue les femmes grosses pour voir le siége de leurs enfans ? " P. 360. White (Mass. of St. Bartholomew, 200) confounds in his account the two brother cardinals, and makes *Lorraine* to have been Archbishop of Sens.

moved to inflict those calamities with which the unhappy realm was every day threatened.[1]

A few days before Condé penned this appeal, the English ambassador had written and implored his royal mistress to seize the golden opportunity to inspirit the frightened Catharine de' Medici, panic-stricken by the violent measures of the Roman Catholic party; assuring her that "not a day passed but that the Spanish ambassador, the Bishop of Rome, or some other papist prince's minister put terror into the queen mother's mind."[2] But Throkmorton's words and Cecil's entreaties were alike powerless to induce Elizabeth to improve her advantage. The opportunity was fast slipping by, and the calamities foretold by Condé were coming on apace.

In truth, few calamities could exceed in horror those that now befell France. In the southeastern corner of the kingdom, above all other parts, civil war, ever prolific in evil passions, was already bearing its legitimate fruits. For several years the fertile, sunny hills of Provence and Dauphiny had enjoyed but little stable peace, and now both sides caught the Disorders in Provence and first notes of the summons to war and hurried to the Dauphiny. fray. Towns were stormed, and their inhabitants, whether surrendering on composition or at the discretion of the conqueror, found little justice or compassion. The men were more fortunate, in being summarily put to the sword; the women were reserved for the vilest indignities, and then shared the fate of their fathers and husbands. The thirst for revenge caused the Protestant leaders and soldiers to perpetrate deeds of cruelty little less revolting than those which disgraced the papal cause; but there was, at least, this to be said in their favor, that not even their enemies could accuse them of those infamous excesses of lewdness of which their opponents were notoriously guilty.[3] Their vengeance was satisfied with the lives, and did not demand the honor of the vanquished.

---

[1] Letter of Condé of April 19th, Mém. de Condé, iii. 300, 301 ; Hist. ecclés. des égl. réf., ii. 246, 247 ; J. de Serres, ii. 40–42.

[2] Throkmorton to Cecil, April 10. 1562. State Paper Office.

[3] I will not sully these pages even by a reference to the unnatural and beastly crimes which De Thou and other trustworthy historians ascribe to the Roman Catholic troops, especially the Italian part.

The little city of Orange, capital of William of Nassau's principality, contained a growing community of Protestants, whom
The city of   the prince had in vain attempted to restrain.   About
Orange.   a year and a half before the outburst of the civil war,
William the Silent, then a sincere Roman Catholic,[1] on receiving complaints from the Pope, whose territories about Avignon
—the Comtât Venaissin—ran around three sides of the principality, had expressed himself " marvellously sorry to see how
those wicked heresies were everywhere spreading, and that they
had even penetrated into his principality of Orange." [2]   And
when he received tidings that the Huguenots were beginning
to preach, he had written to his governor and council, " to see
to it by all means in the world, that no alteration be permitted
in our true and ancient religion, and in no wise to consent that
those wicked men should take refuge in his principality."   As
Protestantism advanced in Orange, he purposed to give instructions to use persuasion and force, " in order to remedy a disorder so pernicious to all Christendom." [3]   While he was unwilling to call in French troops, lest he should prejudice his
sovereign rights, he declared his desire to be authorized to
employ the pontifical soldiers in the work of repression.[4]   But
in spite of these restrictive measures, the reformed population
increased rather than diminished, and the bishop of the city
now called upon Fabrizio Serbelloni, a cousin of Pope Pius the
Fourth, and papal general at Avignon, to assist him by driving
out the Protestants, who, ever since the massacre of Vassy, had
feared with good reason the assault of their too powerful and
hostile neighbors, and had taken up arms in self-defence.   They
had not, however, apprehended so speedy an attack as Serbelloni now made (on the fifth of June), and, taken by surprise,

---

[1] So late as January, 1561, he wrote : " Quant à la religion, que sa Majesté
se peult asseuré que je viveray et moreray en icelle."   Gachard, Correspondance de Guillaume le Taciturne, ii. 6.

[2] " Et suis mervilleusement mari de veoir comme ces méchantes hérésies
se augmente partout," etc.

[3] " Qu'il fasse tout debvoir du monde, tant par puplication, comme par
force (autant qui j'en porrois la avoir) de remédier à telle désordre, qui est si
domagable à tout la christienté."

[4] Letter to Card. Granvelle, Oct. 21, 1560, Gachard, i. 461–463.

were able to make but a feeble resistance. The papal troops entered the city through the breach their cannon had effected. Never did victorious army act more insolently or with greater inhumanity. None were spared; neither the sick on their beds, nor the poor in their asylums, nor the maimed that hobbled through the streets. Those were most fortunate that were first despatched. The rest were tortured with painful wounds that prolonged their agonies till death was rather desired than dreaded, or were hurled down upon pikes and halberds, or were hung to pot-hooks and roasted in the fire, or were hacked in pieces. Not a few of the women were treated with dishonor; the greater part were hung to doors and windows, and their dead bodies, stripped naked, were submitted to indignities for which the annals of warfare, except among the most ferocious savages, can scarcely supply a parallel. That the Almighty might not seem to be insulted in the persons only of living creatures formed in His own image, the fresh impiety was perpetrated of derisively stuffing leaves torn from French Bibles into the gaping wounds of the dead lying on this field of carnage. Nor did the Roman Catholics of Orange fare much better than their reformed neighbors. Mistaken for enemies, they were massacred in the public square, where they had assembled, expecting rather to receive a reward for their services in assisting the pontifical troops to enter, than to atone for their treachery by their own death.[1]

But the time for revenge soon came around. The barbarous warfare initiated by the adherents of the triumvirate in Dauphiny and Provence bred or brought forward a leader and soldiers who did not hesitate to repay cruelty with cruelty. François de Beaumont, Baron des Adrets, was a merciless general, who

François de Beaumont, Baron des Adrets.

affected to believe that rigor and strict retaliation were indispensable to remove the contempt in which the Huguenots were held, and who knew how by bold movements to appear where least expected, and by vigor to multiply the apparent size of his army. Attached to the

---

[1] De Thou (whose graphic account I have principally followed), iii. 226-228; J. de Serres, ii. 183, 184; Hist. ecclés. des égl. réf., iii. 164-167.

Reformation only from ambition, and breathing a spirit far removed from the meekness of the Gospel, he soon awakened the horror of his comrades in arms, and incurred the censure of Condé for his barbarities ; so that, within a few months, becoming disgusted with the Huguenots, he went over to the papal side, and in the second civil war was found fighting against his former associates.[1] Meantime, his brief connection with the Huguenots was a blot upon their escutcheon all the more noticeable because of the prevailing purity;[2] and the injury he inflicted upon the cause of Protestantism far more than cancelled the services he rendered at Lyons and elsewhere. At Pierrelate he permitted his soldiers to take signal vengeance on the garrison for the recent massacre. At Mornas the articles of the capitulation, by which the lives of the besieged were guaranteed, were not observed; for the Protestant soldiers

---

[1] Agrippa d'Aubigné has inserted in his history (i. 154–156) an interesting conversation which he held with the Baron des Adrets, then an old man, a dozen years later, in the city of Lyons. In answer to the question, Why he had resorted to acts of cruelty unbecoming to his great valor ? the baron replied that no one commits cruelty in avenging cruelty; for, if the first measures are *cruelty*, the second are *justice*. His severities, he urged, were needed in order to show proper spirit in view of the past, and proper regard for the future. His soldiers must be forced to commit themselves beyond hope of pardon—they must, especially in a war in which their opponents cloaked themselves with the royal authority, fight without respect of persons. " The soldier cannot be taught," said he with characteristic bluntness, " to carry his sword and his hat in his hand at the same time." When asked what motive he had in subsequently leaving his old comrades in arms, he explained that it was neither fear nor avarice, but disgust at their timid policy and at seeing himself superseded. And to D'Aubigné's third question—a somewhat bold one, it must be confessed—Why success had never attended his recent undertakings, he answered "with a sigh : " "*Mon enfant*, nothing is too warm for a captain who has no greater anxiety for victory than have his soldiers. With the Huguenots I had *soldiers ;* since then I have had only *hucksters*, who cared for nothing but money. The former were moved by apprehension unmingled with fear, and revenge, passion, and honor were the wages they fought for. I could not give those Huguenot soldiers *reins* enough ; the others have worn out my *spurs*."

[2] And yet I agree with Von Polenz, Gesch. des Franz. Calvinismus (Gotha, 1859), ii. 188, 189, note, in regarding the Roman Catholic accounts of Des Adrets's cruelties and perfidy as very much exaggerated, and in insisting upon the circumstance that the barbarity practised at Orange had furnished him not only the example, but the incentive.

from Orange, recognizing among them the perpetrators of the
crimes which had turned their homes into a howling desert, fell
upon them and were not—perhaps could not be—restrained by
their leader.[1] The fatal example of Orange was but too faithfully copied, and precipitating the prisoners from the summit of
a high rock became the favorite mode of execution.[2] Only one
of the unfortunates, who happened to break his fall by catching
hold of a wild fig-tree growing out of the side of the cliff, was
spared by his enemies.[3] A number of the naked corpses were
afterward placed in an open boat without pilot or tiller, and
suffered to float down the Rhône with a banner on which were
written these words: " O men of Avignon! permit the bearers
to pass, for they have paid the toll at Mornas." [4]

The atrocities of Des Adrets and his soldiers in the East
were, however, surpassed by those which Blaise de Montluc
Blaise de   inflicted upon the Huguenots of the West, or which
Montluc.   took place under his sanction. His memoirs, which
are among the most authentic materials for the history of the
wars in which he took part, present him to us as a remorseless
soldier, dead to all feelings of sympathy with human distress,

---

[1] According to Jean de Serres, this leader was the Baron des Adrets in person; according to De Thou, Montbrun commanded by the baron's appointment. So also Histoire ecclés., iii. 171.

[2] So at Montbrison, the Baron des Adrets reserved thirty prisoners from the
common slaughter to expiate the massacre of Orange by a similar method.
One of them was observed by Des Adrets to draw back twice before taking the
fatal leap. " What ! " said the chief, "do you take *two springs* to do it ? "
" I will give you *ten* to do it ! " the witty soldier replied; and the laugh he
evoked from those grim lips saved his life. De Thou (iii. 231, 232) and
others.

[3] J. de Serres, ii. 188; Castelnau, liv., iv. c. ii. But the " Discours des Guerres de la comté de Venayscin et de la Prouence . . . . par le seigneur
Loys de Perussiis, escuyer de Coumons, subiect et uassal de sa saincteté " (dedicated to " Fr. Fabrice de Serbellon, cousin-germain de N. S. P. et son général
en la cité d'Avignon et dicte comté," Avignon, 1563, and reprinted in Cimber
(iv. 401, etc.), makes no mention of the fig-tree, and regards the preservation
as almost miraculous. There is a faithful representation of the ruined Château of Mornas above the frightful precipice, in Count Alexander de Laborde's
magnificent work, Les Monuments de la France (Paris, 1836), plate 179.

[4] Discours des Guerres de la comté de Venayscin, etc., 453; De Thou, iii.
240.

glorying in having executed more Huguenots than any other royal lieutenant in France,[1] pleased to have the people call the two hangmen whom he used to take about with him his "lackeys."[2] It is not surprising that, under the auspices of such an officer, fierce passions should have had free play. At Toulouse, the seat of the most fanatical parliament in France, a notable massacre took place. Even in this hot-bed of bigotry the reformed doctrines had made rapid and substantial progress, and the great body of the students in the famous law-school, as well of the municipal government, were favorable to their spread.[3] The common people, however, were as virulent in their hostility as the parliament itself. They had never been fully reconciled to the publication of the Edict of January, and had only been restrained from interference with the worship of the Protestants by the authority of the government. Of late the Huguenots had discovered on what treacherous ground they stood. A funeral procession of theirs had been attacked, and several persons had been murdered. A massacre had been perpetrated in the city of Cahors, not far distant from them. In both cases the entire authority of parliament had been exerted to shield the guilty. The Huguenots, therefore, resolved to forestall disaster by throwing Toulouse into the hands of Condé, and succeeded so far as to introduce some companies of soldiers within the walls and to seize the "hôtel de ville." They had, however, miscalculated their strength. The Roman Catholics were more numerous, and after repeated con-

Massacre at Toulouse.

---

[1] Mém. de Blaise de Montluc, iii. 393 (Petitot ed.): "pouvant dire avec la vérité qu'il n'y a lieutenant de Roy en France qui ait plus faict passer d'Huguenots par le cousteau ou par la corde, que moy."

[2] "Me deliberay d'user de toutes les cruautez que je pourrois." Ib., iii. 20. "Je recouvray secrettement deux bourreaux, lesquels on appella depuis mes laquais, parce qu'ils estoient souvent apres moy." Ib., iii., 21. Consult the succeeding pages for an account of Montluc's brutality, which could scarcely be credited, but that Montluc himself vouches for it.

[3] Since the publication of the Edict of January at Toulouse (on the 6th of February), the Protestant minister had sworn to observe its provisions before the seneschal, viguier, and capitouls, and, when he preached, these last had been present to prevent disturbance. A place of worship, twenty-four cannes long by sixteen in width (174 feet by 116), had been built on the spot assigned by the authorities. Hist. ecclés. des égl. réf., iii. 1.

flicts they were able to demand the surrender of the building in which the Protestants had intrenched themselves. Destitute alike of provisions and of the means of defence, and menaced with the burning of their retreat, the latter accepted the conditions offered, and—a part on the day before Pentecost, a part after the services of that Sunday, one of the chief festivals of the Reformed Church—they retired without arms, intending to depart for more hospitable cities. Scarce, however, had the last detachment left the walls, when the tocsin was sounded, and their enemies, respecting none of their promises, involved them in a horrible carnage. It was the opinion of the best informed that in all three thousand persons perished on both sides during the riot at Toulouse, of whom by far the greater number were Huguenots. Even this effusion of blood was not sufficient. The next day Montluc appeared in the city. And now, encouraged by his support, the Parliament of Toulouse initiated a system of judicial inquiries which were summary in their character, and rarely ended save in the condemnation of the accused. Within three months two hundred persons were publicly executed. The Protestant leader was quartered. The parliament vindicated its orthodoxy by the expulsion of twenty-two counsellors suspected of a leaning to the Reformation; and informers were allured by bribes, as well as frightened by ecclesiastical menaces, in order that the harvest of confiscation might be the greater.[1]

Such were the deeds which the Roman Catholics of southern France have up to our times commemorated by centenary celebrations;[2] such the pious achievements for which Blaise de

---

[1] De Thou, iii. 294; Hist. ecclés. des égl. réf., iii. 1–32.

[2] Even in 1762, Voltaire remonstrated against a jubilee to "thank God for four thousand murders." Yet a century later, in 1862, Monseigneur Desprez, Archbishop of Toulouse, gave notice of the recurrence of the celebration in these words : "The Catholic Church always makes it a duty to recall, in the succession of ages, the most remarkable events of its history—particularly those which belong to it in a special manner. It is thus that we are going to celebrate this year the jubilee commemorative of a glorious act accomplished among you three hundred years ago." The archbishop was warm in his admiration of the last centennial procession, "at which were present all the persons of distinction—the religious orders, the officiating minister under his

Montluc received from Pope Pius the Fourth the most lavish praise as a zealous defender of the Catholic faith.[1]

Meanwhile, about Paris and Orleans the war lagged. Both sides were receiving reinforcements. The ban and rear-ban were summoned in the king's name, and a large part of the levies joined Condé as the royal representative in preference to Navarre and the triumvirate.[2]   Charles the Ninth and Catharine

Foreign alliances sought.

had consented to publish a declaration denying Condé's allegation that they were held in duress.[3]   The Guises had sent abroad to Spain, to Germany, to the German cantons of Switzerland, to Savoy, to the Pope. Philip, after the abundant promises with which he had encouraged the French papists to enter upon the war, was not quite sure whether he had better answer the calls now made upon him. He was by no means confident that the love of country of the French might not, after all, prove stronger than the discord engendered by their religious differences, and their hatred of the Spaniard than their hatred of their political rivals.[4]   "Those stirrings," writes Sir Thomas Chaloner from Spain, "have here gevyn matter of great consultation day by day to this king and counsaile. One wayes they devise howe the Gwisans may be ayded and assisted by them,

---

canopy, the red robes, and the members of parliament pressing behind the university, the seneschal, the *bourgeoisie*, and finally a company of soldiers." But the French government, not agreeing with the prelate in the propriety of perpetuating the reminiscence, forbade the procession and all out-door solemnities, and declared "the celebration of a jubilee of the 16th to the 23d of May next, enjoined by the Archbishop of Toulouse, to be nothing less than the commemoration of a mournful and bloody episode of our ancient religious discords." See a letter from a correspondent of the New York Evening Post, Paris, April 10, 1862.

[1] Papal brief of April 23, 1562 : "Ista sunt vere catholico viro digna opera, ista haud dubie divina sunt beneficia. Agimus omnipotenti Deo gratias, qui tam præclaram tibi mentem dedit," etc.   Soldan, ii. 61.

[2] De Thou, iii. 149–151.

[3] Ibid., iii. 143, April 7th.

[4] Catharine de' Medici stated to Sir Harry Sydney, the special English envoy, in May, 1562, that her son-in-law, the King of Spain, had offered Charles thirty thousand foot and six thousand horse "payd of his owne charge," besides what the Duke of Savoy and others were ready to furnish. Letter of Sidney and Throkmorton to Queen Elizabeth, May 8, 1562, MSS. State Paper Office.   Duc d'Aumale, Princes de Condé, Pièces justif., i. 363.

esteming for religion sake that the prevaylment of that syde importithe them as the ball of theire eye. Another wayes they stand in a jelousie whither theis nombers thus assembled in Fraunce, may not possibly shake hands, and sett upon the Lowe Countries or Navarre, both peecs, upon confidence of the peace, now being disprovided of garisons. So ferfurthe as they here repent the revocation of the Spanish bands owt of Flanders.
. . . . So as in case the new bushops against the people's mynd shall need be enstalled, the Frenche had never such an opertunyte as they perchauns should fynd at this instant." [1] To the Duke of Würtemberg the Guises had induced Charles and Catharine to write, throwing the blame of the civil war entirely upon Condé; [2] but Christopher, this time at least, had his eyes wide open, and his reply was not only a pointed refusal to join in the general crusade against the Calvinists, but a noble plea in behalf of toleration and clemency. [3]

The Huguenots, on the other hand, had rather endeavored to set themselves right in public estimation and to prepare the way for future calls for assistance, than made any present requisitions. Elizabeth's ambassador, Throkmorton, had been carefully instructed as to the danger that overhung his mistress with all the rest of Protestant Christendom. He wrote to her that the plot was a general one, including England. "It may please your Majesty the papists, within these two days at Sens in Normandy, have slain and hurt two hundred persons—men and women. Your Majesty may perceive how dangerous it is to suffer papists that be of great heart and enterprise to lift up their crests so high." [4] In another despatch he warned her of her danger. "It standeth your Majesty upon, for the conservation of your realm in the good terms it is in (thanks be to God), to countenance the Protestants as much as you may, until they be set afoot again, I mean in this realm ; for here dependeth the great sway of that matter." [5]

Queen Elizabeth's aid invoked.

---

[1] Sir T. Chaloner, ambassador in Spain, to Sir Nicholas Throkmorton, **May** 1, 1562, Haynes, State Papers, 382, 383.
[2] April 17th. Mém. de Condé, iii. 281–284.
[3] May 15th and 16th, Mém. de Condé, iii. 284–287.
[4] Froude, History of England, vii. 404.
[5] Throkmorton to the queen, April 1, 1562, State Paper Office.

Cecil himself adopted the same views, and urged them upon Elizabeth's attention. Not succeeding in impressing her according to his wish, he resorted to extraordinary measures to compass the end. He instructed Mundt, his agent in Germany, to exert himself to induce the Protestant princes to send "special messengers" to England and persuade Elizabeth to join in "a confederacy of all parts professing the Gospel." In fact, the cunning secretary of state went even farther, and dictated to Mundt just what he should write to the queen. He was to tell her Majesty "that if she did not attempt the furtherance of the Gospel in France, and the keeping asunder of France and Spain, she would be in greater peril than any other prince in Christendom," for "the papist princes that sought to draw her to their parts meant her subversion"—a truth which, were she to be informed of by any of the German princes, might have a salutary effect.[1] But the vacillating queen could not be induced as yet to take the same view, and needed the offer of some tangible advantages to move her. No wonder that Elizabeth's policy halted. Every occurrence across the channel was purposely misrepresented by the emissaries of Philip, and the open sympathizers of the Roman Catholic party at the English court were almost more numerous than the hearty Protestants. A few weeks later, a correspondent of Throkmorton wrote to him from home: "Here are daily bruits given forth by the Spanish ambassador, as it is thought, far discrepant from such as I learn are sent from your lordship, and the papists have so great a voice here as they have almost as much credit, the more it is to be lamented. I have not, since I came last over, come in any company where almost the greater part have not in reasoning defended papistry, allowed the Guisians' proceedings, and seemed to deface the prince's quarrel and design. How dangerous this is your lordship doth see."[2] The Swiss Protestant cantons were reluctant to appear to countenance rebellion. Berne sent a few ensigns to Lyons at the request of the Protestants of that city, but wished

Cecil's urgency and schemes.

Divided sympathies of the English.

---

[1] Cecil to Mundt, March 22, 1562, State Paper Office.
[2] Wm. Hawes to Throkmorton, July 15, 1562, State Paper Office.

to limit them strictly to the defensive, and subsequently she yielded to the urgency of the Guises and recalled them altogether.[1] But as yet no effort was made by Condé to call in foreign assistance. The reluctance of Admiral Coligny, while it did honor to the patriotism which always moved him, seems to have led him to commit a serious mistake. The admiral hoped and believed that the Huguenots would prove strong enough to succeed without invoking foreign assistance; moreover, he was unwilling to set the first example of bringing in strangers to arbitrate concerning the domestic affairs of France.[2] And, indeed, had his opponents been equally patriotic, it is not improbable that his expectation would have been realized. For, if inferior to the enemy in infantry, the Huguenots, through the great preponderance of noblemen and gentlemen in their army, were at first far superior in cavalry.

The beaten path of diplomatic manœuvre was first tried. Four times were messengers sent to Condé, in the king's name, Diplomatic requiring his submission. Four times he responded manœuvres. that he could not lay down his arms until Guise should have retired from court and been punished for the massacre of Vassy, until the constable and Saint André should have returned to their governments, leaving the king his personal liberty, and until the Edict of January should be fully re-established.[3] These demands the opposing party were unwilling to concede. It is true that a pretence was made of granting the last point, and, on the eleventh of April, an edict, ostensibly in confirmation of that of January, was signed by Charles, by the advice of Catharine, the King of Navarre, the Cardinals of Bourbon and Guise, the Duke of Guise, the constable, and Aumale. But there was a glaring contradiction between the two laws, for Paris was ex-

---

[1] Hist. ecclés., iii. 143–145 ; De Thou, iii. 233, 234.

[2] Almost all the members of Condé's council favored a call upon the German Protestant princes for prompt support. But "the admiral broke off this plan of theirs, saying that he would prefer to die rather than consent that those of the religion should be the first to bring foreign troops into France." It was, therefore, concluded to send two gentlemen to Germany, to remain there until the conclusion of the war, in order to explain the position of the Huguenots. Hist. ecclés. des égl. réf., ii. 23.

[3] Mém. de Condé, i. 79, 80. Cf. Baum, ii., App., 177.

pressly excepted from the provisions. In or around the capital no exercises of the reformed religion could be celebrated.[1] Such was the trick by which the triumvirs hoped to take the wind out of the confederates' sails. Though the concession could not be accepted by the Protestants, it might be alleged to show foreigners the unreasonableness of Condé and his supporters. Meantime, in reply to the prince's declaration as to the causes for which he had taken up arms, the adherents of Guise published in their own vindication a paper, wherein they gravely asserted that, but for the duke's timely arrival, fifteen hundred Huguenots, gathered from every part of the kingdom, would have entered Paris, and, with the assistance of their confederates within the walls, would have plundered the city.[2]

The month of May witnessed the dreary continuation of the same state of things. On the first, Condé wrote to the queen mother, reiterating his readiness to lay down the arms he had assumed in the king's defence and her's, on the same conditions as before. On the fourth, Charles, Catharine, and Antoine replied, refusing to dismiss the Guises or to restore the Edict of January in reference to Paris, but, at the same time, inviting the prince to return to court, and promising that, after he should have submitted, and the revolted cities should have been restored to their allegiance, the triumvirs would retire to their governments.[3]

On the same day two petitions were presented to Charles. Both were signed by Guise, Montmorency, and Saint André. In the first they prayed his Majesty to interdict the exercise of every other religion save the "holy Apostolic and Roman," and require that all royal officers should conform to that religion or forfeit their positions; to compel the heretics to restore the churches which had been destroyed; to punish the sacrilegious; to declare rebels all who persisted in retaining arms without

---

[1] Hist. ecclés. des égl. réf., ii. 14 ; Mém. de Condé, i. 81–83, and iii. 256 ; De Thou, iii. 143.

[2] "Que sans sa venue à Paris, il fust arrivé vers les Pasques, plus de quinze centz chevaulx de tous costez du royaume, pour saccager la ville," etc. Response à la Déclaration que faict le Prince de Condé, etc. Mém. de Condé, iii. 242.

[3] Mém. de Condé, iii. 388–391 ; Hist. ecclés. des égl. réf., ii. 30, 31 ; Jean de Serres, ii. 63 ; De Thou, iii. 152.

permission of the King of Navarre. Under these conditions they would consent, they said, to leave France—nay, to go to the ends of the world. In the second petition they demanded the submission of the confederates of Orleans, the restitution of the places which had been seized, the exaction of an oath to observe the royal edicts, both new and old, and the enforcement of the sole command of Navarre over the French armies.[1]

Condé's reply (May twentieth) was the most bitter, as well as the ablest and most vigorous paper of the initiatory stage of the war. It well deserves a careful examination. The pretended *petition*, Louis of Bourbon wrote to the queen mother, any one can see, even upon a cursory perusal, to be in effect nothing else than a *decree* concocted by the Duke of Guise, Constable Montmorency, and Marshal Saint André, with the assistance of the papal legate and nuncio and the ministers of foreign states. Ambition, not zeal for the faith, is the motive. In order to have their own way, not only do the signers refuse to have a prince of the blood near the monarch, but they intend removing and punishing all the worthy members of the royal privy council, beginning with Michel de l'Hospital, the chancellor. In point of fact, they have already made a ridiculous appointment of six new counsellors. The queen mother is to be banished to Chenonceaux, there to spend her time in laying out her gardens. La Roche-sur-Yon will be sent elsewhere. New instructors are to be placed around the king to teach him riding, jousting, the art of love—anything, in short, to divert his mind from religion and the art of reigning well. The conspiracy is more dangerous than the conspiracy of Sulla or Cæsar, or that of the Roman triumvirs. Its authors point to their titles, and allege the benefits they have conferred; but their boasts may easily be answered by pointing to their insatiable avarice, and to the princely revenues they have accumulated during their long connection with the public administration. They speak of the present dangerous state of the country. What was it before the massacre of Vassy? After the publication of the Edict of January universal peace prevailed.

Condé's reply to the pretended petition.

[1] J. de Serres, ii. 112–117; Hist. ecclés. des égl. réf., ii. 27–29; Mém. de Condé, iii. 392, 393; De Thou, iii. 153, 154.

That peace these very petitioners disturbed. What means the coalition of the constable and Marshal Saint André? What mean the barbarities lately committed in Paris, but that the peace was to be broken by violent means? As to the obedience the petitioners profess to exhibit to the queen, they showed her open contempt when they refused to go to the provinces which they governed under the king's orders; when they came to the capital contrary to her express direction, and that in arms; when by force they dragged the king, her son, and herself from Fontainebleau to the Louvre. They have accused the Huguenots of treating the king as a prisoner, because these desire that the decree drawn up by the advice of the three estates of the realm should be made irrevocable until the majority of Charles the Ninth; but how was it when three persons, of whom one is a foreigner and the other two are servants of the crown, dictate a *new* edict, and wish that edict to be absolutely irrevocable? There is no need of lugging the Roman Catholic religion into the discussion, and undertaking its defence, for no one has thought of attacking it. The demand made by the petitioners for a compulsory subscription to certain articles of theirs is in opposition to immemorial usage; for no subscription has ever been exacted save to the creed of the Apostles. It is a second edict, and in truth nothing else than the introduction of that hateful Spanish inquisition. Ten thousand nobles and a hundred thousand soldiers will not be compelled either by force or by authority to affix their signatures to it. But, to talk of enforcing submission to a Roman Catholic confession is idle, so long as the Duke of Guise and the Cardinal of Lorraine do not retract their own adhesion to the Augsburg Confession lately given in with such protestations to a German prince. The charge of countenancing the breaking of images the prince would answer by pointing to the penalties he has inflicted in order to repress the irregularity. And yet, if it come to the true desert of punishment, what retribution ought not to be meted out for the crimes perpetrated by the petitioners, or under their auspices and after their examples, at Vassy, at Sens, at Paris, at Toulouse, and in so many other places? For the author of the petition should have remembered that it is nowhere written that a dead image ever cried for vengeance; but the blood of man—God's living image—demands it of heaven, and draws it down, though it tarry long. As for the accusation brought against Condé and the best part of the French nobility, that they are rebels, the prince hopes soon to meet his accusers in the open field and there decide the question whether a foreigner and two others of such a station as they are shall undertake to judge a prince of the blood. To allege Navarre's authority comes with ill-grace from men who wronged that king so openly during the late reign of Francis the Second. Finally, the Prince of Condé would set over against the petition of the triumvirate, one of his own, containing for its principal articles that the Edict of January, which his enemies seek to overturn, shall be observed inviolate; that all the king's subjects of every order and condition shall be maintained in their rights and privileges; that the professors of the reformed faith shall be protected until the majority of Charles; that arms shall be laid down on either side; above all, that *foreign* arms, which he himself, so far from inviting to France, has, up to the present moment, steadfastly declined when voluntarily offered, and which he will never resort to unless compelled by his enemies, shall be banished from the kingdom.[1]

While the clouds of war were thus gathering thick around Orleans, within its walls a synod of the reformed churches of France had assembled on the twenty-fifth of April, to deliberate of matters relating to their religious interests. Important questions of discipline were discussed and settled, and a day of public fasting and prayer was appointed in view of the danger of a declared civil war.[2]

Third National Synod.

---

[1] Jean de Serres, ii. 118–150; Mém. de Condé, iii. 395–416; Hist. ecclés. des égl. réf., ii. 32–46; De Thou, iii. 154–157. It is incredible that, as De Thou suggests, this answer should have been penned by Montluc, Bishop of Valence. On the other hand, it bears every mark of having proceeded from the pen of that learned, eloquent, and sprightly writer, Theodore Beza. As a literary production it fully deserves the warm encomium passed upon it by Professor Baum : "It is a masterpiece in respect both to the arrangement and to the treatment of the matter ; and, with its truly Demosthenian strength, may, with confidence, be placed by the side of the most eloquent passages to which the French language can point." Baum, Theodor Beza, ii. 642.

[2] J. de Serres, ii. 93, etc. ; De Thou, iii. 158. See the acts of the third Na-

The actual war was fast approaching. The army of the Guises, under the nominal command of the King of Navarre, was now ready to march in the direction of Orleans. Before setting out, however, the triumvirs resolved to make sure of their hold upon the capital, and royal edicts (of the twenty-sixth and twenty-seventh of May) were obtained ordering the expulsion from Paris of all known Protestants.[1] Then, with an army of four thousand foot and three thousand horse, the King of Navarre marched toward the city of Châteaudun.[2] On hearing of the movement of his brother's forces, the Prince of Condé advanced to meet him at the head of six thousand foot and two thousand horse. There were those, however, who still believed it to be possible to avert a collision and settle the matters in dispute by amicable discussion. Of this number was Catharine de' Medici. Hastily leaving the castle of Vincennes, she hurried to the front,

Interview of Catharine and Condé.

and at the little town of Toury, between the two armies, she brought about an interview between Condé, the King of Navarre, and herself. Such was the imbittered feeling supposed to animate both sides, that the escorts of the two princes had been strictly enjoined to avoid approaching each other, lest they should be tempted to indulge in insulting remarks, and from these come to blows. But, to the great surprise of all, they had no sooner met than papist and Huguenot rushed into each other's arms and embraced as friends long separated. While the principals were discussing the terms of union, their followers had already expressed by action the accord reigning in their hearts, and the white cloaks of Condé's attendants were to be seen indiscriminately mingled with the crimson cloaks of his brother's escort. Yet, after all, the interview came to nothing. Neither side could accept the only terms the other would offer, and Catharine returned disappointed to Paris, to be greeted by the populace with the most insulting language

---

tional Synod in Aymon, Tous les Synodes, i. 23-31. The Second National synod had been held at Poitiers, on the tenth of March, 1561. Its acts are in Aymon, i. 13-22.

[1] J. de Serres, ii. 170; De Thou, iii. 160; Jehan de la Fosse, 50; Hist ecclés. des égl. réf. ii. 47.

[2] De Thou, iii. 160.

for imperilling the orthodoxy of the kingdom.[1] Not, however,
altogether despairing of effecting a reconciliation, Condé addressed a letter to the King of Navarre, entreating him, before
it should be too late, to listen to his brotherly arguments. The
answer came in a new summons to lay down his arms.[2]

Yet, while they had no desire for a reconciliation on any such
terms as the Huguenots could accept, there were some substantial advantages which the Roman Catholic leaders hoped to reap
under cover of fresh negotiations. All the portion of the valley
of the Loire lying nearest to Paris was in the hands of the confederates of Orleans. It was impossible for Navarre to reach
the southern bank, except by crossing below Amboise, and thus
exposing the communications of his army with Paris to be cut
off at any moment. To attain his end with less difficulty, Antoine now sent word to his brother that he was disposed to conclude a peace, and proposed a truce of six days. Meanwhile,
he requested Condé to gratify him by the "loan" of the town
The "loan" of Beaugency, a few miles below Orleans, where he
of Beaugency. might be more comfortably lodged than in his present inconvenient quarters. The request was certainly sufficiently novel, but that it was granted by Condé may appear even
more strange.

This was not the only act of folly in which the Huguenot
leaders became involved. Under pretence of showing their
readiness to contribute their utmost to the re-establishment of
peace, the constable, Guise, and Saint André, after obtaining a
declaration from Catharine and Antoine that their voluntary
retreat would do no prejudice to their honor,[3] retired from the
royal court, but went no farther than the neighboring city of
Châteaudun. The Prince of Condé, swallowing the bait, did
not hesitate a moment to place himself, the very next day, in
the hands of the queen mother and his brother, and was led
more like a captive than a freeman from Beaugency to Talsy,

---

[1] Journal de Bruslart, Mémoires de Condé, i. 87; Claude Haton, i. 284;
Hist. ecclés. des égl. réf. ii. 48.

[2] See the prince's affectionate letter to Antoine, June 13th, Hist. ecclés. des
égl. réf. ii. 49; De Thou, *ubi supra ;* J. de Serres, ii. 156.

[3] Mém. de Guise, 495.

where Catharine was staying. Becoming alarmed, however, at his isolated situation, he wrote to his comrades in arms, and within a few hours so goodly a company of knights appeared, with Coligny, Andelot, Prince Porcien, La Rochefoucauld, Rohan, and other distinguished nobles at their head, that any treacherous plans that may have been entertained by the wily Italian princess were rendered entirely futile. She resolved,
Futile nego-
tiations. therefore, to entrap them by soft speeches. With that utter disregard for consistency so characteristic both of her actions and of her words, Catharine publicly [1] thanked the Huguenot lords for the services they had rendered the king, who would never cease to be grateful to them, and recognized, for her own part, that her son and she herself owed to them the preservation of their lives. But, after this flattering preamble, she proceeded to make the unpalatable proposition that they should consent to the repeal of the edict so far as Paris was concerned, under the guarantee of personal liberty, but without permission to hold public religious worship. The prince and his associates could listen to no such terms. Indeed, carried away by the fervor of their zeal, they protested that, rather than surrender the rights of their brethren, they would leave the kingdom. "We shall willingly go into exile," they said, "if our absence will conduce to the restoration of public tranquillity." This assurance was just what Catharine had been awaiting. To the infinite surprise of the speakers themselves, she told them that she appreciated their disinterested motives, and accepted their offer; that they should have safe-conducts to whatever land they desired to visit, with full liberty to sell their goods and to receive their incomes; but that their voluntary retirement would last only until the king's majority, which would be declared so soon as he had completed his fourteenth year! [2] It needs scarcely be said that, awkward as was the pre-

---

[1] It was in the presence of seven knights of the order of St. Michael, of the secretaries of state, etc. See Condé's long remonstrance against the judgment of the Parisian parliament, Aug. 8, 1562. Hist. ecclés. des égl. réf., ii. 71; Mém. de Condé, iii. 587.

[2] Unlucky Bishop Montluc has received the doubtful credit of having laid this pretty snare for the Huguenot chiefs, but with what reason it is beyond

dicament in which they had placed themselves, the prince and
his companions had little disposition to follow out Catharine's
plan. On their return to the Protestant camp, the clamor of
the soldiers against any further exposure of the person of their
leader to peril, and the opportune publication of an intercepted
letter said to have been written by the Duke of Guise to his
brother, the Cardinal of Lorraine, on the eve of his departure
for Châteaudun, and disclosing treacherous designs,[1] decided
the Huguenot leaders to break off the negotiations.[2]

The long period of comparative inaction was now succeeded
by a spasmodic effort at energetic conduct. The six days' truce
had scarcely expired when the prince resolved to throw himself
unexpectedly upon the neighboring camp of the Roman Catholics, before Montmorency, Guise, and Saint André had resumed
their accustomed posts. One of those nocturnal attacks, which,
under the name of *camisades*, figure so frequently in the military history of the period, was secretly organized, and the Protestant soldiers, wearing white shirts over their armor, in order
that they might easily recognize each other in the darkness of
the night, started with alacrity, under D'Andelot's command,
on the exciting adventure. But their guides were treacherous,
or unskilful, and the enterprise came to naught.[3] Disappointed
in this attempt, and unable to force the enemy to give battle,

---

my ability to conjecture. The same brain could scarcely have indited the bitter reply to the petition of the triumvirs, and devised the cunning project of
entangling their opponents. Evidently the Bishop of Valence has received
some honors to which he is not entitled.

[1] Mém. de Guise, 494; Hist. ecclés. des égl. réf., ii. 59. "Conclusion,"
says the duke in his confidence in the success of his project, " la religion réformée, en nous conduisant et tenant bon, comme nous ferons jusques au
bout, s'en va aval l'eau, et les admiraux, mal ce qui est possible : toutes nos
forces entièrement demeurent, les leurs rompues, les villes rendues sans parler d'édits ne de presches et administration de sacremens à leur mode." A
memorandum of eight articles from the triumvirs to Navarre, seized at the
same time, showed the intention to arrest the Prince of Condé. Ib., ii. 60.

[2] J. de Serres, ii. 170–180; Hist. ecclés. des égl. réf., *ubi supra ;* De Thou,
iii. 164–168. Harangue of Bishop Spifame to the emperor, Le Laboureur,
Add. aux Mém. de Castelnau, ii. 28–38. Mémoires de Jéhan de l'Archevesque,
Sieur de Soubise, Bulletin, xxiii. (1874) 460, 461.

[3] La Noue, c. v., p. 597; De Thou. iii. 168, 169, etc.

Condé turned his attention to Beaugency, which the King of Navarre had failed to restore, and carried it by storm. He would gladly have followed up the advantage by laying siege to Blois and Tours, which the triumvirate had taken and treated with the utmost cruelty; but heavy rains, and the impossibility of carrying on military operations on account of the depth of the mud, compelled him to relinquish his project, and reduced the main army to renewed inactivity.[1]

The protracted delays and inexcusable sluggishness of the leaders had borne their natural fruits. Many of the Protestant gentlemen had left the camp in disgust at the mistakes committed; others had retired to their homes on hearing that their families were exposed to the dangers of war and stood in need of their protection; a few had been corrupted by the arts of the enemy. For it was a circumstance often noticed by contemporaries, that no envoy was ever sent from Orleans to the court who did not return, if not demoralized, yet so lukewarm as to be incapable of performing any good service in future.[2] Yet the dispersion of the higher rank of the reformed soldiers, and the consequent weakening of Condé's army in cavalry, were attended with this incidental advantage, that they contributed greatly to the strengthening of the party in the provinces, and necessitated a similar division of the opposing forces.[3]

Never, perhaps, was there an army that exhibited such excellent discipline as did the army of the Protestants in this the first stage of its warfare. Never had the morals and religion of soldiers been better cared for. It was the testimony of a soldier, one of the most accomplished and philosophical writers of his times—the brave "Bras de Fer"—that the preaching of the Gospel was the great instrument of imbu-

Huguenot discipline.

---

[1] J. de Serres, ii. 180 ; Hist. ecclés. des égl. réf., ii. 61, 62.

[2] Hist. ecclés. des égl. réf., ii. 62; La Noue, c. iv.

[3] La Noue, c. vii., p. 600. "Ledict seigneur prince de Condé," says Jean Glaumeau of Bourges, in his journal, "voyant qu'il ne pouvoit avoir raison avec son ennemy et qu'il ne le pouvoit rencontrer, ayant une armée de viron trente ou quarante milles hommes, de peur qu'ilz n'adurassent (endurassent) fain ou soif, commence à les séparer et envoya en ceste ville de Bourges, tant de cheval que de pied, viron quatre milles, et y arrivèrent le samedi xie jour de juillet." Bulletin, v. (1857) 387.

ing the army with the spirit of order. Crimes, he tells us, were promptly revealed; no blasphemy was heard throughout the camp, for it was universally frowned upon. The very implements of gambling—dice and cards—were banished. There were no lewd women among the camp-followers. Thefts were unfrequent and vigorously punished. A couple of soldiers were hung for having robbed a peasant of a small quantity of wine.[1] Public prayers were said morning and evening; and, instead of profane or indelicate songs, nothing was heard but the psalms of David. Such were the admirable fruits of the careful discipline of Admiral Coligny, the true leader of the Protestant party; and they made a deep impression upon such enthusiastic youths as François de la Noue and Téligny. Their more experienced author, however, was not imposed upon by these flattering signs. "It is a very fine thing," he told them, "if only it last; but I much fear that these people will spend all their goodness at the outset, and that, two months hence, nothing will remain but malice. I have long commanded infantry, and I know that it often verifies the proverb which says: '*Of a young hermit, an old devil!*' If this army does not, we shall give it a good mark."[2] The prediction was speedily realized; for, although the army of the prince never sought to rival the papal troops in the extent of its license, the standard of soldierly morality was far below that which Coligny had desired to establish.[3]

So far as cruelty was concerned, everything in the conduct of their antagonists was calculated to provoke the Protestants to bitter retaliation. The army of Guise was merciless. If the infuriated Huguenots selected the priests that fell into their hands for the especial monuments of their retribution, it

---

[1] Hist. ecclés. des égl. réf., ii. 61.

[2] "Si celle-cy y faut, nous ferons la croix à la cheminée." Mém. de la Noue, c. vi. 598, 599.

[3] The author of the Hist. ecclés. des égl. réf., ii. 61, regards the failure of the confederates promptly to put to the death—as Admiral Coligny and others had insisted upon their doing—a Baron de Courtenay, who had outraged a village girl, and their placing him under a guard from which he succeeded in making his escape, as "the door, so to speak, through which Satan entered the camp."

was because the priesthood as a body had become the instigators of savage barbarity, instead of being the ministers of peace ;
because when they did not, like Ronsard the poet, themselves
buckle on the sword, or revel in blood, like the monks of Saint
Calais,[1] they still fanned, as they had for years been fanning, the
flame of civil war, denouncing toleration or compromise, wield-
ing the weapons of the church to enforce the pious duty of exterminating heresy and heretics, repeating and exaggerating
every foul calumny invented to the disadvantage of the reformers. No wonder, then, that the ecclesiastical dress itself became the badge of deadly and irreconcilable hostility, and that
in the course of this unhappy war many a priest was cut down
without any examination into his private views or personal history. Parliament, too, was setting the example of cruelty by
reckless orders amounting almost to independent legislation. By a series of " arrêts " succeeding each other
rapidly in the months of June and July, the door was
opened wider and wider for popular excess. When the churches
of Meaux were visited by an iconoclastic rabble on the twenty-
sixth of June, the Parisian parliament, on the thirtieth of
June, employed the disorder as the pretext of a judicial " declaration " that made the culprits liable to all the penalties
of treason, and permitted any one to put them to death without further authorization. The populace of Paris needed no
fuller powers to attack the Huguenots, for, within two or
three days, sixty men and women had been killed, robbed,
and thrown into the river. Parliament, therefore, found it
convenient to terminate the massacre by a second order restricting the application of the declaration to persons taken in
the very act.[2] A few days later (July, 1562), other arrêts
empowered all inhabitants of towns and villages to take up

Severities of the parliament.

---

[1] De Thou, iii. 171.

[2] Abbé Bruslart, Mém. de Condé, i. 90 ; Hist. ecclés. des égl. réf., ii. 66 ;
Journal de Jehan de la Fosse, 52. The latter erroneously calls it an edict " de
par le roi ; " but certainly gives the essence of the order according to the popular estimate when he says " qu'il estoit permis au peuple de tuer tout huguenot qu'il trouveroit, d'où vint qu'il y en eust en la ville de Paris plusieurs tués
et jetés en l'eau."

arms against those who molested priests, sacked churches, or "held conventicles and unlawful assemblies," whether public or secret; and to arrest the ministers, deacons, and other ecclesiastical functionaries for trial, as guilty of treason against God as well as man.[1] Not content with these appeals to popular passion,[2] however, the Parisian judges soon gave practical exemplifications of their intolerant principles; for two royal officers—the "lieutenant général" of Pontoise, and the "lieutenant" of Senlis—were publicly hung; the former for encouraging the preaching of God's word "in other form than the ancient church" authorized, the latter for "celebrating the Lord's Supper according to the Genevese fashion." These were, according to the curate of St. Barthélemi, the first executions at Paris for the simple profession of "Huguenoterie" since the pardon proclaimed by Francis the Second at Amboise.[3] A few days later,

---

[1] Mém. de Condé, i. 91. Text of arrêt of July 13th, ib., iii. 544; of arrêt of July 17th, ib., iii. 547. Hist. ecclés. des égl. réf., *ubi supra;* Recordon, p. 108.

[2] Nicholas Pithou has left in his MSS., which, unfortunately, have not yet been published entire, a thrilling narrative of the savage excesses committed partly by the authorities of Troyes, partly by the soldiers and the rabble, under their eyes and with their approval. There is nothing more abominable in the annals of crime than what was committed at this time with the connivance of the ministers of law. The story of the sufferings of Pithou's sister, Madame de Valentigny, will be found of special interest. See Recordon, 107–129.

[3] Mém de Condé, i. 91, and Hist. ecclés. des égl. réf., *ubi supra.* J. de la Fosse, 53, 54, "pour huguenoterye." Even with these judicial executions the people interfered, cutting off the heads of the victims, using them for footballs, and finally burning them. The contemptuous disobedience of the *people* of Paris and their cruelty are frequent topics touched upon in Throkmorton's correspondence. He acknowledges himself to be afraid, because of "the daily despites, injuries, and threatenings put in use towards him and his by the insolent, raging people." He sees that "neither the authority of the king, the queen mother, or any other person can be sanctuary" for him; for they "daily most cruelly kill every person (no age or sex excepted) whom they take to be contrary to their religion, notwithstanding daily proclamations under pain of death to the contrary." He declares that the king and his mother are, "for their own safety, constrained to lie at Bois de Vincennes, not thinking good to commit themselves into the hands of the furious Parisians;" and that the Chancellor of France, "being the most sincere man of this prince's council," is in as great fear of his life as Throkmorton himself, being lodged hard by the Bois de Vincennes, where he has the protection of

a new and more explicit declaration pronounced all those who had taken up arms, robbed churches and monasteries, and committed other sacrilegious acts at Orleans, Lyons, Rouen, and various other cities mentioned by name, to be rebels, and deprived them of all their offices. Yet, by way of retaliation upon Condé for maintaining that he had entered upon the war in order to defend the persons of the king and his mother, unjustly deprived of their liberty, parliament pretended to regard the prince himself as an unwilling captive in the hands of the confederates; and, consequently, excepted him alone from the general attainder.[1] But the legal fiction does not seem to have been attended with the great success its projectors anticipated.[2] The people could scarcely credit the statement that the war was waged by the Guises simply for the liberation of their mortal enemy, Condé, especially when Condé himself indignantly repelled the attempt to separate him from the associates with whom he had entered into common engagements, not to add that the reputation of the Lorraine family, whose mouth-piece parliament might well be supposed to be, was not over good for strict adherence to truth.

Meanwhile the triumvirs were more successful in their military operations than the partisans of the prince. Their auxiliaries came in more promptly, for the step which Condé now saw himself forced to take, in consequence of his opponents' course, they had long since resolved upon. They had received reinforcements from Germany, both of infantry and cavalry,

---

the king's guards; and yet even there he has been threatened with a visit from the Parisians, and with being killed in his own house. See both of Throkmorton's despatches to the queen, of August 5, 1562, State Paper Office. One of them is printed in Forbes, ii. 7, etc.

[1] Mém. de Condé, i. 91–93; Hist. ecclés. des égl. réf., *ubi supra;* De Thou, iii. 192, 193; J. de La Fosse, 54.

[2] It appears from a letter of the Nuncio Santa Croce (April 29th), that, as early as two months before, the court flattered itself with the hope of deriving great advantages from excluding Condé from the ban, and affecting to regard him as a prisoner (Aymon, i. 152, and Cimber et Danjou, vi. 91). "Con che pensano," he adds, "di quietar buona parte del popolo, che non sentendo parlar di religione, e parendoli ancora che la guerra si faccia per la liberatione del Principe de Condé, stara a vedere."

under command of the Rhinegrave Philip of Salm and the
Count of Rockendorf; while Condé had succeeded in detaching
but few of the Lutheran troopers by a manifesto in which he
endeavored to explain the true nature of the struggle. Soldiers
from the Roman Catholic cantons had been allowed a free
passage through the Spanish Franche-Comté by the regent of
the Low Countries, Margaret of Parma. The Pope himself
contributed liberally to the supply of money for paying the
troops.[1] But the Protestant reinforcements from the Palatinate
and Zweibrücken (Deux-Ponts), and from Hesse, which D'Andelot, and, after him, Gaspard de Schomberg, had gone to
hasten, were not yet ready; while Elizabeth still hesitated to
listen to the solicitations of Briquemault and Robert Stuart,
the Scotchman, who had been successively sent to her court.[2]

After effecting the important capture of the city of Poitiers,
Marshal Saint André, at the head of a Roman Catholic army,
had marched, about the middle of August, toward
Bourges, perhaps the most important place held by
the Protestants in central France. Beneath the walls
of this city he joined the main army, under Navarre's nominal
command, but really led by the Duke of Guise. The siege
was pressed with vigor, for the king was present in person with
the " Guisards." To the handful of Huguenots their assailants
appeared to be " a marvellous army of French, Germans,
reiters, Spaniards, and other nations, numbering in all eighty
or a hundred thousand men, with the bravest cavalry that could
be seen." [3] And, when twenty or twenty-five cannon opened
upon Bourges with balls of forty or fifty pounds' weight, and
when six hundred and forty discharges were counted on a single day, and every building in the town was shaken to its
very foundations, the besieged, numbering only a few hundred

*Military suc-
cesses of the
triumvirs.*

---

[1] " The byshopp off Rome hathe lent these hys cheampions and frends on
hundrethe thousand crowns, and dothe pay monthely besyds six thousand
sowldiers." Throkmorton to the Council, July 27, 1562, Forbes, State
Papers, ii. 5.

[2] De Thou, iii. 191, etc. ; Hist. ecclés. des égl. réf., ii. 64, etc.

[3] The number was, in fact, only about 15,000 foot and 3,000 horse, according to De Thou, iii. 198.

men, would have been excusable had they lost heart. Instead
of this, they obstinately defended their works, repaired the
breach by night, and inflicted severe injury on the enemy by
nocturnal sallies. To add to the duke's embarrassment, Admiral Coligny, issuing from Orleans, was fortunate enough to cut
off an important convoy of provisions and ammunition coming
from Paris to the relief of the besiegers.[1] Despairing of taking
the city by force, they now turned to negotiation. Unhappily,
M. d'Ivoy, in command of the Huguenot garrison, was not
proof against the seductive offers made him. Disregarding the
remonstrances of his companions in arms, who pointed to the
fact that the enemy had from day to day, through discouragement or from sheer exhaustion, relaxed their assaults, he con-
Fall of   sented (on the thirty-first of August) to surrender
Bourges.   Bourges to the army that had so long thundered at its
gates. D'Ivoy returned to Orleans, but Condé, accusing him of
open perfidy, refused to see him; while the Protestants of

---

[1] Although Coligny captured six cannon and over forty wagons of powder,
he was compelled reluctantly to destroy, or render useless, and abandon munitions of war of which he stood in great need; for the enemy had taken
the precaution to kill or drive away the horses, and the wagons could not be
dragged to Orleans, a distance of over twenty miles. It happened that Sir
Nicholas Throkmorton, whose instructive correspondence furnishes so lucid
a commentary upon the events from 1559 to 1563, was travelling under escort
of the royal train, to take leave of Charles IX. at Bourges. In the unexpected
assault of the Huguenots he was stripped of his money and baggage, and
even his despatches. Under these circumstances he thought it necessary to
accompany Coligny to Orleans. Catharine, who knew well Throkmorton's
sympathy with the Protestants, and hated him heartily (" Yt is not th' Ambassador of Englande," he had himself written only a few days earlier,
" which ys so greatlye stomackyd and hatyd in this countreye, but yt ys the
persone of Nicholas Throkmorton," Forbes, ii. 33), would have it that he
had purposely thrown himself into the hands of the Huguenots. His confidential correspondence with Queen Elizabeth does not bear out the charge.
Despatch from Orleans, Sept. 9, 1562, Forbes, State Papers, ii. 36, etc.
Catharine assured Sir Thomas Smith, on his arrival at court as English ambassador, that she wished he had been sent before, instead of Throkmorton,
" for they took him here to be the author of all these troubles," declaring
that Throkmorton was never well but when he was making some broil, and
that he was so " passionate and affectionate " on the Huguenots' side, that
he cared not what trouble he made. Despatch of Smith, Rouen, Nov. 7,
1562, State Paper Office.

Bourges shared the usual fate of those who trusted the promises of the Roman Catholic leaders, and secured few of the religious privileges guaranteed by the articles of capitulation.[1]

With the fall of Bourges, the whole of central France, as far as to the gates of Orleans, yielded to the arms of Guise. Everywhere the wretched inhabitants of the reformed faith were compelled to submit to gross indignities, or seek safety in flight. To many of these homeless fugitives the friendly castle of Montargis, belonging to the Duchess of Ferrara, to which reference will shortly be made, afforded a welcome refuge.[2]

The necessity of obtaining immediate reinforcements had at length brought Condé and the other great Huguenot lords to acquiesce in the offer of the only terms upon which Elizabeth of England could be persuaded to grant them actual support. As the indispensable condition to her interference, she demanded that the cities of Havre and Dieppe should be placed in her hands. These would be a pledge for the restoration of Calais, that old English stronghold which had fallen into the power of the French during the last war, and for whose restoration within eight years there had been an express stipulation in the treaties Cateau-Cambrésis. This humiliating concession the Huguenots reluctantly agreed to make. Elizabeth in turn promised to send six thousand English troops (three thousand to guard each of the cities), who should serve

Help from Queen Elizabeth.

---

[1] Histoire ecclés., ii. 296–306 (the terms of capitulation, ii. 304, 305); Mém. de Castelnau, liv. iii.,.c. xi. (who maintains they were implicitly observed); Throkmorton, in Forbes, State Papers, ii. 41; Davila, bk. iii., p. 71; De Thou, iii. 198, 199. " Bituriges turpiter a duce præsidii prodit sese dediderunt, optimis quidem conditionibus, sed quas biduo post perfidiosissimus hostis infregit." Beza to Bullinger, Sept. 24, 1562, Baum, ii., Appendix, 194. M. Bourquelot has published a graphic account of the capture of Bourges in May, by the Huguenots, under Montgomery, and of the siege in August, from the MS. Journal of Jean Glaumeau, in the National Library (Bulletin de l'hist. du prot. fr., v. 387–389). M. L. Lacour reprints in the same valuable periodical (v. 516–518) a contemporary hymn of some merit, " Sur la prise de Bourges." We are told that a proverb is even now current in Berry, not a little flattering to the Huguenot rule it recalls:

" L'an mil cinq cent soixante et deux
Bourges n'avoit prêtres ny gueux." (Ibid., v. 389.)

[2] Jean de Serres, De statu relig. et reip., ii. 258, 259.

under the command of Condé as the royal lieutenant, and pledged her word to lend the prince and his associates one hundred and forty thousand crowns toward defraying the expenses of the war.[1] On the twentieth of September the Queen of England published to the world a declaration of the motives that led her to interfere, alleging in particular the usurpation of the royal authority by the Guises, and the consequent danger impending over the Protestants of Normandy through the violence of the Duke of Aumale.[2]

The tidings of the alliance and of some of its conditions had already reached France, and they rather damaged than furthered the Protestant cause. As the English queen's selfish determination to confine her assistance to the protection of the three cities became known, it alarmed even her warmest friends among the French Protestants. Condé and Coligny earnestly begged the queen's ambassador to tell his mistress that "in case her Majesty were introduced by their means into Havre, Dieppe, and Rouen with six thousand men, only to keep those places, it would be unto them a great note of infamy." They would seem wantonly to have exposed to a foreign prince the very flower of Normandy, in giving into her hands cities which they felt themselves quite able to defend without assistance. So clearly did Throkmorton foresee the disastrous consequences of this course, that, even at the risk of offending the queen by his presumption, he took the liberty to warn her that if she suffered the Protestants of France

---

[1] This conclusion was arrived at as early as Aug. 29th. Froude, Hist. of England, vii. 433. Seventy thousand crowns were to be paid to the prince's agents at Strasbourg or Frankfort so soon as the news should be received of the transfer of Havre, thirty thousand more within a month thereafter. The other forty thousand were in lieu of the defence of Rouen and Dieppe, should it seem impracticable to undertake it. Havre was to be held until the Prince should have effected the restitution of Calais and the adjacent territory according to the treaties of Cateau-Cambrésis, although the time prescribed by those treaties had not expired, and until the one hundred and forty thousand crowns should have been repaid without interest. The compact, signed by Queen Elizabeth at Hampton Court, Sept. 20, 1562, is inserted in Du Mont, Corps Diplomatique, v. 94, 95, and in Forbes, State Papers, ii., 48–51.

[2] See the declaration in Hist. ecclés. des égl. réf., ii. 415, 416; and Forbes, State Papers, ii. 79, 80. J. de Serres, ii. 261, etc. Cf. Forbes, State Papers, ii. 60, 69–79.

to succumb, with minds so alienated from her that they should
consent to make an accord with the opposite faction, the possession of the cities would avail her but little against the united
forces of the French. He therefore suggested that it might be
quite as well for her Majesty's interests, "that she should serve
the turn of the Huguenots as well as her own."[1] Truly, Queen
Elizabeth was throwing away a glorious opportunity of displaying magnanimous disinterestedness, and of conciliating the affection of a powerful party on the continent. In the inevitable
struggle between Protestant England and papal Spain, the possession of such an ally as the best part of France would be of
inestimable value in abridging the contest or in deciding the
result. But the affection of the Huguenots could be secured by
no such cold-blooded compact as that which required them to
appear in the light of an unpatriotic party whose success would
entail the dismemberment of the kingdom. To make such a
demand at the very moment when her own ambassador was
writing from Paris that the people "did daily most cruelly
use and kill every person, no age or sex excepted, that they took
to be contrary to their religion," was to show but too clearly
that not religious zeal nor philanthropic tenderness of heart, so
much as pure selfishness, was the motive influencing her.[2] And
yet the English queen was not uninformed of, nor wholly insensible to, the calls of humanity. She could in fact, on occasion, herself set them forth with force and pathos. Nothing

---

[1] Throkmorton to the queen, Sept. 24, 1562, Forbes, State Papers, ii. 64, 65.
[2] Froude, *ubi supra*. In fact, Elizabeth assured Philip the Second—and
there is no reason to doubt her veracity in this—that she would recall her
troops from France so soon as Calais were recovered and peace with her
neighbors were restored, and that, in the attempt to secure these ends, she
expected the countenance rather than the opposition of her brother of Spain.
Queen Elizabeth to the King of Spain, Sept. 22, 1562. Forbes, State Papers,
ii. 55. It is not improbable, indeed, that there were ulterior designs even
against Havre. "It is ment," her minister Cecil wrote to one of his intimate
correspondents, "to kepe Newhaven in the Quene's possession untill Cal-
lice be eyther delyvered, or better assurance of it then presently we have."
But he soon adds that, in a certain emergency, "I think the Quene's Majestie
nead not be ashamed to utter her right to Newhaven as parcell of the Duchie
of Normandy." T. Wright, Queen Elizabeth and her Times (London, 1838),
i. 96.

could surpass the sympathy expressed in her autograph letter to Mary of Scots, deprecating the resentment of the latter at Elizabeth's interference—a letter which, as Mr. Froude notices, was not written by Cecil and merely signed by the queen, but was her own peculiar and characteristic composition. "Far sooner," she wrote, "would I pass over those murders on land; far rather would I leave unwritten those noyades in the rivers— those men and women hacked in pieces; but the shrieks of the strangled wives, great with child—the cries of the infants at their mothers' breasts—pierce me through. What drug of rhubarb can purge the bile which these tyrannies engender?"[1]

The news of the English alliance, although not unexpected, produced a very natural irritation at the French court. When Throkmorton applied to Catharine de' Medici for a passport to leave the kingdom, the queen persistently refused, telling him that such a document was unnecessary in his case. But she significantly volunteered the information that "some of his nation had lately entered France without asking for passports, who she hoped would speedily return without leave-taking!"[2]

Meanwhile the English movement rather accelerated than retarded the operations of the royal army. After the fall of Bourges, there had been a difference of opinion in the council whether Orleans or Rouen ought first to be attacked. Orleans was the centre of Huguenot activity, the heart from which the currents of life flowed to the farthest extremities of Gascony and Languedoc; but it was strongly fortified, and would be defended by a large and intrepid garrison. A siege was more likely to terminate disastrously to the assailants than to the citizens and Protestant troops. The admiral laughed at the attempt to attack a city which could throw three thousand men into the breach.[3] Rouen, on the contrary, was weak, and, if attacked before reinforcements were received from England,

---

[1] Froude, History of England, vii. 460, 461.

[2] Catharine to Throkmorton, Étampes, Sept. 21, 1562, State Paper Office.

[3] Mém. de la Noue, c. vii. ; De Thou, iii. 206, 207 (liv. xxxi). Throkmorton is loud in his praise of the fortifications the Huguenots had thrown up, and estimates the soldiers within them at over one thousand horse and five thousand foot soldiers, besides the citizen militia. Forbes, ii. 39.

but feebly garrisoned.   Yet it was the key of the valley of the
Seine, and its possession by the Huguenots was a
Siege of
Rouen, Oc-
tober. perpetual menace of the capital.[1]   So long as it was
in their hands, the door to the heart of the kingdom
lay wide open to the united army of French and English Protestants.   Very wisely, therefore, the Roman Catholic generals
abandoned their original design[2] of reducing Orleans so soon as
Bourges should fall, and resolved first to lay siege to Rouen.
Great reason, indeed, had the captors of such strongholds as
Marienbourg, Calais, and Thionville, to anticipate that a place
so badly protected, so easily commanded, and destitute of any
fortification deserving the name, would yield on the first alarm.[3]
It was true that a series of attacks made by the Duke of
Aumale upon Fort St. Catharine, the citadel of Rouen, had
been signally repulsed, and that, after two weeks of fighting, on
the twelfth of July he had abandoned the undertaking.[4]   But,
with the more abundant resources at their command, a better
result might now be expected.   Siege was, therefore, a second
time laid, on the twenty-ninth of September, by the King of
Navarre.

The forces on the two sides were disproportionate.   Navarre,

---

[1] Cuthbert Vaughan appreciated the importance of this city, and warned
Cecil that " if the same, for lack of aid, should be surprised, it might give the
French suspicion on our part that the queen meaneth but an appearance of
aid, thereby to obtain into her hands such things of theirs as may be most
profitable to her, and in time to come most noyful to themselves."   Forbes,
ii. 90.   Unfortunately it was not Cecil, but Elizabeth herself, that restrained
the exertions of the troops, and she was hard to move.   And so, for lack of
a liberal and hearty policy, Rouen was suffered to fall, and Dieppe was given
up without a blow, and Warwick and the English found themselves, as it were,
besieged in Havre.   Whereas, with those places, they might have commanded
the entire triangle between the Seine and the British Channel.   See Throkmorton's indignation, and the surprise of Condé and Coligny, Forbes, State
Papers, ii. 193, 199.

[2] In a letter to Lanssac, Aug. 17, 1562, Catharine writes: " Nous nous
acheminons à Bourges pour en déloger le jeune Genlis . . . L'ayant levé
de là, comme je n'y espère grande difficulté, nous tournerons vers Orléans
pour faire le semblable de ceux qui y sont."   Le Laboureur, i. 820.

[3] Mém. de François de la Noue, c. viii. (p. 601.)

[4] Hist. ecclés. des égl. réf., ii. 375, 376, 383; J. de Serres, ii. 181; De
Thou, iii. 179–181.

Montmorency, and Guise were at the head of sixteen thousand foot and two thousand horse, in addition to a considerable number of German mercenaries. Montgomery,[1] who commanded the Protestants, had barely eight hundred trained soldiers.[2] The rest of the scanty garrison was composed of those of the citizens who were capable of bearing arms, to the number of perhaps four thousand more. But this handful of men instituted a stout resistance. After frequently repulsing the assailants, the double fort of St. Catharine, situated near the Seine, on the east of the city, and Rouen's chief defence, was taken rather by surprise than by force. Yet, after this unfortunate loss, the brave Huguenots fought only with the greater desperation. Their numbers had been reinforced by the accession of some five hundred Englishmen of the first detachment of troops which had landed at Havre on the third of October, and whom Sir Adrian Poynings had assumed the responsibility of sending to the relief of the beleaguered capital of Normandy.[3] With Killigrew of Pendennis for their captain, they had taken advantage of a high tide to pass the obstructions of boats filled with stone and sand that had been sunk in the river opposite Caudebec, and, with the exception of the crew of one barge that ran ashore, and eleven of whom were hung by the Roman Catholics, "for having entered the service of the Huguenots contrary to the will of the Queen of England," they succeeded in reaching Rouen.[4]

These, however, were not the only auxiliaries upon whom the Huguenot chief could count. The women were inspired

---

[1] It was undoubtedly a Roman Catholic fabrication, that Montgomery bore on his escutcheon *a helmet pierced by a lance* (un heaume percé d'une lance), in allusion to the accident by which he had given Henry the Second his mortal wound, in the joust at the Tournelles. Abbé Bruslart. Mém. de Condé, i. 97, who, however, characterizes it as "chose fort dure à croire."

[2] Mém. de la Noue, c. viii.

[3] When Lord Robert Dudley began to break to the queen the disheartening news that Rouen had fallen, Elizabeth betrayed "a marvellous remorse that she had not dealt more frankly for it," and instead of exhibiting displeasure at Poynings's presumption, seemed disposed to blame him that he had not sent a thousand men instead, for his fault would have been no greater. Dudley to Cecil, Oct. 30, 1562, Forbes, State Papers, ii. 155.

[4] De Thou, iii. 328 ; Froude, vii. 436 ; Sir Thomas Smith to Throkmorton, Paris, Oct. 17, 1562, Forbes, State Papers, ii. 117.

with a courage that equalled, and a determination that surpassed, that of their husbands and brothers. They undertook the most arduous labors; they fought side by side on the walls; they helped to repair at night the breaches which the enemy's cannon had made during the day; and after one of the most sanguinary conflicts during the siege, it was found that there were more women killed and wounded than men. Yet the courage of the Huguenots sustained them throughout the unequal struggle. Frequently summoned to surrender, the Rouenese would listen to no terms that included a loss of their religious liberty. Rather than submit to the usurpation of the Guises, they preferred to fall with arms in their hands.[1] For fall they must. D'Andelot was on his way with the troops he had laboriously collected in Germany; another band of three thousand Englishmen was only detained by the adverse winds; Condé himself was reported on his way northward to raise the siege—but none could arrive in time. The King of Navarre had been severely wounded in the shoulder, but Guise and the constable pressed the city with no less decision. At last the walls on the side of the suburbs of St. Hilaire and Martainville were breached by the overwhelming fire of the enemy. The population of Rouen and its motley garrison, reduced in numbers, worn out with toils and vigils, and disheartened by a combat which ceased on one day only to be renewed under less favorable circumstances on the next, were no longer able to continue their heroic and almost superhuman exertions.

On Monday, the twenty-sixth of October, the army of the triumvirate forced its way over the rubbish into Rouen, and the richest city of France, outside of Paris, fell an unresisting prey to the cupidity of an insubordinate soldiery. Rarely had so tempting a prize fallen into the hands of a conquering army; rarely were the exactions of war more remorsely inflicted.[2] But the barbarities of a licentious army

Fall of Rouen.

---

[1] "But thei will have there preaching still. Thei will have libertie of their religion, and thei will have no garrison wythin the towne, but will be masters therof themselves: and upon this point thei stand." Despatch of Sir Thomas Smith, Poissy, Oct. 20, 1562. Forbes, State Papers, ii. 123.

[2] The plundering lasted eight days. While the Swiss obeyed orders, and

were exceeded in atrocity by the cooler deliberations of the The Norman Norman parliament. That supreme court, always parliament. inimical to the Protestants, had retired to the neighboring city of Louviers, in order to maintain itself free from Huguenot influence. It now returned to Rouen and exercised a sanguinary revenge. Augustin Marlorat, one of the most distinguished among the reformed ministers of France, and the most prominent pastor of the church of Rouen, had been thrown into prison; he was now brought before the parliament, and with others was sentenced to death as a traitor and a disturber of the public repose, then dragged on a hurdle to the place of execution and ignominiously hung.[1]

The ferocity of the Norman parliament alarming the queen mother, she interfered to secure the observance of the edict of amnesty she had recently prepared. But serious results followed in the case of two prominent partisans of Guise who had fallen into Condé's hands, and were in prison when the tidings reached Orleans. On the recommendation of his council, the prince retaliated by sending to the gallows Jean Baptiste Sapin, a member of the Parisian parliament, and the Abbé de Gastines, who had been captured while travelling in company with an envoy whom the court were sending to Spain.[2]

---

promptly desisted, "the French suffered themselves to be killed rather than quit the place whilst there was anything left." Castelnau, liv. iii., c. 13. The *curé* of Mériot waxes jocose over the incidents of the capture : "Tout ce qui fut trouvé en armes par les rues et sur les murailles fut passé par le fil de l'espée. La ville fut mise au pillage par les soldatz du camp, qui se firent gentis compaignons. *Dieu sçait que ceux qui estoient mal habillez pour leur yver* (hiver) *ne s'en allèrent sans robbe neufve.* Les huguenotz de la ville furent en tout maltraictez," etc. Mém. de Claude Haton, i. 288.

[1] On the siege of Rouen, see the graphic account of De Thou, iii. (liv. xxxiii.) 328–335 ; the copious correspondence of the English envoys in France, Forbes, State Papers, vol. ii.; the Hist. ecclés. des égl. réf., ii. 389–396 (and Marlorat's examination and sentence *in extenso*, 398–404); J. de Serres, ii. 259 ; La Noue, c. viii.; Davila (interesting, and not so inaccurate here as usual, perhaps because he had a brother-in-law, Jean de Hemery, sieur de Villers, in the Roman Catholic army, but who greatly exaggerates the Huguenot forces), ch. iii. 73–75 ; Castelnau, liv. iii., c. 13.

[2] It is to be noted, however, that the order of the Prince of Condé, in the case of Sapin (November 2, 1562), makes no mention of the judicial murder of Marlorat, but alleges only his complicity with parliament in imprisoning

The fall of Rouen was followed within a few weeks by the death of the King of Navarre. His painful wound was not, perhaps, necessarily mortal, but the restless and vainglorious prince would not remain quiet and allow it to heal. He insisted on being borne in a litter through the breach into the city which had been taken under his nominal command. It was a sort of triumphal procession, marching to the sound of cymbals, and with other marks of victory. But the idle pageant only increased the inflammation in his shoulder. Even in his sick-room he allowed himself no time for serious thought; but, prating of the orange-groves of Sardinia which he was to receive from the King of Spain, and toying with Rouhet, the beautiful maid of honor by whom Catharine had drawn him into her net, he frittered away the brief remnant of an ignoble life. When visibly approaching his end, he is said, at the suggestion of an Italian physician, to have confessed himself to a priest, and to have received the last sacraments of the Romish Church. Yet, with characteristic vacillation he listened, but a few hours later, with attention and apparent devoutness, to the reading of God's Word, and answered the remonstrances of his faithful Huguenot physician by the assurance that, if he recovered his health, he would openly espouse the Augsburg Confession, and cause the pure Gospel to be preached everywhere throughout France.[1] His death occurred

Death of Antoine de Bourbon, King of Navarre.

---

the king, his mother, and the King of Navarre, in annulling royal edicts by magisterial orders, in constraining the king's officers to become idolaters, in declaring knights of the Order of St. Michael and other worthy gentlemen rebels, in ordering the tocsin to be rung, and inciting to assassination, etc. Hist. ecclés. des égl. réf., ii. 115, 116. See Bruslart, Mém. de Condé, i. 100. When Condé was informed that the Parisian parliament had gone in red robes to the "Sainte Chapelle," to hear a requiem mass for Counsellor Sapin, he laughed, and said that he hoped soon to multiply their *litanies* and *kyrie eleysons*. Hist. ecclés., *ubi supra*.

[1] As early as October 27th, Navarre sent a gentleman to Jeanne d'Albret, then at Pau in Béarn, "desiring to have her now to cherish him, and do the part of a wife;" and the messenger told Sir Thomas Smith, with whom he dined that day in Evreux, "that the king pretendeth to him, that this punishment [his wounds] came to him well-deserved, for his unkindness in forsaking the truth." Forbes, State Papers, ii. 167. The authenticity of the story of Antoine of Navarre's death-bed repentance is sufficiently attested by

on the seventeenth of November, 1562, at Les Andelys, a village
on the Seine. He had insisted, contrary to his friends' advice,
upon being taken by boat from Rouen to St. Maur-des-Fossés,
where, within a couple of leagues of Paris, he hoped to breathe a
purer air; but death overtook him before he had completed
half his journey.[1]

Had Antoine embraced with sincerity and steadfastly maintained either of the two phases of religious belief which divided
between them the whole of western Christendom, his death
would have left a void which could have been filled with difficulty. He was the first prince of the blood, and entitled to the
regency. His appearance was prepossessing, his manners courteous. He was esteemed a capable general, and was certainly
not destitute of administrative ability. If, with hearty devotion, he had given himself to the reformed views, the authority
of his great name and eminent position might have secured for
their adherents, if not triumph, at least toleration and quiet.
But two capital weaknesses ruined his entire course. The love
of empty glory blinded him to his true interests; and the love
of sensual pleasure made him an easy dupe. He was robbed of
his legitimate claims to the first rank in France by the promise
of a shadowy sceptre in some distant region, which every sensible statesman of his time knew from the first that Philip the
Second never had entertained the slightest intention of conferring; while, by the siren voices of her fair maids of honor,
Catharine de' Medici was always sure of being able to lure

---

the letter written, less than a year later (August, 1563), by his widow, Jeanne
d'Albret, to the Cardinal of Armagnac : "Où sont ces belles couronnes que
vous luy promettiés, et qu'il a acquises à combattre contre la vraye Religion
et sa conscience; comme la confession dernière qu'il en a faite en sa mort en
est seur tesmoignage, et les paroles dites à la Royne, en protestation de faire
prescher les ministres par tout s'il guerissoit." Pierre Olhagaray, Histoire
de Foix, Béarn, et Navarre (Paris, 1609), p. 546. See also Brantôme (edition Lalanne), iv. 367, and the account, written probably by Antoine's physician, De Taillevis, among the Dupuy MSS. of the Bibliothèque nationale,
ibid., iv. 419.

[1] Lestoile (Collection Michaud et Poujoulat), 15 ; Hist. ecclés. des égl. réf.,
ii. 397, 406–408 ; De Thou, 336, 337 ; Relation de la mort du roi de Navarre,
Cimber et Danjou, iv. 67, etc.

him on to the most humiliating concessions. Deceived by the emissaries of the Spanish king and the Italian queen mother, Antoine would have been an object rather of pity than of disgust, had he not himself played false to the friends who supported him. As it was, he passed off the stage, and scarcely left a single person to regret his departure. Huguenots and papists were alike gratified when the world was relieved of so signal an example of inconstancy and perfidy.[1] Antoine left behind him his wife, the eminent Jeanne d'Albret, and two children—a son, the Prince of Béarn, soon to appear in history as the leader of the Huguenot party, and, on the extinction of the Valois line, to succeed to the throne as Henry the Fourth; and a daughter, Catharine, who inherited all her mother's signal virtues. The widow and her children were, at the time of Antoine's death, in Jeanne's dominions on the northern slopes of the Pyrenees, whither they had retired when he had first openly gone over to the side of the Guises. There, in the midst of her own subjects, the Queen of Navarre was studying, more intelligently than any other monarch of her age, the true welfare of her people, while training her son in those principles upon which she hoped to see him lay the foundations of a great and glorious career.

The sagacity of the enemy had been well exhibited in the vigor with which they had pressed the siege of Rouen. Condé, with barely seven thousand men, had several weeks before shut himself up in Orleans, after despatching the few troops at his

---

[1] I am convinced that the historian De Thou has drawn of this fickle prince much too charitable a portrait (iii. 337). It seems to be saying too much to affirm that " his merit equalled that of the greatest captains of his age; " and if " he loved justice, and was possessed of uprightness," it must be confessed that his dealings with neither party furnish much evidence of the fact. (I retain these remarks, although I find that the criticism has been anticipated by Soldan, ii. 78). Recalling the earlier relations of the men, it is not a little odd that, when the news of Navarre's death reached the "holy fathers" of the council then in session in the city of Trent, the papal legates and the presidents paid the Cardinal of Lorraine a formal visit to *condole* with him on the decease of his dear relative ! (Acta Conc. Tridentini, *apud* Martene et Durand, Amplissima Collectio, tom. viii. 1299). The farce was, doubtless, well played, for the actors were of the best in Christendom.

disposal for the relief of Bourges and Rouen, and could do nothing beyond making his own position secure, while impatiently
awaiting the long-expected reinforcements from England and
Germany.[1] The dilatoriness that marked the entire conduct of
the war up to this time had borne its natural fruit in the gradual diminution and dispersion of his forces, in the loss of one
important city after another, and almost of entire provinces,
and, worst of all, in the discouragement pervading all classes of
the Huguenot population.[2] Now, however, he was on the eve
of obtaining relief. Two days after the fall of Rouen, on the
twenty-eighth of October, a second detachment of the English
fleet succeeded in overcoming the contrary winds that had detained them ten days in crossing the channel, and landed three
The English thousand troops at the port of Havre.[3] D'Andelot
in Havre.   had finally been able to gather up his German "reiters" and "lansquenets,"[4] and was making a brilliant march
through Alsace, Lorraine, Burgundy, and Champagne, skilfully
avoiding the enemy's forces sent out to watch and intercept him.[5]

---

[1] Letter of Beza to Bullinger, Sept. 1, 1562, Baum, iii., App., 190. The
Huguenots had sustained a heavy loss also in the utter defeat and dispersion
by Blaise de Montluc of some five or six thousand troops of Gascony, which
the Baron de Duras was bringing to Orleans.

[2] The sentiments of well-informed Huguenots are reflected in a letter of Calvin, of September, 1562, urging the Protestants of Languedoc to make col-
lections to defray the expense entailed by D'Andelot's levy. "D'entrer en
question ou dispute pour reprendre les faultes passées, ce n'est pas le temps.
Car, quoy qu'il en soit, Dieu nous a réduicts à telle extrémité que si vous
n'estes secourus de ce costé-là, on ne voit apparence selon les hommes que
d'une piteuse et horrible désolation." Bonnet, Lettres franç., ii. 475.

[3] Hist. ecclés., ii. 421.

[4] See "Capitulation des reytres et lansquenetz levez pour monseigneur le
prince de Condé, du xviii. d'aoust 1562," Bulletin, xvi. (1867), 116–118. The
reiters came chiefly from Hesse.

[5] Claude Haton, no friend to Catharine, makes the Duke d'Aumale, in command of eight or nine thousand troops, avoid giving battle to D'Andelot,
and content himself with watching his march from Lorraine as far as St.
Florentin, in obedience to secret orders of the queen mother, signed with the
king's seal. Mémoires, i. 294, 295. The fact was that D'Andelot adroitly
eluded both the Duke of Nevers, Governor of Champagne, who was prepared
to resist his passage, and Marshal Saint André, who had advanced to meet
him with thirteen companies of "gens-d'armes" and some foot soldiers. Davila, bk. iii. 76 ; De Thou, iii. (liv. xxxiii.) 356.

On the sixth of November, he presented himself before the gates of Orleans, and was received with lively enthusiasm by the prince and his small army.[1]

Now at length, on the seventh of November, Condé could leave the walls which for seven months had sheltered him in almost complete inaction, and within which a frightful pestilence had been making havoc among the flower of the chivalry of France; for, whilst fire and sword were everywhere laying waste the country, heaven had sent a subtle and still more destructive foe to decimate the wretched inhabitants. Orleans had not escaped the scourge. The city was crowded with refugees from Paris and from the whole valley of the Loire. Among these strangers, as well as among the citizens, death found many victims. In a few months it was believed that ten thousand persons perished in Orleans alone; while in Paris, where the disease raged more than an entire year, the number of deaths was much larger.[2]

With the four thousand lansquenets and the three thousand reiters brought him from Germany,[3] Condé was able to leave a force, under command of D'Andelot, sufficient to defend the city of Orleans, and himself to take the field with an army of about fifteen thousand men.[4] " Our enemies,"

Condé takes the field.

---

[1] Hist. ecclés. des égl. réf., ii. 114, 115. The writer ascribes the fall of Rouen to the delay of the reiters in assembling at their rendezvous. Instead of being ready on the first of October, it was not until the tenth that they had come in sufficient numbers to be mustered in.

[2] Eighty thousand, according to the Hist. ecclés. des égl. réf., ii. 91, 92 ; twenty-five thousand, according to Claude Haton, Mémoires, 332, 333.

[3] Letter of Beza to Bullinger, Sept. 1st, Baum, ii., App., 191 ; Hist. ecclés. des égl. réf., ii. 114, 115 ; Davila, bk. iii., 77 ; De Thou, iii. 355, 356.

[4] Letter of Beza to Calvin, Dec. 14, 1562, Baum, ii., App., 196. The authority of Beza, who had recently returned from a mission on which he had been sent by Condé to Germany and Switzerland and who wrote from the camp, is certainly to be preferred to that of Claude Haton, who states the Huguenot forces at 25,000 men (Mémoires, i. 298). The prince's chief captains —Coligny, Andelot, La Rochefoucauld, and Mouy—Haton rates as the best warriors in France after the Duke of Guise. According to Throkmorton's despatches from Condé's camp near Corbeil, the departure from Orleans took place on the 8th of November, and the prince's French forces amounted only to six thousand foot soldiers, indifferently armed, and about two thousand horse. Forbes, State Papers, ii. 195. But this did not include the Germans

he said, "have inflicted two great losses upon us in taking our castles"—meaning Bourges and Rouen—"but I hope that now we shall have their knights, if they move out upon the board."[1]

As he was leaving Orleans, he was waited upon by a deputation of fifty reformed ministers, who urged him to look well to the discipline and purity of the army. They begged him, by salutary punishment, to banish from the camp theft and rapine, and, above all, that more insidious and heaven-provoking sin of licentiousness, which, creeping in, had doubtless drawn down upon the cause such marked signs of the Lord's displeasure, that, of all the congregations in France, only the churches of a few islands on the coasts, and the churches of Montauban, Havre, Orleans, Lyons, and of the cities of Languedoc[2] and Dauphiny, continued to rear their heads through the storm that had prostrated all the rest; and, to this end, they warned him by no means to neglect to afford his soldiers upon the march the same opportunities of hearing God's Word and of public prayer which they had enjoyed in Orleans.[3]

—some seven thousand five hundred men more. Ibid , ii. 196. Altogether, he reckons the army at " 6,000 horsemen of all sorts and nations, and 10,000 footmen." Ibid., ii. 202.

[1] Mém. de La Noue, c. viii., p. 602.

[2] The Protestants of Languedoc held in Nismes (Nov. 2–13, 1562) the first, or at least one of the very first, of those " political assemblies " which became more and more frequent as the sixteenth century advanced. Here the Count of Crussol, subsequently Duke d'Uzès, was urged to accept the office of " head, defender, and conservator " of the reformed party in Languedoc. To the count a council was given, and he was requested not to find the suggestion amiss that he should in all important matters, such as treaties with the enemy, consult with the general assembly of the Protestants, or at least with the council. By this good office he would demonstrate the closeness of the bond uniting him as head to the body of his native land, besides giving greater assurance to a people too much inclined to receive unfounded impressions (" ung puple souvent trop meticulleux et de legiere inpression "). Procès-verbal of the Assembly of Nismes, from MS. Bulletin, xxii. (1873), p. 515.

[3] Hist ecclés. des égl. réf., ii. 117 ; De Thou, iii. 357. Calvin's, or the Geneva liturgy, was probably used but in part. Special prayers, adapted to the circumstances of the army, had been composed, under the title of " Prières ordinaires des soldatz de l'armée conduicte par Monsieur le Prince de Condé, accomodées selon l'occurrence du temps." Prof. Baum cites a simple, but beautiful evening prayer, which was to be said when the sentinels were placed on guard for the night. Theodor Beza, ii. 624, note.

The Huguenot army directed its course northward, and the different divisions united under the walls of Pluviers, or Pithiviers, a weak place, which surrendered after six hours of cannonading, with little loss to the besieging party. The greater part of the garrison was dismissed unharmed, after having been compelled to give up its weapons. Two of the officers, as guilty of flagrant breach of faith and other crimes, were summarily hung.[1] And here the Huguenot cause was stained by an act of cruelty for which no sufficient excuse can be found. Several Roman Catholic priests, detected, in spite of their disguise, among the prisoners, were put to death, without other pretext save that they had been the chief instigators of the resistance which the town had offered. Unhappily, the Huguenot regarded the priest, and the Roman Catholic the reformed minister, as the guilty cause of the civil war, and thought it right to vent upon his head the vengeance which his own religion should have taught him to leave to the righteous retribution of a just God. After the fall of Pithiviers, no resistance was attempted by Étampes and other slightly garrisoned places of the neighborhood, the soldiers and the clergy taking refuge, before the approach of the army, in the capital.

The prince was now master of the country to the very gates of Paris, and it was the opinion of many, including among them the reformer, Beza, that the city itself might be captured by a sudden advance, and the war thus ended at a blow.[2] They therefore recommended that, without delay, the army should hasten forward and attack the terrified inhabitants before Guise and the constable should have

The prince appears before Paris.

---

[1] Throkmorton (Forbes, ii. 195, 197) represents the executions as more general, and as an act of severity, "chiefly in revenge of the great cruelty exercised by the Duke of Guise and his party at Rouen against the soldiers there, but specially against your Majesty's subjects."

[2] Throkmorton was convinced of the practicability of capturing Paris by a rapid movement even from before Corbeil: "The whole suburbes on this syde the water is entrenched, where there is sundry bastions and cavaliers to plante th' artillerye on, which is verey daungerous for th' assaylantes. Nevertheles, if the Prince had used celeritie, in my opinion, with little losse of men and great facilitie he might have woon the suburbes; and then the towne coulde not longe have holden, somme parte of the sayd suburbes havinge domination therof." Forbes, ii. 217.

time to bring the army and the king back from Normandy, where they still lingered. The view was so plausible, indeed, that it was adopted by most of the reformed historians, and, being indorsed by later writers, has caused the failure to march directly against the capital to be regarded as a signal error of Condé in this campaign. But it would certainly appear hazardous to adopt this conclusion in the face of the most skilful strategists of the age. It has already been seen that François de la Noue, one of the ablest generals of whom the Huguenots could ever boast, regarded the idea of capturing Paris at the beginning of the struggle, with the comparatively insignificant forces which the prince could bring to the undertaking, as the most chimerical that could be entertained. Was it less absurd now, when, if the Protestant army had received large accessions, the walls of Paris could certainly be held by the citizens for a few days, until an army of fully equal size, under experienced leaders, could be recalled from the lower Seine? Such, at least, was the conclusion at which Admiral Coligny, the commanding spirit in the council-chamber and the virtual head of the Huguenot army, arrived, when he calmly considered the perils of attacking, with twelve or fifteen thousand men and four pieces of artillery, the largest capital of continental Europe —a city whose population amounted to several hundred thousand souls, among whom there was now not a single avowed Protestant, and whose turbulent citizens were not unaccustomed to the use of arms. He resolved, therefore, to adopt the more practicable plan of making the city feel the pressure of the war by cutting off its supplies of provisions and by ravaging the surrounding country. Thus, Paris—" the bellows by whose blasts the war was kept in flames," and " the kitchen that fed it "—would at last become weary of sustaining in idleness an insolent soldiery, and of seeing its villages given over to destruction, and compel the king's advisers to offer just terms of peace, or to seek a solution of the present disputes on the open field.[1]

---

[1] Mémoires de François de la Noue, c. ix., p. 603 (Collection Michaud et Poujoulat). See also Davila (bk. iii. 77), who represents the advice of the admiral rather to have been to employ the army in recapturing the places

But, whatever doubt may be entertained respecting the propriety of the plan of the campaign adopted by the Prince of Condé, there can be none respecting the error committed in not promptly carrying that plan into execution. The army loitered about Étampes instead of pressing on and seizing the bridges across the Seine. Over these it ought to have crossed, and, entering the fruitful district of Brie, to have become master of the rivers by which the means of subsistence were principally brought to Paris. With Corbeil and Lagny in his possession, Condé would have held Paris in as deadly a grasp as Henry the Fourth did twenty-eight years later, when Alexander of Parma was forced to come from Flanders to its assistance.[1] When, at last, the Huguenot army took the direction of Corbeil, commanding one of the bridges, the news arrived of the death of Antoine of Navarre. And with this intelligence came fresh messengers from Catharine, who had already endeavored more than once by similar means to delay the Huguenots in their advance. She now strove to amuse Condé with the hope of succeeding his brother as lieutenant-general of the kingdom during Charles's minority.[2]

In vain did the soldiers chafe at this new check upon their en-

---

along the Loire, while Condé insisted on trying to become master of Paris. De Thou, iii. 358. Beza, in his letter of Dec. 14th, says : " Quum enim urbs repentino impetu facile capi posset, etc." So also the Hist. ecclés. des égl. réf., ii. 118.

[1] See Motley, United Netherlands, iii. 59.

[2] " The Prince of Condé and his campe having approched the towne of Corbeille, and being ready to batter the same, the queene mother sente her principal escuyer, named Monsieur de Sainte-Mesme, with a lettre to the sayd prince, advertisinge him of the deathe of the kinge, his brother. The sayd de Sainte-Mesme had also in credence to tell the prince from the queene, that she was verey desirous to have an ende of theise troubles : and also that she was willinge that the sayd prince should enjoy his ranke and aucthorité due unto him in this realme. . . . This the queene mother's lettre and sweete words hathe empeached the battrye and warlyke procedings against Corbeill ; the prince therby beeing induced to desist from using any violence against his ennemyes. I feare me, that this delaying will torne much to the prince's disadvantage ; and that there is no other good meaning at this time in this faire speeche, then there was in the treaty of Bogeancy (Beaugency) in the monethe of July last." Throkmorton to the queen, from Essonne, opposite Corbeil, Nov. 22, 1562, Forbes, ii. 209.

thusiasm, in vain did prudent counsellors remonstrate. There was a traitor even in the prince's council, in the person of Jean de Hangest, sieur de Genlis (brother of D'Ivoy, the betrayer of Bourges), whose open desertion we shall soon have occasion to notice, and this treacherous adviser was successful in procuring a delay of four days.[1] The respite was not thrown away. Before the Huguenots were again in motion, Corbeil was reinforced and rendered impregnable against any assaults which, with their feeble artillery, they could make upon it. Repulsed from its walls, after several days wasted in the vain hope of taking it, the prince moved down the left bank of the Seine, and, on the twenty-eighth of November, encamped opposite to Paris in the villages of Gentilly and Arcueil.[2] New proffers came from Catharine; there were new delays on the road. At Port à l'Anglais a conference with Condé had been projected by the queen mother, resulting merely in one between the constable and his nephew Coligny—as fruitless as any that had preceded; for Montmorency would not hear of tolerating in France another religion besides the Roman Catholic, and the Admiral would rather die a thousand deaths than abandon the point.[3]

Under the walls of Paris new conferences took place. The Parisians worked night and day, strengthening their defences, and making those preparations which are rarely completed except under the spur of an extraordinary emergency. Meanwhile, every day brought nearer the arrival of the Spanish and Gascon auxiliaries whom they were expecting. At a windmill near the suburb of St. Marceau, the Prince of Condé, Coligny, Genlis, Grammont, and Esternay met the queen mother, the Prince of La Roche-sur-Yon, the constable, his son Marshal Montmorency, and Gonnor, at a later time known as Marshal Cossé. On both sides there were professions of the most ardent desire for peace, and " Huguenot " and " papist " embraced each other cordially at parting. But the dangerous intimacy soon bore the bitter fruit of open treachery. A *camisade* had been secretly planned by the Huguenots, and the attack was about to

---

[1] Letter of Beza to Calvin, Dec. 14th, Baum, ii., App., 197.
[2] Ib., *ubi supra*.
[3] Hist. ecclés. des égl. réf., ii. 120 ; De Thou, iii. 359.

be made on the enemy's works, when word was brought that one of the chiefs intrusted with the knowledge of all their plans —the same Genlis, who had been the principal advocate of the delays upon the route — had gone over to the enemy, and the enterprise was consequently abandoned.[1]

The deliberations being set on foot by the one party, at least, only in order to gain time, it is not surprising that they accomplished nothing. The court would concede none of the important demands of the prince. It was resolved to exclude Protestantism not only from Paris, but from Lyons, from all the seats of parliaments, from frontier towns, and from cities which had not enjoyed the right of having preaching according to the Edict of January. The exercises of the reformed worship could not be tolerated in any place where the court sojourned—a cunning provision which would banish from the royal presence all the princes and high nobility, such as Renée of France, Condé, and the Châtillons, since these could not consent to live without the ordinances of their faith for themselves and their families and retainers. The triumvirs would not agree to the recall of those who had been exiled. They were willing to have all proceedings against the partisans of Condé suspended; but they would neither consent that all edicts, ordinances, and sentences framed against the Huguenots be declared null and void, nor assent to the restoration of those dignities which had been taken from them. In other words, as the prince remarked, the Protestant lords were to put a halter about their own necks for their enemies to tighten whenever the fancy should take them so to do.[2]

At last the Parisian defences were completed, and the Spanish and Gascon troops, to the number of seven thousand men, arrived. Then the mask of conciliation was promptly laid

---

[1] Hist. ecclés. des égl. réf., ii. 132 ; De Thou, iii. 361 ; Mém. de Castelnau, liv. iv., c. iv. ; Forbes, ii. 227. 228. Even in September, the English ambassador wrote from Orleans, "there is greate practise made by the queene mother and others to winne Monsieur de Janlis and Monsieur de Grandmont from the prince." Forbes, ii. 41.

[2] " Par ce moyen, un chacun de nous trainera son licol, jusques à ce que les dessusdits le serrent à leur appetit." Hist. ecclés. des égl. réf., ii. 126. The details of the conferences, with the articles offered on either side, are given at great length, pp. 121–136.

aside. Two weeks of precious time had been lost, the capital was beyond doubt impregnable, and the unpleasant fact stared the prince in the face that, after leaving a sufficient force to garrison it, the constable and Guise might still march out with an army outnumbering his own.[1] On the tenth of December the Huguenot army broke up its encampment, and moved in the direction of Chartres, hesitating at first whether to lay siege to that city or to press on to Normandy in order to obtain the needed funds and support of the English. The decision was made in a few days to adopt the latter course, and Condé had proceeded as far as the vicinity of Dreux on the river Eure, when he found himself confronted by the enemy, who, enjoying the advantage of possessing the cities and bridges on the route, could advance with greater ease by the principal roads. The triumvirs, so lately declining battle in front of Paris, were now as eager as they had before been reluctant to try their fortunes in the open field. No longer having the King of Navarre behind whose name and authority to take shelter, they desired to cover their designs by the queen mother's instructions. So, before bringing on the first regular engagement, in which two armies of Frenchmen were to undertake each other's destruction, they had sent Michel de Castelnau, the well-known historian, on the fifteenth of December, to inquire of Catharine de' Medici whether they should give the Huguenots battle. But the queen was too timid, or too cunning, to assume the weighty responsibility which they would have lifted from their own shoulders.

---

[1] " The queene mother and hyr councelours," wrote Throkmorton to Elizabeth, four or five days later (Dec. 13, 1562), " have at the length once agayne showed, howe sincerely they meane in their treatyes. For when their force out of Gascoigne together with two thousand five hundred Spainardes were arrived, and when they had well trenched and fortefyed the faulxbourges and places of advantage of Paris; espienge, that the prince coulde remayne no longer with his campe before Paris for lack of victuaill and fourrage, having abused him sufficiently with this treaty eight or ten dayes: the sayd queene mother . . . . refused utterly the condicions before accorded." Forbes, State Papers, ii. 226. It is not strange that the ambassador, after the meagre results of the past five weeks, " could not hope of any great good to be done, until he saw it; " although he was confident that " if matters were handled stoutly and roundly, without delay," the prince might constrain his enemies to accord him favorable conditions.

"Nurse," she jestingly exclaimed, when Castelnau announced his mission, calling to the king's old Huguenot foster-mother who was close at hand, "the generals have sent to ask a woman's advice about fighting; pray, what is your opinion?" And the envoy could get no more satisfactory answer than that the queen mother referred the whole matter to themselves, as experienced military men.[1]

On the nineteenth of December, 1562, the armies met. The enemy had that morning crossed the Eure, and posted himself The battle of with sixteen thousand foot and two thousand horse, Dreux, December 19, and with twenty-two cannon, between two villages 1562. covering his wings, and with the city of Dreux and the village of Tréon behind him as points of refuge in case of defeat. The constable commanded the main body of the army. Guise, to rebut the current charge of being the sole cause of the war, affected to lead only his own company of horse in the right wing, which was under Marshal Saint André. The prince's army was decidedly inferior in numbers; for, although he had four thousand horse,[2] his infantry barely amounted to seven thousand or eight thousand men, and he had only five pieces of artillery. Yet the first movements of the Huguenots were brilliant and effective. Condé, with a body of French horse, fell upon the battalion of Swiss pikes. It was a furious onset, long remembered as one of the most magnificent cavalry charges of the age.[3] Nothing could stand before it. The solid phalanx was pierced through and through, and the German reiters, pouring into the way opened by the French, rode to and fro, making havoc of the brave but defenceless mountaineers. They even penetrated to the rear, and plundered the camp of the enemy, carrying off the plate from Guise's tent. Meanwhile Coligny was even more successful than the prince. With a part of the Huguenot right he attacked and scattered the troops

---

[1] Mém. de Castelnau, liv. iv., c. iv.

[2] Five thousand, according to the Duke d'Aumale (Les Princes de Condé, i. 190).

[3] " Quatre-vingtz salades . . . . lesquels sembloient estre *quatre-vingtz saettes* du ciel ! " Explanation of plan of battle sent by Guise to the king, reprinted in Mém. de Condé, iv. 687.

surrounding his uncle, the constable. In the mêlée Montmorency himself, while fighting with his usual courage, had his jaw fractured by a pistol-shot, and was taken prisoner. But now the tide turned. The Swiss, never for a moment dreaming of retreat or surrender, had promptly recovered from their confusion and closed their ranks. The German infantry, or lansquenets, were brought up to the attack, but first hesitated, and then broke before the terrible array of pikes. D'Andelot, ill with fever, had thus far been forced to remain a mere spectator of the contest. But now, seeing the soldiers whom he had been at such pains to bring to the scene of action in ignominious retreat, he threw himself on his horse and labored with desperation to rally them. His pains were thrown away. The lansquenets continued their course, and D'Andelot, who scarcely escaped falling into the enemy's hands, probably concurred in the verdict pronounced on them by a contemporary historian, that no more cowardly troops had entered the country in fifty years.[1] It was at this moment that the Duke of Guise, who had with difficulty held his impatient horse in reserve on the Roman Catholic right, gave the signal to his company to follow him, and fell upon the French infantry of the Huguenots, imprudently left unprotected by cavalry at some distance in the rear. The move was skilfully planned and well executed. The infantry were routed. Condé, coming to the rescue, was unable to accomplish anything. His horse was killed under him, and, before he could be provided with another, he was taken prisoner by Damville, a son of the constable. The German reiters now proved to be worth little more than the lansquenets. Returning from the pursuit of the fugitives of the constable's division, and perceiving the misfortunes of the infantry, they retired to the cover of a wood, and neither the prayers nor the expostulations of the admiral could prevail on them to face the enemy again that day.[2] But Guise could not follow up his advantage.

---

[1] "Etant chose certaine qu'il n'entra de cinquante ans en France des plus couards hommes que ceux-là, bien qu'ils eussent la plus belle apparence du monde." Hist. ecclés. ii. 144.

[2] It ought perhaps, in justice to the reiters, to be noticed that Coligny attributes their failure not to cowardice, as in the case of both the French

The battle had lasted five hours. Almost the whole of the Huguenot cavalry and the remnants of the infantry had been drawn up by Coligny in good order on the other side of a ravine; and the darkness would not allow the Duke, even had he been so disposed, to renew the engagement.[1]

On either side the loss had been severe. Marshal Saint André, Montbéron—one of the constable's sons—and many other illustrious Roman Catholics, were killed. Montmorency was a prisoner. The Huguenots, if they had lost fewer prominent men and less common soldiers, were equally deprived of their leading general. What was certain was, that the substantial fruits of victory remained in the hands of the Duke of Guise, to whom naturally the whole glory of the achievement was ascribed. For, although Admiral Coligny thought himself sufficiently strong to have attacked the enemy on the following day,[2] if he could have persuaded his crest-fallen German auxiliaries to follow him, he deemed it advisable to abandon the march into Normandy—difficult under any circumstances on account of the lateness of the season—and to conduct his army back to Orleans. This, Coligny—never more skilful than in conducting the most difficult of all military operations, a retreat in the presence of an enemy —successfully accomplished.[3]

---

and the German infantry, but to their not understanding orders, and to the occasional absence of an interpreter.

[1] La Noue in his commentaries (Ed. Mich., c. x., p. 605 seq.) makes some interesting observations on the singular incidents of the battle of Dreux. The author of the Histoire ecclés., ii. 140, and De Thou, iii. 367, criticise both the Roman Catholic and the Protestant generals. They find the former to blame for not waiting to engage the Huguenots until they had reached the rougher country they were approaching, where the superiority of Condé in cavalry would have been of little avail. They censure the latter for leaving his own infantry unprotected, and for attacking the enemy's infantry instead of his cavalry. If this had been routed, the other would have made no further resistance.

[2] He had, according to Beza's letter to Calvin, Dec. 27th (Baum, ii. Appendix, 202), lost only one hundred and fifty of his horsemen; or, according to the Histoire ecclés. (ii. 146), only twenty-seven.

[3] For details of the battle of Dreux, see Hist. ecclés., ii. 140–148; Mém. de Castelnau, liv. ii., c. v.; De Thou, iii. 365, etc.; Pasquier, Lettres (Ed. Feugère), ii. 251–254; Guise's relation, reprinted in Mém. de Condé, iv. 685, etc., and letters subsequently written, ibid. iv. 182, etc.; Coligny's brief account

The first tidings of the battle of Dreux were brought to Paris by fugitives from the constable's corps. These announced the capture of the commanding general, and the entire rout of the Roman Catholic army. The populace, intense in its devotion to the old form of faith, and recognizing the fatal character of such a blow,[1] was overwhelmed with discouragement. But Catharine de' Medici displayed little emotion. " Very well! " she quietly remarked, " *then we shall pray to God in French.*"[2] But the truth was soon known, and the dirge and the *miserere* were rapidly replaced by the loud *Te Deum* and by jubilant processions in honor of the signal success of the Roman Catholic arms.[3]

Recovering from their panic, the Parisian populace continued to testify their unimpeachable orthodoxy by daily murders. It was enough, a contemporary writer tells us, if a boy, seeing a man in the streets, but called out, " Voylà ung Huguenot," for straightway the idle vagabonds, the pedlers, and porters would set upon him with stones. Then came out the handicraftsmen and idle apprentices with swords, and thrust him through with a thousand wounds. His dead body, having been robbed of clothes, was afterward taken possession of by troops of boys, who asked

Riotous conduct of the Parisian mob.

---

written just after the battle, ibid. iv. 178–181 ; the Swiss accounts, Baum, ii. Appendix, 198–202 ; Vieilleville, liv. viii., c. xxxvi. ; Davila, 81, seq. Cf. letter of Catharine, *ubi infra*, and two plans of the engagement, in vol. v. of Mém. de Condé. The Duc d'Aumale gives a good military sketch, i. 189–205.

[1] "Et non sans cause," says Abbé Bruslart ; "d'autant que de ceste bataille despendoit tout l'estat de la religion chrestienne et du royaume." Mém. de Condé, i. 105. A despatch of Smith to the Privy Council, St. Denis, Dec. 20, 1562, gives this first and incorrect account. MS. State Paper Office.

[2] H. Martin, Hist. de France, x. 156. Le Laboureur, ii. 450. Catharine's own account to her minister at Vienna, it is true, is very different. "J'en demeuray près de 24 heures *en une extrême ennuy et fascherie*, et jusques à ce que le S. de Losses arriva par-devers moy, qui fut hier sur les neuf heures du matin." Letter to the Bishop of Rennes, Dec. 23, 1562, *apud* Le Laboureur, Add. aux Mém. de Castelnau, ii. 66–68.

[3] The Council of Trent, on receiving an account of the battle, Dec. 28th, offered solemn thanksgivings. Acta Concil. Trid. *apud* Martene et Durand, Ampl. Coll., t. viii. 1301, 1302 ; Letter of the Card. of Lorraine to the Bishop of Rennes, French ambassador in Germany, *apud* Le Laboureur, Add. aux Mém. de Castelnau, ii. 70.

nothing better than to "trail" him down to the Seine and throw him in. If the victim chanced to be a "town-dweller," the Parisians entered his house and carried off all his goods, and his wife and children were fortunate if they escaped with their lives. With the best intentions, Marshal Montmorency could not put a stop to these excesses; he scarcely succeeded in protecting the households of foreign ambassadors from being involved in the fate of French Protestants.[1] Yet the same men that were ready at any time to imbue their hands in the blood of an innocent Huguenot, were full of commiseration for a Roman Catholic felon. A shrewd murderer is said to have turned to his own advantage the religious feeling of the people who had flocked to see him executed. " Ah! my masters," he exclaimed when already on the fatal ladder, " I must die now for killing a Huguenot who despised our Lady; but as I have served our Lady always truly, and put my trust in her, so I trust now she will show some miracle for me." Thereupon, reports Sir Thomas Smith, the people began to murmur about his having to die for a Huguenot, ran to the gallows, beat the hangman, and having cut the fellow's cords, conveyed him away free.[2]

Of the triumvirs, at whose instigation the war had arisen, one was dead,[3] a second was a prisoner in the hands of the enemy, the third—the Duke of Guise—alone remained. Navarre had died a month before. On the other hand, the Huguenots had lost their chief. Yet the war raged without cessation. As soon as the Duke of Guise had collected his army and had, at Rambouillet, explained to the king and court, who had come out to meet him, the course of recent events, he followed the Admiral toward Orleans. Invested by the king with the supreme command during the captivity of the constable, and leading a victorious army, he speedily reduced Étampes and Pithiviers, cap-

---

[1] Sir Thomas Smith to Cecil, February 4, 1563, State Paper Office.

[2] Same to same, February 26, 1563, State Paper Office.

[3] For Marshal Saint André, who had once gravely suggested in the council the propriety of sewing the queen mother up in a bag and throwing her into the river, it is understood that the Medici shed few tears. Brantôme and Le Laboureur, Add. aux Mém. de Castelnau, ii. 81. The marshal had been shot by a victim whom he had deprived of his possessions by confiscation. Ibid., *ubi supra.*

tured by Condé on his march to Paris.   Meantime, Coligny had
taken a number of places in the vicinity of Orleans, and his
"black riders" had become the terror of the papists of Sologne.[1]
Orleans in- Not long after Guise's approach, fearing that his de-
vested.   sign was to besiege the city of Orleans, Coligny threw
himself into it.   His stay was not long, however.   His German
cavalry could do nothing in case of a siege, and would only be a
burden to the citizens.   Besides, he was in want of funds to
pay them.   He resolved, therefore, to strike boldly for Normandy.[2]   Having persuaded the reiters to dispense with their
heavy baggage-wagons,[3] which had proved so great an incum-
Coligny   brance on the previous march, he started from Orleans
returns to   on the first of February with four thousand troopers,
Normandy.   leaving his brother D'Andelot as well furnished as
practicable to sustain the inevitable siege.   The lightness of his
army's equipment precluded the possibility of pursuit; its
strength secured it an almost undisputed passage.[4]   In a few
days it had passed Dreux and the scene of the late battle, and
at Dives, on the opposite side of the estuary of the Seine from
Havre, had received from the English the supplies of money
which they had long been desirous of finding means to convey

---

[1] "Black devils," Guise calls them in a letter of Jan. 17th.   "M. de Châtillon et ces diables noirs sont à Jerjuau."   Mém. de Guise, 502.

[2] Coligny had notified the English court of his intention early in January,
and Cecil entertained high hopes of the result : "A gentleman is arryved at
Rye, sent from the Admyrall Chastillion, who assureth his purpose to prosecute the cause of God and of his contrey, and meaneth to joyne with our
power in Normandy, which I trust shall make a spedy end of the whole."
Letter to Sir T. Smith, January 14th, Wright, Q. Eliz., i. 121.

[3] How important a matter this was, may be inferred from the fact that the
Admiral took pains to dwell upon it, in a letter to Queen Elizabeth, written
two or three days before his departure : "Advisant au reste vostre Majésté,
Madame, que j'ay faict condescendre les reistres a laisser tous leur bagages
et empechemens en ceste ville (chose non auparavant ouye): de sorte que dedans le dix ou douziesme de ce moys de Febvrier prochain au plus tard, avec
l'aide de Dieu, nous serons bien prez du Havre de Grace," etc.   Letter from
Orleans, Jan. 29, 1563, Forbes, ii. 319.

[4] "En cest equipage, nous faisions telle diligence, que souvent nous préve-
nions la renommée de nous mesmes en plusieurs lieux où nous arrivions."
Mém. de la Noue, c. xi.   La Noue states the force at two thousand reiters,
five hundred French horse, and one thousand mounted arquebusiers.

to the Huguenots.[1] The only considerable forces of the Guise
faction in Normandy were on the banks of the river, too busy
watching the English at Havre to be able to spare any troops to
resist Coligny. Turning his attention to the western shores of
the province, he soon succeeded in reducing Pont-l'Evêque, Caen,
Bayeux, Saint Lo, and the prospect was brilliant of his soon being able, in conjunction with Queen Elizabeth's troops, to bring
all Normandy over to the side of the prince.[2] Meanwhile, however, there were occurring in the centre of the kingdom events
destined to give an entirely different turn to the relations of the
Huguenots and papists in France. To these we must now direct
our attention.

François de Guise, relieved of the admiral's presence, had
begun the siege of Orleans four days after the departure of the
latter for Normandy (on the fifth of February), and manifested
the utmost determination to destroy the capital city, as it might
be regarded, of the confederates. Indeed, when the court, then
sojourning at Blois, in alarm at the reports sent by Marshal de
Brissac from Rouen, respecting Coligny's conquests and his
own impotence to oppose him, ordered Guise to abandon his
undertaking and employ his forces in crushing out the flames
that had so unexpectedly broken forth in Normandy, the duke
declined to obey until he should have received further orders,
and gave so cogent reasons for pursuing the siege, that the king
and his council willingly acquiesced in his plan.[3] From his independent attitude, however, it is evident that Guise was of
Pasquier's mind, and believed he had gained as much of a
victory in the capture of the constable, his friend in arms, but
dangerous rival at court, taken by the Huguenots at Dreux, as

---

[1] "The 8th of that moneth" (February), says Stow, "the said Admirall
came before Hunflew with six thousand horsemen, reisters and others of his
owne retinues, beside footmen, and one hundred horsemen of the countries
thereabout, and about sixe of the clocke at night, there was a great peale of
ordinance shot off at Newhaven (Havre) for a welcome to the sayd Admirall."
Annals (London, 1631), 653. The passage is inaccurately quoted by Wright,
Queen Eliz., i. 125, note.

[2] Hist. des égl. réf., ii. 156, 157; Mém. de Castelnau, liv. iv., c. vii. and
viii.

[3] Mém. de Castelnau, liv. iv., c. ix.

by the capture of the Prince of Condé, his enemy, who had fallen into his hands in the same engagement.[1]

The city of Orleans, on the north bank of the Loire, was protected by walls originally of no great worth, but considerably strengthened since the outbreak of the civil war. On the oppo-

Capture of site side of the river, a suburb, known as the *Porte-*
the Portereau. *reau*, was fortified by weaker walls, in front of which two large bastions had recently been erected. The suburb was connected with Orleans by means of a bridge across the Loire, of which the end toward the Portereau was defended by two towers of the old mediæval construction, known as the "tourelles," and that toward the city by the city wall and a large square tower.[2] Against the Portereau the duke directed the first assault, hoping easily to become master of it, and thence attack the city from its weakest side. His plan proved successful beyond his expectations. While making a feint of assailing with his whole army the bastion held by the Gascon infantry, he sent a party to scale the bastion guarded by the German lansquenets, who, being taken by surprise, yielded an entrance almost without striking a blow. In a few minutes the Portereau was in the hands of Guise, and the bridge was crowded with fugitives tumultuously seeking a refuge in the city. Orleans itself was nearly involved in the fate of its suburb; for the enemy, following close upon the heels of the fleeing host, was at the very threshold of the "tourelles," when D'Andelot, called from his sick-bed by the tumult, posting himself at the entrance with a few gentlemen in full armor, by hard blows beat back the troops, already sanguine of complete success.[3] A few days later the "tourelles" themselves were scaled and taken.[4]

After so poor a beginning, the small garrison of Orleans had sufficient reason to fear the issue of the trial to which they

---

[1] Œuvres (Ed. Feugère), ii. 254; and again, ii. 257.

[2] Davila, bk. iii., p. 85.

[3] Castelnau (liv. iv., c. ix.), who was present, gives a less graphic account than Davila (bk. iii., pp. 85, 86), who was not. Hist. ecclés. des égl. réf., ii. 159–161; La Noue, c. xi. 607–609.

[4] Feb. 9th—the day before Sir Thomas Smith reached Blois. Letter to Privy Council, Feb. 17, 1563, State Paper Office; Hist. ecclés. des égl. réf., ii. 160.

were subjected. But, so far from abandoning their courage, they applied themselves with equal assiduity to their religious and to their military duties. "In addition to the usual sermons and the prayers at the guard-houses, public extraordinary prayers were made at six o'clock in the morning; at the close of which the ministers and the entire people, without exception, betook themselves to work with all their might upon the fortifications, until four in the evening, when every one again attended prayers." Everywhere the utmost devotion was manifested, women of all ranks sharing with their husbands and brothers in the toils of the day, or, if too feeble for these active exertions, spending their time in tending the sick and wounded.[1]

Not only did the Huguenots, when they found their supply of lead falling short, make their cannon-balls of bell-metal—of which the churches and monasteries were doubtless the source—and of brass, but they turned this last material to a use till now, it would appear, unheard of. "I have learned this day, the fifteenth instant, of the Spaniards," wrote the English ambassador from the royal court, which was at a safe distance, in the city of Blois, "that they of Orleans shoot brass which is hollow, and so devised within that when it falls it opens and breaks into many pieces with a great fire, and hurts and kills all who are about it. Which is a new device and very terrible, for it pierces the house first, and breaks at the last rebound. Every man in Portereau is fain to run away, they cannot tell whither, when they see where the shot falls."[2]

"A new and very terrible device."

It could not, however, be denied that there was much reason for discouragement in the general condition of the Protestant cause throughout the country. Of the places so brilliantly acquired in the spring of the preceding year, the greater part had been lost. Normandy and Langue-

Huguenot reverses.

---

[1] Hist. ecclés. des égl. réf., ii. 162.

[2] Sir Thomas Smith to the Privy Council, Feb. 15th and 17th, 1563, State Paper Office, Calendar, pp. 138, 141. It is now known, of course, that *bombs* had been occasionally used long before 1563, by the Arabs in Spain, and others. But this kind of missile was practically a novelty, and was not adopted in ordinary warfare till near a century later.

doc were the only bright spots on the map of France. Lyons still remained in the power of the Huguenots, in the southeast; but, though repeated assaults of the Duke of Nemours had been repulsed, it was threatened with a siege, for which it was but indifferently prepared.[1] Des Adrets, the fierce chieftain of the lower Rhône, had recently revealed his real character more clearly by betraying the cause he had sullied by his barbarous advocacy, and was now in confinement.[2] Indeed, everything seemed to point to a speedy and complete overthrow of an undertaking which had cost so much labor and suffering,[3] when an unexpected event produced an entire revolution in the

---

[1] It was at a most trying moment—when M. de Soubise, the Protestant governor, found that only two weeks' provisions remained in the city, and therefore felt compelled to issue an order to force some 7,000 non-combatants—women, children, and the poor—to leave Lyons, that Viret, the Huguenot pastor, had an opportunity to display the great ascendency which his eminent piety and discretion had secured him over all ranks in society. According to the newly published Memoirs of Soubise, Viret boldly remonstrated against an act which was equivalent to a surrender of thousands of defenceless persons to certain butchery, and declared that the ordinary rules of military necessity did not apply to a war like this, "in which the poorest has an interest, since we are fighting for the liberty of our consciences," adding his own assurance that help would come from some other quarter. Finally the governor yielded, saying : " Even should it turn out ill and my reputation suffer, as though I had not done my duty as a captain, yet, at your word, I will do as you ask, being well assured that God will bless my act." Bulletin, xxiii. (1874), 497. It will be remembered that Pierre Viret had been the able coadjutor of Farel in the reformation of Geneva, twenty-eight years before. The siege of Lyons was made the subject of a lengthy song by Antoine Du Plain (reprinted in the Chansonnier Huguenot, 220 seq.), containing not a few historical data of importance.

[2] " Nous venons maintenans d'estre advertyz de Lion par M. de Soubize, comme le Baron des Adrez, ayant esté practiqué par M. de Nemours, avoit comploté de faire entrer quelque gendarmerie et gens de pied de M. de Nemours dedans Rommans, ville du Daulphiné : dont il a esté empesché par le sieur de Mouvans, et par la noblesse du pays ; qui se sont saisiz de sa personne, et le ont mené prisonnier à Valence, pour le envoyer en Languedoc devers mon frere, naguères cardinal de Chastillon, et Monsieur de Crussol (qui ont presque delivré tout le dict pays de Languedoc de la tyrannie des ennemys de Dieu et du Roy) a fin de le faire punir, et servir d'exemple aux autres deserteurs de Dieu, de leur debvoir, et de la patrie." Admiral Coligny to Queen Elizabeth, Orleans, January 29, 156⅔, Forbes, ii. 320.

[3] The gloomy picture is painted by Henri Martin, x. 158, etc.

THE FIRST CIVIL WAR.

attitnde of the contending parties and in the purposes of the leaders.

This event was the assassination of François de Guise. On the evening of the eighteenth of February, 1563, in company with a gentleman or two, he was riding the round of his works, and arranging for a general attack on the morrow. So confident did he feel of success, that he had that morning written to the queen mother, it is said, that within twenty-four hours he would send her news of the capture of Orleans, and that he intended to destroy the entire population, making no discrimination of age or sex, that the very memory of the rebellious city might be obliterated.[1] At a lonely spot on the road, a man on horseback, who had been lying in wait for him, suddenly made his appearance, and, after discharging a pistol at him from behind, rode rapidly off, before the duke's escort, taken up with the duty of assisting him, had had time to make any attempt to apprehend the assassin. Three balls, with which the pistol was loaded, had lodged in Guise's shoulder, and the wound, from the first considered dangerous, proved mortal within six days. The murderer had apparently made good his escape; but a strange fatality seemed to attend him. During the darkness he became so confused that, after riding all night, he found himself almost at the very place where the deed of blood had been committed, and was compelled to rest himself and his jaded horse at a house, where he was arrested on suspicion by some of Guise's soldiers. Taken before their superior officers, he boldly avowed his guilt, and boasted of what he had done. His name he gave as Jean Poltrot, and he claimed to be lord of Mérey, in Angoumois; but he was better known, from his dark complexion and his familiarity with the Spanish language, by the sobriquet of " L'Espagnolet."

Assassination of François de Guise.

---

[1] This statement does not rest upon any documentary proof that I am aware of. It is, however, vouched for by the Hist. ecclés. des égl. réf., ii. 162. Moreover, Admiral Coligny, in his later defence, expressly states, " on the testimony of men worthy of belief," that Guise "was accustomed to boast that, on the capture of the city, he would spare none of the inhabitants, and that no respect would be paid to age or sex." Jean de Serres, iii. 29; Mém. de Condé, iv. 348.

He was an excitable, melancholy man, whose mind, continually brooding over the wrongs his country and faith had experienced at the hands of Guise, had imbibed the fanatical notion that it was his special calling of God to rid the world of "the butcher of Vassy," of the single execrable head that was accountable for the torrents of blood which had for a year been flowing in every part of France.

After having been a page of M. d'Aubeterre, father-in-law of the Huguenot leader Soubise, Mérey, at the beginning of the civil war, had been sent by the daughter of D'Aubeterre to her husband, then with Condé at Orleans. Subsequently he had accompanied Soubise on his adventurous ride with a few followers from Orleans to Lyons, when the latter assumed command in behalf of the Huguenots. Soubise appears to have valued him highly as one of those reckless youths that court rather than shun personal peril, while he shared the common impression that the lad was little better than a fool. True, for years—ever since the tumult of Amboise, where his kinsman, La Renaudie and another relative had been killed—Mérey had been constantly boasting to all whom he met that he would kill the Duke of Guise; but those who heard him "made no more account of his words than if he had boasted of his intention to obtain the imperial crown."[1]

He had given expression to his purpose at Lyons, in the presence of M. de Soubise, the Huguenot governor, and again to Admiral Coligny before he started on his expedition to Normandy. But the Huguenot generals evidently imagined that there was nothing in the speech beyond the prating of a silly braggart. Soubise, indeed, advised him to attend to his own duties, and to leave the deliverance of France to Almighty God; but neither the admiral nor the soldiers, to whom he often repeated the threat, paid any attention to it. In short, he was regarded as one of those frivolous characters, of whom there is an abundance in every camp, who expect to acquire a cheap notoriety by extravagant stories of their past or prospective achievements, but never succeed in earning more,

---

[1] Mém. de Soubise, Bulletin, xxiii. (1874) 499.

with all their pains, than the contempt or incredulity of their listeners. Still, Poltrot was a man of some value as a scout, and Coligny had employed him [1] for the purpose of obtaining information respecting the enemy's movements, and had furnished him at one time with twenty crowns to defray his expenses, at another with a hundred, to procure himself a horse. The spy had made his way to the Roman Catholic camp, and, by pretending to follow the example of others in renouncing his Huguenot associations, had conciliated the duke's favor to such an extent that he excited no suspicion before the commission of the treacherous act.

But, if Poltrot was a fanatic, he was not of the stuff of which martyrs are made. When questioned in the presence of the queen and council to discover his accomplices, his constancy wholly forsook him, and he said whatever was suggested. In particular he accused the admiral of having paid him to execute the deed, and Beza of having instigated him by holding forth the rewards of another world. La Rochefoucauld, Soubise, and others were criminated to a minor degree. During his confinement in the prisons of the Parisian parliament, to which he was removed, he continually contradicted himself. But his weakness did not save him. He was condemned to be burned with red-hot pincers, to be torn asunder by four horses, and to be quartered. Before the execution of this frightful sentence, he was, by order of the court, put to torture. But, instead of reiterating his former accusations, he retracted almost every point. [2] To purchase a few moments' reprieve, he

Execution of Poltrot.

---

[1] Not without some hesitation, however. So little confidence in his good judgment did his frivolous appearance inspire, that Coligny observed: "I would not trust him, without knowing him better than I do, had not Monsieur de Soubise sent him to me." Mém. de Soubise, Bulletin, xxiii. (1874) 502.

[2] The Procès verbal of Poltrot's examination just before his death, March 18th, is inserted in the Hist. ecclés. des égl. réf., ii. 187–198. In this he declares that his first testimony was *false* and extorted by the fear of death, and exculpates Soubise, Beza, Coligny, etc., from having instigated him. He says that when put to torture he will say anything the questioners want him to. Accordingly, when so tortured, he accuses them, and when released a moment after the horses have begun to rend him in pieces, he conjures up a plot of the Huguenots to sack Paris, etc. May it not properly be asked, what such

sought an interview with the first president of the parliament, Christopher de Thou; and we have it upon the authority of that magistrate's son, the author of an imperishable history of his times, that, entering into greater detail, Poltrot persisted constantly in exculpating Soubise, Coligny, and Beza. A few minutes later, beside himself with terror and not knowing what he said in his delirium, he declared the admiral to be innocent; then, at the very moment of execution, he accused not only him, but his brother, D'Andelot, of whom he had said little or nothing before.[1]

Coligny heard in Normandy the report of the atrocious charges that had been wrung from Poltrot. Copies of the assassin's confession were industriously circulated in the camp, and he thus became acquainted with the particulars of the accusation. With Beza and La Rochefoucauld, who were with him at Caen, he published, on the twelfth of March, a long and dignified defence. The reformer for himself declared, that, although he had more than once seen persons illdisposed toward the Duke of Guise because of the murders perpetrated by him at Vassy, he had never been in favor of proceeding against him otherwise than by the ordinary methods of law. For this reason he had gone to Monceaux to solicit justice of Charles, of his mother, and of the King of Navarre. But the hopes which the queen mother's gracious answer had excited were dashed to the earth by Guise's violent resort to arms. Holding the duke to be the chief author and promoter of the present troubles, he admitted that he had a countless number of times prayed to God that He would either change his heart or rid the kingdom of him. But he appealed to the testimony of Madame de Ferrare (Renée de France, the mother-in-law of Guise), and all who had ever heard him, when he said

Beza and Coligny are accused, but vindicate themselves.

---

testimony as this is worth? For or against Coligny, volumes of it would not affect his character in our estimation.

[1] The direct testimony of Jacques Auguste de Thou, on a matter with which he was evidently intimately acquainted through his father, is unimpeachable, and will outweigh with every unprejudiced mind all the stories of Davila, Castelnau, etc., founded on mere report. De Thou, Histoire univ. (liv. xxxiv.), iii. 403.

that never had he publicly mentioned the duke by name. As for Poltrot himself, he had never met him.

The admiral himself was not less frank. Ever since the massacre of Vassy he had regarded Guise and his party as common enemies of God, of the king, and of the public tranquillity; but never, upon his life and his honor, had he approved of such attacks as that of Poltrot. Indeed, he had steadfastly employed his influence to deter men from executing any plots against the life of the duke; until, being duly informed that Guise and Saint André had incited men to undertake to assassinate Condé, D'Andelot, and himself, he had desisted from expressing his opposition. The different articles of the confession he proceeded to answer one by one; and he forwarded his reply to the court with a letter to Catharine de' Medici, in which he earnestly entreated her that the life of Poltrot might be spared until the restoration of peace, that he might be confronted with him, and an investigation be made of the entire matter before unsuspected judges. "But do not imagine," he added, "that I speak thus because of any regret for the death of the Duke of Guise, which I esteem the greatest of blessings to the realm, to the Church of God, to myself and my family, and, if improved, the means of giving rest to the kingdom." [1]

The admiral's frankness was severely criticised by some of his friends. He was advised to suppress those expressions that were liable to be perverted to his injury, but he declared his resolution to abide by the consequences of a clear statement of the truth. And indeed, while the worldly wisdom of Coligny's censors has received a species of justification in the avidity with which his sincere avowals have been employed as the basis of graver accusations which he repelled, the candor of his defence has set upon his words the indelible impress of veracity which following ages can never fail to read aright. That Catharine recognized his innocence is evident from the very

---

[1] Poltrot's pretended confession of Feb. 26th, at Camp Saint Hilaire, near Saint Mesmin, with the replies signed by Coligny, la Rochefoucauld, and Beza to each separate article, is inserted in full in Mém. de Condé, iv. 285–303, and the Hist. ecclés. des égl. réf., ii. 176–186. Coligny's letter to Catharine, ibid., ii. 186, 187, Mém. de Condé, iv. 303.

act by which she endeavored to make him appear guilty. He had begged that Poltrot might be spared till after the conclusion of peace, that he might himself have an opportunity to vindicate his innocence by confronting him in the presence of impartial judges. It was Catharine's interest, she thought, to confirm her own power by attaching a stigma to the honor of the Châtillons, and so depriving them of much of their influence in the state.[1] Accordingly, on Thursday, the eighteenth of March, Poltrot was put to death and his mouth sealed forever to further explanations. *The next day the Edict of Pacification was signed at Amboise.*[2] After all, it is evident that Coligny's innocence or guilt, in this particular instance, must be judged by his entire course and his well-known character. If his life bears marks of perfidy and duplicity, if the blood of the innocent can be found upon his skirts, then must the verdict of posterity be against him. But if the careful examination of his entire public life, as well as the history of his private relations, reveals a character not only above reproach, but the purest, most beneficent, and most patriotic of all that France can boast in political stations in the sixteenth century, the confused and contradictory allegations of an enthusiast who had not counted the cost of his daring attempt—allegations wrung from him by threats and torture—will not be allowed to weigh for an instant against Coligny's simple denial.[3]

---

[1] That Catharine de' Medici was no very sincere mourner for Guise is sufficiently certain ; and it is well known that there were those who believed her to have instigated his murder (See Mém. de Tavannes, Pet. ed., ii. 394). This is not surprising when we recall the fact that almost every great crime or casualty that occurred in France, for the space of a generation, was ascribed to her evil influence. Still the Viscount de Tavannes makes too great a draft upon our credulity, when he pretends that she made a frank admission of guilt to his father. " Depuis, au voyage de Bayonne, passant par Dijon, elle dit au sieur de Tavannes: ' Ceux de Guise se vouloient faire roys, je les en ay bien gardé devant Orléans.' " The expression " devant Orléans " can hardly be tortured into a reference to anything else than Guise's assassination.

[2] I entirely agree with Prof. Baum (Theodor Beza, ii. 719) in regarding " this single circumstance as more than sufficient to demonstrate both the innocence of Coligny and his associates, and the consciously guilty fabrication of the accusations."

[3] Besides the authorities already referred to, the Journal of Bruslart, Mém.

Of the Duke of Guise the estimates formed by his contemporaries differed as widely as their political and religious views.
With the Abbé Bruslart he was "the most virtuous,
heroic, and magnanimous prince in Europe, who for
his courage was dreaded by all foreign nations." To
the author of the history of the reformed churches his ambition and presumption seemed to have obscured all his virtues.[1]
The Roman Catholic preachers regarded his death as a stupendous calamity, a mystery of Divine providence, which they
could only interpret by supposing that the Almighty, jealous of
the confidence which His people reposed rather in His creature
than in Himself, had removed the Duke of Guise in order to
take the cause of His own divinity, of His spouse the Church, of
the king and kingdom, under His own protection.[2] The Bishop
of Riez wrote and published a highly colored account of the
duke's last words and actions, in the most approved style of
such posthumous records, and introduced edifying specimens
of a theological learning, which, until the moment of his
wounding, Guise had certainly never possessed, making him, of
course, persist to the end in protesting his innocence of the
guilt of Vassy.[3] The Protestants, while giving him credit for
some compunctions of conscience for his persecuting career, and
willingly admitting that, but for his pernicious brother, the
Cardinal of Lorraine, he might have run a far different course,
were compelled to view his death as a great blessing to France.[4]

Various esti-
mates of
Guise.

---

de Condé, i. 123, 124; Davila, bk. iii. 86, 87; Claude Haton, i. 322, etc.;
J. de Serres, ii. 343-345; and Pasquier, Lettres (Œuvres choisies), ii. 258,
may be consulted with advantage.   Prof. Baum's account is, as usual, vivid,
accurate, and instructive (Theodor Beza, ii. 706, etc.).   Varillas, Anquetil, etc.,
are scarcely worth examining.   There is the ordinary amount of blundering
about the simplest matters of chronology.   Davila places the wounding of
Guise on the 24th of February, his death three days later, etc.

[1] Mém. de Condé, i. 124; Hist. ecclés. des égl. réf., ii. 164.

[2] Claude Haton, i. 325, 326.

[3] See Riez's letter to the king, reprinted in Mém. de Condé, iv. 243-265, and
in Cimber and Danjou's invaluable collection of contemporary pamphlets and
documents, v. 171-204; Hist. ecclés. des égl. réf., ii. 164.

[4] Hist. ecclés. des égl. réf. *ubi supra.*   There is extant an affecting letter
from the aged Renée of Ferrara to Calvin, in which she complains with deep
feeling of the reformed, and especially their preachers, for the severity with

A famous incident, illustrating the perils to which the Huguenots of the central provinces were subjected during the siege, is too characteristic to be passed over in silence.　More than once, in the course of the war, the town and castle of Montargis, the Duchess of Ferrara's residence, had been threatened on account of the asylum it afforded to defenceless Protestants flocking thither from all quarters.　When the minds of the Roman Catholics had become exasperated by nine or ten months of civil war, they formed a settled determination to break up this "nest of Huguenots."　Accordingly the Baron de la Garde—Captain Poulain, of Mérindol memory—brought an order, in the king's name, from the Duke of Guise, at that time before the walls of Orleans, commanding Renée to leave Montargis, which had become important for military purposes, and to take up her abode at Fontainebleau, St. Germain,

Renée de France at Montargis.

---

which even after his death they attacked the memory of her son-in-law, and even spoke of his eternal condemnation as an ascertained fact.　"I know," she said, "that he was a persecutor; but I do not know, nor, to speak freely, do I believe that he was reprobated of God; for he gave signs to the contrary before his death.　But they want this not to be mentioned, and they desire to shut the mouths of those who know it."　Cimber et Danjou, v. 399, etc.　Calvin's reply of the 24th of January, 1564, is admirable for its kind, yet firm tone (Bonnet, Lettres franç. de Calvin, ii. 550, etc., Calvin's Letters, Am. edit., iv. 352, etc.).　He freely condemned the beatification of the King of Navarre, while the Duke of Guise was consigned to perdition.　The former was an apostate; the latter an open enemy of the truth of the Gospel from the very beginning.　Indeed, to pronounce upon the doom of a fellow-sinner was both rash and presumptuous, for there is but one Judge before whose seat we all must give account.　Yet, in condemning the authors of the horrible troubles that had befallen France, and which all God's children had felt scarcely less poignantly than Renée herself, sprung though she was from the royal stock, it was impossible not to condemn the duke "who had kindled the fire."　Yea, for himself, although he had always prayed God to show Guise mercy, the reformer avowed, in almost the very words of Beza, that he had often desired that God would lay His hand upon the duke to free His Church of him, unless He would convert him.　"And yet I can protest," he added, "that but for me, before the war, active and energetic men would have exerted themselves to destroy him from the face of the earth, whom my sole exhortation restrained."

Some of the composers of Huguenot ballads were bitter enough in their references to Guise's death and pompous funeral; see, among others, the songs in the Chansonnier Huguenot, pp. 253 and 257.

or Vincennes. The duchess replied that it was idle to say that so weak a place as Montargis could, without extensive repairs, be of any military importance; and that to remove to any place in the vicinity of Paris would be to expose herself to assassination by the fanatical populace. She therefore sent Poulain back to the king for further instructions. Meantime, Poulain was followed by Malicorne, a creature of the duke's, at the head of some partisan troops. This presumptuous officer had the impertinence to demand the immediate surrender of the castle, and went so far as to threaten to turn some cannon against it, in case of her refusal. But he little understood the virile courage of the woman with whom he had to do. "Malicorne," she answered him, "take care what you undertake. There is not a man in this kingdom that can command me but the king. If you attempt what you threaten, I shall place myself first upon the breach, that I may find out whether you will be audacious enough to kill a king's daughter. Moreover, I am not so ill-connected, nor so little loved, but that I have the means of making the punishment of your temerity felt by you and your offspring, even to the very babes in the cradle." The upstart captain was not prepared for such a reception, and, after alleging his commission as the excuse for the insolence of his conduct, delayed an enterprise which the wound and subsequent death of Guise entirely broke off.[1] Montargis continued during this and the next civil wars to be a safe refuge for thousands of distressed Protestants.

A great obstacle to the conclusion of peace was removed by

---

[1] Hist. ecclés. des égl. réf., ii. 285, 286. The story is well told in Memorials of Renée of France, 215-217. De Thou (liv. xxx.), iii. 179, has incorrectly placed this occurrence among the events of the first months of the war. During the second war Brantôme once stopped to pay his respects to Renée, and saw in the castle over 300 Huguenots that had fled there for security. In a letter of May 10, 1563, Calvin speaks of her as "the nursing mother of the poor saints driven out of their homes and knowing not whither to go," and as having made her castle what a princess looking only to this world would regard almost an insult to have it called—"God's hostelry" or "hospital" (ung hostel-Dieu). God had, as it were, called upon her by these trials to pay arrears for the timidity of her younger days. Lettres franç., ii. 514 (Amer trans., iv. 314).

Guise's death. There was no one in the Roman Catholic camp to take his place. The panegyric pronounced upon the duke by the English ambassador, Sir Thomas Smith, may perhaps be esteemed somewhat extravagant, but has at least the merit of coming from one whose sympathies were decidedly adverse to him. " The papists have lost their greatest stay, hope, and comfort. Many noblemen and gentlemen did follow the camp and that faction, rather for the love of him than for any other zeal or affection. He was indeed the best captain or general in all France, some will say in all Christendom ; for he had all the properties which belong [to], or are to be wished in a general : a ready wit and well advised, a body to endure pains, a courage to forsake no dangerous adventures, use and experience to conduct any army, much courtesy in entertaining of all men, great eloquence to utter all his mind. And he was very liberal both of money and honor to young gentlemen, captains, and soldiers ; whereby he gat so much love and admiration amongst the nobility and the soldiers in France, that I think, now he is gone, many gentlemen will forsake the camp; and they begin to drop away already. Then he was so earnest and so fully persuaded in his religion, that he thought nothing evil done that maintained that sect ; and therefore the papists again thought nothing evil bestowed upon him ; all their money and treasure of the Church, part of their lands, even the honor of the crown of France, they could have found in their hearts to have given him. And so all their joy, hope, and comfort one little stroke of a pistolet hath taken away ! Such a vanity God can show men's hope to be, when it pleaseth Him." [1]

Of the four generals on the Roman Catholic side under whose auspices the war began, three were dead and the fourth was in captivity. The treasury was exhausted. The interest of old debts was left unpaid ; new debts had been contracted.

---

[1] Despatch to the queen, Blois, February 26, 156⅔, Forbes, State Papers, ii. 340. "Of the thre things that did let this realme to come to unity and accorde," adds Smith, "I take th' one to be taken away. How th' other two wil be now salved—th' one that the papists may relent somwhat of their pertinacie, and the Protestants have som affiaunce or trust in there doengs, and so th' one live with th' other in quiet, I do not yet se."

Less than half the king's revenues were available on account of the places which the Huguenots held or threatened. The alienation of one hundred thousand livres of income from ecclesiastical property had been recently ordered, greatly to the annoyance of the clergy. The admiral's progress had of late been so rapid that but two or three important places of lower Normandy remained in friendly hands. After the reduction of these he would move down through Maine and Anjou to Orleans, with a better force than had been marshalled at Dreux;[1] the English would gain such a foothold on French soil as it would be difficult to induce them to relinquish. And where could competent generals be secured for the prosecution of hostilities? The post of lieutenant-general, now vacant, had, indeed, been offered to the Duke Christopher of Würtemberg; but what prospect was there that a Protestant would consent to conduct a war against Protestants?[2]

Catharine was urgent for an immediate conclusion of peace. For the purpose of fixing its conditions, Condé was brought, Deliberations for peace. under a strong guard, to the camp of the army before Orleans, and, on the small "Isle aux Bouviers" in the middle of the Loire, he and the constable, released on their honor, held a preliminary interview on Sunday, the seventh of March, 1563.[3] At first there seemed little prospect of harmonizing their discordant pretensions; for, if the question of the removal of the triumvirs had lost all its practical importance, the old bone of contention remained in the re-establishment of the Edict of January. On this point Montmorency was inflexible. He had been the prime instrument in expelling Prot-

---

[1] Mém. de Castelnau, liv. iv., c. xii. ; Davila, bk. iii. 88; Journal de Bruslart, Mém. de Condé, i. 124; Letter of Catharine to Gonnor, March 3d, ibid., iv. 278; Hist. ecclés., ii. 200.

[2] Rascalon, Catharine's agent, proffered the dignity in a letter of the 13th of March, and the duke declined it on the 17th of the same month. At the same time he gave some wholesome advice respecting the observance of the Edict, etc. Hist. ecclés., ii. 165-168.

[3] "La Royne . . . y a si vivement procedé, que ayant ordonné que sur la foy de l'un et de l'autre nous nous entreveorions en l'Isle aux Bouviers, joignant presque les murs de ceste ville, dimenche dernier cela fut executé." Condé to Sir Thomas Smith, Orleans, March 11, 1463, Forbes, ii. 355.

estantism from Paris, and had distinguished himself by burning the places of worship. It could hardly be expected that he should rebuild what he had so laboriously torn down. And, whatever had been his first intentions, Condé proved less tenacious than might have been anticipated from his previous professions. The fact was, that the younger Bourbon was not proof against the wiles employed with so much success against his elder brother. Flattered by Catharine, he was led to suppose that after all it made little difference whether the full demands of the Huguenots were expressly granted in the edict of pacification or not. The queen mother was resolved, so he was assured, to confer upon him the dignity and office of lieutenant-general, left vacant by Navarre's death. When this should be his, it would be easy to obtain every practical concession to which the Huguenots were entitled. So much pleased was the court with the ardor he displayed, that he was at last permitted to go to Orleans on his own princely parole, in order to consult his confederates.

The Huguenot ministers whose advice he first asked, seeing his irresolution, were the more decided in opposing any terms that did not expressly recognize the Edict of January. Seventy-two united in a letter (on the ninth of March, 1563), in which they begged him not to permit the cause to suffer disaster at his hands, and rather to insure an extension, than submit to an abridgment of the liberty promised by the royal ordinance.[1] From the ministers, however, Condé went to the Huguenot "noblesse," with whom his arguments of expediency had more weight, and who, weary of the length and privations of the war, and content with securing their own privileges, readily accepted the conditions reprobated by the ministers. The pacification was accordingly agreed upon, on the twelfth of March, and

---

[1] Hist. ecclés. des égl. réf., ii. 170, 171. Coupled with demands for the restitution of the edict without restriction or modification, the prohibition of insults, the protection of the churches, the permission to hold synods, the recognition of Protestant marriages, and that the religion be no longer styled "new," "inasmuch as it is founded on the ancient teaching of the Prophets and Apostles," we find the Huguenot ministers, true to the spirit of the age, insisting upon "the rigorous punishment of all Atheists, Libertines, Anabaptists, Servetists, and other heretics and schismatics."

officially published in the form of a royal edict, dated at Amboise, on the nineteenth of March, 1563.

Charles the Ninth, by advice of his mother, the Cardinal of Bourbon, the Princes of Condé and La Roche-sur-Yon, the Dukes of Montmorency, Aumale, and Montpensier, and other members of his privy council, grants, in this document, to all barons, châtellains, and gentlemen possessed of the right to administer " haute justice," permission to celebrate in their own houses the worship of "the religion which they call reformed" in the presence of their families and retainers. The possessors of minor fiefs could enjoy the same privilege, but it extended to their families only. In every bailiwick or sénéchaussée, the Protestants should, on petition, receive one city in whose suburbs their religious services might be held, and in all cities where the Protestant religion was exercised on the seventh of March of the present year, it should continue in one or two places *inside* of the walls, to be designated hereafter by the king. The Huguenots, while secured in their liberty of conscience, were to restore all churches and ecclesiastical property which they might have seized, and were forbidden to worship according to their rites in the city of Paris or its immediate neighborhood. The remaining articles of the peace were of a more personal or temporary interest. Foreign troops were to be speedily dismissed; the Protestant lords to be fully reinstated in their former honors, offices, and possessions; prisoners to be released; insults based upon the events of the war to be summarily punished. And Charles declared that he held his good cousin, the Prince of Condé, and all the other lords, knights, gentlemen, and burgesses that had served under him, to be his faithful subjects, believing that what they had done was for good ends and for his service.[1]

Such was the Edict of Amboise—a half-way measure, very different from that which was desired on either side. The English ambassador declared he could find no one, whether Protestant or

Edict of Pacication, March 12, 1563.

---

[1] The text of the edict of Amboise is given by Isambert, Recueil des anc. lois franç., xiv. 135–140 ; J. de Serres, ii. 347–357 ; Hist. ecclés. des égl. réf., ii. 172–176 ; Agrippa d'Aubigné, i. (liv. iii.) 192–195. See Pasquier, Lettres (Œuvres choisies), ii. 260.

papist, that liked the "accord," or thought it would last three
weeks. And he added, by way of warning to Coligny
and Condé: "What you, who are the heads and rulers,
do, I cannot tell; but every man thinketh that it is

Sir Thomas Smith's remonstrance.

but a traine and a deceipt to sever the one of you from another,
and all of you from this stronghold [Orleans], and then thei will
talke with you after another sorte."[1]   He urged the Huguenots
to learn a lesson from the fate of Bourges, Rouen, and other
cities which had admitted the "papists," and to consider that
these fine articles came from the queen mother, the Cardinals
of Bourbon, Ferrara, and Guise, and others like them, who desired to take the Protestants like fish in a net.   And he gave
D'Andelot the significant hint—very significant it was, in view
of what afterwards befell his brother Gaspard—that the report
spread by the enemy respecting Poltrot's confession was only a
preparation that, *in case any of the Huguenot noblemen should
be assassinated, it might be said that the deed had been done in
just revenge by the Guises*, who would not hesitate to sacrifice
them either by force or by treason.[2]

Of the other party, Catharine de' Medici alone was jubilant
over the edict.   On the contrary, the Roman Catholic people
of Paris regarded it as an approval of every sort of impiety and
wicked action, and the parliament would register it only after
repeated commands (on the twenty-seventh of March), and then
with a formal declaration of its reluctance.[3]   But no one was
so much disappointed as the admiral.   Hastening

Coligny's disappointment.

from Normandy to Orleans, he reached that city on
the twenty-third of March, only to find that the peace had been
fully concluded several days before.   In the council of the confederates, the next day, he spoke his mind freely.   He reminded Condé that, from the very commencement of hostilities, the

---

[1] Smith to the queen, April 1, 1563, in Duc d'Aumale, Princes de Condé, i.
Documents, 439.

[2] Smith to D'Andelot, March 13, 1563, State Paper Office.

[3] Journal de Bruslart, Mém. de Condé, i. 125: "de expresso Regis mandato
iteratis vicibus facto." Claude Haton is scarcely more complimentary than
Bruslart: "elle (la paix) estoit faicte du tout au désavantage de l'honneur de
Dieu, de la religion catholicque et de l'authorité du jeune roy et repos public
de son royaume." Mémoires, i. 327, 328.

triumvirs had offered the restoration of the Edict of January
with the exclusion of the city of Paris; and that never had affairs stood on a better footing than now,[1] when two of the three
chief authors of the war were dead, and the third was a prisoner.
But the poor had surpassed the rich in devotion ; the cities had
given the example to the nobles.   In restricting the number of
churches to one in a bailiwick, the prince and his counsellors
had ruined more churches by a single stroke of the pen than all
the forces of their enemies could have overthrown in ten years.
Coligny's warm remonstrance was heard with some regret for
the precipitancy with which the arrangement had been made;
but it was too late.   The peace was signed.   Besides, Condé
was confident that he would soon occupy his brother's place,
when the Huguenots would obtain all their demands.

But while the prince refused to draw back from the articles
of peace to which he had pledged himself, he consented to visit
the queen mother in company with the admiral, and endeavor
to remove some of the restrictions placed upon Protestant worship.   And Catharine was too well satisfied with her success in
restoring peace, to refuse the most pressing of the admiral's requests.   However, she took good care that none of her promises
should be in writing, much less be incorporated in the Edict of
Pacification.   "The prince and the admyrall," wrote the special
envoy Middlemore to Queen Elizabeth, "have bene twice with
the quene mother since my commynge hyther, where the admirall hath bene very earnest for a further and larger lybertye in
the course of religion, and so hath obtayned that there shall be

---

[1] Elizabeth of England was herself, apparently, awakening to the importance of the struggle, and new troops subsidized by her would soon have entered
France from the German borders.   "This day," writes Cecil to Sir Thomas
Smith, ambassador at Paris, Feb. 27, 156$\frac{2}{3}$, "commission passeth hence to
the comte of Oldenburg to levy eight thousand footemen and four thousand
horse, who will, I truste, passe into France with spede and corradg.   He is a
notable, grave, and puissant captayn, and fully bent to hazard his life in the
cause of religion."   Th. Wright, Queen Elizabeth and her Times, i. 125.
But Elizabeth's troops, like Elizabeth's money, came too late.   Of the latter,
Admiral Coligny plainly told Smith a few weeks later: "If we could have
had the money at Newhaven (Havre) *but one xiii daies sooner*, we would have
talked with them after another sorte, and would not have bene contented with
this accord."   Smith to the queen, April 1, 1563, in Duc d'Aumale, i. 439.

preachings within the townes in every balliage, wheras before yt was accordyd but in the suburbs of townes only, and that the gentylmen of the visconte and provoste of Parys shall have in theyr houses the same libertye of religion as ys accordyd elzwhere. So as the sayd admyrall doth now seame to lyke well inoughe that he shewyd by the waye to mislyke so muche, which was the harde articles of religion concludyd upon by the prince in his absence." [1]

On Sunday, the twenty-eighth of March, 1563—the anniversary of that Sunday which they had kept with so much solemnity at Meaux, on the eve of their march to Orleans—the Huguenot nobles and soldiers celebrated the Lord's Supper, in the simple but grand forms of the Geneva liturgy, within the walls of the church of the Holy Rood, long since stripped of its idolatrous ornaments, and on the morrow began to disperse to the homes from which for a year they had been separated. [2] The German reiters, at the same time, set out on their march toward Champagne, whence they soon after retired to their own country.

The war that had just closed undoubtedly constituted a turning-point in the Huguenot fortunes. The alliance between the Results of persecuted reformers, on the one hand, and the princes the war. of the blood and the nobility of France, on the other, had borne fruit, and it was not altogether good fruit. The patient confessors, after manfully maintaining their faith through an entire generation against savage attack, and gaining many a convert from the witnesses of their constancy, had grasped the sword thrust into their hands by their more warlike allies. In truth, it would be difficult to condemn them ; for it was in self-defence, not against rightful authority, but against the tyranny of a foreign and hostile faction. Candidly viewing their circum-

---

[1] Letter from Orleans, March 30, 1563, MSS. State Paper Office, Duc d'Aumale, i. 411.

[2] Hist. ecclés. des égl. réf., ii. 203. Theodore Beza was the preacher on this occasion, and betrayed his own disappointment by speaking of the liberty of religion they had received as " not so ample, peradventure, as they would wish, yet such as they ought to thank God for." Smith to the queen, March 31, State Paper Office.

stances at the distance of three centuries, we can scarcely see how they could have acted otherwise than as they did. Yet there was much that, humanly speaking, was unfortunate in the conjuncture. War is a horrible remedy at any time. Civil war superadds a thousand horrors of its own. And a civil war waged in the name of religion is the most frightful of all. The holiest of causes is sure to be embraced from impure motives by a host of unprincipled men, determined in their choice of party only by the hope of personal gain, the lust of power, or the thirst for revenge—a class of auxiliaries too powerful and important to be altogether rejected in an hour when the issues of life or death are pending, even if by the closest and calmest scrutiny they could be thoroughly weeded out—a process beyond the power of mortal man at any time, much more in the midst of the tumult and confusion of war. The Huguenots had made the attempt at Orleans, and had not shrunk from inflicting the severest punishments, even to death, for the commission of theft and other heinous crimes. They had endeavored in their camp to realize the model of an exemplary Christian community. But they had failed, because there were with them those who, neither in peace nor in war, could bring themselves to give to so strict a moral code any other obedience than that which fear exacts. Such was the misery of war. Such the melancholy alternative to which, more than once, the reformed saw themselves reduced, of perishing by persecution or of saving themselves by exposing their faith to reproach through alliance with men of as little religion or morality as any in the opposite camp.

The first civil war prevented France from becoming a Huguenot country. This was the deliberate conclusion of a Venetian ambassador, who enjoyed remarkable opportunities for observing the history of his times.[1] The practice of the Christian virtue of patience and submission under suffering and insult had made the reformers an incredible number of friends. The waging of war, even in self-defence, and the reported acts of wanton destruction, of cruelty and sacrilege—it mattered little whether they were true

It prevents France from becoming Huguenot.

---

[1] Relazione di Correro, 1569. Rel. des Amb. Vén., ii. 118–120.

or false, they were equally credited and produced the same results—turned the indifference of the masses into positive aversion. It availed the Huguenots little in the estimate of the people that the crimes that were almost the rule with their opponents were the exception with them; that for a dozen such as Montluc, they were cursed with but one Baron des Adrets; that the barbarities of the former received the approbation of the Roman Catholic priesthood, while those of the latter were censured with vehemence by the Protestant ministers. Partisan spirit refused to hold the scales of justice with equal hand, and could see no proofs of superior morality or devotion in the adherents of the reformed faith.

Besides their psalms, hallowed by so many thrilling associations, the Huguenots possessed a whole cycle of song. The meagre portion of this that has come down to us is among the most valuable of the monuments illustrative of their modes of thought and their religious and political aspirations. At the same time it brings vividly before us the great crises of their history. M. Henri Bordier has done a service not easily estimated at its full worth, by the publication of a considerable collection of the popular songs of the Protestants, under the title, "Le Chansonnier Huguenot du XVIe Siècle" (Paris, 1871). These songs are grouped in four divisions: religious songs, polemic and satirical songs, songs of war, and songs of martyrdom.

Huguenot ballads and songs.

The three oldest Huguenot songs known to exist belong to the first two divisions, and have been saved from destruction by the enemies of their authors, in the very attempt to secure their suppression. They have recently been found upon the records of the Parliament of Paris, where they obtained a place, thanks to the zeal of the "lieutenant général" of Meaux in endeavoring to ferret out the composers of anti-papal ballads. They were entered, without regard to metre, as so much prose. A stanza or two of the song entitled *Chanson nouvelle sur le chant:* "*N'allez plus au bois jouer,*" and evidently adapted to the tune of a popular ballad of the day, may suffice to indicate the character of the most vigorous of these compositions. It is addressed to Michel d'Arande, a friend of Farel, whom Bishop Briçonnet had invited to preach the Gospel in his diocese of Meaux, and begins:

> Ne preschez plus la vérité,
> Maistre Michel!
> Contenue en l'Evangille,
> Il y a trop grand danger
> D'estre mené
> Dans la Conciergerie.
> Lire, lire, lironfa.

Il y a trop grand danger
D'estre mené
Dans la Conciergerie
Devant les chapperons fourrez
Mal informez
Par gens plains de menterie.
Lire, lire, lironfa.

The " chants religieux," of which M. Bordier's collection reproduces twenty-five, are partly poetical paraphrases of the Ten Commandments, the Lord's Prayer, etc., and partly original compositions on a variety of themes, such as patient endurance of insult, etc. They display great familiarity with the Holy Scriptures, and sometimes not a little poetic fire.

The " chants polémiques " treat of a number of subjects, prominent among which are the monks and nuns, and the doctrines of the papal church. In one the expiring papacy is represented as summoning to her bedside cardinals, bishops, and other members of the clergy, to witness her last struggles. In another the Sorbonne is held up to ridicule, in company with all the mediæval doctors of theology. In a third the poet more seriously combats the belief in purgatory as unscriptural. But it is the mass that bears the brunt of attack. The Host figures under the designation, current in the literature of the sixteenth century,[1] of *Le Dieu de Pâte*, or *Le Dieu de Farine*. The pompous and complicated ceremonial, with its repetitions devoid of meaning for the illiterate spectator, is, on the whole, the favorite object of satire. In strict accordance with the spirit of the rough controversy of the times, little mercy is shown to religious antagonists. There is a good specimen of this style of treatment in an interesting song dating from about 1564, entitled " Noel nouveau de la description ou forme et manière de dire la Messe, sur ce chant: Hari, bouriquet." Of the fifteen stanzas of which it is composed, two or three may serve as samples. The preliminary service over, the priest comes to the consecration of the wafer :

Un morceau de paste
Il fait adorer ;
Le rompt de sa patte
Pour le dévorer,
Le gourmand qu'il est.
Hari, hari l'asne, le gourmand qu'il est,
Hari bouriquet !

Le Dieu qu'il faict faire,
La bouche le prend ;
Le cœur le digère,
Le ventre le rend,
Au fond du retrait !
Hari, hari l'asne, au fond du retrait,
Hari bouriquet !

---

[1] It appears at least as early as in Farel's Epistre à tous Seigneurs, written in 1530, p. 166 of Fick's edition.

Le peuple regarde
L'yvrongne pinter
Qui pourtant n'a garde
De luy présenter
A boire un seul traict.
Hari, hari l'asne, à boire un seul traict,
Hari bouriquet!

Achève et despouille
Tous ses drapeaux blancs,
En sa bourse fouille
Et y met six blancs.
C'est de peur du frais.
Hari, hari l'asne, c'est de peur du frais,
Hari bouriquet!

A somewhat older song (written before 1555) purports to be the dirge of the Mass uttered by itself—*Désolation de la Messe expirant en chantant.* The Mass in perplexity knows not how to begin the customary service:

Spiritus, Salve, Requiem,
Je ne sçay si je diray bien.
Quel *Introite*, n' *Oremus*
Je prenne ; *Sancti, Agimus.*
Feray-je des Martyrs ou Vierges ?
De ventre ad te clamamus!
Sonnez là, allumez ces cierges :
Y a-t-il du pain et du vin ?

Où est le livre et le calice
Pour faire l'office divin ?
Ça, cest autel, qu'on le tapisse !
Hélas, la piteuse police.
Ame ne me vient secourir.
Sans Chapelain, Moine, Novice,
Me faudra-il ainsi périr ?

Pope and cardinals are summoned in vain. No one comes, no one will bring reliquary or consecrated wafer. The Mass must finally resign all hope and die :

Hélas chantant, brayant, virant,
Tant que le crime romp et blesse
Puis que voy tost l'ame expirant,
Dites au moins adieu la Messe.
A tous faisant mainte promesse
Ore ai-je tout mon bien quitté
Veu qu'a la mort tens et abaisse
Ite Missa est ; donc *Ite,*
Ite Missa est.

The "chants de guerre" furnish a running commentary upon the military events of the last forty years of the sixteenth century, which is not devoid of interest or importance. The hopeful spirit characterizing the earlier ballads is not lost even in the latest; but the brilliant anticipations of a speedy triumph of the truth, found before the outbreak of the first civil war, or immediately thereafter, are lacking in other productions, dating from the close of the reign of Henry the Third. In a spirited song, presumably belonging to 1562, the poet, adopting the nickname of Huguenots given to the Protestants by their opponents, retaliates by applying an equally unwelcome term to the Roman Catholics, and forecasting the speedy overthrow of the papacy :

> Vous appellez Huguenots
> Ceux qui Jesus veullent suivre,
> Et n'adorent vos marmots
> De boys, de pierre et de cuyvre.
>   Hau, Hau, Papegots,
> Faictes place aux Huguenots.
>
> Nostre Dieu renversera
> Vous et vostre loy romaine,
> Et du tout se mocquera
> De vostre entreprise vaine.
>   Hau, Hau, Papegots,
> Faictes place aux Huguenots.
>
> Vostre Antechrist tombera
> Hors de sa superbe place
> Et Christ partout règnera
> Et sa loy pleine de grâce.
>   Hau, Hau, Papegots,
> Faictes place aux Huguenots.

The current expectation of the Protestants is attested in a long narrative ballad by Antoine Du Plain on the siege of Lyons (1563), in which Charles the Ninth figures as another Josiah destined to abolish the idolatrous mass :

> Ce Roy va chasser l'Idole
> Plain de dole
> Cognoissant un tel forfait :
> Selon la vertu Royale,
> Et loyale,
> Comme Iosias a fait.

It is noticeable that the words "va chasser l'Idole" are an anagram of the royal title *Charles de Valois*—an anagram which gave the Huguenots no little comfort. The same play upon words appears with a slight variation in a "Huictain au Peuple de Paris, sur l'anagrammatisme du nom du tres-chrestien Roy de France, Charles de Valois IX. de ce nom" (Recueil des Choses Mémorables, 1565, p. 367), of which the last line is,

> "O Gentil Roy qui *chassa leur idole.*"

But after the massacre of St. Bartholomew's Day the hopes of the Huguenots were blighted.   If the king is not referred to by name, his mother figures as the guilty cause of all the misfortune of France.   She is a second Helen born for the ruin of her adopted country, according to Étienne de Maisonfleur.

> Hélène femme estrangère
> Fut la seule mesnagère
> Qui ruina Ilion,
> Et la reine Catherine
> Est de France la ruine
> Par l'Oracle de Léon.

"Léon" is Catharine's uncle, Pope Leo the Tenth, who was said to have predicted the total destruction of whatever house she should be married into. See also the famous libel "Discours merveilleux de la vie de Catherine de Medicis" (Ed. of Cologne, Pierre du Marteau, 1693), p. 609.

The massacre of St. Bartholomew's Day naturally contributes a considerable fund of laments, etc., to the Huguenot popular poetry of the century.   A poem apparently belonging to a more remote date, discovered by Dr. Roullin, and perhaps the only Breton song of the kind that has come down to us, is as simple and unaffected a narrative as any of the modern Greek *mœrologia* (Vaurigaud, Essaie sur l'hist. des églises réf. de Bretagne, 1870, i. 6).   It tells the story of a Huguenot girl betrayed to the executioner by her own mother. In spite of a few dialectic forms, the verses are easily understood.

> Voulz-vous ouir l'histoire
> D'une fille d'espit
> Qui n'a pas voulu croire
> Chose que l'on lui dit.
>
> —Sa mère dit : "Ma fille,
> A la messe allons donc ! "
> —" Y aller à la messe,
> Ma mère, ce n'est qu'abus.
>
> Apportez-moi mes livres
> Avec mes beaux saluts.
> J'aimerais mieux être brûlée
> Et vantée au grand vent
>
> Que d'aller à la messe
> En faussant mon serment."
> —Quand sa très-chère mère
> Eut entendu c' mot là,
>
> Au bourreau de la ville
> Sa fille elle livra.
> "Bourreau, voilà ma fille !
> Fais à tes volontés ;

Bourreau, fais de ma fille
Comme d'un meurtrier."
Quand elle fut sur l'échelle,
Trois rollons jà montée,

Elle voit sa mère
Qui chaudement pleurait.
"Ho! la cruelle mère
Qui pleure son enfant

Après l'avoir livrée
Dans les grands feux ardents.
Vous est bien fait, ma mère,
De me faire mourir.

Je vois Jesus, mon père,
Qui, de son beau royaume,
Descend pour me quérir.
Son royaume sur terre
Dans peu de temps viendra,
Et cependant mon âme
En paradis ira."

CHAPTER XIV.

THE PEACE OF AMBOISE, AND THE BAYONNE CONFERENCE.

SCARCELY had the Edict of Amboise been signed when a demand was made upon the English queen for the city of Havre, placed in her possession by the Huguenots, as a pledge for the restoration of Calais in accordance with the treaty of Cateau-Cambrésis, and as security for the repayment of the large sums she had advanced for the maintenance of the war. But Elizabeth was in no favorable mood for listening to this summons. Instead of being instructed to evacuate Havre, the Earl of Warwick was reinforced by fresh supplies of arms and provisions, and received orders to defend to the last extremity the only spot in France held by the queen. A formal offer made by Condé to secure a renewal of the stipulation by which Calais was to be given up in 1567, and to remunerate Elizabeth for her expenditures in the cause of the French Protestants, was indignantly rejected; and both sides prepared for open war.[1] The struggle was short and decisive. The French were a unit on the question of a permanent occupation of their soil by foreigners. Within the walls of Havre itself a plot was formed by the French population to betray the city into the hands of their countrymen; and Warwick was forced to expel the natives in order to secure the lives of his own

The restoration of Havre demanded.

---

[1] Froude, Hist. of England, vii. 519. See the courteous summons of Charles, April 30, 1563, Forbes, State Papers, ii 404, 405, and Elizabeth's answer, May 7th, ibid., ii. 409–411 ; Condé's offer in his letter of June 26, 1563, Forbes, ii. 442. See also the extended correspondence of the English envoys, in the inedited documents published by the Duc d'Aumale, Princes de Condé, i. 423–500.

troops.[1] But no vigilance of the besieged could insure the safety of a detached position on the borders of so powerful a state as France. Elizabeth was too weak, or too penurious, to afford the recruits that were loudly called for. And now a new and frightful auxiliary to the French made its appearance. A contagious disease set in among the English troops, crowded into a narrow compass and deprived of their usual allowance of fresh meat and wholesome water. The fearful mortality attending it soon revealed the true character of the scourge. Few of those that fell sick recovered. Gathering new strength from day to day, it reigned at length supreme in the fated city. Soon the daily crowd of victims became too great to receive prompt sepulture, and the corpses lying unburied in the streets furnished fresh fuel for the raging pestilence. Seven thousand English troops were reduced in a short time to three thousand, in a few days more to fifteen hundred men.[2] The hand of death was upon the throat of every survivor. At length, too feeble to man their works, despairing of timely succor, unable to sustain at the same moment the assault of their opponents and the fearful visitation of the Almighty, the English consented to surrender ; and, on the twenty-eighth of July, a capitulation was signed, in accordance with which, on the next day, Havre, with all its fortifications and the ships of war in its harbor, fell once more into the hands of the French.[3]

Fall of Havre.

---

[1] Froude, vii. 520 ; Castelnau, liv. v., c. ii.　Compare Forbes, ii. 422.

[2] " The plage dothe increace here dayly, wherby our nombres are decayde within these fowr days in soche sorte, as we have not remayning at this present (in all our judgements) 1500 able men in this towne.　They dye nowe in bothe these peces upon the point of 100 a daye, so as we can not geyt men to burye theym," etc.　Warwick to the Privy Council, July 11, 1563.　Forbes, ii. 458.

[3] De Thou, iii. (liv. xxxv.) 417–420 ; Mém. de Castelnau, liv. v., c. ii. and iii. ; Cimber et Danjou, v. 229 ; Stow's Annals (London, 1631), 655, 656 ; Agrippa d'Aubigné, liv. iv., c. ii. (i. 198–200) ; Davila, bk. iii. (Eng. trans., London, 1678), p. 89 ; Froude, vii. 519–528.　Consult especially Dr. Patrick Forbes, Full View of the Public Transactions in the Reign of Queen Elizabeth (London, 1741), vol ii. pp. 373–500.　This important collection of letters, to which I have made such frequent reference under the shorter title of " State Papers," ends at this point.　Peace was definitely concluded between France and England by the treaty of Troyes, April 11, 1564 (Mém. de Condé,

The pacification of Amboise, a contemporary chronicler tells us, was received with greater or less cordiality in different localities of France, very much according to the number of Protestants they had contained before the war. "This edict of peace was very grievous to hear published and to have executed in the case of the Catholics of the peaceable cities and villages where there were very few Huguenots. But it was a source of great comfort to the Catholics of the cities which were oppressed by the Huguenots, as well as of the neighboring villages in which the Catholic religion had been intermitted, mass and divine worship not celebrated, and the holy sacraments left unadministered—as in the cities of Lyons and Orleans, and their vicinity, and in many other cities of Poitou and Languedoc, where the Huguenots were masters or superior in numbers. As the peace was altogether advantageous to the Huguenots, they labored hard to have it observed and published."[1]

How the peace was received.

But to secure publication and observance was not always possible.[2] Not unfrequently the Huguenots were denied by the illiberality of their enemies every privilege to which they were entitled by the terms of the edict. At Troyes, the Roman Catholic party, hearing that peace had been made, resolved to

---

v. 79, 80). Sir Nicholas Throkmorton, who had long been a prisoner, held to be exchanged against the hostages for the restitution of Calais, given in accordance with the treaty of Cateau-Cambrésis, now returned home. Before leaving, however, he had an altercation with his colleague, Sir Thomas Smith, of which the latter wrote a full account. Sir Nicholas, it seems, in his heat applied some opprobrious epithets to Smith, and even called him "traitor" —a charge which the latter repudiated with manly indignation. "Nay, thou liest, quoth I; I am as true to the queen as thou any day in the week, and have done her Highness as faithful and good service as thou." Smith to Cecil, April 13, 1564, State Paper Office.

[1] Mém. de Claude Haton, i. 356, 357.

[2] See the order of the fanatical Parliament of Toulouse, which it had the audacity to publish with, or instead of, the king's edict. It contains this clause : "Ce que estant veu par nous, avons ordonné et ordonnons que, en la ville de Thoulouse ni aultres du ressort du parlement d'icelle, ne se fera publicquement ni secrettement aulcun exercice de la nouvelle prétendue religion, en quelque sorte que ce soit, sous peine de la hart. Item, que tous ceux qui vouldront faire profession de laditte prétendue religion réformée ayent à se retirer," etc. Mém. de Claude Haton, i. 358, 359.

employ the brief interval before the edict should be published, and the mayor of the city led the populace to the prisons, where all the Huguenots that could be found were at once murdered.[1] The vexatious delays, and the actual persecution still harder to be borne, which were encountered at Rouen, have

Vexatious delays in Normandy. been duly recorded by an anonymous Roman Catholic contemporary, as well as in the registers of the city hall and of the Norman parliament, and may serve as an indication of what occurred in many other places. From the chapter of the cathedral and the judges of the supreme provincial court, down to the degraded rabble, the entire population was determined to interpose every possible obstacle in the way of the peaceable execution of the new law. Before any official communication respecting it reached them, the clergy declared, by solemn resolution, their intention to reserve the right of prosecuting all who had plundered their extensive ecclesiastical domain. The municipality wrote at once to the king, to his mother, and to others at court, imploring that Rouen and its vicinity might be exempted from all exercise of the "new religion." Parliament sent deputies to Charles the Ninth to remonstrate against the broad concessions made in favor of the Protestants, and, even when compelled to go through the form of a registration, avoided a publication of the edict, in order to gain time for another fruitless protest addressed to the royal government.

When it came to the execution of the law, the affair assumed a more threatening aspect. The Roman Catholics had resolved to resist the return of the "for-issites," or fugitive Huguenots. At first they excused their opposition by alleging that there were bandits and criminals of every kind in the ranks of the exiles. Next they demanded that a preliminary list of their names and abodes should be furnished, in order that their arms might be taken away. Finally they required, with equal perverseness, that, in spite of the express stipulation of the king's rescript, the "for-issites" should return only as private individuals, and should not venture to resume their former

---

[1] Recordon, Le Protestantisme en Champagne, 132, 133.

offices and dignities. Meantime the "for-issites," driven to desperation by the flagrant injustice of which they were the victims, began to retaliate by laying violent hands upon all objects of Roman Catholic devotion in the neighboring country, and by levying contributions upon the farms and villas of their malignant enemies. The Rouenese revenged themselves in turn by wantonly murdering the Huguenots whom they found within the city walls.

The embittered feeling did not diminish at once after the more intrepid of the Huguenots had, under military compulsion, been readmitted into Rouen. There were daily complaints of ill-usage. But the insolence of the dominant party rose to a still higher pitch when there appeared a royal edict—whether genuine or forged has not as yet been settled—by which the cardinal demands of the Huguenots were granted. The alleged concessions may not strike us as very extraordinary. They consisted chiefly in disarming the Roman Catholics equally with the adherents of the opposite creed, and in erecting a new chamber in parliament to try impartially cases in dispute between the adherents of the two communions.[1] This was certainly decreeing but a small measure of the equality in the eye of the law which the Protestants might claim as a natural and indefeasible right. The citizens of the Norman capital, however, regarded the enactment as a monstrous outrage upon society. Charles the Ninth happened at this time to be passing

---

[1] M. Floquet, in his excellent history of the Norman Parliament (ii. 571), repudiates as "une de ces exagérations familières à De Bèze," the statement of the Histoire ecclés. des églises réformées, "that in the Parliament of Rouen, whatever the cause might be, whoever was known to be of the (reformed) religion, whether plaintiff or defendant, was instantly condemned." Yet he quotes below (ii. 571, 573, 574), from Chancellor de l'Hospital's speech to that parliament, statements that fully vindicate the justice of the censure. "Vous pensez bien faire d'adjuger la cause à celuy que vous estiméz plus homme de bien ou meilleur chrestien ; comme s'il estoit question, entre les parties, lequel d'entre eux est meilleur poète, orateur, peintre, artisan, et enfin de l'art, doctrine, force, vaillance, ou autre quelconque suffisance, non de la chose qui est amenée en jugement." And after enumerating other complaints : "Ne trouvez point estrange ce que je vous en dy : car souvent sont apportéz au roy de vos jugements qui semblent, de prime face, fort esloignéz de toute droicture et équité."

through Gaillon, a place some ten leagues distant from Rouen,
on his way to the siege of Havre; and Damours,
the advocate-general, was deputed to bear to him a
protest drawn up by parliament. The tone of the
paper was scarcely respectful to the monarch; it was positively
insulting to the members of the royal council who professed the
Protestant faith. It predicted the possible loss of Normandy,
or of his entire kingdom, in case the king pursued a system of
toleration. The Normans, it said, would not submit to Protestant governors, nor to the return of the exiles in arms, nor to
their resumption of their former dignities. If the "for-issites"
continued their excesses, they would be set upon and killed.
The Roman Catholic burgesses of Rouen even proclaimed a
conditional loyalty. Should the king not see fit to accede to
their demands, they declared themselves ready to place the keys
of their city in his hands to dispose of at his pleasure, at the
same time craving permission to go where they pleased and to
take away their property with them.

Truly the spirit of the "Holy League" was already born,
though the times were not yet ripe for the promulgation of
such tenets. The advocate-general was a fluent speaker, and he
had been attended many a weary mile by an enthusiastic
escort. Parliamentary counsellors, municipal officers, clergy,
an immense concourse of the lower stratum of the population—
all were at Gaillon, ready to applaud his well-turned sentences.
But he had chosen an unlucky moment for his oratorical display. His glowing periods were rudely interrupted by one of
the princely auditors. This was Louis of Condé—now doubly
important to the court on account of the military undertaking
that was on foot—who complained of the speaker's insolent
words. So powerful a nobleman could not be despised. And
so the voluble Damours, with his oration but half delivered,
instead of meeting a gracious monarch's approval and
returning home amid the plaudits of the multitude,
was hastily taken in charge by the archers of the royal guard
and carried off to prison. The rest of the Rouenese disappeared
more rapidly than they had come. The avenues to the city
were filled with fugitives as from a disastrous battle. Even

Protest of the Norman par-liament.

A rude rebuff.

the grave parliament, which the last winter had been exhibiting its august powers in butchering Huguenots by the score, beginning with the arch-heretic Augustin Marlorat, lost for a moment its self-possession, and took part in the ignominious flight. Shame, however, induced it to pause before it had gone too far, and, putting on the gravest face it could summon, it reappeared ere long at Gaillon with becoming magisterial gravity. Never had there been a more thorough discomfiture.[1]   A few days later the Marshal de Bourdillon made his entry into Rouen with a force of Swiss soldiers sufficient to break down all resistance, the " for-issites " were brought in, a new election of municipal officers was held, and comparative quiet was restored in the turbulent city.[2]

So far as a character so undecided could frame any fixed purpose, Catharine de' Medici was resolved to cement, if possible, a stable peace. The Chancellor, Michel de l'Hospital, still retained his influence over her, and gave to her disjointed plans somewhat of the appearance of a deliberate policy. That policy certainly seemed to mean peace. And to prove this, commissioners were despatched to the more distant provinces, empowered to enforce the execution of the Edict of Amboise.[3]   Yet never was the court less in sympathy with the Huguenots than at this moment. If shameless profligacy had not yet reached the height it subsequently attained under the last Valois that sat upon the throne of France, it was undoubtedly taking rapid strides in that direction. For the giddy throng of courtiers, living in an atmosphere that reeked with corruption,[4]

Commission-
ers to enforce
the edict.

Alienation of
a profligate
court.

---

[1] Chron. MS. du xvi. siècle, Registres, etc., apud Floquet, Hist. du parlement de Normandie, ii. 525–547.

[2] Ibid., ii. 548.

[3] The father of Agrippa d'Aubigné was, as his son informs us, one of the commissioners sent on this occasion to Guyenne.   Mémoires d'A. d'Aubigné, ed. Buchon, 474.

[4] What else can be said, in view of such well authenticated statements as the following?   On his progress through France, to which reference will soon be made, Charles the Ninth stopped with his court at Troyes, where no expense was spared in providing tournaments and games for his amusement. Just as he was about to leave the city, and was already booted for his journey,

the stern morality professed by the lips and exemplified in the lives of Gaspard de Coligny and his noble brothers, as well as by many another of nearly equal rank, could afford but few attractions. Many of these triflers had, it is true, exhibited for a time some leaning toward the reformed faith. But their evanescent affection was merely a fire kindled in the light straw: the fuel was soon consumed, and the brilliant flame which had given rise to such sanguine expectations died out as easily as it sprang up.[1] When once the novelty of the simple worship in the rude barn, or in the retired fields, with the psalms of Marot and Beza sung to quaint and stirring melodies, had worn off; when the black gown of the Protestant minister had become as familiar to the eye as the stole and chasuble of the officiating priest, and the words of the reformed confession of sins as familiar to the ear as the pontifical litanies and prayers, the "assemblée" ceased to attract the curious from the salons of St. Germain and Fontainebleau. Besides, it was one thing to listen to a scathing account of the abuses of churchmen, or a violent denunciation of the sins of priest and monk, and quite another to submit to a faithful recital of the iniquities of the court, and hear the wrath of God denounced against the profane, the lewd, and the extortionate. There were some incidents, occurring just at the close of the war, that completed the alienation which before had been only partial. The Huguenots had attempted by stringent regulations to banish swearing, robbery, and other flagrant crimes from their army. They had

he was detained for a little while that he might witness a novel entertainment. He was taken to a garden where a number of young girls, selected for their extraordinary beauty and entirely nude, executed in his presence the most obscene dances. It was two churchmen that are said to have provided the boy-king with this infamous diversion—Cardinal Charles of Bourbon and Cardinal Louis of Guise. Recordon, 143.

[1] "Il est notoire qu'au temps du colloque de Poissy la doctrine evangelique y fut proposée en liberté; ce qui causa que plusieurs, tans grands que petits, prindrent goust à icelle. Mais, tout ainsi qu'un feu de paille fait grand' flamme, et puis s'esteint incontinent d'autant que la matière défaut, après que ce qu'ils avoient receu comme une nouveauté se fut un peu envieilly en leur cœur, les affections s'amortirent, et la pluspart retourna à l'ancienne cabale de la cour, qui est bien plus propre pour faire rire et piaffer, et pour s'enrichir." Mém. de Franç. de la Noue, c. ii. (Ed. Mich. et Pouj., 591).

punished robbery in many instances with death. They had succeeded so far in doing away with oaths, that their opponents had paid unconscious homage to their freedom from the despicable vice. In those days, when in the civil struggle it was so difficult to distinguish friends from foes, there was one proof of unimpeachable orthodoxy that was rarely disputed.

Profanity a test of Catholicity. He must be a good Catholic who could curse and swear. The Huguenot soldier would do neither.[1] So nearly, indeed, did the Huguenot affirmation approach to the simplicity of the biblical precept, that one Roman Catholic partisan leader of more than ordinary audacity had assumed for the motto on his standard the blasphemous device: " 'Double 's death' has conquered 'Verily.' "[2] But the strictness with which theft and profanity were visited in the Huguenot camp produced but a slight impression, compared with that made by the punishment of death inflicted by a stern judge at Orleans, just before the proclamation of peace, on a man and woman found guilty of adultery. Almost the entire court cried out against the unheard-of severity of the sentence for a crime which had never before been punished at all. The greater part of these advocates of facile morals had even the indiscretion to confess that they would never consent to accept such people as the Huguenots for their masters.[3]

Even after the publication of the Edict of Amboise, there was one matter left unsettled that threatened to rekindle the flames of civil war. It will be remembered that the murderer

---

[1] " Quelque chose qu'il sût dire avec blasphèmes horribles—moyen ordinaire à telles gens pour prouver leur religion." Hist. ecclés. des églises réformées, ii. 458. To stuff leaves torn from French Bibles into the mouths or wounds of dying or dead Huguenots, as we have seen, was a diversion not unknown to their opponents. Of course, there is nothing astonishing in the circumstance that the invocation of Calvin's liturgy—" Notre aide soit au nom de Dieu qui a fait le ciel et la terre "—should have been a favorite formula for the beginning of a game of chance, or that the doxology—" Louange à Dieu de tous ses biens "—[" Praise God from whom all blessings flow."]—should have been esteemed a fitting ejaculation for the winner. Ibid., ii. 310, 431.

[2] " 'Double mort Dieu' a vaincu ' Certes '; entendant par ce dernier mot ceux de la religion qui condamnent ces juremens et blasphêmes." Hist. ecclés. des égl. réf., ii. 507.

[3] De Thou, iii (liv. xxxv.) 409.

of the Duke of Guise, overcome by terror in view of his fate,
Admiral Co-
ligny accused. had charged Gaspard de Coligny with having instigated the perpetration of the foul crime ; that, as soon
as he heard the accusation, the admiral had not only answered
the allegations, article by article, but had written, earnestly
begging that Poltrot's execution might be deferred until the
return of peace should permit him to be confronted with his
accuser. This very reasonable demand, we have seen, had been
rejected, and the miserable assassin had been torn into pieces
by four horses, upon the Place de Grève, on the very day preceding that which witnessed the signing of the Edict of Amboise. If, however, the queen mother had hoped to diminish
the difficulties of her position by taking this course, she had
greatly miscalculated. In spite of his protestations, and of a
second and more popular defence which he now made,[1] the
Guises persisted in believing, or in pretending to believe, Coligny to be the prime cause of the murder of the head of their
family. His very frankness was perverted into a proof of his
complicity. The admiral's words, as an eminent historian of
our own day observes, bear the seal of sincerity, and we need go
for the truth nowhere else than to his own avowals.[2] But they
did not satisfy his enemies. The danger of an open rupture
was imminent. Coligny was coming to court from his castle
of Châtillon-sur-Loing, with a strong escort of six hundred gentlemen ; but so inevitable did a bloody collision within the walls
of Paris seem to the queen, that she begged Condé to dissuade
him for the present from carrying out his purpose. Meantime,
His defence
espoused by
Condé and
the Mont-
morencies. Condé and the two Montmorencies—the constable
and his son, the marshal—espoused Coligny's cause as
their own, by publicly declaring (on the fifteenth of
May) his entire innocence, and announcing that any
blow aimed at the Châtillons, save by legal process, they would
regard and avenge as aimed at themselves.[3] Taking excuse

---

[1] Declaration dated Châtillon-sur-Loing, May 5, 1563. Mém. de Condé, iv.
339–349 ; and Jean de Serres, iii. 15–29.

[2] Martin, Hist. de France, x. 164.

[3] De Thou, iii. (liv. xxxv.), 415, 416. Catharine had been the involuntary
instrument of renewing the old friendship between the constable and his

from the unsettled relations of the kingdom with England and at home, the privy council at the same time enjoined both parties to abstain from acts of hostility, and adjourned the judicial investigation until after arms had been laid down.[1]

At length, on the twenty-sixth of September—two months after the reduction of Havre—the Guises renewed their demand

Petition of the Guises. with great solemnity. Charles was at Meulan (on the Seine, a few miles below Paris), when a procession of mourners entered his presence. It was the family of Guise, headed by the late duke's widow, his mother, and his children, coming to sue for vengeance on the murderer. All were clad in the dress that betokened the deepest sorrow, and the dramatic effect was complete.[2] They brought a petition couched in decided terms, but making no mention of the name of Coligny, and signed, not only by themselves, but by three of the Bourbons—the Cardinal Charles, the Duke of Montpensier, and his son—and by the Dukes of Longueville and Nemours.[3] Under the circumstances, the king could not avoid granting their request and ordering inquisition to be made by the peers in parliament assembled.[4] But the friends of the absent admiral saw in the proposed investigation only an attempt on the part of his enemies to effect through the forms of law the ruin of the most prominent Huguenot of France. It was certain, they urged, that he could expect no justice at the hands of the presidents and counsellors of the Parisian parliament. Nor did they find it difficult to convince Catharine that to permit a

---

nephews, when, on Guise's death, she conferred the office of grand master upon his young son, instead of restoring it to Anne de Montmorency, to whom the dignity had formerly belonged. Three months later (Aug. 30, 1563) Condé drew up another paper, assuming the entire responsibility for all the acts of the Châtillon brothers during the war : "Acte par lequel M. le prince de Condé déclare que tout ce que M. l'amiral de Coligny et M. D'Andelot son frère ont fait pendant les troubles, ils ont fait à sa réquisition et par ses ordres." Mém. de Condé, iv. 651.

[1] See Martin, x. 174, 175.

[2] Davila, bk. iii. 92, and D'Aubigné, liv. iv., c. iii. (i. 201), both of whom mistake the place of the occurrence, supposing it to have been Paris.

[3] Copie de la requeste présentée au Roy très-chrestien par ceulx de la mayson de Guyse, etc. Mém. de Condé, iv. 667, 668.

[4] Ibid., iv. 668.

public trial would be to reopen old sores and to risk overturning in a single hour the fabric of peace which for six months she had been laboring hard to strengthen.[1] The king was therefore induced to evoke the consideration of the complaint of the Guises to his own grand council. Here again new difficulties sprang up. The Duchess of Guise was as suspicious of the council as Coligny of the parliament, and challenged the greater number of its members as too partial to act as judges. In fact, it seemed impossible to secure a jury to settle the matter in dispute. After months spent to no purpose in wrangling, Charles determined to remove the question both from the parliament and from the council, and on the fifth of January, 1564, reserved for himself and his mother the duty of adjudication. At the same time, on the ground that the importance of the case demanded the deliberations of a prince of greater age and of more experience than he as yet possessed, and that its discussion at present might prove prejudicial to the tranquillity of the kingdom, he adjourned it for three full years, or until such other time as he might hereafter find to be convenient.[2]

The feud between the Châtillons and the Guises was not, however, the only embarrassment which the government found itself compelled to meet. Catharine was in equal perplexity with respect to the engagements she had entered into with the Prince of Condé. It was part of the misfortune of this improvident princess that each new intrigue was of such a nature as to require a second intrigue to bolster it up. Yet she was to live long enough to learn by bitter experience that there is a limit to the extent to which plausible but lying words will pass current. At last the spurious coin was to be returned discredited to her own coffers. Catharine had enticed Condé into concluding a peace much less

*Embarrass-
ment of Cath-
arine.*

---

[1] "C'est un vray moyen pour destruire et gaster en une heure tout le fondement de ce qu'elle a prins grand' peine de bastir depuis six mois." Mémoire présenté à la Reine-mère, pour empêcher que la maison de Guyse n'allât demander justice au parlement de Paris, de l'assassinat de François duc de Guise. Mém. de Condé, iv. 493–495.

[2] Arrêt du conseil du Roy, par lequel il évoque à sa personne le procès meu entre les maisons de Guyse et de Chastillon, etc. Mém. de Condé, iv. 495.

favorable to the Huguenots than his comrades in arms had expected in view of the state of the military operations and the pecuniary necessities of the court, by the promise that he should occupy the same controlling position in the government as his brother, the King of Navarre, held at the time of his death. We have seen that he was so completely hoodwinked that he assured his friends that it was of little consequence how scanty were the concessions made in the edict. He would soon be able, by his personal authority, to secure to " the religion " the largest guarantees. If we may believe Catharine herself, he went so far in his enthusiastic desire for peace as to threaten to desert the Huguenots, if they declined to embrace the opportunity of reconciliation.[1]

How to get rid of the troublesome obligation she had assumed, was now the problem ; since to fulfil her promise honestly was, for a person of her crooked policy and inordinate ambition, not to be thought of for an instant. The readiest solution was found in abolishing the office of lieutenant-general. This could be done only by declaring the termination of the minority of Charles. For this an opportunity presented itself,

The majority of Charles proclaimed.

when, on the seventeenth of August, 1563,[2] the queen and her children, with a brilliant retinue, were in the city of Rouen, on their return from the successful campaign against Havre. That day Charles the Ninth held a " lit de justice " in the palace of the Parliament of Normandy. Sitting in state, and surrounded by his mother, his younger brothers, and a host of grandees, he proceeded to address the assembled counsellors, pronouncing himself of full age, and, in the capacity of a major king, delivered to them an edict, signed the day before, ordering the observance of his Edict of Amboise and the complete pacification of his kingdom by a univer-

---

[1] " Ne parlez encore à personne," writes Catharine to M. de Gonnor (March 12, 1563), "des conditions, car j'ay toûjours peur qu'ils ne nous trompent; encore que le Prince de Condé leur a déclaré que s'ils n'acceptent ces conditions et s'ils ne veulent la paix, qu'il s'en viendra avec le Roy mon fils, et se déclarera leur ennemy, chose que je trouve très-bonne." Le Laboureur, ii. 241.

[2] Not September 15th, as Davila states, nor September 24th, as D'Aubigné seems to assert; but his narrative is confused.

sal laying down of arms.[1] True, Charles was but a few days more than thirteen years of age; but his right to assume the full powers of government was strenuously maintained by Chancellor L'Hospital, upon whom devolved the task of explaining more fully the king's motives and purposes. Then Catharine, the author of the pageant, rising, humbly approached her son's throne, and bowed to the boy in token that she resigned into his hands the temporary authority she had held for nearly three years. Charles, advancing to meet her, accepted her homage, saying, at the same time, in words that were but too significant and prophetic of the remainder of his reign: " Madame ma mère, you shall govern and command as much or more than ever." [2]

The Parliament of Rouen, flattered at being selected for the instrument in so important an act, published and registered the edict of Charles's majority, notwithstanding some unpalatable provisions. Not so the Parliament of Paris. The counsellors of the capital were even more indignant at the slight put upon their claim to precedence, than at the proposed disarming of the Roman Catholics—a measure particularly distasteful to the riotous population of Paris.[3] The details of their opposition need not, however, find a record here. In the end the firmness

Charles and the refractory Parliament of Paris.

of the king, or of his advisers, triumphed. At Mantes [4] Charles received a deputation from the recalcitrant judges, with Christopher de Thou, their first president, at its head. After hearing their remonstrances, he replied to the delegates that, although young and possessed of little experience, he was as truly king of France as any of his predecessors, and that he intended to make himself obeyed as such. To prove, however, that he had not acted inconsiderately

---

[1] The two documents—address and edict—in Mém. de Condé, iv. 574–581.

[2] Floquet, Hist. du parlement de Normandie, ii. 584. The entire scene is very vividly portrayed, ibid., ii. 561–586. Bruslart, Mém. de Condé, i. 132; De Thou, iii. (liv. xxxv.) 421–424 ; Jean de Serres, iii. 32 ; Mém. de Castelnau, liv. v., c. iv., etc.; Agrippa d'Aubigné, Hist. univ., liv. iv., c. iii. (i. 200–202) ; Davila, bk. iii. 90.

[3] " Les Parisiens furent fort pressés qu'ils eussent à mettres les armes bas," says the metropolitan curate, Jean de la Fosse, under date of May, 1563, " mais ils n'en volurent jamais rien faire." Mém. d'un curé ligueur, 63, 64.

[4] A town on the left bank of the Seine, four leagues beyond Meulan.

in the premises, he called upon the members of his council who were present to speak ; and each in turn, commencing with Cardinal Bourbon, the first prince of the blood, declared that the edict of Amboise had been made with his consent and advice, and that he deemed it both useful and necessary. Whereupon Charles informed the parliamentary committee that he had not adopted this course because he was under any obligation to render to them an account of his actions. " But," said he, " now that I am of age, I wish you to meddle with nothing beyond giving my subjects good and speedy justice. The kings, my predecessors, placed you where you are, in order that they might unburden their consciences, and that their subjects might live in greater security under their obedience, not in order to constitute you my tutors, or the protectors of the realm, or the guardians of my city of Paris. You have allowed yourselves to suppose until now that you are all this. I shall not leave you under the delusion; but I command you that, as in my father's and grandfather's time you were accustomed to attend to justice alone, so you shall henceforth meddle with nothing else." He professed to be perfectly willing to listen to their representations when modestly given ; but he concluded by threatening them that, if they persisted in their present insolent course, he would find means to convince them that they were not his guardians and teachers, but his servants.[1] These stout words were shrewdly suspected to come from " the shop of the chancellor,"[2] whose popularity they by no means augmented. But Charles was himself in earnest. A fresh delegation of counsellors was dismissed from the royal presence with menaces,[3] and the parlia-

---

[1] Mém. de Condé (Bruslart), Sept., 1563, i. 133–135.

[2] Ibid., *ubi supra.* " Ces parolles là sont venues de la boutique de Monsieur le Chancellier et non du Roy."

[3] Ibid., i. 136. Even after Charles's lecture and a still more intemperate address of Montluc, Bishop of Valence, when parliament came to a vote there was a tie. To please Catharine, whose entire authority was at stake, the royal council of state gave the extraordinary command that the minute of this vote should be erased from the records of parliament, and the edict instantly registered. This last was forthwith done. De Thou, iii. (liv. xxxv.) 426, 427. Bruslart (*ubi supra,* i. 136) denies that the erasure was actually made as Charles had commanded.

ment and people of Paris were both finally compelled to succumb. Parliament registered the edict; the people surrendered
their arms—the poor receiving the estimated value of the weapons, the tradesmen and burgesses a ticket to secure their future
restoration. As a matter of course, the nobles do not appear at
all in the transaction, their immemorial claim to be armed even
in time of peace being respected.

Pope Pius the Fourth had been as indignant as Philip the
Second himself at the conclusion of peace with the Huguenots.
He avenged himself as soon as he received the tidings,
by publishing, on the seventh of April, 1563, a bull
conferring authority upon the inquisitors general of
Christendom to proceed against heretics and their favorers—
even to bishops, archbishops, patriarchs and cardinals—and to
cite them before their tribunal by merely affixing the summons
to the doors of the Inquisition or of the basilica of St. Peter.
Should they fail to appear in person, they might at once be condemned and sentenced. The bull was no idle threat. Without
delay a number of French prelates were indicted for heresy, and
summoned to come to Rome and defend themselves. The list
was headed by Cardinal Odet de Châtillon, Coligny's
eldest brother, who had openly espoused the reformed
belief, and St. Romain, Archbishop of Aix. Caraccioli, who had
resigned the bishopric of Troyes and had been ordained a Protestant pastor, Montluc of Valence, and others of less note,
figured among the suspected.[1] As they did not appear, a number of these prelates were shortly condemned.[2] Not content
with this bold infraction of the Gallican liberties, the Roman
pontiff went a step farther, and, through the Congregation of
the Inquisition, cited Jeanne d'Albret, Queen of Navarre, to
appear at Rome within six months, on pain of being held attainted of heresy, and having her dominions given in possession
to the first Catholic occupant.[3]

The Pope's bull against princely here- tics.

Cardinal Châtillon.

---

[1] De Thou, iii. (liv. xxxv.) 441, etc.

[2] Letter of Card. de la Bourdaisière, Rome, Oct. 23, 1563, in which sentence
is said to have been pronounced, the day before, on the Archbishop of Aix,
and the bishops of Uzès, Valence, Oléron, Lescar, Chartres, and Troyes.
Le Laboureur, i. 863, 864.

[3] Monitorium et citatio officii sanctæ Inquisitionis contra illustrissimam et

In other words, not only Béarn, the scanty remnant of her titular monarchy, but all the lands and property to which the Huguenot queen had fallen heir, were to follow in the direction the kingdom of Navarre had taken, and go to swell the enormous wealth and dominion of the Spanish prince,[1] who found his interest to lie in the discord and misfortunes of his neighbors. Surely such an example would not be without significance to princes and princesses who, like Catharine, were wont occasionally to court the heretics on account of their power, and whose loyalty to the papal church could scarcely be supposed, even by the most charitable, to rest on any firmer foundation than self-interest. Nor was the lesson thrown away. Catharine and Michel de l'Hospital, and many another, read its import at a glance. But, instead of breaking down their opposition, the papal bull only forearmed them. They saw that Queen Jeanne's cause was their cause—the cause of any of the Valois who, whether upon the ground of heresy or upon any other pretext, might become obnoxious to the See of Rome. The

The council protests against the papal bull.

royal council of state, therefore, promptly took the matter in hand, in connection with the recent trial of the French prelates, and replied to the papal missive by a spirited protest, which D'Oisel, the French ambassador at Rome, was commissioned to present. In his monarch's name he was to declare the procedure against the Queen of Navarre to be not only derogatory to the respect due to the royal dignity, which that princess could claim to an equal degree with the other monarchs of Christendom, but injurious to the rights and honor of the king and kingdom, and subversive of civil society.

serenissimam dominam Joannam Albretiam, reginam Navarræ, Mém. de Condé, iv. 669–679; and Vauvilliers, Histoire de Jeanne d'Albret, iii. Pièces justif., 221–240. It is dated Tuesday, September 28, 1563. De Thou, iii. (liv. xxxv.) 442. The Card. de la Bourdaisière (*ubi supra*) merely says : " Tout le monde dit à Rome, que la Reine de Navarre fut aussi privée audit Consistoire, mais il n'en est rien, bien est-elle citée." Mém. de Castelnau, liv. v., c. ix.

[1] It needed no very extraordinary penetration to read " Philip " under the words of the monitorium : " Ita ut in casu contraventionis (quod Deus avertat) et contumaciæ, regnum, principatus, ac alia cujuscunque status et dominia hujuscemodi, dentur et dari possint *cuilibet illa occupanti, vel illi aut illis quibus Sanctitati suæ et successoribus suis dare et concedere magis placuerit.*"

It was unjust, for it was dictated by the enemies of France, who sought to take advantage of the youth of the king and his embarrassments arising from civil wars, to oppress a widow and orphans—the widow and orphan children, indeed, of a king for whom the Pope had himself but recently been endeavoring so zealously to secure the restoration of Navarre. The malice was apparent from the fact that nothing similar had been undertaken by the Holy See against any of the monarchs who had revolted from its obedience within the last forty years. Sovereign power had been conferred upon the Pope for the salvation of souls, not that he might despoil kings and dispose of kingdoms according to his caprice—an undertaking his predecessors had engaged in hitherto only to their shame and confusion. Finally, the King of France begged Pius to recall the sentence against Queen Jeanne, otherwise he would be compelled to employ the remedies resorted to by his ancestors in similar cases, according to the laws of the realm.[1] Not content with this direct appeal, Catharine wrote to her son's ambassador in Germany to interest the emperor and the King of the Romans in an affair that no less vitally affected them.[2] So vigorous a response seems to have frightened the papal court, and the bull was either recalled or dropped—at least no trace is said to be found in the Constitutions of Pius the Fourth—and the proceedings against the bishops were indefinitely suspended.[3]

---

[1] Summary of the protest in De Thou, iii. (liv. xxxv.) 441–447; and Vauvilliers, ii. 7–17; in full in Mém. de Condé, iv. 680–684. "Quant au fait de la Reine de Navarre, qui est celuy qui importe le plus, ledit sieur d'Oysel aura charge de luy faire bien entendre," says Catharine in a long letter to Bishop Bochetel (*ubi infra*), "qu'il n'a nulle autorité et jurisdiction sur ceux qui portent titre de Roy ou de Reine, et que ce n'est à luy de donner leur estats et royaumes en proye au premier conquerant."

[2] See the interesting letter of Catharine to Bochetel, Bishop of Rennes, French ambassador at Vienna, Dec. 13, 1563, in which the papal assumption is stigmatized as dangerous to the peace of Christendom. "De nostre part nous sommes délibéréz de ne le permettre ny consentir," she says, and she is persuaded that neither Ferdinand nor Maximilian will consent. Le Laboureur, i. 783.

[3] De Thou, iii. (liv. xxxv.) 447. Castelnau (liv. v., c. ix.) gives a wrong impression by his assertion that "the Pope could never be induced to reverse the sentence against the Queen of Navarre."

But while Catharine felt it necessary, for the maintenance of her own authority and of the dignity of the French crown, to enter the lists boldly in behalf of the Queen of Navarre, she was none the less bent upon confirming that authority by rendering it impossible for the Huguenots ever again to take the field in opposition to the crown. A war for the sake of principle was something of which that cynical princess could not conceive. The Huguenot party was strong, according to her view, only because of the possession of powerful leaders. The religious convictions of its adherents went for nothing. Let the Condés, and the Colignies, and the Porciens, and the La Rochefoucaulds be gained over, and the people, deprived of a head, would subordinate their theology to their interest, and unity would be restored under her own rule. It was the same vain belief that alone rendered possible a few years later such a stupendous crime and folly as the St. Bartholomew's Day massacre. Many an obscure and illiterate martyr, who had lost his life during her husband's reign, might have given her a far juster estimate of the future than her Macchiavellian education, with all its fancied shrewdness and insight into human character and motives, had furnished her.

To overthrow the political influence of the Huguenots she must seduce their leaders. Of this Catharine was sure. With whom, then, should she commence but with the brilliant Condé ? The calm and commanding admiral, indeed, was the true head and heart of the late war—never more firm and uncompromising than after defeat—as reluctant to renounce war without securing, beyond question, the religious liberty he sought, as he had been averse to take up the sword at all in the beginning. Of such a man, however, little hope could be entertained. But Louis of Bourbon was cast in another mould. Excessively small in stature and deformed in person, he was a general favorite ; for he was amiable, witty, and talkative.[1] Moreover, he was fond of pleasure

Catharine's attempt to seduce Condé from the Huguenots.

---

[1] Le Laboureur, ii. 610, 611 ; Brantôme, Hommes illustres (Œuvres, ix. 259). We cannot accept, without much caution, the portraits drawn of the prince by the English while they were still smarting with resentment against him for concluding peace with the king without securing the claims of Eliza-

to an extent that attracted notice even in that giddy court, and
as open to temptation as any of its frivolous denizens.[1] For
such persons Catharine knew how to lay snares. Never did
queen surround herself with more brilliant enticements for the
unwary. Her maids of honor were at once her spies and the
instruments of accomplishing her designs. As she had had
a fair Rouhet to undermine the constancy of Antoine, so she
had now an Isabeau de Limueil to entrap his younger brother.
Nor did Catharine's device prove unsuccessful. Condé became
involved in an amorous intrigue that shook the confidence of
his Huguenot friends in his steadfastness and sincerity; while
the silly girl whom the queen had encouraged in a course
that led to ruin, as soon as her shame became notorious, was
ignominiously banished from court—for no one could surpass
Catharine in the personation of offended modesty.[2] Yet, notwithstanding a disgraceful fall which proved to the satisfaction
of a world, always sufficiently sceptical of the depth of religious
convictions, that ambition had much more to do with the prince's
conduct than any sense of duty, Condé was not wholly lost to
right feelings. The tears and remonstrances of his wife—the
true-hearted Éléonore de Roye—dying of grief at his inconstancy, are said to have wrought a marked change in his char-

---

beth upon Calais. "The Prince of Condé," wrote Sir Thomas Smith, April
13, 1563, " is thought . . . . to be waxen almost a new King of Navarre. So
thei which are most zelous for the religion are marvelously offendid with him;
and in great feare, that shortly all wil be worse than ever it was. Et quia
nunc prodit causam religionis, as they say, διὰ τὴν ῥᾳθυμίαν αὐτοῦ καὶ ψυχρότητα
πρὸς τὰ καλά, and begynnes even now γυναικομανεῖν, as the other did; they
thinke plainly, that he will declare himself, ere it be long, unkiend to God, to
us, and to himself; being won by the papists, either with reward of Balaam,
or ells with Cozbi the Midianite, to adjoigne himself to Baal-peor." Forbes,
State Papers, ii. 385.

[1] " Le bon prince," says Brantôme, " estoit aussi mondain qu'un autre, et
aimoit autant la femme d'autruy que la sienne, tenant fort du naturel de ceux
de la race de Bourbon, qui ont esté fort d'amoureuse complexion." Hommes
illustres, M. le Prince de Condé. Granvelle wrote to the Emperor Ferdinand
from Besançon (April 12, 1564), that word had come from France, " que le
prince de Condé y entendoit au service des dames plus qu'en aultre chose, et
assez froid en la religion des huguenotz." Papiers d'état, vii. 467.

[2] See Bayle's art. on Isabeau de Limueil; J. de Serres, iii. 45, 46; De
Thou, iii. (liv. xxxv.) 42.

acter.' From that time Catharine's power was gone. In vain did she or the Guises strive to gain him over to the papal party by offering him, in second marriage, the widow of Marshal Saint André, with an ample dower that might well dazzle a prince of the blood with but a beggarly appanage;[2] or even by proposing to confer upon him the hand of the yet blooming Queen of Scots,[3] the Prince of Condé remained true to the cause he had espoused till his blood stained the fatal field of Jarnac.

But while the queen mother was plying the great with her seductions, while the Roman Catholic leaders were artfully instilling into the minds of the people the idea that the Edict of Amboise was only a temporary expedient,[4] while royal governors, or their lieutenants, like Damville—the constable's younger son —at Pamiers, were cruelly abusing the Protestants whom they ought to have protected,[5] there was much in the tidings that came especially from southern France to encourage the reformers. In the midst of the confusion and carnage of war the leaven had yet been working. There were even to be found places where the progress of Protestantism had rendered the application of the provisions of the edict nearly, if not quite impossible. The little city of Milhau, in Rouergue,[6] is a striking and very interesting instance.

Huguenot progress.

---

[1] Jean de Serres, iii. 50, 51; De Thou, iii (liv. xxxv.) 412, 413.   Cf. Bolwiller to Cardinal Granvelle, Sept. 4, 1564, Papiers d'état du cardinal de Granvelle, viii. 305.   See, however, the statements in chapter xvi. of this history.

[2] His revenue from his county of Soissons was not 1,000 crowns a year, and he had little from his other possessions (Le Laboureur, ii. 611).   Secretary Courtewille, in his secret report (Dec., 1561), states that the Huguenot nobles of the first rank were in general poor—Vendôme, Condé, Coligny, etc.— and that were it not for a monthly sum of 1,200 crowns, which the Huguenots furnished to Condé, and 1,000 which the admiral received in similar manner, they would hardly know how to support themselves.   Papiers d'état du card. de Granv., vi. 440.

[3] Mary herself, however, writing to her aunt, the Duchess of Aerschot (Nov. 6, 1564), represents the offer of marriage as made by Condé, both to her grandmother and to her uncle the cardinal: "à qui il a fait toutes les belles offres du monde."   Papiers d'état du card. de Granv., viii. 481.

[4] Jean de Serres, iii. 32, 33.

[5] Ibid., iii. 45, 46; De Thou, iii. (liv. xxxv.) 414; D'Aubigné, Hist. univ., i. 197.

[6] On the upper Tarn, in the modern department of the Aveyron.

The edict had expressly directed that all churches should be restored to the Roman Catholics, and that the Protestants should resort for worship to other places, either in the suburbs, or—in the case of cities which the Huguenots had held on the seventh Milhau-en-Rouergue. of March, 1563—within the walls. But, soon after the restoration of peace, the consuls and inhabitants of Milhau presented a petition to Charles the Ninth, in which they make the startling assertion that the entire population has become Protestant ("de la religion"); that for two years or thereabouts they have lived in undisturbed peace, whilst other cities have been the scene of disturbances; and that, at a recent gathering of the inhabitants, they unanimously expressed their desire to live in the exercise of the reformed faith, under the royal permission. By the king's order the petition was referred for examination to the commissioners for the execution of the edict in the province of Guyenne. All its statements were found to be strictly correct. There was not one papist within the city; not one man, woman, or child expressed a desire for the re-establishment of the Roman Catholic ceremonial. The monks had renounced the cowl, the priests their vestments. Of their own free will, some of the friars had married, some had taken up useful trades. The prior had voluntarily resigned the greater part of his revenues; retaining one-third for his own support, he had begged that the remainder might be devoted to the preaching of God's Word and the maintenance of the poor. The two churches of the place had for eighteen months been used for Protestant worship, and there were no other convenient places to be found. Indeed, had the churches been given up, there would have been no one to take possession. A careful domiciliary examination by four persons appointed by the royal judge had incontestably established the point. Over eight hundred houses were visited, constituting the greater part of the city. The occupants were summoned to express their preferences, and the result was contained in the solemn return of the commission: "We have not found a single person who desired or asked for the mass; but, on the contrary, all demanded the preaching of the Word of God, and the administration of His holy sacraments as instituted by Himself in that Word.

And thus we certify by the oath we have taken to God and to the king." [1]

From other places the cry of the churches for ministers to be sent from Geneva was unabated. In one town and its environs, so inadequate was a single minister to the discharge of his pastoral duties, that the peasants of the vicinity were compelled to baptize one another's children, or to leave them unbaptized. [2] At Montpellier it is the consuls that beg that their corps of ministers may be doubled; their two pastors cannot preach every day and three times upon Sunday, and yet visit the neighboring villages. [3]

The cry for ministers.

Nowhere, however, was the advance of Protestantism so hopeful as in the principality of Béarn, whither Jeanne d'Albret had retired, and where, since her husband's death, she had been dividing her cares between the education of her son, Henry of Navarre, and the establishment of the Reformation. A less courageous spirit than hers [4]

Establishment of the Reformation in Béarn.

---

[1] The very important documents which exhibit these facts at great length are in the archives of the "Mairie" of Milhau and in the Bibliothèque nationale, and were inedited until printed in the Bulletin, ix. (1860) 382–392. Among the names of the Huguenots of Milhau figuring here is that of Benoit Ferragut, apothecary.

[2] Graignan, pour l'église de Someyre, à la Vénérable Compagnie, 19 juin, 1563, Gaberel, Hist. de l'église de Genève, i., Pièces justificatives, 153. "Et pourtant, je ne peux pas suffire à tout. Les paysans se baptisent les enfants les ungs les autres, ou sont contraincts de les laisser à baptiser."

[3] Les consuls de Montpellier à la Vén. Comp., 30 janvier, 1563 (1564), ibid., i., Pièces just., 179.

[4] I know of no more beautiful monument of Jeanne's courage and piety than the letter she wrote to the Cardinal of Armagnac, in reply to a letter of the cardinal, dated August 18, 1563, intended to frighten her into a return to the papal church. It was sent by the same messenger who had brought the letter of Armagnac, and it has every mark of having been Jeanne's own composition. Both letters are given in full by Olhagaray, Hist. de Foix, Béarn, et Navarre, 536–543, and 544–551; a summary in Vauvilliers, i. 347–362. The Queen of Navarre boldly avowed her sentiments, but declared her policy to be pacific: "Je ne fay rien par force; il n'y a ny mort ny emprisonnement, ny condemnation, qui sont les nerfs de la force." But she refused to recognize Armagnac—who was papal legate in Provence, Guyenne, and Languedoc —as having any such office in Béarn, proudly writing: "Je ne recognois en Bearn que Dieu auquel je dois rendre conte de la charge qu'il m'a baillée de son peuple." The publication of these letters produced a deep impression favorable to the Reformation.

might well have succumbed in view of the difficulties in her way. Of the nobility not one-tenth, of the magistracy not one-fifth, were favorable to the changes which she wished to introduce. The clergy were, of course, nearly unanimous in opposition.[1] She was, however, vigorously and wisely seconded in her efforts by the eminent reformed pastor, Merlin, formerly almoner of Admiral Coligny, whom Calvin had sent from Geneva at her request.[2] But when, contrary to his advice, the Queen of Navarre had summoned a meeting of the estates of her small territory, she detected unexpected symptoms of resistance. She accordingly abstained from broaching the unwelcome topic of reformation. But the deputies of the three orders themselves introduced it. Taking occasion from a prohibition she had issued against carrying the host in procession, they petitioned her to maintain them in the religion of their ancestors, in accordance with the promise which the princes of the country were accustomed to make.[3] Fortunately a small minority was found to offer a request of an entirely opposite tenor; and Jeanne d'Albret, with her characteristic firmness, declared in reply "that she would reform religion in her country, whoever might oppose." So much discontent did this decision provoke that there was danger of open sedition.[4]

---

[1] Letter of Jehan Reymond Merlin to Calvin, Pau, July 23, 1563, printed for the first time in the Bulletin, xiv. (1865) 233, 234.

[2] Olhagaray, Hist. de Foix, Béarn, et Navarre, p. 535; Vauvilliers, Hist. de Jeanne d'Albret, i. 319.

[3] Letter of Merlin, *ubi supra*, 237, 238; Vauvilliers, i. 320.

[4] Ibid., 238. "Dont plusieurs, voire des grands, s'en allèrent fort mal con tens, et singulièrement quelques-uns qu'elle rabroua plus rudement que je n'eusse désiré." Merlin adds that all now saw the excellence of his advice, for, had it been followed, "il y auroit apparence que la réformation eust esté faite en ce pays par l'authorité des estats; maintenant il faut qu'elle se fasse de seule puissance absolue de la royne, voyre avec danger." In other parts of France, as well as in Béarn, Jeanne's reformatory movements were looked upon with great disfavor. Upon a glass window at Limoges (made about the year 1564, and still in existence, I believe) she is represented, by way of derision, as herself in the pulpit, and preaching to a congregation of eight Huguenots seated. Underneath is the bitter couplet,

"Mal sont les gens endoctrinés
Quand par femme sont sermonés."

These internal obstacles were, however, by no means the only difficulties. The court of Pau was disturbed by an uninterrupted succession of rumors of trouble from without. Now it was the French king that stood ready to seize the scanty remnants of Navarre, or the Spaniard that was all prepared for an invasion from the south; anon it was Montluc from the side of Guyenne, or Damville from that of Languedoc, who were meditating incursions in the interest of the Roman Catholic Church. " In short," exclaims her indefatigable coadjutor, Raymond Merlin, " it is wonderful that this princess should be able to persist with constancy in her holy design!"[1] Then came the papal citation, and the necessity to avoid the alienation of the French court which would certainly result from suddenly abolishing the papal rites, especially in view of the circumstance that Catharine de' Medici had several times begged the Queen of Navarre by letter to refrain from taking that decided step.[2]

It speaks well for the energy and intrepidity of Jeanne d'Albret, as well as for the wisdom of some of her advisers, that she was able to lay in these troublous times such broad foundations for the Protestant system of worship and government as we shall shortly have occasion to see her laying; for she was surrounded by courtiers who beheld in her bold espousal of the Reformation the death-blow to their hopes of advancement at Paris, and were, consequently, resolute in their opposition. An incident occurring some months later demonstrates that the perils from her treacherous neighbors were not purely imaginary. This event was nothing less than the discovery of a plan to kidnap the Queen of Navarre and her young son and daughter, and to give them over into the hands of the Spanish Inquisition. Shortly after Antoine's

A plan to kidnap Jeanne and her children.

M. Hennin, Monuments de l'hist. de France, Paris, 1863, tome ix. (1559–1589) 76. The statement that this and a somewhat similar representation, also described in this work, came from an old abbey, whose monks thus revenged themselves upon the queen for removing their pulpit, seems to be a mistake.

[1] Letter of Merlin, *ubi supra*, 239 : " Brief c'est merveille que ceste princesse puisse persister constamment en son sainct vouloir." Cf. letter of same, Dec. 25, 1563, 245.

[2] Letter of Merlin, Dec. 25, 1563, *ubi supra*, 245.

death, her enemies in France—among whom, despite his subsequent denial, it is probable that Blaise de Montluc was one
—had devised this plot as a promising means of promoting
their interests. They had despatched a trusty agent to prepare
a few of their most devoted partisans in Guyenne for its execution; he was then to pass into Spain, to confer with the Duke
of Alva. The latter part of his instructions had not been fulfilled when the assassination of Guise took place. Nothing
daunted by this mishap, the conspirators ordered their agent to
carry out the original scheme. Alva received it with favor,
and sent the Frenchman, with his own approval of the undertaking, to the Spanish court, where he held at least three mid-
night interviews with Philip. No design was ever more dear
to that prudent monarch's heart than one which combined the
rare attractions of secrecy and treachery, particularly if there
were a reasonable hope in the end of a little wholesome blood-
letting. Fortunately, however, the messenger had not been so
careful in his conversation but that he disclosed to one of
Isabella's French servants all that was essential in his commission. The momentous secret soon found its way to the Spanish
queen's almoner, and finally to the queen herself. The blow
impending over her cousin's head terrified Isabella, and melted
her compassionate heart. She disclosed to the ambassador of
Charles the Ninth the astounding fact that some of the Spanish troops then at Barcelona, on their way to the campaign in
Barbary, were to be quietly sent back from the coast to the
interior. Thence, passing through defiles in the Pyrenees,
under experienced guides, they were to fall upon the unsuspecting court of the Queen of Navarre at Pau. In such a case,
to be forewarned was to be forearmed. The private secretary
of the French envoy was despatched to inform Jeanne d'Albret
of her peril, and to notify Catharine de' Medici of the intended
incursion into the French territories. The premature disclosure
occasioned the abandonment of the plan; but it is said that
Philip the Second never forgave his unfortunate wife her part
in frustrating its execution.[1]

---

[1] " Récit d'une entreprise faite en l'an 1565 contre la Reine de Navarre et
messeigneurs les enfans," etc., etc.; Cimber et Danjou, Archives curieuses,

The month of December, 1563, witnessed the close of that celebrated convocation, the Council of Trent.   This is not the place
for the discussion of its extraordinary history, yet it is
worth while to note the conclusion of an assembly
which exerted so weighty an influence in establishing
the dogmas of the papal church.   Resumed after its long suspension, on the eighteenth of January, 1562, the council from
whose deliberations such magnificent results of harmony had
been expected, began its work by rendering the breach between
the Roman Catholic and the Protestant worlds incurable.   Fortunately for the Roman See, all the leading courts in Christendom, although agreed in pronouncing for the necessity of reform,
were at variance with one another in respect to the particular
objects to be aimed at.   It was by a skilful use of this circumstance that the Pope was enabled to extricate himself creditably
from an embarrassing situation, and to secure every essential
advantage.   At the reopening of the council, the French and
German bishops were not present, and the great majority of the
members being poor Italian prelates dependent almost for their
daily bread upon the good pleasure of the pontiff, it is not surprising that the first step taken was to concede to the Pope or
his legates the exclusive right to introduce subjects for discussion, as well as the yet more important claim of sitting as judge
and ratifying the decisions of the assembled Fathers before
they became valid.   Notwithstanding this disgraceful surrender
of their independence and authority, the Roman See was by
no means sure as to the results at which the prelates of the
Council of Trent would arrive.   France and the empire demanded radical reforms in the Pope and his court, and some
concessions to the Protestants—the permission of marriage for
the priesthood, the distribution of the wine to the laity in the
eucharistic sacrament, and the use of the vernacular tongue in a

The Council of
Trent closes
its sessions.

---

vi. 281–295.   The year should be 1564.   The best authority is, however, that
of De Thou, iii. (liv. xxxvi.) 496–499, who states that he simply gives the
account as he had it from the lips of Secretary Rouleau, who brought the
tidings to France, and from the children of the domestic of Isabella who
detected the conspiracy.   See, also, Léon Feer, in Bulletin, xxvi. (1877), 207.
etc., 279, etc.

portion, at least, of the public services. The arrival of the Cardinal of Lorraine and other bishops, in the month of November, 1562, to reinforce the handful of French prelates in attendance, enhanced the apprehensions of Pius. For, strange as it may appear to us, even Pius suspected Charles of favoring innovation—so far had the arch-hypocrite imposed on friend as well as foe by his declaration of adhesion to the Augsburg Confession! The fact was that there was no lack of dissimulation on any side, and that the prelates who urged reforms were among the most insincere. They had drawn up certain articles without the slightest expectation, and certainly without the faintest desire, to have them accepted. Their sole aim seemed to be to shift the blame for the flagrant disorders of the Church from their own shoulders to those of the Pope. If their suggestions had been seriously entertained and acted upon, no men would have had more difficulty than they in concealing their chagrin.[1] The monarchs—and it was their ambassadors who, with the papal legates, directed all the most important conclusions—were at heart equally averse to the restoration of canonical elections, and to everything which, by relieving the ecclesiastics of their servile dependence upon the crown, might cut off that perennial fountain for the payment of their debts and for defraying the expenses of their military enterprises, which they had discovered in the contributions wrung from churchmen's purses. Thus, in the end, by a series of compromises, in which Pope and king each obtained what he was anxious to secure, and sacrificed little for which he really cared, the council managed to confirm the greater number of the abuses it had been expected to

---

[1] Michel de l'Hospital frankly told Santa Croce that the misfortunes of France came exclusively from the French themselves, "e della vita dei preti, molto sregolata, i quali non vogliono esser riformati, e principalmente quelli del Concilio, e poi nelle loro lettere rejiciunt culpam in Papam." "Io so," adds the nuncio himself, "che sono loro che non vogliono esser riformati, e hanno mandati di quà certi articoli che hanno parimente mandati a Roma, circa gli quali io vi posso dir che se Sua Santita li accordasse, conformamente alle loro petitioni, sariano i più malcontenti del mondo; ma no le hanno fatte ad altro fine che per haver occasione di mostrar di quà, che il Papa è quello che non vuole, mentre che sono loro che non vogliono quella riformatione del clero." Santa Croce to Borromeo, March 28, 1563, Aymon, i. 230, 231; Cimber et Danjou, vi. 138.

remove, and to render indelible the line of demarcation between Roman Catholic and Protestant, which it was to have effaced.

The Cardinal of Lorraine returning to France, after the conclusion of the council (the fourth of December, 1563), made it his first object to secure the ratification of the Tridentine decrees. He had now thrown off the mask of moderation, which had caused his friends such needless alarms, and was quite ready to sacrifice (as the nuncio had long since prophesied he would sacrifice)[1] the interests of France to those of the Roman See. But the undertaking was beyond his strength.

Cardinal Lorraine returns to France,

On Lorraine's arrival at court, then stopping at St. Maur-sur-Marne (January, 1564), Catharine answered his request that the king should approve the conclusions of Trent by saying that, if there was anything good in them, the king would gladly approve of it, even if it were not decreed by the council. And, at a supper, to which he was invited the same evening at the quarters of the Cardinal of Bourbon, he had to put up with a good deal of rough jesting from Condé and his boon companions, who plied him with pungent questions respecting the Pope and the doings of the holy Fathers.[2]

and unsuccessfully seeks the approval of the decrees of Trent.

A few weeks later Lorraine made a more distinct effort to secure recognition for the late council's work. Several of the presidents of parliament, the avocat-général, and the procureur du roi had been summoned to court—which, meanwhile, had removed to Melun (February, 1564)—to give their advice to the privy council respecting this momentous question. The cardinal's proposition met with little favor. Chancellor L'Hospital distinguished himself by his determined opposition, and boldly refuted the churchman's arguments. The cardinal had long been chafing at the intractability

Wrangle between Lorraine and L'Hospital.

---

[1] " Il quale (Cardinal di Lorreno) con la morte del suo fratello, havera manco spiriti, e credo io che terra più conto della satisfattione di Sua Santita che di qua." Santa Croce to Borromeo, Blois, March 28, 1563, shortly after Guise's death. Aymon, i. 233 ; Cimber et Danjou, vi. 140.

[2] " Sed hæ nugæ ipsi nequaquam placebant." Languet, letter of Feb. 3, 1564, Epist. secr., ii. 283.

of the lawyer, who owed his early advancement to the influence of the house of Guise, and now could no longer contain his anger. He spoke in a loud and imperious tone, and used taunts that greatly provoked the illustrious bystanders. "It is high time for you to drop your mask," he said to L'Hospital, "for, as for myself, I cannot discover what religion you are of. In fact, you seem to have no other religion than to injure as much as possible both me and my house. Ingrate that you are, you have forgotten all the benefits you have received at my hands." The chancellor's answer was quiet and dignified. "I shall always be ready, even at the peril of my life, to return my obligations to you. I cannot do it at the expense of the king's honor and welfare." And he added the pointed observation that the cardinal was desirous of effecting, by intrigue, what he had been unable to effect by force of arms. Others took up the debate, the old constable himself disclaiming any intention of disputing respecting doctrines which he approved, but expressing his surprise that Lorraine should disturb the tranquillity of the kingdom, and take up the cause of the Roman pontiff against a king through whose liberality he was in the enjoyment of an annual revenue of three or four hundred thousand francs. Catharine, as usual, did her best to allay the irritation ; but the cardinal, greatly disappointed, retired to Rheims.[1]

A few months after the scene at Melun, the most eminent of French jurists, the celebrated Charles Du Moulin, published an unanswerable treatise, proving that the Council of Trent had

---

[1] Letter of Santa Croce to Borromeo, Melun, Feb. 25, 1564, Aymon, i. 258, 259 ; Letter of Beza to Bullinger, Geneva, March 6, 1564, Simler Coll. (Zurich) MSS. ; Languet, March 6, 1564, Epist. secr., ii. 286, 287. There has been great confusion respecting this altercation between Lorraine and L'Hospital. According to Henri Martin (Histoire de France, x. 194), it took place "à propos d'un nouvel édit qui accordait aux réformés quelques facilités pour l'enseignement et l'exercise de leur religion en maisons privées dans les villes où le culte public leur était interdit." M. Jules Bonnet has kindly made search for me in the Zurich and Paris libraries, and obtained corroborative proof of what I already suspected, that M. Martin and others had confounded the scene at *Melun* in February, 1564, with another quarrel between the same persons in March, 1566, at *Moulins*. See the documents, including the letter of Beza referred to above, published together with my inquiries, in the Bulletin de la Soc. du prot. fr., xxiv. (1875) 409–415.

none of the characteristics of a true œcumenical synod, and that

Opposition of
Du Moulin.
its decrees were null and void.[1]   And the Parliament
of Paris, although it ordered the seizure of the book
and imprisoned the author for some days, could not be induced to consent to incorporate in the legislation of the country the Tridentine decrees, so hostile in spirit to the French
legislation.[2] Evidently parliament, although too timid to say
so, believed, with Du Moulin, that the acceptance of the decrees
in question "would be against God and against the benefit of
Jesus Christ in the Gospel, against the ancient councils, against
the majesty of the king and the rights of his crown, against his
recent edicts and the edicts of preceding kings, against the liberty and immunity of the Gallican Church, the authority of the
estates and courts of parliament of the kingdom, and the secular
jurisdiction."[3]

It was shortly before this time that the report gained currency that Charles the Ninth had received an embassy from
Philip of Spain and the Duke of Savoy, inviting him, it was
said, to a conference with all other "Christian" princes, to be
held on the twenty-fifth of March (1564), to swear submission
in common to the decrees of Trent and devise means for the
repression of heresy.   But neither Charles nor his mother, still
very much under the influence of the tolerant chancellor, was
disposed to enter upon the path of persecution marked out for
them.   The conference was therefore, we are told, gracefully,
but firmly declined.[4] The story was but an idle rumor, the
absurdity of which is clearly seen from this one fact among
many, that Philip had not at this time himself accepted and
published the Tridentine decrees;[5] while, from various docu-

---

[1] "Conseil sur le fait du Concile de Trente," etc.   Mém. de Condé, v. 81–
129.   The dedication to Prince Porcien is dated May 29, 1564.   See De Thou,
iii. (liv. xxxvi.) 501.

[2] Du Moulin was ordered by a royal letter to be set at large, Lyons, June
24, 1564.

[3] Conclusion of "Conseil," etc.   Mém. de Condé, v. 129.

[4] De Thou, iii. (liv. xxxvi.), 499, 500 ; Ag. d'Aubigné, Hist. univ., i. 203
(liv. iv., c. iv.) ; Mém. de Castelnau, liv. v., c. vi.

[5] Prof. Soldan has discussed the matter at great length.   Gesch. des Prot.
in Frank., ii. 197, etc.

ments that have come down to us, it appears that Catharine de' Medici had for some months [1] been projecting a trip that should enable her son to meet several of the neighboring princes, for the purpose of cultivating more friendly relations with them. From this desire, and from the wish, by displaying the young monarch to the inhabitants of the different provinces, to revive the loyalty of his subjects, seriously weakened during the late civil war, apparently arose the project of that well-known "progress" of Charles the Ninth through the greater part of France, a progress which consumed many successive months.

Whether the Cardinal of Lorraine had any direct part, as was commonly reported, in bringing about the journey of the king, is uncertain. He himself wrote to Granvelle that he had neither advocated nor opposed it; [2] but the character of the man has been delineated to little purpose in these pages if the reader is disposed to give any weight to his assertion. Certain, however, it is that the Huguenots looked upon the project with great suspicion, and that its execution was accepted as a virtual triumph of their opponents. Condé and Coligny could see as clearly as the cardinal the substantial advantages which a formal visit to the elder branch of the Lorraine family might secure to the branch of the family domiciled in France ; and they could readily imagine that under cover of this voyage might be concealed the most nefarious designs against the peace of their co-religionists. It is not surprising that many Huguenot nobles accepted it as a mark of the loss of favor, and that few of them accompanied the court in its wanderings. [3] The English ambassador, noting this im-

The "progress" of Charles IX.

---

[1] As early as Dec. 13, 1563, the queen mother had announced to the French ambassador in Vienna her son's expected journey, toward the end of February or the beginning of March, to visit his sister, the Duchess of Lorraine, and her infant son. Letter to Bochetel, Bishop of Rennes, Le Laboureur, i. 784. See, too, Languet's letter of Nov. 16, 1563, Epist. secr., ii. 268.

[2] Lorraine to Granvelle, *ubi infra*. The progress was resolved upon, it will be seen, before Lorraine's return from Trent.

[3] " I am going to meet their Majesties at Châlons," wrote the Cardinal of Lorraine from Tou-sur-Marne, between Rheims and Châlons, April 20, 1564 ; " thence they are to leave for Bar, where they will, I think, remain no more than four or five days. I hope that the voyage will be honorable and profit-

portant fact, made, on his own account, an unfavorable deduction from what he saw, as to the design of the court. "They carry the king about this country now," he observed, "mostly to see the ruins of the churches and religious houses done by the Huguenots in this last war. They suppress the losses and hurts the Huguenots have suffered."[1] On the other hand, the Roman Catholic party received their success as a presage of speedy restoration to full power, and entertained brilliant hopes for the future.[2] The queen mother was beginning to make fair promises to the papal adherents, and the influence of the admiral and his brothers seemed to be at an end.

Leaving the palace of Fontainebleau, the court passed through Sens and Troyes to the city of Bar-sur-Seine, where Charles acted as sponsor for his infant nephew, the son of the Duke of Lorraine. The brilliant *fêtes* that accompanied the arrival of the king here and elsewhere could not, however, hide from the world one of the chief results, if not designs, of the journey. It was a prominent part of the queen mother's plan to seize the opportunity for carrying out the system of repression toward the Huguenots which she had already begun. While there is no reason to suppose that as yet she felt any disposition to lend an ear to the suggestions of Spanish emissaries, or of Philip him-

---

able for our house. . . . As to our court, it was never so empty of persons belonging to the opposite religion as it is now. The few that are there show very great regret at this voyage, in which I can assure you that I have not meddled at all, either to further or to retard it; only a short time after my return from Trent, I succeeded in having Nancy changed for Bar." Papiers d'état du card. de Granvelle, vii. 511.

[1] Smith to Cecil, Tarascon, Oct. 21, 1564, State Paper Office, Calendar.

[2] "Assuredly, sir," wrote the cardinal in the letter just cited, "the queen my mistress shows, daily more and more, a strong and holy affection. This evening I have heard, by the Cardinal of Guise, my brother, who has reached me, many holy intentions of their Majesties, which may God give them grace to put into good execution." Ibid., *ubi supra*. In a somewhat similar strain Granvelle about this time wrote: "I am so strongly assured that religion is going to take a favorable turn in France, that I know not what to say of it. The world in that quarter is so light and variable, that no great grounds of confidence can be assumed. But it is at any rate something that matters are not growing worse." Letter to Bolwiller, April 9, 1564, Papiers d'état, etc., vii. 461.

self, for a general massacre, or at least an open war of extermination, she was certainly very willing by less open means to
preclude the Protestants from ever giving her trouble, or
becoming again a formidable power in the state. The most
unfavorable reports, in truth, were in circulation against the
Huguenots. At Lyons they were accused of poisoning the wells,
or, according to another version of the story, the kitchen-pots,
in order to give the impression that the plague was in the city,
and so deter the king from coming.[1] Catharine had no need,
however, of crediting these calumnious tales in order to be
moved to hostile action. Her desire was unabated to reign under
her son's name, untrammelled by the restraint of the jealous love
of liberty cherished by the Huguenots. Their numbers were large
—though not so large as they were then supposed to be. Even
so intelligent a historian as Garnier regards them as constituting
nearly one-third of the kingdom.[2] M. Lacretelle is undoubtedly
much more correct in estimating them at fifteen or sixteen
hundred thousand souls, or barely one-tenth of the entire population of France—a country at that time much more sparsely
inhabited, and of which a much larger part of the surface was
in inferior cultivation, or altogether neglected, than at present.[3]
But, however small their number in proportion to the papists,
the Huguenots, from their superior industry and intelligence,
from the circumstance that their strength lay in the sturdy
middle class and in the nobility, including little of the rabble
of the cities and none of that of Paris,[4] were a party that
naturally awakened the jealousy of the queen. We need make
little account of any exasperation in consequence of such silly
devices as the threatening letter said to have been put in

---

[1] Letter of Granvelle to the Emperor Ferdinand, May 8, 1564, Papiers d'état,.
vii. 613 ; also 622, 631.

[2] " Les réformés qui formoient presque le tiers du royaume." Garnier,.
Hist. de France, xxx. 453.

[3] " On peut présumer qu'il n'y eut jamais en France plus de quinze on seize
cent mille réformés. . . . La France possédait a peine quinze millions
d'habitans. Ainsi les protestans n'en formaient guère que le dixième."
Lacretelle, Histoire de France pendant les guerres de religion, ii. 169, 170.
The entire passage is important.

[4] Giov. Michiel, Rel. des Amb. Vén., i. 412.

Catharine's bed-room, warning her that if she did not drive the
papists from about her, "she and her L'Aubespine" (secretary
of state) would feel the dagger.[1]   She was too shrewd not to
know that a Roman Catholic was more likely to have penned
it than a Huguenot.

In furtherance of the policy to which she had now committed herself, she caused the fortifications of the cities that
had been strongholds of the Protestants during the late war to
be levelled, and in their place erected citadels whereby the
Huguenots might be kept in subjection.[2]   As Easter approached,
Catharine's new zeal. Catharine revealed the altered tone of her mind by
notifying her maids of honor that she would suffer
none to remain about her but those who were good Catholics
and submitted to the ordinary test of orthodoxy.   There is said
to have been but a single girl who declined to go to mass, and
preferred to return to her home.[3]   Well would it have been if
the queen had been as attentive to the morals[4] as to the orthodoxy of these pleasure-seeking attendants.   But, to belong to
the "religion ancienne et catholique" was a mantle large enough
to cover a multitude of sins.

More direct infringements upon the liberty guaranteed by the
Edict of Amboise had already been made or were yet in store.
The legislation which could not conveniently be repealed by for-
Interpretative declarations infringing upon the Edict. mal enactment could be rendered null by interpretative declarations.   Charles was made to proclaim that
by the Edict he had not intended to permit preaching
in places previously belonging to the patrimony of the Church,

---

[1] Capefigue, from MS., Hist. de la réforme, de la ligue, etc., ii. 408.

[2] Jean de Serres, iii. 47, 48 ; De Thou, iii., liv. xxxvi. 504 ; Mem. de Castelnau, l. v., c. x.; Pasquier, Lettres, iv., 22, *ap.* Capefigue, ii. 410.

[3] Granvelle to the Emperor Ferdinand, April 12, 1564, Pap. d'état, vii. 467.

[4] Of solicitude on this score, the only evidence I have come across is furnished by the following passage of one of the "Occurrences in France," under
date of April 11, 1565, sent to the English Government.   "Orders are also
taken in the court that no gentleman shall talk with the queen's maids,
except it is in the queen's presence, or in that of Madame la Princesse de
Roche-sur-Yon, except he be married ; and if they sit upon a form or stool,
he may sit by her, and if she sit upon the ground he may kneel by her, but
not lie long, as the fashion was in this court."   State Paper Office, Calendar,
331.

or held as benefices. This was aimed at such prelates of doubtful catholicity as Saint Romain, Archbishop of Aix, or the Cardinal Bishop of Beauvais, Odet de Châtillon. He was made to say, that by the places where Protestant worship could be held within the walls, by virtue of its having been exercised on the seventh of March, 1563, were meant only those that had been garrisoned by Protestants, and had undergone a successful siege. This stroke of the pen cut off several cities in which Protestantism had been maintained without conflict of arms. The Huguenot counsellors of the parliament were deprived of the enjoyment of their right to attend the "assemblée," or "Protestant congregation," by a gloss which forbade the inhabitants of Paris from attending the reformed worship in the neighboring districts. When the court reached Lyons, a city which, as we have seen, had been among the foremost in devotion to the Protestant cause, a fresh edict, of the twenty-fourth of June, prohibited the reformed rites from being celebrated in any city in which the king might be sojourning. Five or six weeks later, at the little town of Roussillon, a few miles south of Vienne, on the Rhône, another

Declaration of Roussillon. and more flagrant violation of the letter and spirit of the edict of pacification was incorporated in a declaration purporting to remove fresh uncertainties as to the meaning of its provisions. It forbade the noblemen who might possess the right to maintain Protestant services in their castles, to permit any persons but their own families and their vassals to be present. It prohibited the convocation of synods and the collection of money, and enjoined upon ministers of the gospel not to leave their places of residence, nor to open schools for the instruction of the young. But the most vexatious and unjust article of all was that which constrained all priests, monks, and nuns, who during or since the troubles had forsaken their vows and had married, either to resume their monastic profession and dismiss their consorts, or to leave the kingdom. As a penalty for the violation of this command, the men were to be sentenced to the galleys for life, the women to close confinement in prison. I omit in this list of grievances suffered by the Huguenots some minor annoyances such as that which compelled the artisan to desist from working in his shop with open doors on the festivals of the Roman Catholic Church.[1]

These legal infractions were not all. Everywhere the Huguenots had to complain of acts of violence, committed by their papist neighbors, at the instigation of priests and bishops, and not infrequently of the royal governors. Little more than a year had passed since peace was restored, and already the victims of religious assassination rivalled in number the martyrs of the days of open persecution. At Crevant the Protestants were attacked on their way to their "temple;" at Tours they were attacked while engaged in worship. At Mans the fanatical bishop was the chief instigator of a work of mingled murder and rapine. At Vendôme it was the royal governor himself, Gilbert de Curée, who fell a victim to the hatred of the Roman Catholic noblesse, and was treacherously killed while hunting.[2] If anything more was needed to render the violence insupportable, it was found in the fact that any attempt to obtain judicial investigation and redress resulted not in the condemnation of the guilty, but in the personal peril of the complainant.[3]

Assaults upon unoffending Huguenots.

Smarting under the repeated acts of violence to which at every moment they were liable, and under the successive infringements upon the Edict of Amboise, the Huguenots urged the Prince of Condé to represent their grievances to the monarch, in the excellence of whose heart they had not yet lost confidence. The Protestant leader did not repel the trust. His appeal to Charles and to the queen mother was urgent. He showed that, even where the letter of the edict

Condé appeals for redress.

---

[1] Edict of Vincennes, June 14, 1653, and Declarations of Paris, Dec. 14, 1563; of Lyons, June 24, 1564; and of Roussillon, Aug. 4, 1564. Isambert, Recueil des anc. lois. franç., xiv. 141, 159, 170–172, and Drion, Hist. chronol., i. 102–108. See Jean de Serres, iii. 35–41, 55–63, and after him, De Thou, iii. (liv. xxxv.) 411, 412, 504, 505.

[2] Jean de Serres, iii. 54, 55, 64, 65, etc. De Thou, iii. (liv. xxxvi.) 503, etc.

[3] Ibid., *ubi supra*. There are no similar cases of assassination on the part of Huguenots at this period. That of Charry at court seems to have resulted partly from revenge for personal wrongs, partly from mistaken devotion on the part of one of D'Andelot's followers to his master's interests. See Languet, letter of Feb. 3, 1564, Epist. secr., ii. 284.

was observed, its spirit was flagrantly violated. The edict provided for a place for preaching in each prefecture, to be selected by the king. In some cases no place had yet been designated. In others, the most inconvenient places had been assigned. Sometimes the Huguenots of a district would be compelled to go *twenty or twenty-five leagues* in order to attend divine worship. The declaration affecting the monks and nuns who had forsaken their habit was a violation of the general liberty promised. So also was the prohibition of synods, which, though not expressly mentioned, were implied in the toleration of the religion to which they were indispensably necessary. But it was the prejudice and ill-will, of which the Huguenots were the habitual victims at the hands of royal governors and other officers, which moved them most deeply. The evident desire was to find some ground of accusation against them. The ears of the judges were stopped against their appeals for justice. It was enough that they were accused. Decrees of confiscation, of the razing of their houses, of death, were promptly given before any examination was made into the truth of their culpability. On a mere rumor of a commotion in the Protestant city of Montauban, an order was issued to demolish its walls. The case was far otherwise with turbulent Roman Catholic towns. The people were encouraged to acts of violence toward the Huguenots by the impunity of the perpetrators of similar crimes, and by the evident partiality of those who were set to administer justice. Out of six or seven score murders of Protestants since the peace, not two of the abominable acts had been punished. Under such circumstances it would not be surprising if the victims of inordinate cruelty should at length be driven in desperation to take their defence into their own hands.[1]

The king, or his ministers, fearful of a commotion during his absence from Paris, answered the letter of the prince with tolerable courtesy, and even made a pretence of desiring to

---

[1] Jean de Serres, iii. 65-82; De Thou, iii. (liv. xxxvi.) 505; Lettres de Monseigneur le Prince de Condé à la Roine Mère du Roy, avec Advertissemens depuis donnéz par ledit Seigneur Prince à leurs Majestez, etc. (Aug. 31, 1564, etc.), Mém. de Condé, v. 201-214.

secure justice to his Protestant subjects; but the attempt really effected very little. Thus, for instance, while sojourn-
Conciliatory reply of the king.
ing in the city of Valence (on the fifth of September, 1564), Charles received a petition of the Huguenots of Bordeaux, setting forth some of the grievances under which they were groaning, and gave a favorable answer. He permitted them, by this patent, to sing their psalms in their own houses. He declared them free from any obligation to furnish the "pain bénit," and to contribute to the support of Roman Catholic fraternities. The Protestants were not to be molested for possessing or selling copies of the Bible. They must not be compelled to deck out their houses in honor of religious processions, nor to swear on St. Anthony's arm. They might work at their trades with closed doors, except on Sundays and solemn feasts. Magistrates were forbidden to take away the children of Huguenots, in order to have them baptized according to Romish rites. Protestants could be elected to municipal offices equally with the adherents of the other faith.[1] In a similar tone of conciliation the king published an order from Roussillon, remitting the fines that had been imposed upon the Huguenots of Nantes for neglecting to hang tapestry before their houses on Corpus Christi Day, and permitting them henceforth to abstain from an act so offensive to their religious convictions.[2]

Such local concessions were, however, only the decoys by

---

[1] "Articles respondus par le Roy en son Conseil privé, sur la requeste présentée par plusieurs habitans de la ville de Bourdeaux," etc. The signature of the secretary, Robertet, was affixed Sept. 5, 1564; but such was the obstinacy of the judges of Bordeaux, that the document was not published in the parliament of that city until nearly eight months later (April 30, 1565). Mém. de Condé, v. 214–224. Cimber et Danjou, Archives curieuses, vi. 271–278. The Protestants petitioned for another town in place of St. Macaire, which had been assigned them for their religious worship—the most inconveniently situated in the entire " sénéchaussée." They desired a city which they could go to and return from on the same day. They stated that " la plus grande partie des plus notables familles de la ville de Bordeaux est de la religion réformée." This part of their request the king referred to the judgment of the governor.

[2] Ordonnance du roi Charles IX., 6 août, 1564, Nantes MS., Bulletin, xiii. (1864), 203, 204.

which the queen mother intended to lure the Huguenots on to a fatal security. A few months later, at Avignon, Catharine caused an ordinance to be published in the king's name, which Cardinal Santa Croce characterized as an excellent one. It excluded Protestants from holding judicial seats. Catharine told the nuncio that her counsellors had been desirous of extending the same prohibition to all other charges under government, but that she had deterred them. It would have driven the Huguenots to desperation, and might have occasioned disturbances. "We shall labor, however," she said, "to exclude them little by little from all their offices." At the same time she expressed her joy that everything was succeeding so well, and privately assured the nuncio "that people were much deceived in her."[1]

[margin note: Protestants excluded from judicial posts.]

And yet such are the paradoxes of history, especially in this age of surprises, that, at the very moment the king was depriving his own Protestant subjects of their rights, he was negotiating in behalf of the Protestant subjects of his neighbors! The king would not leave Avignon—so wrote the English envoy—without reconciling the inhabitants of the Comtât Venaissin and the principality of Orange, whom diversity of religion had brought into collision. And, by the articles of pacification which the ambassador enclosed, the king was seen "to have had a care for others also, having provided a certain liberty of religion even to the Pope's own subjects, which he had much difficulty in obtaining."[2]

While the queen mother, under cover of her son's authority, followed the new policy of opposition to the Huguenots upon which she had now entered, an incident occurred at Paris show-

---

[1] Aymon, i. 277, 278, and Cimber et Danjou, Archives cur., vi. 167. As by this time both Papists and Huguenots knew Catharine de' Medici to be a woman utterly devoid of moral principle, it may fairly be considered an open question whether there was any one in France more deceived than she was in supposing that she had deceived others.

[2] Sir Thomas Smith to the queen, from Tarascon (near Avignon), Oct. 21, 1564, enclosing "Articles of pacification for those of the religion in Venaissin and Avignon agreed to by the ministers of the Pope and those of the Prince of Orange, Oct. 11, 1564." Signed by the vice-legate, Bishop of Fermo, and Fabrizio Serbellone. State Paper Office.

ing that even the Roman Catholics were not unanimous in their support of the Guises and their plan of exterminating heresy. The governor of the metropolis was Marshal Montmorency, the most worthy of all the constable's sons. He had vigorously exerted himself ever since the king's departure to protect the Huguenots in accordance with the provisions of the treaty. A Protestant woman, who during the war had been hung in effigy for "huguenoterie," but had returned from her flight since the conclusion of peace, died and was secretly buried by friends, one Sunday night, in the "Cimetière des Innocents." The next morning a rabble, such as only Paris could afford, collected with the intention of disinterring the heretic. And they would have accomplished their design, had not Marshal Montmorency ridden in, sword in hand, and resolved to hang the culprits that very day. "He would assist the Huguenots," he is reported to have been in the habit of saying, "because they were the weaker party." [1] On Monday, the eighth of January, 1565, the Cardinal of Lorraine approached the city in full ecclesiastical dress, with the intention of entering it. [2] He was attended by his young nephew, the Duke of Guise, and by an escort of armed men, whom Catharine had permitted him to retain in spite of the general prohibition, because of the fears he undoubtedly felt for his personal safety. As he neared Paris he was met by a messenger sent by the governor, commanding him to bid his company lay down their arms, or to exhibit his pretended authority. The cardinal, accustomed to domineer over even such old noble families as the Montmorencies, would do neither, and attempted to ride defiantly into the city. But the marshal was no respecter of persons. With the troops at his command he met and dispersed the cardinal's escort. Lorraine fled as for his life into a shop on the Rue Saint Denis. Thence he was secretly con-

Marshal Montmorency checks the Parisian mob.

His encounter with Cardinal Lorraine.

---

[1] Journal d'un curé ligueur (Jehan de la Fosse), 55, 56, 68.

[2] "Lundi passé, viii⁰ du present mois, ung peu avant les trois heures après midy, monsieur le révérendissime cardinal de Lorraine, vestu du robbon et chappeau, ... est entré en Paris." Account written two days after the occurrence by Del Rio, attached to the Spanish embassy in Paris. Papiers d'état du card. de Granvelle, viii. 600–602.

veyed to his own palace, and shortly after he left the city in
utter discomfiture, but breathing dire threats against the marshal.[1] The latter, calling into Paris his cousin the admiral, had
no difficulty in maintaining order. Great was the consternation
of the populace, it is true, for the absurd report was circulated
that Coligny was come to plunder the city, and to seize the
Parliament House, the Cathedral, and the Bastile;[2] and even
the first president, De Thou, begged him, when he came to the
parliament, to explain the reasons of his obeying his cousin's
summons, and to imitate the prudence of Pompey the Great
when he entered the city of Rome, where Cæsar's presence rendered a sedition imminent. The admiral, in reply, gracefully
acknowledged the honor which parliament had done him in
likening him to Pompey, whom he would gladly imitate, he said,
because Pompey was a patriot. Still he saw no appositeness in
the comparison, " as there was no Cæsar in Paris." [3]

Early in the month of June, 1565, Charles the Ninth and his
court reached the neighborhood of the city of Bayonne, where,
on the very confines of France and Spain, a meeting
had been arranged between Catharine and her daughter Isabella, wife of Philip the Second. Catharine's
first proposal had been that her royal son-in-law should himself
be present. She had urged that great good to Christendom
might flow from their deliberations. Philip the Prudent, however, and his confidential adviser, the Duke of Alva, were sus-

The confer-
ence at Bay-
onne, June,
1565.

---

[1] Mém. de Castelnau, liv. vi., c. iii. ; Jean de Serres, iii. 85, 86 ; De Thou,
iii. (liv. xxxvii.) 533–537 ; Mém. de Claude Haton, i. 381–383; Journal de
Jehan de la Fosse, 70–72 ; Condé MSS., in Duc d'Aumale, Princes de Condé,
i. 518 ; Le Livre des Marchands (Ed. Panthéon) 424, 425, where the ludicrous
features of the scene are, of course, most brightly colored. "J'espère bien
aussi m'en resentir ung jour," wrote the cardinal himself, a few weeks later,
from Joinville. Pap. d'état du card. de Granvelle, viii. 681.

[2] Jehan de la Fosse, 72.

[3] Harangue de l'Admiral de France à Messieurs de la Cour de Parlement de
Paris, du 27 janvier 1565, avec la réponse. Papiers d'état du card. de Granvelle, viii. 655–657. M. de Crussol, in a letter of February 4, 1565, alludes to
the admiral's flattering reception by the clergy and by the Sorbonne, "qui
sont allé le visiter et offert infiny service ; " and states that both parties were
gratified by the interview. Condé MSS., in Duc d'Aumale, Princes de Condé,
piéces inédits, i. 520.

picious of the design.   Alva was convinced that Catharine had
only her own private ends in view.[1]   Granvelle observed that
little fruit came of these interviews of princes but discord and
confusion, and judged that, had not the queen mother strenuously insisted upon improving perhaps the only opportunity
which she and her daughter might enjoy of seeing each other,
even the interview between the two queens would have been
declined.[2]   As it was, however, Philip excused himself on the
plea of engrossing occupations.

Such were the circumstances under which the Bayonne conference took place—a meeting which Cardinal Granvelle assured
his correspondents was a simple visit of a daughter to her
mother,[3] but to which contemporaries, both Roman Catholic
and Protestant, ascribed a far deeper significance.   At this
meeting, according to Jean de Serres, writing only four or five
years after the event,[4] a holy league, as it was called, was
formed, by the intervention of Isabella, for the purpose of re-
establishing the authority of the ancient religion and of extirpating the new.   France and Spain mutually promised to render
each other assistance in the good work ; and both pledged
themselves to the support of the Holy See by all the means in
their power.   Philip himself was not present, either, it was conjectured, in order that the league might the better be kept secret,
or to avoid the appearance of lowering his dignity before that
of the French monarch.[5]   The current belief—until recently

---

[1] Philip II. to Alva, Dec. 14, 1563, Pap. d'état du card. de Granvelle, vii.
269 ; Alva to Philip II., Dec. 22, 1563, ib., vii. 286, 287.

[2] Granvelle to the Baron de Bolwiller, March 13, 1565, ib., ix. 61, 62.

[3] Ibid., *ubi supra.*   " Je vous asseure, comme il est véritable, qu'il n'y a
aultre chose en cecy que simple visitation de fille à mère."

[4] Prof. Kluckhohn, strangely enough, speaks of Jean de Serres's Commentarii de statu relig., etc., as " zuerst im Jahre, 1575, erschienen " (Zur Geschichte des angeb. Bündnisses von Bayonne, Abhand. der k. bayer. Akademie,
München, 1868, p. 151).   I have before me the earlier edition of 1571, containing verbatim the passage he quotes, with a single unimportant exception
—" ecclesiarum " instead of " religiosorum."

[5] J. de Serres, Comment. de statu reipublicæ et religionis in Gallia regno,
Carolo IX. rege (1571), iii. 92.   The Prince of Condé, in his long petition sent
to Charles, Aug. 23, 1568, at the outbreak of the Third Civil War, says expressly in reference to events a year preceding the Second War : " Quando-

almost the universal belief of historians—goes farther, and alleges that in this mysterious conference Catharine and Alva, who accompanied his master's wife, concocted the plan of that famous massacre whose execution was delayed by various circumstances for seven years. Alva was the tempter, and the words with which he recommended his favorite method of dealing with heresy, by destroying its chief upholders, were embodied in the ignoble sentence, " Better a salmon's head than ten thousand frogs." [1]

In fact, a general impression that the conference had led to the formation of a distinct plan for the universal destruction of Protestantism gained ground almost immediately. Within about a month after the queen mother and her daughter had ended their interview, the English ambassador wrote to Leicester and Cecil that "they of the religion think that there has been at this meeting at Bayonne some complot betwixt the Pope, the King of Spain, and the Scottish queen, by their ambassadors, and some say also the Papists of England." [2]

Fortunately, however, we are not left to frame by uncertain conjecture a doubtful story of the transactions of this famous interview. A copy of certain letters of Alva himself to King Philip has been preserved among the manuscripts of Cardinal Granvelle, to dispel many inveterate misapprehensions. These letters not only prove that no plan for a massacre of

---

quidem ego et alii Religionis reformatæ viri fuerimus jampridem admoniti de inito Baionæ consilio cum Hispano, ad eos omnes plane delendos atque exterminandos qui Religionem reformatam in tuo regno profiteantur." Ibid., iii. 200.

[1] The remark is said to have been accidentally overheard by Henry of Navarre, afterward Henry the Fourth, of whose presence little account was taken in consequence of his youth. (He was just eleven years and a half old.) But his intimate follower, Agrippa d'Aubigné, would have been likely to give him as authority, had this been the case. He only says : " Les plus licentieux faisoient leur profit d'un terme du Duc d'Alve à Baionne, que dix mille grenouilles ne valloient pas la teste d'un saumon." Hist. univ., liv. iv., c. v. (i. 206). Jean de Serres, *ubi supra*, iii. 125, gives the expression in nearly the same words : " Satius esse unicum salmonis caput, quam mille ranarum capita habere."

[2] Smith to Leicester and Cecil, July 2–29, 1565. State Paper Office, Calendar, 403.

the Huguenots was agreed upon by the two parties, but that
Alva did not even distinctly declare himself in favor
of such a plan. They furnish, however, an instructive view, such as can but rarely be so well obtained,
of the net of treacherous intrigue which the fingers of Philip
and his agents were for many years busy day and night in cautiously spreading around the throne of France.

No plan of massacre agreed upon.

On Thursday, the fourteenth of June, the young Spanish
queen, with her brilliant train of attendant grandees, crossed
the narrow stream forming the dividing line between
the two kingdoms, and was conducted by her mother,
her brothers and sister, and a crowd of gallant French nobles,
to the neighboring town of Saint Jean de Luz. On Friday, Catharine and Charles rode forward to make their solemn
entry into Bayonne, where they were to await their
guests' arrival. Before they started, Alva had already been at
work complimenting such good Catholics as the constable,
Cardinal Bourbon, and Prince La Roche-sur-Yon, flattering
Cardinal Guise (his brother of Lorraine was absent from court,
not yet being fully reinstated in favor), the Duke of Montpensier, and vain old Blaise de Montluc. Nor were his blandish-
ments thrown away. Poor weak Guise—the "cardinal des
bouteilles" he was called, from the greater acquaintance he had
with wine and good living than with religious or political affairs [1]—was overcome with emotion and gratitude, and begged
Alva to implore the Catholic king, by the love of God, to look
in pity upon an unhappy kingdom, where religion was fast
going to ruin. Montpensier threw himself into Alva's arms,

June 14th.

June 15th.

---

[1] "On apelloit ce bon prélat 'le cardinal des bouteilles,'" says Lestoile,
"pource qu'il les aimoit fort, et ne se mesloit guères d'autres affaires que de
celles de la cuisine, où il se connoissoit fort bien, et les entendoit mieux que
celles de la religion et de l'estat." In chronicling the death of Louis, Cardinal
of Guise, at Paris, March 29, 1578, he records the suggestive fact that "he was
the last of the six brothers of the house of Guise; yet died he young, at the
age of forty-eight years." Journal de Henri III., p. 96 (edit. Michaud). So
closely is the scriptural warning fulfilled, that "bloody and deceitful men
shall not live out half their days." Cardinal Guise (not Cardinal Lorraine, as
Mr. Henry White seems to suppose, Massacre of St. Bartholomew, Am. edit.,
187, 188) was the abettor of the massacre of Vassy.

and told him that Philip alone was the hope of all the good in France, declaring for himself that he was willing to be torn in pieces in his behalf, and maintaining the meanwhile, that, should that pleasant operation be performed, " Philip " would be found written on his heart. To Blaise de Montluc's self-conceit Alva laid siege in no very covert manner, assuring him that his master had not given his consent to Catharine's plan for an interview until he had perused a paper written by the grim old warrior's hand, in which he had expressed the opinion that the conference would be productive of wholesome results. The implied praise was all that was needed to induce Montluc to explain himself more fully. He was opposed to the exercise of any false humanity. He ascribed the little success that had attended the Roman Catholic arms in the last struggle to the half-way measures adopted and the attempt to exercise the courtesies of peace in time of war. The combatants on either side addressed their enemies as "my brother" and "my cousin." As for himself, he had made it a rule to spare no man's life, but to wage a war of extermination. To this unburdening of his mind Alva replied by giving Montluc to understand that, as a good Roman Catholic, it should be his task to discover the means of inducing Charles and his mother to perform their duty, and, if he failed in this, to disclose to Philip the course which he must pursue, " since it was impossible to suffer matters to go on, as they were going, to their ruin."

What the duty of the French king was, in Philip's and Alva's view, is evidenced by the advice of the "good" Papists which the minister reports to his master with every mark of approbation. It was, in the first place, to banish from the kingdom every Protestant minister, and prohibit utterly any exercise of the reformed religion. The provincial governors, whose orthodoxy in almost every case could be relied upon, were to be the instruments in the execution of this work.[1] But, besides this, it would be necessary to seize a few of the leaders and cut off their heads. Five or six, it was suggested, would be all the

---

[1] Cartas que el Duque de Alba scrivió, etc. Papiers d'état du cardinal de Granvelle, ix. 296.

victims required.[1] It was, in fact, essentially the plan of operations with which Alva undertook a year or two later the reduction of the Netherlands to submission to Spanish tyranny and
the Papal Church. Treacherous imprisonments of the most suspected, which could scarcely have been confined within such
narrow numerical limits as Alva laid down, together with a
"blood council" to complete the work, or with a massacre in
which the proprieties of judicial investigation would be less
nicely observed—such was the scheme after Philip's own heart.

But this scheme suited the present frame of mind neither of
Charles nor of Catharine. When the crafty Spaniard, cautiously feeling his way, begged the young king to be very careful of his life, "for God, he was convinced, was reserving him
to execute a great work by his hands, in the punishment of the
offences which were committed in that kingdom,"[2] Charles
briskly responded: "Oh! to take up arms does not suit me. I
have no disposition to consummate the destruction of my kingdom begun in the past wars."[3] The duke clearly saw that the
king was but repeating a lesson that had been taught him by
others, and contemptuously dismissed the topic.[4]

Catharine was not less determined than her son to avoid a
resort to arms. It was with difficulty that Alva could get her
to broach the subject of religion at all. Isabella having, at his
suggestion, pressed her mother to disclose the secret communication to make which she had sought this interview, Catharine
referred, with some bitterness, to the distrust of Charles and of
herself evidently entertained by Philip, which would be likely

---

[1] "Con no mas personas que con cinco ó seys que son el cabo de todo esto,
los tomasen á su mano y les cortasen las cabeças," etc. Ibid., ix. 298.

[2] "Que mirase mucho por su salud, pues que della dependia todo el bien de
la christiandad, y creya que le tenia Dios guardado para venir por su mano un
gran servicio, que era el castigo de las offensas que en este su reyno se le ha-
zian." Cartas que el Duque de Alba scrivió a su Magestad . . . . que con-
tienen las vistas en Bayona, etc. Papiers d'état du card. de Granvelle, ix.
291.

[3] "Saltó luego con dezirme : ' ó, el tomar las armas no conviene, que yo de-
struya mi reyno como se començó á hazer con las guerras passadas.' " Ibid.,
ubi supra.

[4] "Como es, descubrí lo que le tenian pedricado ; passé á otras materias,"
etc. Ibid., ubi supra.

to lead in the end to a renewal of war between France and Spain. And she reproached Isabella with having so soon allowed herself to become " Hispaniolized " [1]—a charge from which her daughter endeavored to clear herself as best she could.

Catharine and Alva.   When at last Alva succeeded in bringing up the subject, which was, ostensibly at least, so near what Philip called his heart, Catharine's display of tact was such as to elicit the profound admiration of even so consummate a master in the art of dissimulation as the duke himself. Her circumspection, he declared, he had never seen equalled.[2] She maintained that there was no need of alarm at the condition of religion in France, for everything was going on better than when the Edict of Pacification was published. " It is your satisfaction at being freed from war that leads you to take so cheerful a view," urged Alva. " My master cannot but require the application of a more efficient remedy, since the cause is common to Spain ; for the disease will spread, and Philip has no inclination to lose his crown, or, perhaps, even his head." Catharine now insisted upon Alva's explaining himself and disclosing his master's plan of action. This Alva declined to do. Although Philip was as conversant with the state of France as she or any other person in the kingdom, yet he preferred to leave to her to decide upon the precise nature of the specific to be administered. Catharine pressed the inquiry, but Alva continued to parry the question adroitly. He asks if, since the Edict of Toleration, ground has been gained or lost. Decidedly gained, she replies, and proceeds to particularize. But Alva is confident that she is deceiving herself or him : it is notorious that things are becoming worse every day.

" Would you have me understand," interrupts Catharine, " that we must resort to arms again ? "

" I see no present need of assuming them," answers Alva, " and my master would not advise you to take them up, unless constrained by other necessity than that which I now see."

---

[1] " Que venia muy Española." Ibid., ix. 300.
[2] " Ella començó cierto la plática con el mayor tiento que yo he visto tener jamas á nadie en cosa." Ibid., ix. 303.

"What, then, would Philip have me do?" asks Catharine. "Apply a prompt remedy," answers Alva; "for sooner or later your enemies will, by their own action, compel you to accept the wager of war, and that, probably, under less favorable circumstances than at present. All Philip's thoughts are intent upon the expulsion of that wretched sect of the Huguenots, and upon restoring the subjects of the French crown to their ancient obedience, and maintaining the queen mother's legitimate authority." "The king, my son," responds Catharine, "publishes whatever edicts he pleases, and is obeyed." "Then, if he enjoys such authority over his vassals," breaks in Isabella, "why does he not punish those who are rebels both against God and against himself?"

That question Catharine did not choose to answer. Instead of it she had some chimerical schemes to propose—a league between France, Spain, and Germany, that should give the law to the world, and a confirmation of the bonds that united the royal houses of France and Spain by two more marriages, viz.: of Don Carlos to Margaret, her youngest daughter, and of the Duke of Anjou to the Princess of Portugal. Alva, however, making light of such projects, which could, according to his view, effect nothing more than the bond already connecting the families, was not slow in bringing the conversation back to the religious question. But he soon had reason to complain of Catharine's coldness. She had already expressed her mind fully, she said; and she resented, as a want of the respect due to her, the hint that she was more indifferent than previously. She would not fail to do justice, she assured him. That would be difficult, rejoined Alva, with a chancellor at the head of the judiciary who could not certainly be expected to apply the remedy needed by the unsound condition of France. "It is his personal enemies," promptly replied Catharine, "who, out of hatred, accuse L'Hospital of being a bad Catholic." "Can you deny that he is a Huguenot?" asked the Spaniard. "I do not regard him as such," calmly answered the French queen. "Then you are the only person in the kingdom who is of that opinion!" retorted the duke. "Even before I left France, and during the lifetime of my father, King Henry," said Isabella, interrupting with considerable animation, "your Majesty knows that that was his reputation ; and you may be certain that so long as he is retained in his present office the good will always be kept in fear and in disfavor, while the bad will find him a support and advocate in all their evil courses. If he were to be confined for a few days only in his own house, you would at once discover the truth of my words, so much better would the interests of religion advance."[1] But this step Catharine was by no means willing to take. Nor, when again pressed by Alva, who dwelt much on the importance to Philip of knowing her intentions as to applying herself in earnest to the good work, so as to be guided in his own actions, would she deign to give any clearer indications. Yet she avowed—greatly shocking the orthodox duke thereby[2]—that she designed, instead of securing the acceptance of the decrees of Trent by the French, to convene a council of "good prelates and wise men," to settle a number of matters not of divine or positive prescription, which the Fathers of Trent had left undecided. Alva expressed his extreme astonishment, and reminded her of the Colloquy of Poissy—the source, as he alleged, of all the present disgraceful situation of France.[3] But Catharine threw the whole blame of the failure of that conference upon the inordinate conceit of the Cardinal of Lorraine,[4] and persisted in the plan. The Spaniard came to the conclusion that Catharine's only design was to avoid having recourse to salutary rigor, and indulged in his correspondence with his master in lugubrious vaticinations respecting the future.[5]

So far, then, was the general belief which has been adopted

---

[1] Cartas que el Duque de Alba scrivió, etc. Papiers d'état du card. de Granvelle, ix. 315.

[2] "Yo me alteré *terriblemente* de oírselo, y le dixe que me maravillava mucho." Ibid., ix. 317.

[3] "La junta passada de adonde començáron todas las desverguenças que al presente ay en este reyno." Ibid., ix. 317.

[4] "En la otra el cardenal de Lorena havia sido el que avia hecho todo el daño, pensando poder persuadir á los ministros." Ibid., *ubi supra*.

[5] "Parécenos que quiere con esta semblea (i. e., assemblée), que ellos llaman, remendar lo que falta en el rigor necessario al remedio de sus vasallos, y plega á Dios no sea," etc. Ibid., ix. 318.

by the greater number of historians up to our own days from
being correct—the belief that Catharine framed, at the

Catharine re-
jects all vio-
lent plans. Bayonne conference, with Alva's assistance, a plan for
the extermination of the Protestants by a massacre
such as was realized on St. Bartholomew's Day, 1572—that, on
the contrary, the queen mother refused, in a peremptory manner that disgusted the Spanish fanatics, every proposition that
looked like violence.   That we have not read the correspondence
of Alva incorrectly, and that no letter containing the mythical
agreement of Catharine ever reached Philip, is proved by the tone
of the letters that passed between the great agents in the work
of persecution in the Spanish Netherlands.   Cardinal Granvelle,
who, in his retreat at Besançon, was kept fully in-

Cardinal
Granvelle's
testimony. formed by the King of Spain, or by his chief ministers, of every important event, and who received
copies of all the most weighty documents, in a letter to Alonso
del Canto expresses great regret that Isabella and Alva should
have failed in their endeavor to induce Catharine de' Medici to
adopt methods more proper than she was taking to remedy the
religious ills of France.   She promised marvels, he adds, but
was determined to avoid recourse to arms, which, indeed, was
not necessary, if she would only act as she should.   He was
persuaded that the plan she was adopting would entail the ruin
of religion and of her son's throne.[1]

While the policy of two of the most important nations on the
face of the globe, in which were involved the interests, temporal
and eternal, of millions of men, women, and children, formed
the topic of earnest discussion between two women—a mother
and her daughter, the mother yet to become infamous for her
participation in a bloody tragedy of which she as yet little
dreamed—and a Spanish grandee doomed to an equally unenviable immortality in the records of human suffering and

Festivities and
pageantry. human crime, the city of Bayonne was the scene of
an ephemeral gayety that might well convey the impression that such merry-making was not only the sole object of
the conference, but the great concern of life.[2]   Two nations,

---

[1] Letter of Granvelle, Aug. 20, 1565, Papiers d'état, ix. 481.

[2] " Depuis l'arrivée n'y eust mention que de festins, récréations et passe-

floundering in hopeless bankruptcy, yet found money enough to lavish upon costly but unmeaning pageants, while many a noble, to satisfy an ostentatious display, made drafts which an impoverished purse was little able to honor. The banquets and jousts, the triumphal arches with their flattering inscriptions, the shows in which allegory revelled almost to madness—all have been faithfully narrated with a minuteness worthy of a loftier theme.[1] This is, however, no place for the detailed description which, though entertaining, can be read to advantage only on the pages of the contemporary pamphlets that have come down to us.

Yet, in the discussion of the more serious concerns of a great religious and political party, we may for a moment pause to gaze at a single show, neither more magnificent nor more dignified than its fellows; but in which the youthful figure of a Bearnese destined to play a first part in the world's drama, but

---

temps de diverses manières." Relation du voyage de la reine Isabelle d'Espagne à Bayonne, MSS. Belgian Archives, Compte Rendu de la commission royale d'histoire, seconde série, ix. (1857) 159. This paper was drawn up by the Secretary of State Courteville, and sent to President Viglius.

[1] Over the first triumphal arch was a representation of Isabella (or Elizabeth) trampling Mars under foot, with the mottoes *Sacer hymen pacem nobis contulit* and *Deus nobis hæc otia fecit*, and below the lines :

> Élizabeth, de roy fille excellente,
> Vous avez joint ung jour deux rois puissans ;
> France et l'Espaigne, en gloire permanente,
> Extolleront voz âges triumphans, etc.

Over a second arch at the palace gate, which was reached by a street hung with tapestry and decorated with the united arms of France and Spain, was suspended a painting of Catharine with her three sons and three daughters, and the inscription :

> C'est à l'entour de royalle couronne
> Que le jardin hespérien floronne :
> Ce sont jardins de si belle féconde,
> Qui aujourd'huy ne trouve sa seconde ;
> Ce sont rameaux vigoureux et puissans ;
> Ce sont florons de vertu verdissans.
> Royne sans per (paire), de grâce décorée,
> Vous surmontez Pallas et Cythérée.

Catharine's portraits scarcely confirm the boast of her panegyrist that she surpassed Venus, however well she might match Minerva in sagacity.

up to this time living a life of retirement in his ancestral halls, first makes his appearance among the pomps to which as yet he has been a stranger. The pride of the grandfather whose name he bore, Henry of Navarre had been permitted, at that whimsical old man's suggestion, to strengthen an already vigorous constitution by athletic sports, and by running barefoot like the poorest peasant over the sides of his native hills. "God designed," writes a companion of his later days who never rekindles more of his youthful fire than when descanting upon his master's varied fortunes, "to prepare an iron wedge wherewith to cleave the hard knots of our calamities."[1] Later in childhood, when both father and grandfather were dead, he was the object of the unremitting care of a mother whose virtues find few counterparts or equals in the women of the sixteenth century; and Jeanne d'Albret, in a remarkable letter to Theodore Beza, notes with joy a precocious piety,[2] which, there is reason to fear, was not hardy enough to withstand the withering atmosphere of a court like that with which he was now making his first acquaintance.

One evening there was exhibited in a large hall, well lighted by means of blazing torches, a tournament in which the knights fought on foot.[3] From a castle where they held an enchanted lady captive, the knights challengers issued, and "received all comers with a thrust of the pike, and five blows with the sword." Each champion, on his arrival, endeavored to enter the castle, but was met at the portal by guards "dressed very fantastically in black," and repelled with "lighted instruments." Not a few of the less illustrious were captured here. The more exalted in rank reached the donjon, or castle-keep, but as they thought to set foot within it, a trap-door opened and they too found

---

[1] Agrippa d'Aubigné, Histoire universelle, i. 1.

[2] "Le feu bon homme Monsieur de La Gaucherie y marchoit en rondeur de conscience, et mesme mon filz lui doibt et aux siens cette rasine (racine) de piété qui lui est, par la grasse de Dieu, si bien plantée au cueur par bonnes admonitions, que maintenant, dont je loue ce bon Dieu, elle produit et branches et fruitz. Je lui suplie qu'il luy fasse ceste grasse qu'il continue de bien en mieulx." Letter of Dec. 6, 1566, MSS. Geneva Library, Bulletin de la Soc. de l'hist. du prot. français, xvi. (1867) 65.

[3] "Ung tournoy a pied."

themselves prisoners. It fared better with the princes; for the success of each champion was measured by a rigid heraldic scale. These passed the donjon, but, on a bridge leading to the tower where slept the enchanted lady, a giant confronted them, and in the midst of the combat the bridge was lowered, and they were taken, as had been their predecessors. "The Duke of Vendôme,[1] son of the late duke, whom they call in France the Prince of Navarre—a boy apparently ten or eleven years of age—crossed the bridge, and the giant pretended to surrender ; but he too was afterward repulsed like the rest." The Duke of Orleans—whom the reader will more readily recognize under the title of Duke of Anjou, which he, about this time, received —next entered the lists. Naturally he penetrated further than his namesake of Navarre, and " the giant showed more fear of him than of the other ; " but a cloud enveloped them both, and " thus the duke vanished from sight." King Charles was the last to fight, and for his prowess it was reserved for him to defeat the giant and deliver the lady.[2]

The author of the pompous show had made a serious mistake. The giant " League," before whom so many a champion failed, it was the lot not of Charles, nor of Henry of Valois, but of the other Henry, of Navarre, to overcome. That giant was already in existence, although still in his infancy. For some time past the

The confra- zealous papists, impatient of the sluggish devotion of
ternities. the court, had been forming " confréries," or fraterni-
ties, whose members, bound together by a common oath, were pledged to the support of the Roman Catholic religion.[3] The plan was a dangerous one, and it shortly excited the apprehen-

---

[1] It will be remembered that the Spaniards never acknowledged the claim of Antoine or his wife to the title of sovereigns of Navarre. In all Spanish documents, therefore, such as that which we are here following, their son Henry is designated only by the dukedom of Bourbon-Vendôme which he inherited from his father.

[2] Relation du voyage de la reine Isabelle à Bayonne, MSS. Belgian Archives, *ubi supra*, ix. 161, 162.

[3] See Jean de Serres, iii., 53, for the fraternities of the Holy Ghost in Burgundy. Blaise de Montluc's proposition of a league with the king as its head had been declined ; the monarch needed no other tie to his subjects than that which already bound them together. Agrippa d'Aubigné, Hist. univ., liv. iv., c. v. (i. 206.)

sion of the king and his mother. " I am told," Charles wrote
in July, 1565, to one of his governors, " that in a number of
places in my realm there is a talk of establishing an association
amongst my subjects, who invite one another to join it. I beg
you to take measures to prevent that any be made for any purpose whatsoever ; but keep my subjects so far as possible united
in the desire to render me duty and obedience." [1]   And to prove
the sincerity of his intentions, the French king ordered the late
Edict of Pacification again to be proclaimed by public crier in the
streets of the seditious city of Paris—a feat which was successfully performed under Marshal Montmorency's supervision, by
the city provost, accompanied by so strong a detachment of
archers and arquebusiers, as effectually to prevent popular disturbance.[2]   Already there were restless spirits that saw in
another civil war fresh opportunity for the advancement of their
selfish interests.   Months ago Villegagnon, the betrayer of the
Brazilian colony of Coligny, had written to Cardinal Granvelle,
telling him that he had resigned his dignities and offices in the
French court, and had informed Catharine de' Medici, " that
until Charles was the declared enemy of the enemies of God
and of His church, he would never again bear arms in his
service." [3]   The vice-admiral, of whom modesty was never a
conspicuous virtue, went so far as to draw a flattering portrait
of himself as a second Hannibal, vowing eternal enmity to the
Huguenots.[4]   And Nicole de St. Rémy, whose only claim to
honorable mention was found in her oft-paraded boast that, as a
mistress of Henry the Second, she had borne him a son, and who
held in France the congenial post of a Spanish spy, suggested
the marriage of the Cardinal of Bourbon in view of the possible

---

[1] Letter of Charles IX. to M. de Matignon, July 31, 1565, *apud* Capefigue,
Hist. de la Réforme, de la Ligue, etc., ii. 419, 420. The same letter stipulated
for the better protection of the Protestants by freeing them from domiciliary
visits, etc.

[2] Maniquet to Gordes, August 1, 1565, Condé MSS. in Aumale, i. 528.

[3] Letter of Villegagnon to Granvelle, May 25, 1564, Papiers d'état, vii. 660.
The Huguenots figure as " les *Aygnos*, c'est-à-dire, en langue de Suisse, rebelles
et conjurés contre leur prince pour la liberté."

[4] Letter of May 27, 1564, Ibid., vii., 666.

contingency of the death of all Catharine's sons.[1] The centre of all intrigue, the storehouse from which every part of France was supplied with material capable of once more enkindling the flames of a destructive civil war, was the house of the Spanish resident envoy, Frances de Alava, successor of the crafty Chantonnay, the brother of Granvelle. It was he that was in constant communication with all the Roman Catholic malcontents in France.[2] Catharine endeavored to check this influence, but to no purpose. The fanatical party were bound by a stronger tie of allegiance to Philip, the Catholic king, than to her, or to the Very Christian King her son. Catharine had particularly enjoined upon the Cardinal of Lorraine to have no communication with Granvelle or with Chantonnay, but the prelate's relations with both were never interrupted for a moment.[3]

The fact was that, so far from true was it that a cordial understanding existed between the courts of France and Spain, such as Siege of Malta, the mythical league for the extirpation of heresy preand French supposes, the distrust and hostility were barely veiled civilities to the Sultan. under the ordinary conventionalities of diplomatic courtesy. While Catharine and Philip's queen were exchanging costly civilities at Bayonne, the Turks were engaged in a siege of Malta, which has become famous for the obstinacy with which it was prosecuted and the valor with which it was repelled. Spain had sent a small detachment of troops to the assistance of the grand master, Jean de la Valette, and his brave knights of St. John, and the Pope had contributed ten thousand crowns to their expenses.[4] Yet at this very moment an envoy of the Sul-

---

[1] Letter of N. de St. Rémy, June 5, 1564. Ibid., viii. 24, 25. " Le peuple l'aymeroit trop mieulx pour roy que nul aultre de Bourbon."

[2] Catharine never forgave Ambassador Chantonnay for having boasted that, with Throkmorton's assistance, he could overturn the State. "Jusqu'à dire que Trokmarton, qui estoit ambassadeur d'Angleterre au commencement de ces troubles, pour l'intelligence qu'il a avec les Huguenots, et luy pour celle qu'il a avec les Catholiques de ce royaume, sont suffisans pour subvertir cet Estat." Letter to the Bishop of Rennes, Dec. 13, 1563, La Laboureur, i. 784.

[3] Granvelle to Philip II., July 15, 1565. Papiers d'état, ix. 399, 402, etc.

[4] See Alex. Sutherland's Achievements of the Knights of Malta (Phila., 1846), ii. 121, which contains an interesting popular account of this memorable leaguer.

tan was at the court of the Very Christian King of France, greatly to the disgust of the Spanish visitors and pious Catholics in general,[1] and only waited for the departure of Isabella and Alva to receive formal presentation to the monarch and his mother.[2]

Meantime, although the queen mother continued her policy of depriving the Huguenots of one after another of the privileges to which they were entitled, and replaced Protestant governors of towns and provinces by Roman Catholics, her efforts at repression seemed, for the time at least, to produce little effect. "The true religion is so rooted in France," wrote one who accompanied the royal progress, "that, like a fire, it kindles daily more and more. In every place, from Bayonne hither, and for the most part of the journey, there are more Huguenots than papists, and the most part of men of quality and mark be of the religion." If the writer, as is probable, was over-sanguine in his anticipations, he could not be mistaken in the size of the great gathering of Protestants—full two thousand—for the most part gentlemen and gentlewomen, which he witnessed with his own eyes, brought together at Nantes to listen to the preaching of the eloquent Perucel.[3]   And it was not an insignificant proof of the futility of any direct attempt to crush the Huguenots, that Constable Montmorency pretty plainly intimated that there were limits which religious proscription must not transcend.   The English ambassador wrote from France, late in November, that the Pope's new nuncio had within two days demanded that the red cap should be taken from the Cardinal of Châtillon.   But the latter, who chanced to be at court, replied that "what he enjoyed he enjoyed by gift of the crown of France, wherewith the Pope had nothing to do."   The old constable was even more vehement.   "The Pope," said he, "has often troubled the quiet of this realm, but I trust he shall not be able to trouble it at this time.   I am myself a papist; but if the Pope and his ministers go about

The constable espouses Cardinal Châtillon's defence.

---

[1] Papiers d'état du card. de Granvelle, ix. 545, etc.

[2] Giovambatista Adriani, Istoria de' suoi tempi (Ed. of Milan, 1834), ii. 221.

[3] Sir Thomas Smith to Cecil, Nantes, Oct. 12, 1565, State Paper Office, Calendar.

again to disturb the kingdom, *my sword shall be Huguenot.* My nephew shall leave neither cap nor dignity which he has for the Pope, seeing the edict gives him that liberty." [1]

Early in the following year, Charles the Ninth convoked in the city of Moulins, in Bourbonnais, near the centre of France, an assembly of notables to deliberate on the interests of the kingdom, which had not yet fully recovered from the desolations of the first civil war. The extensive journey, which had occupied a large part of the two preceding years, had furnished him abundant evidence of the grievances under which his subjects in the various provinces were laboring, and he now summoned all that was most illustrious in France, and especially those noblemen whom he had dismissed to their governments when about to start from his capital, to assist him in discovering the best mode of relief. If the Florentine Adriani could be credited, there were other and sinister designs in the mind of the court, or, at least, in that of Catharine. According to this historian, the plan of the second " Sicilian Vespers," resolved upon at Bayonne, was to have been put into execution at Moulins, which, from its strength, was well suited for the scene of so sanguinary a drama; but, although the Huguenot chiefs assembled in numbers, their actions betrayed so much suspicion of the Roman Catholics, and it seemed so difficult to include all in the blow, that the massacre was deferred until the arrival of a more propitious time, which did not come until St. Bartholomew's Day, 1572.[2] I need not stop to refute a story which presupposes the adoption of resolutions in the conference of Bayonne, which we now know, from documentary evidence, were never for a moment entertained by Catharine and her son the king.

So far from having any such treacherous design, in point of fact the assembly of Moulins was intended in no small degree to serve as a means of healing the dissensions existing among

The court at Moulins.

---

[1] Sir Thomas Smith to Leicester, Nov. 23, 1565, State Paper Office.

[2] " Al qual tempo si riservò tale esecuzione per alcuni sospetti, che apparivano negli Ugonotti, e per difficoltà di condurvegli tutti, e ancora perchè più sicuro luogo era Parigi che Molino." Giovambatista Adriani, Istoria de' suoi tempi (lib. decimottavo), ii. 221.

the nobles. The most serious breaches were the feud between the Châtillons and the Guises on account of the suspected complicity of Admiral Coligny in the murder of the late duke, and that between Marshal Montmorency and the Cardinal of Lorraine, arising out of the affray in January, 1565. Both quarrels were settled amicably in the king's presence, with as much sincerity as generally characterizes such reconciliations. Coligny declared on oath, in the royal presence, that he was guiltless of Guise's murder, neither having been its author nor having consented to it; whereupon the king declared him innocent, and ordered the parties to be reconciled. The com-

Feigned reconciliation of the Guises and Coligny. mand was obeyed, for Anne d'Este, Guise's widow, and Cardinal Charles of Lorraine in turn embraced the admiral, in token of renewed friendship. How much of meaning these caresses contained was to be shown six years later by the active participation of the one in the most famous massacre which the annals of modern history present, and by the exultant rejoicings in which the other indulged when he heard of it. Young Henry of Guise, less hypocritical than his mother and his uncle, held aloof from the demonstration, and permitted the beholders to infer that he was quietly biding his time for vengeance.[1]

An event of principal importance that occurred during the stay of the court at Moulins was a fresh altercation between Lorraine and L'Hospital. A tolerant but apparently unauthorized act of the chancellor furnished the occasion. The Edict of Pacification had made provision for the worship of the Huguenots in but a small number of places through the kingdom. If living out of reach of these more favored localities, what were they to do, that they might not be compelled to exist without the restraints of religion during their lifetime, and to die without its consolations, nor leave their children unbaptized and uninstructed in the articles of their faith? L'Hospital proposed to remedy the evil by permitting the Protestants, in such cases, to institute a species of private worship in their houses, and had pro-

---

[1] De Thou, iii. (liv. xxxix.) 660–664; Castelnau, liv. vi., c. ii.; Jehan de la Fosse, 76 ; Davila, bk. iii. 98.

cured the royal signature to an edict permitting them to call

The chancellor introduces a measure for the relief of the Protestants. in, as occasion might require, ministers of the Gospel from other cities where their regular ministrations were tolerated by the law of Amboise.[1] This edict he had sent forthwith to the different parliaments for registration. The Parliament of Dijon, in Burgundy, however, instead of obeying, promptly despatched two counsellors with a remonstrance to the king.[2] On arriving at court, the delegation at first found it impossible to gain the royal ear. In such awe did the "maîtres de requêtes"—to whom petitions were customarily entrusted—stand of the grave and severe chancellor— that venerable old man with the white beard, whom Brantôme likened to another Cato—that none was found bold enough to present the Burgundian remonstrance. At last the delegates went to the newly-arrived cardinal, and Lorraine readily undertook the task. Appearing in the royal council he introduced the matter by expressing "his surprise that the Catholics had no means of making themselves heard respecting their grievances." The objectionable edict was read, and all the members of the council declared that they had never before seen or heard of

---

[1] The edict, of course, is not to be found in Isambert, or any other collection of French laws; but a letter in Lestoile (ed. Michaud, p. 19), to whom we are indebted for much of our knowledge of the event, refers to the very wording of the document (" ce sont les mots de l'édict "). The letter is entitled " Mémoire d'un différend meu à Moulins en 1566, entre le Cardinal de Lorraine et le Chancellier de l'Hôpital," and begins with the words : " Je vous advise que *du jour d'hier*," etc. M. Bonnet has discovered and published, in the Bulletin de la Soc. de l'hist. du prot. franc., xxiv. (1875) 412–415, a second and fuller account, dated Moulins, March 16, 1566 (MS. French Nat. Library, Dupuy, t. lxxxvi., f. 158). As was seen above (p. 155), this altercation has been generally confounded with that of two years earlier. The letter given by Lestoile (see above) is also published in Mém. de Condé, v. 50, but is referred to the wrong event by the editor. Prof. Soldan (Gesch. des Prot. in Fr., ii. 199), follows the Mém. de Condé in the reference.

[2] Not many months before this occurrence a guest at the Prince of Orange's table told Montigny that there were no Huguenots in Burgundy—meaning the Spanish part, or Franche-Comté. " If so," replied the unfortunate nobleman, " the Burgundians cannot be men of intelligence, since those who have much mind for the most part are Huguenots ; " a saying which, reported to Philip, no doubt made a deep impression on his bigoted soul. Pap. d'état du card. de Granvelle, vii. 187, 188. The Burgundians of France were equally intolerant of the reformed doctrines.

it. Cardinal Bourbon was foremost in his anger, and declared that if the chancellor had the right to issue such laws on his own responsibility, there was no use in having a council. " Sir," A new alterca- said L'Hospital, turning to the Cardinal of Lorraine, tion between Lorraine and " you are already come to sow discord among us ! " the chancellor. " I am not come to sow discord, but to prevent you from sowing it as you have done in the past, scoundrel that you are ! " was the reply.[1] " Would you prevent these poor people, whom the king has permitted to live with freedom of conscience in the exercise of their religion, from receiving any consolation at all ? " asked L'Hospital. " Yes, I intend to prevent it," answered the cardinal, " for everybody knows that to suffer such things is to tolerate secret preaching; and I shall prevent it so long as I shall have the power, in order to give no opportunity for the growth of such tyrannical practices. And," continued he, " do you, who have become what you now are by my means, dare to tell me that I come to sow discord among you ? I shall take good care to keep you from doing what you have done heretofore." The council rose in anger, and passed into the adjoining apartment, where Catharine, who had not recovered from a temporary illness, strove to appease them as best she could. Charles ordered a new meeting, and, after hearing the deputies from Dijon, the king, conformably to the advice of the council, revoked the edict, and issued a prohibition of all exercise of the Protestant religion or instruction in its doctrines, save where it had been granted at Amboise. The chancellor was strictly enjoined to affix the seal of state to no papers relating to religious affairs without the consent of the royal council.

For several years the Protestants in the northern provinces of France had been busily communicating the religious views Protestantism they had themselves embraced to their neighbors in on the north-ern frontier. Artois, Flanders, and Brabant. This intercourse became exceedingly close about the beginning of the year 1566 ;

---

[1] " Je ne suis venu pour troubler; mais pour empescher que ne troubliez, comme avez faict par le passé, belistre que vous estes." Lestoile and Mém. de Condé, *ubi supra*.

and its result was a renunciation of the papal church and its worship, which was participated in by such large numbers, and effected so instantaneously, that the friends and the foes of the new movement were almost equally surprised. The story of this sudden outburst of the reformatory spirit in Valenciennes, Tournay, and other places, accompanied—as are all movements that take a strong hold upon the popular feelings—with a certain amount of lawlessness, which expended itself, however, upon inanimate images and held sacred the lives and honor of men and women, has been well told in the histories of the country whose fortunes it chiefly affected.[1] I may be permitted, therefore, to pass over these indirect results of Huguenot influence, and glance at the fortunes of a border town within the present bounds of France, and closely connected with the history of France in the sixteenth century, of which little or no notice has been taken in this connection.[2] Cateau-Cam-

Progress of the reformation at Cateau-Cambrésis.

brésis, famous for the treaty by which Henry the Second bartered away extensive conquests for a few paltry places that had fallen into the hands of the enemy, was, as its name—Chastel, Château or Cateau—imports, a castle and a borough that had grown up about it, both of them on lands belonging to the domain of Maximilian of Bergen, Archbishop and Duke of Cambray, and Prince of the Holy Roman Empire. It was smaller, but relatively far more important three hundred years ago than at the present day. For several years a few "good burgesses," with their families, had timidly studied the Holy Scriptures in secret, restrained

---

[1] See Prescott, Philip II., and Motley, Rise of the Dutch Republic.

[2] M. Charles L. Frossard, of Lille, discovered the MSS. on which the following account is wholly based, in the Archives of the Department du Nord, preserved in that city. As these papers appear to have been inedited, and are referred to, so far as I can learn, by no previous historian, I have deemed it proper to deviate from the rule to which I have ordinarily adhered, of relating in detail only those events that occurred within the ancient limits of the kingdom of France. However, the reformation at Cateau-Cambrésis received its first impulses from France. Mr. Frossard communicated the papers to the Bulletin de la Société de l'histoire du protestantisme français, iii. (1854), 255-264, 396-417, 525-538. They are of unimpeachable accuracy and authenticity.

from making an open profession of their faith by the terrible
executions which they saw inflicted upon the Protestants in the
Netherlands. But, encouraged by the toleration prevailing in
France, they began to cross the frontier, and to frequent the
Huguenot "assemblées" at Crespy, Tupigny, and Chauny. The
distance was not inconsiderable, and the peril was great. The
archbishop had not only written a letter, which was read in
every parish church, forbidding the singing of Marot's psalms
and the frequenting of French conventicles, but he had sent his
spies to the conventicles to discover cases of disobedience. The
Huguenots of Cateau multiplied in spite of these precautions.
"The eyes of the aforesaid spies," writes a witness of the events,
"were so holden that they did not even recognize those with
whom they conversed." Yet, although the Huguenots met at
home to read the Bible and to "sing the psalms which were
most appropriate to the persecution and dispersion of the children of God," the town was as quiet as it had ever been. A
slight incident, however, revealed the intensity of the fire secretly burning below the surface. A Huguenot minister was
discovered on Whitsunday, in an adjoining village, and brought
to Cateau. His captors facetiously told the suspected Protestants whom they met, that they had brought them a preacher,
and that they would have no further occasion for leaving the
town in quest of one. But the joke was not so well appreciated
as it might have been by the adherents of the reformed faith,
who seem by this time to have become extremely numerous.
The excitement was intense. When the bailiff of Cambrésis
was detected, not long after, stealing into the place by night,
accompanied by some sixty men, with the intention of carrying
the preacher off to Cambray, he met with unexpected resistance.
A citizen, on his way to his garden outside the walls, was the
first to notice the guard of strange arquebusiers at the gate, and
ran back to give the alarm. The tocsin was rung, and the inhabitants assembled in arms. It was now the turn of the bailiff
to be astonished, and to listen humbly to the remonstrances of
the people, indignant that he should have presumed to seize
their gates and usurp the functions of the local magistrates.
However, the intruders, after being politely informed that, ac

cording to strict justice, the whole party might have been summarily put to death, were suffered to beat a hasty retreat; not
that so perfect a control could be put upon the ardor of some,
but that they " administered sundry blows with the flat of their
swords upon the back of the bailiff and a few of his soldiers."

The incident itself was of trifling importance, for the Huguenot minister was promptly given up to the baron of the village
where he had been captured, and was taken by his orders to
Cambray. But it led to serious consequences. Threatened by
the archiepiscopal city, the Protestants of Cateau, afraid to go
to the French preaching-places, sent for Monsieur Philippe,
minister of Tupigny, and held the reformed services just out-
Interference side of their own walls. Alarmed at the progress of
of the Arch- Protestant doctrines in his diocese, the Archbishop
bishop of
Cambray. convened the estates of Cambray, and, on the eighteenth of August, 1566, sent three canons of the cathedral to
persuade his subjects of Cateau to return to the Papal Church,
and to threaten them with ruin in case of refusal. Neither
argument nor menace was of any avail. The Protestants, who
had studied their Bibles, were more than a match for the
priests, who had not ; and, as for the peril, the Huguenots
quaintly replied : " Rather than yield to your demand, we
should prefer to have our heads placed at our feet." When
asked if they were all of this mind, they reiterated their determination : " Were the fires made ready to burn us all, we
should enter them rather than accede to your request and return
to the mass." These were brave words, but the sturdy Huguenots made them good a few months later.

Scarcely a week had passed before the news reached Cateau
(on the twenty-fifth of August) that the " idols " had been broken
in all the churches of Valenciennes, Antwerp, Ghent, Tournay,
and elsewhere. Although stirred to its very depths by the
exciting intelligence, the Protestant population still contained
itself, and merely consulted convenience by celebrating Divine
worship within the city walls, in an open cemetery. Unfortunately, however, the minister whom the reformed had obtained
was ill-suited to these troublous times. Monsieur Philippe,
unlike Calvin and the great majority of the ministers of the

French Protestant church, was rash and impetuous.   Early the
next morning he entered the church of St. Martin, in
company with three or four other persons, and commenced the work of destruction.   Altars, statues,
pictures, antiphonaries, missals, graduals—all underwent a common fate.   From St. Martin's the iconoclasts visited in like
manner the other ecclesiastical edifices of the town and its
suburbs.   Upon the ruins of the Romish superstition the new
fabric arose, and Monsieur Philippe preached the same day in
the principal church of Cateau, to a large and attentive audience.

The images and pictures overthrown.

And now began an animated interchange of proclamations on
the one hand, and of petitions on the other.   The archbishop
demanded the unconditional submission of his subjects, and
gave no assurances of toleration.   The Protestants declared
themselves ready to give him their unqualified allegiance, as
their temporal sovereign, but claimed the liberty to worship
God.   Maximilian referred to the laws and constitutions of the
Empire of which they formed an integral part.   The burgesses
answered by showing that they had always been governed in accordance with the "placards" issued by
the King of Spain for his provinces of the Netherlands, and
that, whenever they had appealed in times past to the chamber
of the Empire, as for example at Spires, they had not only been
repelled, but even punished for their temerity.[1]   They claimed,
therefore, the benefit of the "Accord" made by the Duchess
of Parma at Brussels a few days previously, guaranteeing the
exercise of the reformed religion wherever it had heretofore
been practised;[2] while the archbishop, when forced to declare
himself, plainly announced that he would not suffer the least

The Protes-tant claims.

---

[1] Lille MSS., *ubi supra*, 403.

[2] " De sorte qu'ils espèrent que lesdits de la requeste et du compromis les
adsisteront suyvant leur promesse, à ce qu'ils puissent jouyr de la mesme
liberté accordez à Bruxelles, asçavoir, que l'exercice de la religion aye lieu
par tout où il a esté usité auparavant, comme ceulx du Chastel en Cambrésis
ont eue aussy, et ce seulement par manière de provision, jusques à ce que
aultrement il y soict pourveu par le Roy avec l'advis des estatz, estimans que
le Roy ne souffrira rien en son pays qui ne soict conforme ausdites ordon-
nances de l'empire." Lille MSS., *ubi supra*.

deviation from the Roman Catholic faith. In their perplexity, the Protestants had recourse to the Count of Horn, at Tournay, by whom they were received with the utmost kindness. The count even furnished them with a letter to the archbishop, entreating him to be merciful to them.[1]

But nothing was further from the heart of Maximilian than mercy. He was the same blind adherent of Cardinal Granvelle and his policy, whom, a year or two before, Brederode, Hoogstraaten, and their fellow-revellers had grievously insulted at a banquet given to Egmont before his departure for Spain; the same treacherous, sanguinary priest who wrote to Granvelle respecting Valenciennes: "We had better push forward and make an end of all the principal heretics, whether rich or poor, without regarding whether the city will be entirely ruined by such a course."[2] On Monday, the twenty-fourth of March, 1567, the troops of the archbishop appeared before Cateau, and the same day the place was surrendered by the treachery of some of the inhabitants. At once Cateau became a scene of bloody executions. All that had taken part in the Protestant worship were brought before a tribunal, which often tried, condemned, and punished with death upon one and the same day. Monsieur Philippe, the rash preacher, and one of his deacons seem to have been the first victims. There was no lack of food for the gallows. To have been present at the "preachings," to have partaken of the communion, to have maintained that the Protestant was better than the Roman Catholic religion, to have uttered a jest or drawn a caricature reflecting upon the Papal Church and its ceremonies—any of these was sufficient reason for sending a man to be hung or beheaded. The duchess's "moderation" had effected thus much, that no one seems to have been burned at the stake. And so, at last, by assiduous but bloody work, the Reformation was completely extirpated from Cateau Cambrésis. It was, at least, a source of mournful satisfaction that scarce one of the sufferers failed to exhibit great constancy and pious resignation in view of death.[3]

The Archbishop's vengeance.

---

[1] Letter of P. de Montmorency, Sept. 11, 1566, Lille MSS., *ubi supra.*
[2] Motley, Dutch Republic, i. 458–462.   [3] Lille MSS., *ubi supra.*

Let us return from the Flemish borders to France proper, where, notwithstanding attempts at external reconciliation, the breach between the Protestants and their Roman Catholic neighbors was daily widening, where, in fact, the elements of a new war were gathering shape and consistency. It was becoming more and more difficult—especially for a government of temporary shifts and expedients—to control the antagonistic forces incessantly manifesting themselves. The idea of toleration was understood by neither party. The Roman Catholics of Provins were so slow to comprehend the liberty of conscience and religious profession of which the Huguenots had wrung a concession in the last edict by force of arms, that they undertook to prosecute the Protestants for eating roast lamb and capons during Lent. With little more appreciation of the altered posture of affairs, the Archbishop of Sens (Cardinal Guise) initiated a trial against a heretical curate of Courtenay, according to the rules of canon law, and the latter might have stood but a poor chance to recover his freedom had not the Huguenot lord of Courtenay seized upon the archbishop's "official" as he was passing his castle, and held him as a hostage to secure the curate's release.[1]

The idea of toleration is not understood.

It would be asserting too much to say that the Protestants were innocent of any infraction upon the letter or spirit of the Edict of Amboise. They would have been angels, not men, had they been proof against the contagious spirit of raillery that infected the men of the sixteenth century. Where they dared, they not unfrequently held up their opponents to ridicule in the coarse style so popular with all classes.[2] Thus a contemporary Roman Catholic recounts with indignation

Huguenot pleasantries.

---

[1] Mémoires de Claude Haton, i. 416, 417.

[2] The satirical literature of the period would of itself fill a volume. The Huguenot songs in derision of the mass are particularly caustic. See M. Bordier, Le Chansonnier Huguenot, and the note to the last chapter. The Bulletin de la Soc. de l'hist. du prot. franç., x. (1861), 40, reprints a "dizain" commencing—

> " Nostre curé est un fin boulanger,
> Qui en son art est sage et bien appris :
> Il vend bien cher son petit pain léger,
> Combien qu'il ait le froment à bon prix."

how Prince Porcien held a celebration in Normandy, and among
the games was one in which a "paper castle" was assaulted, and
the defenders, dressed as *monks*, were taken prisoners, and were
afterward paraded through the streets on asses' backs.[1] But
these buffooneries were harmless sallies contrasted with the insults with which the Protestants were treated in every town
where they were not numerically preponderating; nor were they
anything more than rare occurrences in comparison with the latter. This page of history is compelled to record no violent
commotion on the part of the reformed population, save in cases
where, as at Pamiers (a town not far south of Toulouse, near
the foot of the Pyrenees), they had been goaded to madness by
the government deliberately trampling upon their rights of
worship, at the instigation of the ecclesiastical authorities.[2]
A trifling accident might then, however, be sufficient to cause
their inflamed passions to burst out; and in the disturbances
that were likely to ensue, little respect was usually paid to the
churches or the monasteries. Such are wont to be the unhappy
effects of the denial of justice according to the forms of established law. They would have been a hundred-fold more frequent had it not been for the persistent opposition interposed by
the Huguenot ministers—many of them with Calvin carrying
the doctrine of passive submission to constituted authority almost to the very verge of apparent pusillanimity.

From month to month the conviction grew upon the Protestants that their destruction was agreed upon. There was no
Alarm of the doubt with regard to the desire of Philip the Second;
Protestants. for his course respecting his subjects in the Netherlands showed plainly enough that the extermination of heretics
was the only policy of which his narrow mind could conceive as
pleasing in the sight of heaven. The character of Catharine—

---

[1] "Chose indigne d'un prince tel qu'il se disoit." Journal d'un curé ligueur
(Jehan de la Fosse), 73.

[2] See the moderate account of the dispassionate Roman Catholic De Thou,
iii. (liv. xxxix.) 666–670. Also Agrippa d'Aubigné, liv. iv., c. vi. (i. 208), and
Discours des troubles advenus en la ville de Pamiers, le 5 juin 1566, Archives
curieuses (Cimber et Danjou), vi. 309–343. The massacre of Protestants at
Foix was caused by an exaggerated and false account of the commotion at
Pamiers, carried thither by a fugitive Augustinian monk.

stealthy, deceitful, regardless of principle—was equally well understood. Between such a queen and the trusted minister of such a prince, a secret conference like that of Bayonne could not be otherwise than highly suspicious. It is not strange that the Huguenots received it as an indubitable fact that the court from this time forward was only waiting for the best opportunity of effecting their ruin; for even intelligent Roman Catholics, who were not admitted into the confidence of the chief actors in that celebrated interview, came to the same conclusion. Those who knew what had actually been said and done might assure the world that the rumors were false; but the more they asseverated the less they were believed. For it is one of the penalties of insincere and lying diplomacy, that when once appreciated in its true character—as it generally is appreciated in a very brief space of time—it loses its persuasive power, and is treated without much investigation as uniform imposture.[1] With a suspicious vigilance, bred of the very treachery of which they had so often been the victims, the Huguenots saw signs of dangers that perhaps were not actually in preparation for them. And certainly there was enough to alarm. Not many months

Attempts to murder the admiral and Prince Porcien. after the assembly of Moulins a cutthroat by the name of Du May was discovered and executed, who had been hired to murder Admiral Coligny, the most indispensable leader of the party, near his own castle of Châtillon-sur-Loing.[2] The last day of the year there was hung

---

[1] The good policy of straightforward dealing on the part of an ambassador is set forth in a noble letter of Morvilliers, Bishop of Orleans, from which I permit myself to quote a few sentences: "Il y en a toutesfois qui pensent que, pour estre habille homme, il fault tousjours aller masqué, laquelle opinion j'estime du tout erronée, et celluy qui la suit grandement déceu. Le temps m'a donné quelque expérience des choses; mais je n'ay jamais veu homme, suivant ces chemins obliques, qui n'ait embrouillé les affaires de son maistre, et, luy, perdre beaucoup plus qu'acquérir de réputation; et au contraire ceux, qui se sont conduits prudemment avec la verité, avoir, pour le moins, rapporté de leur négociation ce fruict et l'honneur d'y avoir faict ce que les hommes, avec le sens et jugement humain, peuvent faire." Correspondance diplomatique de Bertrand de Salignac de la Mothe Fénélon, vii. 97.

[2] Journal de Jehan de la Fosse, 79, 80; Vie de Coligny (Cologne, 1686), 321–323; Gasparis Colinii Vita, 1575, 55; Agrippa d'Aubigné, Hist. univ., 1, 207.

a lackey, who pretended that the Cardinal of Lorraine had tried to induce him to poison the Prince of Porcien; and, although he retracted his statements at the time of his "amende honorable,"[1] his first story was generally credited. The rumor was current that in December, 1566, Charles received special envoys from the emperor, the Pope, and the King of Spain, warning him that, unless he should revoke his edict of toleration, they would declare themselves his open enemies.[2] This was certainly sufficiently incredible, so far as the tolerant Maximilian was concerned; but stranger mutations of policy had often been noticed, and, as to Pius the Fifth and Philip, nothing seemed more probable.

With the opening of the year 1567 the portentous clouds of coming danger assumed a more definite shape. In the neighboring provinces of the Netherlands, after a long period of procrastination, Philip the Second had at length determined to strike a decisive blow. The Duchess of Parma was to be superseded in the government by a man better qualified than any other in Europe for the bloody work assigned him to do. Ferdinando de Toledo, Duke of Alva, in his sixtieth year, after a life full of brilliant military exploits, was to undertake a work in Flanders such as that which, two years before, he had recommended as the panacea for the woes of France— a work with which his name will ever remain associated in the annals of history. The "Beggars" of the Low Countries, like the Huguenots in their last war, had taken up arms in defence of their religious, and, to a less degree, of their civil rights. The "Beggars" complained of the violation of municipal privileges and compacts, ratified by oath at their sovereign's accession, as the Huguenots pointed to the infringement upon edicts solemnly published as the basis of the pacification of the country; and both refused any longer to submit to a tyranny

Alva in the Netherlands.

---

[1] Journal d'un curé ligueur (Jehan de la Fosse), 81.

[2] "December (1566.) Au commencement vinrent plusieurs ambassades à Paris, tant de la part de l'Empereur, que du Pape, que du roy d'Espagne, lesquels mandèrent au roy de France, qu'il eust à faire casser l'esdict de janvier, ou autrement qu'ils se déclareroient ennemys." Ibid., 80. The fanatical party affected to regard the Edict of Amboise, March, 1563, as a mere re-establishment of the edict of January 17, 1562.

that had, in the name of religion, sent to the gallows or the stake thousands of their most pious and industrious fellow-citizens. The cause was, therefore, common to the Protestants of the two countries, and there was little doubt that should the enemy of either prove successful at home, he would soon be impelled by an almost irresistible impulse to assist his ally in completing his portion of the praiseworthy undertaking. It is true that the Huguenots of France were not now in actual warfare with the government; but, that their time would come to be attacked, there was every reason to apprehend. Hence, when the Duke of Alva, in the memorable summer of 1567, set out from Piedmont at the head of ten thousand veterans, to thread his way over the Alps and along the eastern frontiers of France, through Burgundy and Lorraine, to the fated scene of his bloody task in the Netherlands, the Protestants of France saw in this neighboring demonstration a new peril to themselves. In the first moments of trepidation, their leaders in the royal council are said to have acquiesced in, if they did not propose, The Swiss levy. the levy of six thousand Swiss troops, as a measure of defence against the Spanish general; and Coligny, the same contemporary authority informs us, strongly advocated that they should dispute the duke's passage.[1] Even if this statement be true, they were not long in detecting, or believing that they had detected, proofs that the Swiss troops were really intended for the overthrow of Protestantism in France, rather than for any service against the Duke of Alva. Letters from Rome and Spain were intercepted, we learn from François de la Noue, containing evidence of the sinister designs of the court.[2] The

---

[1] Mémoires de Castelnau, liv. vi., c. ii. Castelnau was certainly in a favorable position for learning the truth respecting these matters; and yet even he speaks of the "holy league," formed at Bayonne, as of something beyond controversy. According to a treaty and renewal of alliance between Charles the Ninth and the Roman Catholic cantons of Switzerland, entered into Dec. 7, 1564, for Charles's lifetime, and seven years beyond, the Swiss were to furnish him, when attacked, not less than six nor more than sixteen thousand men for the entire war. The success of the negotiation occasioned great rejoicing at Paris, and corresponding annoyance in the Spanish dominions. Du Mont, Corps diplomatique, v. 129–131; Jehan de la Fosse, 70; Papiers d'état du card. de Granvelle, viii. 599.

[2] Mém. de Fr. de la Noue, c. xi.

Prince of La Roche-sur-Yon, a prince of the blood, a short time before his death, warned his cousin of Condé of the impending danger.[1] Condé, who, within the past few months, had repeatedly addressed the king and his mother in terms of remonstrance and petition for the redress of the oppression under which the Huguenots were suffering, but to no purpose, again supplicated the throne, urging in particular that the levy of the Swiss be countermanded, since, if they should come, there would be little hope of the preservation of the peace;[2] while Admiral Coligny, who found Catharine visiting the constable, his uncle, at his palace of Chantilly, with faithful boldness exposed to them both the impossibility of retaining the Protestants in quiet, when they saw plain indications that formidable preparations were being made for the purpose of overwhelming them. To these remonstrances, however, they received only what they esteemed evasive answers—excuses for not dismissing the Swiss, based upon representations of the danger of some Spanish incursion, and promises that the just requests of the Huguenots should receive the gracious attention of a monarch desirous of establishing his throne by equity.[3]

"The queene returned answer by letters," wrote the English

---

[1] He did more than this, according to the belief of the times, as expressed by Jean de Serres; for, "having been present at the Bayonne affair," he brought him irrefragable proof of the "holy league entered into by the kings of France and Spain for the ruin of the religion." Comment. de statu. rel. et reip., iii. 126.

[2] Yet so much were intelligent observers deceived respecting the signs of the times, that only a little over two months before the actual outbreak of the second civil war (July 4, 1567), Judge Truchon congratulated France on the edifying spectacle of loving accord which the court furnished. "I have this very day," he writes, "seen the king holding, with his left hand, the head of my lord, the prince [of Condé], and with his right the head of my lord the Cardinal of Bourbon, and *playfully trying to strike their foreheads together.* The Duke d'Aumale was paying his attentions to Madame la Mareschale [de Montmorency.] . . . . The Cardinal of Châtillon was not far off. In short, all, without distinction, seemed to me to be so harmonious that I wish there may never be greater divisions in France. It was a fine example for many persons of lower rank," etc. Letter to M. de Gordes, MS. in Archives de Condé, Duc d'Aumale, Princes de Condé, i. 540, Pièces inédites.

[3] Jean de Serres, iii. 128, 129. See, also, Condé's letter of Aug. 23, 1568. Ibid., iii. 201.

ambassador, Norris, to Elizabeth, "assuringe him"—Condé—
" by the faythe of a princesse *et d'une femme de bien* (for so she
termed it), that so long as she might any waies prevayle with
the Kinge, her sonne, he should never breake the sayd edicte,
and therof required him to assure himselfe ; and if he coulde
come to the courte, he shoulde be as welcome as his owne harte
could devise ; if not, to passe the tyme without any suspect or
jealousie, protesting that there was nothing ment that tended to
his indempnitie, what so ever was bruted abrode or conceyved
to the contrary, as he should perceyve by the sequele erst it
were long."[1]

Shall we blame those sturdy, straightforward men, so long
fed upon unmeaning or readily-broken promises of redress, if
they gave little credit to the royal assurances, and to the more
honeyed words of the queen mother ? Perhaps there existed
no sufficient grounds for the immediate alarm of the Huguenots. Perhaps no settled plan had been formed with the connivance of Philip—no "sacred league" of the kind supposed
to have been sketched in outline at Bayonne—no contemplated
massacre of the chiefs, with a subsequent assembly of notables
at Poitiers, and repeal of all the toleration that had been
vouchsafed to the Protestants.[2] All this may have been false ;
but, if false, it was invested with a wonderful verisimilitude, and
to Huguenots and Papists it had, so far as their actions were concerned, all the effect of truth. At all events the promises of the
king could not be trusted. Had he not been promising, again
and again, for four years ? Had not every restrictive ordinance,
every interpretation of the Edict of Amboise, every palpable

---

[1] Norris to Queen Elizabeth, Aug. 29, 1567, State Paper Office, Duc d'Aumale, Pièces inédites, i. 559.

[2] " Sed ne frustra laborare viderentur, de Albani consilio, ' Satius esse unicum
salmonis caput, quam mille ranarum capita habere,' ineunt rationes de inter-
cipiendis optimatum iis, qui Religionem sequerentur, Condæo, Amiralio, An-
delotio, Rupefocaldio aliisque primoribus viris. Ratio videbatur præsentissi-
ma, ut a rege accerserentur, tanquam consulendi de iis rebus quæ ad regnum
constituendum facerent," etc. Jean de Serres, iii. 125. It will be remembered that this volume was published the year before the St. Bartholomew's
massacre. The persons enumerated, with the exception of those that died
before 1572, were the victims of the massacre.

infringement upon its spirit, if not upon its letter, been prefaced by a declaration of Charles's intention to maintain the edict inviolate? In the words of an indignant contemporary, "the very name of the edict was employed to destroy the edict itself." [1]

The Huguenot expeditions to Florida have been so well sketched by Bancroft and Parkman, and so fully set forth by their latest historian, M. Paul Gaffarel, that I need not speak of them in detail. In fact, they belong more intimately to American than to French history. They owed their origin to the enlightened patriotism of Coligny, who was not less desirous, as a Huguenot, to provide a safe refuge for his fellow Protestants, than anxious, as High Admiral of France, to secure for his native country such commercial resources as it had never enjoyed. " I am in my house," he wrote in 1565, " studying new measures by which we may traffic and make profit in foreign parts. I hope shortly to bring it to pass that we shall have the best trade in Christendom " (Gaffarel, Histoire de la Floride française, Paris, 1875, pp. 45, 46).   But, although the project of Huguenot emigration was conceived in the brain of the great Protestant leader, apparently it was heartily approved by Catharine de' Medici and her son. They certainly were not averse to be relieved of the presence of as many as possible of those whom their religious views, and, still more, their political tendencies, rendered objects of suspicion. "If wishing were in order," Catharine (Letter to Forquevaulx, March 17, 1566, Gaffarel, 428) plainly told the Spanish ambassador, on one occasion, "I would wish that all the Huguenots were in those regions" ("si c'estoit souëter, ie voudrois que touts les Huguenots fussent en ce pais-là"). In the discussion that ensued between the courts of Paris and Madrid, the queen mother never denied that the colonists went not only with her knowledge, but with her consent. In fact, she repudiated with scorn and indignation a suggestion of the possibility that such considerable bodies of soldiers and sailors could have left her son's French dominions without the royal privity (Ibid., 427).

The first expedition, under Jean Ribault, in 1562, was little more than a voyage of discovery. The main body promptly returned to France, the same year, finding that country rent with civil war. The twenty-six or twenty-eight men left behind to hold "Charlesfort" (erected probably near the mouth of the South Edisto river, in what is now South Carolina), disheartened and famishing, nevertheless succeeded in constructing a rude ship and recrossing the Atlantic in the course of the next year.

A second expedition (1564), under René de Laudonnière, who had taken part

The Huguenot attempts at colonization in Florida.

1562.

---

[1] " Ita Edicti nomen usurpabatur, dum Edictum revera pessundaretur."
Jean de Serres, iii. 60.

in the first, was intended to effect a more permanent settlement. A strong
earthwork was accordingly thrown up at a spot christened "Caroline," in honor of Charles the Ninth, and the colony was inaugurated under fair auspices. But improvidence and mismanagement soon bore
their legitimate fruits. Laudonnière saw himself constrained to build ships
for a return to Europe, and was about to set sail when the third expedition
unexpectedly made its appearance (August 28, 1565), under Ribault, leader
of the first enterprise.

1564.

Unfortunately the arrival of this fresh reinforcement was closely followed
by the approach of a Spanish squadron, commanded by Pedro Menendez, or
Melendez, de Abila, sent by Philip the Second expressly to destroy
the Frenchmen who had been so presumptuous as to settle in territories claimed by his Catholic Majesty. Nature seemed to conspire with
their own incompetency to ruin the French. The French vessels, having gone
out to attack the Spaniards, accomplished nothing, and, meeting a terrible
storm, were driven far down the coast and wrecked. "Caroline" fell into
the hands of Menendez, and its garrison was mercilessly put to death. The
same fate befell the shipwrecked French from the fleet. Those
who declared themselves Roman Catholics were almost the only
persons spared by their pitiless assailants. A few women and
children were granted their lives; also a drummer, a hornblower, and a few
carpenters and sailors, whose services were valuable. Laudonnière and a
handful of men escaped to the woods, and subsequently to Europe. About
two hundred soldiers, who threatened to entrench themselves and make a formidable resistance, were able to obtain from Menendez a pledge that they
should be treated as prisoners of war, which, strange to say, was observed.
The rest—many hundreds—were consigned to indiscriminate slaughter;
Ribault himself was flayed and quartered; and over the dead Huguenots was
suspended a tablet with this inscription: "Hung, not as Frenchmen, but as
Lutherans" (Gaffarel, 229; De Thou, iv. 113; Ag. d'Aubigné, i. 248). Spain
and Rome had achieved a grand work. The chaplain Mendoza could piously
write: "The greatest advantage from our victory, certainly, is the triumph
our Lord grants us, which will cause His Holy Gospel to be introduced into
these regions" (Mendoza, *apud* Gaffarel, 214).

1565.

*Massacre by
Menendez.*

The report of these atrocities, tardily reaching the Old World, called forth
an almost universal cry of horror. Fair-minded men of both communions
stigmatized the conduct of Menendez and his companions as sheer murder;
for had not the French colonists of Florida been attacked before being summoned to surrender, and butchered in cold blood after being denied even such
terms as were customarily accorded to Turks and other infidels? Among
princes, Philip alone applauded the deed, and seemed only to regret that
faith had been kept with any of the detested Huguenots (Gaffarel, 234, 245).
It has been commonly supposed that whatever indignation was shown by
Catharine de' Medici and her son, was merely assumed in deference to the
popular clamor, and that but a feeble remonstrance was really uttered. This
supineness would be readily explicable upon the hypothesis of the long premeditation of the massacre of St. Bartholomew's Day. If the treacherous

murder of Admiral Coligny and the other great Huguenot leaders had indeed been deliberately planned from the time of the Bayonne conference in 1565, and would have been executed at Moulins in 1566, but for unforeseen circumstances, no protests against the Florida butchery could have been sincere. On the other hand, if Catharine de' Medici was earnest and persistent in her demand for the punishment of Menendez, it is not conceivable that her mind should have been then entertaining the project of the Parisian matins. The extant correspondence between the French queen mother and her envoy at the court of Madrid may fairly be said to set at rest all doubts respecting her attitude. She was indignant, determined, and outspoken.

So slowly did news travel in the sixteenth century, that it was not until the eighteenth of February, 1566, that Forquevaulx, from Madrid, despatched to the King of France a first account of the events that had occurred in Florida nearly five months before. The ambassador seems to have expressed becoming indignation in the interviews he sought with the Duke of Alva, repudiating with dignity the suggestion that the blame should be laid upon Coligny, for having abused his authority as admiral to set on foot a piratical expedition into the territories of a friendly prince; and holding forth no encouragement to believe that Charles would disavow Coligny's acts. He told Alva distinctly that Menendez was a butcher rather than a good soldier (" plus digne bourreau que bon soldat," Forquevaulx to Charles IX., March 16, 1566, Gaffarel, 425). He declared to him that the Turks had never exhibited such inhumanity to their prisoners at Castelnovo or at Gerbes —in fact, never had barbarians displayed such cruelty. As a Frenchman, he assured the Spaniard that he shuddered when he thought of so execrable a deed, and that it appeared to him that God would not leave it unpunished (Ibid., 426).

Catharine's own language to the Spanish ambassador, Don Francez de Alava, was not less frank. " As their common mother," she said, " I can but have an incredible grief at heart, when I hear that between princes so closely bound as friends, allies, and relations, as these two kings, and in so good a peace, and at a time when such great offices of friendship are observed between them, so horrible a carnage has been committed on the subjects of my son, the King of France. I am, as it were, beside myself when I think of it, and cannot persuade myself that the king, your master, will refuse us satisfaction " (Catharine to Forquevaulx, Moulins, March 17th, Gaffarel, 427). Not content with this plain talking to Alava, she " prayed and ordered " Forquevaulx to make Philip himself understand her desires respecting " the reparation demanded by *so enormous an outrage.*" He was to tell his Catholic Majesty that Catharine would never rest content until due satisfaction was made ; and that she would feel " marvellous regret " should she not only find that all her pains to establish perpetual friendship between the two kings had been lost, but one day be reproached by Charles for having suffered such a stain upon his reputation " (" que . . . j'aye laissé faire une telle escorne à sa reputation." Gaffarel, 429).

Forquevaulx fulfilled his instructions to the very letter, adding, on his own account, that in forty-one years of military service he had never known so execrable an execution. He seems also to have disposed effectually of the Spanish claim to Florida through right of ancient discovery, by emphasizing the circumstance that Menendez, after his victory, thought it necessary to take formal possession of the land. He informed Philip that no news could be more welcome to the Huguenots than that the subjects of Charles had been murdered by those very persons who were expected to strengthen him by their friendship and alliance (Forquevaulx to Catharine, April 9th, Gaffarel, 432). His words had little effect upon any one at the Spanish court, save the young queen, who felt the utmost solicitude lest her brother and her husband should become involved in war with each other. ("Me sembla qu'il tint à peu qu'elle ne pleurast son soul de crainte qu'il ne survienne quelque alteration." Forquevaulx, *ubi supra*, 430.)

But, although no progress was made toward obtaining justice, the French government did not relax its efforts. Charles wrote from Saint Maur, May 12, 1566, that his will was that Forquevaulx should renew his complaint and insist with all urgency upon a reparation of the wrong done him. "You will not cease to tell them," said the king, "that they must not hope that I shall ever be satisfied until I see such a reparation as our friendship demands." (Gaffarel, 437.)

The French ambassador continued to press his claim, and, in particular, to demand the release of the French prisoners, even up to near the time when a private citizen, Dominique de Gourgues, undertook to avenge his country's wrongs while satisfying his thirst for personal revenge. De Gourgues was not, as has usually been supposed, a Huguenot; he had even been an adherent of Montluc and of the house of Guise (Gaffarel, 265). But, having been captured in war by the Spaniards, in 1566, he had been made a galley-slave. From that time he had vowed irreconcilable hatred against the Catholic king. He obtained a long-deferred satisfaction when, in April, 1568, he surprised the fort of Caroline, slew most of the Spanish soldiers, and placed over the remainder—spared only for the more ignominious punishment of hanging upon the same trees to which Huguenots had been suspended—the inscription, burned with a hot iron on a pine slab : "I do this not as to Spaniards, nor as to seamen, but as to traitors, robbers, and murderers." (The words are given with slight variations. See "La Reprinse de la Floride par le Cappitaine Gourgue," reprinted by Gaffarel, 483–515 ; Agrippa d'Aubigné, i. 354–356 ; De Thou, iv. 123–126.)

Sanguinary revenge of De Gourgues, April, 1568.

CHAPTER XV.

THE SECOND CIVIL WAR AND THE SHORT PEACE.

A TREACHEROUS peace or an open war was now apparently the only alternative offered to the Huguenots. In reality, however, they believed themselves to be denied even the unwelcome choice between the two. The threatening preparations made for the purpose of crushing them were indications of coming war, if, indeed, they were not properly to be regarded, according to the view of the great Athenian orator in a somewhat similar case, as the first stage in the war itself. The times called for prompt decision. Within a few weeks three conferences were held at Valéry and at Châtillon. Ten or twelve of the most prominent Huguenot nobles assembled to discuss with the Prince of Condé and Coligny the exigencies of the hour. Twice was the impetuosity of the greater number restrained by the calm persuasion of the admiral. Convinced that the sword

Coligny's pacific counsels. is a fearful remedy for political diseases—a remedy that should never be applied except in the most desperate emergency—Coligny urged his friends to be patient, and to show to the world that they were rather forced into war by the malice of their enemies than drawn of their own free choice. But at the third meeting of the chiefs, before the close of the month, they were too much excited by the startling reports reaching them from all sides, to be controlled even by Coligny's prudent advice. A great friend of "the religion" at court had

Rumors of plots to destroy the Huguenots. sent to the prince and the admiral an account of a secret meeting of the royal council, at which the imprisonment of the former and the execution of the latter was agreed upon. The Swiss were to be distributed in equal de-

tachments at Paris, Orleans, and Poitiers, and the plan already
indicated—the repeal of the Edict of Toleration and the proclamation of another edict of opposite tenor—was at once to be carried into effect. "Are we to wait," asked the more impetuous,
"until we be bound hand and foot and dragged to dishonorable death on Parisian scaffolds? Have we forgotten the more
than three thousand Huguenots put to violent deaths since the
peace, and the frivolous answers and treacherous delays which
have been our only satisfaction?" And when some of the leaders
expressed the opinion that delay was still preferable to a war
that would certainly expose their motives to obloquy, and entail
so much unavoidable misery, the admiral's younger brother,
D'Andelot, combated with his accustomed vehemence
a caution which he regarded as pusillanimous, and
pointedly asked its advocates what all their innocence
would avail them when once they found themselves in prison
and at their enemy's mercy, when they were banished to foreign
countries, or were roaming without shelter in the forests and
wilds, or were exposed to the barbarous assaults of an infuriated
populace.[1] His striking harangue carried the day. The admiral reluctantly yielded, and it was decided to anticipate the attack of the enemy by a bold defensive movement. Some advocated the seizure of Orleans, and counselled that, with this
refuge in their possession, negotiations should be entered into
with the court for the dismissal of the Swiss; others that the
party should fortify itself by the capture of as many cities as
possible. But to these propositions the pertinent reply was
made that there was no time for wordy discussions, the controversy must be settled by means of the sword;[2] and that, of a

D'Andelot's warlike coun-sels prevail.

---

[1] The most authentic account of these important interviews is that given
by François de la Noue in his Mémoires, chap. xi. It clearly shows how much
Davila mistakes in asserting that "the prince, the admiral, and Andelot persuaded them, without further delay, to take arms." (Eng. trans., London,
1678, bk. iv., p. 110.) Davila's careless remark has led many others into the
error of making Coligny the advocate, instead of the opposer, of a resort to
arms. See also De Thou, iv. (liv. xlii.) 2–7, who bases his narrative on that
of De la Noue, as does likewise Agrippa d'Aubigné, l. iv., c. vii. (i. 209), who
uses the expression: "L'Amiral voulant endurer toutes extremitez et se con-
fier en l'innocence."   [2] "Ains avec le fer."

hundred towns the Protestants held at the beginning of the last
war, they had found themselves unable to retain a
dozen until its close. Finally, the prince and his
companions resolved to make it the great object of
their endeavors to drive the Cardinal of Lorraine from
court and liberate Charles from his pernicious influence. This
object was to be attained by dispersing the Swiss, and by conducting hostilities on a bold plan—rather by the maintenance
of an army that could actively take the field,[1] than by seizing
any cities save a few of the most important. On the twenty-
ninth of September, the feast-day of St. Michael, the Huguenots having suddenly risen in all parts of France, Condé and
Coligny, at the head of the troops of the neighboring provinces,
were to present themselves at the court, which would be busy
celebrating the customary annual ceremonial of the royal order.
They would then hand to the king a humble petition for the
redress of grievances, for the removal of the Cardinal of Lorraine, and for the dispersion of the Swiss troops, which, instead
of being retained near the frontiers of the kingdom which they
had ostensibly come to protect, had been advanced to the very
vicinity of the capital.[2] It might be difficult to prevent the
enterprise from wearing the appearance of a plot against the
king, in whose immediate vicinity the cardinal was; but the
event, if prosperous, would demonstrate the integrity of their
purpose.[3]

The plan was well conceived, and better executed than such
schemes usually are. The great difficulty was to keep so impor-

Cardinal Lor-
raine to be
seized and
King Charles
liberated.

---

[1] " Une armée gaillarde." La Noue, *ubi supra.*

[2] Mém. de Castelnau, liv. vi., c. iv., c. v. ; La Noue, c. xi. ; De Thou, iv.
(liv. xlii.) 5, 6. Davila, l. iv., p. 110, alludes to the accusation, extorted from
Protestant prisoners on the rack, that " the chief scope of this enterprise was
to murder the king and queen, with all her other children, that the crown
might come to the Prince of Condé," but admits that it was not generally
credited. The curate of Saint Barthélemi is less charitable ; describing the rising of the Protestants, he says : " En ung vendredy 27ᵉ se partirent de toutes
les villes de France les huguenots, sans qu'on leur eust dit mot, mais ils craig-
noient que si on venoit au dessein de leur entreprise qui estoit de prendre ou
tuer le roy Charles neuvième, qu'on ne les saccagea ès villes." Journal d'un
curé ligueur (J. de la Fosse), 85.

[3] La Noue, and De Thou, *ubi supra.*

tant a secret. It was a singular coincidence that, as in the case
of the tumult of Amboise, over seven years before,
the first intimations of their danger reached the
Guises from the Netherlands.[1] But the courtiers,
whose minds were taken up with the pleasures of the chase, and
who dreamed of no such movement, were so far from believing
the report, that Constable Montmorency expressed vexation
that it was imagined that the Huguenots could get together one
hundred men in a corner of the kingdom—not to speak of an
army in the immediate vicinity of the capital—without the
knowledge of himself, the head of the royal military establishment; while Chancellor de l'Hospital said that "it was a
capital crime for any servant to alarm his prince with false
intelligence, or give him groundless suspicions of his fellow-
subjects." [2]

The secret slowly leaks out.

The news, however, being soon confirmed from other sources,
a spy was sent to Châtillon-sur-Loing to report upon the admiral's movements. He brought back word that he had found
Coligny at home, and apparently engrossed in the labors of the
vintage—so quietly was the affair conducted until within forty-
eight hours of the time appointed for the general uprising.[3] It
was not until hurried tidings came from all quarters that the
roads to Châtillon and to Rosoy—a small place in Brie, where
the Huguenots had made their rendezvous—were swarming
with men mounted and armed, that the court took the alarm.

It was almost too late. The Huguenots had possession of

---

[1] The historian, Michel de Castelnau, sieur de Mauvissière, had been sent
as a special envoy to congratulate the Duke of Alva on his safe arrival, and
the Duchess of Parma on her relief. As he was returning from Brussels, he
received, from some Frenchmen who joined him, a very circumstantial account of the contemplated rising of the Huguenots, and, although he regarded
the story as an idle rumor, he thought it his duty to communicate it to the king
and queen. Mémoires, liv. vi., c. iv.

[2] Mém. de Castelnau, *ubi supra.* It is probable that the French court partook of Cardinal Granvelle's conviction, expressed two years before, that the
Huguenots would find it difficult to raise money or procure foreign troops for
another war, not having paid for those they had employed in the last war,
nor holding the strongholds they then held. Letter of May 7, 1565, Papiers
d'état, ix. 172.

[3] Mém. du duc de Bouillon (Ancienne Collection), xlvii. 421.

Lagny and of the crossing of the river Marne. The king and queen, with their suite, at Meaux, were almost entirely unprotected, the six thousand Swiss being still at Château-Thierry, Flight of the thirty miles higher up the Marne. Instant orders court to Paris. were sent to bring them forward as quickly as possible, and the night of the twenty-eighth of September witnessed a scene of abject fear on the part of the ladies and not a few of the gentlemen that accompanied Charles and his mother. At three o'clock in the morning, under escort of the Swiss, who had at last arrived, the court started for Paris, which was reached after a dilatory journey that appeared all the longer because of the fears attending it.[1] The Prince of Condé, who had been joined as yet only by the forerunners of his army, engaged in a slight skirmish with the Swiss; but a small band of four or five hundred gentlemen, armed only with their swords, could do nothing against a solid phalanx of the brave mountaineers, and he was forced to retire. Meanwhile Marshal Montmorency, sent by Catharine to dissuade the prince, the admiral, and Cardinal Châtillon from prosecuting their enterprise, had returned with the message that " the Huguenots were determined to defeat the preparations made to destroy them and their religion, which was only tolerated by a conditional edict, revocable by the king at his pleasure." [2]

The Cardinal of Lorraine did not share in the flight of the court to Paris. Never able to boast of the possession of overmuch courage, he may have feared for his personal safety; for it was not impossible that he might be sacrificed by a queen rarely troubled with any feelings of humanity, to allay the storm raging about the ship of state; or he may have hoped to be of greater service to his party away from the capital.[3] However this may be, the Cardinal betook himself in hot haste to the city of Rheims, but reached his palace only after an almost

---

[1] La Fosse, p. 86, represents Charles as exclaiming, when he entered the Porte Saint Denis : " Qu'il estoit tenu à Dieu, et qu'il y avoit quinze heures qu'il estoit à cheval, et avoit eust trois alarmes."

[2] Mém. de Castelnau, liv. vi., c. v. ; La Noue, c. xiii. (Anc. Coll., xlvii. 180–185 ; De Thou, iv. 8 ; J. de Serres, iii. 129–131 ; La Fosse, 86 ; Agrippa d'Aubigné, Hist. univ., i. 210.

[3] " Ravi d'avoir allumé le feu de la guerre," says De Thou, iv. 9.

miraculous escape from capture by his enemies.[1] Once in safety, he despatched two messengers in rapid succession[2] to Brussels, and begged Alva to send him an agent with whom he might communicate in confidence. The proposals made when that personage arrived at Rheims were sufficiently startling; for, after calling attention to Philip's rightful claim to the throne of France, in case of the death of Charles and his brothers, he offered in a certain contingency to place in the Spanish monarch's hands some strong places that might prove valuable in substantiating that claim. In return, the Cardinal wished Philip to assume the defence of the papal church in France, and particu-

Cardinal Lorraine invites Alva to invade France. larly desired him to undertake the protection of his brothers and of himself. The message was not unwelcome either to Alva or to his royal master. They were willing, they said, to assist the King of France in combating the Huguenots,[3] and they made no objection to accepting the cities. At the worst, these cities would serve as pledges for the repayment of whatever sums the King of Spain might expend in maintaining the Roman Catholic faith in France. With respect to the propriety of Philip's becoming the formal guardian of the Guises, Alva felt more hesitation, for who knew how matters might turn out? And Philip, never quite ready for any important decision, praised his lieutenant's delay, and inculcated further procrastination.[4] But the succession to the throne of France was worthy of deep consideration. As Alva intimated, the famous Salic law, under which Charles's sister Isabella was excluded from the crown, was merely a bit of pleasantry, and force of arms would facilitate the acknowledgment of her claims.[5]

---

[1] De Thou, *ubi supra*.

[2] The circumstance of two messengers, each bearing letters from the same person, while the letters made no allusion to each other, following one another closely, struck Alva as so suspicious, that he actually placed the second messenger under arrest, and only liberated him on hearing from his own agent on his return that the man's credentials were genuine.

[3] Alva proposed to detach 5,000 men to prevent the entrance of German auxiliaries into France, and protect the Netherlands.

[4] Letter of Alva to Philip, Nov. 1, 1567, Gachard, Correspondance de Philippe II., i., 593.

[5] " Que la ley sálica, que dizien, es baya, y las armas la allanarian." Ibid, i. 594.

The blow which the Huguenots had aimed at the tyrannical government of the Cardinal of Lorraine had missed its mark, through premature disclosure ; but they still hoped to accomplish their design by slower means.   Shut up in Paris, the court might be frightened or starved into compliance before the Roman Catholic forces could be assembled to relieve the capital.   With this object the Prince of Condé moved around to the north side of the city, and took up his quarters, on the second of October, in the village of Saint Denis.   With the lower Seine, which, in one of its serpentine coils, here turns back upon itself, and retreats from the direction of the sea, in his immediate grasp, and within easy striking distance of the upper Seine, and its important tributary the Marne—the chief sources of the supply of food on which the capital depended—the Prince of Condé awaited the arrival of his reinforcements, and the time when the hungry Parisians should compel the queen to submit, or to send out her troops to an open field.   At the same time he burned the windmills that stretched their huge arms on every eminence in the vicinity.   It was an ill-advised measure, as are all similar acts of destruction, unless justified by urgent necessity. If it occasioned some distress in Paris,[1] it only embittered the minds of the people yet more, and enabled the municipal authorities to retaliate with some color of equity by seizing the houses of persons known or suspected to be Huguenots, and selling their goods to defray part of the expense incurred in defending the city.[2]

Condé at Saint Denis.

The attempt " to seize the person of the king "—for such the movement was understood to be by the Roman Catholic party— was even more unfortunate.   It produced in Charles an alienation [3]

---

[1] The price of wheat, Jehan de la Fosse tells us (p. 86) advanced to fifteen francs per " septier."

[2] Journal d'un curé ligueur (J. de la Fosse), 86.

[3] In one of Charles's first despatches to the Lieutenant-Governor of Dauphiny, wherein he bids him restrain, and, if necessary, attack any Huguenots of the province who might undertake to come to Condé's assistance, there occurs an expression that smacks of the murderous spirit of St. Bartholomew's Day: "You shall cut them to pieces," he writes, "without sparing a single person; for the more dead bodies there are, the less enemies remain (car tant plus de mortz, moins d'ennemys !)" Charles to Gordes, Oct. 8, 1567, MS. in Condé Archives, D'Aumale, i. 563.

which the enemies of the Huguenots took good care to prevent

The Huguenot movement alienates the king. him from ever completely forgetting. They represented the undertaking of Meaux as aimed, not at the counsellors of the monarch, but at the " Sacred Majesty " itself, and Condé and Coligny, with their associates, were pictured to the affrighted eyes of the fugitive boy-king as conspirators who respected none of those rights which are so precious in the view of royalty.

Meantime Catharine was not slow in resorting to the arts by which she was accustomed to seek either to avert the evil consequences of her own short-sighted policy, or to gain time to defeat the plans of her opponents.[1] The Huguenots received a deputation consisting of the chancellor, the Marshal de Vieilleville, and Jean de Morvilliers—three of the most influential and

Negotiations opened. The Huguenots gradually abate their demands. moderate adherents of the court — through whom Charles demanded the reason of the sudden uprising which causelessly threatened his own person and the peace of the realm. The Huguenot leaders replied by denying any evil design, and showing that they had armed themselves only in self-defence against the manifested malice of their enemies.[2] Subsequent interviews between Condé and the envoys of Charles seemed to hold forth some hopes of peace. The king declared himself ready to furnish the Protestants with proofs of the uprightness of his intentions, and L'Hospital even exhibited the draft of an edict in which their rights should be guaranteed. As this proved unsatisfactory, the prince, at the chancellor's suggestion, submitted the requests of his associates. These related to the banishment of the foreign troops, the permission to come and present their petitions to the king, the confirmation and maintenance of the past edicts, with the repeal of all restrictive interpretations, the assembling of the states gen-

---

[1] Davila (i. 113) makes the latter her distinct object in the negotiations : " The queen, to protract the time till supplies of men and other necessary provisions arrived, and to abate the fervor of the enemy, being constrained to have recourse to her wonted arts, excellently dissembling those so recent injuries, etc."

[2] Of course " Sieur Soulier, prêtre " sees nothing but perversity in these grounds. " Ils n'alleguèrent que des raisons frivolles pour excuser leur armement." Histoire des édits de pacification, 64.

eral, and the removal of the burdensome imposts under which
the people groaned, and which were of advantage only to the
crowd of Italians and others enjoying extraordinary credit at
court.[1] If the first of these demands were sufficiently bold, the
last demand was little calculated to conciliate Catharine, who
naturally conceived herself doubly insulted by the covert allusion to her own prodigality and by the reference to her countrymen. She found no difficulty in inducing Charles to answer
through a proclamation sent by a herald to the confederates, commanding Condé, Coligny, D'Andelot, La Rochefoucauld, Genlis,
and the other leaders, by name, to lay down the arms which
they had taken up without his consent.[2] Perceiving the mistake they had committed in making requests which, although
just and appropriate, were in part but ill-suited to the times, the
Protestants began to abate their demands. Confining themselves
to the matter of religion, they now petitioned only for an unrestricted liberty of conscience and worship, confirmed by the
repeal of all ordinances or parliamentary decisions conflicting
with it. Their moderation inspired fresh hopes of averting the
resort to arms, and a new conference was held, between the Huguenot position and the city of Paris, at the hamlet of La Chapelle Saint Denis. It was destined to be the last. Constable
Montmorency, the chief spokesman on the Roman
Catholic side, although really desirous of peace, could
not be induced to listen to the only terms on which
peace was possible. " The king," he said, " will never
consent to the demand for religious toleration throughout
France without distinction of persons or places. He has no
intention of permanently tolerating two religions. His edicts
in favor of the Protestants have been intended only as temporary measures; for his purpose is to preserve the old faith by
all possible means. He would rather be forced into a war with
his subjects than avoid it by concessions that would render him
an object of suspicion to neighboring princes." [3]

Constable Montmorency the mouth-piece of intolerance.

---

[1] Davila is certainly incorrect in stating that the Huguenots demanded " that
the queen mother should have nothing to do in the government " (p. 113).

[2] October 7th, Soulier, Hist. des édits de pacification, 65.

[3] De Thou, iv. (liv. xlii.) 10–15 ; Jean de Serres, iii. 131, 132 ; Davila, bk.

The simultaneous rising of the Huguenots in every quarter of the kingdom, and the immediate seizure of many important cities, had surprised and terrified the court; but it had also stimulated the Roman Catholic leaders to put forth extraordinary efforts to bring together an army superior to that of their opponents. Besides the Parisian militia and the troops that flocked in from the more distant provinces, it was resolved to call for the help repeatedly promised by Philip of Spain and his minister, the Duke of Alva, when urging Charles to break the compacts he had entered into with his reformed subjects. But the assistance actually furnished fell far short of the expectations held forth. When Castelnau, after two efforts, the first of which proved unsuccessful,[1] reached Brussels by a circuitous route, he found Alva lavish of good wishes, and urgent, like his master, that no arrangement should be made with the rebels before they had suffered condign punishment. But the envoy soon convinced himself that all these protestations meant little or nothing, and that the Spaniards were by no means sorry to see the French kingdom rent by civil war. Ostensibly, Alva was liberal above measure in his offers. He wished to come in person at the head of five thousand horse and fifteen thousand foot, and make short work of the destruction of Condé and his followers—a proposition which Castelnau, who knew that Catharine was quite as jealous of Spanish as of Huguenot interference in her schemes, felt himself compelled politely to decline; especially as the very briefest term within which Alva professed himself ready to move was a full month and a half. For seven or eight days the duke persisted in refusing the Spanish troops that were requested,[2]

Insincerity of Alva's offers of aid.

---

iv. 113–115; Agrippa d'Aubigné, Hist. universelle, l. iv., c. 6, 7 (i. 211, 212); Castelnau, l. vi., c. 6.

[1] So closely was Paris invested on the north, that, although accompanied by an escort of sixty horse, Castelnau was driven back into the faubourgs when making an attempt by night to proceed by one of the roads leading in this direction. He was then forced to steal down the left bank of the Seine to Poissy, before he could find means to avoid the Huguenot posts. Mémoires, l. vi., c. 6.

[2] Castelnau was instructed to ask for three or four regiments of Spanish or Italian foot, and for two thousand cavalry of the same nations.

and in insisting upon his own offer—precious time which, had it been husbanded, might have changed the face of the impending battle before the walls of Paris. When, at length, pressed by the envoy for a definite answer or for leave to return, the duke offered to give him, in about three weeks' time, a body of four or five thousand German lansquenets—troops that would have been quite useless to Charles, who already had at his disposition as many pikemen as he needed, in the six thousand Swiss. All that Castelnau was finally able to bring home was an auxiliary force of about seventeen hundred horse, under Count Aremberg. Even now, however, the officer in command was bound by instructions which prevented him from taking the direct road to the beleaguered capital of France, and compelled him to pass westward by Beauvais and Poissy.[1]

The impatience of the Parisians, who for more than a month had been inactive spectators, while their city was besieged by an insignificant force and they were deprived of the greater part of their ordinary supplies of food, could scarcely be restrained. They were the more anxious for battle since they had received encouragement by the recapture of a few points of some military importance along the course of the lower Seine. Unable to resist the pressure any longer, Constable Anne de Montmorency led out his army to give battle to the Huguenots on the tenth of November, 1567. Rarely has such an engagement been willingly entered into, where the disproportion between the contending parties was so considerable. The constable's army consisted of sixteen thousand foot soldiers (of whom six thousand were

Battle of
Saint Denis,
Nov. 10, 1567.

---

[1] I have deemed it important to go into these details, in order to exhibit in the clearest light the insincerity of Philip the Second—a prince who could not be straightforward in his dealings, even when the interests of the Church, to which he professed the deepest devotion, were vitally concerned. My principal authority is the envoy, Michel de Castelnau, liv. vi., c. 6. Alva's letter to Catharine de' Medici, Dec., 1567, Gachard, Correspondance de Philippe II., i. 608, 609, sheds some additional light on the transactions. I need not say that, where Castelnau and Alva differ in their statements, as they do in some essential points, I have had no hesitation in deciding whether the duke or the impartial historian is the more worthy of credit. See, also, De Thou, iii. (liv. xli.) 755.

Swiss, and the remainder in part troops levied in the city of Paris) and three thousand horse, and was provided with eighteen pieces of artillery. To meet this force, Condé had barely fifteen hundred hastily mounted and imperfectly equipped gentlemen, and twelve hundred foot soldiers, gathered from various quarters and scarcely formed as yet into companies. He had not a single cannon. Of his cavalry, only one-fifth part were provided with lances, the rest having swords and pistols. The greater number had no defensive armor; and not a horse was furnished with the leathern *barbe* with which the knight continued, as in the middle ages, to cover his steed's breast and sides. The constable had wisely chosen a moment when the prince had weakened himself by detaching D'Andelot, with five hundred horse and eight hundred arquebusiers, to seize Poissy and intercept the Count of Aremberg.[1] In the face of such a disparity of numbers and equipment, the Huguenots exhibited signal intrepidity.[2] With Coligny thrown forward on the right, in front of the village of Saint Ouen, and Genlis on the left, near Aubervilliers, they opened the attack upon the overwhelming numbers of the enemy, who descended from higher ground to meet them. Marshal de Montmorency, the constable's eldest son, commanding a part of the royal army, alone was successful, and had the valor of his troops been imitated by the rest, the defeat of the Huguenots would

---

[1] Mem. de Fr. de la Noue, c. xiv. (Ancienne coll., xlvii. 189); Davila, bk. iv. 116; Agrippa d'Aubigné, Hist. universelle, i. 212, 213; De Thou, iv. 22; Martin, Hist. de France, x. 246. There is some discrepancy in numbers. There is, however, but little doubt that those given in the text are substantially correct. D'Aubigné blunders, and more than doubles the troops of the constable.

[2] Agrippa d'Aubigné relates an incident which has often been repeated. Among the distinguished spectators gathered on the heights of Montmartre, overlooking the plain, was a chamberlain of the Turkish sultan, the same envoy who had been presented to the king at Bayonne. When he saw the three small bodies of Huguenots issue in the distance from Saint Denis, and the three charges, in which so insignificant a handful of men broke through heavy battalions and attacked the opposing general himself, the Moslem, in his admiration of their valor, twice cried out: "Oh, that the grand seignior had a thousand such men as those soldiers in white, to put at the head of each of his armies! The world would hold out only two years against him." Hist. univ., i. 217.

have been decisive; but the "Parisian regiment," despite its
gilded armor,[1] yielded at the first shock of battle and fled in
confusion to the walls of Paris. Their cowardice uncovered
the position of the constable, and the cavalry of the Prince
penetrated to the spot where the old warrior was still fighting
hand to hand, with a vigor scarcely inferior to that which he
had displayed more than fifty years earlier, in the first Italian
campaign of Francis the First.[2] A Scottish gentleman, according to the most probable account—for
the true history of the affair is involved in unusual
obscurity—Robert Stuart by name, rode up to Montmorency
and demanded his surrender. But the constable, maddened at
the suggestion of a fourth captivity,[3] for all reply struck Stuart
on the mouth, with the hilt of his sword, so violent a blow that
he broke three of his teeth. At that very moment he received,
whether from Stuart or from another of the Scottish gentlemen is uncertain,[4] a pistol-shot that entered his shoulder and
inflicted a mortal wound. At a few paces from him, Condé,
with his horse killed under him, nearly fell into the hands of
the enemy. At last, however, his partisans succeeded in rescuing him, and, while he retired slowly to Saint Denis, the dying
constable was carried to Paris, whither the Roman Catholic
army returned at evening.[5]

The constable is mortally wounded.

---

[1] "Autant de volontaires Parisiens bien armez et *dorez comme calices.*"
Agrippa d'Aubigné, l. iv., c. 8 (i. 213). "Tenans la bataille desjà achevée,
tout ce gros si bien doré print la fuitte." (Ibid., i. 215.)

[2] At Marignano, in 1515.

[3] He was taken prisoner by the Emperor Charles V. at Pavia, in company
with Francis I. ; at the battle of Saint Quentin, in 1557 ; and in 1562, at the
battle of Dreux, by the Huguenots. It was rather hard that the story should
have obtained currency, according to the curé of Mériot, that Constable
Montmorency was shot by a royalist, who saw that he was purposely allowing himself to be enveloped by the troops of Condé, in order that he might be
taken prisoner, " comme telle avoit jà esté sa coustume en deux batailles ! "
Mém. de Claude Haton, i. 458.

[4] Even Henry of Navarre, in a letter of July 12, 1569, published by Prince
Galitzin (Lettres inédites de Henry IV., Paris, 1860, pp. 4–11) states that he
is unable to say whether it was Stuart, " pour n'en sçavoir rien ; " but asserts that " il est hors de doubte et assez commung qu'il fut blessé en pleine
bataille et combattant, et non de sang froid."

[5] Mémoires de Fr. de la Noue, c. xiv. ; Jean de Serres, iii. 137, 138 ; De

The battle of Saint Denis was indecisive, and the victory was claimed by both sides. The losses of the Huguenots and the Roman Catholics were about equal—between three and four hundred men—although the number of distinguished Huguenot noblemen killed exceeded that of the slain belonging to the same rank in the royal army. If the possession of the field at the end of the day, and the relief of Paris, be taken as sufficient evidence, the honor of success belonged to the Roman Catholic army. But the loss of their chief commander far more than counterbalanced any advantage they may have gained. Not that Anne de Montmorency was a general of remarkable abilities. Although he had been present in a large number of important engagements ever since the reign of Louis the Twelfth, and had proved himself a brave man in all, he was by no means a successful military leader. The late Duke of Guise had eclipsed his glory, and in a much briefer career had exhibited much more striking tactical skill. The battle of Saint Denis, it was alleged by many, had itself been marred by his clumsy disposition of his troops. Proud and overbearing in his deportment, he alienated even those with whom his warm attachment to the Roman Catholic Church ought to have made him popular. Catharine de' Medici, we have seen, had long been his enemy. In like manner, even the bigoted populace of Paris forgot the pious exploits that had earned him the surname of "le Capitaine Brûlebanc," and remembered only his suspicious relationship to Cardinal Châtillon, Admiral Coligny, and D'Andelot, those three intrepid brothers whose uncompromising morality and unswerving devotion to their religious convictions made them, even more than the Prince of Condé, true representatives of the dreaded Huguenot party.[1]

Character of Anne de Montmorency.

Thou, iv. 22, etc. ; Agrippa d'Aubigné, Hist. univ., i. 214–217 ; Castelnau, liv. vi., c. 7 ; Claude Haton, i. 457 ; Jean de la Fosse, 88, 89 ; Charles IX. to Gordes, Nov. 11, 1567, Condé MSS., D'Aumale, i. 564.

[1] " La mort dudit connestable fut plaincte de peu de gens du party des catholicques, à cause de la huguenotterie de l'admiral, du card. de Chastillon, et d'Andelot, ses nepveux, qui estoient, après le Prince de Condé, chefz des rebelles huguenotz françoys et des plus meschant ; et avoient plusieurs personnes ceste oppinion du connestable, qu'il les eust bien retirez de ceste rebellion

But the loss of the principal general at this important juncture in military affairs dealt a severe blow to the Roman Catholic cause. There was no other leader of sufficient prominence to put forth an indisputable claim to succeed him. Catharine, not sorry to be relieved of so formidable a rival, was resolved that he should have no troublesome successor. Accordingly she induced the king to leave the office of constable vacant, and to confer upon her second surviving son, Henry, Duke of Anjou, whose unscrupulous character had already made him her favorite, the supreme command of the army, with the less ambitious title of royal lieutenant-general.[1]

The death of the constable, who survived his wound only a single day, and the subsequent divisions of the court, furnished the Prince of Condé with an immunity from attack, of which, in view of his great inferiority in number of troops, he deemed it most prudent to take advantage by promptly retiring from his exposed position. Besides this, he had now an imperative summons to the eastern frontier of the kingdom.

At the very commencement of the war the Protestants had sent a deputation to the German princes to solicit their support in a struggle in which the adherents of the Augsburg Confession were no less vitally interested than the reformed. But Bochetel, Bishop of Rennes, the envoy of Charles the Ninth, had so skilfully misrepresented the true character of the contest, that the Landgrave of Hesse, and the Electors of Saxony and Brandenburg, persuaded that political motives, rather than zeal for religion, were the occasion of the revolt, had refused to assist the Huguenots, while permitting William of Saxony and the Marquis of Baden to levy troops for the king. To the Elector Palatine, Frederick the Third, surnamed "the Pious," who from a Lutheran had become a Calvinist, a special ambassador was despatched in the person of M. de Lansac. This gentleman, by more than usually reckless misstatements, sought to persuade the elector to abandon

The Protestant princes of Germany determine to aid the Huguenots.

---

s'il eust voulu, attendu que tous avoient esté avancez en leurs estatz par le feu roy Henry, par son moyen." Claude Haton, i. 458.

[1] Charles IX. to Gordes, Nov. 17, 1567, Condé MSS., Duc d'Aumale, i. 565.

the enterprise of assistance which he had intended to intrust to his second son, John Casimir. But his falsehoods were refuted by the straightforward exposé of the prince's agents,[1] and Lansac was only so far successful that the elector consented to delay the departure of the troops until he had sent a messenger to France to acquaint himself with the true state of the case. It needed no more than this to determine him; for the minister whom the elector had intrusted with the commission, after visiting successively the court of the king and the camp of the prince of Condé, returned with certain proofs that the representations of Bochetel and of Lansac were altogether false.[2] Consequently the army which John Casimir had gathered was speedily despatched to furnish Condé the support the Huguenots so much needed.

In the letter which the elector palatine sent about the same time to the King of France, the motives of this apparently inimical action are vividly set forth. His envoy, the Councillor Zuleger, says the elector, has made a careful examination. Lansac and his companion have industriously circulated throughout Germany the report that the Edict of Toleration is kept entire, that Condé and the Protestants have no other object in view but a horrible rebellion against Charles to deprive him of his crown, and that the prince has had money struck as if he were king himself.[3] But Zuleger has, on the contrary, reported that when,

---

[1] This exposé, committed to writing by the elector palatine's request, and translated for Frederick's convenience into German, is published by Prof. A. Kluckhohn, in a monograph read before the Bavarian Academy of Sciences: "Zur Geschichte des angeblichen Bündnisses von Bayonne, nebst einem Originalbericht über die Ursachen des zweiten Religionskriegs in Frankreich." (Abhandlungen, iii. Cl., xi. Bd., i. Abth.) Munich, 1868. The Huguenot envoys were Chastelier Pourtaut de Latour and Francour. The document is probably from the pen of the former (p. 13).

[2] De Thou, iv. 28. 29; Castelnau, liv. vi., c. 8; Jean de Serres, iii. 144, 146. Agrippa d'Aubigné, Hist. univ., i. 217, 218. Wenceslaus Zuleger's Report is printed in full by F. W. Ebeling, Archivalische Beiträge, 48–73, and by A. Kluckhohn, Zwei pfälzische Gesandtschaftsberichte, etc. Abhandl. der Bayer. Akad., 1868, 189–205.

[3] It is needless to say that no authentic coins or medals bearing Condé's head, with the designation of "Louis XIII.," have ever been found. After the direct contradiction by Catharine de' Medici, no other testimony is neces-

in the presence of the royal council, he asked for proofs of Condé's intention to make himself king, Catharine de' Medici replied that it was a "mockery," and that, though Condé had struck money, both in the late and in the present troubles, it was with the king's inscription and arms, and not as though he were himself king. So far from that, Zuleger declares that, during the eleven days of his stay in the prince's camp, he heard prayers offered morning and night for the preservation of the state and for the king's safety. As to the maintenance of the edict, the constable before his death openly affirmed that Charles would not permit a free exercise of religion, and never intended the Edict of Orleans to be other than *provisional*. Indeed, the queen-mother remarked to Zuleger that it is a privilege of the French monarchs never to make a perpetual edict; to which Charles, who was present, promptly responded, "Pourquoi non?" [1]

It was to form a junction with the force brought by John Casimir that the prince now raised the siege of Paris, two or three days subsequently to the battle of Saint Denis,[2] and after that D'Andelot, disappointed in having had no share in the engagement, had scoured the field, driving back into Paris an advanced guard of the enemy, and burning, by way of bravado, some windmills in the very suburbs.[3]

The purpose of the Huguenot leaders could not be mistaken, and Catharine was determined to frustrate it. The chief object at which all her intrigues now aimed was to delay the Prot-

---

sary. The Jesuits, however, impudently continued to speak of Condé's treason as an undoubted truth, and even gave the legend of the supposed coin as "Ludovicus XIII., Dei gratia, Francorum Rex primus Christianus." See "Plaidoyé de Maistre Antoine Arnauld, Advocat en Parlement, pour l'Université de Paris . . . . contre les Jesuites, des 12 et 13 Juillet, 1594." Mémoires de la ligue, 6, 164. Arnauld stigmatizes the calumny as "notoirement fausse."

[1] Frederick, Elector Palatine, to Charles IX., Heidelberg, Jan. 19, 1568. Printed in full in F. W. Ebeling, Archivalische Beiträge, 74–82.

[2] Agrippa d'Aubigné, *ubi supra*.

[3] November 13th, " Hier au soyr, vers les sept heures," says Charles to Gordes, Nov. 14, 1567, MS. Condé Arch., D'Aumale, i. 565. The king naturally represents the movement as confused—" une bonne fuyte "—and confidently states that he will follow, and, by a *second* victory, put a speedy end to the war.

estant army in its march toward Lorraine, until the Duke of
The Hugue- Anjou, at the head of a force which was daily gain-
nots go to
meet the Ger- ing new accessions of strength from the provinces,
mans.   should be able to overtake Condé and bring on a
general and decisive action. From Saint Denis the Huguenots
had first followed the course of the upper Seine to Montereau.
Crossing the stream at this point, Coligny, as usual commanding the vanguard, had, at Pont-sur-Yonne, received a powerful
detachment, under the Count of La Rochefoucauld, which had
made its way from the provinces of Poitou, Saintonge, and
Guyenne, across the valley of the Loire, to reinforce the Prince
of Conde's army.[1] Having effected a junction, the united body
had changed its course, recrossed the Seine, and counter-
marched to the river Marne, at Épernay and Châlons. Coligny's skilful manœuvre had disappointed the queen's plan, and
she resorted to her accustomed arts of negotiation. So flattering, indeed, were her promises, that Condé, had he not been
restrained by the more prudent counsels of his associates (among
whom the Vidame of Chartres was most urgent in his protests
against so suicidal a policy), would instantly have relaxed the
Treacherous sinews of war.[2] A petty act of treachery served to
diplomacy.   open his eyes, and to prevent the Protestants from
involving themselves in more serious disaster; for the Count de
Brissac took advantage of a three days' armistice to fall unexpectedly upon an outpost of the prince's army and gain an
advantage, which was duly magnified by report at Paris into a
brilliant victory.[3] Unabashed by this incident, Catharine soon

---

[1] Agrippa d'Aubigné, liv. iv., c. 11 (i. 219).

[2] Ibid., i. 219, 220.

[3] La Noue, c. xiv.; De Thou, iv. 37; Jehan de la Fosse, 89, 90; Agrippa
d'Aubigné, i. 227. Davila, bk. iv., pp. 119, 120, represents Brissac's attack
(which, according to him, was not made till after the expiration of the truce)
as a part of a projected general assault. Anjou's main body failed to come
up, and so Condé was saved. The blame was thrown on Marshal Gonnor
(Cossé) and on M. de Carnavalet, the king's tutor, whom some suspected of
unwillingness to allow so much noble blood to be shed. Others accused the
one of too much friendship with the Châtillons, the other of a leaning to
heresy (" de sentir le fagot ") Agrippa d'Aubigné, i. 227. See also Cl.
Haton, i. 503. These two noblemen were accused of advocating other designs
which were very obnoxious to the Roman Catholic party. " La vérité est,"

after renewed her seductive offers (on the twentieth of December, 1567). She invited a conference with the Cardinal of Châtillon and other Protestant leaders, and herself went so far as Châlons to meet them. Thence the scene of the negotiations was transferred to Vincennes, in the vicinity of Paris, and for a time the prospect of reconciliation was bright and encouraging. The king's envoys consented to the re-establishment of the Edict of Amboise, without any past or future restrictions, until the decision of the religious question by that mythical assembly which, like a mirage of the desert, ever and anon arose to entrance and disappoint the longing eyes of thoughtful men in this century—a free, universal, and legitimate council of the Church. But the hopes founded on these promises were as illusory as any previously conceived. Instead of a formal and unambiguous ratification of the terms by Charles himself, the Cardinal of Châtillon was treated only to complaints about the causeless rising of the Protestants, and expressions of astonishment that Condé had not instantly countermanded the approach of the German auxiliaries on receiving the king's gracious proffers.[1]

Meantime Catharine was not idle in soliciting foreign aid. The Duke d'Aumale—who had also marched to Lorraine, in order to meet the Germans coming to the assistance of the Roman Catholics, under command of the Marquis of Baden— not being strong enough to block the passage of Condé's troops,

Catharine implores Alva's assistance.

Catharine wrote to Alva, begging him to send to the duke, in this emergency, two thousand arquebusiers. She warned him that if, through the failure to procure them, the German reiters of John Casimir should be permitted to enter the kingdom, she would hold herself exonerated, in the sight of God and of all Christian princes, from the blame that might otherwise attach to her for the peace which she

---

says Jehan de la Fosse, in his journal, p. 90, under date of December, 1567, "que aulcuns grands seigneurs entre lesquels on nomme Gonor [et] Carnavallet donnoient à entendre que si Monsieur, frère du roy, voloit prendre une partie de ces gens et les joindre avec le camp des huguenots, qui [qu'ils] le feroient comte de Flandre."

[1] De Thou, iv. 37-41; Castelnau, liv. vi., c. 8; La Fosse, 91.

would be compelled to make with the heretics.[1]   Alva, in reply, declined to send the Spanish arquebusiers, who, he said, were needed by him, and could do little good in France; but he added that, if Aumale, who was a soldier, would guarantee with this accession to stop the reiters, he would let them go, useful as they were in the Netherlands.   As to the accommodation

Alva's view of accommodations with heretics.   with the Huguenots, which Catharine suggested, he viewed it as a frightful evil, and exclaimed "that it was better to have a kingdom ruined in preserving it for God and the king, than to retain it whole, but without religion, for the advantage of the devil and his partisans, the heretics."[2]

About the beginning of the new year the foot-sore Huguenot army, after nearly two months of tedious marches through a hostile country, and no less tedious negotiations, reached Lorraine, only to find that their German allies had not yet arrived. Sick at heart, with a powerful enemy hanging on their rear, and seeking only an opportunity to make a sudden descent upon them, many of the Huguenots were disposed to take advantage of the proximity of the German cities to disperse and find a refuge there.   But Condé, with his never-failing vivacity and cheerfulness, and Coligny, with his "grave words," succeeded in checking their despondency until the welcome news of John

Condé and John Casimir meet in Lorraine.   Casimir's approach was announced.   He brought six thousand five hundred horse, three thousand foot, and four cannon of moderate size.   His arrival did not, however, prove an occasion of unmingled satisfaction.   The reiters, serving from purely mercenary motives, demanded the immediate payment of one hundred thousand crowns, promised as a first instalment on account of their wages, and were resolved to go no farther without receiving it.   The Prince of Condé had but two thousand crowns to meet the engagement. In this new perplexity the Huguenots, from the leaders down to the very lowest, gave a noble illustration of devotion to their

---

[1] Catharine de' Medici to Alva, Dec. 4, 1567, Gachard, Correspondance de Philippe II., i. 607.

[2] Alva to Catharine de' Medici, Dec., 1567, Gachard, Correspondance de Philippe II., i. 608, 609.

religion's cause. Condé and Coligny set the example by giving up their plate to replenish the empty coffers of the army. The *Generosity of the Huguenot troops.* captains urged, the ministers of the gospel preached, a generous sacrifice of property in the common interest. Their exhortations did not fall upon dull ears. Money, gold chains, silver, articles of every description, were lavishly contributed. An unpaid army sacrificed its own private property, not only without a murmur, but even joyfully. The very camp-servants vied with their masters, and put them to shame by their superior liberality.[1] In a short time a sum was raised which, although less than what had been pledged, contented the reiters, who declared themselves ready to follow their Huguenot fellow-soldiers into the heart of the kingdom.[2] Well might an army capable of such heroic contempt for personal gain or loss be deemed invincible !

And now, with feelings widely different from those which had possessed them in the journey toward Lorraine—a move *The march toward Orleans.* ment too nearly akin to a flight to inspire anything but disgust—the Huguenot soldiers, over twenty thousand strong, turned their faces once more westward. Their late pursuers, no longer seeking an engagement where the result might be worse than doubtful, confined themselves to watching their progress from a safe distance. As all the cities upon their route were in the hands of the Roman Catholics, the Huguenots were forced to take more circuitous and difficult paths through the open country. But the dispositions made by Coligny are said to have been so thorough and

---

[1] It is told of one lackey that he contributed twenty crowns.

[2] The scene is described in an animated manner by François de la Noue, c. xv. (Ancienne Collection, xlvii. 199–201) ; De Thou, iv. 41. "Marque le lecteur," writes Agrippa d'Aubigné, in his nervous style, "un trait qui n'a point d'exemple en l'antiquité, que ceux qui devoient demander paye et murmurer pour n'en avoir point, puissent et veuillent en leur extreme pauvreté contenter une armée avec 100,000 livres à quoi se monta cette brave gueuserie ; argument aux plus sages d'auprès du roi pour prescher la paix; tenans pour invincible le parti qui a la passion pour difference, et pour solde la necessité." Hist. univ., i. 228. D'Aubigné is mistaken, however, in making the army contribute the entire 100,000. Davila and De Thou say they raised 30,000 ; La Noue, over 80,000.

masterly, that they travelled safely and in comfort.[1]   Not that
the soldiers, dispersed at night through the villages, were freed
from the necessity or the temptation to pillage;[2] for the poor
farmers, robbed of the fruits of their honest toil, frequently had
good reason to complain that those who had recently dispensed
their own treasure with so liberal a hand were even more lavish
of the property of others.   But they were far more merciful
and considerate toward their enemies than the Roman Catholic army to its friends.   Even a curate of Brie—no very
great lover of the Huguenots, who relates with infinite gusto
the violation of Huguenot women by Anjou's soldiers[3]—admits that, excepting in the matter of the plundering of the
churches and the distressing of priests, the Roman Catholics
were a little worse than the heretics.[4]

Leaving the Huguenot army on its march toward Orleans,
let us glance at the operations of the party in other quarters of
the kingdom.   Southern France, where the Protestants were
most numerous, and where the excitable character of the people disposed them more easily than elsewhere to sudden outbreaks, was not behind the north in rising at the appointed time (September, 1567).   At Nismes, indeed,
a furious commotion broke out—the famous "Michel-
ade," as it was called, because it immediately followed the feast-
day of St. Michael—a commotion whose sanguinary excesses
gave it an unenviable notoriety, and brought deep disgrace upon
the Protestant cause.   Here the turbulent populace was encouraged by the report that Lyons was in friendly hands, and maddened by the intelligence that, besides the common dangers impending over all the Huguenots of France, the Huguenots of
Nismes had more particular occasion for fear in the troops of

The "Michel-
ade" at
Nismes.

---

[1] Mém. de Fr. de la Noue, c. xv.

[2] Ibid., *ubi supra*.

[3] Mémoires de Claude Haton, i. 500–503.

[4] Ibid., ii. 517.   "Et dès lors fut le pillage mis sus par les gens de guerre
des deux partis; et firent tous à qui mieux pilleroit et rançonneroit son hoste,
jugeant bien en eux que qui plus en pilleroit plus en auroit.   Les gens de
guerre du camp catholicque, excepté le pillage des églises et saccagemens
des prebstres, estoient au reste aussi meschans, et quasi plus que les huguenotz."

the neighboring Comtât Venaissin. These troops, it was said, had been summoned by the bishop and chapter of the cathedral of Nismes. The mob accordingly took possession of the city, closing the gates, and imprisoning a large number of persons— consuls, priests, and other obnoxious characters. That night the cathedral and the chapter-house witnessed a wild scene of destruction. Pictures of the saints, and altars, including everything associated with Roman Catholic worship, were ruthlessly destroyed. But the most terrible event occurred in the episcopal palace. The bishop was saved from capture and certain death by the intervention of a courageous man, himself a Protestant; but others were less fortunate. No fewer than eighty prisoners, brought in detachments to the court of the palace, were butchered in rapid succession, and their corpses thrown promiscuously into a well. The next morning the Protestant pastors and elders assembled, and, sending to the ringleaders a minister and a deacon, begged them to discontinue their horrible work. Already, however, had returning shame made everybody unwilling to avow his complicity in the crime. Quiet was restored. The Protestant seneschal and council released such prisoners as had escaped the fate of their comrades, and the bishop himself was sent away under an escort to a place of safety, by order of the very judge whom the clergy had, a year before, sought to deprive of his office as a heretic.[1] Nismes remained in the hands of the Protestants through the war.

Meanwhile more important movements took place. René of Savoy, son of the Count de Tende, but better known as Cipierre,

---

[1] Ménard, Hist. de Nismes, apud Cimber et Danjou, vii. 481, etc. ; Bouche, Histoire gén. de Languedoc, v. 276, 277.   Prof. Soldan, Geschichte des Protestantismus in Frankreich, ii. 274–276, whose account of an event too generally unnoticed by Protestant historians is fair and impartial, calls attention to the following circumstances, which, although they do not excuse in the least its savage cruelties, ought yet to be borne in mind : 1st, That no woman was killed ; 2d, that only those *men* were killed who had in some way shown themselves enemies of the Protestants ; and, 3d, that there is no evidence of any premeditation. To these I will add, as important in contrasting this massacre with the many massacres in which the Huguenots were the victims, the fact that the Protestant ministers not only did not instigate, but disapproved, and endeavored as soon as possible to put an end to the murders.

was Condé's agent in assembling the Huguenots of Provence;
Huguenot but Paul de Mouvans, whom we have met with be-
successes in fore in this history, was the real hero of the region.
the south
and west. In Dauphiny, Montbrun commanded. In Bourbonnais and the neighboring provinces west of the Rhône, Parcenac
and Verbelai raised three thousand foot and five hundred horse,
but sustained so severe a loss while passing through Forez, that
the number was soon reduced to barely twelve hundred. Nearer
the Pyrenees, seven thousand men were assembled, known as
"the army of the viscounts," to which further reference will
shortly be made. Lyons, one of the Huguenot strongholds in
the first war, the Protestants failed to capture.[1] But Orleans
was secured by the skill of François de la Noue, a young champion whose name was destined long to figure in the most brilliant deeds of arms of his party, both in France and in the Low
La Rochelle Countries.[2] In the west, too, the Huguenots made the
secured for most important gain of the war in the city of La
Condé. Rochelle, for the next half-century and more their
secure refuge on approach of danger.

This place, strong by nature, surrounded by low, marshy
grounds, rendering it almost unapproachable from the land side,
save by the causeways over which the roads ran, with a large
and convenient harbor and with easy access to the sea, was
already rich and populous. The citizens of La Rochelle were
noted for their independent spirit, engendered or fostered by
their maritime habits. Although the great importance of the
city dates from the civil wars, when its wharves received the
commerce driven from older ports, and when its privateers swept
the shores of Brittany and the bosom of the English channel, it
had long boasted extraordinary privileges, among which the
most highly prized was the right to refuse admission to a royal
garrison.[3] Besides this, the citizens were accustomed to choose

---

[1] De Thou, iv. 33–35.

[2] Agrippa d'Aubigné, i. 211.

[3] Henri Martin (Histoire de France, x. 255), on the authority of Coustureau,
Vie du duc de Montpensier, states that the Rochellois had, after the peace of
1563, bought from Catharine de' Medici, for 200,000 francs, the suppression of
the garrison placed in their city by the Duke of Montpensier, and remarks:
"Ces 200,000 francs coutèrent cher!" The authority, however, is very slen-

three candidates for the office of mayor, from whom the king or
the royal governor made his selection ; and the magistrate thus
appointed enjoyed an authority which the Rochellois would
scarcely concede to their monarch.[1] La Rochelle—whose former
orthodoxy Father Soulier attempts to establish by instancing the
sentence which the "présidial" of the city pronounced in 1552
against some Protestants, condemning them to be dragged on a
hurdle with a fagot of sticks bound to their backs, and afterward
to be burned, one of them alive [2]—had been so far affected by the
progress of the Reformation, that it was perhaps only the fear
of losing its trade and privileges that prevented it from openly
siding with Condé in the first religious war.[3] By this time,
however, Protestantism had struck such deep roots, that one of
the three candidates for the mayoralty, at the Easter elections
of 1567, was Truchares, a political Huguenot. The king was,
indeed, warned of his sentiments; but the royal governor, M. de
Jarnac, supported his claims, and Truchares received the requisite confirmation.[4] Still La Rochelle hesitated to espouse the
Protestant side. It was not until midwinter,[5] that Condé, re-

---

der in the absence of all corroborative evidence, and Arcère, more than a century ago, showed (Histoire de la Rochelle, i. 625) how improbable, or, rather,
impossible the story is. If any gift was made to Catharine by the city, it
must have been far less than the sum, enormous for the times and place, of
200,000 crowns ; and, at any rate, it could not have been for the purchase of
a privilege already enjoyed for hundreds of years. See the illustrative note at
the end of this chapter.

[1] Agrippa d'Aubigné, i. 218. "Plus absolument et avec plus d'obeïsance
que les Rochellois, qui depuis ont tousjours tenu le parti réformé, n'en ont
voulu deferer et rendre aux princes mesmes de leur parti, contre lesquels ils
se sont souvent picquez, en resveillant et conservant curieusement leurs privileges."

[2] Others were beaten and banished, and suffered the other penalties denounced by the Edict of Châteaubriant, as Soulier goes on to show with much
apparent satisfaction. Hist. des édits, etc., 67, 68. The text of the joint
sentence of Couraud, Constantin, and Monjaud is interesting. It is given by
Delmas, L'Église réformée de la Rochelle (Toulouse, 1870), pp. 19–25.

[3] Martin, Hist. de France, x. 254.

[4] Agrippa d'Aubigné, *ubi supra ;* Davila, bk. iv. 122 ; De Thou, iv. 27 seq.;
Soulier, 69. According to Arcère, Hist. de la Rochelle, i. 352, the mayor's
correct name was Pontard, Sieur de Trueil-Charays.

[5] The commission was dated from Montigny-sur-Aube, January 27, 1568,

turning from Lorraine, commissioned M. de Sainte-Hermine to assume command of the city in his name; and on the tenth of February, 1568, the mayor and échevins of La Rochelle opened their gates to their new friends, with protestations of their purpose to devote their lives and property to the advancement of the common cause. "The sequel proved only too clearly," writes a Roman Catholic historian, "that they were very sincere in their promises; for, having soon after demolished all the churches, they employed the materials to fortify this city in such a manner that it served from this time forward as a citadel for the Protestants, and as a secure retreat for all the apostates and malcontents of the kingdom until it was reduced by Louis the Thirteenth." [1]

Meantime the irresolute queen mother, always oscillating between war and peace, had again begun to treat with the Huguenots. Between the fifth and twentieth of January she held repeated interviews with Cardinal Châtillon, D'Esternay, and Téligny. The bigots took the alarm. The Papal Nuncio and the ambassadors of Spain and Scotland did their utmost "to impeach the accord." A post arrived from Philip the Second, offering a hundred thousand crowns of gold if Charles would continue the war. The doctors of the Sorbonne remonstrated. All united in a common cry that "it was impossible to have two religions in one realm without great confusion." Poor Charles was so moved by the stale falsehood, as well as by the large promises made him, that he sent the Protestant envoys word that he would treat no further unless Condé and his "complices" would send the reiters back to Germany, and, wholly disarming, come to him with their ordinary retinues to purge themselves of the attempt made at Meaux.

Spain and Rome oppose the negotiations for peace.

Even this amount of complaisance on the part of the weak monarch, however, did not satisfy Cardinal Santa Croce, who, on one occasion entering the council chamber (on the twentieth

---

Soulier, 70.   De Thou's expression (*ubi supra*), "peu de temps après," is therefore unfortunate.

[1] Soulier, Hist. des édits de pacification, 70.

of January), boldly demanded the fulfilment of the queen mother's promise to surrender Cardinal Châtillon into
the Pope's hands.   Catharine did not deny the promise, but interposed the plea that the present was a very
unsuitable time, since Châtillon had come to court upon
the king's safe-conduct.   To this the churchman
replied that no respect ought to be had toward the Cardinal, for
he was "an excommunicate person," condemned of schism, and
dead in the eyes of the law.   Up to this point the Duke de
Montmorency, who was present, had kept silence; but now,
turning to the queen mother, he is reported by the English
ambassador to have made a pungent address.   "But, madam,"
he said, "is it possible that the Cardinal Châtillon's
delivery should come in question, being warranted by
the king and your Majesty to the contrary, and I
myself being made a mean therein?   Wherefore this matter is
odious to be talked of, and against the law of arms and all good
civil policy; and I must needs repute them my enemies who
go about to make me falsify my promise once made."   After
these plain words Santa Croce "departed without attaining his
most cruel request."[1]

Cardinal Santa Croce demands that Cardinal Châtillon be surrendered to the Pope.

Retort of Marshal Montmorency.

During the first few months after the assumption of arms,
the Huguenots of southern France, surrounded by domestic
enemies, had confined themselves to attempting to secure their
own safety and that of their neighbors, by taking the most important cities and keeping in check the forces of the provincial
governors—an undertaking in which they met with more success in the districts bordering upon the Mediterranean than in
those adjoining the Bay of Biscay.   These events, although in
themselves important and interesting, would usurp a dispropor-

---

[1] Norris to Queen Elizabeth, January 23, 1568, State Paper Office.   I retain the quaint old English form in which Norris has couched the marshal's
speech.   It is plain, in view of the perfidy proposed by Santa Croce, even in
the royal council, that Condé was not far from right in protesting against the
proposed limitation of Cardinal Châtillon's escort to twenty horse, insisting
" que la qualité de mondict sieur le Cardinal, qui n'a acoustumé de marcher
par païs avecques si peu de train, ny son eage (age) ne permectent pas maintenant de commencer."   Condé to the Duke of Anjou, Dec. 27, 1567, MS. Bibl.
nat., Aumale, Prince de Condé, i. 568.

tionate place in this history. While Condé was absent from the vicinity of the capital, however, a body of six thousand troops, drawn from the army of the *viscounts*, under Mouvans and other experienced southern leaders, undertook a hazardous march from Dauphiny, intending to join the prince's army at Orleans.[1] The cities were in the possession of the enemy, the fords were carefully guarded, the entire country was hostile. But the perils which might have deterred less resolute men only enhanced the glory of the success of the gallant Huguenots. Abandoned by a considerable number of their comrades, who preferred a life of plunder to a fatiguing journey under arms, they met (on the eighth of January, 1568) and defeated, with a force consisting almost exclusively of infantry, the cavalry which the governor of Auvergne and the local nobility had assembled near the village of Cognac[2] to dispute their passage. Continuing their march, they reached Orleans in time to relieve that city, to whose friendly protection against the Roman Catholic bands of Martinengo and Richelieu that infested its neighborhood and threatened its capture Condé and the other Huguenot leaders of the north had entrusted their wives and children.[3]

Having stopped a brief time to rest the soldiers after the protracted march, the viscounts turned their victorious arms against the city of Blois. After the surrender of this place, they had

March of the viscounts to meet Condé.

---

[1] The " seven viscounts "—often referred to about this period—were the viscounts of Bourniquet, Monclar, Paulin, Caumont, Serignan, Rapin, and Montagut, or Montaigu. They headed the Protestant gentry of the provinces Rouergue, Quercy, etc., as far as to the foot of the Pyrenees. Mouvans held an analogous position in Provence, Montbrun in Dauphiné, and D'Acier, younger brother of Crussol, in Languedoc. Agrippa d'Aubigné, i. 220, 221; De Thou, iv. 33; Duc d'Aumale, Princes de Condé, i. 327. When " the viscounts " consented, at the earnest solicitation of the second Princess of Condé, to part with a great part of their troops, they confided them to Mouvans, Rapin, and Poncenac.

[2] The *village* of Cognac, or Cognat, near Gannat, in the ancient Province of Auvergne (present Department of Allier), must not, of course, be confounded with the important *city* of the same name, on the river Charente, nearly two hundred miles further west.

[3] Jean de Serres, iii. 146, 147; De Thou, iv. 48–51; Agrippa d'Aubigné, ι. 226.

proceeded down the valley of the Loire, and were about to take Montrichard, on the Cher, when recalled by Condé. The prince had by forced marches anticipated the army of Anjou, resolving to strike a blow which should be felt at the hostile capital itself, Siege of and had selected Chartres, an important city about Chartres. fifty miles in a south-westerly direction from Paris, as the most convenient place to besiege.[1] Rapid, however, as had been his advance—and a part of his army had travelled sixty miles in two days—the enemy had sufficient notice of his inten- tion to throw into the city a small force of soldiers; and when Condé arrived before the walls (on the twenty-fourth of February, 1568), he found the place prepared to sustain an attack, in which the courage of the assailants was equalled by the skill and reso- lution of the defenders.　As usual, the Huguenots were badly off for artillery ; the united armies could only muster five siege- pieces and four light culverines.　"For, although the Catholics esteem the Huguenots to be 'fiery' men," says a quaint old writer, who was as ready with his sword as with his pen, "they have always been poorly provided with such implements.　Nor have they, like the former, a Saint Anthony, who, they say, presides over the element in question."[2]

The operations of the siege of Chartres were interrupted by fresh negotiations for peace.　Half a year had the flames of war been desolating the fairest parts of France; yet the court was no nearer the attainment of its ends than at the outbreak of hostilities.　If the Roman Catholic forces had been swollen to about forty thousand men, they were confronted by a Huguenot army of twenty-eight or thirty thousand men in the very neighborhood of the capital.　The voice of prudence

---

[1] Opinions differed respecting the propriety of the movement. According to La Noue, Chartres in the hands of the Huguenots would have been a "thorn in the foot of the Parisians ;" while Agrippa d'Aubigné makes it "a city of little importance, as it was neither at a river crossing, nor a sea-port ;" "but," he adds, "in those times places were not estimated by the standard now in vogue."

[2] "Car encore que les Catholiques estiment les Huguenots estre *gens à feu*, si sont-il toujours mal pourveus de tels instrumens," etc.　Mém. de la Noue, c. xviii.　For the siege of Chartres, besides La Noue, see Jean de Serres, iii. 148 ; De Thou, iv., 51–53 ; Agrippa d'Aubigné, i. 229–232.

dictated an immediate settlement of the dispute before more lives were sacrificed, more towns and villages destroyed, more treasure squandered. Catharine, reigning supreme under her son's name, with her usual inconstancy of purpose, was ready to exchange the war, into which she had plunged France by lending too willing an ear to the suggestions of Philip of Spain, as they came to her through the Cardinal of Lorraine and others, and which had produced only bloodshed, devastation of the kingdom, and deeper depression of the finances, for the peace to which Michel de l'Hospital, her better genius, was constantly urging her by every consideration of policy and justice.

In a paper, wherein about this time the chancellor committed to writing the arguments he had often ineffectually employed to persuade the king and his mother, he combats with patriotic indignation the flimsy pretexts of which the priests and the Spaniard made use in pressing the continuance of hostilities. "'The king has more men than the Huguenots.' True, but we find twice as many battles on record gained by the smaller as by the greater number; in consequence of which fact all princes and nations have recognized the truth that victory is the gift of God. 'The king's cause is the more just.' Grant it—yet God makes use of such instruments as He wills to punish our iniquities—the Babylonians, for instance, of old, the Turks in our own days. The Huguenots have thus far succeeded beyond all expectation. They have little money, but what they have they use well, and they can get more. Their devotion to their cause is conspicuous. They are not a rabble hastily gotten together, which has risen imprudently, in disorder, without a leader, without discipline. They are experienced, resolute, desperate warriors, with plans formed long ago—men ready to risk everything for the attainment of their matured designs. Necessity and despair render them docile and wonderfully subject to discipline; and with this co-operates the high esteem they have conceived of their leaders, whose ambition is restrained, whose union is cemented by the same necessity which the ancients called 'the bond of concord.' On the contrary, the king's camp is rent by quarrels, envy, and rivalry; ambition is unbridled, avarice reigns supreme. With

Chancellor Michel de l'Hospital's memorial.

the termination of so wretched a war, there will shine forth a joyous and blessed peace, which I can justly term a 'precious conquest,' since it will render his Majesty redoubtable to all Europe, which has learned the greatness of the two powers which the king will restore to his own subjection.

"The true method of breaking up the leagues of the Huguenots is to remove the necessity for forming them. This must be done by treating the Huguenots no longer as enemies, but as friends. For, if we examine carefully into the matter, we shall find that hitherto they have been dealt with as rebels; and this has compelled them to resort to all means of self-preservation. This has placed arms in their hands; this has engendered the horrible desolation of France. For the intrigues set on foot against them in all quarters were conducted with so little attempt at secrecy—the disfavor was so evident, the disdain was so apparent, the threats of the rupture of the Edict of Pacification and of the publication of the decrees of the Council of Trent were so open, and the injustice of their handling was so manifest, that they had been too dull and stupid, had they not avoided the treachery in store for them.[1] Even brute beasts perceive the coming of the storm, and seek the covert; let us not find fault if men, perceiving it, arm themselves for the encounter. Our menaces have been the messengers of our plots, as truly as the lightning is the messenger of the thunderbolt. We have shown them our preparatives; let us, therefore, cease to wonder that they stand ready to start on the first intimation of danger.[2] When they see that they have no longer anything to fear, they will certainly return to their accustomed occupations."[3]

---

[1] "Ils eussent esté par trop lourds et stupides, s'ils n'en eussent évité la feste."

[2] "Cessons donc de nous esbahir s'ils ont un pied en l'air et l'œil en la campagne."

[3] The whole of this remarkable memorial is inserted in the older Collection universelle de mémoires, xlv. 224–260. Its importance is so great, as reflecting the views of a mind so impartial and liberal as that of Chancellor L'Hospital, that I make no apology for the prominence I have given to it. Besides the omission of much that might be interesting, I have in places rather recapitulated than translated literally the striking remarks of the original.

L'Hospital was right. The Huguenots wanted nothing but security of person and conscience—the latter even more than the former. And they were ready to lay down their arms so soon as the court could bring itself to concede the restoration of the Edict of Amboise, without the restrictive ordinances and interpretations which had shorn it of most of its value. On this basis negotiations now recommenced. The more prudent Huguenots suggested that the party ought to receive at the king's hands some of the cities in their possession, to be held as pledges for the execution of the articles of the compact. But Charles and his counsellors resented the proposal as insulting to the dignity of the crown,[1] and the Huguenots, not yet fully appreciating the fickleness or treachery of the court, did not press the demand—a fatal weakness, soon to be atoned for by the speedy renewal of the war on the part of the Roman Catholics.[2] After brief consultation the terms of peace were agreed upon, and were incorporated in the royal edict of the twenty-third of March, 1568, known, from the name of the place where it was signed, as the "Edict of Longjumeau." The cardinal provisions were few : they re-established the supremacy of the Edict of Amboise, expressly repealing all the interpretations that infringed upon it ; and permitted the nobles, who under that law had been allowed to have religious exercises in their castles, to admit strangers as well as their own vassals to the services of the reformed worship. Condé and his followers were, at the same time, recognized as good and faithful servants of the crown, and a general amnesty was pronounced covering all acts of hostility, levy of troops, coining of money, and similar offences. On the other hand, the Huguenots bound themselves to disband and lay down their arms, to surrender the places they held, to renounce foreign alliances, and to eschew in future all meetings other than those religious

Edict of Pacification, Longjumeau, March 23, 1568.

---

[1] La Noue, c. xviii.

[2] Castelnau, who was behind the scenes, assures us that had "the Huguenots insisted upon keeping some places in their own hands, for the performance of what was promised, it would have been granted, and, in all probability, have prevented the war from breaking out so soon again," etc. Mém., liv. vi., c. 11.

gatherings permitted under the last peace. The new edict was not a final and irrevocable law, but was granted " until, by God's grace, all the king's subjects should be reunited in the profession of one and the same religion." [1]

The Huguenots gained by this peace all their immediate demands, and so far the edict might be deemed satisfactory. But what better security had they for its observance more than they had had for the observance of that which had preceded it? Coligny, prudent and far-sighted, had shown himself as averse to concluding it without sufficient guarantees for its faithful execu-

Condé favors and Coligny opposes the peace. tion, as he had been opposed to beginning the war a half-year before. The peace, he urged, was intended by the court only as a means of saving Chartres, and of afterward overwhelming the reformers; [2] and he attempted to prove his assertions by the signal instances of bad faith which had provoked the recourse to arms. But Condé was impatient. If we may believe Agrippa d'Aubigné, his old love of pleasure was not without its influence; [3] but he covered his true motives under the specious pretext afforded him by the Huguenot nobles, who, fatigued with the incessant toils of the campaign, reduced to straits by a warfare which they had carried on at their own expense, and longing to revisit homes which had been repeatedly threatened with desolation, had abandoned their standards and scattered to their respective provinces at the first mention of peace. [4] François de la Noue, more charitable to the prince, regards the universal desire for peace, without much concern respecting its conditions, as the wild blast of a hurricane which the Huguenot captains could not resist if they would. [5] When whole cornets of cavalry started without leave, before the siege of Chartres was actually raised, what could generals, deserted

---

[1] Jean de Serres, iii. 149–154; De Thou, iv. 54, 55; Davila, bk. iv. 124; Castelnau, *ubi supra ;* Agrippa d'Aubigné, i. 260, etc.

[2] " L'Amiral maintenoit et remonstroit que cette paix n'estoit que pour sauver Chartres, et puis pour assommer separez ceux qu'on ne pourroit vaincre unis." Agrippa d'Aubigné, i. 232.

[3] " Le Prince de Condé plus facile, desireux de la cour, où il avoit laissé quelque semence d'amourettes, se servit de ce que plusieurs quittoient l'armée," etc. Ibid., *ubi supra.*

[4] La Noue, c. xviii.   [5] La Noue, c. xix.

by volunteers who had come of their own accord and had served
for six months without pay, expect to accomplish?

Was the peace of Longjumeau—"the patched-up peace," or
"the short peace," as it was called; that "wicked little peace,"
as La Noue styles it[1]—a compact treacherously entered into by
Was the court sincere? the court? This is the old, but constantly recurring
question respecting every principal event of this un-
happy period; and it is one that rarely admits of an easy or
a simple answer. So far as the persons who had been chiefly
instrumental in forwarding the negotiations which ended in the
peace of Longjumeau were concerned, they were Chancellor
L'Hospital and the Bishops of Orleans and Limoges—the most
moderate members of the royal council,[2] whose fair spirit was
so conspicuous that for years they had been exposed to insult
and open hostility as supposed Huguenots. Nothing is clearer
than that the purpose of these men was the sincere and entire
re-establishment of peace on a lasting foundation. The arguments of L'Hospital which I have laid before the reader furnish
sufficient proof. This party had, through the force of circumstances, temporarily obtained the ascendancy in the council,
and now had the ear of the queen mother. But there were by
the side of its representatives at the council-board men of an
entirely different stamp—advocates of persecution, of extermination; a few, from conscientious motives, preferring, with
Alva, a kingdom ruined in the attempt to root out heresy, to
one flourishing, with heresy tolerated; a larger number—and
Cardinal Lorraine, who had now resumed his seat and his influence, must be classed with these—counting upon deriving personal advantage from the supremacy of the papal faction. It
is equally manifest that this party could have acquiesced in the

---

[1] "La paix fourrée," Soulier, Histoire des édits de pacification, 73. "Ceste
meschante petite paix," La Noue, c. xix.   Agrippa d'Aubigné, Hist. universelle, i. 260, and, following him, Browning, Hist. of the Huguenots, i. 220,
and De Félice, Hist. of the Protestants of France, 190, say that this peace
was wittily christened "La paix boiteuse et mal-assise;" but, as we shall see,
this designation belongs to the peace of Saint Germain-en-Laye, in 1570, concluding the third religious war.

[2] Leopold Ranke, Civil Wars and Monarchy in France in the Sixteenth and
Seventeenth Centuries (New York, 1853), 234.

peace, which again formally acknowledged the principle of religious toleration, only with the design of embracing the first favorable opportunity for crushing the Huguenots, when scattered and disarmed. Their desires, at least, deceived no one of ordinary perspicacity. Indeed, the peace came near failing to go into effect at all, in consequence of the discovery of the fact that a "privy council" had been held in the Louvre, to which none but sworn enemies of the Huguenots were admitted, "wherein was conspired a surprise of Orleans, Soissons, Rochelle, and Auxerre," to be executed by four designated leaders, while the Protestants were laying down their arms. In an age of salaried spies, it is not astonishing that by ten o'clock the next morning the whole plot was betrayed to Cardinal Châtillon, who immediately sent word to stay the publication of the peace. When Charles heard of it, we are told that he swore, by the faith of a prince, that, if there had been any such conspiracy, it had been formed wholly without his knowledge, and, laying his hand on his breast, said: "This is the cardinal and Gascoigne's practice. In spite of them, I will proceed with the peace;" and, commanding pen and ink to be brought, he wrote Condé a letter promising a good and sincere observance of the articles agreed upon.[1]

A treacherous plot detected. The king indignant.

But, besides the two parties, and wavering between them—fluctuating in her own purposes, as false to her own plans as she was to her promises, with no principles either of morality or of government, intent only on grasping power, the enemy of every one that stood in the way of this, even if it were her son or her daughter—was that enigma, Catharine de' Medici, whose secret has escaped so many simply because they looked for something deep and recondite, when the solution lay almost upon the very surface. Was Catharine sincerely in favor of peace? She was never sincere. Her Macchiavellian training, the enforced hypocrisy of her married life, the trimming policy she had thought herself compelled to pursue during the minority of the kings, her two sons, had eaten from her soul, even to

---

[1] Norris to Cecil, Paris, March 30, 1568, State Paper Office.

its root, truthfulness—that pure plant of heaven's sowing. Loving peace only because it freed her from the fears, the embarrassments, the vexations of war—not because she valued human life or human happiness—she embraced it as a welcome expedient to enable her to escape the present perplexities of her position. It is improbable that Catharine distinctly premeditated a treacherous blow at the Huguenots, simply because she rarely premeditated anything very long. I am aware that this estimate of the queen is quite at variance with the views which have obtained the widest currency; but it is the estimate which history, carefully read, seems to require us to adopt.

Short-sightedness of Catharine.

Catharine's plans were proverbially narrow in their scope, never extending much beyond the immediate present. After the catastrophe, which had perhaps been the result of the impulse of the moment, she was not, however, unwilling to accept the homage of those who deemed it a high compliment to her prudence to praise her consummate dissimulation. She probably entered upon the peace of Longjumeau without any settled purpose of treachery—unless that state of the soul be in itself treachery that has no fixed intention of upright dealing. But she had not, in adopting the advice of Chancellor de l'Hospital, renounced the policy of the Cardinal of Lorraine, in case that policy should at some future time appear to be advantageous; and it was much to be feared that the contingency referred to would soon arrive. Catharine, not less than Charles himself, resented "the affair of Meaux" of the preceding September. It was studiously held up to their eyes by the enemies of the Huguenots as an attempt upon the honor, and indeed even upon the personal liberty and life of their Majesties. Might not Catharine and Charles be tempted to retaliate by trying the effect of a surprise upon the Huguenots themselves?

The Huguenots had certainly been grossly imprudent in putting themselves at the mercy of a woman whom they had greatly offended, and whose natural place, according to those mysterious sympathies which bind men of similar natures, was with their adversaries. They had been warned by their secret friends at court, some of them by Roman

Imprudence of the Huguenots.

Catholic relatives.[1]   But the caution was little heeded.   It was not long[2] before those who had been the most strenuous advocates of peace began to admit that the draught they had put to their own lips, and now must needs drink, was likely to prove little to their taste.[3]

The parliaments made serious objections to the reception of the edict.   Toulouse was, as usual, pre-eminent for its intolerance.   The king sent Rapin, a Protestant gentleman who had served with distinction under Condé in Languedoc, to carry the law to the parliament, and require its official recognition.   The choice was unfortunate, for it awakened all the hatred of a court proverbial for its hostility to the Reformation.   An accusation of matters quite foreign to his mission was trumped up against Rapin, and, contrary to all the principles of justice, and notwithstanding the privileged character he bore as the king's envoy, he was arrested, condemned to death, and executed.   So atrocious a crime might perhaps have been punished, had not the new commotions to which we shall soon be obliged to pay attention, intervened and screened the culprits from their righteous retribution.[4]   Not

Judicial murder of Rapin, at Toulouse.

---

[1] La Noue, c. xviii. (Anc. coll., 214).

[2] A fortnight had not elapsed since the date of the Edict of Pacification when Condé was compelled to call the king's attention to a flagrant outrage committed by Foissy, a royalist, against the Sieur d'Esternay.   After having burned Esternay's residence at Lamothe during the preliminary truce, Foissy subsequently to the conclusion of peace returned and completed his work of devastation.   Condé to Charles IX., April 5, 1568, MS., Archives du dép. du Nord, *apud* Duc d'Aumale, i. 572.

[3] "Nous avons fait la folie, ne trouvons donc estrange si nous la beuvons. Toutefois il y a apparence que le breuvage sera amer." La Noue, *ubi supra*.

[4] De Thou, iv. 55, 56; Jean de Serres, Comm. de statu, etc., iii. 160; Condé's petition of Aug. 23d, ibid., iii. 218; Mém. de Claude Haton, i. 357–359, who, however, makes the singular blunder of placing the incident of Rapin's death after the peace of Amboise in 1563.   The curé's description of the zeal of the Toulouse parliament for the Roman Catholic Church confirms everything that Protestant writers have said on the subject: "Laditte court de parlement avoit tousjours résisté à laditte prétendue religion et faict exécuter ceux qui en faisoient profession, nonobstant édict à ce contraire faict en faveur d'iceux huguenotz."   See also Raoul de Cazenove, Rapin-Thoyras, sa famille, sa vie, et ses œuvres (Paris, 1866), 47–49—a truly valuable work, and a worthy tribute to a distinguished ancestry.

content with murdering Rapin, the Parliament of Toulouse still refused to register the edict, and not less than four successive orders were sent by the king before his refractory judges yielded an unwilling consent, even then annexing restrictive clauses which they took care to insert in their secret records.[1]

Again Roman Catholic pulpits resounded, as they did whenever any degree of toleration was accorded the Protestants, with denunciations of Catharine, of Charles, of all in the council who had advocated such pernicious views.

Seditious preachers and mobs.

Again Ahab and Jezebel appear; but while Catharine is always Jezebel, it is Charles that now figures, in place of poor Antoine of Navarre, as Ahab.[2]   Again, in the struggle of royalty with priests and monks breathing sedition, it is the churchman who by his arrogance carries off the victory with the common people, while from the sensible he receives merited contempt.[3] So fine a text as the edict afforded for spirited Lenten discourses did not present itself every day, and the clergy of France improved it so well that the passions of their flocks were inflamed to the utmost.[4]   Except where their numbers were so large as to command respect, the Protestants scarcely dared to return to their homes.

The very mention of the peace, with its favorable terms for the Protestants, was enough to stir up the anger of the ignorant populace.   When the Parliament of Rouen, after agreeing to the Edict of Longjumeau in private session, threw open its doors

---

[1] "Edictum promulgant, hac addita exceptione, *Reservatis clausulis quæ secreto Senatus commentario continentur.*"   J. de Serres, iii. 160, 161; De Thou, *ubi supra.*   See the petition of Condé of Aug. 23d.   J. de Serres, iii. 220, etc.

[2] Mém. de Claude Haton, ii. 527, etc.

[3] "Sire," said a nobleman, after listening to the arguments against the peace made by some of the remonstrants, and to Charles's replies, "it is too much to undertake to dispute with these canting knaves; it were better to have them strapped in the kitchen by your turnspits."   Ibid., ii. 530.

[4] Playing upon the chancellor's name, Sainte Foy, one of the court preachers, exclaimed in the pulpit: "Be not astonished if the Huguenots demolish the churches, for they have turned all France into a *hospital* instead"—"donnant à entendre que par le chancelier nommé Hospital, la France estoit pauvre, pourtant qu'il a par trop encore de douceur pour les huguenots qui ont ruiné le pais de France."   Jehan de la Fosse, 93, 94.

(on the third of April, 1568) to give it official publication, a
Riot when the edict is published at Rouen. rabble that had come purposely to create a tumult, interrupted the reading with horrible imprecations against the peace, the Huguenots, the edicts, the "prê-ches," and the magistrates who approved such impious acts. The presidents and counsellors fled for their lives. The populace, as though inspired by some evil spirit, raged and committed havoc in the "palais de justice." The mob opened the prisons and liberated eight or ten Roman Catholics; then flocked to the ecclesiastical dungeons and would have massacred the Protestants that were still confined there, had these not found means to ransom their lives with money. It was not until six days later that the royal edict was read, in the presence of a large military force called in to preserve order.[1]

In spite of the provisions of the edict, the Huguenots wandered about in the open country, avoiding the cities where they Treatment of the returning Huguenots. were likely to meet with insult and violence, if not death. The Protestants of Nogent, Provins, and Bray hesitated for three months, and then we are told that each man watched his opportunity and sought to enter when his Roman Catholic friends might be on guard to defend him from the insolence of others.

But the sufferings of the Huguenot burgess were not ended when he was once more in his own house. He was studiously treated as a rebel. Every movement was suspicious. A Roman Catholic chronicler, who has preserved in his voluminous diary many of the details that enable us to restore something of its original coloring to the picture of the social and political condition of the times, vividly portrays the misfortunes of At Provins. the unhappy Huguenots of Provins. They were not numerous. One by one, thirty or forty had stealthily crept into town, experiencing no other injury than the coarse raillery of their former neighbors. Thereupon the municipal government met and deliberated upon the measures of police to be taken "in order to hold the Huguenots in check and in fear, and to avoid any treachery they might intend to put into prac-

---

[1] Floquet, Hist. du parlement de Normandie, iii. 36–42.

tice by the introduction of their brother Huguenots into the
city to plunder and hold it by force." The determination
arrived at was that each of the four captains should visit the
Huguenot houses of his quarter, examine the inmates, and take
all the weapons he found, giving a receipt to their owners.
This was not the only humiliation to which the Protestants
were subjected. A proclamation was published forbidding them
from receiving any person into their houses, from meeting
together under any pretext, from leaving their houses in the
evening after seven o'clock in summer, or five in winter,
from walking by day or night on the walls, or, indeed, from
approaching within two arquebuse shots' distance of them—all
upon pain of death! They could not even go into the country
without a passport from the bailiff and the captain of the gate,
the penalty of transgressing this regulation being banishment.
No wonder that the Huguenots were irritated, and that most of
them wished that they had not returned.[1] Since, however, a
royal ordinance of the nineteenth of May expressly enjoined
upon all fugitive Huguenots to re-enter the cities to which they
belonged, and in case of refusal commanded the magistrates
to raise a force and attack them as presumptive robbers and
enemies of the public peace,[2] they were perhaps quite as safe
within the walls as roaming about outside of them.

Early in the summer an event occurred on the northern
frontier, which, although in itself of little weight, augmented
the suspicions which the Protestants began to entertain of the Spanish tendencies of the government.

Expedition
and fate of De
Cocqueville.

One Seigneur de Cocqueville, with a party of French
and Flemish Huguenots, had crossed the northern boundary and
invaded Philip's Netherland provinces. He had, however, been
driven back into France. As he was believed to have acted
under Condé's instructions, that prince was requested by Charles
to inform him whether Cocqueville were in his service. When
Condé disavowed him, and declined all responsibility for the

---

[1] Mémoires de Claude Haton, ii. 533, 534. Similar regulations were made
in many other places "cumplurimis in locis." Jean de Serres, iii. 156.

[2] Jean de Serres, iii. 158, 159.

movement, Marshal Cossé was directed to march against Cocque-ville, and, on the eighteenth of July, the Huguenot chieftain was captured at the town of Saint Valéry, in Picardy, where he had taken refuge. Of twenty-five hundred followers, barely three hundred are said to have been spared. In order to please Alva, the Flemings received no quarter. The leaders, Coc-queville, Vaillant, and Saint Amand, were brought to Paris and gibbeted on the Place de Grève.[1]

The central government itself gave the gravest grounds for fear and suspicion. The Huguenots had promptly disbanded. They had lost no time in dismissing their German allies, who, Attitude of the government suspicious. retiring with well-filled pockets to the other side of the Rhine, seemed alone to have profited by the intestine commotions of France.[2] On the contrary, the Roman Catholic forces showed no disposition to disarm. It is true that, in the first fervor of the ascendancy of the peace party, Catharine countermanded a levy of five thousand Saxons, much to the annoyance of Castelnau, who had by his unwearied diligence brought them in hot haste to Réthel on the Aisne, only to learn that the preliminaries of peace were on the point of being concluded, and that the troopers were expected to retrace their steps to Saxony.[3] But the Swiss and Italian soldiers, as well as the French gens-d'armes, were for the most part retained. To Humières, who commanded for the king in Péronne, Charles wrote an explanation of his course: "Inasmuch as there are sometimes turbulent spirits so constituted that they neither can

---

[1] De Thou, iv. 77, 78 ; Castelnau, l. vii., c. 1 ; D'Aubigné, i. 260 ; La Fosse, 97 ; Motley, Dutch Republic, ii. 184.

[2] Charles was, however, near experiencing trouble with the reiters of Duke Casimir. He had, by the terms of the agreement with the Huguenots, under-taken to advance the 900,000 francs which were due, and on failing to fulfil his engagements his unwelcome guests threatened to turn their faces toward Paris. Mém. de Castelnau, liv. vi., c. 11. At last, with promises of payment at Frankfort, the Germans were induced to leave France. Du Mont, Corps diplomatique, v. 164, gives a transcript of Casimir's receipt, May 21, 1568, for 460,497 livres, etc.

[3] Mémoires de Castelnau, liv. vi., c. 9, c. 10. Duke John William of Saxe-Weimar was even more vexed at the issue of his expedition than Castelnau himself. It was with difficulty that he could be persuaded to accept an invi-tation to make a visit to the French court.

nor desire to accommodate themselves so soon to quiet, it has appeared to me extremely necessary to anticipate this difficulty, and act in such a manner that, force and authority remaining on my side, I may be able to keep in check those who might so far forget themselves as to set on foot new disturbances and be the cause of seditious uprising."[1] Large garrisons

Garrisons and interpretative ordinances.

were thus provided for those towns which had rendered themselves conspicuous in the defence of the Huguenots during the late war, and the sufferings of the Protestants, upon whom, in preference to their Roman Catholic neighbors, the insolent soldiers were quartered, were terrible beyond description.[2] The horrors of the "dragonnades" of the reign of Louis the Fourteenth were rivalled by these earlier military persecutions. Multitudes were despoiled of their goods, hundreds lost their lives at the hands of their cruel guests. France assumed the aspect of a great camp, with sentries posted everywhere to maintain it in peace against some suspected foe. The sea-ports, the bridges, the roads were guarded; the Huguenots themselves were placed under a species of surveillance. Nor were the old resorts of the court forgotten. Again interpretative ordinances were called in to abrogate a portion of the law itself. Charles declared in a new proclamation that he had not intended by the Edict of Longjumeau to include Auvergne, nor any district belonging as an appanage to his mother, to Anjou, Alençon, or the Bourbon princes, in the toleration guaranteed by the edict. And thus a very considerable number of Protestants were by a single stroke of the pen stripped

---

[1] Paris MS., *apud* Soldan, Gesch. des Prot. in Frankreich, ii. 300. Rumor, as is usual in such cases, outstripped even the unwelcome truth, and Norris wrote to Queen Elizabeth that the king had sent secret letters to two hundred and twelve places, charging the governors " to runne uppon them [the Huguenots] and put them to the sword." "Your Majestie will judge," adds Norris, "ther is smale place of surety for them of the Religion, either in towne or felde." Letter of June 4, 1568, *apud* D'Aumale, Les Princes de Condé, ii. 363, Pièces inédites.

[2] When the Protestants at Rouen begged protection, the king sent four companies of infantry, which the citizens at first refused to admit. At last they were smuggled in by night, *and quartered upon the Huguenots.* Floquet, Hist. du parlement de Normandie, iii. 43.

of the privileges solemnly accorded to them but a few weeks before.[1] Other pledges were as shamelessly broken. The Huguenot gentlemen whom the court had attempted to punish by declaring them to have forfeited their honors and dignities, were not reinstated according to the terms of the edict.[2]

The conduct of individual governors furnished still greater occasion for complaint and alarm. The Duke of Nemours, who, in marrying Anne of Este, Guise's widow, two years before, seemed also to have espoused all the hatred which the Lorraines felt for Protestantism, and for the family of the Châtillons, its most prominent and faithful defenders, was governor of the provinces of Lyonnais and Dauphiny. This insubordinate nobleman loudly proclaimed his intention to disregard the Edict of Longjumeau, as opposed to the Roman Catholic Church and to the king's honor. In vain did the Protestants, who were numerous in the city of Lyons, demand to be allowed to enjoy the two places of worship they had possessed, before the late troubles, within the city walls. The duke would not listen to their just claims, and the court, in answer to their appeals, only responded that the king did not approve of the holding of Protestant services inside of cities, and that a place would shortly be assigned for their use in the vicinity.[3] Unrebuked by the queen or her son for his flagrant disobedience, Nemours received nothing but plaudits from the fanatical adherents of the religion he pretended to maintain, and was honored by the Pope, Pius the Fifth (on the fifth of July, 1568), with a special brief, in which he was praised for being the first to set a resplendent example of resistance to the execution of an unchristian peace.[4]

Marshal Tavannes, in Burgundy, earned equal gratitude for his opposition to the concession of Protestant rights. Not content with remonstrance respecting a peace which had excited every one "to raise his voice against the king and Catharine," and with dark hints of the danger of handling so carelessly a

Oppression by royal governors.

[1] Jean de Serres, iii. 157, 158.
[2] Ibid., *ubi supra*.
[3] Jean de Serres, iii. 161; Soldan, ii. 303.
[4] Soldan, ii. 306.

border province like Burgundy,[1] he openly favored the revival
of those "Confraternities of the Holy Ghost" which Charles
had so lately condemned and prohibited. Being himself detained by illness, two of his sons were present at a meeting
of one of these seditious assemblages, held in Dijon, the provincial capital, where, before a great concourse of people, the
most inflammatory language was freely uttered.[2]

At Troyes, the capital of Champagne, a similar association
assumed the designation of "the Christian and Royal League."
The document, containing the oath taken by the clergy
whom the king's lieutenant had associated with the
nobility and the provincial estates in the "holy"
bond, is still extant, with the signatures of the bishop, the
deans, canons, and inferior ecclesiastics appended.[3] The pri-
mary object was the maintenance of "the true Catholic and
Roman Church of God;" and after this the preservation of the
crown for the house of Valois was mentioned. It was to be
sustained "against all persons, without excepting any, save the
persons of the king, his sons and brothers, and the queen their
mother, and without regard to any relationship or alliance,"
and "so long as it might please God that the signers should
be governed according to the Roman and Apostolic Church."[4]
In less public utterances the spirit of insubordination to the regal authority made itself understood even more clearly. When
the formation of such associations was objected to, on the
ground of the king's prohibition, the response given by those

The "Chris-
tian and Royal
League."

---

[1] Letter to Catharine, April 27, 1568, MS., *apud* Soldan, ii. 303.

[2] Jean de Serres, iii. 163, 164. Petition of Condé of Aug. 23d. Ibid., iii.
215, etc.

[3] MS. Bibl. nat., *apud* Mém. de Claude Haton, ii. App., 1152, 1153. Less
correctly given in Lestoile's Mémoires. The title is "Sermens des Associez
de la Ligue Chrestienne et Roiale," and the date is June 25, 1568.

[4] Prof. Soldan is certainly right (ii. 305) in his interpretation of the passage, "tant et si longuement qu'il plaira à Dieu que nous serons *par eux*
régis en nostredicte religion apostolique et romaine," which Ranke (Civil
Wars and Monarchy, p. 236), and, following him, Von Polenz (Gesch. des
franz. Calvinismus, ii. 361), have construed as referring to "la maison de
Valois." Involved as is the phraseology, I do not see how the word "eux"
can designate any other person or persons than "ledit s\ lieutenant avec
mesditz sieurs de la noblesse de cedit gouvernement et autres associez."

who pretended to be better informed than the rest was that the Cardinal of Lorraine could make the matter agreeable to his Majesty. Others more boldly announced the intention of
Insubordination to royal authority. the Roman Catholic party, in case Charles should refuse to sanction its course, to send him to a monastery for the rest of his days, and elect another king in his place. Three months' time was all that these blatant boasters allowed for the utter destruction of the Huguenots in France. An end would be made of them as soon as the harvest and vintage were past.[1]

If the Roman Catholics had resolved upon a renewal of the war, they certainly had reason to desire a better combination of their forces than they had effected in the late contest. They had been startled and amazed at the rapidity with which, although embracing but an inconsiderable minority of the pop-
Admirable organization of the Huguenots. ulation, the Huguenots had succeeded in massing an army that held at bay that of the king. They admired the completeness of the organization which enabled the Prince of Condé and the admiral to summon the gentry of the most distant provinces, and bring them to the very vicinity of the court before the movement was suspected even by Constable Montmorency, who believed himself to be kept advised of the most trifling occurrences that took place in any part of France. The triumph of the Huguenots—for was it not a triumph which they had achieved in securing such terms as the Edict of Longjumeau conceded?—was a disgrace to the papists, who had not known how to use their overwhelming preponderance in numbers. Never had a more signal example been given of the superiority of united and zealous sympathy over discordant and soulless counsels.[2] While their

---

[1] Jean de Serres, iii. 164.

[2] "Den Erfolg des letzten Krieges," well observes Prof. Soldan, "hatten die Hugenotten nicht ihrer Anzahl, sondern der Organisation und dem Geiste ihres Gemeindewesens zu verdanken. Diese bewegliche, weitverzweigte, aus einem festen Mittelpunkte gleichmässig gelenkte und von Eifer für die gemeinsame Sache belebte Vereinsgliederung hatte über den lahmen und stockenden Mechanismus vielfach grösserer, aber in sich selbst uneiniger Kräfte einen beschämenden Triumph erlangt." Geschichte des Protestantismus in Frankreich, ii. 303.

enemies, with nothing in common but their hatred of Protestantism, were hampered by the want of concert between their leaders, or cheated of their success by their positive jealousies and quarrels, the Huguenots had in their common faith, in their well-ordered form of church government, combining the advantages of great local efficiency with those of a representative union, and in their common danger, the instruments best adapted to secure the ends they desired. "They were so closely bound together by this order and by these objects," wrote the Venetian ambassador Correro, "that there resulted a concordant will and so perfect a union that it made them prompt in rendering instant obedience and in forming common designs, and most ready to execute the commands of their superiors." [1]

With such associations as "the Confraternities of the Holy Ghost," and "the Christian and Royal League" springing up in various parts of France, under the express sanction of the provincial governors, and publishing as their chief aim the extirpation of heresy from the realm; with priests and monks, especially those of the new order of Jesus, inflaming the passions of the people by seditious preaching, and persuading their hearers that any toleration of heretics was a compact with Satan, it is not strange that murder held high carnival wherever the Protestants were not so numerous as to be able to stand on the defensive. The victims were of every rank and station, from the obscure peasant to the distinguished Cipierre, son of the Count de Tende and a relative of the Duke of Savoy, the orders for whose assassination were confidently believed to have issued from the court. [2] At Auxerre,

Murder runs riot throughout France.

---

[1] Relations des Amb. Vén., ii. 116.

[2] Cipierre, a young nobleman only twenty-two years of age, was returning, with a body-guard of about thirty-five men, from a visit to his cousin, the duke, at Nice, where he had been treated with great honor. When approaching Fréjus he perceived signs of treachery in a body of men lurking under cover of a grove, and betook himself for safety into the city, now, since his father's death, a part of the province of which his eldest brother was royal governor. The tocsin was rung, and his enemies, originally a band of three hundred men, being swollen by constant accessions to four times that number, the house in which Cipierre had taken refuge was assailed. After a heroic defence the small party of defenders surrendered their arms, on assurance that their opponents would at once retire. The papists, however,

which had been given up by the Huguenots in accordance with
the provisions of the peace, one hundred and fifty Protestants
paid with their lives the price of their good faith. Their bodies
were thrown into the public sewers. In the city of Amiens
one hundred and fifty persons were slaughtered at one time.
Instead of punishment, the rioters obtained their object: the
reformed worship was forbidden in Amiens, or within three
leagues of the city.[1] At Clermont the assassins, after plundering the wares of a wealthy merchant, who had refused to hang
tapestry before his house at the time of the procession on Corpus Christi Day—La Fête-Dieu—burned him in a fire made of
furniture taken from his own house.[2] At Ligny, in Champagne,
a Huguenot was pursued into the very bed-chamber of a royal
officer, and there killed. Troyes, Bourges, Rouen, and a host
of other places, witnessed the commission of atrocities which it
would be rather sickening than profitable to narrate.[3] In Paris
itself the murders of Huguenots were frequent. " On Sunday
last," wrote Norris, the English envoy, to his royal mistress,
" the Prince of Condé sent a gentleman to the king, to beseech
his Majesty to administer justice against such as murder them
of the religion, and as he entered into the city there were five
slain in St. Anthony's street, not far from my lodging."[4] The
aggregate of homicides committed within the brief compass of
this so-called peace was enormous. Jean de Serres and Agrippa
d'Aubigné may possibly go somewhat beyond the mark when

---

scarcely made a pretence of fulfilling their compact, for they speedily returned
and massacred every one whom they found in the house. Cipierre himself
was not among the number. To secure him a new breach of faith was necessary. The captain of the murderers pledged his own word to the magistrate
that if Cipierre would come forth from his hiding-place he would spare his
life. He discharged the obligation, so soon as Cipierre presented himself, by
plunging a dagger into his breast. J. de Serres, iii. 166–168 ; Agrippa d'Aubigné, i. 262.

[1] Petition of Condé, Aug. 23, 1568, J. de Serres, iii. 210, 211.

[2] Vie de Coligny (Cologne, 1686), 349, 350 ; J. de Serres, iii. 166.

[3] Ibid., iii. 165 ; Recordon, from MSS. of N. Pithou, 155–157 ; MS. Mém.
historiques des Antiquités de Troyes, by Duhalle, *apud* Bulletin de l'hist. du
prot. fr., xvii. (1868) 376. Of the royal edicts guaranteeing the Protestants,
the last author remarks that " ils firent plus de bruit que de fruit."

[4] Duc d'Aumale, Princes de Condé, ii. 364, Pièces justificatives.

they state the number of victims in three months—April, May, and June, 1568—at over ten thousand; [1] but they are substantially correct in saying that the number far exceeded that of the armed Huguenots slain during the six months of the preceding war; [2] for the Venetian ambassador, who certainly had no motive for exaggeration, asserts that "the principal cities of the kingdom, notwithstanding the conditions of the peace, refused to readmit 'the preachings' to their territories, and slew many thousands of Huguenots who dared to rise and complain." [3]

While the majority of the cities held by the Protestants had, as we have seen, promptly opened their gates to the king, a number, perceiving the dangers to which they were exposed, alarmed by the attitude of the Roman Catholics, and doubtful of the good faith of the court, declined to allow the garrisons to enter. This was the case with La Rochelle, which defended its course by appealing to its privileges, and with Montauban, Albi, Milhau, Sancerre, Castres, Vézelay, and other less important towns. [4] The events of a few

Rochelle and other cities refuse to receive garrisons.

---

[1] J. de Serres, iii. 168; Agrippa d'Aubigné, i. 262.

[2] Jean de Serres does not expressly state that he refers to the combatants, but I presume this to be his meaning.

[3] Relazione di Correro, Rel. des Amb. Vén., ii. 120.

[4] "Montauban, etc., faisoient conter les cloux de leurs portes aux garnisons qu'on leur envoyoit." Agrippa d'Aubigné, i. 261. It was the *garrisons* only that were refused ; the royal governors were promptly accepted. M. de Jarnac, for instance, had no difficulty in securing recognition at La Rochelle ; but he was not permitted to introduce troops to distress and terrify the citizens. See the letters of the "Maire, Echevins, Conseilliers et Pairs," of La Rochelle to Charles the Ninth, April 21st, June 6th and 30th, etc. Le Laboureur, Add. aux Mém. de Castelnau, ii. 547–551. They deny the slanderous accusation that the Roman Catholics have not been permitted to return since the peace, asserting, on the contrary, that they have greeted them as brethren and fellow-citizens. They appeal to M. de Jarnac himself for testimony to the good order of La Rochelle. "Meanwhile," they say, "we are preserving this city of yours in all tranquillity, and maintain it, under your obedience, with much greater security, devotion, affection, fidelity and loyalty, such as we have received from our predecessors, than would do all others who were strangers and mercenaries, and not its natural subjects and inhabitants." Norris to Queen Elizabeth, June 23, 1568: "The towne of Rochelle hathe now the thirde time bin admonished to render itself to the king." State Paper Office, Duc d'Aumale, ii. 367.

weeks had amply vindicated the wisdom and justice of their refusal. La Rochelle even began to repair its fortifications, confident that the papal faction would never rest until it had made
the attempt to destroy the great Huguenot stronghold in the
west. Evidently there was no safety for a Protestant under
the ægis of the Edict of Longjumeau. The Prince of Condé
dared not resume the government of the province
Condé and
Coligny re- nominally restored to his charge, and retired to Noyers,
tire.
a small town in Burgundy, belonging to his wife's
dower, where he would be less exposed than in the vicinity of
Paris to any treacherous attempt upon his person. Admiral
Coligny was not slow in following his example. He abandoned
his stately manor of Châtillon-sur-Loing, where, with a heart
saddened by recent domestic affliction,[1] he had been compelled
to exercise a princely hospitality to the crowds that daily
thronged to consult with him and to do him honor,[2] and took

---

[1] His wife, Charlotte de Laval, whose brave Christian injunctions, as we
have seen, decided the reluctant admiral to take up arms in the first religious
war (see ante, chapter xiii., p. 35), lay dying of a disease contracted in
her indefatigable labors for the sick and wounded soldiers at Orleans, whilst
the admiral was at the siege of Chartres. On the conclusion of the peace he
hastened to her, but was too late to find her alive. In a touching letter, written to her husband after all hope of seeing him again in this world had fled,
a letter the substance of which is preserved by one of his biographers (Vie
de Coligny, Cologne, 1686, p. 342), she lamented the loss of a privilege that
would have alleviated the sufferings of her last hours, but consoled herself with
the thought of the object for which he was absent. She conjured him, by the
love he bore her and to her children, to fight to the last extremity for God
and religion; warning him, lest through his habitual respect for the king—a
respect which had before made him reluctant to take up arms—he should
forget the obligations he owed to God as his first Master. She begged him to
rear the children she left him in the pure religion, that they might one day
be capable of taking his place; and, for their sakes, implored him not
to hazard his life unnecessarily. She bade him beware of the house of
Guise. "I do not know," she added, "whether I ought to say the same
thing of the queen mother, as we are forbidden to judge evil of our neighbor;
but she has given so many marks of her ambition that a little distrust is excusable." The earlier biographer of Coligny (Gasparis Colinii Vita, 1575, p.
63, etc.) gives an affecting picture of the deep sorrow and pious resignation
of the admiral.

[2] Somewhat hyperbolically, the biographer of the admiral (Vie de Coligny,
p. 346) says that the concourse at Châtillon and Noyers was so great that the

up his abode in the castle of Tanlay, belonging to his brother
D'Andelot, and within a few miles of the prince's retreat.[1]
D'Andelot himself had recently started for Brittany, where his
first wife, Claude de Rieux, had held extensive possessions.[2]
D'Andelot's Before leaving, however, he had written to Catha-
remonstrance. rine de' Medici, a letter of remonstrance full of noble
sentiments. The occasion was the murder of one of his gentlemen, whom he had sent to the neighboring city of Auxerre;
but his letter embraced a complete view of "the calamitous
state of the poor kingdom," whose misery "was such as to
cause the hair of all that heard to stand on end." "Not only,"
said D'Andelot, "can we feel no doubt that God will not leave
unpunished so much innocent blood, which continues to cry before Him for vengeance, as well as so many violations of women
and maidens; so many robberies; so much oppression—in one
word, every species of iniquity. But, besides this, we can look
for nothing else than the near-approaching desolation and ruin
of this state: for no one that has read sacred and profane history will be able to deny that such things have always preceded
the overthrow of empires and monarchies. I am well aware,

Louvre was a desert in comparison! When ten gentlemen left by one gate,
twenty entered by another. The churches raised a purse of 100,000 crowns,
one-half of which was to go to him, and the other half to the Prince of
Condé; but, though nearly ruined by the enormous expenses of his hospitality, he declined to receive his portion.

[1] Noyers and Tanlay are ten or twelve miles from each other, in the modern
department of the Yonne.

[2] Jean de Serres, *ubi supra*. Cf. De Thou, iv. 142; Bulletin de la Soc. de
l'hist. du prot. fr. (1854), iii. 239. This valuable periodical is mistaken in
stating, vii. (1858) 120, that "D'Andelot s'était retiré dans ses terres de
Bretagne à la conclusion de la paix." He did not leave Tanlay until after
writing the letter referred to below, and shortly before Coligny's arrival:
"partant de chez lui, pour se rendre chez son frère Andelot, il trouva qu'il
étoit allé en Bretagne." Vie de Coligny, 350. D'Andelot was in Brittany
at the outbreak of the third war. His adventures in escaping to La Rochelle
will be narrated in the next chapter. Mr. Henry White is, of course, equally
wrong when he says (Massacre of St. Bartholomew, New York, 1868, p. 291):
"The admiral had gone to this charming retreat [Tanlay], to consult with
his brother, to whom it belonged, *and who had joined him there*," and when
he mentions D'Andelot as in the suite of Condé and Coligny in their celebrated flight (p. 292); "besides which, he (the prince) was accompanied by
the admiral and his family, *by Andelot* and his wife," etc.

madam, that there will be those who, on seeing this letter, will ridicule me, and will say that I am playing the part of prophet or preacher. I am neither the one nor the other, since God has not given me this calling. But I will yet say, with truth, that there is not a man in the kingdom, of any rank or quality, who loves his king and his kingdom better than I do, or who is more grieved at seeing those disorders that I see, which can, in the end, result only in general confusion. I know full well that I shall be met with the taking up of arms, in which I participated, with so many others, on the eve of last St. Michael's Day, as if we had intended to attack the persons of your Majesties, or anything belonging to you, or this state, as was published wherever it was possible, and as is still daily asserted. But, not to undertake other justification, I will only say that, if such wickedness had entered into my heart, though I might conceal it from men, I could not hide it from God, from whom I never have asked forgiveness for it, nor ever shall I." D'Andelot proceeded to show that the movement in question had been caused by absolute necessity, and that this was rendered evident to all men by that which was now occurring in every part of France. He told her that it was sufficiently manifest that this universal oppression was only designed to provoke "those of the religion" to such a point that they would lose patience, and to obtain a pretext for attacking and exterminating them. He reminded her that he had often insisted "that opinions in matters of religion can be changed neither by fire nor by force of arms, and that those deem themselves very happy who can lay down their lives for the service of God and for His glory." He warned her of those who, unlike the Huguenots, would sacrifice the interests of the state to their own individual ends of ambition or revenge. In conclusion, after alluding to a recent sudden death which much resembled a mark of the divine displeasure upon the murderous assault that had called forth this letter, he exclaimed: " I do not mean to be so presumptuous as to judge the dealings of God; but I do mean to say, with the sure testimony of His word, that all those who violate public faith are punished for it." [1]

---

[1] Lettre de François d'Andelot à la Royne mère du Roy, de Tanlay, ce 8ᵐᵉ juillet, 1568. MS. Library of Berne. This letter has been twice printed

That salutary warning had been rung in Catharine's ears more than once, and was destined to be repeated again and again, with little effect : "All those who violate public faith are punished for it." L'Hospital had but a few months before been urging to a course of political integrity, and pointing out the rock on which all previous plans of pacification had split. There was but one way to secure the advantages of permanent peace, and that was an upright observance of the treaties formed with the Huguenots. But Catharine was slow to learn the lesson. Crooked paths, to her distorted vision, seemed to be the shortest way to success. Her Italian education had taught her that deceit was better, under all circumstances, than plain dealing, and she could not unlearn the long-cherished theory. Whether L'Hospital's views were originally the chief motives that influenced her in consenting to the peace of Longjumeau, or whether she had acquiesced in it as a cover to treacherous designs, certain it is that she now began to side openly with the chancellor's enemies, and that the Cardinal of Lorraine regained his old influence in the council. The fanatical sermons that had been a premonitory symptom of the previous wars were again heard with complacency in the court chapel ; for, about the month of June, the king appointed as his preachers four of the most blatant advocates of persecution : Vigor, a canon of Notre Dame ; De Sainte Foy ; the gray friar, Hugonis ; and Claude de Sainctes, whose acquaintance the reformers had made at the Colloquy of Poissy.[1]

Catharine takes side with the chancellor's enemies.

There had been a desperate struggle in the royal council ever since the conclusion of the peace. The extreme Roman Catholics, recognizing the instability of Catharine, had long since

in the Bulletin de la Soc. de l'hist. du prot. français, iv. (1856) 329–331, and vii. (1858) 121–123. The first reproduction is in one important part more correct than the second. It is not impossible, after all, that the author of the letter was not D'Andelot, but his brother, Admiral Coligny himself ; for M. J. Tessier mentions (Bulletin, xxii. (1873) 47, that it exists in manuscript in the Paris National Library (MSS. Vc. Colbert, 24, f. 161), in the admiral's own handwriting, and signed with his usual signature, *Chastillon.* The whole tone, I must confess, seems rather to be his.

[1] Journal d'un curé ligueur (Jehan de la Fosse), 96.

begun to base their hopes upon Henry of Anjou's influence. Their opponents accepted the issue, and resolved to circumscribe the duke's inordinate powers. Three of the marshals of

Remonstrance of the three marshals.
France—Montmorency, his brother Damville, and Vieilleville—presented themselves at a meeting of the royal council held in the queen mother's sick-chamber (on the second of May, 1568), to remonstrate against Anjou's retaining the office of lieutenant-general. Even Cardinal Bourbon supported their movement, and, sinking for the time his extreme religious partisanship, threatened to leave the court, and give the world to understand how much he had at heart the honor of his house and the welfare of his friends. The object of the marshals could not be mistaken : it was nothing less than the overthrow of the Cardinal of Lorraine, who sought supreme power under cover of Anjou's name. The end of the war, remarked the ambassador, Sir Henry Norris, had brought no end to the mortal hatred between the houses of Guise and Montmorency. The prospect of permanent peace was dark. The king was easy to be seduced, his mother bent upon maintaining these divisions in the court, and Anjou so much under the cardinal's influence that it was to be feared that the Hugue-

Catharine's intrigues.
nots would in the end be forced to have recourse once more to arms. In the midst of these perils, the queen mother had been exercising her ingenuity in playing off one party against the other; now giving countenance to the Guises, now to the Montmorencies. At one time she used Limoges, at another Morvilliers or Sens, in her secret intrigues. Presently she resorted to Lorraine, and, when jealous of his too great forwardness, would turn to the chancellor himself, " undoing in one day what the cardinal had intended long afore." Besides these prominent statesmen, she had not scrupled to take up with meaner tools—men whose elevation boded no good to the commonwealth, and with whom she conferred about the imposition of those onerous taxes which had cost her the forfeiture of the good-will of the people. To add to the confusion, the jealousy between the king and his brother Anjou had reappeared, and the chancellor had lost his characteristic courage and avowed his utter despair of being able to stem

the fierce tide of human selfishness and passion. Cardinal Lorraine was realizing his long-cherished hope: "for this one man's authority had been the greatest countermand of his devices." [1]

The Huguenot leaders had entered into engagements to repay to the king the nine hundred thousand francs advanced by him to the German reiters of Count Casimir. This sum—a large one for the times—Charles now called upon Condé and Coligny to refund, and he expressly commanded that it should not be levied upon the Protestant churches, but be raised by those who had taken up arms in the late contest.[2] It was a transparent attempt to array the masses that had suffered little pecuniarily in the war against the brave men who had not only impoverished themselves, but hazarded their lives in defence of the common cause. Nothing less than the financial ruin of the prince and the admiral, who had voluntarily become sureties, seemed likely to satisfy their enemies.

The court tries to ruin Condé and Coligny.

The Prince of Condé despatched young Téligny to carry his spirited reply to this extraordinary demand, and, not confining himself to the exhibition of its flagrant injustice, he recapitulated the daily multiplying infractions upon the edict. The Protestants were treated as enemies, he said, and were safe neither at home nor abroad. An open war could not be more bitter.[3] Besides countless general massacres, he complained of the recent assassination of two of his own dependants, and of the surveillance exercised over all the great noblemen "of the religion," who were closely watched in their castles by the commanders of neighboring forces. Against

Téligny sent to carry a reply.

---

[1] Norris to Queen Elizabeth, May 12, 1568, State Paper Office.

[2] Jean de Serres, iii. 170; Davila, bk. iv. 128; Condé to the king, Noyers, June 11, 1568, MS. Paris Lib., *apud* D'Aumale, ii. 351-353.

[3] As the prince had described the state of affairs in a letter to the king, of July 22, 1568: "Nous nous voions tuez, pillez, saccagez, les femmes forcées, les filles ravies des mains de leurs pères et mères, les grands mis hors de leurs charges," etc. All this injustice had been committed with complete impunity. In fact, to use his own forcible words, were the king to attempt to punish the outrages done to the Protestants, "the trees in France would have more men than leaves upon them"—"tous les arbres seroient plus couvertz d'hommes que de feuilles." MS. Paris Lib., *apud* D'Aumale, ii. 355, 356.

himself the unparalleled insult had been shown of placing a garrison in the palace of a prince of the blood. Nay, he had arrested a spy caught in the very act of measuring the height of the fortifications of Noyers, and sounding the depth of the moat, with a view to a subsequent assault, and the capture not only of the prince, but of the admiral, who frequently came there to see him. He rehearsed the grounds of just alarm which the Protestants had in the threats their indiscreet enemies were daily uttering, and in " the confraternities of the Holy Ghost," defiantly instituted with the approval of the king's own governors. What safety was there for the Huguenots when a counsellor of a celebrated parliament had lately asserted, in the presence of an assembly of three thousand persons, " that he had commands from the leading men of the royal council admonishing the Catholics that they ought to give no credence to any edicts of the king unless they contained a peculiar mark of authenticity." And he was induced to believe him right, by noticing the fact that, since the establishment of peace, no one had obeyed the royal letters. Finally, in decided but respectful language, he remonstrated against the pernicious precedent which the court was allowing to become established, when the express commands of the monarch were set at naught with impunity.[1]

As the time approached for the blow to be struck that should forever put an end to the exercise of the reformed faith in France, the conspirators began to betray their anxiety lest their nefarious designs might be anticipated and rendered futile by such a measure of defence as that which the Huguenots had taken on the eve of Michaelmas. They resolved, therefore, if possible, to bind their victims hand and foot ; and no more convenient method presented itself than that of involving them in obligations of implicit obedience which would embarrass, if they did not absolutely preclude, any exercise of their wonderful system of combined action. About the beginning of August, Charles despatched to all parts of his dominions the form of an oath which was to be demanded of every Protestant subject, and the royal officers and magistrates

An oath to be exacted of the Huguenots.

---

[1] J. de Serres, iii. 171–173 ; Davila, bk. iv. 128.

were directed to make lists of those who signed as well as of those who refused to sign it.[1] " We protest before God, and swear by His name "—so ran the oath—" that we recognize King Charles the Ninth as our natural sovereign and only prince . . . . and that we will never take up arms save by his express command, of which he may have notified us by his letters patent duly verified; and that we will never consent to, nor assist with counsel, money, food, or anything else whatsoever, those who shall arm themselves against him or his will. We will make no levy or assessment of money for any purpose without his express commission ; and will never enter into any secret leagues, intrigues, or plots, nor engage in any underhand practices or enterprises, but, on the contrary, we promise and swear to notify him or his officers of all that we shall be able to learn and discover that is devised against his Majesty . . . . Moreover, we protest that we will not leave the city, whatever necessity may arrive, but will join our hearts, our wills, and our abilities with our fellow-citizens in defence of that city, to which we will always entertain the devotion of true and faithful citizens, whilst the Catholics will find in us sincere and fraternal affection : awaiting the time when it may please God to put an end to all troubles, to which we hope that this reconciliation will be a happy prelude." [2]

The trap was not ill contrived, and its bars were strong enough to hold anything that might venture within.   Fortunately, however, the bait did not conceal the cruel design lurking behind it. Why, it might be asked, this new test ? Was Condé, whom the king had only four or five months ago recognized by solemn edict as his " dear cousin and faithful servant and subject," a friend or a foe?   Had peace been concluded with the Hugue-

---

[1] The Bulletin de la Soc.. de l'hist. du prot. français, ix. (1860) 217-219, published from MSS. in the Library of the British Museum, the letter of Charles the Ninth to the first president of the Parisian parliament, dated '' du château de Bolongne, ce premier jour d'aoust,'' enclosing the formula. The pretext is '' afin d'oster tout ce doubte et différend qui règne aujourd'huy parmi nos subjectz.'' The president is to associate with himself the seigneur de Nantouillet, provost of the city, and the seigneur de Villeroy, '' prévôt des marchands.''

[2] Bulletin, etc., ix. (1860) 218, 219 ; Jean de Serres, iii. 175, etc.

nots only that they might anew be treated as rebels and enemies? What had become of the prescribed amnesty? Was it at all likely that private citizens would bury in oblivion their former dissensions and abstain from mutual insults, when the monarch officially reminded them that there was one class of his subjects whose past conduct made them objects of grave suspicion? While, therefore, the Huguenots professed themselves ready to give the king all possible assurances of their loyal devotion, they declined to swear to a form that bore on its face the proof that it was composed, not in accordance with Charles's own ideas, but by an enemy of the crown and of public tranquillity. They requested that it might receive such modifications as would permit them to sign it with due regard to their own self-respect and to their religious convictions, and they entreated Charles to confirm their liberty of conscience and of religious observance; for, without these privileges, which they valued above their own existence, they were ready to forsake, not only their cities, but their very lives also.[1]

At this critical moment the destiny of France was wavering in the balance, and the decision depended upon the answer to be given to the question whether Chancellor L'Hospital or Cardinal Lorraine should retain his place in the council. The tolerant policy of the former is too well understood to need an explanation. The designs of the latter are revealed by an intercepted letter that fell into the hands of the Huguenots about this time. It was written (on the ninth of August) at the little country-seat named Madrid,[2] whose ruins are still pointed out, near the banks of the Seine, on the edge of the Bois de Boulogne, and not far from the walls of the city of Paris. The writer, evidently a devoted partisan of the house of Guise, had been entrusted by the Cardinal of Lorraine[3] with a glimpse at the designs of the party of which the latter

The plot disclosed by an intercepted letter.

---

[1] Jean de Serres (Comm. de statu rel. et reipublicæ, iii. 174–183) inserts the reply of the Protestants to the proposed oath, article by article.

[2] Built by Francis I., and so named because constructed on the plan of the palace in which he lived when a captive in Spain.

[3] It is true the writer carefully avoids mentioning the cardinal's name, but there is no difficulty in discovering that he is intended.

was the declared chief. A proclamation was soon to be made in the king's name, through Marshal Cossé, to the Protestant nobles, assuring them of the monarch's intention to deal kindly and peaceably with them, to preserve their religious liberties, and to treat them as his faithful subjects; and explaining the design of the movement which he was now setting on foot to be merely the reduction of the inhabitants of some insolent cities (those that, like La Rochelle, had refused to admit garrisons) to his authority. This announcement, the cardinal proceeded to say, might disturb some good Catholics, who would think that their labors and the dangers they had undergone were all in vain. In reality, however, it was only intended to secure the power in the hands of the king, and to take away from the Protestant leaders all occasion for assembling, until, being reduced to straits, that rabble, so hostile to the king and the kingdom, should be wholly destroyed. Thus the very remnants would be annihilated; for the seed would assuredly spring up again, unless the same course should be pursued as that of which the French had resplendent examples shown them by their neighbors.[1] Meanwhile, until these plans could be carried into effect, as they would doubtless be within the present month, the Protestant nobles must be carefully diverted, as some were already showing signs of security, and others of falling into the snare prepared for them. The cardinal, so he informed the writer, was confident, with God's favor, of an easy and most certain victory over the enemies of the faith.[2]

Such were the cardinal's intentions as expressed by himself and reported almost word for word[3] in a letter to which I shall

---

[1] "Uti nimirum detur opera ut vires penes Regem sint, primoresque religionis illius occupentur, omnes conveniendi rationes illis demantur: ut ad illas angustias redacti, quemadmodum facillimum erit, possit hujusmodi colluvies regi regnoque adversaria, plane pessundari, omnesque adeo reliquiæ profligari: quoniam semen profecto esset in dies egerminaturum, nisi ea ratio observaretur, cujus a vicinis nostris adeo luculenta exempla demonstrentur." Jean de Serres, iii. 187.

[2] The letter is given entire, with the exception of some matters of no general interest, in the valuable chronicle of this period, by Jean de Serres (s. l. 1571), iii. 185–190.

[3] "Hæc sunt propemodum ipsa illius verba, quæ conatus sum memoriæ

presently have occasion again to direct the reader's attention. It was the policy advocated persistently both by Pius the Fifth and by Philip the Second, and embodied in counsel which would have been resented by a court possessed of more self-respect than the French court, as impertinent advice. For, in the report made to Catharine by one of her servants at the Spanish capital, there is a wonderful similarity in the language employed to that used at the conference of Bayonne. Isabella of France is again *Isabella of France again her husband's mouth-piece.* the speaker, though much suspected of uttering rather the sentiments of Philip, her husband, who was present,[1] than her own. Again, after expressing the most vehement zeal for the welfare of her native country, she advocated rigorous measures against the Huguenots, in phrases almost identical with those which, as the Duke of Alva relates, she had addressed to her mother three years before. " She told me among other things," says the queen's agent, " that she would never believe that either the king her brother, or you, will ever execute the design already entered into between you (although, by your command, I had notified the king [Philip] and herself of your good-will respecting this matter), until she saw it performed; for you had often before made them the same promises, but no result had ever followed. She feared that your Majesties might be dissuaded from action by the smooth speeches of certain persons in your court, until the enemy gained the opportunity of forming new designs, not only against the king's authority, but even against yourselves. The apprehension kept her in a constant state of alarm." [2]

But, although Catharine had now given in her adhesion to the Spanish and Lorraine party, the success of that party was as yet incomplete. L'Hospital was still in the privy council, and Charles himself greatly preferred the conciliation and peace ad-

---

mandare, ut possem ad te de rerum omnium statu certius perscribere." Ib., iii. 188.

[1] " Et quoniam tunc vehementius quam assuevisset, rem illam mihi commemoravit, et fortasse regis domini sui, qui ibi tunc erat, mandatu, volui hac de causa te istarum rerum facere certiorem."

[2] This letter, which was also intercepted by the Huguenots, is preserved by Jean de Serres, iii. 184, 185. It bears unmistakable marks of authenticity.

vocated by the chancellor. The same letter from the pleasure-palace of " Madrid," on the banks of the Seine, whose contents have already occupied our attention, makes important disclosures respecting the attitude of the unhappy prince, of whom it may be questioned whether his greatest misfortune was that he had so unprincipled a mother, or that he had not sufficient strength of will to resist her pernicious designs. " I observed," wrote this correspondent still further in reference to the Cardinal of Lorraine, " that he was very much excited on account of a conversation which the king had recently had with the queen, and which he believed to have been suggested to him by others.

King Charles entreats his mother to avoid war. For the king entreated his mother, almost as a suppliant, 'to take the greatest care lest war should again break out, and that the edict should everywhere be observed : otherwise he foresaw the complete ruin of his kingdom.'[1] And when the queen alleged the rebellion of the inhabitants of La Rochelle, he replied, as he had been instructed beforehand, 'that the Rochellois only desired to retain their ancient privileges. Their demand was not unreasonable ; and even if it were, it was better to make a temporary sacrifice to the welfare of the realm than to plunge in new turmoil. As to the nobles, he was persuaded that they would live peaceably if the edict were properly executed. In short, he was earnestly desirous that matters should be restored to their best and most quiet state.' The queen and very many other illustrious persons have but one object of fervent desire, and that is to see the kingdom of France return to the condition it was in under Francis and Henry. The queen mother knows that this speech was dictated to him by certain men, and she owes the authors of it no good-will. So much the more anxiously does she desire, in common with a vast multitude of good Catholics, to prove to

---

[1] Condé himself alludes to these words of Charles the Ninth to his mother, in his letter of August 23d. Referring to the king's aversion to a resort to violence, he says : "Quod mihi repetitis literis sæpissime demonstrasti, et nuper quidem Reginæ matri, ex eo sermone quem cum illa habebas, quo significabas quantum odiosa tibi esset turbarum renovatio : cum nimirum illam orabas, daret operam ut omnia pacificarentur, efficeretque ne rursus ad bella civilia rediretur, quæ non possent non extremum exitium afferre." Jean de Serres, iii. 193.

the king that whatever is done in this affair has for its sole object to liberate him from servitude and make him a king in reality, and to expel the pestilence and those infected by it— a result utterly unattainable in any other way." [1]

Catharine could not doubt that it was Michel de l'Hospital that had infused into Charles his own just and pacific spirit.

Catharine's animosity against L'Hospital. From the moment she had come to this conclusion the chancellor's fall was inevitable. The particular occasion of it, however, seems to have been the opposition which he offered to the reception of a papal bull. To relieve the royal treasury, the court had applied to Rome for permission to alienate ecclesiastical possessions in France yielding an income of fifty thousand crowns (or one hundred and fifty thousand francs), on the plea that the indebtedness had been incurred in defence of the Roman Catholic faith. Pius the Fifth granted the application, but in his bull of the first of August, 1568, he not only made it a condition that the funds should be exclusively employed under the direction of a trustworthy person—and as such he named the Cardinal of Lorraine —in the extermination of the heretics of France, or their reconciliation with the Church of Rome, but he ascribed to Charles in making the request the declared purpose of continuing a work for which his own means had proved inadequate. The reception of the document was in itself an act of bad faith, and the chancellor resisted it to the utmost of his power, urging that the pontiff should be requested to alter its objectionable form. [2]

Another of those painful scenes occurred in the privy council (on the nineteenth of September), of which there had

Another quarrel between Lorraine and the chancellor. been so many within the past four or five years. Again the disputants were the Cardinal of Lorraine and the chancellor. The former angrily demanded the reason why L'Hospital had refused to affix his signature to the bull; whereupon the latter alleged, among many other

---

[1] Letter *apud* J. de Serres, iii. 188–190.

[2] De Thou, iii. 136 ; Castelnau, liv. vii., c. 1, where the sum is erroneously trebled ; Davila, bk. iv., p. 130. See also Soldan, ii., 324, and Von Polenz, ii. 365.

grounds, that to revoke the Edict of Pacification, as demanded by the Pope, "was the direct way to cause open wars, and to bring the Germans into the realm." The cardinal was "much stirred." He called L'Hospital a hypocrite; he said that his wife and daughter were Calvinists. "You are not the first of your race that has deserved ill of the king," he added. "I am sprung from as honest a race as you are," retorted the other. Beside himself with fury, Lorraine "gave him the lie, and, rising incontinently out of his chair," would have seized him by the beard, had not Marshal Montmorency stepped in between them. "Madam," said the cardinal, "in great choler," turning to the queen mother, in whose presence the angry discussion took place, "the chancellor is the sole cause of all the troubles in France, and were he in the hands of parliament his head would not tarry on his shoulders twenty-four hours." "On the contrary, Madam," rejoined L'Hospital, "the cardinal is the original cause of all the mischiefs that have chanced as well to France, within these eight years, as to the rest of Christendom. In proof of which I refer him to the common report of even those who most favor him." [1]

But the chancellor accomplished nothing. Catharine had overcome her weak son's partiality for the grave old counsellor by persuading him that, as the chancellor's wife, his daughter, his son-in-law, and indeed his entire house, were avowedly Huguenots, it was impossible but that he was himself only restrained from making an open profession of Protestantism by the fear of losing his present position. [2] Finding himself not only stripped of all influence, and compelled to witness the enactment of measures repugnant to his very nature, but an object of hatred to his associates, Michel de l'Hospital withdrew from a council board where, as he asserted, even Charles himself did not dare to express his opinions freely. [3] Subsequently retiring altogether from the court to his country-seat of Vignai, not far from Étampes, he surrendered his insig-

The chancellor's fall.

---

[1] Norris, in a letter to Cecil, Sept. 25, 1568, gives almost the very words of the angry contestants. State Paper Office.

[2] Davila, bk. iv. 130 ; De Thou, iv. (liv. xliv.) 136.

[3] Ranke, Civil Wars and Monarchy in France, 236, 237.

nia of office to a messenger of Catharine, who came to recommend him, in the king's name, to take that rest which his
advanced years demanded. Monsieur de Morvilliers succeeded
him, with the title of keeper of the seals, but the full powers
of chancellor.[1] In quiet retirement, the venerable judge and
legislator lingered more than four years, unhappy only in being
spared to see the melancholy results of the rejection of his prudent counsels, the desolation of his native land, and the transfor-
mation of an amiable king into a murderer of his own subjects.
Few days in this eventful reign were more lasting in their consequences than that which beheld the final removal from all
direct influence upon the court of the only leading politician or
statesman who could have forestalled the horrors of a generation
of inhuman wars.

The crisis now rapidly approached. The Huguenot chiefs
were widely separated from each other—Montgomery in Normandy, Genlis and Mouy in Picardy, Rochefoucauld
at Angoulême, D'Andelot in Brittany, Condé and
Coligny in Burgundy. The royal court, now entirely in the
interest of the Guises, resolved to execute the plan which the
Roman Catholic nobles of this faction had sketched to Alva
three years before at Bayonne, by the seizure of five or six of
the leaders, as a measure preliminary to the total suppression

The plot.

---

[1] Davila and De Thou, *ubi supra*. De Thou seems certainly to be wanting
in his accustomed accuracy when he represents—iv. (liv. xliv.) 136, 137—the
submission of the test-oath to the Protestants as posterior to, and consequent
upon the fall of L'Hospital : "La reine délivrée du Chancelier, et n'ayant
plus personne qui s'opposât à ses volontés, ne songea plus qu'à brouiller les
affaires, etc." I have shown that the papal bull which L'Hospital opposed
was dated at Rome on the same day (August 1, 1568) on which Charles sent
his orders to the president of the Parisian parliament to administer the oath
to the Protestants of the capital. Yet, as early as on the 12th of May, 1568,
the English ambassador, Norris, wrote to Cecil that Anjou, a cruel enemy
of the Protestants, had a privy council of which Cardinal Lorraine was the
"chiefest" member, and his own chancellor, who sealed everything submitted
to him, "which thing he [the good olde chauncelor of the Kinges] hathe so to
harte as he is retirid him to his owne house in the towne of Paris ; and wheras
the King's chauncelor I meane, who nether for love nor dread wolde seal eny-
thing against the statutes of the realme, or that might be prejudiciall to the
same, this of Mr. d'Anjou's refusithe nothing that is proferid to him." State
Paper Office, Duc d'Aumale, ii. 360.

of Protestantism in France.   Gaspard de Tavannes was entrusted with the execution of the most important part of the
scheme—the arrest of the prince and the admiral.   Fourteen
companies of gens-d'armes and as many ensigns of infantry
stood under his orders, and Noyers was closely beset on all
sides.[1]   It was at this moment, when secrecy was all important
to the success of the plot, that the tidings of the threatening
storm reached its destined victims.   It has long been believed
and reported that Tavannes, unwilling to lend himself to unworthy machinations whose execution would
have wounded his soldierly pride, took measures to
warn Condé and Coligny of their danger.   Unfortunately, the
story rests on no better authority than his "Mémoires," written by a son who has often shown a greater desire to vindicate
his father's memory than to maintain historical truth, and who,
writing under the rule of the Bourbons, had in this case, as in
that of the pretended deliverance of Henry of Navarre and
Henry of Condé, at the great Parisian massacre four years
later, sufficient inducements for endeavoring to represent the
reigning family as indebted to his father for its preservation.[2]
Brantôme is consistent with the entire mass of contemporary
documents in representing Tavannes as the author of the whole
scheme ; and certainly one who was so deeply implicated in the
massacre of St. Bartholomew's Day cannot have been too humane to think of capturing, or even assassinating, two nobles,
although one of them was a prince of the blood.   A more
probable story is that Tavannes was the unintentional instrument of the disclosure, a letter of his having fallen into
Huguenot hands, containing the words: "The deer is in the

*Marshal Ta-
vannes its
author.*

---

[1] Jean de Serres, iii. 191 ; Davila, bk. iv., p. 128.

[2] See Soldan, Gesch. des Prot. in Frankreich, ii. 327, note 63.   Yet Condé
himself, shortly before the flight from Noyers, expressed himself in striking-
ly confident terms as to Tavannes's probity.   In a letter to the king, complaining of the treacherous plots formed against himself, July 22, 1568, the
prince says he is sure that Tavannes is not privy to these designs, "car je le
cognois de trop longue main ennemy de ceulx qui ne veullent qu'entretenir
les troubles.   Parquoy je croy que cecy se faict à son desceu."   MS. Paris
Lib., *apud* D'Aumale, ii. 356.

net; the game is ready."[1] But, in point of fact, the Huguenots needed no such hints. With their perfect organization, in the face of so treacherous a foe, after so many violations as they had of late witnessed of the royal edict, they were already on their guard, and the hostile preparations had not escaped their notice.

When the news first reached him that the troops sent ostensibly to besiege La Rochelle were recalled, Condé, alarmed by what he heard from every quarter, had begged his mother-in-law, the Marchioness de Rothelin, to go to the court and entreat the king, in his name, to maintain the sanctity of his engagements, confirmed by repeated oaths. Scarcely had she departed, however, before he received fresh and reiterated warnings that his safety depended upon instant escape. He determined, nevertheless, to make a last attempt to avert the horrid prospect of a war which, from the malignant hatred exhibited by all classes of Roman Catholics, he rightly judged would exceed the previous contests both in duration and in destructiveness. He addressed to his young sovereign a letter explaining the necessity of the step he was about to take, accompanied by a long appeal, of which it would be impracticable to give even a brief summary. Every point in the multitudinous grievances of which the Huguenots complained was recapitulated. Every counter-charge with which the court had endeavored to parry the force of previous remonstrances was satisfactorily answered. In eloquent terms the prince indicted Charles, Cardinal of Lorraine, as the enemy alike of the royal dignity and of the liberties of the people, as the author of all the troubles of France, and the advocate and defender of robbers and murderers.[2] He reminded the king of

Condé's last appeal to the king.

---

[1] "Le cerf est aux toiles, la chasse est préparée." See Anquetil, Esprit de la ligue, i. 278.

[2] "Turbarum causas imputamus adversario illi tuo ac tuæ dignitatis hosti Cardinali Lotharingo et sociis, quorum nimirum pravis consiliis et arcta necessitudine et familiaritate quam cum Hispano habent, dissensiones et simultates inter tuos subjectos ab hinc sex annis continuantur, et misere foventur atque aluntur per cædes atque strages, quæ ipsorum nutu quotidie ubique perpetrantur." Jean de Serres, iii. 194. "Impurusne Presbyter, tigris, tyrannus," etc., ibid., iii. 196. "Cardinalis Lotharingus, quasi sicariorum ac prædorum patronus," etc., ibid., iii., 210.

the declaration of Maximilian, the present Emperor of Germany, in a letter written before his election to Charles himself: "All the wars and all the dissensions that are to-day rife among the Christians have originated from two cardinals— Granvelle and Lorraine."[1] And he closed the long and eloquent document by protesting, in the sight of God and of all foreign nations, that the Huguenot nobles sought the punishment of Lorraine and his associates alone, as the guilty causes of all the calamities that portended destruction to the French crown, and would pursue them as perjured violators of the public faith and capital enemies of peace and tranquillity. He therefore hoped that no one would be astonished if he and his allies should henceforth refuse to receive as the king's commands anything that might be decided upon by the royal council, so long as the cardinal might be present at its sessions, but should regard them as fabrications of the cardinal and his fellows. The causes of the misfortunes that might arise must be attributed, not to himself and his Huguenot allies, but to the cardinal and his Roman Catholic confederates.[2]

Having despatched " this testimony of the innocence, integrity, and faith " of himself and of his associates, " to be transmitted to posterity in everlasting remembrance," the Prince of Condé set out on the same day (the twenty-third of August) from Noyers. Coligny had joined him, bringing from Tanlay his daughter, the future bride of Téligny—and, after that nobleman's assassination on St. Bartholomew's Day, of William of Orange, the hero of the revolt of the Netherlands—and his young sons, as well as the wife and

The flight of the prince and the admiral

---

[1] " Quodnam item de illo judicium tulerit Cæsar Maximilianus hodie imperans, cum ad te prescripsit, omnia bella et omnes dissensiones, quæ inter Christianos hodie vagantur, proficisci a Granvellano et Lotharingo Cardinalibus." Jean de Serres, iii. 234.

[2] This petition or protestation of Condé is among the longest public papers of the period, occupying not less than forty-three pages of the invaluable Commentarii de statu religionis et reipublicæ of Jean de Serres. It well repays an attentive perusal, for it contains, in my judgment, the most important and authentic record of the sufferings of the Huguenots during the peace. The reader will notice that I have made great use of its authority in the preceding narrative.

infant son of his brother D'Andelot. Condé was himself accompanied by his wife, who was expecting soon to be confined, and by several children. His own servants and those of the admiral, with a few noblemen that came in from the neighborhood, swelled their escort to about one hundred and fifty horse.[1] With such a handful of men, and embarrassed in their flight by the presence of those whom their age or their sex disqualified for the endurance of the fatigues of a protracted journey, Condé and Coligny undertook to reach the friendly shelter of the walls of La Rochelle. It was a perilous attempt. The journey was one of several hundred miles, through the very heart of France. The cities were garrisoned by their enemies. The bridges and fords were guarded. The difficulties, in fact, were apparently so insurmountable, that the Roman Catholics seem to have expected that any attempt to escape would be made in the direction of Germany, where Casimir, their late ally, would doubtless welcome the Protestant leaders. This mistake was the only circumstance in their favor, for it diminished the number and the vigilance of the opposing troops.

Proves wonderfully successful.

The march was secret and prompt. Contrary to all expectation, an unguarded ford was discovered not far from the city of Sancerre,[2] by which, on a sandy bottom, the fugitive Huguenots crossed the Loire, elsewhere deep and navigable as far as Roanne.[3] If the drought which had so reduced the stream as to render the passage practicable was justly regarded as a providential interposition of Heaven in their behalf, the sudden

---

[1] Jean de Serres, iii. 241.

[2] The place is sufficiently designated by Ag. d'Aubigné (Hist. univ., i. 263) "à Bonni près Sancerre;" by Jean de Serres (iii. 242) "ad Sangodoneum vicum (Saint Godon) qui tribus ferme milliaribus distat ab ea fluminis parte, qua transiit Condæus;" by Hotman, Gasparis Colinii Vita, 1575 (p. 68), "ad flumen accessit, quo Sancerrani collis radices alluuntur," and by the "Vie de Coligny" (p. 351), "vis à vis de Sancerre." It will surprise no one accustomed to the uncertainties and perplexities of historical investigation, that while one author, quoted by Henry White (Mass. of St. Bartholomew, 292), puts the crossing "near les Rosiers, four leagues below Saumur," Davila (p. 129) places it at Roanne. The two spots are, probably, not less than 230 miles apart in a straight line.

[3] See De Thou, etc.

rise of the river immediately afterward, which baffled their pursuers, was not less signal a blessing.[1]   Other dangers still confronted them, but their prudence and expedition enabled them to escape them, and on the eighteenth of September[2] the weary travellers, with numbers considerably increased by reinforcements by the way, entered the gates of La Rochelle amid the acclamations of the brave inhabitants.

The escape of the prince and the admiral rendered useless all further attempt at the concealment of the treacherous designs of the papal party; and the third religious war dates from this moment.

The third civil war opens.

The city of La Rochelle, said to have become a walled place about 1126, had received many tokens of favor at the hands of its successive masters before the accession of Queen Alienor, or Éléonore, last Duchess of Aquitaine.   It was by a charter of this princess, in 1199, that the municipality, or " commune," was established.   (Arcère, Hist. de la Rochelle, ii., Preuves, 660, 661.)   The terms of the charter are vague ; but, as subsequently constituted, the " commune " consisted of one hundred prominent citizens, designated as " pairs," or peers, in whom all power was vested.   The first member in dignity was the " maire " or mayor, selected by the Seneschal of Saintonge from the list of three candidates yearly nominated by his fellow-members.   The historian of the city compares him, for power and for the sanctity attaching to his person, to the ancient tribunes of Rome.   Next were the twenty-four " échevins," or aldermen, one-half of whom on alternate years assisted the mayor in the administration of justice. Last of all came seventy-five " pairs " having no separate designation, who took part in the election of the mayor, and voted, on important occasions, in the " assemblée générale."   (See a historical discussion, Arcère, i. 193–199.)

The city of La Rochelle and its privileges.

From King John Lackland, of England, the Rochellois are said to have received express exemption from the duty of marching elsewhere in the king's service, without their own consent, and from admitting into their city any troops from abroad.   (P. S. Callot, La Rochelle protestante, 1863, p. 6.) When, in 1224, after standing a siege of three weeks, La Rochelle fell into the hands of Louis VIII. of France, its new master engaged to maintain all its privileges—a promise which was well observed, for not only did the city lose

---

[1] Recueil des choses mém. (Hist. des Cinq Rois), 336.   The Life of Coligny (1575), p. 68, states that the rise took place within *three* hours after the Huguenots crossed.

[2] Jean de Serres, iii. 192, and De Thou, iv. (liv. xliv.) 140.   The dates of Condé's departure from Tanlay and arrival at La Rochelle are, as usual, given differently by other authorities.

nothing, but it actually received new favors at the king's hands. (Arcère, i. 212; Callot, 6.) In 1360, the disasters of the French, consequent upon the battle of Poitiers, compelled the monarch to surrender the city of La Rochelle to his captors in order to regain his liberty. The concession was reluctantly made, with the most flattering testimony to the past fidelity of the inhabitants (see letters of John II. of France, to the Rochellois, Calais, Oct., 1360, Arcère, ii., Preuves, 761), and it was with still greater reluctance that the latter consented to carry it into effect. "They made frequent excuses," says Froissard, "and would not, for upwards of a year, suffer any Englishman to enter their town. The letters were very affecting which they wrote to the King of France, beseeching him, by the love of God, that he would never liberate them of their fidelity, nor separate them from his government and place them in the hands of strangers; for they would prefer being taxed every year one-half of what they were worth, rather than be in the hands of the English." (Froissard, i. c. 214, Johnes's Trans.) When compelled to yield, it was with the words : " We will honor and obey the English, but our hearts shall never change." Edward the Third had solemnly confirmed their privileges (Callot, 8).

But La Rochelle's unwilling subjection to the English crown was of brief duration. By a plot, somewhat clumsily contrived, but happily executed (Aug., 1372), the commander of the garrison, who did not know how to read, was induced to lead his troops outside of the castle wall for a review. The royal order that had been shown him was no forgery, but had been sent on a previous occasion, and the attesting seal was genuine. At a preconcerted signal, two hundred Rochellois rose from ambush, and cut off the return of the English. The latter, finding their antagonists reinforced by two thousand armed citizens under the lead of the mayor himself, soon came to terms, and, withdrawing the few men they had left behind in the castle, accepted the offer of safe transportation by a ship to Bordeaux. (See the entertaining account in Froissard, i. c. 311.) The wary Rochellois took good care, before even admitting into their city Duguesclin, Constable of France, with a paltry escort of two hundred men-at-arms, to stipulate that pardon should be extended to those who immediately after the departure of the English had razed the hateful castle to the ground, and that no other should ever be erected; that La Rochelle and the country dependent upon it should henceforth form a particular domain under the immediate jurisdiction of the king and his parliament of Paris; that its militia should be employed only for the defence of the place ; and that La Rochelle should retain its mint and the right to coin both "black and white money." (Froissard, *ubi supra,* corrected by Arcère, i. 260.) Not only did the grateful monarch readily make these concessions, and confirm all La Rochelle's past privileges, but, for its "immense services," by a subsequent order he conferred nobility upon the "mayor," "échevins" and "conseillers" of the city, both present and future, as well as upon their children forever. (Letters of January 8, 137⅔, Arcère, ii., Preuves, 673-675.)

The extraordinary prerogatives of which this was the origin were recognized and confirmed by subsequent monarchs, especially by Louis the Eleventh, Charles the Eighth, Louis the Twelfth, and Francis the First. (Callot, 11.)

The resistance of the inhabitants to the exaction of the obnoxious "gabelle," or tax upon salt, did indeed, toward the end of the reign of the last-named king (1542), bring them temporarily under his displeasure ; but, with the exception of a modification in their municipal government, made in 1530, and revoked early in the reign of Henry the Second, the city retained its quasi-independence without interruption until the outbreak of the religious wars.

As we have seen (*ante*, p. 227), La Rochelle was in 1552 the scene of the judicial murder of at least two Protestants. The constancy of one of the sufferers had been the means of converting many to the reformed doctrines, and among others Claude d'Angliers, the presiding judge, whose name may still be read at the foot of their sentence. (Arcère, i. 329.) So rapidly had those doctrines spread, that on Sunday, May 31, 1562, the Lord's Supper was celebrated according to the fashion of Geneva, not in one of the churches, but on the great square of the hay-market, in a temporary enclosure shut in on all sides by tapestries and covered with an awning of canvas. More than eight thousand persons took part in the exercises. But if the morning's services were remarkable, the sequel was not less singular. "As the disease of image-breaking was almost universal," says an old chronicler, "it was communicated by contagion to the inhabitants of this city, in such wise that, that very afternoon about three or four o'clock, five hundred men, who were under arms and had just received the same sacrament, went through all the churches and dashed the images in pieces. Howbeit it was a folly conducted with wisdom, seeing that this action passed without any one being wounded or injured." (P. Vincent, *apud* Callot, 34, and Delmas, 61.) As usual, the whole affair was condemned by the ministers.

Although La Rochelle had steadily refused, during the earlier part of the first religious war, to declare for the Prince of Condé, and had maintained a kind of neutrality, the court was in constant fear lest the weight of its sympathies should yet draw it in that direction. It was therefore a matter of great joy when, in October, 1562, the Duke of Montpensier succeeded, by a ruse meriting the designation of treachery, in throwing himself into La Rochelle with a large body of troops. With his arrival the banished Roman Catholic mass returned, and the Protestant ministers were warned to leave at once. (Arcère, i. 339.)

For two months after the restoration of peace, the Huguenots of La Rochelle, embracing almost the entire population, held their religious services, in accordance with the terms of the Edict of Pacification, in the suburbs of the city. But, on the 9th of May, 1563, Charles the Ninth was prevailed to give directions that one or two places should be assigned to the Huguenots within the city. This gracious permission was ratified with greater solemnity in letters patent of July 14th, in which the king declared the motive to be the representations made to him of "the inconveniences and eminent dangers that might arise in our said city of La Rochelle, if the preaching and exercise of the pretended reformed religion should continue to be held outside of the said city, being, as it is, a frontier city in the direction of the English, ancient enemies of the inhabitants of that city, where it would be easy for them, by this means, to execute some evil enterprise." (Commission of Charles IX., to M. de Jarnac. This valuable MS., with other MSS., carried to Dublin at the revocation of the Edict of Nantes, by M. Elie Bouhereau, and placed in the Marsh Library, has recently been restored to La Rochelle, in accordance with M. Bouhereau's written directions.   Delmas, 369.)

Two years later, Charles and his court, returning from their long progress through France, came to La Rochelle, and spent three days there (Sept., 1565). A noteworthy incident occurred at his entry.   The jealous citizens had not forgotten an immemorial custom which was not without significance.   A silken cord had been stretched across the road by which the monarch was to enter, that he might stop and promise to respect the liberties and franchises of La Rochelle.   Constable Montmorency was the first to notice the cord, and in some anger and surprise asked whether the magistrates of the city intended to refuse their sovereign admission.   The symbolism of the pretty custom was duly explained to him, but for all response the old warrior curtly observed that "such usages had passed out of fashion," and at the same instant cut the cord with his sword.   (Arcère, i. 349 ; Delmas, 80, 81.)   Charles himself refused the request of the mayor that he should swear to maintain the city's privileges.   After so inauspicious a beginning of his visit, the inhabitants were not surprised to find the king, during his stay, reducing the "corps-de-ville" from 100 to 24 members, under the presidency of a governor invested with the full powers of the mayor ; ordering that the artillery should be seized, two of the towers garrisoned by foreign troops, and the magistrates enjoined to prosecute all ministers that preached sedition ; or banishing some of the most prominent Protestants from La Rochelle.

It was characteristic of the government of Catharine de' Medici—always destitute of a fixed policy, and consequently always recalling one day what it had done the day before—that scarcely two months elapsed before the queen mother put everything back on the footing it had occupied before the royal visit to La Rochelle.

CHAPTER XVI.

THE THIRD CIVIL WAR.

HAVING narrowly escaped falling into the hands of their treacherous enemies, and finding themselves compelled once more to take up arms in defence of their own lives and the liberties of their fellow-believers, the Prince of Condé and Admiral Coligny resolved to institute a vigorous contest. A single glance at the situation, the full dangers of which were now disclosed by the tidings coming from every quarter, was sufficient to convince them that in a bold and decided policy lay their only hope of success. The Roman Catholics had, it is true, enjoyed rare opportunities for maturing a comprehensive plan of attack ; although the sequel seemed to prove that they had turned these opportunities to little practical use. But the Huguenots possessed countervailing advantages, in close sympathy with each other, in fervid zeal for their common faith, as well as in an organization all but perfect. Simultaneously with their flight from Noyers, the prince and the admiral had sent out a summons addressed to the Protestants in all parts of the kingdom, and this was responded to with enthusiasm by great numbers of those who had been their devoted followers in the two previous wars. Multitudes of young men, also, with imaginations inflamed by the recital of the exploits of their fathers and friends, burned to enroll themselves under such distinguished leaders. Many were the stratagems resorted to by these aspirants for military honors. Among others, the eminent historian, Theodore Agrippa d'Aubigné, has left an amusing account of the adventures he passed through in reaching the

Relative advantages of the Roman Catholics and Huguenots.

Enthusiasm of Huguenot youth.

Huguenot recruiting station. His prudent guardian had taken the precaution to remove Agrippa's clothes every evening, in order to prevent him from carrying out his avowed purpose of entering the army; but one night, on hearing the report of the

Enlistment of Agrippa d'Aubigné.

arquebuse—which a number of his companions, bent on the same course, had fired as a signal near his place of confinement—the youth boldly lowered himself to the ground by the sheets of his bed, and, with bare feet and no other clothing than a shirt, made his way to Jonzac. There, after receiving an outfit from some Protestant captains, he jotted down at the bottom of the receipt which he gave them in return, the whimsical declaration "that never in his life would he blame the war for having stripped him, since he could not possibly leave it in a sorrier plight than that in which he entered it."[1]

The resolution and enthusiasm of the Huguenots were greatly augmented by the imprudent course of the court. Notwithstanding their own guilty designs, Catharine and the Cardinal of Lorraine were taken by surprise when the news reached them that Condé and Coligny had escaped, and that the Huguenots were everywhere arming. So sudden an outbreak had not been expected; and, while awaiting the muster of that portion of the troops that had been dismissed, but was now summoned to assemble at Étaples on the 10th of September,[2] it was thought best to quiet the agitated minds of the people. A declaration was accordingly published, assuring all the adherents of the reformed faith who remained at home and furnished no assistance to the enemy, of the royal protection, Charles promising, at the same time, to give a gracious hearing to their grievances.[3] But, as soon as the Roman Catholic forces

The court proscribes the reformed religion.

began to collect in large numbers, and the apprehension of a sudden assault by the Huguenots died away, the court threw off the mask of conciliation, and Charles was made to sign two laws unsurpassed for intolerance. The first purported to be "an irrevocable and perpetual edict."

---

[1] Mémoires d'Aprippa d'Aubigné (Ed. Buchon), 475.

[2] Jean de Serres, iii. 247.

[3] Mém. de Claude Haton, ii. 541 ; De Thou, iv. (liv. xliv.) 145.

It rehearsed the various steps taken by Charles the Ninth and his brother Francis in reference to the "so-called reformed religion," from the time of the tumult of Amboise. It alluded to the edicts of July and of January—the latter adopted by the queen mother, by advice of the Cardinals of Bourbon and Tournon, of the constable, of Saint André, and others, because less objectionable than an edict tolerating the worship of that religion *within* the walls of the cities. None of these concessions, it asserted, having satisfied the professors of the new faith, who had collected money and raised troops with the intent of establishing another government in place of that which God had instituted, the king now repealed the edicts of toleration, and henceforth prohibited his subjects, of whatever rank and in all parts of his dominions, on pain of confiscation and death, from the exercise of any other religious rites than those of the Roman Catholic Church. All Protestant ministers were ordered to leave France within fifteen days. Quiet and peaceable laymen were promised toleration until such time as God should deign to bring them back to the true fold ; and pardon was offered to all who within twenty days should lay down their arms.[1] The second edict deprived all Protestant magistrates of the offices they held, reserving, however, to those who did not take part in the war, a certain portion of their former revenues.[2]

In order to give greater solemnity to the transaction, Charles, clothed in robes of state and with great pomp, repaired to the parliament house, to be present at the publication of the new edicts, and with his own hands threw into the fire and burned up the previous edicts of pacification. "Thus did his Royal Highness of France," writes a contemporary German pam-

---

[1] The text of the edict is given by Jean de Serres, iii. 272–281. See also De Thou, iv. (liv. xliv.) 145, 146 ; Castelnau, liv. vii., c. ii. La Fosse (Journal d'un curé ligueur, 98), gives the correct date : "Septembre. *La veille du Saint Michel* (i. e., *Sept.* 28th) fut rompu l'esdict de janvier, et publié dedans le palais esdict au contraire ; " while the ambassador La Mothe-Fénélon alludes to it in a despatch to Catharine as " votre édict du xxxᵉ de Septembre." Correspondance diplomatique, i. 28.

[2] J. de Serres, iii. 281, 282 ; De Thou and Castelnau, *ubi supra*, Recordon, Le protestantisme en Champagne, 158, 159.

phleteer with intense satisfaction, "as was seemly and becoming to a Christian supreme magistrate, *pronounce sentence of death upon all Calvinistic and other heresies.*" [1]

Nothing devised by the papal party could have been better adapted to further the Huguenot cause than the course it had

Impolicy of this course. adopted. The wholesale proscription of their faith united the Protestants, and led every able-bodied man to take up arms against a perfidious government, whose disregard of treaties solemnly made was so shamefully paraded before the world. "These edicts," admits the candid Castelnau, "only served to make the whole party rise with greater expedition, and furnished the Prince of Condé and the admiral with a handle to convince all the Protestant powers that they were not persecuted for any disaffection to the government, but purely for the sake of religion." [2]

Efforts were not spared by the Guisard party to make capital abroad out of the new proscriptive measures. Copies of the edicts, translated from the French, were put into circulation

Attempts to make capital of the proscriptive measures. beyond the Rhine, accompanied by a memorial embodying the views presented by an envoy of Charles to some of the Roman Catholic princes of the empire. The king herein justified himself for his previous clemency by declaring that he had entertained no other idea than that of allowing his subjects of the "pretended" reformed faith time and opportunity for returning to the bosom of the only true church. Lovers of peace and good order among the Germans were warned that they had no worse enemies than the insubordinate and rebellious Huguenots of his Very Christian Majesty's dominions, while the adherents of the Augsburg Confession were distinctly given to understand that Lutheranism was safer with the Turk than where Calvin's doctrines were professed. [3]

---

[1] Zway Edict, u. s. w., *ubi infra*, p. 38.

[2] Castelnau, *ubi supra*.

[3] I have before me this interesting publication, of which the first lines of the title-page (inordinately long and comprehensive, after the fashion of the times) run as follows: "Zway Edict, sampt einer offnen Patent der Königlichen Würden in Franckreich, durch welche alle auffrurische Predigten, ver-

To influence the princes the offices of skilled diplomatists were called into requisition, but to no purpose. When Blandy requested the emperor, in Charles's name, to prevent any succor from being sent to Condé from Germany, Maximilian replied by counselling his good friend the king to seek means to restore concord and harmony among his subjects, and professing his own inability to restrain the levy of auxiliary troops. And from Duke John William, of Saxony, the same envoy only obtained expressions of regret that the war so lately suppressed had broken out anew, and of discontent on the part of the German princes at the rumor that Charles had been so ill advised as to join in a league made by the Pope and the King of Spain, with the view of overwhelming the Protestants.[1]

On the other hand, the new direction taken by Catharine met with the most decided favor on the part of the fanatical populace, and the pulpits resounded with praise of the complete abrogation of all compacts with heresy. The Roman Catholic party in Toulouse acted so promptly, anticipating even the orders of the royal court, as to make it evident that they had been long preparing for the struggle. On Sunday, the twelfth of September, a league for the extermination of heresy was published, under the name of a *crusade*. A priest delivered a sermon with the consent of the Parliament of Toulouse. Next day all who desired to join in the bloody work met in the cathedral dedicated to St. Stephen— the Christian protomartyr having, by an irony of history, more than once been made a witness of acts more congenial to the spirit of his persecutors than to his own—and prepared themselves for their undertaking by a common profession of their faith, by an oath to expose their lives and property for the maintenance of the Roman Catholic religion, and by confession and communion. This being done, they adopted for their motto the words, " Eamus nos, moriamur cum Christo," and attached to their dress a white cross to distinguish them from

A " crusade " preached at Toulouse.

---

samblungen unnd ubung der newen unchristlichen Secten und vermainten Religion gantz und gar abgeschafft und allain die Römische und Bäpstische Catholische ware Religion gestattet werden sollen. . . . . 1568."

[1] De Thou, iv. (liv. xliv.) 160, 161.

their Protestant fellow-citizens. Of success they entertained no misgivings. Had not Attila been defeated, with his three hundred thousand men, not far from Toulouse? Had not God so blessed the arms of "our good Catholics" in the time of Louis the Eighth, father of St. Louis, that eight hundred of them had routed more than sixty thousand heretics? "So that we doubt not," said the new crusaders, "that we shall gain the victory over these enemies of God and of the whole human race; and if some of us should chance to die, our blood will be to us a second baptism, in consequence of which, without any hinderance, we shall pass, with the other martyrs, straight to Paradise." [1] A papal bull, a few months later (on the fifteenth of March, 1569), gave the highest ecclesiastical sanction to the crusade, and emphasized the complete extermination of the heretics. [2]

The faithful, but somewhat garrulous chronicler, who has left us so vivid a picture of the social, religious, and political condition of the city of Provins during a great part of the second half of this century, describes a solemn procession in honor of the publication of the new ordinance, which was attended by over two thousand persons, and even by the magistrates suspected of sympathy with the Protestants. Friar Jean Barrier, when pressed to preach, took for his text the song of Moses: "I will sing unto the Lord, for He hath triumphed gloriously: the horse and his rider hath He thrown into the sea." His treatment of the verse was certainly novel, although the exegesis might not find much favor with the critical Hebraist. The Prince of Condé was the *horse*, on whose

Fanaticism of the Roman Catholic preachers.

---

[1] "Notre sang nous sera ung secong baptême, par quoy sans aucun empeschement, nous irons avec les autres martyrs droit en paradis." Publication de la croisade, Hist. de Languedoc, v. (Preuves) 216, 217. See the account, ibid., v. 290.

[2] Ibid., v. (Preuves) 217. The laborious author of the Hist. de Languedoc, v. 290, makes a singular mistake in saying "that this bull is dated March 15th, of the year 1568, which proves that the project had been formed several months before its execution." The date of the bull is, indeed, given as stated at the close of the document; but the addition, "pontificatus nostri anno quarto," furnishes the means for correcting it. Pius V. was not created Pope until January 7, 1566. See De Thou, iii. (liv. xxxix.) 622.

back were mounted the Huguenot ministers and preachers—the *riders* who drove him hither and thither by their satanic doctrine. Although they were not as yet drowned, like Pharaoh and his army in the Red Sea, France had great reason to rejoice and praise God that the king had annulled the Edict of January, and other pernicious laws made during his minority. As for himself, said the good friar, he was ready to die, like another Simeon, since he had lived to see the edicts establishing "the Huguenotic liberty" repealed, and the preachers expelled from France.[1]

Similar rejoicings with similar high masses and sermons by enthusiastic monks, were heard in the capital[2] and elsewhere. But the jubilant strains were sounded rather prematurely; for the victory was yet to be won. The Huguenot nobles, invited by Condé, were flocking to La Rochelle; the Protestant inhabitants of the towns, expelled from their homes, were generally following the same impulse. But others, reluctant, or unable to traverse such an expanse of hostile territory, turned toward nearer places of refuge. Happily they found a number of such asylums in cities whose inhabitants, alarmed by the marks of treachery appearing in every quarter of France, had refused to receive the garrisons sent to them in the king's name. It was a wonderful providence of God, the historian Jean de Serres remarks. The fugitive Huguenots of the centre and north found the gates of Vézelay and of Sancerre open to them. Those of Languedoc and Guyenne were safe within the walls of Montauban, Milhau, and Castres. In the southeastern corner of the kingdom, Aubenas, Privas, and a few other places afforded a retreat for the women and children, and a convenient point for the muster of the forces of Dauphiny.[3]

The Huguenot places of refuge.

Meantime, the Queen of Navarre, with young Prince Henry and his sister Catharine, started from her dominions near the Pyrenees. The court had in vain plied her with conciliatory letters and messages sent in the king's name. Gathering her

---

[1] Mémoires de Claude Haton, ii. 541, 542.   [2] Jehan de la Fosse, 99.
[3] Jean de Serres, iii. 249.

troops together, and narrowly escaping the forces despatched Jeanne d'Al- to intercept her, she formed a junction with a very bret and D'An- considerable body of troops raised in Périgord, Au- delot reach La Rochelle. vergne, and the neighboring provinces, under the Seigneur de Piles, the Marquis de Montamart, and others, and, after meeting the Prince of Condé, who came as far as Cognac to receive her, found safety in the city of La Rochelle.[1]

From an opposite direction, François d'Andelot, whom the outbreak of hostilities overtook while yet in Brittany, was warned by Condé to hasten to the same point. With his accustomed energy, the young Châtillon rapidly collected the Protestant noblemen and gentry, not only of that province, but of Normandy, Touraine, Maine, and Anjou, and with such experienced leaders as the Count of Montgomery, the Vidame of Chartres, and François de la Noue, had reached a point on the Loire a few miles above Angers. It was his plan to seize and hold the city and bridge of Saumur, and thus secure for the Huguenots the means of easy communication between the two sides of the important basin intervening between the smaller basins of the Seine and the Garonne. His expectations, however, were frustrated principally by the good fortune of M. de Martigues, who succeeded in making a sudden dash through D'Andelot's scattered divisions, and in conveying to the Duke of Montpensier at Saumur so large a reinforcement as to render it impossible for the Huguenots to dream of dislodging him.[2] For a time D'Andelot was in great peril. With only about fifteen hundred horse and twenty-five hundred foot,[3] he stood on the banks of a river swollen by autumnal rains and supposed

---

[1] Jean de Serres, iii. 255, 256; De Thou, iv. (liv. xlix.) 141. De Serres (iii. 256–266) gives interesting extracts of the letters which Jeanne wrote to Charles, to his mother, to the Duke of Anjou, and to her brother-in-law, the Cardinal of Bourbon. She urged the latter, by every consideration of blood and honor, to shake off his shameful servitude to the counsels of the Cardinal of Lorraine, whom she openly accused of having conspired to murder Bourbon, with Marshal Montmorency and Chancellor L'Hospital, during a recent illness of the queen.

[2] Jean de Serres, iii. 267–269; De Thou, iv. (liv. xliv.) 142, 143; D'Aubigné, liv. v., c. 2, 3 (i. 264–268).

[3] J. de Serres, *ubi supra*.

to be utterly impassable, and in the midst of a country all whose cities were in the hands of the enemy.   He had even formed the desperate design of retiring twenty or thirty miles north-ward, in hope of being able to entice Montpensier to follow him so incautiously that he might turn upon him, and, after winning a victory, secure for himself a passage to the sources of the Loire or to his allies in Germany.   At this moment the joyful announce-ment was made by Montgomery that a ford had been discovered. The news proved to be true.   The crossing was safe and easy. Not a man nor a horse was lost.   The interposition of heaven in their behalf was so wonderful, that, as the Huguenot troopers reached the southern bank, the whole army, by common and irresistible impulse, broke forth in praise to Almighty God, and sang that grand psalm of deliverance—the seventy-sixth.[1]   Never had those verses of Beza been sung by more thankful hearts or in a nobler temple.[2]

Full of courage, the exultant troops of D'Andelot now pressed southward.   First the city of Thouars fell into their hands; then the more important Partenay surrendered itself
Success in Poitou, An-goumois, etc. to the Huguenots.   Here, according to the cruel rules of warfare of the sixteenth century, they deemed themselves justified in hanging the commander of the place, who had thrown himself into the castle, for having too obstinately insisted upon standing an assault in a spot incapable of defence,

---

[1]   " C'est en Judée proprement
        Que Dieu s'est acquis un renom ;
        C'est en Israël voirement
        Qu'on voit la force de son Nom :
        En Salem est son tabernacle,
        En Sion son sainct habitacle."
I quote from an edition of the unaltered Huguenot psalter (1638).

[2] Jean de Serres, iii. 270 ; De Thou, iv. (liv. xliv.) 144, 145 ; Agrippa d'Au-bigné, Hist. univ. liv. v., c. 4 (i. 269) states the circumstance that the river fell a foot and a half during the four hours consumed in the crossing, and then rose again as opportunely : " Mais il s'en fust perdu la pluspart sans un heur nompareil ; ce fut que la riviere s'estant diminuée d'un pied et demi durant le passage de quatre heures, se r'enfla sur la fin ; " adding in one of those nervous sentences which constitute a principal charm of his writings : "Nous dirions avec crainte *ces courtoisies de Loire*, si nous n'avions tous ceux qui ont escrit pour gariment."

together with some priests who had shared his infatuation.[1] Admiral Coligny now met his brother, and the united army, with three cannon brought from La Rochelle, forming his entire siege artillery, demanded and obtained the surrender of Niort, the size and advantageous position of which made it a bulwark of La Rochelle toward the east. Angoulême, Blaye, Cognac, Pons, and Saintes, were still more valuable acquisitions. In short, within a few weeks, so large a number of cities in the provinces of Poitou, Angoumois, and Saintonge had fallen under the power of the Protestants, that they seemed fully to have retrieved the losses they had experienced through the treacherous peace of Longjumeau. " In less than two months," writes La Noue of his fellow-soldiers, " from poor vagabonds that they were, they found in their hands sufficient means to continue a long war."[2] And the veteran Admiral Coligny, amazed at the success attending measures principally planned by himself, was accustomed to repeat with heartfelt thankfulness the exclamation attributed to Themistocles : "I should be lost, if I had not been lost!"[3]

Meantime, in the south-eastern part of France, the provinces of Dauphiny, Provence, and Lower Languedoc, the Huguenots had not been slow in responding to the call of the Prince of Condé. The difficulty was rather in assembling their soldiers than in raising them ; for there was little lack of volunteers after the repeal of the royal edicts in favor of the Protestants. With great trouble the contingents of Dauphiny and Provence were brought across the Rhône, and at Alais the Baron d'Acier[4] mustered an army to go to the succor of the Prince of Condé at La Rochelle. A Roman Catholic historian expresses his profound astonishment that the Huguenots of this part of the kingdom, when surprised

Affairs in Dauphiny, Provence, and Languedoc.

---

[1] Jean de Serres, iii. 270, 271 ; De Thou, iv. (liv. xliv.) 147 ; Agrippa d'Aubigné, i. 269.

[2] La Noue, c. xx.

[3] Ibid., *ubi supra ;* De Thou, iv. (liv. xliv.) 150.

[4] Jacques de Crussol, Baron d'Acier (or, Assier), afterwards Duke d'Uzès, lieutenant-general of the royal armies in Languedoc, etc. According to the Abbé Le Laboureur (iii. 56–60), it was interest that induced him, a few years later, to become a Roman Catholic.

by the violation of the peace, should so speedily have been able to mass a force of twenty-five thousand men, well furnished and equipped, and commanded by the most excellent captains of the age—Montbrun, Mouvans, Pierre-Gourde, and others.[1] The abbé's wonder was doubtless equalled by the consternation which the news spread among the enemies of the Huguenots. The Roman Catholics could bring no army capable of preventing the junction of D'Acier's troops with those of Condé; but the Duke of Montpensier succeeded, on the twenty-fifth of October, in inflicting a severe loss upon one of the divisions at Messignac, near Périgueux. Mouvans and Pierre-Gourde, who were distant from the main body, were attacked in their quarters, by a force under Brissac, which they easily repulsed. D'Acier, suspecting the design of the enemy, had commanded the Huguenot captains to make no pursuit, and to await his own arrival. But brave Mouvans was as impatient of orders as he was courageous in battle. Disregarding the authority which sat so lightly upon him, he fell into an ambuscade, where he atoned for his rashness by the loss of his own life and the lives of more than a thousand of his companions. After this disaster, D'Acier experienced no further opposition, and, on the first of November, he met the advancing army of Condé at Aubeterre, on the banks of the Dronne.[2]

With the new accessions to his army, the prince commanded

Powerful Huguenot army in the south.

It effects a junction with Condé's forces.

---

[1] Le Laboureur, Add. aux Mém de Castelnau, ii. 588. The same author elsewhere (ii. 56–60) states the army as only 20,000. Jean de Serres, iii. 284, 285, and De Thou, iv. (liv. xliv.) 150–152, give an account of the difficulties encountered in bringing these troops to the place of rendezvous, and enumerate the leaders and contingents of the three provinces. According to the latter, the total was 23,000 men. See Agrippa d'Aubigné, liv. v., c. 5 (i. 271).

[2] Jean de Serres, iii. 286, 291, 292; De Thou, iv. (liv. xliv), 153, 154; Agrippa d'Aubigné, *ubi supra;* Davila, bk. iv., p. 132, 133; Le Laboureur, ii. 588, 589. It is more than usually difficult to ascertain the loss of the Huguenots at Messignac. Jean de Serres, who states it at 600, and Davila, who says that it amounted to 2,000 foot and more than 4,000 horse, are the extremes. De Thou sets it down at more than 1,000; D'Aubigné at 1,000 or 1,200; Castelnau at 3,000 foot and 300 horse; and Le Laboureur, following him, at over 3,000 men.

a force very considerably larger than any he had led in the previous wars. Among the conflicting statements, we may find it
difficult to fix its numbers. Agrippa d'Aubigné says that, after
the losses consequent upon the defeat of Messignac and those
resulting from camp diseases, Condé's army consisted of only
seventeen thousand foot soldiers, and two thousand five hundred
horsemen.[1] A Huguenot bulletin, sent from La Rochelle for
the information of Queen Elizabeth and the Protestants of
England, may have given somewhat too favorable a view of the
prince's prospects, but was certainly nearer the truth, in assigning him twenty-five thousand arquebusiers and a cavalry force
of five or six thousand men.[2] On the other hand, Henry of
Anjou, who had been placed in nominal command of the Roman
Catholic army, had not yet been able to assemble a much superior, probably not an equal, number of soldiers. The large
forces which, according to his ambassador at the English court,
Charles the Ninth could call out,[3] existed only on paper. The
younger Tavannes, whose father was the true head of the royal
army, gives it but about twenty thousand men.[4]

It was already nearly winter when the armies were collected,
and their operations during the remainder of the campaign
were indecisive. In the numerous skirmishes that occurred
the Huguenots usually had the advantage, and sometimes inflicted considerable damage upon the enemy. But the Duke
of Anjou, or the more experienced leaders commanding in his
name, studiously avoided a general engagement. The instructions from the court were to wear out the courage and enthusi-

---

[1] Hist. univ., liv. v., c. 6 (i. 273).

[2] "Discours envoyé de la Rochelle," accompanying La Mothe Fénélon's
despatch of January 20, 1569. Correspondance diplomatique, i. 137, 138.
Another letter of a later date gives even larger figures—30,000 foot (25,000
of them arquebusiers) and 7,000 or 8,000 horse, besides recruits expected
from Montauban. Ibid., i. 147.

[3] Upwards of 23,000 horse and 200 ensigns of foot (which we may perhaps
reckon at 40,000 men). Despatch of La Mothe Fénélon, Dec. 5, 1568, Corresp.
diplomatique, i. 29.

[4] Mémoires de Tavannes, iii. 38. De Thou, iv. 154, assigns 18,000 foot and
3,000 horse to Condé ; and 12,000 foot and 4,000 horse, exclusive of the Swiss
(who, according to Tavannes, numbered 6,000), to Anjou.

asm of Condé's adherents by protracting a tame and monoto-
nous warfare.[1] The prince's true policy, on the contrary, lay in
decided action. His soldiers were inferior to none in France.
The flower of the higher nobility and the most substantial of
the middle classes had flocked to his standard so soon as it was
unfurled. But, without regular commissariat, and serving at
their own costs, these troops could not long maintain themselves
in the field.[2] The nobles and country gentlemen, never too
provident in their habits, soon exhausted their ready funds,
with their crowd of hungry retainers, and became a more pitia-
ble class than even the burgesses. The latter, whom devotion
to their religious convictions, rather than any thirst for personal
distinction, had impelled to enter the service, could not remain
many months away from their workshops and counting-rooms
without involving their families in great pecuniary distress. It
was not, however, possible for Condé and Coligny to bring about
a combat which the duke was resolved to decline, and the unparalleled severity of the season suspended, at the same time,
their design of wresting from his hands the city of Saumur,
a convenient point of communication with northern France.
Early in December the vines were frozen in the fields,[3] disease
broke out in either camp, and the soldiers began to murmur at
a war which seemed to be waged with the elements rather than
with their fellow-men. While Anjou's generals, therefore,
drew off their troops to Saumur, Chinon on the Vienne, and
Poitiers, Condé's army went into winter quarters a little farther
west, at Montreuil-Bellay, Loudun and Thouars, but afterward
removed, for greater commodity in obtaining provisions, to
Partenày and Niort.[4]

It was while the Huguenots lay thus inactive that their leaders
deliberated respecting the best means of providing for their sup-

---

[1] Jean de Serres, iii. 295, 296.

[2] "Resolution qui sembloit la plus nécessaire aux Réformez, pource que
difficilement pouvoient-ils maintenir une telle troupe sans solde et sans
magazins reglez." Agrippa d'Aubigné, liv. v., c. 6 (i. 273).

[3] See "Tableau des phénomènes météorologiques, astronomiques, etc.,
mentionnés dans les Mémoires de Claude Haton."

[4] Jean de Serres, iii. 304, 305; De Thou, iv. (liv. xliv.) 159.

port during the coming campaign. Jeanne d'Albret, whose

Huguenot reprisals and negotiations. masculine vigor [1] had never been displayed more conspicuously than during this war, was present, and assisted by her sage counsels. It was determined, in view of the cruelties exercised upon the Protestants in those parts of the kingdom where they had no strongholds, and of the confiscation of their property by judicial decisions, to retaliate by selling the ecclesiastical possessions in the cities that were now under Huguenot power, and applying the proceeds to military uses. The order of sale was issued under the names of the young Prince of Navarre, of Condé, Coligny, D'Andelot and La Rochefoucauld, and a guarantee was given by them. As a reprisal the measure was just, and as a warlike expedient nothing could be more prudent; for, while it speedily filled the coffers of the Huguenot army, it cut off one great source of the revenues of the court, which had been authorized both by the Pope and by the clergy itself to lay these possessions under contribution.[2]

Already the temper of the Protestant leaders had been sounded by an unaccredited agent of Catharine de' Medici, who found Condé at Mirebeau, and entreated him to make those advances toward a peace which would comport better with his dignity as a subject than with that of Charles as a king. But the prince, who saw in the mission of an irresponsible mediator only a new attempt to impede the action of the confederates, had dismissed him, after declaring, in the presence of a large number of his nobles, that he had been compelled to resort to arms in order to provide for his own defence. The war was, therefore, directed not against the king, but against those capital enemies of the crown and of the realm, the Cardinal of Lorraine and his associates. All knew his own vehement desire for peace, of which his late excessive compliance was a sufficient proof; but, since the king was surrounded by his ene-

---

[1] "Cette Roine, n'aiant de femme que le sexe, l'âme entière aux choses viriles, l'esprit puissant aux grands affaires, le cœur invincible aux adversitez." Agrippa d'Aubigné, ii. 8.

[2] Jean de Serres, iii. 306, 307.

mies, he intended, with God's favor, to come and present his petitions to his Majesty in person.[1]

Abroad the Huguenots had not been idle in endeavoring to secure the support of advantageous alliances. So early as in the month of August, after the disastrous defeat of Louis of Nassau at Jemmingen, the Prince of Orange had contemplated the formation of a league for common defence with the Prince of Condé and Admiral Coligny. A draft of such an agreement has been preserved; but it is unsigned, and may be regarded rather as indicative of the friendly disposition of the French and Dutch patriots than as a compact that was ever formally adopted.[2] That same autumn William of Orange had undertaken an expedition intended to free the Netherlands from the tyranny of Alva. He had been met with consummate skill. The duke refused to fight, but hung remorselessly on his skirts. The inhabitants of Brabant extended no welcome to their liberator. The prince's mercenaries, vexed at their reception, annoyed by the masterly tactics of their enemy, and eager only to return to their homes, clamored for pay and for plunder. Orange, outgeneralled, was compelled to abandon the campaign, and would gladly have turned his arms against the oppressors of his fellow-believers in France; but his German troops had enlisted only for the campaign in the Netherlands, and peremptorily declined to transfer the field of battle to another country. However, the depth of the Meuse, which had become

William of Orange attempts to aid the Huguenots.

----

[1] Jean de Serres, iii. 296, 297 ; Relation sent from La Rochelle, La Mothe Fénélon, i. 173. The Prince of Condé had also made a solemn protestation in writing, and before a large assembly, before entering upon any belligerent acts. The substance of these frequent documents is so similar that I have deemed it unnecessary to do more than refer to it. See J. de Serres, iii. 249, 250. The Huguenot soldiers had, at the same time, taken an oath to support the cause until the achievement of a peace securing the undisturbed enjoyment of life, honors and religious liberty, and to submit to a careful military discipline. Ibid., iii. 251, 252–255, where the oath and a summary of the rules of discipline are inserted.

[2] " Projet d'alliance du Prince d'Orange avec l'Amiral de Coligny et le Prince de Condé pour obtenir entière liberté de conscience dans les Pays-Bas et en France. Le — aout l'an 1568." Groen Van Prinsterer, Archives de la Maison d'Orange-Nassau, iii. 282–286.

unfordable, furnished more persuasive arguments than could be
brought forward by Genlis and the Huguenots who with him
had joined the Prince of Orange, and the army of the patriots
was forced to direct its course southward and to cross the
French frontier.

Great was the consternation at the court of Charles. Paris
trembled for its safety, and vigorous were the efforts made to
get rid of such dangerous guests. Marshal Cossé, who commanded for his Majesty on the Flemish border, was
too weak to copy successfully the tactics of Alva; but
he employed the resources of diplomacy. His secretary, the Seigneur de Favelles, not content with remonstrating
against the prince's violation of the territory of a king with whom
he was at peace, endeavored to terrify him by exaggerating the
resources of Charles the Ninth and by fabricating accounts of
Huguenot reverses. Condé, he said, had been forced to recross
the river Vienne in great confusion ; and there was a flattering
prospect that he would be compelled to shut himself up in La
Rochelle ; for " Monseigneur the Duke of Anjou " had an irresistible army of six thousand horse and twenty-five or thirty
thousand foot, besides the forces coming from Provence under
the Count de Tende, the six thousand newly levied Swiss
brought by the Duke d'Aumale, and other considerable bodies
of troops.[1] Gaspard de Schomberg[2] was despatched on a similar errand by Charles himself, and offered the prince, if he
came merely desiring to pass in a friendly manner through the
country, to furnish him with every facility for so doing. In
reply, William of Orange, although the refusal of his soldiers to
fight against Charles[3] left him no alternative but to embrace the

*Consterna-
tion and de-
vices of the
court.*

---

[1] Letter of Favelles (Dec., 1568), Groen Van Prinsterer, Archives, etc.,
iii. 312–316.

[2] He was not a " maréchal," as Mr. Motley inadvertently calls him (Dutch
Republic, ii. 261), but a very prominent and successful negotiator, whose
eulogy M. de Thou, an intimate friend, has pronounced in the 122d book of
his history (ix. 285). Henry, the first Count of Schomberg made Marshal of
France, was not born until 1583.

[3] It was generally believed that Schomberg, gaining access to the Germans
through one of the principal officers, to whom he was related, was the occasion of their disaffection. Jean de Serres, iii. 298. " Il mesnagea si bien

course marked out for him, did not disguise his hearty sympathy
with his suffering brethren in France. In view of the
attempts made, according to his Majesty's edict of September last, to constrain the consciences of all who
belonged to the Christian religion, and in view of the king's
avowed determination to exterminate the pure Word of God,
and to permit no other religion than the Roman Catholic—a
thing very prejudicial to the neighboring nations, where there
was a free exercise of the Christian religion—the prince declared
his inability to credit the assertions of his Majesty, that it was
not his Majesty's intention to constrain the conscience of any one.
He avowed his own purpose to give oppressed Christians everywhere all aid, comfort, counsel, and assistance ; asserting his
conviction that the men who professed " the religion " demanded nothing else than the glory of God and the advancement of His Word, while in all matters of civil polity they were
ready to render obedience to his Majesty. He averred, moreover, that if he should perceive any indications that the Huguenots were pursuing any other object than liberty of conscience and security for life and property, he would not only
withdraw his assistance from them, but would use the whole
strength of his army to exterminate them.[1] After this declaration, the prince prosecuted his march to Strasbourg, where he
disbanded his troops, pawning his very plate and pledging his
principality of Orange, to find the means of satisfying their
demands. Great was the delight of the royalists, great the
disappointment of the Huguenots, on hearing that the expedition had vanished in smoke. " The army of the Prince of
Orange," wrote an agent of Condé in Paris, " after having
thrice returned to the king's summons a sturdy answer that it
would never leave France until it saw religion re-established,

Declaration of the Prince of Orange.

---

la plus part des capitaines," says Agrippa d'Aubigné, i. 340, " que quand le
Prince leur parla d'aller joindre le Prince de Condé, *il les trouva tous bons
théologiens et mauvais partisans ;* discourans de la justice des armes, sans
oublier le droit des rois et les affaires qu'ils avoient en leur païs. Schomberg
s'en revint aiant reçeu quelques injures par Genlis."

[1] Letter of December 3, 1568, Cissonne, in Motley, Rise of the Dutch Republic, ii. 261, 262.

has retreated, in spite of our having given it notice of your intention to avow it. I know not the cause of this sudden movement, for which various reasons are alleged." [1] William the Silent had not, however, relinquished the intention of going to the assistance of the Huguenots, whose welfare, next to that of his own provinces, lay near his heart. Retaining, therefore, twelve hundred horsemen whom he found better disposed than the rest, he patiently awaited the departure of the new ally of the French Protestants, Wolfgang, Duke of Deux-Ponts (Zweibrücken), in whose company he had determined to cross France with his brothers Louis and Henry of Nassau. [2]

The Prince of Condé received more immediate and substantial assistance from beyond the Channel. When Tavannes undertook to capture Condé and Coligny at Noyers, it was in contemplation to seize Odet, Cardinal of Châtillon, the admiral's elder brother, [3] in his episcopal palace at Beauvais. He received, however, timely warning, and made his escape through Normandy to England, where Queen Elizabeth received him at her court with marks of distinguished favor. [4] His efforts to enlist the sympathies and assistance of

Aid sought from England.

---

[1] News-letter from Paris, from the Huguenot physician of the Duke of Jarnac, discovered in the gauntlet of the Prince of Condé, and sent by Anjou, with other papers found on his dead body, to King Charles. Duc d'Aumale, Princes de Condé, Pièces inéd., ii. 391.

[2] Jean de Serres, iii. 299; Groen Van Prinsterer, Archives, etc., iii. 316; Motley, Dutch Republic, ii. 263; Ag. d'Aubigné, liv. v., c. 26 (i. 340).

[3] Mr. Froude falls into a very natural error, in calling him (History of England, Am. edit., ix. 334) "the *younger* Châtillon." With the exception of a brother who died in early youth, he was the oldest of the family; but his quiet and more sluggish character inclined him to accept the cardinal's hat, when offered to him by his uncle, the constable; and, rich with the revenues of bishoprics and abbeys, he subsequently renounced all his rights as eldest son to his brother Gaspard. Froude is, however, in good company. Even the usually accurate Tytler-Fraser says of Cardinal Châtillon: "This high-born ecclesiastic was in most things the reverse of his *elder* brother D'Andelot." England under Edward VI. and Mary, i. 36.

[4] Lodged by Elizabeth in Sion House, not far from Hampton Court, he was accorded more honor than usually fell to the lot of an envoy of royalty. Never, says Florimond de Ræmond, did the queen meet him but she greeted him with a kiss, and it became a popular saying that Condé's ambassador was a much more important personage than the envoy of the King of France. De ortu, progressu, et ruina hæreseon (Cologne, 1614), ii. 284 (l. vi., c. 15).

the English monarch in behalf of his persecuted countrymen were seconded by Cavaignes, who soon arrived as an envoy from Condé. Cavaignes was instructed to ask material aid—money to meet the engagements made with the Duke of Deux-Ponts, and ships with their armaments to increase the small flotilla of privateersmen, which the Protestants had, for the first time, sent out from La Rochelle. Soon after appeared the vice-admiral, Chastelier-Pourtaut de Latour, under whose command the flotilla had been placed, bearing a letter from the Queen of Navarre to her sister of England, in which she was entreated to espouse a quarrel that had arisen not from ambition or insubordination, but from the desire, in the first place, to defend religion, and, next, to rescue a king who was being hurried on to ruin by treacherous advisers.[1] To these reiterated appeals, and to the solicitations for aid addressed to them by other refugees from papal violence who had found their way to the shores of Great Britain, the subjects of the queen returned a more gracious answer than the queen herself. The exiled Huguenot ministers were received with open arms by men who regarded them as champions of a common Christianity,[2] and some Protestant noblemen had in a few

Generous response of the English people.

---

[1] The letter of Jeanne to Elizabeth, Oct. 15, 1568, is inserted in Jean de Serres, iii. 288–291.

[2] There were many English clergymen with whom the diversity of order in public worship created no prejudice against the reformed churches of France. Of this number was William Whittingham, Dean of Durham, who, when he accompanied the Earl of Warwick, upon the occupation of Havre in 1562, conformed the service of the English garrison to that of the resident Protestants. Understanding that some of his countrymen had made "frivolous" complaints of his action, the Dean justified himself by Saint Augustine's counsel in such matters, and by alleging the disastrous consequences a different course would have produced on the minds of the French Protestants, who, he said, "as they had conceived evil of the infinity of our rites and cold proceedings in religion, so if they should have seen us (but in form only, though not in substance), to use the same or like order in ceremonies which the papists had a little afore observed (against whom they now venture goods and body), they would to their great grief have suspected our doings as not sincere, and have feared in time the loss of that liberty which after a sort they had purchased with the bloodshedding of many thousands." And the dean maintains the wisdom of the course pursued, having "perceived that it wrought here a marvellous conjunction of minds between the French and us, and brought

weeks after their arrival raised for their relief, the sum—considerable for those days—of one hundred pounds sterling. Not only the laity, but even the clergy of the Church of England, took a tender pride in receiving the "few servants of God"—some three or four thousand—whom Providence had thrown upon their shores. They welcomed them to their cities, and resented the attempts of Pope and king to secure their extradition. Could the Pope, who harbored six thousand usurers and twenty thousand courtesans in his own city of Rome, call upon the Queen of England to deny the right of asylum to "the poor exiles of Flanders and France, and other countries, who either lost or left behind them all that they had—goods, lands, and houses—not for adultery, or theft, or treason, but for the profession of the Gospel?" "It pleased God," wrote Bishop Jewel, "here to cast them on land: the queen of her gracious pity hath granted them harbor. Is it become so heinous a thing to show mercy?" "They are our brethren," continued their noble-minded advocate, "they live not idly. If they have houses of us, they pay rent for them. They hold not our grounds but by making due recompense. They beg not in our streets, nor crave anything at our hands, but to breathe our air, and to see our sun. They labor truly, they live sparefully. They are good examples of virtue, travail,

Bishop Jewel's noble plea.

---

singular comfort to all our people." The Bishop of London seems to have concurred in these views, as well as Cuthbert Vaughan, and probably Warwick himself. Whittingham to Cecil, Newhaven (Havre), Dec. 20, 1562, State Paper Office. It ought to be added that Whittingham, in this letter, expresses in fact a preference for the French forms to the English, as "most agreeable with God's Word, most approaching to the form the godly Fathers used, best allowed of the learned and godly in these days, and according to the example of the best reformed churches." Dean Whittingham, who had married the sister of John Calvin, was a leader of the Puritan party in the Church of England, and the editor and principal translator of the "Genevan" version of the English Bible. His opponents maintained that he was "a man not in holy orders, either according to the Anglican or the Presbyterian rite." (History of the Church of England, by G. G. Perry, Canon of Lincoln, New York, 1879, p. 303.) But a commission appointed by the queen to look into the matter, after the dean had been excommunicated by the Archbishop of York, reported that "William Whittingham was ordained in a better sort than even the archbishop himself." (Historic Origin of the Bible, by Edwin Cone Bissell, New York, 1873, p. 57.)

faith, and patience. The towns in which they abide are happy, for God doth follow them with His blessings." [1]

Queen Elizabeth was less decidedly in their favor. Her court swarmed with creatures of the Spanish king, who openly gloried in the victories of the Guises. The ambassadors of Charles and Philip strove to the utmost to render the Huguenots odious to her mind, and to give a false coloring to the war raging in France. Her jealousy of the royal prerogative was appealed to, by the repeated declaration that the Protestants of France were turbulent men, who, for the slightest occasion and upon the most slender suspicion, were ready to have recourse to arms—enthusiasts, who could not be dissuaded from rash enterprises; sectaries, who employed their consistories and their organized form of church government to levy men, to collect arms, munitions of war, and money—rebels, in fine, who could at any moment rise within an hour, and surprise his most Christian Majesty's cities and provinces. The abrogation of religious liberty was, therefore, not merely advisable, but absolutely necessary. Elizabeth was reminded, also, of her own intolerant measures toward the Roman Catholics of her dominions; and she was assured that her fears of a combined attack on all the Protestants were devoid of foundation—that Charles had neither taken up arms, nor revoked the edicts of toleration at the desire of any other prince, still less because of the instance of any private individuals, but of his own free will, in order to secure his kingdom.[2] These arguments, if they did not convince Elizabeth, gave her a fair excuse for trying to maintain an appearance of non-intervention, which the perilous position of England seemed to her to dictate. With the problem of Scotland and Mary Stuart yet unsolved—with a very considerable part of the lords and commons of her own kingdom scarcely con-

Marginal note: Misgivings of Queen Elizabeth.

---

[1] " A view of a seditious bull sent into England from Pius Quintus, Bishop of Rome, 1569," etc.   Works of Bishop Jewel, edited by R. W. Jelf, vii. 263–265.

[2] Despatch of La Mothe Fénélon, Dec. 5, 1568, detailing the justification of Charles, which he had made in an interview with Queen Elizabeth, Correspondance diplomatique, i. 28–33.

cealing their affection for the Romish faith—she deemed it hazardous to provoke too far the enmity of Philip the Second, her brother-in-law, and a late suitor for her hand. As if any better way could be found of warding off from her island the assaults of Philip than by rendering efficient aid to Condé and Orange! As if England's dissimulation and refusal to support the "Huguenots" and the "Gueux" in any other than an underhand way were likely to retard the sailing of the great expedition that was to turn the Pope's impotent threats against the "bastard of England" into fearful realities! As if Protestantism, everywhere menaced, could hope for glorious success in any other path than a bold and combined defence![1]

Her double-dealing and effrontery.
Unfortunately Elizabeth was fairly launched on a sea of deceitful diplomacy, and not even Cecil could hold her back. She gave La Mothe Fénélon, the French envoy, assurances that would have been most satisfactory could he have closed his eyes to the facts that gave these assurances the lie direct. At one time, with an appearance of sincerity, she told the Spanish ambassador, it is true, that she could not abandon the family of Châtillon, who had long been her friends, whilst she saw the Guises, the declared enemies of her person and state, in such authority, both in the council and the field; that she could not feel herself secure, especially since a member of the French council had inadvertently dropped the hint that, after everything had been settled at home, Charles would turn his arms against England. She had rather, consequently, anticipate than be anticipated.[2] But to La Mothe Fénélon himself she maintained unblushingly that, so far from helping the French Protestants, "there was nothing in the world of which she entertained such horror as of seeing a body

---

[1] Yet no one could speak more courageous words than Elizabeth in her own interests. In December, 1560, she requested the ambassador of Francis II. "to write to his master frankly what she was about to say, viz., that she meant to do her best to defend herself: that she was not of such poverty, nor so void of the obedience of her subjects, but she trusted to be able to do this. *She came of the race of lions, and therefore could not sustain the person of a sheep.*" Communication with the French Ambassador, December 13, 1560, State Paper Office.

[2] Despatch of La Mothe Fénélon, Dec. 21, 1568, Corresp. dipl., i. 55, 56.

rising in rebellion against its head, and that she had no notion
of associating herself with such a monster."[1] And again and
again she protested that she was not intriguing in France—that
she had sent the Huguenots no assistance.[2] At the same time
Admiral Winter had been despatched with four or five ships of
war and a fleet of merchantmen, to carry to La Rochelle, in
answer to the request of Condé and of the Queen of Navarre,
100,000 "angelots" and six pieces of cannon and ammunition.[3] When the ambassador was commissioned to lay before the
queen a remonstrance against this flagrant breach of neutrality,
and to demand an answer, within fifteen days, respecting her
intentions,[4] Elizabeth, in declaring for peace, had the effrontery to assert that the assistance in cannon and powder (for she
denied that any money was left at La Rochelle) was involuntary, not only with her, but even with the admiral himself.
Having dropped into the harbor to obtain the wine and other
commodities with which his fleet of merchantmen were to be
freighted, Admiral Winter was approached by the governor of
the city, who so strongly pressed him to sell or lend them some
pieces of artillery and some powder, which they could not do
without, that, considering that he, as well as the ships, were in
their power, he thought it necessary to comply with a part of
their requests, although it was against his will.[5] Such were the

---

[1] "Qu'elle n'avoit rien en si grand horreur, en ce monde, que de voir ung
corps s'esmouvoir contre sa teste, et qu'elle n'avoit garde de s'adjoindre à ung
tel monstre." Ibid., i. 60.

[2] Ibid., i. 36–130.

[3] Mém. de Castelnau, liv. vii., c. 2; Agrippa d'Aubigné, liv. v., c. 10 (i. 283) ;
De Thou, iv. (liv. xliv.) 160. La Mothe Fénélon's despatch of January 24,
1569 (Corr. dipl. i. 153, 154), states the assistance at 6 cannon and furniture,
300 barrels of powder, 4,000 balls, and £7,000.

[4] Despatch to La Mothe Fénélon, March 8, 1569, and "Articles presentez
à la royne d'Angleterre par le Sr de la Mothe, etc," Corresp. diplom., i. 224,
237–241.

[5] "Considérant luy-mesmes et toute la flotte des marchands estre en leur
pouvoir, il trouva nécessaire pour luy de condescendre en partie à leurs demandes, combien que ce fût contre sa volonté." Coppie du messaige qui a esté
declairé par la Majesté de la Royne et son conseil, par parolle de bouche,
à l'amb. du Roy de France, par Jehan Somer, clerc du signet de sa Majesté
le IIIe jour de mars, 1568. Corresp. diplom., i. 242–251.

paltry falsehoods to which Elizabeth's insincere course naturally
and directly led.   La Mothe Fénélon was well aware that Admiral Winter, besides his public commission, had been furnished with a secret order, authorizing him to assist La Rochelle, signed by Elizabeth's own hand, without which the
wary old seaman absolutely refused to go, doubtless fearing
that he might be sacrificed when it suited his mistress's crooked
policy.   What the order contained was no mystery to the French
envoy.[1]   Neither party in this solemn farce was deceived, but
both wanted peace.   Catharine would have been even more
vexed than surprised had Elizabeth confessed the truth, and so
necessitated a resort to open hostilities.[2]   As the honor of the
government was satisfied, even by the notoriously false story of
Winter's compulsion, there was no necessity for pressing the
question of its veracity to an inconvenient length.

The cold winter of 1568–1569 passed without signal events,
excepting the great mortality among the soldiers of both camps
from an epidemic disease—consequent upon exposure to the
extraordinary severity of the season—and the fruitless siege of
the city of Sancerre by the Roman Catholics.   Five

Fruitless
sieges and   weeks were the troops of Martinengo detained before
plots.
the walls of this small place, whose convenient proximity to the upper Loire rendered it valuable to the Huguenots,
not only as a means of facilitating the introduction of their
expected German auxiliaries into central France, but still more
as a refuge for their allies in the neighboring provinces.   The
bravery of the besieged made them superior to the forces sent
to dislodge them.   They repulsed, with great loss to their enemies,
two successive assaults on different parts of the works, and, at
last, gaining new courage from the advantages they had obtained,
assumed the offensive, and forced Martinengo and the captains
by whom he had been reinforced to retire humiliated from the

---

[1] Despatch of Dec. 5, 1568, Corresp. diplom., i. 32, 33.

[2] In his despatch of March 25, 1569, La Mothe Fénélon admits to Catharine
his great perplexity as to how he should act, so as neither to show too little
spirit nor to provoke Elizabeth to such a declaration as would compel the
king, his master, to declare war at so inopportune a time.   Corresp. diplom.,
i. 281.

hopeless undertaking.[1] Meantime, in not less than three important cities which the Huguenots hoped to gain without striking a blow, the plans of those who were to have admitted the Protestants within the walls failed in the execution; and Dieppe, Havre, and Lusignan remained in the power of the Roman Catholic party.[2]

At the opening of the spring campaign the Prince of Condé found his position relatively to his opponents by no means so favorable as at the close of the previous year. His loss by disease equalled, his loss by desertion exceeded, that of the Duke of Anjou; for it was impossible for troops serving at their own expense, however zealous they might be for the common cause, to be kept together, especially during a season of inaction, so easily as the forces paid out of the royal treasury. Besides this, the Duke of Anjou had received considerable reinforcements. Two thousand two hundred German reiters, under the Rhinegrave and Bassompierre, had arrived in his camp. They were the first division of a force of five thousand six hundred men who had crossed the Rhine, near the end of December, under Philibert, Marquis of Baden, and others. The young Count de Tende brought three thousand foot soldiers from Provence and Dauphiny, and smaller bodies came in from other parts of France.[3] Condé, on the contrary, had received scarcely any accessions to his troops. The "viscounts," whose arrival had turned the scale at the conclusion of the last war, lingered in Guyenne, with an army of six thousand foot soldiers and a well-appointed cavalry force, preferring to protect the Protestant territories about Montauban and Castres, and to ravage the lands of their enemies, as far as to the gates of Toulouse, rather than leave their homes unprotected and join Condé. A dispute respecting precedence had not been without some influence in causing the delay, and M. de Piles, who had been twice sent to urge them forward, had only succeeded in

Growing superiority of Anjou's forces.

---

[1] Jean de Serres, iii. 307, 308; De Thou, iv. (liv. xlv.) 169, 170; Castelnau, liv. vii., c. 3.

[2] De Thou, iv. 171, 172; Castelnau, *ubi supra.*

[3] Jean de Serres, iii. 302, 309; Du Thou, iv. 161; Agrippa d'Aubigné, i. 277.

bringing a corps of one thousand two hundred arquebusiers and
two hundred horse.[1] It was now expected, however, that realizing the vital importance of opposing to Anjou a powerful Protestant army, the viscounts would abandon their short-sighted
policy ; and it was the intention of Condé and Coligny, after
effecting a junction, to march with the combined armies to meet
the Duke of Deux-Ponts. Anticipating this plan, the court had
despatched the Dukes of Aumale and of Nemours to guard the
entrance into France from the side of Germany. There seemed
to be danger that the precaution would prove ineffectual through
the jealousy existing between the two leaders ; but this danger
Catharine attempted to avert by removing the royal court to
Metz, where she could exert her personal influence in reconciling
the ambitious rivals.[2] In order to prevent the threatened union
of Condé and the viscounts, the Duke of Anjou now left his
winter quarters upon the Loire and moved southward. On the
other hand, the Prince of Condé left Niort, and, pursuing a
course nearly parallel, passed through St. Jean d'Angely to
Saintes, thence diverging to Cognac, on the Charente.[3]

The Charente, although by no means one of the largest rivers
of France, well deserves to be called one of the most capricious.
For about a quarter of its length it runs in a north-
westerly direction. At Civray it abruptly turns southward and flows in a meandering course as far as Angoulême, receiving on the way the waters of the Tardouère
(Tardoire), and with it almost completely inclosing a considerable tract of land. At Angoulême, the old whim regaining

*The armies
meet on the
Charente.*

---

[1] De Thou, iv. (liv. xlv.) 174, 175.
[2] The Earl of Leicester gives Charles a more direct part in the war. "The
king hathe bene these two monethes about Metz in Lorrayne, to empeache
the entry of the Duke of Bipounte, who is set forward by the common assent
of all the princes Protestants in Germany, with twelve thousand horsemen,
and twenty-five thousand footemen, to assiste the Protestants in France, and
to make some final end of their garboyles." Letter to Randolph, ambassador
to the Emperor of Muscovy, May 1, 1569, Wright, Queen Elizabeth, i. 313.
The facilities, even for diplomatic correspondence, with so distant a country
as Muscovy, were very scanty. Leicester's despatch is accordingly an interesting résumé of the chief events that had occurred in Western Europe during
the past sixty days.
[3] Agrippa d'Aubigné, i. 277 ; De Thou, iv. 172, etc.

supremacy, the Charente again bends suddenly westward, and finally empties into the ocean below Rochefort, through a narrow arm of the sea known as the Pertuis d'Antioche. The tract of country included between the river and the shores of the Bay of Biscay, comprising a large part of the provinces of Aunis and Saintonge, was in the undisputed possession of the Huguenots. They held the right bank of the river, and controlled the bridges. Here they intended to await the arrival of the viscounts. Jarnac, an important town on this side, a few miles above Cognac, Admiral Coligny with the advance guard of the prince's army had wrested from the enemy. They had also recovered Châteauneuf, a small place situated higher up, and midway between Jarnac and Angoulême.

In pursuance of his plan, the Duke of Anjou, after crossing the Charente near Ruffec, had moved around to the south side, determined to prevent the junction of the two Huguenot armies. Once more Châteauneuf fell into his hands; but the garrison, after retreating to the opposite bank, had destroyed the bridge behind them. This bridge the Roman Catholics set themselves at once to repair. At the same time they began the construction of a bridge of boats in the immediate vicinity. While these constructions were pushed forward with great vigor, the royal army marched down as far as Cognac and made a feint of attack, but retired after drawing from the walls a furious cannonade. It was now that prudence demanded that the Protestant army should withdraw from its advanced position with only the Charente between its vanguard and the far superior forces of the enemy. This was the advice of Coligny and of others in the council of war. But Condé prevented its prompt execution, exclaiming: "God forbid that it should ever be said that a Bourbon fled before his enemies!"[1]

The bridges being now practicable, almost the whole army of Anjou was thrown across the Charente under cover of the dark-

---

[1] "Ja Dieu ne plaise qu'on die jamais que Bourbon ait fuyt devant ses ennemis." Lestoile, 21. It is probably to this circumstance that the Earl of Leicester alludes, when he says that " the Prince of Condé, through his overmuche hardines and little regard to follow the Admirall's advise had his arme broken with a courrire shotte," etc. Wright, Queen Elizabeth, i. 313, 314.

ness, during the night of the twelfth and thirteenth of March,
only a small force remaining on the left bank to protect
Châteauneuf and the passage. So skilfully was this movement
effected that it escaped the observation even of those divisions
of the Protestant army that were close to the point of crossing.
When at length the admiral was advised that the enemy were in
force on the northern bank, he at once issued the order to fall
back toward Condé and the main body of the Huguenots. Unfortunately, the divisions of Coligny's command were scattered;
some had been discontented with the posts assigned them, and
had on their own responsibility exchanged them for others that
better suited their fancy. The very command to concentrate
was obeyed with little promptness, and the afternoon was more
than half spent before Coligny, and D'Andelot, who was with
him, could begin the retreat. Never was dilatoriness more ill-
timed. The handful of men with the admiral, near the abbey
and hamlet of Bassac, fought with desperation, but
could not ward off the superior numbers of the enemy.

Battle of Jar-
nac, March
13, 1569.

La Noue, in command of the extreme rear, with great
courage drove back the foremost of the Roman Catholics, but
was soon overpowered and taken prisoner. His men were
thrown in disorder upon D'Andelot, who, by an almost superhuman effort, not only sustained the shock, but retook and for
a short time held the abbey. D'Andelot was, however, in turn
forced to yield the ground.

Meantime Coligny had called upon Condé for assistance, and
the prince, leaving his infantry to follow, had hurried back with
the few horse that were within reach, and now took position on
the left. But it was impossible for so unequal a struggle to
continue long. The Huguenots were outflanked and almost enclosed between their adversaries and the Charente. It was a
time for desperate and heroic venture. Coligny's forces had
lost the ground which they had been contesting inch by inch
about a raised causeway.

Condé himself had but three hundred knights. One of his
arms he carried in a sling, because of a recent injury. To
render his condition yet more deplorable, his thigh had just
been broken, as he rode up, by a kick from the unmanageable

horse of his brother-in-law, La Rochefoucauld. The prince was
no coward. Turning to his little company of followers, he exclaimed: "My friends, true noblesse of France, here is the
opportunity we have long wished for in vain! Our God is the
God of Battles. He loves to be so called. He always declares
Himself for the right, and never fails to succor those who serve
Him. He will infallibly protect us, if, after having taken up
arms for the liberty of our consciences, we put all our hope in
Him. Come and let us complete what the first charges have
begun; and remember in what a state Louis of Bourbon entered
into the combat for Christ and for his native land!" Thus
having spoken, he bent forward, and, at the head of his devoted
band, and under an ensign bearing for device the figure of the
Roman hero Marcus Curtius and the singularly appropriate
motto, "Doux le peril pour Christ et le Pays," he dashed upon
a hostile battalion eight hundred strong.[1]

The conflict was, in the judgment of that scarred old Huguenot warrior, Agrippa d'Aubigné, the sharpest and most obstinate
in all the civil wars.[2] At last Condé's horse was killed under
him, and the prince was unable to extricate himself. The day
was evidently lost, and Condé, calling two of the enemies'
knights with whom he was acquainted, and the life of one of
whom he had on a former occasion saved, raised his visor, made
himself known, and surrendered. His captors pledged him
their word that his life should be spared, and respectfully endeavored to raise him from the ground. Just at that moment
another horseman rode up. It was Montesquiou, captain of
Anjou's guards, who came directly from his master, and was
charged—so it was said—with a secret commission. He drew a
Death of   pistol as he approached, and, without inquiring into
Louis, Prince the terms of the capture, shot Condé in the back.
of Condé.   The shot penetrated between the joints of his armor,
and caused almost instantaneous death.

---

[1] Agrippa d'Aubigné, Hist. univ., liv. v., c. 8 (i. 280); De Thou, iv. 175.

[2] D'Aubigné, ubi supra. A Huguenot patriarch, named La Vergne, was
noticed by Agrippa himself fighting in the midst of twenty-five of his nephews
and kinsmen. The dead bodies of the old man and of fifteen of his followers
fell almost on a single heap, and nearly all the survivors were taken prisoners.

So perished a prince even more illustrious for his courage
and intrepidity than for his exalted rank—a prince who had
conscientiously espoused the reformed faith, and had felt himself constrained by his duty to his God and to his fellow-
believers to assert the rights of the oppressed Huguenots against
illegal persecution. "Our consolation," wrote Jeanne d'Albret a
few weeks later, "is that he died on the true bed of honor, both
for body and soul, for the service of his God and his king, and
the quiet of his fatherland."[1] So magnanimous a hero could
not be insensible to the invasion of his claims as the representative of the family next in the succession to the Valois; but
I cannot agree with those who believe that, in his assumption of
arms in three successive wars, he was influenced solely, or even
principally, by selfish or ambitious motives. His devotion to
the cause which he had espoused was sincere and whole-souled.
If his love of pleasure was a serious blot upon his character, let
charity at least reflect upon the fearful corruption of the court
in which he had been living from his childhood, and remember that if Condé yielded too readily to its fascinations, and
fell into shameful excesses, he yet bore with meekness the
pointed remonstrances of faithful friends, and in the end shook
off the chains with which his enemies had endeavored to bind
him fast.[2] As a soldier, no one could surpass Condé for bra-

[1] Jeanne d'Albret to Marie de Clèves, April, 1569, Rochambeau, Lettres
d'Antoine de Bourbon et de Jehanne d'Albret (Paris, 1877), 297.

[2] I regret to say that the current representations as to the termination of
Condé's dishonorable attachment to Isabeau de Limueil are proved by contemporary documents to be erroneous. The tears and remonstrances of his wife
Éléonore de Roye (see *ante*, chapter xiv.) may have had some temporary effect.
But an anonymous letter among the Simancas MSS., written March 15, 1565
(and consequently more than six months after Éléonore's death, which occurred
July 23, 1564), portrays him as " hora più che mai passionato per la sua Limo-
lia." Duc d'Aumale, Pièces justif., i. 552. Just as Calvin (letter of September 17, 1563, Bonnet, Lettres franç., ii. 539) had rebuked the prince with his
customary frankness, warning him respecting his conduct, and saying that
" les bonnes gens en seront offenséz, les malins en feront leur risée," so now
Coligny and the Huguenot gentlemen of his suite united with the Protestant
ministers in begging him to renounce his present course of life, and contract
a second honorable marriage. The latter held up to him "il pericolo et
infamia propria, et il scandalo commune a tutta la relligione per esserne lui
capo ; " the former threatened to leave him. I have seen no injurious reports

very.[1] If his abilities as a general were not of the very first
order, he had at least the good sense to adopt the plans of Gaspard de Coligny, the true hero of the first three civil wars. The
relations between these two men were well deserving of admiration. On the part of Condé there was an entire absence of jealousy of the resplendent abilities and well-earned reputation of
the admiral. On the part of Coligny there was an equal freedom from desire to supplant the prince either in the esteem of
his followers or in military rank. Coligny was inflexible in his
determination to accept no honors or distinctions that might
appear to prejudice the respect due by a Châtillon to a prince
of royal blood.[2]

The Prince of Condé was, unfortunately, not the only Huguenot leader murdered in cold blood at the battle of Jarnac.
Chastelier-Pourtaut de Latour, who, having lately brought his
flotilla back in safety to La Rochelle, had hastened to take the
field with the Protestants, was recognized after his capture as
the same nobleman who, five years before, had killed the Sieur
de Charry at Paris, and was killed in revenge by some of
Charry's friends. Robert Stuart, the brave leader descended
from the royal house of Scotland, who was said to have slain
Constable Montmorency in the battle of St. Denis, was assassinated after he had been talking with the Duke of Anjou,
within hearing and almost in sight of the duke, by one of the
constable's adherents.[3]

These flagrant violations of good faith incurred severe ani-

affecting Condé's morals after his marriage, November 8, 1565, to Françoise
Marie d'Orléans Longueville. Duc d'Aumale, Princes de Condé, i. 263-278.

[1] Long the idol of the Huguenots, both of high or of low degree, he enjoyed
a popularity perpetuated in a spirited song (" La Chanson du Petit Homme "),
current so far back as the close of the first war, 1563, the refrain of which,
alluding to the prince's diminutive stature, is: "*Dieu gard' de mal le Petit
Homme!*" Chansonnier Huguenot, 250, etc.

[2] The author of the Vie de Coligny (Cologne, 1686) gives more than one
instance of a deference on the part of the subject of his biography which may
seem to the reader excessive, but which alone could satisfy the chivalrous
feeling of the loyal knight of the sixteenth century.

[3] Brantôme (Hommes illustres, Œuvres, viii. 163, 164) relates that Honorat
de Savoie, Count of Villars, begged the Duke of Anjou to have Stuart given
over to him, and, having gained his request, murdered him.

madversion. A letter is extant, written by young Prince Henry
of Navarre, or in his name, to Henry of Anjou, on
the twelfth of July, 1569, about four months after the
battle of Jarnac. He begins by answering the asper-
sions cast upon his mother and himself, and by asserting that, if his age (which, however, is not much less than that
of Anjou) disqualifies him from passing a judgment upon the
present state of affairs, he has lived long enough to recognize
the instigators of the new troubles as the enemies of the public
weal. It is not Henry of Navarre, whose honors and dignities
are all dependent upon the preservation of France, who seeks
the ruin of the kingdom; but, rather, they seek its ruin who,
in their eagerness to usurp the crown, have gone the length of
making genealogical searches to prove their possession of a title
superior to that of the Valois, "and have learned how to sell
the blood of the house of France against itself,[1] *constraining
the king*, as it were, *to make use of his left arm to cut off his
right*, so as more easily to wrest his sceptre from him afterward." In reply to the statement of Anjou that Stuart alone
was killed in cold blood, Henry of Navarre affirms that he can
enumerate many others.[2] " But I shall content myself with
merely reminding you of the manner in which the late Prince
of Condé was treated, inasmuch as it touches you, Sir, and
because it is a matter well known and free of doubt. For his
death has left to posterity an example of as noted treachery,
bad faith and cruelty as was ever shown, seeing that those, Sir,
who murdered him could not be deterred from the perpetration
of so wicked an act by the respect they owed to the greatness
of your blood, to which he had the honor of being so nearly

Henry of Navarre remonstrates against the perfidy.

---

[1] " Qui par artifices merveilleusement subtils ont bien sceu vandre le sang
de la maison de France contre soy-mesmes." ·

[2] The Earl of Leicester wrote to Randolph : " Robert Stuart, Chastellier,
and certaine other worthy gentlemen, to the number of six, were lykewise
taken and slayne, as the Frenche tearme it, de sang froid." Wright, Queen
Elizabeth, i. 314. See also Cardinal Châtillon's letter to the Elector Palatine, June 10, 1569, in which the writer declares significantly of Condé's
murder by Montesquiou, " ce qu'il n'eust osé entreprendre sans en avoir
commandement *des plus grands*." Kluckholn, Briefe Friedrich des Frommen, ii. 336.

related, and that they dealt with him as they would have done
with the most miserable soldier of the whole army." [1]

The Huguenot loss in the battle of Jarnac was surprisingly
small in the number of men killed.   It is probable that, including prisoners, they lost about four hundred men, or about twice
as many as the Roman Catholics.[2]   But the loss was in effect
much more considerable.   The dead and the prisoners were the
flower of the French nobility.   Among those that had fallen
into the enemy's hands were the bastard son of Antoine of
Navarre, François de la Noue, Soubise, La Loue, and others of
nearly equal distinction.   Of infantry the Huguenot army lost
but few men, as the regiments, with the exception of that of
Pluviaut, did not enter the engagement at all.   Coming up too
late, and finding themselves in danger of falling into the hands
of the enemy's victorious cavalry, they evacuated Jarnac, crossed
to the left bank of the Charente, and, after breaking down the
bridge, retreated leisurely toward Cognac.   Admiral Coligny,
meantime, upon whom the command in chief now devolved,
diverged to the right, and conducted the cavalry in safety to
Saintes.   The Roman Catholic army, apparently satisfied with
the success it had gained, made no attempt at pursuit.

The Duke of Anjou entered Jarnac in triumph.   With him
was brought the corpse of the Prince of Condé, tied to an ass's
back, to be afterward exposed by a pillar of the house where
Anjou lodged—the butt of the sneers and low wit of the sol-

---

[1] Letter of Henry of Navarre to the Duke of Anjou, " escript au Camp
d'Availle le xii⁰ jour de juillet 1569." Lettres inédites de Henry IV. re-
cueillies par le Prince Augustin Galitzin (Paris, 1860), 4–11.

[2] The Huguenot loss is given by Jean de Serres (iii. 316) at 200 killed and
40 taken prisoners. Agrippa d'Aubigné states it at 140 gentilhommes (Hist.
univ., i. 280). The Earl of Leicester's words are : " In which conflicte was
slayne on both sydes, as we heare, not above foure hundred men " (Wright.
Queen Elizabeth, i. 313, 314). Castelnau speaks of over a hundred Huguenot
gentlemen slain and an equal number taken prisoners (liv. vii., c. 4). The
" Adviz donné par Mᵣ Norrys, ambassadeur pour la royne d'Angleterre, prins
de ses lettres, envoyées de Metz, le 18 d'Avril " (La Mothe Fénélon, i. 362),
agrees with Leicester, but is unique in making Anjou's loss greater than that
of the Huguenots. De Thou makes the Protestants lose 400. The untruth-
ful Davila says, " the Huguenots lost not above seven hundred men, but they
were most of them gentlemen and cavaliers of note."

diers.[1] In the first glow of exultation over a victory, the real
credit of which belonged to Gaspard de Tavannes,[2] Anjou contemplated erecting a chapel on the spot where Condé fell. The
better counsels of M. de Carnavalet, however, induced him to
abandon a design which would have confirmed all the sinister
rumors respecting his complicity in the assassination.[3] The
prince's dead body was given up for interment to the Prince
of Navarre, and found a resting-place in the ancestral tomb at
Vendôme.[4]

Henry of Anjou was not inclined to suffer his victory to pass
unnoticed. Almost as soon as the smoke of battle had
cleared away, a careful description of his exploit was
prepared for circulation, and it was no fault of the compiler if

Exaggerated bulletins.

---

[1] Agrippa d'Aubigné, i. 281. La Fosse and others have preserved one of
the good Catholic stanzas composed on this occasion :

> L'an mil cinq cent soixante et neuf
> Entre Congnac et Châteauneuf
> Fust apporté sur une ânesse
> Le grand ennemi de la messe.
>
> (Journal d'un curé ligueur, 104.)

[2] " On donna l'honneur de cette défaicte à M. de Tavannes." La Fosse, 104.

[3] De Thou, iv. (liv. xlv.) 177. Claude de Sainctes, afterward Bishop of
Evreux, who, it will be remembered, figured at the colloquy of Poissy, is
credited with the suggestion of the chapel.

[4] The principal authorities consulted for the battle of Jarnac, or of Bassac,
as it is also frequently called, from the abbey near which it raged, are : Jean
de Serres, iii. 309–315 ; De Thou, iv. (liv. xlv.) 173–176 ; Castelnau, liv. vii.,
c. 4; Ag. d'Aubigné, i. 278–281 ; Le vray discours de la bataille donnée par
monsieur le 13. iour de Mars, 1569, entre Chasteauneuf et Jarnac, etc., avec
privilege (Cimber et Danjou, Archives curieuses, vi. 365, etc.) ; Discours de la
bataille donnée par Monseigneur, Duc d'Anjou et de Bourbonnoys, . . .
contre les rebelles . . . entre la ville d'Angoulesme et Jarnac, près d'une
maison nommée Vibrac appartenant à la Dame de Mezières; an inaccurate
official account, drawn up at Metz by Neufville on the first reception of the
news, and sent by the Spanish ambassador, Alava, to Philip II. ; La Mothe
Fénélon, Corr. dip., vii. 3–11 ; Davila, bk. iv. ; the " Relation originale " in
Documents inédits tirés des coll. MSS. de la bibliothèque royale (Fr. gov.),
iv. 483, etc. Compare the excellent narratives of the Duc d'Aumale and
Prof. Soldan. The Bulletin de la Soc. de l'hist. du prot. fr., i. (1853) 429, gives
a representation of a monument, in the form of an obelisk, about eleven feet
in height, erected by the Department of the Charente, in 1818, on the spot
where Condé fell. A somewhat similar monument, raised in 1770 by the
Count de Jarnac, was destroyed during the first French revolution.

the account he gave was not sufficiently flattering to the young prince's vanity. Condé's body had not been four days in the hands of the Roman Catholics, before Anjou wrote to his brother, the King of France, announcing the fact that he had already despatched messengers with the precious document to the Pope and the Duke of Florence, to the Dukes of Savoy, Ferrara, Parma, and Urbino, to the Republic of Venice and the Duke of Mantua, and to Philip of Spain; while copies were also under way, intended for the French ambassadors in England and Switzerland, for the Parliaments of Paris, Bordeaux, and Toulouse, the "prevôt des marchands," and the "échevins" of the capital, and others.[1]

The exaggerated bulletins of the Duke of Anjou were received with great demonstrations of joy by all the Roman Catholic allies of France. Pope Pius the Fifth in particular sent warm congratulations to the "Most Christian King" and to Catharine de' Medici. But he was very careful to couple his expressions of thanks with an earnest recommenda- tion to pursue the work so auspiciously begun, even to the extermination of the detested heretics. "The more kindly God has dealt with you and us," he promptly wrote to Charles, "the more vigorously and diligently must you make use of the present victory to pursue and destroy the remnants of the enemy, and wholly tear up, not only the roots of an evil so great and which had gathered to itself such strength, but even *the very fibres* of the roots. Unless they be thoroughly extirpated, they will again sprout and grow up (as we have so often heretofore seen happen), where your Majesty least expects it." Pius pledged his word that Charles would succeed in his undertaking, "if no respect for men or for human considerations should be powerful enough to induce him to spare God's enemies, who had spared neither God nor him." "In no other way," he added, "will you be able to appease God, than by avenging the injuries done to God with the utmost severity, by the merited punishment of most accursed men." And he set as a warning before the

The Pope's sanguinary injunctions.

---

[1] Anjou to Charles IX., March 17, 1569, Duc d'Aumale, Les Princes de Condé, ii. 399.

eyes of the French monarch the example of King Saul, who,
when commanded by God, through Samuel the Prophet, so to
smite the Amalekites, an infidel people, that none should escape,
neither man nor woman, neither infant nor suckling, incurred
the anger and rejection of the Almighty by sparing Agag and
the best of the spoil, instead of utterly destroying them.[1]

Two weeks later the pontiff received the unwelcome tidings
that some of the Huguenot prisoners taken in the battle of
Jarnac had been spared. La Noue, Soubise, and other gentlemen had actually been left alive, and were likely to escape without paying the forfeit due to their crimes. At this dreadful
intelligence the righteous indignation of Pius was kindled. On
one and the same day (the thirteenth of April) he wrote long
letters to Catharine, to Anjou, to the Cardinal of Lorraine, to
the Cardinal of Bourbon, as well as to Charles himself.[2] Of all
these letters the tenor was identical. Such slackness to execute
vengeance would certainly provoke God's patience to anger;
the king must visit condign punishment upon the enemies of
God and the rebels against his own authority. To the victor
of Jarnac he was specially urgent, supplicating him to counteract any leanings that might be shown to an impious mercy.
" Your brother's rebels have disturbed the public tranquillity of
the realm. They have, so far as in them lay, subverted the
Catholic religion, have burned churches, have most cruelly slain
the priests of Almighty God, have committed numberless other
crimes; consequently they deserve to receive those extreme
penalties (*supplicia*) that are ordained by the laws. And if any
of their number shall attempt, through the intercession of your
nobles with the king your brother, to escape the penalties they
deserve, it is your duty, in view of your piety to God and zeal
for the divine honor, to reject the prayers of all that intercede
for them, and to show yourself equally inexorable to all." [3]

Was it in consequence of the known desire of the occupant
of the Holy See that the policy of the French courts of justice

---

[1] Apostolicarum Pii Quinti, P. M., Epistolarum libri quinque.   Antverpiæ,
1640, 152.
[2] Pii Quinti Epist., 157–166.
[3] Ibid., 160, 161.

became more and more sanguinary ? We can scarcely doubt that
the Pope's injunctions had much to do with these increasing severities. Beginning in March, 1569, the
Parliament of Bordeaux issued a series of decrees
condemning a crowd of Protestants to death. The
names that appear upon the records within the compass of one
year number not less than *twelve hundred and seventeen*. The
victims were taken out of all grades of society—from noblemen,
military men, judges, priests and monks, down to humble
mechanics and laborers. The lists made out by their enemies
prove at least one fact which the Huguenots had long maintained : that they counted in their ranks representatives of the
first families of the country, as well as of every other class of
the population. Happily sentence was pronounced generally
upon the absent, and the barbarous punishment of beheading,
quartering, and exposing to the popular gaze, remained unexecuted. But the incidental penalty of the confiscation of the
property of reputed Huguenots, which, so far from being a
mere formal threat, was in fact the principal object contemplated by the prosecution, proved to be sober reality, and the goods
of the banished Protestants afforded rich plunder to the informers.[1]

The sanguinary action of the Parliament of Bordeaux.

Upon Elizabeth of England the first effect of the reported
victory at Jarnac was clearly marked. Her favorite, the Earl
of Leicester, assured the French ambassador that, although the queen was sorry to see those professing
her religion maltreated, yet, as queen, she would arm
in behalf of Charles when fighting against his own subjects.[2]
Her own declarations, however, were not so strong, or perhaps,
after a little reflection, she took a more hopeful view of the
fortunes of the Huguenots. For, although she exhibited curiosity to hear the "true" account, which a special messenger
from Charles the Ninth was commissioned to bring her, and received the tidings in a manner satisfactory to the French am-

Queen Eliza-beth becomes colder.

---

[1] Boscheron des Portes, Hist. du Parlement de Bordeaux (Bordeaux, 1877),
i. 214, 216. As the Huguenots were condemned, not for heresy, but for rebellion, sacrilege, etc., the learned author finds no mention of fagot and flame.

[2] La Mothe Fénélon, i. 288–294.

bassador, she would not rejoice at the death of Condé, whom she held to be a very good and faithful servant of his Majesty's crown, and deplored a war which, whether victory inclined to one side or the other, must lead to the diminution of Charles's best forces and the ruin of his noblesse.[1]

In point of fact, however, the defeat which the royalists had flattered themselves would terminate the war, and over which they had sung Te Deums, weakened the Huguenots very little.[2]

Spirit of the Queen of Navarre.

The Queen of Navarre, on hearing the intelligence, hurried to Cognac, where she presented herself to the army, and reminded the brave men who heard her voice that, although the Prince of Condé, their late leader, was dead, the good cause was not dead; and that the courage of such good men ought never to fail. God had provided, and ever would provide, fresh instruments to uphold His own chosen work. Her brief address restored the flagging spirits of the fugitives. When she returned to La Rochelle, to devise new means of supplying the necessities of the army, she left behind her men resolved to retrieve their recent losses. They did not wait long for an opportunity. The Roman Catholics, advancing, laid siege to Cognac, confident of easy success. But the garrison, which included seven thousand infantry newly levied, received them with determination. Sallies were frequent and bloody, and when, at last, the siege was raised, the army of Anjou had sacrificed nearly as many men before the walls of a small provincial city as the Huguenots had lost on the much vaunted field of Jarnac.[3]

The events of the next two or three months certainly exhibited no diminution in the power or in the spirit of the

---

[1] Despatch of April 12, 1569, ibid., i. 303.

[2] It is evident that the results of the battle were designedly exaggerated by the Roman Catholics at the time, and have been overrated ever since. Agrippa d' Aubigné alleges that, out of 128 cornets of cavalry in the Huguenot army, only fifteen were engaged; and that of over 200 ensigns of infantry, barely *six*—those under Pluviaut—came within a league of the battlefield. Hist. univ., *ubi supra*.

[3] Jean de Serres, iii. 317, 318 ; De Thou, iv. (liv. xlv.) 178, 179. De Thou reckons the losses of the Roman Catholics before Cognac at more than 300 men.

Huguenots.   St. Jean d'Angely, into which Count Montgomery

The Hugue-
nots recover
strength.
had thrown himself, defied the entire army of Anjou, and the siege was abandoned.   Angoulême, an equally tempting morsel, he tried to obtain, but failed.   At Mucidan, a town somewhat to the southwest of Périgueux, he was more successful.   But he effected its capture at the expense of the life of Brissac, one of his bravest officers —a loss which he attempted to avenge by murdering the garrison, after it had surrendered on condition that life and property should be spared.[1]   Within a month or two after the battle of Jarnac the Protestants at La Rochelle wrote, for Queen Elizabeth's information, that they were more powerful than ever, that Piles had brought them 4,000 recruits, that D'Andelot was soon to bring the viscounts with a large force.[2]

But the course of that indefatigable warrior was now run. D'Andelot's excessive labors and constant exposure had brought on a fever to which his life soon succumbed.   There were not wanting those, it is true, who ascribed his sudden death, like most of the deaths of important personages in the latter part of

Death of
D'Andelot.
this century, to poison ; and Huguenot and loyal pamphleteers alike laid the crime at the door of Catharine de' Medici.[3]   But there is no sufficient evidence to

---

[1] De Thou, iv. 180, 181; Agrippa d'Aubigné, i. 282 ; J. de Serres, iii. 318, 319.

[2] La Mothe Fénélon, i. 367.   And now, to the insulting *quatrain* already quoted à propos of Condé's death, the Huguenot soldiers of Angoumois replied in rough verses of their own :

> Le Prince de Condé
> Il a été tué ;
> Mais Monsieur l'Amiral
> Est encore à cheval,
> Avec La Rochefoucauld
> Pour achever tous ces Papaux.

V. Bujeaud, Chronique protestante de l'Angoumois, 40.

[3] Discours merveilleux de la vie de Catherine de Medicis (Cologne, 1683), 645.   See the atrocious letter to Catharine, which the queen found upon her bed, Nov. 8, 1575, and which purports to have been written from Lausanne. In the copy published by Le Laboureur (ii. 425–429), it is signed "Grand Champ ; " in that which the editor of Claude Haton gives in an appendix (p. 1111–1115) the name is " Emille Dardani."   The date is doubtful.   Le Labou-

substantiate the accusation, and we must not unnecessarily
ascribe this base act to a woman already responsible for too
many undeniable crimes.[1] The death of so gallant and true-
hearted a nobleman, a faithful and unflinching friend of the
Reformation from the time when it first began to spread exten-
sively among the higher classes of the French population, and
who had amply atoned for a momentary act of weakness, in the
time of Henry the Second, by an uncompromising profession
of his religion on every occasion during the reigns of that monarch's two sons, was deeply felt by his comrades in arms. As
"colonel-general of the French infantry," he had occupied the
first rank in this branch of the service,[2] and his experience
was as highly prized as his impetuous valor upon the field of
battle. The brilliancy of his executive abilities seemed to all
beholders indispensable to complement the more calm and deliberative temperament of his elder brother. It was natural,
therefore, that the admiral, while pouring out his private grief
for one who had been so dear to him, in a touching letter to
D'Andelot's children,[3] should experience as deep a sorrow for

reur is apparently more correct in giving it as "le troisième mois de la qua-
trième année après la trahison" (St. Bartholomew's Day).

[1] The Vie de Coligny (Cologne, 1686), p. 360, 361, says nothing to indicate
that the author regarded D'Andelot's death as other than natural. But Hotman's Gasparis Colinii Vita (1575), p. 75, mentions the suspicion, and considers
it confirmed by the saying attributed to Birague, afterward chancellor, that
"the war would never be terminated by arms alone, but that it might be
brought to a close very easily by *cooks*." Cardinal Châtillon, in a letter to the
Elector Palatine, June 10, 1569, alludes to his brother's having died of poison
as a well-ascertained fact, "comme il est apparent tant par l'anatomie," etc.
Kluckholn, Briefe Frederick des Frommen, ii. 336.

[2] Since the outbreak of the present war, the court had undertaken to
deprive D'Andelot of his rank, and had divided his duties between Brissac and
Strozzi. Brissac had been killed, and Strozzi was now recognized by the court
as colonel-general.

[3] The letter written from Saintes, May 18, 1569, is inserted in Gasparis Colinii
Vita (1575) pp. 75–78, the author remarking, "quam ipsius manum, atque
chirographum præ manibus jam habeo." The possession of so many family
manuscripts on the part of the anonymous writer of this valuable contemporary account, is explained by the fact that he was no other than the distinguished Francis Hotman, in whose hands the admiral's widow, Jaqueline d'Entremont, or Antremont, had placed all the documents she possessed, entreating
him to undertake the pious task of compiling a life of her husband. In a re-

the loss of his wise and efficient co-operation. He might be pardoned a little despondency as he recalled the prophetic words that had dropped from D'Andelot's lips during a brief respite from his burning fever: "France shall have many woes to suffer with you, and then without you; but all will in the end fall upon the Spaniard!"[1] The prospect was not bright. Peace was yet far distant—peace, which Coligny preferred a thousand times to his own life, but would not purchase dishonorably by the sacrifice of civil liberty and of the right to worship his God according to the convictions of his heart and conscience. The burden of the defence of the Protestants had appeared sufficiently heavy when Condé, a prince of the blood, was alive to share it with him. But now, with the entire charge of maintaining the party against a powerful and determined enemy, who had the advantage of the possession of the person of the king, and thus was able to cloak his ambitious designs with the pretence of the royal authority, and deprived of a brother whom the army had appropriately surnamed "le chevalier sans peur,"[2] the task might well appear to demand herculean strength.

Henry of Navarre had, indeed, just been recognized as general-in-chief, and he was accompanied by his cousin, Henry of Condé; but Navarre was a boy of little more than

New responsibility imposed on Admiral Coligny.

fifteen, and his cousin was not much older. Nothing could for the present be expected from such striplings; and the public, ever ready to look upon the comical side of even the most serious matters, was not slow in nicknaming them the "admiral's two pages."[3] Coligny, however, was not crushed by the new responsibility which devolved upon him. No longer

---

markable letter which has but lately come to light, dated January 15, 1572 (new style 1573), after an exordium full of those classical allusions of which the age was so fond, she writes: "Ne trouvez étrange, je vous supplie, si j'ai essayé de réveiller vostre plume pour laisser à la postérité autant de témoignages de la vertu de feu monseigneur et mari, que nos ennemis la veulent désigner," etc. Bulletin, vi. 29.

[1] "La France aura beaucoup de maux avec vous, et puis sans vous; mais en fin tout tombera sur l'Espagnol." Agrippa d'Aubigné, i. 283.

[2] Agrippa d'Aubigné, ubi supra.

[3] Berger de Xivrey, Lettres missives de Henri IV. (Paris, 1843), i. 7.

hampered by the authority of one whose counsels often verged
on foolhardiness, he soon exhibited his consummate abilities so
clearly, that even his enemies were forced to acknowledge that
they had never given him the credit he deserved. "It was
soon perceived," observes an author by no means friendly to
the Huguenots, "that the accident (of Condé's death) had
happened only in order to reveal in all its splendor the merits
of the Admiral de Châtillon. The admiral had had during
his entire life very difficult and complicated matters to unravel,
and, nevertheless, he had never had any that were not far below his abilities, and in which, consequently, he had no need
of exerting his full capacity. Thus those qualities that were
rarest, and that exalted him most above others, remained hidden, through lack of opportunity, and would apparently have
remained always concealed during the lifetime of the Prince of
Condé, because the world would have attributed to the prince
all those results to whose accomplishment it could not learn that
the admiral had contributed more than had the former. But,
after the battle of Jarnac had permitted the admiral to exhibit
himself fully on the most famous theatre of Europe, the Calvinists perceived that they were not so unhappy as they thought,
since they still had a leader who would prevent them from
noticing the loss they had experienced, so many singular qualities had he to repair it."[1]

Wolfgang, Duke of Deux Ponts, had at length entered France,
and was bringing to the Huguenots their long-expected succor.

The Duke of
Deux Ponts
comes with
German aux-
iliaries.
He had seven thousand five hundred reiters from
lower Germany, six thousand lansquenets from upper
Germany, and a body of French and Flemish gentle-
men, under William of Orange and his brother, Mouy,
Esternay and others, which may have swelled his army to about

---

[1] Histoire de Charles IX. par le sieur Varillas (Cologne, 1686), ii. 161, 162.
I am glad to embrace this opportunity of quoting a historian in whose statements of facts I have as seldom the good fortune to concur as in his general
deductions of principles. M. de Thou (iv. 182) remarks in a similar spirit:
" Il fit voir à la France (et ses ennemis même en convinrent) qu'il étoit capable
de soutenir lui seul tout le parti Protestant dont on croyoit auparavant qu'il
ne soutenoit qu'une partie."

seventeen thousand men in all.[1] In vain did his cousin, the Duke of Lorraine, attempt to dissuade him, offering to reimburse him the one hundred thousand crowns he had already spent upon the preparations for the expedition. Even Condé's death did not discourage him. He came, he said, to fight, not for the prince, but for "the cause."[2] When about entering his Most Christian Majesty's dominions, he had published the reasons of his coming to assist the Huguenots. In this paper he treated as pure calumnies the accusations brought by their enemies against Condé, Coligny, and their associates, and proved his position by quoting the king's own express declaration, in the recent edicts of pacification, " that he recognized everything they had attempted as undertaken by his orders and for the good of the kingdom." [3] The point was certainly well taken. Charles's various declarations were not remarkably consistent. In one, Condé was "his faithful servant and subject," and his acts were prompted by the purest of motives. In the next, he and his fellow-Huguenots were incorrigible rebels, with whom every method of conciliation had signally failed. But Charles did not trouble himself to attempt to smooth away these contradictions. He is even said to have replied to the envoy whom Deux Ponts sent him (April, 1569), demanding the restitution of the Edict of January and the payment of thirty thousand crowns due to Prince Casimir, that " Deux Ponts was too insignificant a personage (*trop petit compagnon*) to undertake to dictate laws to him, and that, as to the money, he would deliberate about *that* when the duke had laid down his arms." [4]

---

[1] Ranke (Civil Wars and Monarchy), 241 ; the statement of Jean de Serres, iii. 325, would make the total number a little larger ; the accounts of Agrippa d'Aubigné, i. 285, and De Thou, iv. 185, make it somewhat smaller.

[2] Adviz, etc., La Mothe Fénélon, i. 363.

[3] De Thou, iv. 184 ; Jean de Serres, iii. 320–323. This was in February. It was the more natural for Wolfgang to defend his course, as he was himself an ancient ally of the King of Spain. In the Papiers d'état du card. de Granvelle, ix. 567, we have the text of a compact formed Oct. 1, 1565 : " Lettres de Service accordées par le roi d'Espagne à Wolfgang, comte Palatin et duc de Deux Ponts." According to this document, the duke was bound for three years to obey Philip's summons, although he refused to pledge himself to do anything directly or indirectly against the Augsburg Confession or its supporters.

[4] Journal d'un curé ligueur (Jehan de la Fosse), 104.

The secret of this arrogant demeanor is found in the fact that the court believed it impossible for the Germans to join Coligny. Even so late as the middle of May, when Deux Ponts had penetrated to Autun in Burgundy, Charles regarded the attempt as well nigh hopeless. The fortunes of the Huguenots were desperate. "There remains for them as their last resort," he wrote to one of his ambassadors, "but the single hope that the Duke of Deux Ponts will venture so far as to go to find them where they are. But there is little likelihood that an army of strangers, pursued by another of about equal strength—an army destitute of cities of its own, without means of passing the rivers, favored by no one in my kingdom, dying of hunger, so often harassed and put to inconvenience—should be able to make so long a journey without being lost and dissipated of itself, even had I no forces to combat it." "The duke," continued the king, "will soon repent of his mad project of entering France, and attempting to cross the Loire, where such good provision has been made to obstruct him." [1]

Charles had not exaggerated the difficulties of the undertaking; but Deux Ponts, under the blessing of Heaven, surmounted them all. The discord between Aumale and Nemours rendered weak and useless an army that might, in the hands of a single skilful general, have checked or annihilated him. [2] Mouy and his French comrades were good guides. The Loire was reached, while Aumale and Nemours followed at a respectful distance. Guerchy, an officer lately belonging to Coligny's army, discovered a ford by which a part of the Germans crossed. The main body laid siege to the town of La Charité, which was soon reduced (on the twentieth of May), the Huguenots thus gaining a bridge and stronghold that proved of great utility for their future operations. Six days

They overcome all obstacles and join Coligny.

---

[1] Letter of Charles IX. to La Mothe Fénélon, May 14, 1569, Corresp. dipl., vii. 20, 21. The same incredulity respecting the possibility of Deux Ponts's enterprise is expressed by the anonymous author of a memorandum of a journey through France, in Documents inédits tirés des MSS. de la bibl. royale, iv. 493. It is alluded to in the "Remonstrance" of the Protestant princes presented after the junction of the armies. Jean de Serres, iii. 337.

[2] Castelnau, liv. vii., c. 5.

after the king had demonstrated the impossibility of the enterprise, Deux Ponts was on the western side of the Loire.[1] Meantime, Coligny and La Rochefoucauld were advancing to meet
him with the élite of their army and with all the artillery they
had. On approaching Limoges on the Vienne, they learned
that the Germans had crossed the river and were but two
leagues distant. Coligny at once took horse, and rode to their
encampment, in order to greet and congratulate their leader.
He was too late. The general, who had conducted an army
Death of   five hundred miles through a hostile country, was in
Deux Ponts.   the last agonies of death, and on the next day (the
eleventh of June) fell a victim to a fever from which he had for
some time been suffering. "It is a thing that ought for all time
to be remarked as a singular and special act of God," said a bulletin sent by the Queen of Navarre to Queen Elizabeth, "that
He permitted this prince to traverse so great an extent of country, with a great train of artillery, infantry, and baggage, and in
full view of a large army; and to pass so many rivers, and
through so many difficult and dangerous places, of such kind
that it is not in the memory of man that an army has passed
through any similar ones, and by which a single wagon could
not be driven without great trouble, so that it appears a dream
to those who have not seen it; and that being out of danger,
and having arrived at the place where he longed to be, in order
to assist the churches of this realm, God should have been
pleased, that very day, to take him to Himself; and, what is
more, that his death should have produced no change or commotion in his army."[2]

Duke Wolfgang of Deux Ponts was quietly succeeded in the
command of the German troops by Count Wolrad of Mansfeld.
A day later the two armies met with lively demonstrations of
joy. In honor of the alliance thus cemented a medal was struck,
bearing on the one side the names and portraits of Jeanne and
Henry of Navarre, and on the other the significant words, "*Pax*

---

[1] De Thou, iv. 185–188; Agrippa d'Aubigné, i. 285; Anquetil, Esprit de la
ligue, i. 297.

[2] Discours envoyé de La Rochelle à la Royne d'Angleterre. La Mothe Fénélon, ii. 158, etc.

certa, victoria integra, mors honesta "—the triple object of their desires.[1]

The combined army, now numbering about twenty-five thousand men, soon came to blows with the enemy. The Duke of Anjou, whose forces were somewhat superior in numbers, had approached within a very short distance of Coligny, but, unwilling to risk a general engagement, had intrenched himself in an advantageous position. A part of his army, commanded by Strozzi, lay at La Roche Abeille, where it was furiously assaulted by the Huguenots. Over four hundred royalists were left dead upon the field, and Strozzi himself was taken prisoner. The disaster had nearly proved still more serious; but a violent rain saved the fugitives by extinguishing the lighted matches upon which the infantry depended for the discharge of their arquebuses, and by seriously impeding the pursuit of the cavalry.[2]

Although the Duke of Anjou had recently received considerable reinforcements—about five thousand pontifical troops and twelve hundred Florentines, under the command of Sforza, Count of Santa Fiore [3]—it was now determined in a military

Huguenot success at La Roche Abeille.

---

[1] De Thou, iv. 188 ; Lestoile, 22 ; J. de Serres, iii. 524 ; Castelnau, liv. vii., c. 6.

[2] Castelnau, liv. vii., c. 7 ; De Thou, iv. 192 ; Jean de Serres, iii. 327 (who states the Roman Catholic loss as higher than given in the text). Brantôme ascribes the defeat of Strozzi to the circumstance that the matches of *his* troops were put out by the rain, and that his infantry, unsupported by cavalry, was at the mercy of Mouy and the Huguenot troopers. Colonnels fr., Œuvres, ed. Lalanne, vi. 60. But the " Discours envoyé de la Rochelle à la Royne d'Angleterre " (La Mothe Fénélon, ii. 160) states that the Huguenots would have done much greater execution and perhaps put an end to the dispute, " n'eust été que, tout ce jour là, la pluye fut si extréme et si grande que noz harquebouziers ne pouvoient plus jouer." La Roche Abeille, or La Roche l'Abeille, is a hamlet seventeen miles south of Limoges.

[3] According to J. A. Gabutius, the biographer of Pius V. (sec. 120, p. 646), the Pope sent 4,500 foot and 1,000 horse, and Cosmo, Duke of Florence, 1,000 foot and 200 horse. Besides these, many nobles attached themselves to the expedition as volunteers. Santa Fiore was instructed to leave France *the moment he should perceive that the heretics were treated with.* " Quod si ipse summus copiarum Dux, vel de pace vel de rerum compositione quidquam Catholicæ religioni damnosum præsentiret ; [Pius V.] imperavit e vestigio aut converso itinere in Italiam remearet, aut ad Catholicum exercitum in Belgic cum hæreticis bellantem sese conferret et adjungeret."

council to disband the greater part of the army, giving to the
French forces a short furlough, and, for the most part,
trusting to the local garrisons to maintain the royal
supremacy in places now in the possession of the Roman Catholics. In adopting this paradoxical course, the generals seem to
have been influenced partly by a desire to furnish the "gentilhommes," serving at their own expense, an opportunity to
revisit their homes and replenish their exhausted purses, and
thus diminish the temptation to desertion which had thinned
the ranks; partly, also, by the hope that the new German auxiliaries of the Huguenots would of themselves melt away in a
climate to which they were unaccustomed.[1]

Furlough of Anjou's troops.

Meanwhile, the admiral, whose power had never been so great
as it now was, exhibited the utmost anxiety to avert, if possible,
any further effusion of blood. Under his auspices a
petition was drawn up in the name of the Queen of
Navarre, and the Princes, Seigneurs, Chevaliers, and
gentlemen composing the Protestant army. A messenger was
sent to the Duke of Anjou to request a passport for the deputies
who were to carry it to the court. But the duke was unwilling
to terminate a war in which he had (whether deservedly or not)
acquired so much reputation, and reluctant to be forced to
resume the place of a subject near a brother whose capricious
and jealous humor he had already experienced. He therefore
either refused or delayed compliance with the admiral's demand.[2]
Coligny succeeded, however, in forwarding the document to his
cousin Francis, Marshal of Montmorency—a nobleman who,
although he had not taken up arms with the Huguenots, virtually maintained, on his estates near Paris, a neutrality which,
from the suspicion it excited, was not without its perils. Montmorency laid the petition before Catharine and the king.

Huguenot petition to the king.

---

[1] De Thou, iv. 192; Vie de Coligny, 364; Gasparis Colinii Vita, 81; Jean de
Serres, iii. 331.   Charles IX. in a letter to La Mothe Fénélon, from St. Ger-
mains des Prés, July 27, 1569, alludes to the successes of the Huguenots,
whom Anjou cannot resist, "ayant donné congé à la pluspart de sa gendar-
merye de s'en aller faire ung tour en leurs maisons." Corresp. diplom., vii.
35, 36. The furlough, which was to expire on the 15th of August, was afterward extended by Anjou to the 1st of October.

[2] See Vie de Coligny, 364; De Thou, iv. 192; Jean de Serres, iii. 345, 346.

The voluminous state papers of the period would possess little
claim to our attention, were it not for the singleness of purpose
which they exhibit as animating the patriotic party through a
long succession of bloody wars. The Huguenots were no rebels
seeking to undermine the authority of the crown, no obstinate
democrats striving to carry into execution an impracticable
scheme of government,[1] no partisans struggling to supplant a
rival faction. They were not turbulent lovers of change. They
had for their leaders princes and nobles with interests all on the
side of the maintenance of order, men whose wealth was wasted,
whose magnificent palaces were plundered of their rich contents,[2] whose lives, with the lives of their wives and children,
were jeoparded in times of civil commotion. Even the unauthorized usurpations of the foreigners from Lorraine[3] would not

---

[1] Yet the "Guisards" were never tired of asserting the contrary. Sir
Thomas Smith tells us that Cardinal Lorraine maintained to him that "they
[the Huguenots] desired to bring all to the form of a republic, like Geneva."
Smith records the conversation at length in a letter to Cecil, wishing his correspondent to perceive "how he had need of a long spoon that should eat
potage with the Devil." The discussion must have been an earnest one. Sir
Thomas was not disposed to boast of being a finished courtier. In fact, he declares that, as to framing compliments, he is "the verriest calf and beast in the
world," and threatens to get one Bizzarro to write him some, which he will get
translated (for all sorts of people), and learn them by heart. He managed
on this occasion to speak his mind to Lorraine pretty freely respecting the
real origin of the war (the conversation took place in 1562), and told the
churchman the uncomplimentary truth, that his brother's deed at Vassy was
the cause of all the troubles. Smith to Cecil, Rouen, Nov. 7, 1562, State
Paper Office.

[2] Not to speak of Noyers, belonging to Condé, Coligny's stately residence at
Châtillon-sur-Loing fell into the hands of the enemy. In direct violation of
the terms of the capitulation, the palace was robbed of all its costly furniture, which was sent to Paris and sold at auction. Château-Renard, which
also was the property of Coligny, was taken by the Roman Catholics, and
became the nest of a company of half-soldiers, half-robbers, under an Italian—
one Fretini—who laid under contribution travellers on the road to Lyons. De
Thou, iv. 198, 199; Agrippa d'Aubigné, i. 292.

[3] How deeply the Guises felt the taunt that they were strangers in France,
appears from a sentence of the cardinal's to the Bishop of Rennes (Trent,
Nov. 24, 1563), wherein, alluding to the recent birth of a son to the Duke of
Lorraine and Catharine de' Medici's daughter, he says that he is "merveilleusement aise . . . . pource que sera occasion aux Huguenots de ne
nous dire plus princes estrangers." Le Laboureur, ii. 313.

have been sufficient to move the greater part of them to a resort
to the sword. Their one purpose, the sole object
which they could not renounce, was the securing of
religious liberty. The Guises—even that cruel and
cowardly cardinal with hands dripping with the blood of the
martyrs of a score of years—were nothing to them, except as
impersonations of the spirit of intolerance and persecution.
Liberty to worship their God in good conscience was their
demand alike after defeats and after successes, under Louis de
Bourbon or under Gaspard de Coligny. They did, indeed,
sympathize with the first family of the blood, deprived of the
position near the throne to which immemorial custom entitled
it—and what true Frenchman did not? But Admiral Coligny,
rather than the Prince of Condé, was the type of the Huguenot
of the sixteenth century—Coligny, the heroic figure that looms
up through the mist of the ages and from among the host of
meaner men, invested with all the attributes of essential greatness—pious, loyal, truthful, brave, averse to war and bloodshed,
slow to accept provocation, resolute only in the purpose to
secure for himself and his children the most important among
the inalienable prerogatives of manhood, the freedom of professing and practising his religious faith.

The single purpose of the Huguenots.

The present petition differed little from its predecessors. It
reiterated the desire of the Huguenots for peace—a desire evidenced on so many occasions, sometimes when prudence might
have dictated a course opposite to that which they adopted.
The return they had received for their moderation could be
read in broken edicts, and in "pacifications" more sanguinary
than the wars they terminated. The Protestant princes and
gentlemen, therefore, entreated Charles "to make a declaration
of his will respecting the liberty of the exercise of the reformed
religion in the form of a solemn, perpetual, and irrevocable
edict." They begged him "to be pleased to grant universally
to all his subjects, of whatever quality or condition they might
be, the free exercise of that religion in all the cities, villages,
hamlets, and other places of his kingdom, without any exception,
reservation, modification, or restriction as to persons, times, or
localities, with the necessary and requisite securities." True,

however, to the spirit of the age, which dreaded unbridled
license of opinion as much as it did the intolerance of the papal
system, the Huguenots were careful to preclude the "Libertines"
from sheltering themselves beneath this protection, by calling
upon Charles to require of all his subjects the profession of the
one or the other religion [1]—so far were even the most enlightened
men of their country and period from understanding what spirit
they were of, so far were they from recognizing the inevitable
direction of the path they were so laboriously pursuing!

It scarcely needs be said that the petition received no attention from a court not yet tired of war. Marshal Montmorency
was compelled to reply to Coligny, on the twentieth of July,
that Charles refused to take notice of anything emanating from
the admiral or his associates until they should submit and return
to their duty. Coligny answered in a letter which closed the
negotiations; protesting that since his enemies would listen to
no terms of accommodation, he had, at least, the consolation of
having done all in his power to avert the approaching desolation of the kingdom, and calling upon God and all the princes
of Europe to bear witness to the integrity of his purpose.[2]

The Huguenots now took some advantage of the temporary
weakness of the enemy in the open field. On the one hand they
reduced the city of Châtellerault and the fortress of Lusignan,
hitherto deemed impregnable.[3] On the other, they despatched
into Béarn the now famous Count Montgomery, who, joining
the "viscounts," was successful in wresting the greater part of
that district from the hands of Terrides, a skilful captain sent
by Anjou, and in restoring it to the Queen of Navarre.[4] Respecting their plan of future operations a great diversity of
opinion prevailed among the Huguenot leaders. Admiral Co-

---

[1] "Copie d'une Remonstrance que ceulx de la Rochelle ont mandé avoyr
envoyée au Roy, après l'arrivée du duc de Deux Ponts." La Mothe Fénélon,
ii. 179–188. In Latin, Jean de Serres, iii. 333–345. Gasparis Colinii Vita, 80.

[2] Mém. de Castelnau, liv. vii., c. 6; Jean de Serres, iii. 345, 346; De Thou,
ubi supra.

[3] "Lusignan la pucelle." De Thou, iv. 197; Jean de Serres, iii. 331;
Agrippa d'Aubigné, i. 290.

[4] Agrippa d'Aubigné, i. 294; De Thou, iv. (liv. xlv.) 200–202; Jean de
Serres, iii. 347.

ligny was strongly in favor of pressing on to the north, and laying siege to Saumur.   With this place in his possession, as it
Coligny's   was reasonable to suppose it soon might be, he would
plans over-   enjoy a secure passage across the river Loire into Brit-
ruled.   tany, Anjou, and more distant provinces, as he already
had access by the bridge of La Charité to Burgundy, Champagne, and the German frontier.   Unfortunately the majority
of the generals regarded it as a matter of more immediate
importance to capture Poitiers, a rich and populous city, said at
that time to cover more ground than any other city in France,
with the single exception of Paris.   They supposed that their
recent successes at Châtellerault and Lusignan, on either side of
Poitiers, and the six pieces of cannon they had taken at Lusignan would materially help them.   Coligny reluctantly yielded
to their urgency, and the army which had appeared before
Poitiers on the twenty-fourth of July, 1569,[1] began the siege
Disastrous   three days later.   It was a serious blunder.   The
siege of   Huguenots succeeded, indeed, in capturing a part of
Poitiers.   the suburbs, and in reducing the garrison to great
straits for food ; but they were met with great determination,
and with a singular fertility of expedient.   The Count de Lude
was the royal governor.   Henry, Duke of Guise (son of the
nobleman assassinated near Orleans in 1563), with his brother
Charles, Duke of Mayenne, and other good captains, had
thrown himself into Poitiers two days before Coligny made
his appearance.   It was Guise's first opportunity to prove to the
world that he had inherited his father's military genius ; and
the glory of success principally accrued to him.   He met the
assailants in the breach, and contested every inch of ground.
Their progress was obstructed by chevaux-de-frise and other
impediments.   Boiling oil was poured upon them from the
walls.   Burning hoops were adroitly thrown over their heads.
Pitch and other inflammable substances fell like rain upon their
advancing columns.   They were not even left unmolested in
their camp.   A dam was constructed on the river Clain, and the

---

[1] Agrippa d'Aubigné, i. 298 : " Pressé par les interests et murmures des
Poictevins, il sentit en cet endroit une des incommoditez qui se trouve aux
partis de plusieurs testes ; sa prudence donc cedant à sa nécessité," etc.

inundation spread to the Huguenot quarters. To these difficulties raised by man were added the ravages of disease. Many
of the Huguenot generals, and the admiral himself, were disabled, and the mortality was great among the private soldiers.

In spite of every obstacle, however, it seemed probable that
Coligny would carry the day. " The admiral's power exceedeth
the king's," wrote Cecil to Nicholas White : "he is sieging of
Poitiers, the winning or losing whereof will make an end of the
cause. He is entered within the town by assault, but the Duke
of Guise, etc., are entrenched in a stronger part of the town ;
and without the king give a battle, it is thought that he cannot
escape from the admiral." [1] Just at this moment, the Duke of
Anjou, assembling the remnants of his forces, appeared before
Châtellerault ; and the peril to the Huguenot city seemed so
imminent, that Coligny was compelled to raise the siege of
Poitiers, on the ninth of September, and hasten to its relief.
Seven weeks of precious time had been lost, and more than two
thousand lives had been sacrificed by the Huguenots in this ill-
advised undertaking. The besieged lost but three or four
hundred men. [2] Great was the delight manifested in Paris,
where, during the prevalence of the siege, solemn processions
had gone from Notre Dame to the shrine of Sainte Geneviève,
to implore the intercession of the patron of the city in behalf
of Poitiers. [3]

Meanwhile the Huguenots had been more fortunate on the
upper Loire, where La Charité sustained a siege of four weeks
by a force of seven thousand Roman Catholics under Sansac.
Its works were weak, its garrison small, but every assault was
bravely met. In the end the assailants, after severe losses experienced from the enemy and from a destructive explosion of
their own magazine, abandoned their enterprise in a panic, on
hearing an ill-founded rumor of Coligny's approach. [4]

It was fortunate for the Protestants of the north and east

---

[1] Letter of Sept. 8, 1569, Wright, Queen Elizabeth, i. 323.
[2] Jean de Serres, iii. 348, etc. ; Castelnau, liv. vii., c. 7 ; De Thou, iv.
205–214 ; Agrippa d'Aubigné, i. 297, etc.
[3] Journal d'un curé ligueur (Jehan de la Fosse), 109.
[4] Jean de Serres, iii. 332 ; Agrippa d'Aubigné, i. 292 ; De Thou, etc.

that they still had Sancerre and La Charité as asylums from the violence of their enemies. Far from their armed companions, there was little protection for their lives or their property. The edict of the preceding September, assuring to peaceable Protestants freedom from molestation in their homes, was as much a dead letter as any of its predecessors. The government, the courts of justice, and the populace, were equally eager to oppress them. At Orleans the "lieutenant-general" placed all the Huguenots of the city, without distinction of age or sex, in the public prisons, upon pretext of providing for the public security. A few days after (on the twenty-first of August) the people, inflamed to fanaticism by seditious priests, attacked these buildings. They succeeded in breaking into the first prison, and every man, woman, and child was murdered. The door of the second withstood all their attempts to gain admission. But the bloodthirsty mob would not be balked of its prey. The whole neighborhood was ransacked for wood and other combustible materials, and willing hands kindled the fire. As the flames rose high above the doomed house, parents who had lost all hope of saving their own lives sought to preserve the lives of their infant children by throwing them to relatives or acquaintances whom they recognized among their persecutors. But there are times when the heart of man knows no pity. The laymen who had been taught that heretics must be exterminated, even to the babe in the cradle, now put into practice the savage lesson they had learned from their spiritual instructors. Fathers and brothers took a cruel pleasure in receiving the hapless infants on the point of their pikes, or in despatching them with halberds, reserving the same fate for any of more mature age who might venture to appeal from the devouring flames to their merciless fellow-men. The number of the victims of sword and fire is said to have reached two hundred and eighty persons.[1]

Cruelties to the Huguenots in the prisons of Orleans.

The tragic end of the Huguenots at Orleans warned the Protestants of the villages and open country of the dangers to which

---

[1] Agrippa d'Aubigné, liv. v., c. 13 (i. 293) ; De Thou, iv. (liv. xlv.) 204 ; Jehan de la Fosse, 108.

they were exposed. Many fled with their wives and children
Montargis a to Montargis, where the aged Renée of Ferrara was
safe refuge. still living, the unwilling spectator of commotions
which she had foreseen and predicted, and which she had
striven to prevent. Her palace was still what Calvin had called
it in the time of the first war, "God's hostelry." Renée's royal
descent, her connection by marriage with the Guises—for
Henry, the present duke, was her grandson—her well-known
aversion to civil war,[1] and, added to these, that demeanor which
ever betrayed a consciousness that she was a king's daughter,
had thus far protected her from direct insult, staunch and
avowed Protestant as she was, and had enabled her to extend to
a host of fugitives for religion's sake a hospitality which had not
yet been invaded. But, the rancor entertained by the two parties increasing in bitterness as the third conflict advanced, it
became more and more difficult to repress the impatience felt
by the fanatics of Paris to rid themselves of an asylum for the
adherents of the hated faith within so short a distance—about
seventy miles—of the orthodox capital. Montargis was narrowly watched. Early in March the duchess was warned, in a
letter, of pretended plans formed by the refugees on her lands
to succor their friends elsewhere in the vicinity—the writer
being no other than the adventurer Villegagnon, the former

---

[1] That Renée was, like all the other prominent Huguenots, from the very
first opposed to a resort to the horrors of war, is certain. Agrippa d'Aubigné
goes farther than this, and asserts (i. 293) that she had become estranged
from Condé in consequence of her blaming the Huguenots for their assumption of arms : "blasmant ceux qui portoient les armes, jusques à estre deve-
nus ennemis, le Prince de Condé et elle, sur cette querelle." I can scarcely
credit this account, of which I see no confirmation, unless it be in a letter to
an unknown correspondent, in the National Library (MSS. Coll. Béthune,
8703, fol. 68), of which a translation is given in Memorials of Renée of France
(London, 1859), 263, 264. It is dated Montargis, Aug. 20, 1569 : "Praying
you . . . . to employ yourself, as I know you are accustomed to do, in
whatsoever way shall be possible to you, in striving to arrive at a good peace,
in which endeavor I, on my part, shall put forth all my power, if it shall
please God. And if it cannot be a general one, *at least it shall be to those who
desire it, and who belong to us.*" Who, however, was the correspondent? The
subscription, "Your good cousin, Renée of France," would appear to point
to Admiral Coligny or some one of equal rank. Louis de Condé was no
longer living.

vice-admiral, the betrayer of Coligny's Huguenot colony to Brazil, who was now in the Roman Catholic service, under the Duke of Anjou.[1] But the fresh flood of refugees to Montargis rendered further forbearance impossible. The preachers stirred up the people, and the people incited the king. Renée was told that she must dismiss the Huguenot preachers, or submit to receiving a Roman Catholic garrison in her castle ; that the exercise of the Protestant religion could no longer be tolerated, and the fugitives must find another home. The duchess could no longer resist the superior forces of her enemies, and tearfully she provided the miserable Huguenots for their journey with such wagons as she could find. The company consisted of four hundred and sixty persons, two-thirds women and infants in the arms of their mothers. Scarcely knowing whither to direct their steps, they fled toward the Loire, and hastened to place the river between them and their pursuers. The precaution availed them little. They had barely reached the vicinity of Châtillon-sur-Loire,[2] when the approach of Cartier with a detachment of light horse and mounted arquebusiers was announced ; and the defenceless throng, knowing that no pity could be expected from men whose hands had already been imbrued in the blood of their fellow-believers, and being exhorted by their ministers to meet death calmly, knelt down upon the ground and awaited the terrible onset. At that very instant, between the hillocks in another direction, and somewhat nearer to the fugitives, a band of cavalry made its appearance. They numbered some one hundred and twenty men, and, as they rode up, were taken for the advance guard of their persecutors. But, on coming nearer and recognizing some of the kneeling suppliants, the knights threw off their cloaks and displayed their white cassocks, the badge of the

Flight of the refugees to Sancerre.

---

[1] Letter of Villegagnon to the Duchess of Ferrara, Montereau, March 4, 1569, *apud* Mém. de Claude Haton, ii. Appendix, 1109.

[2] It must be remembered that this was a different place from Châtillon-sur-Loing, Admiral Coligny's residence, which was not more than fifteen miles distant. The places are frequently confounded with each other. The Loing is a tributary of the Seine, into which it empties below Montereau, after flowing by Châtillon-sur-Loing, Montargis, and Nemours.

adherents of the house of Navarre. They were two cornets of
Huguenot horse, on their way from Berry to La Charité, under
the command of Bourri, Teil, and other captains. In the midst
of the tearful acclamations of the women, their new friends
turned upon the exultant pursuers, and so bravely did they fight
that the Roman Catholics soon fled, leaving eighty men and
two standards on the field. The Huguenot knights, who had
so providentially become their deliverers, escorted the fugitives
from Montargis to Sancerre and La Charité, where they remained in safety until the conclusion of peace.[1]

Meantime the courts of justice emulated the example of cruelty
set them by the government and the mob. In May they began
by sending to the gallows on the Place Maubert, in Paris, a student barely twenty-two years of age, for having taught some
children the Huguenot doctrines (huguenoterie), "without any
other crime," the candid chronicler adds. After so fair a beginning there was no difficulty in finding good subjects for
hanging. Accordingly, on the thirtieth of June, three victims
more were sacrificed on the old Place de Grève, "partly for
heresy and for celebrating the Lord's Supper in their house;
partly"—so it was pretended—"for having assisted in demolish-
ing altars." In the great number of similar executions
with which the sanguinary records of Paris abound,
the fate of Nicholas Croquet and the two De Gastines—father
and son—would have been forgotten, but for the extraordinary
measures taken in respect to the house where the impiety had
been committed of celebrating the Lord's Supper according to
the simple scheme of its first institution. The Parisian parliament ordered that "the house of the Five White Crosses, belonging to the De Gastines, situated in the Rue Saint Denis,"
should be razed to the ground, and that upon the site a stone
cross should be placed, with an inscription explanatory of the
occasion of its erection. That spot was to serve as a public

The "Croix de Gastines."

---

[1] The fullest and most graphic account of this interesting incident I find in
Agrippa d'Aubigné, i. 293 (liv. v., c. 13). See De Thou, iv. (liv. xlv.) 204,
and Memorials of Renée of France (London, 1859), 261-263. The Huguenot
horsemen numbered not eight hundred, as the author last quoted states, but
about one hundred and twenty—"six vingts."

square for all time, and a fine of 6,000 livres, with corporal punishment, was imposed upon any one who should ever undertake to build upon it.[1]   It was not foreseen that military exigencies might presently render imperative a reconciliation with the Huguenots, and that the "perpetual" decree of parliament, like the "irrevocable" edicts of the king, might be somewhat abridged by stern necessity.

The work of blood continued.   In July two noblemen were decapitated—the Baron de Laschêne and the Baron de Courtène —and denunciation of reputed heretics was vigorously prosecuted, by command of parliament and of the city curates.[2]   Two months later a cowardly but impotent blow was struck at a more distinguished personage.   Parliament undertook to try Gaspard de Coligny, and, having found him guilty of treason (on the thirteenth of September), pronounced him infamous, and offered a reward of fifty thousand gold crowns for his apprehension, with full pardon for any offences the captor might have committed.   Lest the exploit, however, should be deemed too difficult for execution, a few days later (on the twenty-eighth of September) the same liberal terms were held out to any one who should murder him.   As it was not

Ferocity of parliament against Coligny and others.

A price set on the head of the admiral.

---

[1] The "Discours de ce qui avint touchant la Croix de Gastines, l'an 1571, vers Noel" (Mémoires de l'état de France sous Charles IX., and Archives curieuses, vi. 475, etc.), contains the quaint decree of the parliament.   See Journal d'un curé ligueur (Jehan de la Fosse), 107.   As actually erected, the monument consisted of a high stone pyramid, surmounted by a gilt crucifix. Besides the decree in question, there were engraved some Latin verses of so confused a construction that it was suggested that the composer intended to cast ridicule both on the Roman Catholics and on the Huguenots.   M. de Thou, who was a boy of sixteen at the time—and who, as son of the first President of Parliament, and himself, at a later time, a leading member and president à mortier of that body, enjoyed rare advantages for arriving at the truth—declares (iv. 488) that the elder Gastines was a venerable man, beloved by his neighbors, and, indeed, by the entire city ; and that the execution was compassed by a cabal of seditious persons, who, by dint of soliciting the judges, of exciting the people, of inducing them to congregate and follow the judges with threats as they left parliament, succeeded in causing to be punished with death, in the persons of the Gastines, an offence which, until then, had been punished only with exile or a pecuniary fine.

[2] Jehan de la Fosse, 107, 108.

so easy to capture or assassinate a general who was at that
moment in command of an army not greatly inferior to that
of the Duke of Anjou, the court gave the Parisian populace
the cheaper spectacle of a hanging of the admiral in effigy. It
was the eve of the festival of "the Exaltation of the Cross"
—Tuesday, the thirteenth of September—and the time was
deemed appropriate for the execution of so determined an
enemy of the worship of that sacred emblem. While Coligny's escutcheon was dragged in dishonor through the streets by
four horses, the hangman amused the mob by giving to his
effigy the traditional tooth-pick, which he was said to be in
the habit of continually using—a facetious trait which the
curate of St. Barthélemi, of course, does not forget to insert in
his brief diary.[1] Nevertheless, that the decree of parliament
setting a price upon the admiral's head was no child's play, appeared about this time from the abortive plot of one Dominique
d'Albe, who confessed that he had been hired to poison the
Huguenot chief, and was hanged by order of the princes.[2]
Nor was it without practical significance that the decree itself
had been translated into Latin, Italian, Spanish, German,
Flemish, English, and Scotch, and scattered broadcast through
Europe by the partisans of Guise.

Meantime the condition of the rival armies in western France
promised again, in the view of the court, a speedy solution of the

---

[1] Journal d'un curé ligueur, 110; Mém. de Castelnau, liv. vii., c. 8; De
Thou, iv. (liv. 1.) 216; Gasp. Colinii Vita (1569), 87 ; Memoirs of G. de
Coligny, 140, etc. The arrêt of the parliament is in Archives curieuses, vi.
377, etc. The Latin life of Coligny (89–91) inserts a manly and Christian
letter, in the author's possession, written (Oct 16, 1569) by the admiral to
his own children and those of his deceased brother, D'Andelot, who were
studying at La Rochelle, shortly after receiving intelligence of this judicial
sentence and of the wanton injury done to his palace at Châtillon-sur-Loing.
" We must follow our Head, Jesus Christ, who himself leads the way," he
writes. " Men have deprived us of all that it was in their power to take
from us, and if it be God's will that we never recover what we have lost, still
we shall be happy, and our condition will be a good one, inasmuch as these
losses have not arisen from any harm done by us to those who have brought
them upon us, but solely from the hatred they bear toward me for the reason
that it has pleased God to make use of me in assisting His Church."

[2] Jean de Serres, iii. 356, 357; Mem. of Coligny, 136 ; De Thou, iv. 216,
217 ; Agrippa d'Aubigné, i. 302.

military problem. The Duke of Anjou had of late been heavily
reinforced. With the old troops that had returned to his standard, and the new troops that poured in upon him, he had a well-
appointed army of about twenty-seven thousand men, of whom
one-third were cavalry. Coligny, on the contrary, had been so
weakened by his losses at the siege of Poitiers, and
by the desertion of those whom disappointment at
the delays and the expense of the service had rendered it impossible to retain, that he was inferior to his antagonist by nine or ten thousand men. He had only eleven or
twelve thousand foot and six thousand horse.[1] The Roman
Catholic general resolved to employ his preponderance of forces
in striking a decisive blow. This appeared the more desirable,
since it was known that Montgomery was returning from the
reduction of Béarn, bringing with him six or seven thousand
veterans—an addition to the Huguenot army that would nearly
restore the equilibrium.

*The Hugue-
nots weak-
ened.*

Leaving Chinon, where he had been for some time strengthening himself, the Duke of Anjou crossed the swollen river
Vienne, on the twenty-sixth of September, and started in pursuit of the Huguenots. Coligny had been resting his army at
Faye, a small town about midway between Chinon and Châtellerault. It was here that the attempt upon his life, to which
allusion has just been made, was discovered. And it was from
this point that the Prince of Orange started in disguise, and
undertook, with forty mounted companions, a perilous journey
across France by La Charité to Montbéliard, for the purpose
of raising in Germany the fresh troops of which the admiral
stood in such pressing need.[2]

The Huguenot general had moved westward, secretly averse
to giving battle before the arrival of Montgomery, but forced
to show a readiness to fight by the open impatience
of his southern troops, and by the murmurs of the
Germans, who openly threatened to desert unless they
were either paid or led against the enemy. Within a couple of

*Battle of
Moncontour,
October 3,
1569.*

---

[1] Jean de Serres, iii. 363 ; De Thou, iv. (liv. xlvi.) 221 ; Castelnau, vii., c. 8.
[2] De Thou, iv. 216 ; Agrippa d'Aubigné, i. 302. The place was also known
by the name of Foie la Vineuse.

leagues of the town of Moncontour, soon to gain historic renown, Coligny, believing the Roman Catholics to be near, drew
up his own men in order of battle (on the thirtieth of September); but, receiving from his scouts the erroneous information that there were no considerable bodies of the enemy in
the neighborhood, he resumed his march toward the town of
which La Noue had rendered himself master. The army was
scarcely in motion before Mouy, commanding the rear, was
attacked by a heavy detachment of the Duke of Anjou's vanguard, under the Duke of Montpensier. Mouy's handful of
men stood their ground well, now facing the enemy and driving him off, now slowly retreating, and gave the rest of the
Huguenot army the opportunity of gaining the opposite side of
a marshy tract, through which there flowed a small stream.
Then they themselves crossed, after losing about a hundred of
their number. Anjou neglected the chance here afforded him
of gaining an entire victory; and Coligny, after halting for a
short time, drew off toward Moncontour, which he reached on
the next day without further obstruction. The duke spent the
night on the battle-field in token of victory, and then started in
pursuit; but, in order to avoid attack while crossing the short,
but deep river Dive, a tributary of the Loire which flows by
the walls of Moncontour, he turned to the left, and, rapidly
ascending to its sources, descended again on the opposite bank.

The admiral might still have succeeded in avoiding a capital
engagement, and in reaching Partenay or some other point of
safety, had he not been again embarrassed by the mutiny of
the Germans, who, as usual, were most urgent for pay on the
eve of battle. As it was, before they could be quieted, the
duke had made up for his considerable détour, and overtook
the Protestants a short distance beyond Moncontour. Coligny,
having given command of the right wing to Count Louis of
Nassau, interposed the left, of which he himself assumed command, between the main body and the enemy, hoping to get off
with a mere skirmish.[1] In this he was disappointed. Attacked
in force, his troops made a sturdy resistance. The fight resem-

---

[1] Agrippa d'Aubigné, i. 305.

bled in some of its incidents the conflicts of the paladins of a
past age. The elder rhinegrave rode thirty paces in front
of his Roman Catholic knights; Coligny as far in advance
of the Protestants. The two leaders met in open field. The
rhinegrave was killed on the spot. The admiral received a
Coligny
wounded. severe injury in his face. The blood, gushing freely from the wound, nearly strangled him before his
visor could be raised. Reluctantly he was compelled to retire
to the rear of the army. Still the tide of battle ran high. The
Swiss troops of Anjou displayed their accustomed valor. It
was matched by that of the Huguenots, who several times
seemed on the point of winning the day, and already shouted,
" Victory! Victory!" The Duke of Anjou, who, however
little he was entitled to the credit of planning the engagement,
certainly displayed great courage in the contest itself, was at
one time in extreme peril, and the Marquis of Baden was killed
while riding near him. On the other side, the Princes of Béarn
and Condé, who had come to the army from Partenay, to encourage the soldiers by their presence, endeavored by word and
example to sustain the courage of the outnumbered Huguenots.[1]
But at the critical moment, when the Roman Catholic line had
begun to give way, Marshal Cossé, who as yet had not been
engaged, advanced with his fresh troops and changed the fortunes of the day. The personal valor of Louis of Nassau was
unavailing. The German reiters, routed and panic-stricken,
fled from the field. Encountering their own countrymen, the
lansquenets or German infantry, they broke through their
ranks and threw them into confusion. Into the breach thus
made the Swiss poured in an irresistible flood. Inveterate

---

[1] In the heat of the engagement, the excited imaginations of the combatants even saw visions of celestial champions, as Theseus was fabled to have
appeared at Marathon. A renegade Protestant captain afterward assured
the Cardinal of Alessandria that on that eventful day he had seen in mid-air
an array of warriors with refulgent armor and blood-red swords, threatening
the Huguenot lines in which he fought; and he had instantly embraced the
Roman Catholic faith, and vowed perpetual service under the banners of the
pontiff. There were others, we are told, to corroborate his account of the
prodigy. Joannis Antonii Gabutii Vita Pii Quinti Papæ (Acta Sanctorum,
Maii 5), § 125, pp. 647, 648.

hatred now found ample opportunity for satisfaction. The
helpless lansquenets were slaughtered without mercy. No

Heavy losses
of the Hu-
guenots.

quarter was given. One of the German colonels,
who had been the foremost cause of the morning's
mutiny, and who had prevented his soldiers from
fighting until their wages were paid, now made them tie handkerchiefs to their pikes to show that they surrendered; but they
fared no better than the rest.[1] Others kneeled and begged for
mercy of their savage foes, crying in broken French, *"Bon
papiste, bon papiste moi!"* It was all in vain. Of four thousand lansquenets that entered the action, barely two hundred
escaped with their lives. Three thousand French, enveloped
by Anjou's cavalry, were spared by the duke's express command, but not before one thousand of their companions had
been killed. In all, two thousand French foot soldiers and
three hundred knights perished on the field, while with the
valets and camp-followers the loss was much more considerable.
La Noue was again a prisoner in the enemy's hands. So also
was the famous D'Acier. His captor, Count Santa Fiore, received from Pius the Fifth a severe letter of rebuke for " having failed to obey his commands *to slay at once every heretic
that fell into his hands.*"[2]

The battle of Moncontour, fought on Monday, the third of
October, 1569, was a thorough success on the side of the Guises
and of Catharine de' Medici. Compared with it, the battle of
Jarnac was only an insignificant skirmish. Although, under
the skilful conduct of Louis of Nassau and of Wolrad of Mans-

---

[1] Agrippa d'Aubigné, i. 307. "Ne se trouva oncques gens plus fidelles au
camp catholicque que lesditz estrangers, et singulièrement les Suisses, lesquelz ne pardonnèrent à ung seul de leur nation germanique de ceux qui
tombèrent en leurs mains." Mém. de Claude Haton, ii. 582.

[2] "Che non avesse il comandamanto di lui osservato d'ammazzar subito
qualunque heretico gli fosse venuto alle mani." Catena, Vita di Pio V.,
apud White, Mass. of St. Bartholomew, 305, and De Thou, iv. (liv. xlvi.)
228. With singular inconsistency—so impossible is it generally to carry out
these horrible theories of extermination—the Roman pontiff himself afterward liberated D'Acier without exacting any ransom. De Thou, *ubi supra.*
" Si Santafiore lui avoit obéï," says an annotator, " Jacques de Crussol
(D'Acier) ne se seroit pas converti, et n'auroit pas laissé une si illustre pos-
terité."

feld, the remnants of the army drew off to Airvault and thence to Partenay, escaping the pursuit of Aumale and Biron, the Huguenot losses were enormous, and the spirit of the soldiers was, for the time, entirely crushed.[1]   The Roman Catholics, on the contrary, had lost scarcely any infantry, and barely five hundred horse, although among the cavalry officers were several persons of great distinction.

Fame magnified the exploit, and exalted the Duke of Anjou into a hero.   Charles himself became still more jealous of his brother's growing reputation.   Pius the Fifth, on re-

The Roman Catholics ex-ulting.

ceipt of the tidings, sent the latter a brief, congratulating him upon his success, renewing his advice to make thorough work of exterminating the heretics, and warning him against a mercy than which there was nothing more cruel.[2] To foreign courts—especially to those which betrayed a leaning to the Protestant side—the most exaggerated accounts of the victory were despatched.   A "relation" of the battle of Moncontour, with which Philip the Second was furnished, stated the Huguenot loss at fifteen thousand men, eleven cannon, three thousand wagons belonging to the reiters, and eight hundred or nine hundred horses.[3]   For a moment the court believed that the Protestants were ruined, and that their entire submission

---

[1] On the battle of Moncontour, consult J. de Serres, iii. 357–362 ; De Thou, iv. 224–228 ; Castelnau, liv. vii., c. 9 ; Agrippa d'Aubigné, liv. v., c. 17 ; a Roman Catholic relation in Groen van Prinsterer, Archives de la Maison d'Orange Nassau, iii. 324–326.

[2] " Nihil est enim ea pietate misericordiaque crudelius, quæ in impios et ultima supplicia meritos confertur." Pius V. to Charles IX., Oct. 20, 1569. Pii V. Epistolæ (Antwerp, 1640), 242.   The French victories of Jarnac and Moncontour were celebrated by a medal struck at Rome, with the legend, " Fecit potentiam in bracchio suo, dispersit superbos," and a representation of Pius kneeling and invoking the aid of heaven against the heretics. In the distance is seen a combat, and above it appears the Divine Being directing the issue.   Figured in " Le Trésor de Numismatique et de Glyptique, par Paul Delaroche " (Medailles des Papes, plate 15, No. 5), Paris, 1839.

[3] La Mothe Fénélon, vii. 65, etc., from Simancas MSS.   So Claude Haton, who is rarely behindhand in such matters, makes the Protestants lose fifteen thousand or sixteen thousand men.   Mémoires, ii. 582.   Admiral Coligny was for a time believed by the court to be dead or mortally wounded, " mais ne fut rien." Ibid., ubi supra.

must inevitably ensue.[1]   The Parisian parliament, in the excess
Extravagance of its joy, added the third of October to the number,
of parliament. already excessive, of its holidays, declaring that henceforth no pleadings should be held on the anniversary of so glorious a triumph.[2] About the same time, in order to exhibit
more clearly the spirit by which it was animated, the same dignified tribunal gave the order that the bodies of Francis D'Andelot and his wife should be disinterred and hanged upon a
a gibbet![3]

The Roman Catholics were, nevertheless, entirely mistaken
in their anticipations of the speedy subjugation of their opponents. The latter were disheartened for a few days, but not in
the least disposed to give over the struggle. "The reformed
were too numerous," a modern historian well remarks, "too
well organized, and had struck their roots too deeply, to be sub-
dued by the loss of a few pitched battles."[4] The prospect at
first was, indeed, very dark. It seemed almost impossible for
the Huguenots to maintain themselves in the region which for
a whole year had been the chief field of operations. As Anjou
advanced southward, Partenay was abandoned without a blow,
and after occupying it he pushed on toward Niort. Of this
Murder of   important place the intrepid De Mouy had been
De Mouy by. placed by Coligny in command. Not content with a
Maurevel.
bare defence, he sallied out and repulsed the enemy.
But his boldness proved fatal to him. There was a Roman Catholic "gentilhomme," Maurevel by name, who, allured by the
reward of fifty thousand crowns offered by parliament for the
capture or assassination of Admiral Coligny, had entered the
Protestant camp with protestations of great disgust with his
former patrons the Guises, and had vainly sought an opportu-

---

[1] If we may credit the curate Claude, Catharine de' Medici alone was vexed at
the completeness of the rout and the number of Huguenots slain, "inasmuch
as she gave them as much support as possible, and encouraged them in rebellion, that the civil wars might continue, in which she took pleasure because of
the management of affairs they threw into her hands"—"pour le maniment
des affaires qu'elle entreprenoit et manioit." Mémoires, ii. 583.

[2] Journal d'un curé ligueur (Jehan de la Fosse), 110.

[3] Jehan de la Fosse, 112. The date is stated as "about Oct. 17th."

[4] Ranke, Civil Wars and Monarchy in France, i. 241.

nity to take the great chieftain's life. Three years later that
opportunity was to present itself in the streets of Paris itself.
Loth to return to his friends without accomplishing any noteworthy exploit, Maurevel joined De Mouy, with whom he so
ingratiated himself that the general not only supplied him
from his purse, but made him a companion and a bed-fellow.
As the Huguenots were returning to Niort, the traitor found
the conjuncture he desired. Chancing to be left alone with De
Mouy, he drew a pistol and shot him in the loins; then putting
spurs to his horse, reached with ease the advancing columns of
Anjou. De Mouy was taken back to Niort mortally wounded.
His friends, contrary to his earnest desire, insisted on taking
him by boat down the Sèvre to La Rochelle, where he died.
Meanwhile Niort, in discouragement, surrendered to the Roman
Catholic army.[1] The assassin was well rewarded. A letter is
extant, written by Charles the Ninth to the Duke of Anjou,
The assassin from Plessis-lez-Tours, on the tenth of October, 1569,
rewarded with in which the king begs his brother to confer on
the collar of
the order. "Charles de Louvier, sieur de Moureveil, being the
person who killed Mouy," the collar of the royal order of Saint
Michael, to which he had been elected by the knights companions, as a reward for "his signal service;" and to see that he
receive from the city of Paris a present commensurate with his
merits![2]

Catharine de' Medici and the Cardinal of Lorraine came from
Tours, where they had been watching the course of the war, to
Fatal error Niort, and the plan of future operations was discussed
of the court. in their presence. Almost every place of importance
previously held by the Huguenots toward the north and east of
La Rochelle had fallen, even to the almost impregnable Lusig-

---

[1] De Thou, iv. 230; Agrippa d'Aubigné, i. 310. The murderer's name is
variously written Maurevel, Moureveil, Montrevel, etc.

[2] This letter, respecting which I confess that I find some difficulties, possesses a history of its own. On the 13th of Ventôse, in the second year of the
republic, the original was sent to the national convention, which, the next
day, ordered its insertion in the official bulletin, and its preservation in the
national library, as emanating "from one of the Neros of France." See App.
to Journal de Lestoile, ed. Michaud, pt. i., p. 307, 308, and the revolutionary
bulletins.

nan. Saint Jean d'Angely, on the Boutonne, was the only remaining outwork, whose capture must precede an attack on the
citadel itself. Should the victorious army of the king lay siege
to Saint Jean d'Angely, or should it continue the pursuit of Coligny and the princes, who, in order to divert it from the undertaking, had retired from Saint Jean d'Angely to Saintes, and
thence, not long after, in the direction of Montauban? This
was the question that demanded an instant answer. Jean de
Serres informs us that the Protestant leaders were extremely
anxious that their enemies should adopt the latter course; [1] yet
the best military authorities on both sides declare without hesitation that the failure of the Roman Catholics to follow it was
the one capital error that saved the Huguenots, perhaps, from
utter destruction. "Hundreds of times have I been amazed,"
says the Roman Catholic Blaise de Montluc, "that so many
great and wise captains who were with Monsieur (the Duke of
Anjou) should have adopted the bad plan of laying sieges, instead of pursuing the princes, who were routed and reduced to
such extremities that they had no means of getting to their feet
again." And the Protestant François de la Noue devotes an
entire chapter of his "discourses" to the proof of the assertion
that "as the siege of Poitiers was the beginning of the mishaps
of the Huguenots, so that of Saint Jean was the means of ar-
resting the good fortune of the Catholics."

What, it may be asked, led to the commission of so fatal an
error? The memoirs of Tavannes, who advocated the immediate pursuit of the admiral, ascribe it to the reluctance of the
Montmorencies to permit their cousin to be overwhelmed; to
the jealousy felt by Cardinal Lorraine of the military successes
which threw his brother, the Duke of Aumale, and his nephew,
the Duke of Guise, into obscurity; and to the suggestions of
De Retz, the king's favorite, who persuaded Charles that it
was dangerous to permit the renown of Anjou to increase yet
further. [2] It must, however, be remembered that the younger

---

[1] "Ut sese Montalbani cum Vicecomitibus conjungerent, et sperantes An-
dium, dum se persequeretur, ab San-Jani oppugnandæ instituto destiturum."
De statu rel. et reip., iii. 365.

[2] See Soldan, iii. 372, 373 ; Anquetil, Esprit de la ligue, i. 317, etc.

Tavannes is not always a good authority ; and that where, as in the present instance, the glory of his father is affected, he becomes altogether untrustworthy. If we reject his account as apocryphal, which apparently we must do, there still remains good reason to believe that the siege of Saint Jean d'Angely was agreed to by the majority of the Roman Catholic leaders from the sincere conviction that its reduction, to be followed by the still more important capture of La Rochelle, would annihilate the Huguenot party in the west, its stronghold and refuge, and that it could then subsist but little longer in other parts of the kingdom.

The defence of Saint Jean d'Angely had been intrusted by Coligny to competent hands. De Piles had found

Siege of
Saint Jean the fortifications weak and imperfect ; he completed
d'Angely. and strengthened them.[1] With a small garrison of Huguenots he repaired by night the breaches made by the enemy's cannon during the day, and repelled every attempt to storm the place. When the siege had advanced about two weeks, Charles himself, who was resolved not to suffer Henry of Anjou any longer to win all the laurels of the war, made his appearance in the Roman Catholic camp, on the twenty-sixth of October, and summoned the garrison to surrender. De Piles, however, declined to listen to the commands of the king, even as he had disobeyed those of the duke, taking refuge in the feudal theory that he could give up the place only to the Prince of Navarre, the royal governor of the province of Guyenne, at whose hands he had received it. Yet the position of the Protestants was growing extremely perilous. During one of the assaults upon the wall, De Piles himself became so thoroughly convinced that Saint Jean would be carried, that he caused a breach to be made in the fortifications in his rear, in order to facilitate the withdrawal of his troops. Happily, he had no need of this mode of escape on the present occasion. Meanwhile the most honorable terms were offered him. These he refused to accept ; but, finding his stock of ammunition rapidly

---

[1] With his usual inaccuracy, Davila speaks of Saint Jean d'Angely as "excellently fortified " (Eng. trans., p. 166).

becoming exhausted, he agreed to a truce of ten days, that he might have time to send a messenger to the princes to obtain their orders; promising, in case he received no succor in the interval, to surrender the city on condition that the garrison should be permitted to retire with their horses, arms and personal effects, and that religious liberty should be granted to all the residents. But, before the armistice had quite expired, Saint Surin, and forty other brave horsemen from Angoulême, succeeded in piercing the enemy's lines, and relieved De Piles from an engagement into which he had entered with great reluctance. The hostages on both sides were given up, and the siege was renewed with greater fury than ever. In the end, seeing no prospect of sufficient reinforcement to enable him to maintain his position, De Piles capitulated (on the second of December) on similar terms to those that he had before declined, and the garrison marched out with flying banners. Seven weeks had they detained the entire army of the victors of Moncontour before an ill-fortified place. More than six thousand men had died under its walls, by the casualties of war and by the scarcely less destructive diseases that raged in the camp.[1] One of the ablest and most enterprising of the royal generals—Sebastian of Luxemburg, Viscount of Martigues and governor of Brittany —had been killed.[2] Of the Protestants, only about a hundred and eighty persons perished, nearly the half of them inhabitants of the town; for the men of Saint Jean d'Angely, and even the

---

[1] This number, given by Agrippa d'Aubigné, i. 313, and by De Thou, iv. (liv. xlv.) 242, seems the most probable. La Popelinière swells it to near 10,000 (Soldan, ii. 375), while Castelnau, liv. vii., c. 10, reduces it to "over 3,000." Strange to say, Jean de Serres, who, writing and publishing this portion of his history within a year after the conclusion of the third civil war, almost uniformly gives the highest estimates of the Roman Catholic losses, here makes them about 2,000, or lower than any one else.

[2] Agrippa d'Aubigné, who was generous enough to appreciate valor even in an enemy, calls him "celui qui entamoit toutes les parties difficiles, à qui rien n'estoit dur ny hazardeux, qui en tous les exploits de son temps avoit fait les coups de partie" (i. 312). Lestoile in his journal (p. 22, Ed. Mich.) affirms that he was killed just as he had uttered a blasphemous inquiry of the Huguenots, where was now their "Dieu le Fort," and taunted them with his having become "à ceste heure leur Dieu le Faible." "Le Dieu, le Fort, l'Éternel parlera," was the first line of a favorite Huguenot psalm.

women and children, had labored industriously in defending their firesides.

It was a part of the compact, that, while neither De Piles nor his soldiers should serve on the Huguenot side for four months, they should be safely conducted without the Roman Catholic lines. The Duc d'Aumale and other leaders seem to have endeavored conscientiously to execute the stipulation ; but their followers could not resist the temptation to attack the Huguenots as they were traversing the suburbs. Nearly all were robbed, and a considerable number—as many, according to Agrippa d'Aubigné, as fell during the siege — were murdered. De Piles, on his arrival at Angoulême, wrote to demand the punishment of those who had committed so flagrant a breach of faith, and, when he could obtain no satisfaction, sent a herald to the king to declare that he held himself and his fellow-combatants absolved from all obligations, and that they would at once resume their places in the Huguenot army.[1]

Nearly three months of precious time elapsed since the disastrous rout of Moncontour before the royalists completed the reduction of the region adjoining La Rochelle. Outside of that citadel of French Protestantism only the little town of Tonnay, on the Charente, still held for the Prince of Navarre. Yet so long as La Rochelle itself stood firm, the Duke of Anjou had accomplished little ; and La Rochelle had made good use of the respite to strengthen its works. Every effort to gain a lodgement in its neighborhood had signally failed. The end of December came, and with it cold and discouragement. Anjou's army was dwindling away. The King of Spain and the Pope recalled their troops, as if the battle of the third of October had ended the war, and Santa Fiore, the pontifical general, sent to Rome twenty-six standards, taken by the Italians at Moncontour—a present from Charles the Ninth, which Pius accepted with great delight, and dedicated as a

---

[1] On the siege of Saint Jean d'Angely, see J. de Serres, iii. 369, 370 ; Agrippa d'Aubigné, i. 311-313 ; De Thou, iv. 238-242 ; Castelnau, liv. vii., c. 10. It scarcely needs to be mentioned that Davila, bk. v., p. 166, knows nothing of any treachery on the part of the Roman Catholics, but duly mentions that De Piles did not observe his promise.

trophy in the Basilica of St. John Lateran.[1] Henry of Anjou
himself was ill, or was unwilling any longer to endure separa-
tion from a court of whose pleasures he was inordinately fond;
and, resigning the command of the army into the hands of the
eldest son of the Duke of Montpensier, François de Bourbon—
generally known as the prince dauphin—he hastened, at the
beginning of the new year, to join Charles and Catharine de'
Medici at Angers. The French troops, meantime, were either
furloughed or scattered, and the generals condemned to inaction, while the German reiters and lansquenets and the Swiss
pikemen were permitted to return to their own homes.[2] Such
was the suicidal policy of the Roman Catholic party—a policy
which saved the Huguenots from prostration; for it may with
truth be affirmed that the errors committed in the siege of
Saint Jean d'Angely, and in disbanding the powerful army
of Anjou, completely obliterated the advantage which had
been won on the bloody field of Moncontour.[3]

While the Protestants had been forced to abandon one important place after another in Poitou, Saintonge and Aunis,
they had in other parts of the kingdom been displaying their
old enterprise, and had obtained considerable success. Vézelay in Burgundy, the birthplace of the reformer Theodore
Beza, passed through a fiery ordeal. This ancient town, built
upon the brow of a hill, and strong as well by reason of its
situation as of its walls constructed in a style that was now becoming obsolete in France, had been captured at the beginning
of the war by some of the neighboring Huguenot noblemen,

---

[1] Davila, bk. v. (Eng. tr., p. 163 and 167); De Thou, iv. (liv. xlvi.) 250.
Gabutius, in his life of Pius V., transcribes the exultant inscription, dictated
by the pontiff himself (§ 126, p. 648), and claims for the canonized subject
of his panegyric the chief credit of the victory. According to him the
Italians were the first to engage with the heretics, and the last to desist from
the pursuit.

[2] Davila, bk. 5th (Eng. tr., p. 167); Mém. de Claude Haton, ii. 591.

[3] " L'hiver arriva, il fallut mettre les troupes en quartier ; et le fruit d'une
victoire si complette, l'effort d'une armée royale si formidable, fut la prise de
quelques places médiocres, pendant que La Rochelle, la plus utile de toutes,
restoit aux vaincus, et que les princes rétablissoient les affaires, à l'aide d'un
délai qu'ils n'avoient point osé se promettre." Anquetil, L'Esprit de la
ligue, i. 317.

who scaled the walls and surprised the garrison. One of the few points the Protestants held in the eastern part of the kingdom, it was regarded as a place of the greatest importance to their cause.

Within a few weeks Vézelay was twice besieged by a Roman Catholic army under Sansac. A vigorous sortie, in which the Huguenots destroyed almost all the engines of war of the assailants, on the first occasion caused the siege to be raised. When Sansac renewed his attempt he fared no better. The soldiers who had thrown themselves into the place, with the enthusiastic citizens, repelled every attack, and promptly suppressed treacherous plots by putting to death two persons whom they found engaged in revealing their secrets to the enemy. Sansac next undertook to reduce Vézelay by hunger; but the Huguenots broke his lines, aided by their friends in La Charité and Sancerre, and supplied themselves abundantly with provisions. When, on the sixteenth of December, Sansac finally abandoned the fruitless and inglorious undertaking, he had lost, since October, no fewer than fifteen hundred of his soldiers.[1]

The Huguenots of Sancerre in turn made an attempt to enter Bourges, the capital of the province of Berry, by promising a large sum of money to the officer second in command of the citadel; but he revealed their plan to his superior, M. de la Chastre, governor of the province, and the advanced party which had been admitted within the gates (on the twenty-first of December) fell into the snare prepared for them.[2] . The capture of Nismes—

Marginal note: Huguenot successes. Vézelay.

---

[1] J. de Serres, iii. 372 ; De Thou, iv. (liv. xlvi.) 234, 235, who makes the loss in the first siege 300 men, and in the second over 1,000 horsemen ; Agrippa d'Aubigné, Hist. univ., l. v., c. 19 (i. 315, 316), who states the total at 1,400 foot and near 400 horse ; while Castelnau, l. vii., c. 10, speaks of but 300 in all. Vézelay, famous in the history of the Crusades (see Michaud, Hist. des Croisades, ii. 125) as the place where St. Bernard in 1146 preached the Cross to an immense throng from all parts of Christendom, is equidistant from Bourges and Dijon, and a little north of a line uniting these two cities.

[2] De Thou, iv. (liv. xlvi.) 246, 247 ; Agrippa d'Aubigné, liv. v., c. 19 (i. 317); J. de Serres, iii. 370. About twenty prisoners were taken, to whom their captors promised their lives. Afterward there were strenuous efforts made, especially by the priests, to have them put to death as rebels and traitors. M. de la Chastre resisted the pressure, disregarding even a severe order of the

"the city of antiquities"—more than compensated for the failure
at Bourges. Rarely has an enterprise of equal diffi-
Brilliant capture of Nismes. culty been more patiently prosecuted, or been crowned
with more brilliant success. The exiled Protestants, a
large and important class, had now for many months been subjected to the greatest hardships, and were anxiously watching an
opportunity to return to their homes. At last a carpenter presented himself, who had long revolved the matter in his mind,
and had discovered a method of introducing the Huguenots
into the city which promised well. There was a fountain, a
short distance from the walls of Nismes, known to the ancients
by the same name as the city itself—Nemausus—whose copious

Parliament of Paris, accompanied by the threat of the enormous fine of 2,000
marks of gold, which bade him send them to the capital. (Hist. du Berry, etc.,
par M. Louis Raynal, 1846, iv, 104, *apud* Bulletin de la Soc. de l'hist. du prot.
fr., iv. (1856) 27.) Even Charles IX. wrote to him, but the governor was inflexible. His noble reply has come to light, dated Jan. 21, 1570, just one month
after the failure of the Protestant scheme. After urging the danger of retaliation by the Huguenots of La Charité and Sancerre upon the prisoners they
held, to the number of more than forty, and the inexpediency of accustoming
the people of Bourges to bloody executions which they would not fail to repeat,
he concludes his remonstrance in these striking words : " Nevertheless, Sire,
if you should find it expedient, for the good of your service, to put them to
death, the channel of the courts of justice is the most proper, without recom-
pensing my services, or sullying my reputation with a stain that will ever be
a ground of reproach against me. And I beg you, Sire, to make use of me in
other matters more worthy of a gentleman having the heart of his ancestors,
who for five hundred years have served their king without stain of treachery
or act unworthy of a gentleman." Inedited letter, *apud* Bulletin, *ubi supra*,
28, 29. M. de la Chastre became one of the marshals of France. He conducted, three years later, the terrible siege of Sancerre, famous in history. He
had the reputation among the Huguenots of being very severe, if not bloodthirsty—a reputation which he deserved, if he was, as Henry of Navarre styles
him, "un des principaux exécuteurs de la Sainct Barthélemy." (Deposition
in the trial of La Mole, Coconnas, etc. Archives curieuses, viii. 150.) La
Chastre tried to clear himself of the imputation, by recalling the events of
1569. To Jean de Léry he maintained " qu'il n'est point sanguinaire, ainsi
qu'on a opinion, comme aussi il l'avoit desjà bien monstré aux autres troubles,
lorsqu'il avoit en sa puissance les sieurs d'Espeau, baron de Renty, et le capitaine Fontaine, qui est en son armée : car encores que la cour du parlement
de Paris luy fist commandement de les représenter, à peine de 2,000 marcs
d'or, il ne le voulut faire." Jean de Léry, Discours de l'extrème famine
. . . . . dans la ville de Sancerre," Archives curieuses, viii. 67.

stream, put to good service by the inhabitants, turned a number of mills within the municipal limits. To admit the waters a canal had been built, which, where it pierced the fortifications, was protected by a heavy iron grating. Through this wet channel the carpenter resolved that the Huguenots should enter Nismes. It so happened that a friend of his dwelt in a house which was close to the wall at this spot; with his help he lowered himself by night from a window into the ditch. A cord, which was slackened or drawn tight according as there was danger of detection or apparent security, served to direct his operations. The utmost caution was requisite, and the water-course was too contracted to permit more than a single person to work at once. Provided only with a file, the carpenter set himself to sever the stout iron bars. The task was neither pleasant nor easy. Night after night he stood in the cold stream, with the mud up to his knees, exposed to wind and rain, and working most industriously when the roar of the elements covered and drowned the noise he made. It was only for a few minutes at a time that he could work; for, as the place was situated between the citadel and the " porte des Carmes," a sentry passed it at brief intervals, and was scarcely out of hearing except when he went to ring the bell which announced a change of guard. Fifteen nights, chosen from the darkest of the season, were consumed in this perilous undertaking; and each morning, when the approach of dawn compelled him to suspend his labors, the carpenter concealed his progress by means of wax and mud. All this time he had been prudent enough to keep his own counsel; but when, on the fifteenth of November, his work was completed, he called upon the Huguenot leaders to follow him into Nismes. A detachment of three hundred men was placed at his disposal. When once the foremost were in the town, and had overpowered the neighboring guards, the Huguenots obtained an easy success. The clatter of a number of camp-servants, who were mounted on horseback, with orders to ride in every direction, shouting that the city was in the hands of the enemy, contributed to facilitate the capture. Most of the soldiers, who should have met and repelled the Protestants, shut themselves up in their houses and refused to leave them. In a few minutes, all Nismes, with the exception of the castle, which held out a few months longer, was taken.[1]

When Admiral Coligny, wounded and defeated, was borne on a litter from the field of Moncontour, where the hopes of the
Coligny encouraged. Huguenots had been so rudely dashed to the ground, his heart almost failed him in view of the prospects of the war and of his faith. Two persons seemed at this critical juncture to have exercised on his mind a singular influence in restoring him to his accustomed hopefulness. L'Estrange, a simple gentleman, was being carried away in a plight similar to his own, when, having been brought to the admiral's side, he looked intently upon him, and then gave expression to his gratitude to Heaven, that, in the midst of the chastisements with which it had seen fit to visit his fellow-believers, there was yet so much of mercy shown, in the words, "Yet is God very gentle!"[2]—a friendly reminder, which, the great leader was wont to say, raised him from gloom and turned his thoughts to high and noble resolve.[3] Nor was the heroic Queen of Navarre found wanting at this crisis. No sooner had she heard of the disaster than she started from La Rochelle, and at Niort met the admiral, with such remnants of the army as still clung to him. Far from yielding to despondency, Jeanne d'Albret urged the generals to renew the contest; and, having communicated to them a part of her own enthusiasm, returned to La Rochelle to watch over the defence of the city, and to lend still more important assistance to the cause, by writing to Queen Elizabeth and the other allies of the Huguenots, correcting the exaggerated accounts of the defeat of Moncontour which had been studiously disseminated by the Roman Catholic party, and imploring fresh assistance.

As for Coligny, his plans were soon formed. The troops of Dauphiny and Provence, always among the most reluctant to

---

[1] De Thou, iv. (liv. xlvi.) 235-237 ; Agrippa d'Aubigné, liv. v., c. 19 (i. 316, 317); Jean de Serres, iii. 368, 369.

[2] " Si est-ce que Dieu est très-doux."

[3] Agrippa d'Aubigné, l. v., c. 18 (i. 309). The words were, as M. Douen reminds us (Clément Marot et le Psautier huguenot, 1878, 13) the first line of the seventy-third psalm of the Huguenot psalter.

leave their homes, had long been clamoring for permission to
return. It was now impossible to retain them. On
the fourteenth of October they started from Angoulême, whither they had gone without consulting the

Withdrawal of the troops of Dauphiny and Provence.

Protestant generals, and, under the leadership of Montbrun and
Mirabel, directed their course toward their native provinces. In
two days they reached the river Dordogne at Souillac, where
a part of their body, while seeking to cross, was attacked by the
Roman Catholics, and suffered great loss. The rest pushed forward to Aurillac, in Auvergne, which had recently been captured
by a Huguenot captain, and soon found their way to Privas,
Aubenas, and the banks of the Rhône.[1] Thence, after refresh-
ing themselves for a few days, they crossed into Dauphiny to
renew the struggle for their own firesides.[2]

On the eighteenth of October, four days after the departure
of the Dauphinese troops from Angoulême, Coligny set forth
from Saintes upon an expedition as remarkable for boldness of
conception as for its singularly skilful and successful execution—
an expedition which is entitled to rank among the most remarkable military operations of modern times.[3] In the face of
an enemy flushed with victory, and himself leading an army
reduced to the mere shadow of its former size, the admiral
deliberately drew up the plan of a march of eight or nine
months, through a hostile territory, and terminating
in the vicinity of the capital itself. As sketched by

Plan of the admiral's bold march.

Michel de Castelnau from the admiral's own words in
conversation with him, the objects of the Protestant general
were principally these: to satisfy the claims of his mutinous
German mercenaries by the reduction of some of the enemy's
rich cities in Guyenne; to strengthen himself by forming a
junction with the army of Montgomery and such fresh troops
as " the viscounts " might be able to raise; to meet on the lower
Rhône the recruited forces of Montbrun and Mirabel; thence

---

[1] De Thou, iv. (liv. xlvi.) 232; Jean de Serres, iii. 366.

[2] Ibid., iii. 372, etc.

[3] Even in December, Languet could scarcely imagine that Coligny would
not return and winter at La Rochelle. Letter of Dec. 12, 1569, Epist. aecr.,
i. 130.

to turn northward, and, having reached the borders of Lorraine, to welcome the Germans whom the Elector Palatine and William of Orange would hold in readiness; and, at last, to bring the war to an end by forcing the Roman Catholics to give battle, under circumstances more advantageous to the reformed, in the immediate vicinity of Paris.[1]

Coligny's army was chiefly composed of cavalry; of infantry he had but three thousand men.[2] The young Princes of Navarre and of Condé, whom he wished to accustom to the fatigues of the march and of the battle-field, while endearing them to the Huguenots by their participation in the same perils with the meanest private soldier, were his companions, and had commands of their own. He had left La Rochefoucauld in La Rochelle to protect the city and the Queen of Navarre. The admiral's course was first directed to Montauban, that city which has been the stronghold of Protestantism in southern France down to the present time. But the difficulties of the way, and, particularly, the improbability of finding easy means of crossing so near their mouths the successive rivers, which, rising in the mountainous region of Auvergne and the Cevennes, all flow westward and empty into the Garonne, or its wide estuary, the Gironde, compelled Coligny to make a considerable deflection to the left. He effected the passage of the Dordogne at Argentat, a little above the spot where Montbrun had sustained his recent check, and, after making a feint of throwing himself into Auvergne, crossed the Lot below Cadenac, and reached Montauban in safety.[3] The Count of Montgomery, returning from his victorious campaign in Béarn, had been ordered to be in readiness in this city. But learning that, by an unaccountable delay, he was still in Condom, south of the Garonne, Coligny marched westward to

He sweeps through Guyenne.

---

[1] Mém. de Castelnau, liv. vii., c. 12.

[2] At least, so says Agrippa d'Aubigné, liv. v., c. 18 (i. 309).

[3] De Thou, iv. (liv. xlvi.) 233; Agrippa d'Aubigné, i. 309, 318 (liv. v., cs. 18 and 20). The two authorities are not in exact agreement, De Thou stating that Coligny went to Montauban before his march to meet Montgomery, while D'Aubigné makes him follow the left bank of the Dordogne down to Aiguillon. Gasparis Colinii Vita (1575), 91, 92, supports De Thou.

Aiguillon, at the confluence of the Lot and the Garonne. Near this place he constructed, with great trouble, a substantial bridge across the Garonne, with the intention of transporting his army to the left bank, and ravaging the country far down in the direction of Bordeaux. This bold movement was prevented by Blaise de Montluc, who, adopting the suggestion of another, and appropriating the credit due to the sagacity of this nameless genius, detached one of the numerous floating windmills that were moored in the Garonne, and having loaded it with stones, sent it down with the current against Coligny's bridge. Not only were the chains that bound the structure broken, but the very boats on which it rested were carried away as far as to Bordeaux itself. It was with great difficulty that the admiral brought back to the right bank the division of his army that had already crossed, and with it the troops of Count Montgomery.[1]

The united army now returned to Montauban, where, in the midst of a rich district in part friendly to the Huguenots, it spent the last days of 1569 and the greater part of the month of January, 1570. Its numbers had by this time received such large accessions, that Coligny wrote to Germany that he had six or seven thousand horse and fifteen thousand foot.[2] As the reformed population of Montauban had contributed enough money to satisfy the prince's indebtedness to the importunate reiters and lansquenets,[3] the troops were enthusiastic in their

---

[1] De Thou, iv. (liv. xlvi.) 249; Agrippa d'Aubigné, liv. v., c. 20 (i. 318); Gasparis Colinii Vita (1575), 94. The author of this valuable and authentic life of the admiral gives a full description of the bridge. Professor Soldan is mistaken in saying that the bridge was not yet completed (Geschichte des Prot. in Frank., ii. 377). It had been completed, and two days had been spent in taking over the German cavalry ("opere effecto, biduoque in traducendis Germanis equitibus consumpto") when the disaster occurred.

[2] Languet, Letter of January 3, 1570, Epist. secretæ, i. 133.

[3] Gasparis Colinii Vita (1576), 91 ; Vie de Coligny (Cologne, 1686), 378, where the account of the expedition, however, is full of blunders. Mr. Browning, following this untrustworthy authority, makes Admiral Coligny cross the Garonne and pass through Béarn, on his way from Saintes to Montauban! A glance at the map of France will show that this would have required a much greater bend to the right than he in reality made to the left, since Béarn lay entirely south of the river Adour. To reach Béarn by land *before* crossing the Garonne,

devotion to the cause, and pushed their raids under the intrepid La Loue south of the Garonne toward the Bay of Biscay, as far as Mont de Marsan and Roquefort in the "Pays des Landes."[1]

The Huguenots now proceeded towards Toulouse, but that city was too strongly fortified and garrisoned to tempt them to make an attack. They inflicted, however, a stern retribution upon the vicinity, devoting to destruction the villas and pleasure-grounds of the members of a parliament that had rendered itself infamous for its injustice and blind bigotry. The cruel fate of Rapin, murdered according to the forms of law, simply because he was a Protestant and brought from the king an edict containing too much toleration to suit the inordinate orthodoxy of these robed fanatics, was yet fresh in the memory of the soldiers, and fired their blood. On ruined and blackened walls, in more than one quarter, could be read subsequently the ominous words, written by no idle braggarts: "*Vengeance de Rapin!*" Leaving the marks of their passage in a desolated district, the Huguenots swept on to the friendly city of Castres, and thence through lower Languedoc, by Carcassonne and Montpellier, which they made no attempt to reduce, to Uzès and Nismes. Meanwhile Piles had from Castres made a marauding expedition with a body of picked troops to the very foot of the Pyrenees, and, in retaliation for the aid which the Spaniards had furnished Charles the Ninth, had penetrated to Perpignan, and ravaged the County of Roussillon.[2]

Thus the Huguenots—of whom Charles had contemptuously written to his ambassador at London, in January, that they were in so miserable a plight that, even since Anjou had dismissed all his men-at-arms after the capture of Saint Jean d'Angely, they dared not show their faces[3]

Marginal notes: "Vengeance de Rapin." · Coligny pushes on to the Rhône. · His singular success and its causes.

as the "Vie" evidently imagines he did, would almost have required Aladdin's lamp. In fact, the entire passage is a jumble of the exploits of Montgomery and Coligny.

[1] La Popelinière, *apud* Soldan, ii. 378.

[2] De Thou, iv. (liv. xlvii.) 303-306 ; Agrippa d'Aubigné, liv. v., c. 20 (i. 319, 320); Davila, bk. v., p. 168 ; Raoul de Cazenove, "Rapin-Thoyras, sa famille," etc., 49, 50.

[3] La Mothe Fénélon, vii. 81.

—had pushed an army from the mouth of the Gironde to the mouth of the Rhône. If Viscount Monclar had fallen mortally wounded near Castres, and brave La Loue had been surprised and killed near Montpellier, the Protestants had, nevertheless, sustained little injury. They had been largely reinforced on the way, both by the local troops that joined them and by chivalric spirits such as M. de Piles, who followed them so soon as he was forced to surrender Saint Jean d'Angely; or, like Beaudiné and Renty, who had been left with La Rochefoucauld to guard La Rochelle, but who, impatient of long inaction, at length obtained permission to attach themselves to the princes, and caught up with them at Castres, after a journey full of hazardous adventures. The Huguenot army, says La Noue, had been but an insignificant snow-ball when it started on its adventurous course; but the imprudence of its opponents permitted it to roll on, without hinderance, until it grew to a portentous size.[1] The jealousy existing between Montluc and Marshal Damville, who commanded for the king—the former as lieutenant-general in Gascony, and the latter as governor in Languedoc—undoubtedly removed many difficulties from the way of Admiral Coligny; and Montluc openly accused his rival, who was a Montmorency, of purposely furthering the designs of his heretical cousin. The accusation was a baseless fabrication; yet it obtained, as such stories generally do, a wide currency among the prejudiced and the ignorant, who could explain Damville's failure to impede Coligny's progress in no more satisfactory way than as the result of collusion between the son and the nephew of the late constable.[2]

Coligny had not yet accomplished his main object. Turning northward, and hugging the right bank of the Rhône, he prosecuted his undertaking of carrying the war to the very gates of

---

[1] "L'imprudence des Catholiques, lesquels laissant rouler, sans nul empeschement, ceste petite pelote de neige, en peu de temps elle *se fit grosse comme une maison.*" Mém. de la Noue, c. xxix.

[2] Of course, Davila (bk. v., p. 167, 168), who rarely rejects a good story of intrigue, especially if there be a dainty bit of treachery connected with it, adopts unhesitatingly the popular rumor of Marshal Damville's infidelity to his trust.

Paris. The few small pieces of artillery the Protestants possessed,
it was now found difficult to drag over rugged hills
that descended to the river's edge. They were, therefore, at first transported to the other side, and finally
left behind in some castles garrisoned by the Huguenots. The
recruits that had been expected from Dauphiny came in very
small numbers, and it was with diminished forces that Coligny
and the princes, on the twenty-sixth of May, reached Saint
Étienne, at that time a small town, which modern enterprise and
capital has transformed into a great manufacturing city.[1] A little
farther, at St. Rambert on the Loire, an incident occurred which
threatened to blight all the fair hopes the Protestants had now
again begun to conceive of a speedy and prosperous conclusion of
the war. Admiral Coligny fell dangerously ill, and for a time
serious fears were entertained for his life. It was a
moment of anxious suspense. Never before had the
reformed realized the extent to which their fortunes
were dependent on a single man. The lesson was a useful one
to the young companions of the princes, who, in the midst of the
stern discipline of the camp, had shown some disposition to complain of the loss of the more congenial gayety of the court.[2]
Louis of Nassau, brother of William of Orange, and next in
command, was the only person among the Protestants that could
have succeeded to Coligny in his responsible position; but even
Louis of Nassau could not exact the respect enjoyed by the
admiral, both with his own troops and with the enemy. Indeed,
it was the conduct of the Roman Catholics at this juncture that
furnished the clearest proof of the indispensable importance to
the Huguenots of their veteran leader. The negotiations, which
must soon be adverted to, had for some time been in progress,
and the court displayed considerable anxiety to secure a peace;
but the moment it was announced that Coligny was likely to

The admiral turns toward Paris.

His illness interrupts negotiations.

---

[1] St. Étienne possessed already, at the time the "Vie de Coligny" was
written, that branch of industry which still constitutes one of its chief
sources of wealth. It was described as a "petite ville fameuse par la quantité
d'armes qui s'y fait, et qui se transportent dans les païs étrangers, en sorte
que c'est ce qui nourrit presque toute la province." P. 381.

[2] Agrippa d'Aubigné, liv. v., c. 21 (i. 322).

die, the deputies from the king broke them off and waited to see the issue. Being asked to explain so singular a course, and being reminded that the Huguenots had other generals with whom a treaty might be formed in case of Coligny's death, it is said that the deputies replied by expressing their surprise that the Protestants did not see the weight and authority possessed by their admiral. "Were he to die to-day," said they, "to-morrow we should not offer you so much as a glass of water. As if you did not know that the admiral's name goes farther in giving you consideration than had you another army equal in size to that you have at present!"[1]

But Gaspard de Coligny was destined to die a death more glorious for himself, and to leave behind him a name more illustrious than it would have been had he died on the eve of the return of peace to his desolated country. He recovered, and once more advanced with his brave Huguenots. And now the distance between the Protestant camp and the Roman Catholic capital was rapidly diminishing. To meet the impending danger, the king ordered Marshal Cossé, who had succeeded the prince dauphin in command of the new army, to cross into Burgundy, check the admiral's course, and, if possible, defeat him. The two armies met on the twenty-fifth of June, in the neighborhood of the small town of Arnay-le-Duc.[2] Great was the disparity of numbers. Cossé had four thousand Swiss, six thousand French infantry, three thousand French, German, and Italian horse, and twelve cannon. Coligny's army had lost so much during its incessant marches through a thousand difficult places, and in a country where desertion or straying from the main body was so easy, that it consisted of but twenty-five hundred arquebusiers and two thousand horsemen, besides a few recruits from Dauphiny.

The Germans, who constituted about one-half of the cavalry, were ill-equipped; but the French horse were as well armed as any corps the Huguenots had been able to set on foot. All were

Engagement of Arnay-le-Duc.

---

[1] Gasparis Colinii Vita, 97, 98.

[2] Arnay-le-Duc, or René-le-Duc, as the place was indifferently called, is situated about thirty miles south-west of Dijon, on the road to Autun.

hardened by toil and well disciplined.   Of artillery the admiral
was entirely destitute.

The armies took position upon opposite hills, separated by a
narrow valley, in which flowed a brook fed by some small ponds.
Cossé made the attack, and attempted to cross the stream ; but,
after an obstinate fight of seven hours, his troops were compelled
to abandon the undertaking with considerable loss.   Next the
entrenchments thrown up by the Huguenots in the neighborhood of the ponds were assaulted.   Here the Roman Catholics
were subjected to a galling fire, and began to yield.   Afterward,
receiving reinforcements, they seemed to be on the point of
succeeding, when Coligny brought up M. de Piles, the hero of
Saint Jean d'Angely, who, supported by Count Montgomery,
soon restored the superiority of the Huguenots.   The enemy
was equally unfortunate in the attempt, simultaneously made,
to turn the admiral's position ; and, foiled at every point, he
retired for the day.   On the morrow, both armies reappeared
in the same order of battle, but neither general was eager to
renew a contest in which the advantage was all with those who
stood on the defensive, and, after indulging in a brief and in-
effective cannonade, the order was given to the Roman Catholic
troops to return to camp.[1]

After this indecisive combat, Coligny, who had no desire to
bring on a general engagement before receiving the considerable
accession of troops of which he was in expectation, slipped
away from Cossé, and though hotly pursued by the enemy's
cavalry, made his way to the friendly walls of La Charité upon
the Loire.   Here he busied himself with preparations for further
undertakings, and was engaged particularly in providing his
army with a few cannon and mortars, of which he had greatly
felt the need, when activity was interrupted by a ten days'
truce, dating from the fourteenth of July, the precursor of a
definite treaty of peace.[2]   At the expiration of the armistice,

---

[1] De Thou, iv. (liv. xlvii.) 312–314; Agrippa d'Aubigné, liv. v., c. 22 (i.
321–325) Castelnau, liv. vii., c. 12 ; Davila, bk. v. 169.
[2] De Thou, iv. (liv. xlvii.) 315.   Davila attributes to the connivance of
Marshal Cossé the escape of the Protestants from Arnay-le-Duc.   This is
consistent with the same writer's statement that it was the marshal's inten-

Coligny advanced, toward the end of July, to his castle of
Châtillon-sur-Loing, and distributed his troops in the
vicinity of Montargis, still nearer Paris. Marshal
Cossé, at the same time, moved in a parallel line
through Joigny, and took up his position at Sens, where he
could at once protect the capital and prevent the Huguenots
from making raids in that fertile and populous province, the
"Île de France," from which the whole country had derived its
name. Leaving the admiral and his brave followers here, at
the conclusion of an adventurous expedition of over twelve hundred miles, which had consumed more than nine months, let us
glance at the negotiations for peace which had long been in
progress, and were now at length crowned with success.

*Coligny ap-
proaches
Paris.*

So true was it of the combatants in the French civil wars,
that they rarely carried on hostilities but they were also treating
for peace, that since the battle of Moncontour there
had hardly elapsed a month without the discussion of
the terms on which arms could be laid aside by both
parties. Scarcely had the first startling impression made by
the defeat of the Huguenots passed away before Catharine de'
Medici sent that skilful diplomatist, Michel de Castelnau, to
assure the Queen of Navarre, at La Rochelle, of her personal
esteem and affection, as well as of her fervent desire to employ
her influence with the king, her son, in effecting a pacification
based upon just and honorable conditions. Jeanne replied in
courteous language ; but, while she insisted upon her own hearty reciprocation of the queen mother's wish, she also expressed
the suspicion which all the reformed entertained of the sincerity
of the leading ministers in the French cabinet, whose relations
with Spain and with the Pope showed that they were intent on
nothing less than the utter ruin of the Huguenots.[1] In November the matter took a more definite shape, through Marshal
Cossé, who appeared in La Rochelle with propositions of peace.
This statesman, otherwise moderate in his counsels, was imbued
with the notion that the Protestants were so discouraged by

*Progress of
the negotia-
tions.*

---

tional slowness that enabled Coligny to seize upon Arnay-le-Duc and post himself so advantageously.

[1] Castelnau, liv. vii., c. 10.

their late defeat, that they would gladly accept any terms. But the Huguenots, having understood that he was empowered merely to offer them liberty of conscience, without the right to the public worship of God, promptly broke off the negotiations.[1] A month or two later they were induced to believe that the court was disposed to larger concessions, or, if not, that they might at least justify themselves in the eyes of the world by showing that they were neither unreasonable nor desirous of prolonging the horrors of war. Two deputies—Jean de la Fin, Sieur de Beauvoir la Nocle, and Charles de Téligny: the one sent by the Queen of Navarre, the other sent by Coligny and the princes, who were already far on their journey through the south of France—came to the king at Angers, and presented the demands of the Huguenots. These demands certainly did not breathe a spirit of craven submission. The Huguenots called not only for complete liberty of conscience, but also for the right to hold their religious assemblies through the entire kingdom, without prejudice to their dignities or honors. They stipulated for the annulling of all sentences pronounced against them; the approval of all that they had done, as done for the welfare of the realm; the restitution of their dignities and property, and the giving of good and sufficient securities for the execution of the edict of pacification.[2] Catharine and her counsellors had undoubtedly gained some wholesome experience since Cossé's first proposals. They had already discovered that a single pitched battle had not ruined the Huguenots; and they now suspected that a number of additional battles might be required to effect that desirable result. It is not astonishing, however, that the queen mother was not yet ready to grant terms which could scarcely have been conceded even on the morrow of an overwhelming defeat. The articles sent by the king to the Protestant leaders as a counter-proposal were therefore of a very different character from those which they had submitted. Charles offered to the Queen of Navarre, the Princes of Navarre and Condé, the admiral, and their followers, entire amnesty, and consented to annul all judicial proceedings made against them

---

[1] De Thou, iv. (liv. xlvii.) 301.   [2] De Thou, iv. (liv. xlvii.) 302.

during these or the late troubles. He would exact no punishment for any treaties which they might have formed with foreign princes, and would restore their goods, honors, and estates. As to the religious question, he would allow them to hold two cities, in which they might do as they pleased, the king placing in each city a capable " gentilhomme " to maintain his authority and the public tranquillity. Elsewhere in France he would tolerate no reformed minister, no exercise of any other religion than his own. Neither would he guarantee the restitution of the judicial and other offices once held by Protestants, since others had bought them, and the money proceeding from the sale had been spent in defraying the expenses of the war ; especially as the clergy must look to the courts for the enforcement of their claims for indemnification for the destruction of the churches and other ecclesiastical property. The king professed himself willing to give all reasonable securities for the performance of his promises, but neglected to make any specification of the nature of those securities.[1] Such were the hard conditions offered—all that Catharine and the Guises were willing to concede at a time when it was hoped that the Huguenots would lose the assistance of one of their secret supporters, Elizabeth of England ; for the Earls of Westmoreland and Northumberland had risen in the north, and they had not only the best wishes, but the ready co-operation of every Spanish and French sympathizer. Charles himself was writing to his ambassador at London a letter meant to meet the queen's eye, instructing him to congratulate Elizabeth on the progress made in suppressing the insurrection ; and Catharine, by the same messenger, sent a secret letter of the same date, ordering the same diplomatic agent, in case the re-

The English rebellion affects the terms offered.

---

[1] The articles, a copy of which was sent to the ambassador at the court of Elizabeth, in a letter from Angers, Feb. 6, 1570, are printed in La Mothe Fénélon, vii. 86–88. I omit reference in the text to the articles prohibiting foreign alliances and the levy of money, prescribing the dismissal of foreign troops, etc. The two cities referred to in the fifth article are rather to be regarded as places of worship—the only places in the kingdom where Protestant worship would be tolerated—than as pledges for the performance of the projected edict, as Prof. Soldan apparently regards them chiefly, if not exclusively. Geschichte des Prot. in Frankreich, ii. 379.

bellion was not at an end, to give aid and comfort to the rebels.[1] Catharine and the Guises had not lost heart. Moved by repeated supplications, Pius the Fifth at last decided to excommunicate the heretical daughter of Henry and Anne Boleyn. But, as the bull of the twenty-fifth of February, 1570, had been procured solely by the entreaties of the rebel earls, enforced by the intercessions of the Guises, and as it was known that Philip the Second, so far from desiring it, was strongly opposed to the imprudent policy of the pontiff, the document, which pretended to relieve all the queen's subjects of the obligations of their allegiance, was committed to the charge of the Cardinal of Lorraine, to launch at Elizabeth's devoted head whenever the convenient moment should arrive.[2]

At Montréal, near Carcassonne, the admiral was again overtaken by a royal messenger, who on this occasion was Biron, equally distinguished on the field and in the council-chamber. While the Protestants replied to his offer that with heartfelt satisfaction they greeted the king's disposition to restore peace to France, and sent to Charles, who was then at Châteaubriand, in Brittany, a delegation consisting of Téligny, Beauvoir la Nocle, and La Chassetière, they distinctly stated that no terms could be entertained which should not include liberty of worship. For they declared that "the deprivation of the exercise of their religion was more insupportable to them than death itself."[3] But, in fact, the Huguenot princes and nobles placed little reliance upon the sincerity of the court, and had no hope of peace so long as they treated at a distance from the capital. Accordingly, Coligny, in his march up the valley of the Rhône, when again approached in the king's name by Biron, accompanied by Henry de Mesmes, Sieur de Malassise, peremptorily declined to enter into a truce which should interrupt the efficiency of his movement.[4]

---

[1] Charles to ambassador, Jan. 14th; letter of Catharine, same date; La Mothe Fénélon, vii. 77, 78.

[2] See Froude, History of England, x. 9, etc.

[3] De Thou, iv. (liv. xlvii.) 305. Cf. Soulier, Hist. des édits de pacification, 92.

[4] De Thou, iv. 311. It was at St. Étienne in Forez, that the incident occurred.

But when at last the admiral reached the Loire, and, at La Charité and Châtillon, was within a few hours of Paris, the attitude of the court in relation to the peace seemed to undergo an entire change, and it became evident that the negotiations, which had previously been employed for the mere purpose of amusing the Huguenots, were now resorted to with the view of ending a war already protracted far beyond expectation. Nor is it difficult to discover some of the circumstances that tended to bring about this radical mutation of policy.[1] The resources of the kingdom were exhausted. It was no longer possible to furnish the ready money without which the German and other mercenaries, of late constituting a large portion of the royal troops, could not be induced to enter the kingdom. The Pope and Philip were lavish of nothing beyond promises and exhortations that above all things Charles should make no peace with the heretical rebels. Indeed, Philip had few men, and no money, to spare. The French troops were in great straits. The gentlemen, who, in return for their immunity from all taxation, were bound to serve the monarch in the field at their own expense, had exhausted their available funds in so long a contest, and it was impossible to muster them in such numbers as the war demanded. Charles himself had always been averse to war. His tastes were pacific. If he ever emulated the martial glory which his brother Anjou had so easily acquired, the feeling was but of momentary duration, and met with little encouragement from his mother. He had, undoubtedly, consented to the initiation of the war only in consequence of the misrepresentations made by those who surrounded him, respecting its necessity and the ease of its prosecution. He had now the strongest reasons for desiring the immediate return of peace. His marriage with the daughter of the emperor had for some months been arranged, but Maximilian refused to permit Elizabeth to become the queen of a country rent with civil commotion. Catharine de' Medici, also, from the advocate of war, had become anxious for peace

Better conditions proposed.

Charles and his mother for peace.

---

[1] For a fuller discussion of these circumstances than the limits of this history will permit me to give, I must refer the reader to the work of Prof. Soldan, Geschichte des Protestantismus in Frankreich, ii. 385.

—tardily returning to the conviction which she had often expressed in former years, that the attempt to exterminate the Huguenots by force of arms was hopeless. After two years she was no nearer her object than when the Cardinal of Lorraine persuaded her to endeavor to seize Condé at Noyers. Jarnac had accomplished nothing; Moncontour was nearly as barren a victory. A great part of what had been so laboriously effected by Anjou's army in the last months of 1569, La Noue had been undoing in the first half of 1570.[1] The Protestants, who were, a few months since, shut up in La Rochelle, had defeated their enemies at Sainte Gemme, near Luçon, and had retaken Fontenay, Niort, the Isle d'Oléron, Brouage, and other places. The Baron de la Garde, who had lately, in the capacity of "general of the galleys," been infesting the seas in the neighborhood of La Rochelle, was compelled to retire to Bordeaux.[2] Saintes had been besieged and captured, and the Huguenots were advancing to the reduction of St. Jean d'Angely, not long since so dearly won by the Roman Catholics.[3] Montluc had, it is true, met with success in Béarn, where Rabasteins was taken and its entire garrison massacred.[4] But what were these advantages at the foot of the Pyrenees, when an army under Gaspard de Coligny, after sweeping four hundred leagues through the southern and western provinces, was now

The war fruitless for its authors.

---

[1] La Noue was one of the most modest, as well as one of the most capable of generals. "I have felt myself so much the more obliged to speak of it," writes the historian De Thou respecting the battle of Sainte Gemme, "as La Noue, the most generous of men, who has written on the civil wars with as much fidelity as judgment, always disposed to render conspicuous the merit of others, and very reserved respecting his own, has not said a word of this victory." De Thou, iv. (liv. xlvii.) 320.

[2] Brantôme has written the eulogy of this personage, whose true name was Antoine Escalin. He was first ambassador at Constantinople, where his good services secured his appointment as general of the galleys. After undergoing the displeasure of the king, and a three years' imprisonment for his participation in the massacre of the Vaudois, he was reinstated in office. Subsequently he was temporarily displaced by the grand prior, and by the Marquis of Elbeuf. It is an odd mistake of Mr. Henry White (Mass. of St. Bartholomew, p. 14, note) when he says : "In the religious wars he sided with the Huguenots." Brantôme says : "Il haïssoit mortellement ces gens-là."

[3] De Thou, iv. 316–325 ; Agrippa d'Aubigné, i. 325–335.

[4] Ibid., *ubi supra.*

in the immediate vicinity of Paris? His forces, indeed, were small in numbers, but would speedily grow formidable. The French ambassador sent from London the intelligence that letters of credit had been sent from England to Hamburg in order to hasten the entrance into France of some twelve or fifteen thousand Germans under Duke Casimir; that twenty-five hundred men were to be despatched from La Rochelle to make a descent on some point in Normandy or Brittany, in conjunction with the ships of the Prince of Orange; and that the English were to be invited to co-operate.[1] If it had proved impracticable to prevent the Duc de Deux Ponts from marching across France to join the confederates near the ocean, what hope was there that the king would be able to hinder the union of Coligny and Casimir? Or, why might not both be reinforced by the troops of La Noue, who had been accomplishing such exploits in Aunis and Saintonge?

The princes of Germany added their intercessions to the stern logic of the conflict. During the festivities in Heidelberg, attending the marriage of John Casimir, Duke of Bavaria, and Elizabeth, daughter of the Elector of Saxony, in June, 1570, the Elector Palatine, the Elector of Saxony, the Margraves George Frederick of Brandenburg and Charles of Baden, Louis, Duke of Würtemberg, the Landgraves William, Philip and George of Hesse, and Adolphus, Duke of Holstein, wrote a joint letter to Charles the Ninth of France, in which they drew his attention to the injury which the long war he was carrying on with his subjects was inflicting upon the states of the empire, and to the necessity of speedily terminating it if he would retain their goodwill and friendship. And they assured him that there was no way of accomplishing this result except by permitting the exercise of the reformed religion throughout the kingdom, and abolishing all distinctions between his Majesty's subjects of different faiths.[2]

When the war had so signally failed, it is not strange that the king and his mother should have turned once more to the advocates of peace, with whose return to favor the retirement

---

[1] La Mothe Fénélon, iii. 210, 215. Despatch of June 21st.
[2] De Thou, iv. 287, 288; Kluckhohn, Briefe Friedrich des Frommen, ii. 398.

of the Guises from court was contemporaneous. Yet the Protestants, who knew too well from experience the malignity of that hated family, could not but shudder lest they might be putting themselves in the power of their most determined enemies. The Queen of Navarre wrote to Charles urging him to use his own native good sense, and assuring him that she feared " marvellously " that these well-known mischief-makers would lure him into " a patched-up-peace "—*une paix fourrée*—like the preceding pacifications. The object they had in view was, indeed, the ruin of the Huguenots ; but the first disaster, she warned him, would fall on the monarch and his royal estate.[1] Cardinal Châtillon, when sounded by the French ambassador in England, expressed his eagerness for peace. On selfish grounds alone he would be glad to exchange poverty in England for his revenues of one hundred and twenty thousand a year in France. But he had his fears. " Remembering that the king, the queen, and monsieur (the Duke of Anjou), to confirm the last peace, did him the honor to give him their word, placing their own hands in his, and that those who induced them to break it were those very persons with whom he and his associates now had to conclude the proposed peace," he said, " his hair stood upon end with fear." All that the Protestants wanted was security. They would be glad to transfer the war elsewhere—a thing his brother the admiral had always desired ; and, if admitted to the king's favor, they would render his Majesty the most notable service that had been done to the crown for two hundred years.[2]

Anxiety of Cardinal Châtillon.

The terms of the long-desired peace were at last decided upon by the commissioners, among whom Téligny and Beauvoir la Nocle were most prominent on the Protestant side, while Biron and De Mesmes represented the court. On the eighth of August, 1570, they were officially promulgated in a royal edict signed at St. Germain-en-Laye.

Royal Edict of pacification, St. Germain, August 8, 1570.

There were in this document the usual stipulations respecting

---

[1] La Mothe Fénélon, iii. 256, 257.

[2] Letter of April 17, 1570, Rochambeau, Lettres d'Antoine de Bourbon et de Jehanne d'Albret (Paris, 1877), 299.

amnesty, the prohibition of insults and recriminations, and kindred topics. The liberty of religious profession was guaranteed. Respecting worship according to the Protestant rites, the provision was of the following character. All nobles entitled to "high jurisdiction"[1] were permitted to designate one place belonging to them, where they could have religious services for themselves, their families, their subjects, and all who might choose to attend, so long as either they or their families were present. This privilege, in the case of other nobles, was restricted to their families and their friends, not exceeding ten in number. To the Queen of Navarre a few places were granted in the fiefs which she held of the French crown, where service could be celebrated even in her absence. In addition to these, there was a list of cities, designated by name—two in each of the twelve principal governments or provinces—in which, or in the suburbs of which, the reformed services were allowed; and this privilege was extended to all those places of which the Protestants had possession on the first of the present month of August. From all other places—from the royal court and its vicinity to a distance of two leagues, and especially from Paris and its vicinity to the distance of ten leagues—Protestant worship was strictly excluded. Provision was made for Protestant burials, to take place in the presence of not more than ten persons. The king recognized the Queen of Navarre, the prince her son, and the late Prince of Condé and his son, as faithful relations and servants; their followers as loyal subjects; Deux Ponts, Orange, and his brothers, and Wolrad Mansfeld, as good neighbors and friends. There was to be a restitution of property, honors, and offices, and a rescission of judicial sentences. To protect the members of the reformed faith in the courts of justice, they were to be permitted to challenge four of the judges in the Parliament of Paris; six—three in each chamber—in those of Rouen, Dijon, Aix, Rennes, and

---

[1] Chassanée in his "Consuetudines ducatus Burgundiæ, fereque totius Galliæ" (Lyons, 1552), 50, defines the "haute justice" by the possession of the power of life and death: "De secundo vero gradu meri imperii, seu altæ justiciæ, est habere gladii potestatem ad animadvertendum in facinorosos homines."

Grenoble; and four in each chamber of the Parliament of Bordeaux. They were to be allowed a peremptory appeal from the Parliament of Toulouse. To defend the Huguenots from popular violence, four cities were to be intrusted to them for a period of two years—La Rochelle, Montauban, Cognac, and La Charité—to serve as places of refuge; and the Princes of Navarre and Condé, with twenty of their followers, were to pledge their word for the safe restoration of these cities to the king at the expiration of the designated term.[1]

Such were the leading features of the edict of pacification that closed the third religious war, by far the longest and most sanguinary conflict that had as yet desolated France. That the terms would be regarded as in the highest degree offensive by the intolerant party at home and abroad was to be expected. The Parisian curate, Jehan de la Fosse, only spoke the common sentiment of the clergy and of the bigoted Roman Catholics when he said that " it contained articles sufficiently terrible to make France and the king's faithful servants tremble, seeing that the Huguenots were reputed as faithful servants, and what they had done held by the king to be agreeable." [2]   It was not astonishing, therefore, that, although the publication of the edict was effected without delay under the eyes of the court at Paris, it gave rise in Rouen to a serious riot.[3] The Papal Nuncio and the Spanish ambassador were indignant. Both Pius and Philip had bitterly opposed the negotiations of the early part of the year. Now their ambassadors made a fruitless attempt to put off the evil day of peace; the Spanish ambassador not only offering three thousand horse and six thousand foot to extirpate the Huguenots, but affirming that " there were no conditions to which he was not ready to bind himself, provided that the king would not make peace with the heretics and rebels." [4]

Dissatisfaction of the clergy.

---

[1] See the edict itself in Jean de Serres, iii. 375–390; summaries in De Thou, iv. (liv. xlvii.) 328, 329, and Agrippa d'Aubigné, i. 364, 365.

[2] Journal d'un curé ligueur, 120.

[3] Ibid., *ubi supra.*

[4] Castelnau, liv. vii., c. 12. The work of this very fair-minded historian terminates with the conclusion of the peace. De Thou, iv. (liv. xlvii.) 327.

For the first time in their history, the relations of the Huguenots of France to the state were settled, not by a royal declaration which was to be of force until the king should attain his majority, or until the convocation of a general council of the Church, but by an edict which was expressly stated to be "*perpetual and irrevocable.*" Such the Protestants, although with many misgivings, hoped that it might prove. It was "The limping and unsettled peace." not, however, an auspicious circumstance that the popular wit, laying hold of the fact that one of the Roman Catholic commissioners that drew up its stipulations— Biron—was lame, while the other—Henri de Mesmes—was best known as Lord of Malassise, conferred upon the new compact the ungracious appellation of "*the limping and unsettled peace*" —"la paix boiteuse et mal-assise." [1]

---

[1] " On la disoit boiteuse et mal-assise," says Henri de Mesmes himself in his account of these transactions, adding with a delicate touch of sarcasm: " Je n'en ay point vû depuis vingt-cinq ans qui ait guère duré." Le Laboureur, Add. aux Mém. de Castelnau, ii. 776.   Prof. Soldan has already exposed the mistake of Sismondi and others, who apply the popular nickname to the preceding peace of Longjumeau.   See *ante*, chap. xv.

CHAPTER XVII.

THE PEACE OF SAINT GERMAIN.

A PROBLEM of cardinal importance here confronts us, in the inquiry whether the peace which had at length dawned upon France was or was not concluded in good faith by the young king and his advisers. Was the treaty a necessity forced upon sincerity of the court by the losses of men and treasure sustained the peace. during three years of almost continual civil conflict? Were the queen mother and those in whose hands rested the chief control of affairs, really tired of a war in which nothing was to be gained and everything was in jeopardy, a war whose most brilliant successes had been barren of substantial fruits, and had, in the sequel, been stripped of the greater part of their glory by the masterly conduct of a defeated opponent? Or, was the peace only a prelude to the massacre—a skilfully devised snare to entrap incautious and credulous enemies?

The latter view is that which was entertained by the majority of the contemporaries of the events, who, whether friends or foes of Charles and Catharine, whether Papists or Protestants, could not avoid reading the treaty of pacification in the light of the occurrences of the "bloody nuptials." The Huguenot author of the "Tocsin against the murderers" and Capilupi, author of the appreciative "Stratagem of Charles the Ninth" —however much they may disagree upon other points—unite in regarding the royal edict as a piece of treachery from beginning to end. It was even believed by many of the most intelligent Protestants that the massacre was already perfected in the minds of its authors so far back as the conference of Bayonne, five years before the peace of St. Germain, in accordance with the suggestions of Philip the Second and of Alva. This last supposition, however, has been overthrown by the discovery of the correspondence of Alva himself, in which he gives an account of the discussions which he held with Catharine de' Medici on that memorable occasion. For we have seen that, far from convincing the queen mother of the necessity for adopting sanguinary measures to crush the Huguenots, the duke constantly deplores to his master the obstinacy of Catharine in still clinging to her own views of toleration. It seems equally clear that the peace of St. Germain was no part of the project of a contemplated massacre of the Protestants. The Montmorencies, not the Guises, were in power, and were responsible for it. The influence of the former had become paramount, and that of the latter had waned. The Cardinal of Lorraine had left the court in disgust and retired to his archbishopric of Rheims, when he found that the policy of war, to which he and his family were committed, was about to be abandoned. Even in the earlier negotiations he had no part, while the queen mother and the moderate Morvilliers were omnipotent.[1] And when Francis Walsingham made his appearance at the French court, to congratulate Charles the Ninth upon the restoration of peace, he found his strongest reasons of hope for its permanence, next to the disposition and the necessities of the king, in the royal "misliking toward the house of Guise, who have been the nourishers of these wars,"[2] and in the increase of the royal "favor to Montmorency, a chief worker of this peace, who now carrieth the whole sway of the court, and is restored to the government of Paris."[3]

---

[1] "La Royne et mons. de Morvillier trettent eus deus seulz avecques eus, ce sont aujourdhuy les grans cous." See two important letters of Lorraine to his sister-in-law, the Duchess of Nemours, April 24th and May 1, 1570, in Soldan, Geschichte d. Prot. in Frank., ii. Appendix, 593, 594, from MSS. of the Bibliothèque nationale.

[2] "Though of late the Cardinal of Lorrain hath had access to the king's presence, yet is he not repaired in credit, neither dealeth he in government." Walsingham to Leicester, Aug. 29, 1570, Digges, Compleat Ambassador, p. 8.

[3] Ibid., ubi supra. Yet it is but fair to add that Walsingham notes that "the great conference that is between the queen mother and the cardinal breedeth some doubt of some practise to impeach the same."

At home and abroad, the peace was equally opposed by those who could not have failed to be its warmest advocates had it been treacherously designed. We have already seen that both Pope Pius the Fifth, and the King of Spain insisted upon a continuance of the war, and offered augmented assistance, in case the government would pledge itself to make no compact with the heretical rebels. The pontiff especially was unremitting in his persuasions and threats; denouncing the righteous judgment of God upon the king who preferred personal advantage to the claims of religion, and reminding him that the divine anger was wont to punish the sins of rulers by taking away their kingdoms and giving them to others.[1] The project of a massacre of Protestants, had it in reality been entertained by the French court while adopting the peace, could scarcely have been kept so profound a secret from the king and the pontiff who had long been urging a resort to such measures, nor would Pius and Philip have been suffered through ignorance to persist in so open a hostility to the compact which was intended to render its execution feasible.

If the Massacre of St. Bartholomew's Day, as enacted on the fatal Sunday of August, was not premeditated in the form it then assumed—if the peace of St. Germain was not, as so many have imagined, a trick to overwhelm the Huguenots taken unawares—are we, therefore, to believe that the idea of such a deed of blood was as yet altogether foreign to the mind of Catharine de' Medici? I dare not affirm that it was. On the contrary, there is reason to believe that the conviction that she might some day find herself in a position in which she could best free herself from entanglement by some such means had long since lodged in her mind.

The designs of Catharine de' Medici.

It was not a strange or repulsive notion to the careful student of the code of morality laid down in "Il Principe." Alva had familiarized her with it, and the civil wars had almost invested it in her eyes with the appearance of justifiable retaliation. She had gloated in secret over the story of the Queen Blanche, mother of Louis the Ninth, and her successful struggle with her

[1] Letter of April 23, 1570, Pii Quinti Epistolæ, 272.

son's insubordinate nobles, telling her countryman, the Venetian ambassador Correro, with a significant laugh such as she was wont occasionally to indulge in, that she would be very sorry to have it known that she had been reading the old manuscript chronicle, for they would at once infer that she had taken the Castilian princess as her pattern.[1]   More unscrupulous than the mother of St. Louis, she had revolved in her mind various schemes for strengthening her authority at the expense of the lives of a few of the more prominent Huguenot chiefs, convinced, as she was, that Protestantism would cease to exist in France with the destruction of its leaders.   But, despite pontifical injunctions and Spanish exhortations, she formed no definite plans; or, if she did, it was only to unravel on the morrow what she had woven the day before.   What Barbaro said of her at one critical juncture was true of her generally in all such deliberations : " Her irresolution is extreme; she conceives new plans from hour to hour ; within the compass of a single day, between morning and evening, she will change her mind three times.[2] "

While it is scarcely possible to believe Catharine to have been more sincere in the adoption of this peace than in any other event of her life, we may feel some confidence that her son was really in favor of peace for its own sake.   He was weary of the war, jealous of his brother Anjou, disgusted with the Guises, and determined to attempt to conciliate his Huguenot subjects, whom he had in vain been trying to crush.   Apparently he wished to make of the amnesty, which the edict formally proclaimed, a veritable act of oblivion of all past offences, and intended to regard the Huguenots, in point of fact as well as in law, as his faithful subjects. An incident which occurred about two months after the conclusion of peace, throws light upon the king's new disposition.   Cardinal Odet de Châtillon, deprived by the Pope of his seat in the Roman consistory, had, on motion of Cardinal Bourbon, been declared by the Parisian parliament to have lost his bishopric

Charles the Ninth in earnest.

---

[1] Relations des Amb. Vén. (Tommaseo), ii. 110.   Correro's relation is of 1569.

[2] Baschet, La diplomatie vénitienne, p. 518.

of Beauvais, on account of his rebellion and his adoption of Protestant sentiments. All such judicial proceedings had indeed been declared null and void by the terms of the pacification, but the parliaments showed themselves very reluctant to regard the royal edict. In October, 1570, Charles the Ninth happening to be a guest of Marshal Montmorency at his palace of Écouen, a few leagues north of Paris, sent orders to Christopher de Thou, the first president, to wait upon him with the parliamentary records. Aware of the king's object, De Thou, pleading illness, sent four of his counsellors instead; but these were ignominiously dismissed, and the presence of the chief judge was again demanded. When De Thou at last appeared, Charles greeted him roughly. "Here you are," he said, "and not very ill, thank God! Why do you go counter to my edicts? I owe our cousin, Cardinal Bourbon, no thanks for having applied for and obtained sentence against the house of Châtillon, *which has done me so much service, and took up arms for me.*" Then calling for the records, he ordered the president to point out the proceedings against the admiral's brother, and, on finding them, tore out with his own hand three leaves on which they were inscribed; and on having his attention directed by the marshal, who stood by, to other places bearing upon the same case, he did not hesitate to tear these out also.[1]

He tears out the record against Cardinal Châtillon.

To all with whom he conversed Charles avowed his steadfast purpose to maintain the peace inviolate. He called it his own peace. He told Walsingham, "he willed him to assure her Majesty, that the only care he presently had was to entertain the peace, whereof the Queen of Navarre and the princes of the religion could well be witnesses, as also generally the whole realm."[2] And the shrewd diplomatist believed that the king spoke the truth;[3] although, when

His assurances to Walsingham.

---

[1] The only account of this striking occurrence which I have seen is given by Jehan de la Fosse, p. 122.

[2] Walsingham and Norris to Elizabeth, Jan. 29, 1571, Digges, 24.

[3] "The best ground of continuance," he writes to Leicester, "that I can learn, by those that can best judge, is the king's own inclination, which is thought sincerely to be bent that way." Jan. 28, 1571, Digges, 28.

he looked at the adverse circumstances with which Charles was surrounded, and the vicious and irreligious education he had received, there was room for solicitude respecting his stability.¹ There was, indeed, much to strengthen the hands of Charles in his new policy of toleration. On the twenty-sixth of November he married, with great pomp and amid the display of the popular delight, Elizabeth, daughter of the Emperor Maximilian the Second. This union, far from imperilling the permanence of the peace in France,² was likely to render it more lasting, if the bridegroom could be induced to copy the conciliatory and politic example of his father-in-law. Not long after Charles received at Villers-Cotterets an embassy sent by the three

Gracious an-
swer to the
German elec-
tors.

Protestant electors of Germany and the other powerful princes of the same faith. They congratulated him upon the suppression of civil disorder in France, and entreated him to maintain freedom of worship in his dominions such as existed in Germany and even in the dominions of the Grand Turk ; lending an ear to none who might attempt to persuade him that tranquillity could not subsist in a kingdom where there was more than one religion. Charles made a gracious answer, and the German ambassadors retired, leaving the friends of the Huguenots to entertain still better hopes for the recent treaty.³

It cannot be denied, however, that the Huguenots could see much that was disquieting and calculated to prevent them from laying aside their suspicions. There were symptoms of the old constitutional timidity on the part of Catharine de' Medici. She showed signs of so far yielding to the inveterate enemies

Catharine
warned by
the Hugue-
nots.

of the Huguenots as to abstain from insisting upon the concession of public religious worship where it had been accorded by the Edict of St. Germain. No wonder that the Huguenots, on their side, warned her, with friendly sincerity and frankness, that, should she refuse to

---

¹ " Thus, sir, you see, for that he is not settled in religion, how he is carried away with worldly respects, a common misery to those of his calling." Ibid., 30.

² Walsingham to Leicester, Aug. 29, 1570, Digges, 8.

³ De Thou, iv. 330–333. See Digges, 30.

entertain their just demands, *the present peace would be only a brief truce, the prelude to a relentless civil war.* " We will all die," was their language, " rather than forsake our God and our religion, which we can no more sustain without public exercise than could a body live without food and drink." [1] Not only did the courts throw every obstacle in the way of the formal recognition of the law establishing the rights of the Huguenots, but the outbreaks of popular hatred against the adherents of the purer faith were alarming evidence that the chronic sore had only been healed over the surface, and that none of the elements of future disorder and bloodshed were wanting. Thus, in the little city and principality of Orange, the Roman Catholic populace, taking advantage of the supineness of the governor and of the consuls, introduced within the walls, under cover of a three days' religious festival, a large number of ruffians from the adjoining Comtât Venaissin. This was early in February, 1571. Now began a scene of rapine and bloodshed that might demand detailed mention, were it not that at the frequent repetition of such ghastly recitals the stoutest heart sickens. Men, and even mere boys, of the reformed faith were butchered in their homes, in the arms of their wives or their mothers. The goods of Protestants were plundered and openly sold to the highest bidder.

Infringement on the edict at Orange.

---

[1] Letter of the Queen of Navarre to the queen mother, Dec. 17, 1570, Rochambeau, Lettres d'Antoine de Bourbon et de Jehanne d'Albret (Paris, 1877), 306. A few lines of this admirable paper (which is, however, much mutilated) may be quoted as having an almost prophetic significance : " Et vous diray, Madame, les larmes aus yeulx, avecq une afection pure et entière que, s'il ne plaist au Roy et à vous nous aseureur nos tristes demandes, que je ne puis espérer qu'une treve . . . en ce royaulme par ceste guerre siville, car nous y mourrons tous plustost que quiter nostre Dieu et nostre religion, laquelle nous ne pouvons tenir sans exersise, non plus qu'un corps ne sauré vivre sans boire et manger. . . . Je vous en ay dit le seul moyen ; ayés pitié de tant de sang répandu, de tant d'impiétés commises en la . . . de ceste guerre et *que vous ne pourrez bien d'un seul mot faire cesser.*" " Et sur cella, Madame, je supliray Dieu qui tient les cueurs des Roys en sa main disposer celui du Roi et le vostre à mectre le repos en ce royaulme à sa gloire et contentement de Vos Majestés, *maugré le complot de M. le Cardinal de Lorrayne,* dont il a descouvert la trame à Villequagnon," etc.

Of many, a ransom was exacted for their safety. The work went on for two weeks. At last a deputy from Orange reached the Huguenot princes and the admiral at La Rochelle, and Count Louis of Nassau, who was still there, wrote to Charles with such urgency, in the name of his brother, the Prince of Orange, that measures were taken to repress and punish the disorder.[1]

A much more serious infringement upon the protection granted to the Protestants by the edict, took place at Rouen about a month later. Unable to celebrate their worship within the city walls, the Protestants had gone out one Sunday morning to the place assigned them for this purpose in the suburbs. Meantime a body of four hundred Roman Catholics posted themselves in ambush near the gates to await their return. When the unsuspecting Huguenots, devoutly meditating upon the solemnities in which they had been engaged, made their appearance, they were greeted first with imprecations and blasphemies, then with a murderous attack. Between one hundred and one hundred and twenty are said to have been killed or wounded. The punishment of this audacious violation of the rights of the Protestants was at first left by parliament to the inferior or presidial judges, and the investigation dragged. The judges were threatened as they went to court: "Si l'on sçavoit que vous eussiez informé, on vous creveroit les yeux; si vous y mectez la main, on vous coupera la gorge!" The people broke into the prisons and liberated the accused. The civic militia refused to interfere. It was evident that no justice could be obtained from the local magistrates. The king, however, on receiving the complaints of the Huguenots, displayed great indignation, and despatched Montmorency to Rouen with twenty-seven companies of soldiers, and a commission authorized to try the culprits. The greater part of these, however, had fled. Only five persons received the punishment of death; several hundred fugitives were hung in effigy. Montmorency attempted to secure the Protestants against fur-

The Protestants at Rouen attacked, March 4, 1571.

---

[1] Discours du massacre fait à Orange, from the Mém. de l'état de France sous Charles IX., Archives curieuses, vi. 459–470 ; De Thou, iv. 483.

ther aggression by disarming the entire population, with the
exception of four hundred chosen men, and by compelling the
parliament, on the fifteenth of May, to swear to observe the
Edict of Pacification—precautions whose efficacy we shall be able
to estimate more accurately by the events of the following year.[1]

The strength of the popular hatred of the Huguenots was
often too great for even the government to cope with. The
rabble of the cities would hear of no upright execution of the
provisions respecting the oblivion of past injuries, and resisted
with pertinacity the attempt to remove the traces of the old
conflict. The Parisians gave the most striking evidence of their unextinguished rancor in the matter of
the "Croix de Gastines," a monument of religious
bigotry, the reasons for whose erection in 1569 have been sufficiently explained in a previous chapter.[2]

The "Croix
de Gastines"
again.

More than a year had passed since the promulgation of the
royal edict of pacification annulling all judgments rendered
against Protestants since the death of Henry the Second; and
yet the Croix de Gastines still stood aloft on its pyramidal base,
upon the site of the Huguenot place of meeting. Several times,
at the solicitation of the Protestants, the government ordered its
demolition. The municipal officers of Paris declined to obey, because it had not been erected by them; the parliament, because,
as they alleged, the sentence was just and they could not retract;
the Provost of Paris, because he was not above parliament,
which had placed it there.[3] Charles himself wrote with his own
hand to the provost: "You deliberate whether to obey me, and
whether you will have that fine pyramid overturned. I forbid
you to appear in my presence until it be cast down."[4] The end
was not yet. The monks preached against the sacrilege of
lowering the cross. Maître Vigor, on the first Sunday of
Advent, praised the people of Paris for having opposed the

---

[1] Floquet, Histoire du Parlement du Normandie, iii. 87–112, whose account
is in great part derived from the registers of the parliament and the archives
of the Hôtel de Ville of Rouen. De Thou, iv. (liv. 1.) 483, certainly greatly
underestimates the number of Protestants killed, when he limits it to *five*.

[2] See *ante*, chapter xvi.

[3] Jehan de la Fosse (Sept., 1571), 132.

[4] Ibid. (Nov., 1571), 133.

demolition, maintaining that they had acted "only from zeal for God, who upon the cross suffered for us." "The people," he declared, "had never murmured when they had taken down Gaspard de Coligny, who had been hung in effigy, and *would soon, God willing, be hung in very deed!*" [1] Meantime, the mob of Paris exhibited its zeal for the honor of the cross by assailing the soldiers sent to tear down the "Croix de Gastines," and by breaking open and plundering the contents of several Huguenot houses. It was not until the provost had called in the assistance of Marshal Montmorency, and the latter had killed a few of the seditious Parisians who opposed his progress, and hung one man to the windows of a neighboring house, that the disturbance ceased. The pyramid was then destroyed, and the cross transferred to the Cimetière des Innocents, where it is said to have remained until the outbreak of the French Revolution.[2] The "plucking down of the cross" was a distasteful draught to the fanatics. "The common people," wrote an eyewitness, "ease their stomacks onely by uttering seditious words, which is borne withal, for that was doubted. The Protestants by the overthrow of this cross receive greater comfort, and the papists the contrary." [3]

---

[1] Jehan de la Fosse (Dec., 1571), 134.

[2] Agrippa d'Aubigné, ii. 4 (liv. i., c. 1); De Thou, iv. (liv. l.) 487–489; Discours de ce qui avint touchant la Croix de Gastines (from Mém. de l'état de Charles IX.), in Cimber et Danjou, Arch. cur., vi. 475, 476; Jehan de la Fosse, *ubi supra*. According to the recently published journal of La Fosse, Charles the Ninth expressed himself to the preachers of Paris, who had come to remonstrate with him in language which may at first sight appear somewhat suspicious: " attestant ledict roy vouloir vivre et mourir en la religion de ses prédécesseurs roys, religion catholique et romaine, toutefois qu'il avoit fait abattre la croix pour certaine cause laquelle il vouloit taire et avoir faict plusieurs choses contre sa conscience, toutefois par contrainte à cause du temps, et supplioit les prédicateurs n'avoir mauvaise opinion de luy" (pp. 138, 139). There is good reason, however, to believe that the secret reason which the king was unwilling to name was not a contemplated massacre of the Protestants, but rather the Navarrese and English marriages, and the war with Spain in the Netherlands.

[3] Walsingham to Burleigh, Dec. 7, 1571, Digges, p. 151. "Marshal Montmorency repaired to this town the third of this moneth accompanied with 300 horse. The next day after his arrival he and the Marshal de Coss conferred with the chief of this town about the plucking down of the cross, which was

The Huguenot leaders, rejoicing at any evidence of the royal favor, desired to strengthen it and render it more stable. For

Projected marriage of Anjou to Queen Elizabeth.

this purpose they found a rare opportunity in projecting matrimonial alliances. Queen Elizabeth, of England, was yet unmarried, a princess of acknowledged ability, and reigning over a kingdom, which, if it had not at that time attained the wealth of industry and commerce which it now possesses, was, at least, one of the most illustrious in Christendom. Where could a more advantageous match be sought for Henry of Anjou, the French monarch's brother? True, the Tudor princess was no longer young, and her personal appearance was scarcely praised, except by her courtiers. She had been a candidate for many projected nuptials, but in none had the disparity of age been so great as in the present case, for, being a maiden of thirty-seven, she lacked but a single year of being twice as old as Anjou.[1] Besides these objections, and independently of the difference of creed between the queen and Anjou, she had the unenviable reputation of being irresolute, fickle, and capricious. And yet, in spite of all these difficulties, the match was seriously proposed and entertained in the autumn and winter succeeding the ratification of peace.

It is worthy of notice that the scheme originated with the French Protestants. Cardinal Châtillon, the admiral's brother, and the Vidame of Chartres, both of them zealous partisans of the Reformation, and at this time engaged in negotiations in England, were the first to make mention of the plan, and probably it took its rise in their minds. Their object was manifest : if France could be united to Protestant England by so distinguished a marriage, the permanence of the peace of St. Germain might be regarded as secure. Under such auspices, the Huguenots, long proscribed and persecuted, might hope for such favor and toleration as they had never yet enjoyed.

Catharine de' Medici, when approached on the subject, gave

resolved on, and the same put in execution, the masons employed in that behalf being guarded by certain harquebusiers."

[1] Queen Elizabeth was born September 7, 1533 ; Henry was born in September, 1551 (the day is variously given as the 18th, 19th, and 21st), and was just nineteen.

indications of hearty acquiescence. Of late there had been a growing estrangement between the French and Spanish courts. The selfishness and arrogance of Philip and his ministers had been particularly evident and offensive during the late war. It was sufficiently clear that the Catholic king opposed the peace less from hatred of heresy or of rebellion, than because of his scarcely disguised hope of profiting by the misfortunes of France. The queen mother was consequently quite inclined to tighten the bonds of amity and friendship with England, when those that had previously existed with Spain were loosened. The prospect of a crown for her favorite son was an alluring one—doubly so, because of Nostradamus's prophecy that she would see all her sons upon the throne, to which she gave a superstitious credence, trembling lest it should involve in its fulfilment their untimely death. It is true that, in view of Elizabeth's age, she would have preferred to marry the Duke of Anjou to some princess of the royal house of England, whom Elizabeth might first have proclaimed her heir and successor.[1] However, as the English queen was, perhaps, even more reluctant than the majority of mankind to be reminded of her advancing years and of her mortality, Catharine's ambassador may have deemed it advisable to be silent regarding the suggestion of so palpable a " memento mori," and contented himself with offering for her own acceptance the hand of one whom he recommended as " the most accomplished prince living, and the most deserving her good graces." [2]   Elizabeth received the proposal with courtesy, merely alluding to the great difference between her age and Anjou's, but admitted her apprehension lest, since " she was already one whose kingdom rather than herself was to be wedded," she might marry one who would honor her as a queen rather than love her as a woman. In fact, the remembrance of the amours of the father and grandfather made her suspicious of the son, and the names of Madame d'Estampes and of Madame de Valentinois (Diana of Poitiers) inspired her with

---

[1] Letter of Catharine to La Mothe Fénélon, Oct. 20, 1570, Correspondance diplomatique, vii. 143–146.

[2] Despatch of La Mothe Fénélon, Dec. 29, 1570. Ibid., vol. iii. 418, 419.

no little fear. All which coy suggestions La Mothe Fénélon, astute courtier that he was, knew well how to answer.[1]

Soon, however, the difficulty threatened to be the unwillingness of the suitor, rather than the reluctance of the lady. Henry of Anjou was the head of the Roman Catholic party in France. Charles's orthodoxy might be suspected ; there was no doubt of his brother's. His intimacy with the Guises, his successes as general of the royal forces in what was styled a war in defence of religion, were guarantees of his devotion to the papal cause. All his prestige would be lost if he married the heretical daughter of Henry the Eighth and Anne Boleyn. Hence desperate efforts were made to deter him —efforts which did not escape the Argus-eyed Walsingham. " The Pope, the King of Spain, and the rest of the confederates, upon the doubt of a match between the queen, my mistress, and monsieur, do seek, by what means they can, to dissuade and draw him from the same. They offer him to be the head and chief executioner of the league against the Turk, a thing now newly renewed, though long ago meant ; which league is thought to stretch to as many as they repute to be Turks, although better Christians than themselves. The cause of the Cardinal of Lorraine's repair hither from Rheims, as it is thought, was to this purpose." [2]

Machinations to dissuade Anjou.

Charles the Ninth was indignant at this interference, and said : " If this matter go forward, it behooveth me to make some counter-league," having his eye upon the German Protestant princes and Elizabeth.[3] Besides, there were at this juncture other reasons for displeasure, especially with Spain. Charles and his mother had received a rebuff from Sebastian of Portugal, to whom they had offered Margaret of Valois in marriage. The young king had replied,

Charles indignant at the interference.

---

[1] And with a freedom which might be mistaken for Arcadian simplicity, did we not know that innocence was no characteristic of either court in that age. " J'en cognoissoys ung," he told her, " qui estoit nay à tant de sortes de vertu, qu'il ne failloit doubter qu'elle n'en fût fort honnorée et singulièrement bien aymée, et dont j'espèrerois qu'au bout de neuf mois après, elle se trouveroit mère d'ung beau filz," etc. La Mothe Fénélon, iii. 439, 454, 455.

[2] Despatch to Cecil, Jan. 28, 1571, Digges, 26.

[3] Ibid., 27.

through Malicorne, "that they were both young, and that therefore about eight years hence that matter might be better talked
of," "which disdainful answer," the English ambassador wrote
from the French court, " is accepted here in very ill part, and is
thought not to be done without the counsel of Spain." [1]

With Henry of Anjou, however, much to the disgust and disappointment of his mother, the "league" succeeded too well.
Scarcely had a month passed, before Catharine was compelled
to write to the envoy in England, telling him that Henry had
heard reports unfavorable to Elizabeth's character, and positively declined to marry her. [2] In her extreme perplexity at
Alençon to be this unexpected turn of events, the queen mother
substituted as suggested to La Mothe Fénélon · that perhaps the
suitor.
Duke of Alençon would do as well, and might step
into the place which his brother had so ungallantly abandoned. [3]
Now, as this Alençon was a beardless boy of sixteen, and, unlike
Charles and Henry, small for his age, it is not surprising that
La Mothe declared himself utterly averse to making any mention of him for the present, lest the queen should come to the
very sensible conclusion that the French were "making sport
of her." [4]

But there was at present no need of resorting to substitution.
For a time the ardor of Anjou was rekindled, and rapidly in-
Anjou's new creased in intensity. Catharine first wrote that Anjou
ardor.
"condescended" to marry Elizabeth ; [5] presently, that
"he desired infinitely to espouse her." [6]   A month or two later
he declared to Walsingham : "I must needs confess that, through
the great commendation that is made of the queen your mistress, for her rare gifts as well of mind as of body, being (as
even her very enemies say) the rarest creature that was in

---

[1] Digges, 27.
[2] Catharine to La Mothe Fénélon, Feb. 2, 1571, Corresp. diplom., vii. 179 ;
and Walsingham to Cecil, Feb. 18, 1571, Digges, 43.
[3] Catharine, *ubi supra*.
[4] La Mothe Fénélon, March 6, 1571, ibid., iv. 11, 12. The ambassador
exhibits his own incredulity respecting the stories circulated to the queen's
disadvantage.
[5] To La Mothe Fénélon, Feb. 18, 1571, ibid., vii. 183.
[6] To the same, March 2, 1571, ibid., vii. 190.

Europe these five hundred years; my affection, grounded upon
so good respects, hath now made me yield to be wholly hers."[1]
On the other hand, Elizabeth began to exhibit such coldness
that her most intimate servants doubted her sincerity in the
entire transaction. With more candor than courtiers usually
exhibit in urging a suit which they suspect to be distasteful to
their sovereign, Lord Burleigh, the Earl of Leicester, and Sir
Francis Walsingham used every means of persuading the queen
to decisive action. "My very good Lord," wrote Walsingham,
on the fourteenth of May, 1571, "the Protestants here do so
earnestly desire this match; and on the other side, the papists
do so earnestly seek to impeach the same, as it maketh me the
more earnest in furthering of the same. Besides, when I particularly consider her Majesty's state, both at home and abroad,
so far forth as my poor eyesight can discern; and how she is
beset with foreign peril, the execution whereof stayeth only
upon the event of this match, I do not see how she can stand if
this matter break off."[2] Lord Burleigh, in perplexity on account of Elizabeth's conduct, exclaimed that "he was not able
to discern what was best;" but added: "Surely I see no continuance of her quietness without a marriage, and therefore I remit
the success to Almighty God."[3] The situation of Elizabeth's
servants was, indeed, extremely embarrassing. Their mistress
had laid an insuperable obstacle in the way. She did
not, indeed, require Anjou to abjure his faith, but her
demands virtually involved this. Not only did she
refuse to grant the duke, by the articles of marriage, public or
even private worship for himself and his attendants, according to
the rites of the Roman Catholic Church, but she wished to bind
him to make no request to that effect after marriage.[4] In vain
did Catharine protest that this was to require him to become an

*Elizabeth
interposes
obstacles.*

---

[1] Walsingham to Burleigh, May 25, 1571, Digges, 101.

[2] Digges, 96.

[3] Ibid., 55.

[4] "So it doth appear, if he would omit that demand, and put it in silence,
yet will her Majestie straitly capitulate with him, that he shall in no way
demand it hereafter at her hands. Which scruple, I believe, will utterly
break off the matter; wherefore I am in small hope that any marriage will
grow this way." Leicester to Walsingham, July 7, 1571, Digges, 116.

atheist, and her own advisers solemnly warn her that this could but lead to an entire rupture of the negotiations.   Under the pretence of excluding all exercise of Popery from England, the queen disappointed the ardent hopes of thousands of sincere and thorough Protestants in France and of many more in England, who viewed the marriage as by far the most advisable cure—far better than a simple treaty of peace—for the ills of both kingdoms.   " If you find not in her Majesty," wrote Walsingham to Leicester, " a resolute determination to marry—a thing most necessary for our staggering state—then were it expedient to take hold of amity, which may serve to ease us for a time, though our disease requireth another remedy ; " and again, a few days later (on the third of August, 1571): " My lord, if neither marriage nor amity may take place, the poor Protestants here do think then their case desperate.   They tell me so with tears, and therefore I do believe them.   And surely, if they say nothing, beholding the present state here, I could not but see it most apparent." [1]

The fears of the Protestants were not baseless.   As the marriage, and the consequent close friendship with England, seemed to insure the growth and spread of the reformed faith,[2] the failure of both was an almost unmistakable portent of the triumph of the opposite party and of the renewal of persecution and bloodshed.   And so also the fanatical Roman Catholics read the signs of the times, and again they plied Anjou with their seductions.   " Great practices are here for the impeachment of this match," wrote the English ambassador, near the end of July, 1571.   " The Papal Nuncio, Spain, and Portugal, are daily courtiers to dissuade this match.   The clergy here have offered Monsieur a great pension, to stay him from proceeding.   In conclusion, there is nothing left undone, that may be thought fit to hinder." [3]

Papal and Spanish efforts.

---

[1] Digges, 119, 120.

[2] A league with France, Walsingham maintained, would be an advancement of the Gospel there and everywhere, and " though it yieldeth not so much *temporal* profit, yet in respect of the *spiritual fruit* that thereby may insue, I think it worth the imbracing."   Ibid., p. 121.

[3] Digges, 120.

And these intrigues were not fruitless. Anjou now declared to his mother that he would not go to England without public assurances that he should enjoy the liberty to exercise his own religion. He was unwilling even to trust the queen's word, as Vexation of Catharine at Anjou's fresh scruples. Catharine and Charles would have wished him to do. Catharine meantime expressed her vexation in her despatches to La Mothe Fénélon.[1] "We strongly suspect," she said, "that Villequier, Lignerolles, or Sarret, or possibly all three, may be the authors of these fancies. If we succeed in obtaining some certainty respecting this matter, I assure you that they will repent of it."[2] But she added that, should the negotiation unfortunately fail, she was resolved to put forth all her efforts in behalf of her son Alençon, who would be more easily suited.[3]

In fact, while Anjou was indifferent, or perhaps disgusted at the obstacles raised in the way of the marriage, and was unwilling to sacrifice his attachment to the party in connection with which he had obtained whatever distinction he possessed; and while Elizabeth, who was by no means blind, saw clearly enough that she was likely to get a husband who would regard his bride rather as an incumbrance than as an acquisition,[4] there were

---

[1] Anjou's humor, she told him, "me faict bien grande peyne." Letter of July 25, 1571, Corresp. diplom., vii. 234.

[2] Ibid., *ubi supra.* This expression deserves to be noticed particularly, inasmuch as it effectually disposes of the story—which can scarcely be regarded otherwise than as a fable—that the assassination of Lignerolles, a little over four months later (December, 1571), was compassed by Charles IX. and his mother, because they discovered that he had become possessed of the secret of the projected massacre of St. Bartholomew. If these royal personages had anything to do with the murder, which is very improbable, they hated Lignerolles for marring the plan of the English match, which they so much desired.

[3] "Je suis résolue de faire tous mes efforts pour réheussir pour mon fils d'Alençon, qui ne sera pas si difficile." Ibid., vii. 235.

[4] It must be admitted that some indignation on Queen Elizabeth's part was pardonable, if, as we learn from La Mothe Fénélon (despatch of May 2, 1571), she had heard that a certain person of high rank in the French court had recommended Anjou to marry the English "granny"—"ceste vieille"—and administer to her, under some pretext, a "French potion"—"un breuvage de France"—so as to become a widower within six months of the wedding day. Then he might marry Mary, Queen of Scots, and reign with her peace-

two persons who were as eager as Elizabeth's advisers, or the Huguenots themselves, to see the match effected. These were Charles the Ninth and Catharine de' Medici, both of whom just now gave abundant evidence of their disposition to draw closer to England and to the Huguenots of France and the Gueux of Holland, while suffering the breach between France and Spain to become more marked.

Count Louis of Nassau, ever since the conclusion of peace, had remained with the Huguenots within the walls of La Rochelle. At the repeated solicitations of his brother, the Prince of Orange, he had entered into correspondence with the king, and urged him to embrace an opportunity such as might never return, to endear himself to the Netherlanders, and add materially to the extent and power of France by espousing the cause of constitutional rights. His advances were so favorably received that he now came in disguise, accompanied by La Noue, Téligny, and Genlis, to confer with Charles upon the subject. They met at Lumigny-en-Brie, whither the king had gone to indulge in his favorite pastime of the chase, and on several consecutive days held secret conferences.[1] Louis was a nobleman whose history and connections entitled him to respect; but his frank and sincere character was a still more powerful advocate in his behalf.[2] He proved to the king how justly he might interfere in defence of the Low Countries, where Philip was seeking "to plant, by inquisition, the foundation of a most horrible tyranny, the overthrow of all

Louis of Nassau confers with the king.

---

ably over the whole island!   Correspondance diplomatique, iv. 84.   However sincere or zealous Elizabeth may have been previously, I doubt whether she ever forgave the suggestion, or the fair princess whose charms were thus exalted above her own.

[1] De Thou, iv. (liv. l.) 492.

[2] "I would your lordship knew the gentleman," enthusiastically writes Walsingham (August 12th, 1571) to the Earl of Leicester. "For courage abroad and counsell at home they give him here the reputation to be another [name in cipher]. He is in speech eloquent and pithy; but which is chiefest, he is in religion, as religious in life as he is sincere in profession. I hope God hath raised him up in these days, to serve for an instrument for the advancement of His glory." Digges, 128. In another letter, without date, the ambassador speaks of him as "surely the rarest gentleman which I have talked withal since I came to France." Ibid., 176.

freedoms and liberties." He traced the course of events since the humiliating treaty of Cateau-Cambrésis, and added: " If you think in conscience and honor you may not become the protector of this people, you should do well to forbear, for otherwise the success cannot be gained. If you think you may, then weigh in policy how beneficial it will be for you, and how much your father would have given, to have had the like opportunity offered unto him that is now presented unto you gratis ; which, if you refuse, the like you must never look for."

Both Charles and his mother appeared well pleased with the proposal, and the king, who had listened attentively to the recital of the follies into which Philip had fallen in consequence of listening to evil advice, exclaimed : " Similar counsellors, by violating my edict, well-nigh brought me into like terms with my subjects, wherefrom ensued the late troubles; but now, thank God, He has opened my eyes to discern what their meaning was." Next, Louis showed that success was not difficult. The Roman Catholics and the Protestants in the Netherlands equally detested the tyranny of the Spaniards. The towns were ready to receive garrisons. Philip had not in the whole country over three thousand troops upon whose fidelity he could rely. The addition of a dozen ships to those already possessed by the patriots would enable them effectually to prevent the landing of Spanish reinforcements. In short, the Netherlands were ripe for a division which would amply recompense France and the German princes, as well as Queen Elizabeth, should she, as was hoped, consent to take part in the enterprise : for the provinces of Flanders and Artois, which had once belonged to the French crown, would gladly give themselves up to Charles; Brabant, Gelderland, and Luxemburg would be restored to the empire; and Holland, Zealand, and the rest of the islands would fall to the share of the queen.[1]

So favorably did Charles and his mother, with those counsellors to whom the secret was intrusted, receive the count's advances, that it was clearly advisable to bring them into com-

---

[1] The substance of Louis of Nassau's secret interviews is best given by Walsingham in a long communication, of August 12, 1571, to Lord Burleigh, Digges, 123-127.

munication with Admiral Coligny, to whose conduct the enterprise, if adopted, must be confided, and for whom the
young king expressed great esteem.   Indeed, so ur-
gently was the admiral invited, and so intimately
did the success or failure of the attempt to enlist France in
the Flemish war seem to be dependent upon his personal influence, that Gaspard de Coligny, despite the ill-concealed solicitude of many of his more suspicious friends, consented to
trust himself in the king's hands.   As for himself, the admiral
had little desire to leave the secure retreat of La Rochelle.
Here he was surrounded by friends.   Here his happiness had
been enhanced by two marriages which promised to add greatly
to the wealth and influence he already possessed.   Jacqueline
d'Entremont, the widow of a brave officer killed in the
civil wars, had long entertained an admiration, which
she made no attempt to disguise, for the bravery and
piety of the stern leader of the Huguenots.   Possessed of very
extensive estates in the dominions of the Duke of Savoy, she
had also the qualities of mind and disposition which fitted her
to become the wife of so upright and magnanimous a man.
The proposals of marriage are said to have come from her relatives, nor did the lady herself hesitate to express the wish before her death to become the Marcia of the new Cato.[1]   The
nuptials were celebrated with great pomp at La Rochelle,
whither Jacqueline, after having been married by proxy,[2] was
escorted by a goodly train of Huguenot nobles.   Great were
the rejoicings of the people, but not less great the anger of the
Duke of Savoy, who, as Jacqueline's feudal lord, claimed the
right to dispose of her hand, and had peremptorily forbidden
her to marry the admiral.   The barbarous revenge which Emmanuel Philibert too soon found it in his power to inflict upon

*Admiral Co-
ligny con-
sulted.*

*He marries
Jacqueline
d'Entremont.*

---

[1] "Contre les deffences et proscriptions de son duc, qui à plat avoit refusé
le Roi de souffrir ce mariage, elle s'en vint à la Rochelle pour avoir nom avant
de mourir (ainsi qu'elle disoit) la Martia de Caton." Agrippa d'Aubigné, ii. 5.

[2] "A quoi ses ennemis trouvèrent à redire, publiant qu'il n'apartenoit
qu'aux *princes* d'épouser par procurateur.   Mais ceux qui parloient des choses
sans passion, imputoient ces sortes de discours à médisance, soûtenant de
leur côté qu'il ne pouvoit faire autrement, puisqu'il n'y avoit pas de sureté
pour lui à l'aller épouser," etc.   Vie de Coligny, 386.

the unfortunate widow of Coligny forms the subject for one of the darkest pages of modern history.[1] Under no less auspicious circumstances was consummated the union of Coligny's daughter, Louise de Châtillon, to Téligny, a young noble whose skill as a diplomatist seemed to have destined him to hold a foremost rank among statesmen. Scarcely less unhappy, however, than her step-mother, Louise was to behold both her father and her husband perish in a single hour by the same dreadful catastrophe.

Was it foolish rashness or overweening presumption that led the admiral to leave the new home he had made within the strong defences of La Rochelle; or was he moved solely by a conscientious persuasion that he had no right to consider personal danger when the great interests of his country and his faith were at stake? The former view has not been without its advocates, some of whom have gloried in finding the proofs of a judicial blindness sent by Heaven to hasten the self-induced destruction of the Huguenots. A more careful consideration of all the circumstances of the case, illustrated by a better appreciation of Coligny's character, rather induces me to adopt the opposite conclusion. Certainly the noble language of Coligny in reply to the warnings of his friends, both now and later, when he was about to venture within the walls of Paris, displayed no unconsciousness of the perils by which he was environed. "Better, however, were it," he said, "to die a thousand deaths, than by undue solicitude for life to be the occasion of keeping up distrust throughout an entire kingdom."

About the beginning of September, 1571, Charles and his court repaired to Blois, on the banks of the Loire.[2] The avowed

Accepts the invitation to court.

---

[1] A very interesting account of the long imprisonment of Coligny's widow is to be found in Count Jules Delaborde's monograph, "Jacqueline d'Entremont," *apud* Bulletin de la Société de l'hist. du prot. fr., xvi. (1867) 220–246.

[2] A few months before the admiral's departure from La Rochelle, there had been held in this Huguenot asylum a convocation of historical importance. The sessions of the seventh national synod, lasting from the second to the eleventh of April, 1571, were consumed in important deliberations respecting the doctrines and discipline of the reformed church (see Aymon, Tous les synodes, i. 98–111). The Queen of Navarre, the Princes of Navarre

object of the movement was to meet Coligny and the Protestant princes. "There are many practices (intrigues) to overthrow this journey," wrote Walsingham, about the middle of the preceding month, " but the king sheweth himself to be very resolute. I am most constantly assured that the king conceiveth of no subject that he hath, better than of the admiral, and great hope there is that the king will use him in matters of greatest trust; for of himself he beginneth to see the insufficiency of others—some, for that they are more addicted to others than to himself; others, for that they are more Spanish than French, or else given more to private pleasures than public. There is none of any account within this realm, whose as well imperfections as virtues, he knoweth not. Those that do love him, do lament that he is so much given to pleasure : they hope the admiral's access unto the court will yield some redress in that case. Queen mother, seeing her son so well affected towards him, laboreth by all means to cause him to think well of her. She seemeth much to further the meeting." [1]

and Condé, Count Louis of Nassau, and Admiral Coligny were present. At the request of the synod, they added their signatures to those of the ministers and elders, upon three copies of the Confession of Faith, engrossed on parchment, which were to be kept at La Rochelle, in Béarn, and at Geneva respectively (see the eighth general article). The moderator on this occasion was Theodore Beza, who had been specially invited to France. The reformer was certainly not destitute of courage, for he could not have forgotten the dangers to which he had been exposed on previous visits to France. They were even greater than Beza himself probably knew. In June, 1563, after the conclusion of the first civil war, there was a rumor at Brussels that Beza could not return to Geneva, because of a quarrel he had had with Calvin. Thereupon, the Duchess of Parma, Regent of the Netherlands, suspecting that he might be tempted to come through the Spanish dominions, issued secret orders that the frontiers should be watched, and offered a reward of one thousand florins to any one who should bring him, dead or alive. He was described as "homme de moïenne stature, ayant barbe à demy blanche, et le visage hault et large." Letters of the Duchess of Parma, June 11th and 25th, 1563, *apud* Charles Paillard, Histoire des troubles religieux de Valenciennes (Paris and Brussels, 1875, 1876), iii. 339, 340, 356.

[1] Walsingham to Burleigh, Aug. 12, 1571, Digges, 122. The ambassador informs Elizabeth, in this letter, of the intense desire of the French Protestants that she should express to the French envoy her approval of the invitation extended to the princes and Coligny, and should say " that so rare a subject as the admiral is was not to be suffered to live in such a corner as

Nothing could surpass the honorable reception of the admiral, when, on the twelfth of September, he arrived with a small His honorable retinue at court in the city of Blois. On first com-reception. ing into the royal presence, he humbly kneeled, but Charles graciously lifted him up, and embraced him, calling him his father, and protesting that he regarded this as one of the happiest days of his life, since he saw the war ended and tranquillity confirmed by Coligny's return. "You are as welcome," said he, "as any gentleman that has visited my court in twenty years." And in the same interview, he expressed his joy in words upon which subsequent events placed a sinister construction, but which nevertheless appear to have been uttered in good faith: "At last we have you with us, and you will not leave us again whenever you wish." [1] Nor was Catharine behind her son in affability. She surprised the courtiers by honoring the Huguenot leader with a kiss. And even Anjou, who chanced to be indisposed, received him in his bedchamber with a show of friendliness. More substantial tokens of favor followed. The same person, who, as the principal general of the rebels, had been attainted of treason, his castle and possessions being confiscated or destroyed by decree of the first parliament of France, and a reward of fifty thousand gold crowns being set upon his head, now received from the king's private purse the unsolicited gift of one hundred thousand livres, to make good his losses during the war. Moreover, he was presented with the revenues of his lately deceased brother, the Cardinal Odet de Châtillon, for the space of one year, and was intrusted with the lucrative office of guardian of the house of Laval during the minority of its heir. Indeed, throughout his stay at Blois, which was protracted through several weeks, Coligny was the favored confidant of Charles, who sometimes even made him preside in the royal council. [2]

Rochelle." It was thought that her commendations would greatly advance his credit with the king.

[1] I know not on what authority Miss Freer states (Henry III. of France, his Court and Times, i. 70) that "even Coligny was startled at the ominous significance of these words; the shadow, however, vanished before the warmth and frankness of Charles's manner." Compare Agrippa d'Aubigné, ii. 5.

[2] Walsingham's account in a letter of La Mothe Fénélon (Corresp. dipl., iv.

Moreover, it was doubtless at Coligny's suggestion that the king at this time wrote to the Duke of Savoy interceding for those Waldenses who in the recent wars had aided the French Protestants in arms, and who since their return to the ducal dominions had experienced severe persecution on that account. " I desire," he says in this letter, " to make a request of you, a request of no ordinary character, but as earnest as you could possibly receive from me—that, just as for the love of me you have treated your subjects in this matter with unusual rigor, so you would be pleased, for my sake, and by reason of my prayer and special recommendation, to receive them into your benign grace, and reinstate them in the possessions which have for this cause been confiscated." He added that he desired not only to exhibit to his Protestant subjects his intention to execute his edict, but to extend to their allies from abroad the same love and protection.[1]

These and other marks of honorable distinction shown to the acknowledged head of the Huguenots, must have been excessively distasteful both to the Guises and to the Spaniard.

Disgust of the Guises and of Alva. The former now retired from court, and left Charles completely in the hands of the Montmorencies and the admiral.[2] Earlier in the year, the Duke of Alva had met with a signal rebuff at the hands of the French, when, in return for the aid furnished to Charles by his Catholic Majesty during the late wars, he requested him to supply him with German reiters, to allow him to levy in France troops to serve against the Prince of Orange, and to detain the fleet which was said to be preparing for the prince at La Rochelle. The first two demands were peremptorily refused, while the ships, it was re-

---

245, 246), its accuracy being vouched for by a letter of Charles IX. himself (ibid., vii. 268); Tocsain contre les massacreurs, Cimber et Danjou, vii. 34, 35 ; De Thou, iv. (liv. l.) 493.

[1] Charles IX. to Emmanuel Philibert, Blois, Sept. 28, 1571, *apud* Leger, Hist. gén. des églises vaudoises (Leyden, 1669), i. 47, 48.

[2] " Durant ce moys, Gaspard de Coligny, remis par l'édit de pacification en l'estat d'admiral, fut mandé par le roy et vint de la Rochelle trouver le Roy à Bloys, et se retira hors de la cour toute la maison de Guise, de sorte que le Roy estoit gouverné par ledit admiral et Montmorency." Jehan de la Fosse, Journal d'un curé ligueur, 132.

plied, were intended merely to make reprisals upon the Spaniards, who had taken some Protestant vessels, drowned a part of
their crew in the ocean, and delivered others into the power of
the Inquisition, and could not be interfered with.[1] The Spanish
ambassador had borne with the offensiveness of this answer; but
the favor with which the Huguenots were now received, and
the openness with which the Flemish war was discussed, rendered his further stay impossible. It is true that the interviews
of Louis of Nassau with the king were held with great secrecy,
and that Charles even had the effrontery to deny that he had
met the brother of Orange at all.[2] It was impossible to deny
that Philip's subjects were despoiled by vessels which issued
with impunity from La Rochelle. But, although the ambassador declared that these grievances must be redressed, or war
would ensue, he was bluntly informed by Charles that "Philip
might not look to give laws to France." Catharine partook of
her son's indignation, the more so as she seems at this time to
have shared in the current belief that her daughter Elizabeth
had been poisoned by her royal husband.[3] At last, in November, the ambassador withdrew from court, without taking leave
of the king, after having, in scarcely disguised contempt,[4] given
away to the monks the silver plate which Charles had presented
to him.

While the new policy of conciliation and toleration thus disgusted one, at least, of those foreign powers which had spurred
Charles gratified. on the government to engage in suicidal civil contests,
it was at home producing the beneficent results hoped
for by its authors. Charles himself appeared to be daily more

---

[1] Walsingham to Cecil, March 5, 1571, Digges, 48, 49.

[2] "And as for conference had with the Count Lewis of Nassau, he told
him, that he was misinformed;" first letter of Walsingham to Burleigh, of
Aug. 12th, Digges, 122. Yet the second letter of the same date gives a detailed account of this conference. It must be admitted that the diplomacy of
the sixteenth century was sufficiently barefaced in its impostures. Louis of
Nassau told Walsingham of an enterprise of Strozzi against Spain, determined
upon by Charles IX. "onely to amaze the king there;" but, as to Strozzi,
"the king here meaneth notwithstanding to disallow [him] openly." Ibid.,
125.

[3] Digges, 122.   [4] Jehan de la Fosse, 134.

convinced of its excellence. In a letter to President Du Ferrier, the French envoy at Constantinople, written during the admiral's stay at Blois, he exposed for the sultan's benefit the reasons for the mutation in his treatment of the Huguenots, and for the cordial reception he had given Coligny at his court. " You know," he said, "that this kingdom fell into discord and division, in which it still is involved. I forgot no prescription which I thought might cure it of this ulcerous wound ; at one time trying mild remedies, at others applying the most caustic, without sparing my own person, or those whom nature made most dear to me. . . . But, having at length discovered that only time could alleviate the ill, and *that those who were at the windows were very glad to see the game played at my expense*,[1] I had recourse to my original plan, which was that of mildness ; and by good advice I made my Edict of Pacification, which is the seal of public faith, under whose benign influence peace and quiet have been restored." And referring to Coligny's arrival, he added : " You know that experience is dearly bought and is worth much. I must therefore tell you that the chief result which I hoped from his coming begins already to develop, inasmuch as the greater part of my subjects, who lately lived in some distrust, have by this demonstration gained such assurance of my kindness and affection, that all partisan feeling and faction are visibly beginning to fade away." [2]

Besides the Flemish project, an important domestic affair engaged the attention of the king and his counsellors at the time of Coligny's visit. This was the proposed marriage of young Henry, the Prince of Béarn, and after his mother's death heir of the crown of Navarre, to Margaret of Valois, the youngest sister of Charles the Ninth. Margaret, who had lately entered upon her twen-

Proposed marriage of Henry of Navarre and the king's sister.

---

[1] " Et que ceulx qui estoient à la fenestre estoient bien aises de veoir jouer le jeu à mes despens." It is scarcely necessary to say that this characteristic expression alludes primarily to the King of Spain and the Duke of Alva in the Netherlands.

[2] Charrière, Négociations de la France dans le Levant, Documents inédits (publ. by the Imperial Government), Paris, 1853, iii. 200. Cf. Sir James Mackintosh, Hist. of England, vol. iii., App. A., pp. 345, 346, audience of Sr. de la Bourdaizière at Rome, cir. Sept., 1571.

tieth year, was a year and a half older than the prince.[1] In a
court and a state of society where the birth of a daughter was
the signal for the initiation of an unlimited number of matrimonial projects, it is not surprising that this match, among
many others, was talked of in the very infancy of the parties,
perhaps with little expectation that anything would ever come
of it. The prince was a sprightly boy, and, it is said, so delighted his namesake, Henry the Second, that the monarch
playfully asked him whether he would like to be his son-in-
law—a question which the boy found no difficulty in answering
in the affirmative. In fact, the matter went so far that, when
the young Bearnese was little over three years of age, Antoine
of Bourbon wrote to his sister, the Duchess of Nevers, with
undisguised delight, of "the favor the king has been pleased to
show me by the agreement between us for the marriage of
Madam Margaret, his daughter, with my eldest son—a thing
which I accept as so particular a token of his good grace, that
I am now at rest and satisfied with what I could most ardently
desire in this world."[2] But the boy's mother had not been
inclined to accept the king's offer to take and educate him with
his own children.[3] She was not very familiar with the disorders of the royal court ; but she had seen enough to convince
her that the quiet plains at the foot of the Pyrenees could
furnish a safer school of manners and morals. More than once
the idea of the connection between the crowns of France and
Navarre was revived, and in 1562 Catharine bethought herself
of it as a means of detaching the unfortunate Antoine from the
triumvirs, whose cause he had espoused with such strange in-

---

[1] Margaret being born May 14, 1552, and Henry of Navarre, Dec. 13,
1553.

[2] Letter of March 21, 155⅖, Rochambeau, Lettres d'Antoine de Bourbon et
de Jehanne d'Albret (Paris, 1877), 145. The story of the promise of Margaret by her father to Henry of Navarre is confirmed by a letter of Charles
IX., now in the National Library, dated October 5, 1571. "The Queen of
Navarre," he writes to Ferralz (Ferrails), at Rome, "has several times invited
me to do her son the honor to marry him to my sister, *whereby also the promise would be fulfilled which my father gave to the late King of Navarre.*" Fr.
von Raumer, Briefe aus Paris (Leipsic, 1830), i. 290.

[3] Mlle. Vauvilliers, Hist. de Jeanne d'Albret (Paris, 1818), i. 106.

fatuation.[1] But other plans soon diverted the ambitious mind
of the Italian queen. Moreover, the civil wars between Protestants and Roman Catholics made the marriage of the daughter of the " Very Christian King " to the son of the most obstinate Huguenot in France appear to be out of the range of
propriety or likelihood. Meantime, Margaret's union with
Sebastian of Portugal was seriously discussed.[2] The tiresome
negotiations ended in January, 1571, with a haughty refusal of
her hand, dictated, as we have seen, by Philip himself. A few
weeks later, as Margaret informs us in her Mémoires—which
may generally be credited, except where the fair author's love
affairs are concerned—the Prince of Navarre began again to be
mentioned as an available candidate for her hand. She expressly states that it was from the Montmorencies that the first
suggestion came [3]—that is, from François de Montmorency, the
constable's oldest son. This nobleman, while he had inherited
a great part of his father's influence, as the head of one of the
most honorable feudal families in France, having its seat in
the very neighborhood of the capital, had ranged himself with
the party opposed to that with which Anne had been identified,
and, although in outward profession a Roman Catholic, was in
full sympathy with the liberal political views of his cousin,
Admiral Coligny. This fact effectually disposes of the story
that the marriage was proposed, however much it may subsequently have been entertained, as a trap to ensnare the Huguenots, thus thrown off their guard.

Marshal Biron, another statesman of the same type, was the
messenger to carry the royal proposals to La Rochelle. He
pictured to the Queen of Navarre in glowing colors the advantages that would flow from this alliance, the strength it would
impart to the friends of mutual toleration, the consternation

---

[1] Soldan, Gesch. des Prot. in Frankreich, ii. 413.

[2] " I thinke," wrote Sir Thomas Smith, as early as January 17, 1563,
" your Majestie hath understood of the marriage practized betwixt the Prince
of Portugall and Madame Margaret, the king's sister." Forbes, State Papers, ii. 287.

[3] Mémoires et Lettres de Marguerite de Valois, edited by M. F. Guessard
(Publications of the French Historical Society), Paris, 1842, 23.

and dismay it would carry into the camp of the enemy. At the same time he declared that Charles the Ninth felt confident that, although he had not as yet obtained from the Pope the dispensation which the relationship subsisting between the parties, as well as their religious differences, rendered necessary, Pius the Fifth would ultimately place no obstacle in the way. Jeanne d'Albret gratefully acknowledged the honor offered by the king to her son, but, before accepting it, professed herself compelled to consult her spiritual advisers respecting the question whether such a marriage might in good conscience be entered into by a member of the reformed church.[1] As for Margaret herself, she gives us in her Mémoires little light as to the state of her own feelings at this time. If we may imagine her so indifferent, she demurely expressed her acquiescence in whatever her mother might decide, but begged her to remember that " she was very Catholic," and that " she would be very sorry to marry any one who was not of her religion."[2] A few months later, however, when the prospects of the marriage became less bright, because of the difficulties arising from religion, it would seem that, with a perversity not altogether

---

[1] De Thou, iv. (liv. l.) 491, 492. Notwithstanding the frequent assertions in royal letters (as, for instance, in one which I have already quoted), that the Queen of Navarre herself urged the marriage, it is certain that she did not initiate it, while it is even maintained that she was only brought to consent by threats. " La reine fut ouïe un temps sans vouloir approuver ledit mariage, jusqu'à cette extrémité qu'on la menaça de faire déclarer son fils illegitime, à cause du mariage qui avoit été contracté entre elle et le Duc de Cleves. Enfin vaincue, elle declare qu'elle n'en esperait que tout malheur." Fr. von Raumer, Briefe aus Paris, i. 291.

[2] Mémoires de Marg. de Valois, 24. The absurdity of the story that Margaret was averse to this marriage, because of a romantic attachment to young Henry of Guise, is sufficiently clear from the circumstance that the Duke of Guise had been married for some time when the match between the Prince of Navarre and Margaret of Valois was first talked of in earnest. He married, on the 17th of September, 1570, Catharine of Cleves, widow of Prince Porcien. (" Hodie celebrantur Lutetiæ Ducis Guisii, qui ducit in uxorem viduam principis Portiani," etc. Languet, Sept. 17, 1570, Epist. secr., i. 163.) It is not probable that Margaret would object to the advantageous marriage with Henry of Navarre on account of her affection for a former lover, who, at the time of her nuptials, had been for two years married to another woman.

unexampled, Margaret became more anxious to have it consummated. At least, Francis Walsingham writes to Lord Burleigh : " The gentlewoman, being most desirous thereof, falleth to reading of the Bible, and to the use of the prayers used by them of the religion." [1]

Meanwhile, the project of a marriage between Elizabeth and Anjou had, as we have seen, been virtually abandoned. The matter of religion was the ostensible stumbling-block ; it can scarcely have been the real difficulty on either side. As to Anjou, the sincerity of his religious convictions is certainly not above suspicion. But he was the head of a party in his brother's kingdom, a party that professed unalterable devotion to the " Holy See " and the old faith. If the eternal rewards of his fidelity to the papacy were at all problematical, there was no doubt whatever in his mind of the advantage of so powerful support as that which the ecclesiastics of France could give him. He was resolved not to throw away this advantage by openly agreeing to renounce all exercise of his own religion in England, and this, too, without the certainty that the concession would secure to him the hand of the queen. And, unfortunately, it was impossible for him to gain this certainty. Elizabeth was already pretty well understood. Her fancies and freaks it was beyond the power of the most astute of her ministers to predict or to comprehend. If the barrier of religion were demolished, there was no possibility of telling what more formidable works might be unmasked. And so Henry, rather more sensible upon this point than even Catharine and Charles, who would have had him shrink from no concessions, made a virtue of necessity, definitely withdrew from competition for the hand of a woman for whose personal appearance it was impossible for him to entertain any admiration ; whose moral character, he had often been told and he more than half suspected, was bad ; [2] and told his friends, and probably believed,

The Anjou match abandoned.

---

[1] Digges, 122.

[2] " La Reyna mi madre," said Anjou one day to a lady, " muestra tener pena de que esta desbaratado mi casamiento, y yo estoy el mas contento hombre del mundo de haber escapado de casar con una puta publica." Francis de Alava to Philip, May 11, 1571, *apud* Froude, Hist. of Eng., x. 224.

that he had had a narrow escape.   The queen, on the other hand, was perhaps not conscious of insincerity of purpose. She must marry, if not from inclination, for protection's sake—the protection of her subjects and herself—so all the world told her; and a marriage that would secure to England the support of France against Spain was the best. But that she sought excuses for not taking the Duke of Anjou is evident, even though she strove to make it appear to others, as well as to herself, that the refusal came at last from him.[1] And she had her advisers— subjects who in secret aspired to her hand, or others—who, in an underhand way, stimulated her aversion to Henry. It is not unlikely that the Earl of Leicester, despite his ardent protesta- tions of zealous support of the match, was the most insidious of its opponents.   " While ' the poor Huguenots ' were telling Walsingham in tears that an affront from England would bring back the Guises, and end in a massacre of themselves, Leicester was working privately upon the queen, who was but too willing to listen to him, feeding her through the ladies of the bedcham- ber with stories that Anjou was infected with a loathsome dis- ease, and assisting his Penelope to unravel at night the web which she had woven under Cecil's direction in the day." [2]

So the negotiation of a marriage between Queen Elizabeth and the Duke of Anjou, after being virtually dead for about a half-year, breathed its last in January, 1572. But the full accord between the two kingdoms was too important to the interests of both, and the opportunity of obtaining a crown for one of her sons too precious in the eye of Catharine. Accordingly the dis- cussion of the terms of the treaty of amity was pressed with still greater zeal, while the French envoy to England was instructed to offer Alençon to Elizabeth in place of his brother. And now were the wits of the statesmen on both sides of the

---

[1] She gravely proposed to her council to have a stipulation for the restitu- tion of Calais inserted in the articles of marriage, and Burleigh, Sussex, and Leicester had some difficulty in persuading her to omit the mention. Lord Burleigh, June 5, 1571, Digges, 104.

[2] Froude, Hist. of England, x. 230. This statement, in itself sufficiently credible in view of Leicester's subsequent career, rests on a passage in a MS. from Simancas, which Mr. Froude inserts in a foot-note.

channel exercised to find good reasons why the match would
The praise of Alençon. be no incongruous one. Unfortunately, Alençon, as
already stated, was short even for his age; but this
was no insuperable obstacle. " Nay," said Catharine de' Medici to Sir Thomas Smith, when she was sounding him respecting his mistress's disposition, " he is not so little; he is so
high as you, or very near." " For that matter, madam," replied
Smith, " I for my part make small account, if the queen's
majestie can fancie him. For *Pipinus Brevis*, who married
Bertha, the King of Almain's daughter, was so little to her,
that he is standing in Aquisgrave, or Moguerre, a church in Almain, she taking him by the hand, and his head not reaching
to her girdle; and yet he had by her Charlemain, the great
Emperor and King of France, which is reported to be almost a
giant's stature." [1]   It was not so easy to dispose of the disparity
in years,[2] and perhaps still less of Alençon's disfigurement by
small-pox ; for that unlucky prince added this to the long cata-
logue of his misfortunes. The course of the treaty for mutual
defence was, happily, somewhat smoother than that of the match-
making. On the eighteenth of April the treaty was formally
concluded,[3] and shortly after, Marshal Montmorency and M. de
Foix were despatched to administer the oath to Queen Elizabeth. This solemn ceremony was performed on Sunday, the fifteenth of June. The deputies were received with every mark
of distinction, and the marshal was publicly presented by the

---

[1] Despatch of March 22, 1572, Digges, 197.

[2] Unless by means of La Mothe Fénélon's arithmetic, who, in conversation
with Queen Elizabeth, maintained that, since her majesty was at least *nine*
years younger in her *disposition*, and Alençon *eight* years older *in manly
vigor*, both parties were of precisely the same age, namely, twenty-seven !
Corresp. diplom., v. 91, etc.

[3] La Mothe Fénélon, vii. 289 ; Dumont, Corps diplomatique, v., 211-215. It
cannot but be regarded as a singular instance of Elizabeth's irresolution and of
that perversity with which she was wont to try the patience of her council
almost beyond endurance, that she gravely proposed to include in the treaty
an article providing for the *protection* of the King of Spain—a stipulation
against which Walsingham earnestly protested as the climax of folly, since it
was certain " that the end of this league is onely to bridle his greatness."
Digges, 175.

queen with the insignia of the Order of the Garter.[1] The commission of the French envoys instructed them to press upon Elizabeth the Alençon marriage as a powerful means of cementing the alliance; and it empowered them to expend money to the extent of ten or twelve thousand crowns in buying the consent of those lords who had hitherto opposed the union. The Earl of Leicester, whose straightforwardness may have been suspected, was to be tempted by the special offer of some French heiress in marriage, the name of Mademoiselle de Bourbon being suggested.[2] But the marriage was not destined to be accomplished, although the negotiations were kept up until the very time of the massacre, and Elizabeth sent to Catharine de' Medici her hearty acknowledgment of the honor she had done her *in offering her all her sons successively.*[3] At the very moment when the fearful blow fell which was to render any such marriage impossible, Catharine was planning and proposing an interview between Elizabeth on the one side, and herself and Alençon on the other. That the dignity of neither party might be compromised, it was suggested that the meeting might take place some calm day on the water between Dover and Boulogne.[4] Elizabeth had reconsidered her partial refusal, and encouraged the project; the nobles, the ladies of the court, the council, all favored it; and in a letter written four days after the streets of Paris flowed with blood, but before the appalling intelligence had reached him, the French ambassador wrote to Catharine: "All who are well affected cry to us, 'Let my Lord the Duke come!'"[5]

It cannot be supposed that such a leaning could be manifested toward the Huguenot party, and such amity concluded with the Protestant kingdom of England, without arousing grave soli-

---

[1] "The like hath not been seen in any man's memory," wrote Lord Burleigh. Montmorency received "a Cupboard of Plate Gilt," "a great cup of gold of 111 ounces," etc. Digges, 218; De Thou, iv. (liv. li.) 537, 538.

[2] La Mothe Fénélon, vii. 292.

[3] Ibid., v. 13.

[4] Ibid., vii. 317–319.

[5] "Que Monseigneur le Duc vienne!" Despatch of Aug. 28, 1872. Corresp. diplom., v. 111.

citude on the part of the Pope and other Roman Catholic sovereigns of Europe. Pius the Fifth determined, if

Pope Pius the Fifth alarmed. possible, to deter Charles from permitting the hateful
marriage between his sister and the heretical Prince
of Navarre. He therefore promptly despatched his nephew,
the Cardinal of Alessandria,[1] first to Sebastian of Portugal,

The Cardinal of Alessandria sent to Paris. whom he found no great difficulty in persuading again
to entertain the project of a marriage with Mar-
garet of Valois, and thence, with the utmost haste, to
the court of Charles the Ninth.[2] The legate, when admitted to
an audience, unfolded at great length the grievances of the
pontiff—the mission of a heretic, formerly a bishop, as envoy
to Constantinople, the rumored opposition of the king to the
Holy League against the Turk, but especially the contemplated
nuptials of a daughter of France with the son of Jeanne d'Albret. Charles replied to these charges in the most politic man-

The king's assurances. ner. He prayed that the earth might open and swal-
low him up, rather than that he should stand in the
way of so illustrious and holy league as that against the infidel.
As to his zeal for the Christian faith, he demonstrated it—
albeit some might object that the fraternal affection which was
reported to subsist between the parties hardly rendered this
argument convincing—by the fact of his having exposed, in its

---

[1] Pius the Fifth—Saint Pius, for his name is commemorated in the prayers
of the Church on the 5th of May—was, we are told by his biographer, a model
of severity to his own kindred ; and, if the fact that he elevated his grand-
nephew, Michael Bonelli, to the sacred college should be alleged as casting
some doubt upon this characteristic of his, we must hasten to add that he did
so, we are assured, only in consequence of the urgent solicitations of Cardinal Farnese and others. He deserves the credit, however, of yielding to
their persuasions with reasonable promptness, for the nomination of his
nephew took place within two months of the Pope's accession. Michael,
being like his uncle a native of the vicinity of Alessandria, in Piedmont,
naturally succeeded to the designation of "il cardinale Alessandrino," which
Pius relinquished on assuming the tiara. Gabutius, Vita Pii Quinti Papæ,
apud Acta Sanctorum (Bolandi) Maii, § 48, p. 630.

[2] The Guises, in the same spirit, had at one time proposed as a candidate
for Margaret's hand the Cardinal of Este, for whom they hoped easily to obtain from the Pope a dispensation from his vow of celibacy. Walsingham to
Cecil, Feb 18, 1571, Digges, 42.

defence, his dearest brother, the Duke of Anjou, to all the perils of war. By civil war the resources of his kingdom had been so weakened that they barely sufficed for its protection. He justified the Navarrese marriage by alleging the remarkable traits which made Henry superior to any other prince of the Bourbon family, and by the great benefit which religion would gain from his conversion. In short, Charles was profuse in protestations of his sincere determination to maintain the Catholic faith ; and, drawing a valuable diamond ring from his finger, he presented it to the legate as a pledge, he said, of his unalterable fidelity to the Holy See, and a token that he would more than redeem his promises. The cardinal legate, however, declined to receive the gift, saying that he was amply satisfied with the plighted word of so great a king, a security more firm than any other pledge that could be given to him.[1] Such seem to have been the assurances given by Charles on this celebrated occasion, vague and indefinite, but calculated to allay to a cer-tain extent the anxiety of the head of the papal church.[2] There is good reason to believe that the king's intention of fulfilling them, not to say his plan for doing so, was equally undefined ; although, so far as his own faith was concerned, he had no thought of abandoning the church of his fathers. The expres-sions by means of which Charles is made to point with unmis-takable clearness to a contemplated massacre,[3] of which, how-

---

[1] Capilupi, Lo stratagema di Carlo IX., 1573, Orig. edit., p. 11 ; Gabutius, Vita Pii Quinti, *ubi supra*, § 244-246, p. 676.

[2] So also says Tavannes : "Il est renvoyé avec paroles générales que Sa Majesté ne feroit rien au prejudice de l'obéissance de Sa Saincteté." Mé-moires (ed. Petitot), iii. 198. Tavannes is explicit in his declarations that the massacre was not premeditated. "Tant s'en faut que l'on pensast faire la Sainct Barthélemy à ces nopces, que sans Madame, fille du Roy, qui y avoit inclination, il se deslioit " (iii. 194). "L'entreprise de la Sainct Barthélemy, qui n'estoit pas seulement pourpensée, et dont la naissance vint de l'impru-dence huguenotte." Ibid., iii. 198.

[3] *E. g. :* "Si j'avois quelque autre moyen de me vanger de mes ennemis, je ne ferois point ce mariage ; mais je n'en ai point d'autre moyen que cetui-ci." Cardinal D'Ossat's letter of Sept. 22, 1599, to Villeroy, Lettres (ed. of 1698), ii. 100. It must be noticed that D'Ossat had a particular purpose in produc-ing testimony to show that Charles IX. *constrained* his sister to marry, as it would assist him in obtaining a divorce for Henry IV. If, as D'Ossat affirms, the Cardinal of Alessandria exclaimed, on hearing of the massacre, "God be

ever the case may stand with respect to his mother, it is all but
certain that he had at this time no idea, can only be regarded
as fabulous additions of which the earliest disseminators of the
story were altogether ignorant.   The fact that the cardinal
legate's rejection of the ring was publicly known[1] seems to be
a sufficient proof that it was offered simply as a pledge of the
king's general fidelity to the Holy See, not of his intention to
violate his edict and murder his Protestant subjects. • The government made the attempt in like manner to quiet the people,
whom even the smallest amount of concession and favor to the
Huguenots rendered suspicious; and the words uttered for

---

praised ! The King of France has kept his word to me," this would agree
equally well with the supposition that Charles IX. had contented himself with
general promises.

[1] " *The foolish cardinal*," wrote Sir Thomas Smith, English ambassador at
the French court during Walsingham's temporary absence (March 3, 157½),
" went away as wise as he came ; he neither brake the marriage with Navarre,
nor got no dismes of the Church of France, nor perswaded the King to enter
into the League with the Turk, nor to accept the Tridentine, or to break off
Treaty with us ; and *the foolishest part of all, at his going away, he refused a
diamond which the King offered him of* 600 *crowns*, yet he was here highly
feasted.   He and his train cost the King above 300 crowns a day, as they
said." Digges, 193.   Gabutius adds that after the death of Pius V.—probably after the massacre—Charles IX. sent the ring to the cardinal with this
inscription upon the bezel : " Non minus hæc solida est pietas, ne pietas possit mea sanguine solvi." Vita Pii Quinti, *ubi supra*, § 246, p. 676.   The inscription had doubtless been cut since the first proffer of the ring.   It appears
to me most probable that the ring was offered by Charles to the cardinal with
the idea that its acceptance would bind him to support the king in his suit for
a dispensation for the marriage of Henry and Margaret, and that the prudent
churchman declined it for the same reason.   Subsequently, with the same
view, Charles sent it to his ambassador at Rome, M. de Ferralz, instructing
him to give it to the Cardinal of Alessandria.   But Ferralz, on consultation
with the Cardinal of Ferrara and others in the French interest, came to the
conclusion that the gift would be useless, and so retained it, at the same time
notifying his master.   The reason may have been either that Alessandria had
too little influence, since his uncle's death, to effect what was desired, or that
the matter was of less consequence when once Charles had resolved to go on
with the marriage without waiting further for the dispensation.   So I understand Charles's words to Ferralz (Aug. 24, 1572) : " J'ai aussi sceu par vostre
dicte mémoire, que par l'avis de mon cousin le cardinal de Ferrare, *vous avez
retenu le diamant que je vous avois envoyé pour le donner de ma part au cardinal Alexandrin*, puisque mon dict cousin et mes autres ministres trouvent
que *le don seroit inutile et perdu*." Mackintosh, iii., App. C., p. 348.

this purpose were often so flattering to the Roman Catholics, that, in the light of subsequent events, they seem to have a reference to acts of treachery to which they were not intended to apply.

The doubt propounded by Jeanne d'Albret to the reformed ministers, respecting the lawfulness of a mixed marriage, hav-

Jeanne d'Albret becomes more favorable to her son's marriage. ing been satisfactorily answered, and the devout queen being convinced that the union of Henry and Margaret would rather tend to advance the cause to which she subordinated all her personal interests, than retard it by casting reproach upon it, the project was more warmly entertained on both sides. Yet the subject was not without serious difficulty. Of this the religious question was the great cause. To the English ambassadors, Walsingham and Smith, Jeanne declared (on the fourth of March, 1572) in her own forcible language, "that now she had the wolf by the ears, for that, in concluding or not concluding the marriage, she saw danger every way; and that no matter (though she had dealt in matters of consequence) did so much trouble her as this, for that she could not tell how to resolve." She could neither bring herself to consent that her son with his bride should reside at the royal court without any exercise of his own religion —a course which would not only tend to make him an atheist, but cut off all hope of the conversion of his wife—nor that Margaret of Valois should be guaranteed the permission to have mass celebrated whenever she came into Jeanne's own domains in Béarn, a district which the queen "had cleansed of all idolatry." For Margaret would by her example undo much of that which had been so assiduously labored for, and the Roman Catholics who had remained would become "more unwilling to hear the Gospel, they having a staff to lean to."[1]

It was this uncertainty about Margaret's course, and the con-

Her solicitude. sequent gain or loss to the Protestant faith, that rendered it almost impossible for Jeanne d'Albret to master her anxiety. "In view," she wrote to her son, "of Mar-

[1] Despatch of March 29, 1572, Digges, 182, 183. It must be noticed that the permission to have mass celebrated in Béarn had been purposely left out in the original basis.

garet's judgment and the credit she enjoys with the queen her
mother and the king and her brothers, if she embrace 'the
religion,' I can say that we are the most happy people in the
world, and not only our house but all the kingdom of France
will share in this happiness. . . . If she remain obstinate in her religion, being devoted to it, as she is said to be, it
cannot be but that this marriage will prove the ruin, first, of our
friends and our lands, and such a support to the papists that,
with the goodwill the queen mother bears us, we shall be ruined
with the churches of France." It would almost seem that a
prophetic glimpse of the future had been accorded to the Queen
of Navarre. "My son, if ever you prayed God, do so now, I
beg you, as I pray without ceasing, that He may assist me in
this negotiation, and that this marriage may not be made in
His anger for our punishment, but in His mercy for His own
glory and our quiet."[1]

But there were other grounds for solicitude. Catharine de'
Medici was the same deceitful woman she had always been.
She would not allow Jeanne d'Albret to see either Charles or
Margaret, save in her presence. She misrepresented the queen's
words, and, when called to an account, denied the report with
the greatest effrontery. She destroyed all the hopes Jeanne
had entertained of frank discussion.

"You have great reason to pity me," the Queen of Navarre
wrote to her faithful subject in Béarn, "for never was I so
disdainfully treated at court as I now am. . . .
Everything that had been announced to me is changed.
They wish to destroy all the hopes with which they
brought me."[2] Catharine showed no shame when
detected in open falsehood. She told Jeanne d'Albret that her
son's governor had given her reason to expect that Henry would
consent to be married by proxy according to the Romish ceremonial. But when she was hard pressed and saw that Jeanne
did not believe her, she coolly rejoined: "Well, at any rate, he
told me something." "I am quite sure of it, madam, but it was

The Queen of
Navarre is
treated with
tantalizing
insincerity.

---

[1] Jeanne d'Albret to Henry of Navarre, Tours, Feb. 21, 1572, Rochambeau,
Lettres d'Antoine de Bourbon et de Jehanne d'Albret (Paris, 1877), 340.
[2] Jeanne d'Albret to M. de Beauvoir, Blois, March 11, 1572, ibid., 345.

something that did not approach that!" "Thereupon," writes Jeanne in despair, "she burst out laughing; for, observe, she never speaks to me without trifling."[1]

But it was particularly the abominable immorality of the royal court that alarmed the Queen of Navarre for the safety of her only son, should he be called to sojourn there. The lady Margaret, she wrote—and her words deserve the more notice on account of the infamy into which the life as yet apparently so guileless was to lead—"is handsome, modest, and graceful; but nurtured in the most wicked and corrupt society that ever was. I have not seen a person who does not show the effects of it. Your cousin, the marquise, is so changed in consequence of it, that there is no appearance of religion, save that she does not go to mass; for, as for her mode of life, excepting idolatry, she acts like the papists, and my sister the princess still worse. . . . I would not for the world that you were here to live. It is on this account that I want you to marry, and your wife and you to come out of this corruption; for although I believed it to be very great, I find it still greater. Here it is not the men that solicit the women, but the women the men. Were you here, you would never escape but by a remarkable exercise of God's mercy. . . . I abide by my first opinion, that you must return to Béarn. My son, you can but have judged from my former letters, that they only try to separate you from God and from me; you will come to the same conclusion from this last, as well as form some idea respecting the anxiety I am in on your account. I beg you to pray earnestly to God; for you have great need of His help at all times, and above all at this time. I pray to Him that you

She is shocked at the morals of the court.

---

[1] "'Il m'a donc dit quelque chose.' 'Je croy bien qu'ouy, Madame, mais c'est quelque chose qui n' approche point de cela.' Elle se prist à rire, car nottez qu'elle ne parle à moy qu'en badinant." Same letter, ibid., 348. How keenly Jeanne felt this treatment may be inferred from a characteristic sentence: "Je vous diray encores que je m'esbahis comme je peux porter les traverses que j'ay, car *l'on me gratte, l'on me picque, l'on me flatte, l'on me brave, l'on me veult tirer les vers du nez*, sans se laisser aller, bref je n'ay que Martin *seul qui marche droict*, encores qu'il ait la goutte, et M. le comte (Nassau) qui me faict tous les bons offices qu'il peut." Same letter, ibid., 353.

may obtain it, that He may give you, my son, all your desires." [1]

Such were the anxieties of the Queen of Navarre in behalf
of a son whom she had carefully reared, hoping to see in
him a pillar of the Protestant faith. She was to be spared
the sight both of those scenes in his life which might have
flushed her cheek with pride, and of other scenes which would
have caused her to blush with shame. At length the last difficulties in the way of Henry of Navarre's marriage, so far as
the court and the queen were concerned, were removed. [2]
Charles and Catharine no longer insisted that Margaret should
be allowed the mass when in Béarn; while Jeanne reluctantly
abandoned her objections to the celebration of the marriage
ceremony in the city of Paris. Accordingly, about the middle
of May the Queen of Navarre left Blois and came to the capital for the purpose of devoting her attention to the final arrangements for the wedding. She had not, however, been long
in Paris before she fell sick of a violent fever, to which it became evident that she must succumb. We are told by a writer
who regards this as a manifest provocation of Heaven, that one
of her last acts before her sudden illness had been a visit to the
Louvre to petition the king that, on the approaching festival of
Corpus Christi (Fête-Dieu), the "idol," as she styled the wafer,
might not be borne in solemn procession past the house in
which she lodged; and that the king had granted her request. [3]
During the short interval before her death she exhibited the
same devotion as previously to the purer Christianity she
had embraced, mingled with affectionate solicitude for her
son and daughter, so soon to be left orphans. Her constancy

---

[1] The letter is inserted entire in La Laboureur, Additions aux Mém. de
Castelnau, i. 859–861. There is much in this letter that lends probability to
Miss Freer's view (Henry III., i. 89) that Catharine had at this time begun
to be opposed to an alliance which she feared might result in the diminution
of her influence at court, and that she therefore "sought, by denying all that
had before been conceded, and by proposing in lieu conditions which she knew
Jeanne could not accept, to throw the odium of a rupture on the Queen of
Navarre."

[2] The contract of marriage was signed at Blois, April 11th.

[3] Jehan de la Fosse (Journal d'un curé ligueur), 143, 144.

and fortitude proved her worthy of all the eulogies that
were lavished upon her.[1] On Monday, the ninth of
June, she died, sincerely mourned by the Huguenots,
who felt that in her they had lost one of their most
able and efficient supports, the weakness of whose sex had not
made her inferior to the most active and resolute man of the
party. Even Catharine de' Medici, who had hated her with
all her cowardly heart, made some show of admiring her virtues, now that she was no longer formidable and her straightforward policy had ceased to thwart the underhanded and shift-
ing diplomacy in which the queen mother delighted. Yet the
report gained currency that Jeanne had been poisoned at Catharine's instigation. She had, it was said, bought gloves of
Monsieur René, the queen mother's perfumer[2]—a man who
boasted of his acquaintance with the Italian art of poisoning—
and had almost instantly felt the effects of some subtle powder
with which they were impregnated. To contradict this and
other sinister stories, the king ordered an examination of her
remains to be made; but no corroborative evidence was discovered. It is true that the physicians are said to have avoided,
ostensibly through motives of humanity, any dissection of the
brain, where alone the evidence could have been found.[3] Be
this as it may, the charge of poisoning is met so uniformly in
the literature of the sixteenth century, on occasion of every
sudden death, that the most credulous reader becomes sceptical
as to its truth, and prefers to indulge the hope that perhaps the

Marginal note: Death of Jeanne d'Al- bret, June 9, 1572.

---

[1] See an interesting account of the Queen of Navarre's last days, her will, etc., in Vauvilliers, Hist. de Jeanne d'Albret, iii. 179–188.

[2] He is said already to have obtained the surname of " l'empoisonneur de la reine." Vauvilliers, iii. 193.

[3] Vauvilliers, Hist. de Jeanne d'Albret, *ubi supra.* Unfortunately for the " glove " theory, the Reveille-Matin des Massacreurs, written within the next year (see p. 172, Cimber and Danjou, " du mois d'aoust *dernier passé* "), makes Jeanne to have died in consequence of a drink (un boucon) given her at a festival at which Anjou was present. So in the Eusebii Philadelphi Dialogi, 1574 (the same book virtually), Jeanne dies, " veneno in quibusdam epulis propinato, quibus Dux Andegavensis intererat, ut quidem mihi a do- mestico ipsius aliquo narratum est," i. 25, 26. The testimony of the physi- cians, who seem to have been unprejudiced, is given in a note in Cimber et Danjou, Archives curieuses, vii. 170, 171.

age may not have been quite so bad as it was represented by contemporaries.

The Prince of Béarn now became King of Navarre; and, as the court went into mourning for the deceased queen, his nuptials with Margaret of Valois were deferred until the month of August.

Admiral Coligny, instead of returning to La Rochelle after his friendly reception at the court at Blois, had gone to Châtil-

Coligny and the boy king.

lon, where his ruined country-seat and devastated plantations had great need of his presence.[1] Here he was soon afterward joined by his wife, travelling from La Rochelle with a special safe-conduct from the king, the preamble of which declared Charles's will and intention to retain Coligny near his own person, "in order to make use of him in his most grave and important affairs, as a worthy minister, whose virtue is sufficiently known and tried."[2] Coligny was not left long in his rural retirement. Charles expressed, and probably felt, profound disgust with his former advisers, and knew not whom to trust. On one occasion, about this time, he held a conversation with Téligny respecting the Flemish war. Téligny had just entreated his Majesty not to mention to the queen mother the details into which he entered—a promise which Charles readily gave, and swore with his ordinary profanity to observe. And then the poor young king, with a desperation which must enlist our sympathy in his behalf, undertook to explain to Coligny's son-in-law his own solitude in the

---

[1] It is said that Charles IX. suggested to him the propriety of this visit, accompanying the suggestion by the words: " I know that you are fond of gardening"—a sly reference to the occasion when Coligny, just before the explosion of the second civil war, was found by the royal spies busily engaged in his vineyards, pruning-hook in hand, and, by his apparent engrossment in the labors of the field, dispelled the suspicions of a Huguenot rising. It was ominous, according to these writers, that Charles should at this moment recall the circumstances of that narrow escape at Meaux from falling into the hands of the Huguenots. Agrippa d'Aubigné, Hist. univ., ii. 6.

[2] " Estant nostre vouloir et intention le retenir près de nous pour nous servir de luy en nos plus graves et importans affaires, comme ministre digne, la vertu duquel est assez cogneue et expérimentée." MS. passport dated September 24, 1571, Biblioth. nat., apud Bulletin de la Soc. de l'hist. du prot français, xvi. (1867) 220.

midst of a crowded court. There was no one, he said, upon whom he could rely for sound counsel, or for the execution of his plans. Tavannes was prudent, indeed; but, having been Anjou's lieutenant, and almost the author of his victories, would oppose a war that threatened to obscure his laurels. Vieilleville was wedded to his cups. Cossé was avaricious, and would sell all his friends for ten crowns. Montmorency alone was good and trustworthy, but so given to the pleasures of the chase that he would be sure to be absent at the very moment his help was indispensable.[1] It is not strange, under these circumstances, that Charles should have turned with sincere respect, and almost with a kind of affection, to that stern old Huguenot warrior, upright, honorable, pious, a master of the art of war, never more to be dreaded than after the reverses which he accepted as lessons from a Father's hands.

As for Coligny himself, his task was not one of his own seeking. But he pitied from his heart the boy-king—still more boyish in character than in years—as he pitied and loved France. Above all, he was unwilling to omit anything that might be vitally important for the progress of the Gospel in his native land and abroad. His eyes were not blind to his danger. When, at the king's request, he came to Paris, he received letters of remonstrance for his imprudence, from all parts of France. He was reminded that other monarchs before Charles had broken their pledges. Huss had been burned at Constance notwithstanding the emperor's safe conduct, and the maxim that no faith need be kept with heretics had obtained a mournful currency.[2] To these warnings Admiral Coligny replied at one moment with some annoyance, indignant that his young sovereign should be so suspected; at another, with more calmness, magnanimously dismissing all solicitude for himself in comparison with the great ends he had in view. When he was urged to consider that

---

[1] Le Tocsain contre les massacreurs (orig. ed., Rheims, 1579), 77.

[2] Le Reveille-Matin des François et de leurs voisins. Composé par Eusebe Philadelphe Cosmopolite, en forme de Dialogues. A Edinbourg, de l'imprimerie de Jaques James. Avec permission. 1574. *Apud* Cimber et Danjou, Archives curieuses, vii. 171. Dialogi Euseb. Philadelphi. Edimburgi, 1574, i. 26.

other Huguenots, less hated by the papists than he was, had been treacherously assassinated—as was the general opinion then— Andelot, Cardinal Châtillon, and lately the Queen of Navarre— his reply was still the same : " I am well aware that it is against me principally that the enmity is directed. And yet how great a misfortune will it be for France, if, for the sake of my individual preservation, she must be kept in perpetual alarm and be plunged on every occasion into new troubles ! Or, what benefit will it be to me to live thus in continual distrust of the king? If my prince wishes to slay me, he can accomplish his will in any part of the realm. As a royal officer, I cannot in honor refuse to comply with the summons of the king, meantime committing myself to the providence of Him who holds in his hand the hearts of kings and princes, and has numbered my years—nay, the very hairs of my head. If I succeed in going in arms to the Low Countries, I hope that I may do signal service, and change hatred into good-will. But, if I fall there, at least the enmity against me will cease, and perhaps men will live in peace, without its being needful to set a whole world in commotion for the protection of the life of a single man." [1]

The juncture was critical, although the future still looked auspicious. Charles was resolved that the marriage of his sister should go forward, and seemed almost as resolute, when he had thus secured peace at home between Papist and Huguenot, to embark in a war against Spain—the natural enemy of French The dispensa- repose and greatness. Gregory the Thirteenth—for tion delayed. Pius the Fifth had died on the first of May, 1572, although his maxims and his counsels were unhappily still alive, and endowed with a mischievous activity—refused to grant the dispensation for the marriage except on impossible conditions. [2]

---

[1] Le Tocsain contre les massacreurs, 40 (Archives curieuses). So Jean de Tavannes—a writer certainly not prejudiced in Coligny's favor—gives him credit for preferring to hazard his life rather than renew the civil war. Yet he adds : " Il ne voyoit ny ne prevoyoit ce qui n'estoit pour lors, d'autant plus qu'il n'y avoit encor rien de resolu contre luy, quoy que les ignorans des affaires d'estat ayent escrit ou dit." Mémoires de Gaspard de Tavannes (Ed. Petitot), iii. 257.

[2] These were four in number: that Navarre should make a secret profession of the Catholic faith, express a desire for the dispensation, restore eccle-

But Charles was too impatient to await his caprice. "My dear
The king's earnestness. aunt," he once said to the Queen of Navarre, a short
time before her death, "I honor you more than the
Pope, and I love my sister more than I fear him. I am not
indeed a Huguenot, but neither am I a blockhead; and if the
Pope play the fool too much, I will myself take Margot," his
common nickname for his sister, "by the hand, and give her
away in marriage in full prêche." [1]

Charles was apparently equally in earnest in his intention to
maintain his edict for the advantage of the Huguenots. Accordingly he published a new declaration to this effect, and sent it to
his governors, accompanied with a letter expressive of his great
gratification that the spirit of distrust was everywhere giving
place to confidence, a proof of which was to be found in the
recent restitution of the four cities of La Rochelle, Montauban,
La Charité, and Cognac, by those in whose hands they were
intrusted by the edict of St. Germain. [2] And Charles's correspondence shows still further that the projects urged by Coligny,
Louis of Nassau, and other prominent patriots, had made a deep
impression upon his imagination, now that for the first time the
prospect of a truly noble campaign opened before him. In
carrying out the extensive plan against the Spanish king, it was
indispensable—so thought the wisest politicians of the time—
to secure the co-operation of the Turk. The extent of Philip's
dominions in the Old and the New World, the prestige of his
successes, the enormous treasure he was said to derive yearly
from his colonial establishments in the Indies, all gave him a
reputation for power which a more critical examination would
have dissipated; but the time for this had not yet arrived.

---

siastical property in his domains, and marry Margaret before the Church.
Charles IX. to Ferralz (Ferrails), July 31, 1572, *apud* Mackintosh, iii., Appendix III.; Fr. von Raumer, Briefe aus Paris (Leipsic, 1831), i. 292.

[1] Journal de Lestoile, p. 24 ; Le Reveille-Matin des Français, etc. ; Arch.
curieuses, vii. 172 ; Dialogi Eusebii Philadelphi, i. 31 ; Vauvilliers, iii. 177 ;
Agrippa d'Aubigné, ii. 12 :—"Ce vieux bigot avec ses cafarderies fait perdre
un bon temps à ma grosse sœur Margot."

[2] Charles IX. to Mandelot, Blois, May 3, 1572, Correspondance du roi Charles
IX. et du sieur de Mandelot, Gouverneur de Lyons, edited by P. Paris (Paris,
1830), pp. 9–11. Also Charrière, Négociations du Levant, iii. 228.

Consequently Charles had sent his ambassador to Constantinople, intending through him to conclude an alliance offensive and defensive with the Moslems. And his declarations to the half-Protestant prelate were explicit enough: "All my humors conspire to make me oppose the greatness of the Spaniards, and I am deliberating how I may therein conduct myself the most skilfully that I can."[1] "I have concluded a league with the Queen of England—a circumstance which, with the understanding I have with the Princes of Germany, puts the Spaniards in a wonderful jealousy."[2] Not only so, but he instructs the ambassador to inform the Grand Seignior that he has a large number of vessels ready, with twelve or fifteen thousand troops about to embark, ostensibly to protect his own harbors, "but in reality intended to keep the Catholic king uneasy, and to give boldness to those Beggars of the Netherlands to bestir themselves and form such enterprises as they already have done."[3] If these assurances had been addressed to a Protestant prince, it would readily be comprehended that they might have had for their object to lull his co-religionists into a fatal security. But, as they were intended only for a Mohammedan ruler, I can see no room for the suspicion that Charles was at this time animated by anything else than an unfeigned desire to realize the plan of Coligny, of a confederacy that should shatter the much-vaunted empire of Philip the Second.

An event now occurred which for a time raised high the hopes of the French Huguenots. This was the capture of the important cities of Mons and Valenciennes. To Count Louis of Nassau the credit of this bold and successful stroke was due. With the secret connivance of Charles, he had recruited in France a body of five hundred horsemen and a thousand foot soldiers, among whom, as was natural, the Huguenot element predominated. With these he

Mons and Valenciennes captured.

---

[1] "Toutes mes fantaisies sont bandées pour m'opposer à la grandeur des Espagnols," etc.   Henri de Valois et la Pologne en 1572, par le Marquis de Noailles (3 vols., Paris, 1867), i. 8.

[2] De Noailles, i. 10.

[3] "De tenir le Roy Catholique en cervelle, et donner hardiesse à ces gueulx des Païs-Bas de se remuer et entreprendre," etc.   Ibid., i. 9.

now set foot again in the Netherlands. The success that first attended his enterprise was owing, however, rather to a well executed trick than to any practical exhibition of generalship; for the gates of Mons were opened from within by a party that had entered on the previous day in the disguise of wine-merchants.[1] Nevertheless the capture of Mons, the capital of the province of Hainault (on Saturday, the twenty-fourth of May), was so brilliant an exploit, coming as it did close upon the heels of other reverses of the Duke of Alva, that the French Huguenots and all who sympathized with them may be pardoned for having indulged even in somewhat extravagant demonstrations of joy. They seem to have believed that it was pretty nearly over with that hated instrument of Spanish tyranny. They fancied that, with his five hundred horse, Louis might penetrate the country by a rapid movement, and either take Alva prisoner, or, if the duke should retire to Antwerp, raise the whole country in revolt.[2]

For the next two months the Huguenot leaders were indefatigable in their efforts to persuade Charles to take open and decided ground against Spain; but they were met by Anjou and the party in his interest with arguments drawn from the difficulty or injustice of the undertaking, and by the suggestion that Elizabeth, as was her wont, would be likely to withdraw so soon as she saw France once engaged in war with her powerful neighbor, and to use Charles's embarrassments as a means of securing private advantages. In point of fact, Charles was personally unwilling to commit himself until sure of England's support. Meanwhile, Catharine, from whose Argus-eyed inspection nothing that was debated in the royal presence, openly or secretly, ever escaped notice, awaited with

Catharine's indecision.

---

[1] De Thou, iv. 674; Motley, Dutch Republic, ii. 369, etc.

[2] " Thence with great celerity the Count Lodovick should send 500 horse to Bruxels under the conduct of M. de la Nue (Noue), where if he hap to find the Duke of Alva, it will grow to short wars, in respect of the intelligence they have with the town, who undertook with the aid of 100 soldiers to take the duke prisoner. If he retires to Antwerp, as it is thought he wil, then it is likely that all the whole country will revolt. I the rather credit this news for that it agreeth with the plot laid by Count Lodovick, before his departure hence," etc. Walsingham to Burleigh, Paris, May 29, 1572, Digges, 204.

her accustomed irresolution Elizabeth's decision, before herself deciding whether to throw her influence into the scale with Coligny (of whose growing favor with her son she had begun to entertain some suspicion), or with Anjou and the Spaniards. But Elizabeth was as ever a riddle, not only to her allies, but even to her most confidential advisers. Certainly she was no friend to Philip and Alva; yet she would not abruptly enter into war against them. She could not help seeing that the interests of her person and of her kingdom, to say nothing of her Protestant faith, were bound up in the success of the Prince of Orange, who was about to cross the Rhine with twenty-five thousand Germans for the relief of Mons, now invested by Alva. For the duke wisely regarded the recapture of this place as the first step in extricating himself from his present embarrassments. In such a strife as that upon which Elizabeth must before long enter, whether with or without her consent, the cordial alliance of France would be valuable beyond computation. And yet, with a fatal perversity, she dallied with the proposal of marriage. One day she would not hear of Alençon, alleging that his age and personal blemishes placed the matter out of all consideration. On another she gave hopes, and agreed to take a month's consideration.[1] Thus she tantalized her suitor. Thus she convinced the cunning Italian woman who, although she made no present show of holding the reins of power in France, was ready at any moment to resume them, that there was no reliance to be placed on England's promise of support against Philip.[2]

The golden opportunity was in truth fast slipping away. Alva had struck promptly at that opponent whose thrust was likely to be most deadly. Mons must soon fall. A French Huguenot force, under command of Jean de Hangest, Sieur de

Queen Eliza- beth inspires no confidence.

---

[1] Queen Elizabeth to Walsingham, July 23, 1572, Digges, 226–230.

[2] "More tremendous issues," Mr. Froude forcibly remarks, "were hanging upon Elizabeth's decision than she knew of. But she did know that France was looking to her reply—was looking to her general conduct, to ascertain whether she would or would not be a safe ally in a war with Spain, and that on her depended at that moment whether the French government would take its place once for all on the side of the Reformation." History of England, x. 370.

Genlis, was sent forward to relieve it. But the Frenchman was no match for the cooler prudence of his antagonist,[1] and Rout of suffered himself, on the march, to be surprised (on Genlis. the nineteenth of July) and taken prisoner by Don Frederick of Toledo and Chiappin Vitelli. Of his army, barely one hundred foot soldiers found their way into the beleaguered town. Twelve hundred were killed on the field of battle— almost in sight of Mons—and a much larger number butchered by the peasantry of the neighborhood.[2] A handful of officers and men, scarcely more fortunate, shared the captivity of their commander, and were destined to have their fortunes depend for a considerable time upon the fluctuating interests of two un-principled courts.[3]

The rout of Genlis was not in itself a decisive event. While Coligny could bring forward a far more numerous army, and Orange was in command of a considerable German force, the loss of this small detachment was but one of those many re-verses that are to be looked for in every war. But, happening under the peculiar circumstances of the hour, it was invested with a consequence disproportioned to its real importance. The fate of the French Huguenots was quivering in the balance. The papal party was known to be bitterly opposed to the war against Spain, and to be merely awaiting an opportunity to strike a deadly blow at the heretics whom the royal edict still protected. Catharine was undecided ; but, with her, indecision was the ordinary prelude to the sudden adoption of some one of many conflicting projects, which had been long brooded over, but between which the choice was, in the end, the result rather

---

[1] In fact, he was acting in violation of the instructions of Louis of Nassau, by whom he had been despatched for aid to France. Apprehending danger, Nassau repeatedly bid him avoid the direct road to Mons, and make a circuit through the territory of Cambray, and effect a junction with the Prince of Orange. Genlis justified his neglect of these directions by alleging the orders of Admiral Coligny. De Thou, iv. 680.

[2] Motley, Dutch Republic, ii. 383, 384 ; De Thou, iv. 680, etc.

[3] It may be noted, by way of anticipation, that Genlis, after an imprison-ment of over a year, was secretly strangled by Alva's command, in the castle of Antwerp. With characteristic mendacity, the duke spread the report that the prisoner had died a natural death. Ibid., *ubi supra.*

of accident, caprice, or temporary impressions, than of calm deliberation.

This reverse at Mons, limited in its extent as it was, would be likely, so the Huguenot leaders of France foresaw—and they were not mistaken—to determine Catharine to take the Spanish side. With the queen mother in favor of Spain and intolerance, experience had taught them that there was little to expect from her weak son's intentions, however good they might be. The only ground of hope for Orange and the Netherlands, and the only prospect for security and religious toleration at home, lay in the success of the Flemish project at Paris; and of this but a single chance seemed to remain—in Elizabeth's finally espousing their cause with some good degree of resolution. " Such of the religion," wrote Walsingham to Lord Burleigh, inclosing the particulars of the disaster of Genlis, " as before slept in security, begin now to awake and to see their danger, and do therefore conclude that, unless this enterprise in the Low Countries have good success, their cause groweth desperate." [1] To the Earl of Leicester Walsingham was still more explicit in his warnings: " The gentlemen of the religion, since the late overthrow of Genlis, weighing what dependeth upon the Prince of Orange's overthrow, have made demonstration to the king, that, his enterprise lacking good success, it shall not then lie in his power to maintain his edict. They therefore desire him to weigh whether it were better to have foreign war with advantage, or inward war to the ruin of himself and his estate.[2] The king being not here, his answer is not yet received. They hope to receive some such resolution as the danger of the cause requireth. In the mean-

It determines Catharine to take the Spanish side.

Loss of the golden opportunity.

---

[1] Walsingham to Burleigh, July 26, 1572, Digges, 225.

[2] It was such arguments as these that afterward, when everything that might be so employed as to justify or palliate the atrocity of Coligny's assassination was eagerly laid hold of, were construed as threats of a Huguenot rising, in case Charles should refuse to engage in the Flemish war. Compare, e. g., the unsigned extract found by Soldan (ii. 433) in the National Library of Paris, No. 8702, fol. 68. But does it need a word to prove that the reference was to a *papal* rising, or, at least, papal compulsion to violate the edict of toleration ?

time, the marshal (Montmorency) desired me to move your lordship to deal with her Majesty to know whether she, upon overture to be made to the king, cannot be content to join with him in assistance of this poor prince." And the faithful ambassador did not forget to remind his mistress that the success of Philip in Flanders was still more dangerous for Elizabeth than for Charles.[1]

Meantime, Admiral Coligny, although disappointed at the rout of the vanguard of the expedition which was to have been fitted out for the liberation of the Netherlands, and yet more at the coolness which it had occasioned among those who up to this moment had been not unfriendly, did not yield to despondency, but labored all the more strenuously to engage Charles in an undertaking fitted to call forth the nobler faculties of his soul, and to free him from the thraldom under narrow-minded and interested counsellors to which he had been subject all his life long. Even before Genlis's defeat (in June, 1572), the admiral had presented an extended paper, wherein the justice and the fair prospects of the war had been set forth with rare force and cogency.[2] It may be that now, under the influence of a sincere and unselfish devotion that took no account of personal risks, the admiral distinctly told his young master that he could never be a king in the true sense until he should emancipate himself from his mother's control, and until he should find, outside of France, some occupation for his brother Henry of Anjou, such as the vacancy of the Polish throne

The admiral retains his courage.

---

[1] Walsingham to Leicester, July 26, 1572, Digges, 225, 226.

[2] This document was written by the illustrious Philippe du Plessis Mornay, then a youth twenty-three years of age, and bears the impress of his vigorous mind. De Thou gives an excellent summary (iv., liv. li., 543–554) ; and it may be found entire in the Mémoires de Du Plessis Mornay (ii. 20–37). Morvilliers, Bishop of Orleans, and keeper of the seals until Birague's appointment in January, 1571, was requested by the king to prepare the answer of the opposite party in the royal council—a task which he discharged with great ability. Summary in De Thou, iv. (liv. li.) 555–563, and Agrippa d'Aubigné, ii. 9, 10. Jean de Tavannes's memoirs of his father contain arguments of Marshal Tavannes and of the Duke of Anjou, dictated by the marshal, against undertaking the Flemish war, as both unjust and impolitic.

seemed to offer.[1] Such frankness would have been patriotic
and timely, although a politician, influenced only by a regard
for his own safety, would have regarded it as foolhardy in the
extreme.

This advice, promptly and faithfully reported to Catharine by
the spies she kept around the king's person,[2] was the last drop
in the cup of Coligny's offences. Charles, at the time of her
discovery of this fact, was absent from court, seeking a few days'
recreation at Montpipeau. Thither his mother, now
really alarmed for the continuance of her influence,
pursued him in precipitate haste.[3] Shutting herself
up with him apart from his followers, she burst into tears and
plied Charles with an artful harangue. For this woman, who
had a masculine will and a heart as cold and devoid of pity as
the most utter scepticism could make it, had the ability to
counterfeit the feminine tenderness which she did not possess.
" I had not thought it possible," she said amid her sobs to her
son, who trembled like a culprit detected in his crime, " I had
not thought it possible that, in return for my pains in rearing
you—in return for my preservation of your crown, of which
both Huguenots and Catholics were desirous of robbing you,
and after having sacrificed myself and incurred such risks in
your behalf, you would have been willing to make me so miserable a requital. You hide yourself from me, your mother, and
take counsel of your enemies. You snatch yourself from my
arms that saved you, in order to rest in the arms of those who
wished to murder you. I know that you hold secret deliberations with the admiral. You desire inconsiderately to plunge
into a war with Spain, and so to expose your kingdom, as well

*Charles and
Catharine at
Montpipeau.*

---

[1] Mémoires de Tavannes (Ed. Petitot), iii. 290.

[2] In this case the chief spy, according to the Tocsain contre les massacreurs, p. 78, and the younger Tavannes, was Phizes, sieur de Sauve, the
king's private secretary for the Flemish matter ; and Tavannes is certainly
correct in making a chief element in Catharine's influence, " la puissance que
ladicte Royne a sur ses enfans par ses créatures qu'elle leur a donné pour ser-
viteurs dez leur enfance." Mémoires, 290, 291.

[3] In fact, Catharine, who spared neither herself nor her attendants in her
furious driving in her "coche" on such occasions, lost one or more of the
horses, which dropped dead. Tocsain contre les massacreurs, p. 78.

as yourself and us, a prey to 'those of the religion.' If I am so miserable, before compelling me to witness such a sight, give me permission to withdraw to my birthplace,[1] and send away your brother, who may well style himself unfortunate in having employed his life for the preservation of yours. Give him at least time to get out of danger and from the presence of enemies made in your service—the Huguenots, who do not wish for a war with Spain, but for a French war and a subversion of all estates, which will enable them to gain a secure footing."[2]

Such was a portion of the queen mother's crafty speech. But there was another point upon which she doubtless touched, and which she used to no little purpose. A report had reached

Rumors of Elizabeth's desertion of her allies.

her from England to the effect that Queen Elizabeth had decided to issue a proclamation recalling the English who had gone to Flushing to assist the patriots. The story was false; so the secretary, Sir Thomas Smith, subsequently assured Walsingham. Elizabeth neither had done so, nor intended anything of the kind.[3] But it was wonderfully like the usual practice of Henry the Eighth's daughter, and Catharine believed it, and looked with horror at the precipice before which she stood. Deserted by her faithless ally, France was entering single-handed a contest of life or death with the world-empire of Spain. In fact, the English ambassador ascribed to the receipt of this intelligence alone both the queen mother's tears and entreaties at Montpipeau and the king's altered policy.

---

[1] Or, only to her estates in Auvergne, according to the Tocsain, pp. 78, 79. It will be remembered that Catharine's mother was a French heiress of the famous family of La Tour d'Auvergne.

[2] The younger Tavannes, in the memoirs of his father (Edit. Petitot), iii. 291, 292, gives the most complete summary of this remarkable conversation; but it is substantially the same as the briefer sketch in the Tocsain contre les massacreurs de France, Rheims 1579, pp. 78, 79—a treatise of which the preface (L'Imprimeur aux lecteurs, dated June 25, 1577) shows that it was written before the death of Charles IX., but the publication of which was from time to time deferred in the vain hope that the authors of the inhuman massacre might yet repent. The new and "more detestable perfidy, fury, and impetuosity" of which the Huguenots were the victims in the first years of Henry III.'s reign, finally brought it to the light. The *Archives curieuses* contain only a part of the treatise.

[3] Smith to Walsingham, Aug. 22, 1572, Digges, 236.

"Touching Flemish matters," he wrote to Lord Burleigh, "the king had proceeded to an open dealing, had he not received advertisement out of England, that her Majesty meant to revoke such of her subjects as are presently in Flanders; whereupon such of his council here as incline to Spain, have put the queen mother in such a fear, that the enterprise cannot but miscarry without the assistance of England, as she with tears had dissuaded the king for the time, who otherwise was very resolute."[1]

Catharine had not mistaken her power over the feeble intellect and the inconstant will of her son. Terrified less by the prospect of a Huguenot supremacy which she held forth, than by the menace of her withdrawal and that of Anjou, Charles, who was but too well acquainted with their cunning and ambition, admitted his fault in concealing his plans, and promised obedience for the future.[2]

It was a sore disappointment to Admiral Coligny. The young king had, until this time, shown himself so favorable, that "commissions were granted, ready to have been sealed, for the levying of men in sundry provinces." But he had now lost all his enthusiasm, and spoke coldly of the enterprise.[3] Gaspard de Coligny did not, however, even now lose courage or forsake the post of duty to which God and his country evidently called him. In truth, the superiority of his mental and moral constitution, less evident in prosperity, now became resplendent, and chained the attention of every beholder. "How perplexed the admiral is, who foreseeth the mischief that is like to follow, if assistance come not

Charles thoroughly cast down.

---

[1] Walsingham to Burleigh, Aug. 10, 1572, Digges, 233. This news and the interview, which must have taken place about the first week of August, are the burden of three letters written by Walsingham on the same day. "Herein nothing prevailed so much as the tears of his mother," he wrote to Leicester, "who without the army of England cannot consent to any open dealing. And because they are, as I suppose, assured by their ambassadors that her Majesty will not intermeddle, they cannot be induced to make any overture" (p. 233). Walsingham was disheartened at the loss of so critical an opportunity. "Pleasure and youth will not suffer us to take profit of advantages, and those who rule under [over] us are fearfull and irresolute."

[2] Mém. de Tavannes, iii. 291.

[3] Walsingham to Leicester, Aug. 10, 1572, Digges, 233.

from above," wrote Walsingham, full of admiration, to the Earl of Leicester, "your lordship may easily guess. And surely to say truth, he never showed greater magnanimity, nor never was better followed nor more honored of those of the religion than now he is, which doth not a little appal the enemies. In this storm he doth not give over the helm. He layeth before the king and his council the peril and danger of his estate, and though he cannot obtain what he would, yet doth he obtain somewhat from him." [1]

So wrote that shrewd observer, Sir Francis Walsingham, just two weeks before the bloody Sunday of the massacre, and eight days before the marriage of Navarre, little suspecting, in spite of his anxiety, the flood of misery which was so soon to burst upon that devoted land. To all human foresight there was still hope that Charles, weak, nerveless, addicted to pleasure, but not yet quite lost to a sense of honor, might yet be induced to adopt a policy which would place France among the foremost champions of intellectual and civil liberty, and transfer to the north of the Pyrenees the prosperity which the Spanish monarchs had misused and had employed only as an instrument of oppression and degradation. And, indeed, Coligny was partially successful; for the impression made upon Charles by his mother's complaints and menaces at Montpipeau gradually wore away, and again he listened with apparent interest to the manly arguments of the great Huguenot leader.

Coligny partially succeeds in reassuring him.

Could Elizabeth at this moment have brought herself to a more noble course, could she for once have forgotten to "deal under hand," and help secretly while in public she disavowed— could she, in short, have realized for a single instant her responsibility as a great Protestant princess, and been willing to expose even her own life to peril in order to secure to the Reformation a chance of fair play, it might not even now have been too late. But what was she doing at this very moment? According to the admission of her own secretary, she was engaged in detaining volunteers from the Netherlands, on the pre-

---

[1] "I am requested to desire your lordship to hold him excused in that he writeth not," he adds, " for that at this time he is overwhelmed with affairs." Walsingham to Leicester, Aug. 10, 1572, Digges, 234.

text of "fearing too much disorder there through lack of some
good head;" and "gently answering with a dilatory and doubtful answer" the Duke of Alva, when he demanded the revocation of the queen's subjects in Netherlands.¹ Was she projecting anything still more dishonorable? The Spanish envoy in
England, Anton de Guaras, affirms it, in a letter of the thirtieth
of June to the Duke of Alva; and we have no means of dis-
proving his assertions.   In his account of a private audience
granted him by Queen Elizabeth, the ambassador
writes: "She told me that emissaries were coming
every day from Flushing to her, proposing to place
the town in her hands.   If it was for the service of
his Majesty, and if his Majesty approved, she said that she
would accept their offer.   With the English who were already
there, and with others whom she would send over for the purpose, it would be easy for her to take entire possession of the
place, and she would then make it over to the Duke of Alva
or to any one whom the duke would appoint to receive it."²
Guaras can scarcely be suspected of misrepresenting the conversation upon so important a topic and in a confidential communication to the Spanish Governor of the Netherlands.   The
most charitable construction of Elizabeth's words seems to be
that they were a clumsy attempt to propitiate the duke "with a
dilatory answer," as Sir Thomas Smith somewhat euphemistic-
ally expresses it, and that she had no intention of making good
her engagements.   But it was a sad blunder on her part, and

Elizabeth toys with dishonorable proposals from Netherlands.

---

¹ Sir Thomas Smith's plea in her behalf is interesting and plausible, but
will not receive the sanction of any one who takes into account the vast difference in the positions of Elizabeth and Charles, or considers the principles
of which the former was, or should have been, the advocate.   The good
secretary, I need not remind my reader, was never reluctant to parade his
Latinity : "If you there [in France] do *tergiversari* and work *tam timide* and
underhand with open and outward edicts, besides excuses at Rome and at
Venice by your ambassadors, you, I say, which have Regem expertem otii,
laboris amantem, cujus gens bellicosa jampridem assueta est cædibus tam
exterioris quam vestri sanguinis, quid faciemus gens otiosa et paci assueta,
quibus imperat Regina, et ipsa pacis atque quietis amantissima."   Smith to
Walsingham, Aug. 22, 1572, Digges, 237.
² Puntos de Cartas de Anton de Guaras al Duque de Alva, June 30th : MS.
Simancas, *apud* Froude, x. 383.

likely to be ruinous to her friends, the French Protestants. Alva was not slow in concluding that Elizabeth's offer was of greater value as documentary proof of her untrustworthy character, than as a means of recovering Flushing. " There is no positive proof," remarks the historian to whom we are indebted for an acquaintance with the letter of Guaras, " that Alva communicated Elizabeth's offers to the queen mother and the King of France, but he was more foolish than he gave the world reason to believe him to be if he let such a weapon lie idle in his writing-desk." [1] And so that inconstant, unprincipled Italian

Fatal results.

woman, on whose fickle purpose the fate of thousands was more completely dependent than even her contemporaries as yet knew, at last reached the definite persuasion that Elizabeth was preparing to play her false, at the very moment when Coligny was hurrying her son into war with Spain. Even if France should prove victorious, Catharine's own influence would be thrown into perpetual eclipse by that of the admiral and his associates. This result the queen mother resolved promptly to forestall, and for that purpose fell back upon a scheme which had probably been long floating dimly in her mind.

The *Mémoires inédits de Michel de la Huguerye*, of which the first volume was recently published (Paris, 1877), under the auspices of the National Historical Society, present some interesting points, and deserve a special reference. At first sight, the disclosures, with which the author tells us he was favored, would seem to establish the bad faith of the court in entering upon the peace of St. Germain, and the long premeditation of the succeeding massacre. A closer examination of the facts, assuming La Huguerye's thorough veracity, shows that this is a mistake. La Huguerye may, indeed, have been informed by companions on the way to Italy, who supposed him to be a partisan of the Guises, that a great blow would be struck at the Huguenots when the proper time arrived ; and La Huguerye may have been confident that he was telling the truth, when, about Martinmas (November 11th), 1570, he stated to De Briquemault, that "the king, seeing that he could not attain his object by way of arms without greatly weakening—nay, endangering his kingdom, had resolved upon taking

Mémoires de Michel de la Huguerye.

---

[1] Froude, x. 385.

another road, by which, in a single day, he would cleanse his whole state."
He may have been assured, on what he deemed good authority, that the
Pope was in the plot, and would keep the King of Spain from doing anything
that might interfere with the execution, and have inferred that, the peace
being a treacherous one, the only hope of the Huguenots lay in skilfully en-
listing Charles in its maintenance, contrary to his original purpose. So he
was confirmed in his belief by the contents of the despatches of the Spanish
ambassador at the French court, treacherously submitted to the Huguenots
by an unfaithful agent of the envoy. But the former statements were, at
most, little better than rumors, to which the circumstances of the hour gave
color. The air was full of dark hints; but, apparently, they had no more solid
foundation than the fact that, in an age abounding in perfidious schemes, the
Protestants had already placed themselves partially in the power of their
great enemies, and were likely soon to be more completely in their hands.
The information received by La Huguerye was a very different thing from an
authoritative avowal of a concealed purpose made by Catharine or by Charles
himself. On the other hand, the assurances in the Spanish despatches were
just of the same general nature as others with which the French government
endeavored to quiet Philip, Alva, and the Roman pontiff himself.

The only other peculiarity of La Huguerye to which I shall allude is his
studied misrepresentation of the character of Jeanne d'Albret, Queen of Navarre. Contrary to the uniform portraiture given by contemporaries of both
religious parties, she here appears as "an inconsiderate woman (femme
légère), with little forethought," "known to be jealous of the authority of
the admiral," "whom she thwarted by her authority as much as was possible,
at whatever cost or danger it might be." She had "intermeddled with affairs
in the last war, unsolicited and of her own accord, not so much for conscience' sake, as because of the hatred her house bore to the popes, sole cause
of the loss of the kingdom of Navarre, and especially through jealousy of the
late Prince of Condé, whom she saw to be in the enjoyment of such credit,
and to be so well followed, that she suspected great injury might result to her
son in the event of his succession to the throne." She was, consequently,
"not very sorry" to hear of Condé's death at Jarnac. Having been disappointed in securing for her son the sole (nominal) command of the Huguenots,
she vented her vengeance upon Coligny, whom she held responsible for the
association of the young Condé in the leadership with his cousin. From that
time forward she took every opportunity to cross the admiral, with the view
of compelling him to retire in disgust from the management of affairs. In
one of the speeches—Sallustian, I suspect—in which the Mémoires abound,
Count Louis of Nassau is represented as lamenting: "It is a great pity to
have to do with a woman who has no other counsel than her own head, which
is too little and light (légère) to contain so many reasons and precautions,
and who is of such weight in matters of so great consequence. And the mischief is that she has such an aversion to the admiral through foolish jealousy,"
etc. At last the admiral is goaded on to unpardonable imprudence. In the
spring of 1572 he yields to the importunities of Marshal Cossé, and goes from
La Rochelle to the royal court at Blois: "weary of being near this princess,

he exposed himself to the evident peril, of which he had had advices and arguments enough."

To all this misrepresentation, the remarks of La Huguerye's editor, the Baron de Ruble, are a sufficient answer: "No other historian of the period, Catholic or Huguenot, has accused the Queen of Navarre of so much jealousy, frivolity, and spite. To the calumnies of La Huguerye we should oppose the verdict which every impartial judge can pronounce respecting this princess, in accordance with the letters published by the Marquis de Rochambeau and the testimony of contemporaries."

CHAPTER XVIII.

THE MASSACRE OF ST. BARTHOLOMEW'S DAY.

THE marriage of Henry of Navarre and Margaret of Valois had been delayed in consequence of the death of the bridegroom's mother, but could now no longer be deferred.

The Huguenot nobles reach Paris. The young queen of Charles the Ninth was soon to become a mother, and it was desirable that she should have the opportunity to leave the crowded and unhealthy capital as soon as possible. Jeanne d'Albret's objection to the celebration of the wedding in Paris had been overruled. The bride herself, indifferent enough, to all appearance, on other points, was resolute as to this matter—she would have her nuptials celebrated in no provincial town. Accordingly, the King of Navarre, followed by eight hundred gentlemen of his party, as well as by his cousin the Prince of Condé, and the admiral, made his solemn entry into the city, which so few of his adherents were to leave alive. Although still clad in mourning for the loss of the heroic Queen of Navarre, they bore no unfavorable comparison with the gay courtiers, who, with Anjou and Alençon at their head, came out to escort them into Paris with every mark of respect.[1]

The betrothal took place in the palace of the Louvre, on Sunday the seventeenth of August. Afterward there was a supper and a ball ; and when these came to an end, Margaret Betrothal of Henry and Margaret. was conducted by her mother, her brothers, and a stately retinue, to the episcopal palace, on the Île de la Cité, adjoining the cathedral, there, according to the immemorial custom of the princesses of the blood, to pass the night

---

[1] Mémoires de Marguerite de Valois, 25, 26.

before her wedding. No papal dispensation had arrived. Gregory XIII. was as obstinate as his predecessor in the pontifical chair, in denying the requests of the French envoys to Rome.[1] But Charles was determined to proceed ; and, in order to silence the opposition of the Cardinal of Bourbon, who still refused to perform the ceremony without the pope's approval, a forged letter was shown to him, purporting to come from the Cardinal of Lorraine, or the royal ambassador at Rome, and announcing that the bull of dispensation had actually been sealed, and would shortly arrive.[2]

Preparations had been made for the wedding in a style of magnificence extraordinary even for that age of reckless expenditure. To show their cordial friendship and fidelity, Charles and his brothers, Anjou and Alençon, and Henry and his cousin of Condé, assumed a costume precisely alike—a light yellow satin, covered with silver embroidery, and enriched with pearls and precious stones. Margaret wore a violet velvet dress with fleurs-de-lis. Her train was adorned with the same emblems. She was wrapped in a royal mantle, and had upon her head an imperial crown glittering with pearls, diamonds, and other gems of incalculable value. The queens were resplendent in cloth of gold and silver.[3] A lofty platform had been erected in front of the grand old pile of Notre Dame. Hither Margaret was brought in great pomp, from the palace of the Bishop of Paris, escorted by the king, by Catharine de' Medici, by the Dukes of Anjou and Alençon, and by the Guises, the marshals, and

---

[1] No dispensation was ever granted until *after* the marriage, and after Henry of Navarre's simulated conversion to Roman Catholicism. Then, of course, there was no need of further hesitation, and the document was granted, of which a copy is printed in Documents historiques inédits, i. 713–715. The bull is dated Oct. 27, 1572. There is, then, no necessity for Mr. Henry White's uncertainty (Massacre of St. Bartholomew, 370): " The new pope, Gregory XIII., appears to have been more compliant, or the letter stating that a dispensation was on the road must have been a forgery."

[2] De Thou, iv. (liv. lii.), 569 ; Lo stratagema di Carlo IX. rè di Francia, contro gli Ugonotti, rebelli di Dio e suoi ; descritto dal signor Camillo Capilupi, e mandato di Roma al signor Alfonzo Capilupi. Ce stratageme est cy après mis en François avec un avertissement au lecteur. 1574. Orig. ed., p. 22.

[3] Mémoires de l'estat de France sous Charles IX. (Cimber et Danjou, vii. 78).

other great personages of the realm.   Upon the platform she met Henry of Navarre, with his cousins Condé and Conty, Admiral Coligny, Count de la Rochefoucauld, and a numerous train of Protestant lords from all parts of the kingdom.   In the sight of an immense throng, the nuptial ceremony was performed by the Cardinal of Bourbon, Henry's uncle, according to the form which had been previously agreed upon.[1]   The bridal procession then entered the cathedral by a lower platform, which extended through the nave to the choir.   Here Henry, having placed his bride before the grand altar to hear mass, himself retired with his Protestant companions to the episcopal palace, and waited for the service to be over.   When notified of its conclusion by Marshal Damville, Henry and his suite returned to the choir, and with his bride and all the attending grandees soon sat down to a sumptuous dinner in the episcopal palace.

Among those who had been admitted to the choir of Notre Dame after the close of the mass, was the son of the first president of parliament, young Jacques Auguste de Thou, the future historian.   Happening to come near Admiral Coligny, he looked with curious and admiring gaze upon the warrior whose virtues and abilities had combined to raise the house of Châtillon to its present distinction.   He saw him point out to his cousin Damville the flags and banners taken from the Huguenots on the fields of Jarnac and Moncontour, still suspended from the walls of the cathedral, mournful trophies of a civil contest.   "These will soon be torn down," De Thou heard Coligny say, "and in their place others more pleasing to the eye will be hung up."   The words had unmistakable reference to the victories which he hoped soon to win in a war against Spain.   It is not strange, however, that the malevolent endeavored to prove that they contained an allusion to the renewal of a domestic war, which it is certain that the admiral detested with his whole heart.[2]

---

[1] " Avec certain formulaire que les uns et les autres n'improuvoyent point." Mém. de l'estat, *ubi supra*, vii. 79.

[2] As De Thou here speaks as an eye-witness of the marriage, I follow his description very closely.   Histoire univ., iv. (liv. lii.) 469, 470.   Agrippa d'Aubigné was not in Paris (Mémoires, édit. Panthéon, p. 478), and his account is meagre and deficient in originality.   Hist. univ., ii. 12 (liv. i., c. 3).   It is quite in keeping with the brave Gascon's character, that, having come to

Later in the day, a magnificent entertainment was given by Charles in the Louvre to the municipality of Paris, the members of parliament, and other high officers of justice.

Entertainment in the Louvre.

Supper was succeeded by a short ball, and this in turn by one of those allegorical representations in which French fancy and invention at this period ran wanton. Through the great vaulted saloon of the Louvre a train of wonderful cars was made slowly to pass. Some were rocks of silver, on whose summits sat in state the king's brothers, Navarre, Condé, the prince dauphin, Guise, or Angoulême. On others sea-monsters disported themselves, and the pagan gods of the water, somewhat incongruously clothed in cloth of gold or various colors, serenely looked on. Charles himself rode in a chariot shaped like a sea-horse, the curved tail of which supported a shell holding Neptune and his trident. When the pageant stopped for a moment, singers of surpassing skill entertained the guests. Étienne le Roy, the king's especial favorite, distinguished himself by the power and beauty of his voice.[1]

The entertainment was prolonged far into the night; but Admiral Coligny, before giving himself repose, snatched from sleep

---

Paris some days before, in order to obtain a commission to command a company of soldiers which he had raised for the war in Flanders, he had been obliged to leave almost instantly upon his arrival, because he had acted as the second of a friend in a duel, and wounded in the face an archer who endeavored to arrest him. Tavannes makes Coligny suggest the removal of the ensigns taken from the Protestants as "marques de troubles," and playfully claim for himself the 50,000 crowns promised to any one who should bring the admiral's head. Mémoires, éd. Petitot, iii. 293.

[1] Mémoires de l'État, *ubi supra*, pp. 79, 80; De Thou, *ubi supra*. I have not deemed it out of place to describe some of the diversions with which the French court occupied itself on the eve of the massacre. The connection between reckless merriment and cold-blooded cruelty is often startlingly close. Besides this, the finances of the country were so hopelessly involved, as the consequence of the late civil wars, that this lavish expenditure was particularly ill-timed. If old Gaspard de Tavannes was as blunt as his son represents him to have been, he gave Charles some good, but, like most good, unheeded advice. "Sire," said he, à propos of the extravagance of the court at Guise's marriage in 1570, "you should make a feast, and instead of the singers who are brought in artificial clouds, you should bring those who would tell you this truth: 'You are dolts! You spend your money in festivals, in pomps and masks, and do not pay your men-at-arms nor your soldiers; foreigners will beat you!'" Mémoires, éd. Petitot, iii. 183.

a few minutes to write a letter to his wife, whom he had left in Châtillon. It is the last which has been preserved, and is otherwise important because of the light it throws upon the hopes and fears of the great Huguenot at this critical time.

" My darling," he said, " I write this bit of a letter to tell you that to-day the marriage of the king's sister and the King of Coligny's let- Navarre took place.   Three or four days will be spent ter to his wife. in festivities, masks, and mock combats.   After that the king has assured me and given me his promise, that he will devote a few days to attending to a number of complaints which are made in various parts of the kingdom, touching the infraction of the edict.   It is but reasonable that I should employ myself in this matter, so far as I am able ; for, although I have infinite desire to see you, yet should I feel great regret, and I believe that you would likewise, were I to fail to occupy myself in such an affair with all my ability.   But this will not delay so much the departure from this city, but that I think that the court will leave it at the beginning of next week.   If I had in view only my own satisfaction, I should take much greater pleasure in going to see you, than in being in this court, for many reasons which I shall tell you.   But we must have more regard for the public than for our own private interests.   I have many other things to tell you, when I am able to see you, for which I am so anxious that you must not think that I waste a day or an hour.   What remains for me to say is that to-day, at four o'clock after noon, the bride's mass was said.   Meanwhile, the King of Navarre walked about in a court with all those of the religion who accompanied him.   Other incidents occurred which I will reserve to relate to you ; but first I must see you. And meantime I pray our Lord, my darling, to keep you in His holy guard and protection.   From Paris, this eighteenth day of August, 1572.   *Mandez-moy comme se porte le petit ou petite.* . . .   I assure you that I shall not be anxious to attend all the festivities and combats that are to take place during these next days.   Your very good husband and friend, Châtillon." [1]

---

[1] I had translated this letter from the copy given by the Mémoires de l'estat de France (*apud* Archives curieuses, vii. 80, 81), which agrees substantially with, and was probably derived from, the version given in Hotman's Gasparis

The festivities and combats—so distasteful to a statesman who recognized the critical condition of French affairs, and re-

Festivities
and mock
combats.

garded this merry-making as ill-timed—pursued their uninterrupted course through Tuesday, Wednesday, and Thursday of that eventful week. But the description of most of the elaborate pageants would contribute little to the value of our conceptions of the character of the age. An exception may perhaps be made in favor of an ingenious tournament that took place on Wednesday in the Hôtel Bourbon. Here the Isles of the Blessed, the Elysian Fields, and Tartarus were represented by means of costly mechanisms. Charles and his brothers figured as knights defending Paradise, which Navarre and others, dressed as knights-errant, endeavored to enter by force of arms, but were repulsed and thrust into Tartarus. After some time the defeated champions were rescued from their perilous situation by the compassion of their victors, and the performance terminated in a startling, but harmless display of fireworks.[1] As the assailants were mostly Protestants, the defenders Roman Catholics, it was not strange that a sinister interpretation was soon put upon the strange plot;

Colinii Vita (1575), 106, 107. On comparing it, however, with the transcript of the original autograph in the remarkable collection of the late Col. Henri Tronchin, given by M. Jules Bonnet in the Bulletin de la Soc. de l'hist. du prot. français, i. (1853), 369, I discover extraordinary discrepancies, and find that, in addition to a different phraseology in every sentence, one clause is inserted by Hotman of which there is not a trace in the Tronchin MS. I refer to the words: "Soyez asseurée de ma part que, parmi ces festins et passe-temps, *je ne donneray fascherie à personne*"—which would, of course, point to the prevailing fears of a collision between the admiral and the young Duke of Guise, or his retainers, whose hatred of Coligny was so well known that Charles IX. had issued a special injunction to the parties to keep the peace. The letter contains at the commencement of the postscript a playful allusion to the hope of his wife soon to be a mother.

[1] Mém. de l'estat, *ubi supra*, 88, 89 ; De Thou, iv. (liv. lii.) 570. The mechanical part of these exhibitions was well executed. In the "*enfer*" there were " un grand nombre de diables et petis diabloteaux faisans infinies singeries et tintamarres avec une grande roue tournant dedans ledit enfer, toute environnée de clochettes." The singer, Étienne le Roy, was again the " deus ex machina," coming from heaven and returning thither, in the character of Mercury mounted upon a gigantic bird. The final explosion inspired so much consternation among the spectators, that it effectually cleared the hall.

but, unless we are to suppose the authors of the massacre, whose success depended upon the surprise of the victims, so infatuated as to wish to forewarn them of their fate, it is scarcely credible that they intended to prefigure the ruin of the reformed faith in France.

The time that had been allotted to pleasure was fast passing. The king was soon to meet Coligny, according to his promise, for the transaction of important business relating both to the internal and to the foreign affairs of France. There were religious grievances to be redressed. The admiral was particularly anxious to bring to the king's notice the flagrant outrage recently perpetrated in Troyes, where a fanatical Roman Catholic populace, indignant that the Huguenots, through the kindness of Marie de Clèves, the betrothed of the Prince of Condé,[1] had been permitted to hold their worship so near the city as her castle of Isle-au-Mont, scarcely three leagues distant,[2] had met the Protestants on their return from service with aggravated insult, and had killed in the arms of its nurse an infant that had just been baptized according to the reformed rites.[3] Catharine and her son Anjou

Huguenot grievances to be redressed.

---

[1] They were married at Blandy, a castle belonging to the Marquise de Rothelin, near Melun, where its ruins are still to be seen (Saint-Fargeau, Dict. des communes de France, s. v.), about a week before the marriage of Navarre, August 10, 1572. Tocsain contre les massacreurs (Arch. curieuses), vii. 42). Marie of Cleves was a daughter of the Duke of Nevers, and sister of Catharine of Cleves, Prince Porcien's widow, whom Henry of Guise had married in Sept., 1570. Journal de Jehan de la Fosse, 146.

[2] It is astonishing to see what considerable distances the Protestants were obliged to go in order to enjoy any religious privileges, and what fatigue they willingly underwent in order to avail themselves of them. In 1563, immediately after the close of the first civil war, instead of being assigned a place for worship in the suburbs, according to the terms of the edict, the Protestants of Troyes were told to go to Céant-en-Othe—full *eight leagues,* or about *twenty-four miles ;* nor could they obtain justice by any remonstrances with the court ! As they went to Céant, in spite of its inconvenient distance, and of the death of several children taken thither to be baptized, the Romanists, in 1570, actually proposed to remove the Protestant *prêche* still farther off, to Villenauxe, *thirteen leagues from Troyes!* Happily, after a while, they availed themselves of the hospitality of a feudal lord nearer by. Recordon, Le protestantisme en Champagne (MSS. of N. Pithou), 136, etc., 149, 163.

[3] Ibid., pp. 168, 169. The Roman Catholics of Troyes sent, about the

saw with consternation that the impression made by the " tears
of Montpipeau " was already in a great degree obliterated, and
feared the complete destruction of their influence if Charles
were longer permitted to have intercourse with Coligny. In
that case a Flemish war would be almost inevitable. Charles's
anger against the Spaniards had kindled anew when he heard
of Alva's inhumanity to Genlis and his fellow-prisoners. But,
when he was informed that Alva had put French soldiers to
the torture, in order to extract the admission of their monarch's
complicity in the enterprise, his passion was almost ungovern-
able, as he asked his attendants again and again : " Do you
know that the Duke of Alva is putting me on trial?"[1] It
seems to have been at this juncture that Catharine and her
favorite son came to the definite determination to put the great
Huguenot out of the way. Henry of Anjou is here his own
accuser. In that strange confession which he made to his physician, Miron,[2] shortly after his arrival in Cracow—a confession
made under the influence, not so much of remorse, as of the
annoyance occasioned by the continual reminders of the massacre which were thrown in his way as he travelled to assume
the throne of Poland—he gives us a partial view of the development of the murderous plot.

Several times had Anjou and Catharine perceived that, when-
Jealousy of
Catharine
and Anjou.
ever Charles had conversed in private with the admiral, his demeanor was visibly changed toward
them. He no longer exhibited his accustomed respect for his

middle of August, two deputies to get the Protestant place of worship removed from Isle-au-Mont, who were present at the massacre.

[1] Baschet, La diplomatie vénitienne, p. 540.

[2] This confession exists in manuscript in the National Library of Paris
(Fonds de Bouhier, 59), under the heading : " Discours du Roy Henry
troisiesme à un personnage d'honneur et de qualité estant près de sa majesté, sur les causes et motifs de la St. Barthélemy." It is printed in an appendix to the Mémoires de Villeroy (Petitot ed., xliv. 496–510). Its authenticity is vouched for by Matthieu, the historiographer of Louis XIII., and is
corroborated by its remarkable agreement with what we can learn from other
sources. Cf., especially, Soldan, Frankreich und die Bartholomäusnacht,
224–226. Some suppose that M. de Souvré, and not Miron, was the person
with whom the conversation at Cracow was held. Martin, Hist. de France,
x. 315.

mother or his wonted kindness for his brother. Once, in particular—and it was, so Anjou tells us, only a few days before St. Bartholomew's Day—Henry happened to enter the room just after Coligny had gone out. Instantly the king's countenance betrayed extreme anger. He began to walk furiously to and fro, taking great strides, and keeping his eyes fixed upon his brother with an expression that boded no good, but without uttering a word. Again and again he placed his hand on his dagger, and Anjou expected nothing less than that his brother would attack him. At last, taking advantage of an opportunity when Charles's back was turned, he hastily retreated from the room. This circumstance led Catharine and Anjou to compare their observations and their plans. " Both of us," says Henry, " were easily persuaded, and became, as it were, certain that it was the admiral who had impressed some evil and sinister opinion of us upon the king. We resolved from that moment to rid ourselves of him, and to concert the means of doing so with the Duchess of Nemours. To her alone we believed that we might safely disclose our purpose, on account of the mortal hatred which we knew that she bore to

The Duchess of Nemours and Henry of Guise.

him."[1] The Duchess of Nemours was born of an excellent mother; for she was Anne d'Este, daughter of Renée of France, the younger child of Louis the Twelfth. In her youth, at the court of her father, the Duke of Ferrara, and in society with that prodigy of feminine precocity, Olympia Morata, she had shown evidences of extraordinary intellectual development and of a kindly disposition.[2] Although she subsequently married Francis of Guise, the leading persecutor of the Protestants, she had not so lost her sympathy with the oppressed as to witness without tears and remonstrances the atrocious executions by which the tumult of Amboise was followed. But the assassination of her husband turned any affection or compassion she may have entertained for Protestantism into violent hatred. Against Coligny, whom, in spite of his protestations, she persisted in believing to be the

[1] Discours du Roy Henry III., Mém. de Villeroy, 499, 500.
[2] See J. Bonnet, Vie d'Olympia Morata (Paris, 1850), 20, etc.

instigator of Poltrot's crime, she bore an implacable enmity; and now, having so often failed in obtaining satisfaction from the king by judicial process, she eagerly accepted the opportunity of avenging herself by a deed more dastardly than that which she laid to the charge of her enemy. Entering heartily into the project which Catharine and Anjou laid before her, the Duchess of Nemours enlisted the co-operation of her son, Henry of Guise, and her brother-in-law, the Duke of Aumale, and herself arranged the details of the plan, which was at once to be put into execution.[1]

Such was the germ of the massacre as yet not resolved upon, which, rapidly developing, was to involve the murder of thousands of innocent persons throughout France. In opposition to the opinion that became almost universal among the Protestants, and gained nearly equal currency among the Roman Catholics—that the butchery had long been contemplated, and that Charles was privy to it—and notwithstanding the circumstances that seem to give color to this opinion,[2] I am compelled to acquiesce in the belief expressed by the Papal Nuncio, Salviati, who, in his despatches, written in cipher to the cardinal secretary of state, could certainly have had no motive to disguise his real sentiments, and whom it is impossible to suppose ignorant of any scheme for the general extirpation of the Protestants, had such a scheme existed for any considerable length of time: "As to all the statements that will be made respecting the firing upon the admiral and his death, different from that which I have written to you, you will in time find out how true they are. Madame the regent, having come to be at variance with him [the admiral], and having decided upon this step a few

Was the massacre long premeditated?

Salviati's testimony.

---

[1] Discours du Roy Henry III., ibid., p. 501. The nuncio, Salviati, informs us that young Guise urged his mother herself to kill Coligny.

[2] The article on the massacre in the North British Review for October, 1869—an article to which I shall have occasion more than once to refer—brings forward a number of passages in the diplomatic correspondence, especially of the minor Italian states, pointing in this direction. They can all, I am convinced, be satisfactorily explained, without admitting the conclusion, to which the writer evidently leans, of a *distinct*, though not a *long* premeditation.

days before, caused him to be fired upon. This was *without the knowledge of the king*, but with the participation of the Duke of Anjou, the Duchess of Nemours, and her son, the Duke of Guise. If the admiral had died at once, no others would have been slain. But, inasmuch as he survived, and they apprehended that some great calamity might happen should he draw closer to the king, they resolved to throw aside shame, and to have him killed together with the rest. And this was put into execution that very night." [1]

As the hour approached, Coligny exhibited no apprehension of special danger. Others, however, more suspicious, or possessed of less faith in Heaven, felt alarm ; and some acted upon their fears. The very " goodness " of the king terrified one. Another said that he had rather be saved with fools than perish with the wise, and hastily forsook the capital. Dark hints had been thrown out by courtiers—such surmises were naturally bred by the defenceless position of the Protestants in the midst of a population so hostile to their faith as the population of Paris—that more blood than wine would be spilled at this wedding. And there were rumors of some mysterious enterprise afloat ; so, at least, it was said after the occurrence. But Coligny moved not from the post which he believed had been assigned to his keeping. On Wednesday

The king's cordiality.

---

[1] " Mad. la Regente venuta in differenza di lui, risolvendosi pochi giorni prima, gli la fece tirare, e senza saputa del Re, ma con participatione di M. di Angiu, di Mad. de Nemours, e di M. di Guisa suo figlio ; e se moriva subito non si ammazzava altri," etc. Salviati, desp. of Sept. 22, 1572, *apud* Mackintosh, Hist. of England, vol. iii., Appendix K. It will be remembered that these despatches were given to Sir James Mackintosh by M. de Châteaubriand, who had obtained them from the Vatican. I need not say how much more trustworthy are the secret despatches of one so well informed as the nuncio, than the sensational " Stratagema " of Capilupi, which pretends (ed. of 1574, p. 26) that *Charles* placed Maurevel in the house from which he shot at Coligny, on discovering that the admiral had formed the plan of firing Paris the next night. To believe these champions of orthodoxy, the Huguenots were born with a special passion for incendiary exploits. It does not seem to strike them that burning and pillaging Paris would not be likely to appear to Coligny a probable means of furthering the war in Flanders. Besides, what need is there of any such Huguenot plot, even according to Capilupi's own view, since he carries back the premeditation of the massacre on the part of Charles at least four years ?

Charles assured him, with laughing countenance, that if the admiral would but give him four days more for amusement, he would not stir from Paris until he had contented him;[1] and the sturdy old Huguenot made no objection when the king, in order to prevent any disturbance which the partisans of Guise might occasion in seeking a quarrel with the followers of the house of Châtillon, proposed to introduce a considerable force of soldiers into the city. "My father," said Charles, with his usual appearance of affection, "you know that you have promised not to give any cause of offence to the Guises so long as you remain here; and they have in like manner promised to respect you and all yours. I am fully persuaded that you will keep your word; but I am not so well assured of their good faith as of yours; for, besides the fact that it is they that would avenge themselves, I know their bravadoes and the favor this populace bears to them."[2]

On Friday morning, the twenty-second of August, Admiral Coligny went to the Louvre, to attend a meeting of the royal council, at which Henry of Anjou presided. It was between ten and eleven o'clock, when, according to the more primitive hours then kept, he left the palace to return home for dinner.[3] Meeting Charles just coming out

Coligny is wounded, August 22.

---

[1] Le Reveille-Matin des François, etc., Archives curieuses, vii. 173; Eusebii Philadelphi Dialogi (1574), i. 33. It has been customary to interpret this language and similar expressions as covertly referring to the massacre which was then four days off. But this seems absurd. Certainly, if Charles was privy to the plan for Coligny's murder, he must have expected him to be killed on Friday—that is, within less than two days. If so, what peculiar significance in the *four* days? For, if a general massacre had been at first contemplated, no interval of two days would have been allowed. Everybody must have known that if the arquebuse shot had done its work, and Coligny had been killed on the spot, every Huguenot would have been far from the walls of Paris long before Sunday. As it was, it was only the admiral's confidence, and the impossibility of moving him with safety, that detained them.

[2] Capilupi, Lo stratagema di Carlo IX., 1574. Orig. ed., pp. 24, 25, and the concurrent French version, pp. 42, 43. This version is incorporated *verbatim* in the Mémoires de l'estat de France sous Charles IX. (Archives curieuses), vii. 89, 90. In like manner the "Mémoires," which are in great part a mere compilation, take page after page from the "Reveille-Matin."

[3] "Ainsi qu'il sortoit présentement du Louvre, pour aller disner en son logis." Charles's letter of same day to La Mothe Fénélon, Corresp. dipl., vii. 322.

of a chapel in front of the Louvre, he retraced his steps, and accompanied him to the tennis-court, where he left him playing with Guise, against Téligny and another nobleman. Accompanied by about a dozen gentlemen, he again sallied forth, but had not proceeded over a hundred paces when from behind a lattice an arquebuse was fired at him.[1] The admiral had been walking slowly, intently engaged in reading a petition which had just been handed to him. The shot had been well aimed, and might have proved fatal, had not the victim at that very moment turned a little to one side. As it was, of the three balls with which the arquebuse was loaded, one took off a finger of his right hand, and another lodged in his left arm, making an ugly wound. Supported by De Guerchy and Des Pruneaux, between whom he had previously been walking, Coligny was carried to his house in the little Rue de Béthisy,[2] only a few steps farther on. As he went he pointed out to his friends the house from which the shot had been fired. To a gentleman who expressed the fear that the balls were poisoned, he replied with composure : " Nothing will happen but what it may please God to order." [3]

The attempted assassination had happened in front of the cloisters of St. Germain l'Auxerrois. The house was recognized as one belonging to the Duchess Dowager of Guise, in which Villemur, the former tutor of young Henry of Guise, had lodged.

---

[1] It is of little moment whether the assassin at his window was screened by a lattice, or by a curtain, as De Thou says, or by bundles of straw, as Capilupi states. I prefer the account of the " Reveille-Matin," as the author tells us that he was one of the twelve or fifteen gentlemen in Coligny's suite— " entre lesquels j'estoy " (p. 174). So the Latin ed., Euseb. Philad. Dialogi, i. 34.

[2] The Rue de Béthisy was the continuation of the Rue des Fossés Saint Germain l'Auxerrois, through which he was walking when he was shot. In the sixteenth century the street bore the former name, beginning at the Rue de l'Arbre Sec, at the corner of which Coligny appears to have lodged. In later times the name was confined to the part east of Rue de Roule. Dulaure, Histoire de Paris, iv. 259. The extension of the Rue de Rivoli, under the auspices of Napoleon III., has not only destroyed the house in which Coligny was murdered, but obliterated the Rue de Béthisy itself.

[3] " Qu'il n'aviendroit que ce qu'il plairoit à Dieu." Reveille-Matin, 175 ; Euseb. Philad. Dialogi (1574), i. 35 ; Mémoires de l'estat, 94.

The door was found locked; but the indignant followers of Coligny soon burst it open. They found within only a woman and a lackey. The assassin, after firing, had fled to the rear of the house. There he found a horse awaiting him; this he exchanged at the Porte Saint Antoine for a fresh Spanish jennet. He was out of Paris almost before pursuit was fairly undertaken. Subsequent investigation left no doubt as to his identity. It was that same Maurevel of infamous memory, who during the third civil war had traitorously shot De Mouy, after insinuating himself into his friendship, and sharing his room and his bed. The king's assassin, "le tueur du roi"—a designation he had obtained when Charles or his advisers gave a special reward for that exploit [1]—had been selected by Catharine, Anjou and the Guises, as possessing both the nerve and the experience that were requisite to make sure of Coligny's death. It was found that he had been placed in the house by De Chailly, "maître d'hôtel" of the king, and that the horse by means of which he effected his escape had been brought to the door by the groom of the Duke of Guise. [2]

Charles was still in the tennis-court, when De Piles came in, sent by Coligny, to inform him of the bloody infraction of the Edict of Pacification. On hearing the intelligence, the king was violently agitated. Throwing down his racket, he exclaimed: " Am I, then, never to have peace? What! always new troubles?" and retired to his room in the Louvre, with a countenance expressive of great dejection. [3] And when, later in the day, the King of Navarre, the Prince of Condé, and La Rochefoucauld, after seeing Coligny's wounds dressed, came to the palace and begged him for permission to leave a city in which there was no security for their lives,

Agitation of the king.

---

[1] See *ante*, chapter xvi.

[2] Reveille-Matin, *ubi sup.*, 175 ; and Euseb. Philad. Dialogi, i. 34, 35 ; Mémoires de l'estat, *ubi sup.*, 93, etc. ; Jean de Serres (1575), iv. fol. 25 ; Tocsain contre les Massacreurs (orig. ed.), 113, etc. ; Registres du Bureau de la ville de Paris (Archives curieuses, vii. 211) ; despatch of Salviati of Aug. 22. App. F to Mackintosh, Hist. of England, iii. 354 ; De Thou, iv. (liv. lii.) 574; Jehan de la Fosse, 147, 148 ; Baschet, La diplomatie vénit., 548.

[3] Mémoires de l'estat, *ubi sup.*, 94 ; Jean de Serres (1575), iv., fols. 25, 26 ; Reveille-Matin, 176 ; Euseb. Philad. Dial., i. 35 ; De Thou, iv. (liv. lii.) 574.

Charles swore to them, with his accustomed profanity, that he would inflict upon the author and abettors of the crime so signal a punishment that Coligny and his friends would be satisfied, and posterity have a warning example. Coligny had received the wound, he said, but the smart was *his*. Catharine, who was present, chimed in, and declared the outrage so flagrant, that just retribution must speedily be meted out, or insolence would be pushed so far as that the king would be attacked in his own palace.[1]

Meantime the admiral bore his sufferings with serenity, and, far from needing any comfort his friends could give him, himself administered consolation to the noblemen around his bed. His sufferings were acute. Amboise Paré, the famous surgeon of the king, himself a Huguenot, was called in; but the instruments at hand were dull, and it was not until the third attempt that he could satisfactorily amputate the wounded finger. "My friends," said Coligny to Merlin, his minister, and to other friends, "why do you weep? As for me, I think myself happy in having received these wounds for the name of God." And when Merlin exhorted him "to thank God for His mercy in preserving his mental faculties sound and entire, and to continue to divert his thoughts and feelings from his assassin and his wounds, and to turn them, as he was doing, from all things else to God, since it was from His hands that he had received them," the admiral's reply was, that sincerely and from the heart he forgave the person who had wounded him, and those who had instigated him, holding it for certain that it was beyond their power to injure him, since, should they even kill him, death would be an assured passage to life.[2] Thus, with quiet submission, and with edifying prayers which it would be too long to insert, the Admiral de Coligny passed those hours which his enemies subsequently, in their desperate attempts to justify or palliate the most abominable of crimes, represented as given up to infamous plots against king and state.

Coligny courageous.

---

[1] Tocsain contre les massacreurs, Archives cur., vii. 45 ; Reveille-Matin, 177; Mémoires de l'estat, 98.

[2] Gasparis Colinii Vita (1574), 108–110 ; Mémoires de l'estat de Charles IX., *ubi supra*, 94–98. The two accounts are evidently from the same hand.

That afternoon, between two and three o'clock, Charles visited the wounded man, at the suggestion of Téligny and

He is visited by the king and his mother.

Damville; for Coligny had expressed a desire to see the monarch, that he might communicate certain matters which concerned him greatly, but of which he feared there was no one else that would inform him.[1] The king came, accompanied by his mother, his brothers, the Duke of Montpensier, Cardinal Bourbon, Marshals Damville, Tavannes and Cossé, Count de Retz, and the younger Montmorencies, Thoré and Méru.[2] The interview was kind and reassuring. The admiral, who lay upon his bed, heartily thanked the king for the honor he had deigned to do him, and for the measures he had already taken in his behalf. And Charles praised the patience and magnanimity exhibited by Coligny, and bade him be of good courage. Then more important topics were introduced. There were three points respecting which the admiral wished to speak to Charles. The first was his own loyalty, which, however much it had been maligned by his enemies, he desired now solemnly to reaffirm, in the presence of Him before whose bar he might soon be called to stand, and he declared that the sole cause of the hostility he had aroused was his attempt to set bounds to the fury of those who presumed to violate royal edicts. Next, he commended to the king the Flemish project. Never had any predecessor of Charles enjoyed so splendid an opportunity as now offered, when several cities of the Netherlands had declared their desire for his favor and protection. But these advances were openly derided by some of the courtiers about the king; while state secrets were so badly kept, that "one could not turn an egg, nor utter a word in the

---

[1] Mémoires de l'estat, *ubi supra*, 98.

[2] Damville, Méru and Thoré, were sons of the constable. Their eldest brother, Marshal Francis de Montmorency, whose greatest vice was his sluggishness and his devotion to his ease, had left Paris a few days before, on the pretext of going to the chase. His absence at the time of the massacre was supposed to have saved not only his life, but that of his brothers. The Guises would gladly have destroyed a family whose influence and superior antiquity had for a generation been obnoxious to their ambitious designs; but it was too hazardous to leave the head of the family to avenge his murdered brothers.

council, but it was forthwith reported to the Duke of Alva."
And, indeed, what else could be expected, since those who were
present, and even his own brothers, communicated to foreigners
and enemies the king's most confidential deliberations? He
earnestly begged Charles to apply a prompt remedy to this
matter in future. The last point was the observance of the
Edict of Pacification. What opinion would foreign nations form
of the king, if he suffered a law solemnly made, and frequently
confirmed by oath, to be openly trampled upon? In proof of
this assertion, he alleged the recent attack upon the Protestants
of Troyes returning from their place of worship, the tragic termination of which has already been noticed.

To that part of Coligny's remarks which related to the war
in Flanders, it is said that Charles made no direct reply; but
he declared that he had never suspected the admiral's loyalty,
and that he accounted him a good man, and a great and generous captain. There was not another man in the kingdom whom
he would prefer to him. And he again asseverated his intention
to enforce a religious observance of his edicts; for which purpose, indeed, he had recently despatched commissioners into all
the provinces, as the queen could inform him. "That is true,
Monsieur l'amiral," said Catharine, "and you know it." "Yes,
madam," he replied, "commissioners have been sent, among
whom are some that condemned me to be hung, and set a price
of fifty thousand crowns on my head." "Then," rejoined
Charles, "we must send others who are open to no suspicion."
Again he promised with his accustomed oath to see that the
attempt upon the admiral's life should be so punished that the
retribution would be forever remembered;[1] after which he
inquired whether Coligny were satisfied with the judges whom
he had appointed to conduct the investigation. Coligny replied
that he committed himself in this matter to the king's prudence,
but suggested that Cavaignes, the recently appointed maître de
requêtes, and two other Huguenots be added to the commission.

---

[1] There was no need of going far, Coligny responded, to discover the author.
"Qu'on en demande à Monsieur de Guise, il dira qui est celuy qui m'a presté
une telle charité; mais Dieu ne me soit jamais en aide si je demande vengeance d'un tel outrage." Mém. de l'estat, *ubi supra*, 104, 105.

The king and De Retz both endeavored to persuade the admiral to permit himself to be transported, for safety's sake, to the Louvre; but Coligny's friends would not consent to a removal which might endanger his life. Charles requested, before he left, to see the ball extracted from the wounded arm, and examined it with apparent curiosity. Catharine took it next, and said that she was glad that it had been removed, for she remembered that, when the Duke of Guise was shot, the physicians repeatedly said that, even if the ball were poisoned, there was no danger to be apprehended when once the ball was taken out. Many afterward regarded it as a significant circumstance that the queen mother's mind should have reverted on this occasion to the murder of which the Lorraine family still persisted in accusing Coligny of having been the instigator.[1]

Such was, according to the solitary Huguenot who was present by Coligny's bed, and who survived the subsequent massacre, the substance of the conversation at this celebrated interview. But, if we may credit the account which purports to have been given by Henry of Anjou, there was an incident which he failed to mention. At a certain point in the conversation Coligny asked to be allowed to speak to the king in private, a request which Charles willingly granted, motioning Henry and Catharine to withdraw. They accordingly retired to the middle of the room, where they remained standing during the suspicious colloquy. Meanwhile their apprehensions were awakened as they noticed that there were more than two hundred gentlemen and captains of the admiral's party in this and an adjacent room and below stairs. The sad looks of the Huguenots, their gestures expressive of discontent, their suppressed whispers, as they passed to and fro, before and behind the queen and her favorite son, with less respect than the latter thought was due to them, impressed

Catharine attempts to break up the conference. them with the idea that they were objects of distrust. Catharine afterward admitted to Henry that never in her life was she so glad to get out of any other place. Her impatience soon impelled her to cut short the con-

[1] Gasparis Colinii Vita, 114–121 ; Mémoires de l'estat, *ubi supra*, 102–106. The two accounts agree almost word for word. There is a briefer narrative in Reveille-Matin, 178, 179; and Euseb. Philad. Dialogi, i. 37.

ference between Charles and Coligny—much to the regret of Charles—on the pretext that longer conversation might retard the sick man's recovery.

Scarcely had the royal party left the admiral's lodgings, when Catharine began to ply Charles with questions respecting Coligny's private communication. Several times he absolutely refused to satisfy her curiosity. But at last, losing all patience, he roughly answered her with an oath: " What the admiral told me was true : kings are recognized as such in France only so far as they have the power to reward or punish their subjects and servants ; and this power and the management of the affairs of the entire state have insensibly slipped into your hands. But this authority of yours, the admiral told me, may some day become highly prejudicial both to me and to my whole kingdom, and I ought to look upon it with suspicion, and to be on my guard. Of this he had desired, as one of my best and most faithful subjects, to warn me before he died. Well then, *mon Dieu*, since you will know it, this is what the admiral was telling me." " This was uttered," Anjou subsequently said, " with so much passion and fury, that the speech cut us to the heart. We concealed our emotion as best we could, and vindicated ourselves. This discourse we pursued from the admiral's lodgings to the Louvre. There, after having left the king in his own room, we retired to that of the queen, my mother, who was nettled and offended in the highest degree by this language of the admiral to the king, and still more by the credit the king seemed to give it, fearing that this might occasion some change in our affairs and in the conduct of the state. To be frank, we found ourselves so unprovided with counsel and understanding, that, being unable to come to any determination at that time, we separated, deferring the matter until the morrow." [1]

Meantime, Charles, not content with closing all the gates of Paris, save two, which were to be strictly guarded,
and with ordering a speedy judicial investigation, despatched, on the very day of the attempt on Coligny's life, a circular letter to all the governors of the provinces, and

Charles writes letters expressing his displeasure.

---

[1] Discours du roy Henry III., *ubi supra*, 502-505.

a similar letter to his ambassadors at foreign courts, declarative of his profound displeasure at this audacious crime. In the former he said: "I am at once sending in every direction in pursuit of the perpetrator, with a view to catch him and inflict such punishment upon him as is required by a deed so wicked, so displeasing, and, moreover, so inconvenient; for the reparation of which I wish to forget nothing." And lest any persons, whether Protestants or Roman Catholics, should be aroused by this news to make a disturbance of the peace, he called upon all the governors to explain the full circumstances of the case. "Assure every one," he wrote, "that it is my intention to observe inviolate my edict of pacification, and so strictly to punish those who contravene its provisions, that men may judge how sincere is my will." [1] In a similar strain he wrote to his ambassador in England, that he was "infinitely sorry" (infiniment marry), and that he desired him to acquaint Queen Elizabeth with his determination to cause such signal justice to be executed, that every one in his realm might take example therefrom. "Monsieur de la Mothe Fénélon," he added in a postscript, "I must not forget to tell you that this wicked act proceeds from the enmity between his [the admiral's] house and the Guises. I shall know how to provide that they involve none of my subjects in their quarrels; for I intend that my edict of pacification be observed in all points." [2]

Not long after the king had left Coligny's room, the admiral was visited by Jean de Ferrières, Vidame de Chartres, a leading Huguenot, who came to condole with him. He also

The Vidame de Chartres advises the Huguenots to leave Paris. had a more practical object in view. In a conference of the great nobles of the reformed faith, held in the room adjoining the admiral's, he advocated the instant departure of the Protestants from Paris, and urged it at considerable length. He saw in the event of the day the first act of a tragedy whose catastrophe could not be long deferred. The Huguenots had thrust their head into the very jaws of the lion; it were prudent to draw it out while it was yet time. But

---

[1] Le roi à Mandelot, 22 août, Correspondance du roi Charles IX. et du sieur de Mandelot (Paris, 1830), 36, 37.

[2] Corresp. dipl. de La Mothe Fénélon, vii. 322, 323.

this sensible advice, based less upon any distinct evidence of a plot for their destruction than upon the obvious temptation which their defenceless situation offered to a woman proverbially unscrupulous, was overruled by the majority of those present. Téligny, in particular, the accomplished and amiable son-in-law of Coligny, opposed a scheme which not only might endanger the admiral's life, but would certainly displease the king, by betraying distrust of his ability or his inclination to defend his Protestant subjects.[1]

Saturday morning came, and with it a report from Coligny's physicians, announcing that his wounds would not prove serious. Meanwhile the investigation into the attempted assassination was pursued, and disclosed more and more evidence of the complicity of the Guises. The young duke and his uncle Aumale, conscious of the suspicion in which they were held, and fearful perhaps of the king's anger, should the part they had taken become known, prepared to retire from Paris, and came to Charles to ask for leave of absence, telling him at the same time that they had long noticed that their services were not pleasing to him. Charles, with little show of courtesy, bade them depart. Should they prove guilty, he said, he would find means to bring them to justice.[2]

And now the time had arrived when Catharine and the Duke of Anjou must come to a final decision respecting the means of extricating themselves from their present embarrassments. Maurevel's shot had done no execution. Coligny was likely to recover, to be more than ever the idol of the Huguenots, to become more than ever the favorite of the king. In that case the influence of Catharine and her younger son would be irretrievably lost; especially if the judicial investigation now in progress should reveal the fact that they were the prime movers in the plan of assassination. Certainly neither Henry of Guise nor his mother would consent to bear the entire responsibility. More than that, the Huguenots were uttering loud demands for justice, which to guilty consciences sounded like threats of retribution.

Catharine and Anjou come to a final decision.

---

[1] Mémoires de l'estat, *ubi supra*, 106, 107.   [2] Ibid., 108.

We must here recur to Henry of Anjou's own account of this critical period; for that strange confession throws the only gleam of light upon the process by which the young king was moved to the adoption of a course whereby he earned the reputation—of which it will be difficult to divest him—of a monster of cruelty. "I went," says Anjou, "to see my mother, who had already risen. I was filled with anxiety, as also she was on her side. We adopted at that time no other determination than to despatch the admiral by whatever means possible. As artifice and cunning could no longer be employed, we must proceed by open measures. But, to do this, we must bring the king to this same resolution. We decided that we would go in the afternoon to his private room, and would bring in the Duke of Nevers, Marshals Tavannes and Retz, and Chancellor Birague, solely to obtain their advice as to the means we should employ in executing the plan upon which my mother and I had already agreed.

" As soon as we had entered the room in which the king my brother was, my mother began to represent to him that the party of the Huguenots was arming against him on account of the wounding of the admiral, the latter having sent several despatches to Germany to make a levy of ten thousand horse, and to the cantons of Switzerland for another levy of ten thousand foot; that most of the French captains belonging to the Huguenot party had already left in order to raise troops within the kingdom; and that the time and place of assembling had been fixed upon. Let so powerful an army as this once be joined to their French troops—a thing which was only too practicable—and the king's forces would not be half sufficient to resist them, in view of the intrigues and leagues they had, inside and outside of the kingdom, with many cities, communities, and nations. Of this she had good and certain advices. Their allies were to revolt in conjunction with the Huguenots under pretext of the public good; and for him (Charles), being weak in pecuniary resources, she saw no place of security in France. And, indeed, there was besides a new consequence of which she wished to warn him. It was that all the Catholics, wearied by so long a war, and vexed by so many

They ply Charles with arguments.

sorts of calamities, were determined to put an end to them. In case he refused to follow their counsel, they also had determined among themselves to elect a captain-general to undertake their protection, and to form a league offensive and defensive against the Huguenots. Thus he would remain alone, enveloped in great danger, and without power or authority. All France would be seen armed by two great parties, over which he would have no command, and from which he could exact just as little obedience. But, to ward off so great a danger, a peril impending over him and his entire state, so much ruin, and so many calamities which were in preparation and just at hand, and the murder of so many thousands of men—to avert all these misfortunes, a single thrust of the sword would suffice—the admiral, the head and author of all the civil wars, alone need be put to death. The designs and enterprises of the Huguenots would perish with him; and the Catholics, satisfied with the sacrifice of two or three men, would remain obedient to him (the king)."

Such arguments, and many more of a similar character, does Henry tell us that he and his wily mother addressed to the unhappy Charles. At first their words irritated him, and, without convincing, drove him into a frenzy of excitement. A little later, giving credit to the oft-repeated assertions of his false advisers, and his imagination becoming inflamed by the picture of the dangers surrounding him which they so skilfully painted, he would, nevertheless, hear nothing of the crime to which he was urged, but began anxiously to consult those who were present whether there were no other means of escape. Each man gave his opinion in succession; and each supported Catharine's views, until it came to the turn of Retz, who, contrary to the expectation of the conspirators, gave expression to more noble sentiments.[1] If any one were justified in hating Coligny and his faction, he said, it was himself, maligned, as he had

---

[1] There is here, however, a direct contradiction, which I shall not attempt to reconcile, between the account of Henry and that of the younger Tavannes, who represents Retz as one of the most violent in his recommendations. According to Tavannes, it was his father, Marshal Tavannes, that advocated moderation. In other respects the two accounts are strongly corroborative of each other.

been, both in France and abroad; but he was unwilling, in avenging private wrongs, to involve France and its royal family in dishonor. The king would justly be taxed with perfidy, and all confidence in his word or in public faith would be lost. Henceforth it would be impossible to treat for terms of peace in those new civil wars in which the French must be involved, and of which their children would not see the end.

These wholesome words at first struck speechless the advocates of murder. Then they undertook, by repeating their arguments, to destroy the effect of the prophetic warn-

The king consents reluctantly.

ing to which the king had just listened. They succeeded but too well. "That instant," says Henry of Anjou, " we perceived a sudden change, a strange and wonderful metamorphosis in the king. He placed himself on our side, and adopted our opinion, going much beyond us and to more criminal lengths; since, whereas before it was difficult to persuade him, now we had to restrain him. For, rising and addressing us, while imposing silence upon us, he told us in anger and fury, swearing by God's death that, ' since we thought it good that the admiral should be killed, he would have it so; but that with him all the Huguenots of France must be killed, in order that not one might remain to reproach him hereafter; and that we should promptly see to it.' And going out furiously, he left us in his room, where we deliberated the rest of the day, during the evening, and for a good part of the night, and decided upon that which seemed advisable for the execution of such an enterprise." [1]

This is the strange record of the change by which Charles, from being the friend of Admiral Coligny, became the accomplice in his murder and in countless other assassinations throughout France. The admission of his guilt by one of the principal actors in the tragedy is so frank and undisguised that we find it difficult to believe that the narrative can have emanated from his lips. But the freaks of a burdened conscience are not to be easily accounted for. The most callous or reticent criminal sometimes is aroused to a recognition of his wicked-

---

[1] Discours du roy Henry III., 505–508.

ness, and burns to communicate to another the fearful secret whose deposit has become intolerable to himself. And fortunately the confession of the princely felon does not stand alone. The son of another of the wretches who persuaded Charles to imbrue his hands in the blood of his subjects has given us the account which he undoubtedly received from his father shortly before his death, and we find the two statements to be in substantial agreement. Tavannes says: " The king notified (of the attempt upon Coligny's life), is offended, and threatens the Guises, not knowing whence the blow came. After a while, he is appeased by the queen, assisted by the sieur de Retz. They make his Majesty angry with the Huguenots—a vice peculiar to his Majesty, who is of choleric humor. They induce him to believe that they have discovered an enterprise of the Huguenots directed against him. He is reminded of the designs of Meaux and of Amboise. Suddenly gained over, as his mother had promised herself that he would be, he abandons the Huguenots, and remains sorry, with the rest, that the wound had not proved mortal." [1]

And now, the assassination of the admiral having received the king's approval, it only remained to decide upon the number of Protestants who should be involved with him in a common destruction, and to perfect the arrangements for the execution of the murderous plot. How many, and who were the victims whose sacrifice was predetermined? This is a question which, with our present means of information, we are unable to answer. Catharine, it is true, used to declare in later times that she contemplated no general massacre; that she took upon her conscience the blood of only five or six persons; [2] and, although the unsupported assertion of so perfidious a woman is certainly not entitled to any great consideration, we can readily see that the heads of half a dozen leaders might have fully contented her. She was not seeking

Few victims selected at first.

---

[1] Mémoires de Gaspard de Saulx, seigneur de Tavannes, by his son, Jean de Saulx, vicomte de Tavannes (Petitot edition), iii. 293, 294.

[2] " Reginam quidem certum est dictitare solitam, edita strage, ' se tantum *sex* hominum interfectorum sanguinem in suam conscientiam recipere.' " Jean de Serres (ed. of 1575), iv., fol. 29. The whole passage is interesting.

for revenge so much as paving the way for her ambition. There were few Huguenots who were apparently so powerful as to interfere with her projects. Coligny, their acknowledged head ; the Count of Montgomery, personally hated as the occasion of the death of her husband, Henry the Second, in the ill-fated tournament; the Vidame of Chartres; and La Rochefoucauld —these were doubtless of the number. Would she have desired to include the King of Navarre and the Prince of Condé ? Not the former, on account of his recent marriage with her daughter. Yet to whom the Bourbons were indebted for the omission of their names from the proscriptive roll we cannot tell. After the accession of Henry the Fourth, it became the interest of all the families concerned to put the conduct of their ancestors in the most favorable light. Thus, Jean de Tavannes states that his father saved the life of the Bearnese in that infamous conclave ; but so little did the latter believe him, that, on the contrary, he persistently refused to confer upon him the marshal's baton, which he would otherwise have received, on the ground that Gaspard de Tavannes was an instigator of the massacre.[1]

Thus much must be held to be clearly established : that fancied political exigencies demanded the assassination of only very few persons ; that personal hatred, on the part of the principal or of the minor conspirators, added many more ; that a still greater number were murdered in cold blood, simply that their spoils might enrich the assassins. What part must be assigned to religious zeal ?[2] To any true outgrowth of religion, none at all ; but much to the malice and the depraved moral teachings

---

[1] " Le roy Henry quatriesme disoit que ce qu'il ne m'avoit tenu promesse estoit en vengeance des services faicts par le sieur de Tavannes mon père aux batailles de Jarnac et Montcontour, mais le principal, parce qu'il l'accusoit d'avoir conseillé la Sainct Barthelemy ; ce qu'il disoit à ses familiers, et à tort, parce que ledict sieur de Tavannes en ce temps-là fut cause qu'il ne courust la mesme fortune que le sieur admiral de Coligny." Mémoires de Tavannes (Petitot edit.), iii. 222.

[2] To ascribe the conduct of Catharine de' Medici herself to any such motive is the extreme of absurdity. Even the author of the " Tocsain contre les massacreurs " rejects the supposition without hesitation. (Original edition, p. 157.) Catharine was certainly a free-thinker, probably an atheist.

of its professed representatives. The hatred of Protestantism,
Religious   engendered in the minds of the people by long years
hatred.   devoted to traducing the character and designs of
the reformers, now bore fruit after its own kind, in revolting
crimes of every sort; while the lesson, sedulously inculcated by
priests, bishops, and monks, that obstinate heretics might right-
eously be, and ought to be exterminated from the face of the
earth, permitted many a Parisian burgess to commit acts from
which any but the most diabolic nature would otherwise have
recoiled in horror. But of the measure of the responsibility of
the Roman pontiff and his clergy for this stupendous crime, it
will be necessary to speak in the sequel.

In devising the plan for the destruction of the Huguenots,
the queen mother and her council were greatly assisted by the
course pursued by the Huguenots themselves, and by the very
Precaution-   circumstances of the case. Under pretence of taking
ary measures. measures to secure the safety of the Protestants, the
" quarteniers " could go, without exciting suspicion, from house
to house, and make a complete list of all belonging to the reformed church.[1] The same excuse served to justify the court
in posting a body of twelve hundred arquebusiers, a part along
the river, a part in the immediate neighborhood of Coligny's
residence.[2] And now the Protestants themselves, startled by
the unusual commotion which they noticed in the city, and by
the frequent passage to and fro of men carrying arms, sent a
gentleman to the Louvre to ask the king for a few guards to
protect the dwelling of their wounded leader. The request
was only for five or six guards; but Charles, feigning astonishment and deep regret that there should be any reason for such
apprehensions, insisted, at the suggestion of his brother Anjou,
who stood by, upon despatching fifty, under command of Cosseins. So well known was the captain's hostility to Coligny
and the Protestants, that Thoré, Montmorency's brother, whispered to the Huguenot messenger as he withdrew : " You could
not have been given in guard to a worse enemy; " but the
royal direction was so positive that no remonstrance seemed

---

[1] Mémoires de l'estat, *ubi supra*, 108.   [2] Ibid., 109.

possible. Accordingly, Cosseins and his arquebusiers took possession, in the king's name, of two shops adjoining Coligny's abode.[1] With as little ceremony, Rambouillet, the "maréchal des logis," turned the Roman Catholic gentlemen out of the lodgings he had previously assigned them in the Rue de Béthisy, and gave the quarters to the Protestant gentlemen instead.[2] The reason assigned for this action was that the Huguenots might be nearer to each other and to the admiral, for mutual protection; the real object seems to have been to sweep them more easily into the common net of destruction.

And yet the majority of the Huguenot leaders were not alive to the dangers of their situation. In a second conference held late on Saturday, the Vidame of Chartres was almost alone in urging instant retreat. Navarre, Condé, and others thought it sufficient to demand justice, and the departure of the Guises, as possessing dangerous credit with the common people. Téligny again dwelt upon the wrong done to Charles in distrusting his sincerity, and deprecated a course that might naturally irritate him. One Bouchavannes was noticed in the conference—a professed Protestant, but suspiciously intimate with Catharine, Retz, and other avowed enemies of the faith. He said nothing, but listened attentively. So soon as the meeting was over, Bouchavannes went to the Louvre and related the discussion to the queen mother.[3] The traitor's report, doubtless grossly exaggerated, is supposed to have decided Catharine to prompt action. It is certain, at least, that the calumnious perversion of the speeches and resolutions of the Huguenot conference was employed to inflame the passions of the mob, as well as to justify the atrocities of the morrow in the eyes of the world.

It was now late in the evening of Saturday, the twenty-third of August. Coligny had been writing to his friends throughout France, recommending them to be quiet, and informing them of the investigations now in progress. God and the king, he said, would do justice. His wounds were not mortal, thank God. If

---

[1] Mémoires de l'estat, *ubi supra*, 110, 111.
[2] Ibid., 111; Gasparis Colinii Vita (1575), 124.
[3] Mémoires de l'estat, *ubi supra*, 112.

his *arm* was wounded, his *brain* was yet sound.[1] Meantime,
the original framers of the murderous plot had called in the
Guises, who in reality had not left Paris.[2] It had been arranged
that the execution should be intrusted to them, in conjunction
with the Bastard of Angoulême, Charles's natural brother, and
Marshal Tavannes. And now at last we emerge from the mist
that envelops many of the preliminaries of the night of horrors.
The records of the Hôtel de Ville contain the first documentary
evidence of the coming massacre. There is no longer any doubt,
unfortunately, of Charles's approval and complicity. " This
day, the twenty-third day of August, very late in the evening,"
Orders issued to the prévôt des marchands. Charles sends for Charron, " prévôt des marchands,"
to come to the Louvre. Here, in the presence of the
queen mother, the Duke of Anjou and other princes
and lords, his Majesty " declares that he has received intelligence that those of the new religion intend to make a rising by
conspiracy against himself and his state, and to disturb the
peace of his subjects and of his city of Paris ; and that this
very night some great personages of the said new religion and
rebels have conspired against him and his said state, going to
such lengths as to send his Majesty some arrogant messages
which sounded like menaces." Consequently, in order to protect
himself and the royal family, Charles directs the prévôt to seize
the keys of all the gates of the city, and to keep them carefully
closed, in order to prevent any one from entering or leaving
Paris. He also commands him to remove all the boats moored
along the Seine, so as to prevent any one from crossing the river ;
and to put under arms all captains, lieutenants, ensigns, and
burgesses capable of doing military duty.[3] The orders were
faithfully and promptly obeyed. Long before morning dawned
they had been transmitted successively to the lower municipal
officers, quarteniers, dizainiers, etc. ; the wherry-men had been
stopped, and the troops and burgesses of Paris having armed
themselves as best they could, were assembled ready for action

---

[1] Reveille-Matin, *ubi supra*, 179 ; Mémoires de l'estat, *ubi sup.*, 113.

[2] Capilupi, 30, 31 ; Mém. de l'estat, *ubi sup.*, 107, 108.

[3] Extrait des Registres et Croniques du Bureau de la ville de Paris, Archives curieuses, vii. 213.

in front of the Hôtel de Ville, on that famous Place de Grève,
so often drenched in martyr's blood.[1]

To the guilty plotters that was a sleepless night.   Unable to
rest quietly, at a little before dawn, Catharine with her two elder
sons found her way to the portal of the Louvre, adjoining the
tennis court.   There, in a chamber overlooking the "bassecour,"
they sat down to await the beginning of their treacherous enterprise.   If we may believe Henry of Anjou, none of them as yet
realized its full horrors; but as they quietly watched in that
hour of stillness for the first signs of the coming outbreak, the
report of a pistol-shot reached their ears.   Instantly
it wrought a marvellous revulsion in their feelings.
Whether the shot wounded or killed any one, they
knew not; but it brought up vividly to their imaginations the
results of the terrible deluge of blood whose flood-gates they
had raised.   Hastily they send a servant to the Duke of Guise,
and countermand the instructions of the evening, and bid him
do no injury to the admiral.   It is too late!   The messenger
soon returns with the tidings that Coligny is already dead, that
the work is about to begin in all the rest of the city.   This news
produces a fresh change.   With one of those fluctuations which
are so easy for souls that have no firm or established principles,
but shift according to the deceptive, ever-varying tide of apparent interest, the mother and her sons return heartily to their
former purpose.   The die is cast, the deed is half done; let it
be fully and boldly consummated.   No room now for pity or
regret.[2]

The first shot and the bell of St. Germain l'Auxerrois.

It was a Sunday morning, the twenty-fourth of August—a day
sacred in the Roman calendar to the memory of Saint Bartholomew.   Torches and blazing lights had been burning all night
in the streets, to render the task easy.   The houses in which
Protestants lodged had been distinctly marked with a white
cross.   The assassins themselves had agreed upon badges for
mutual recognition—a white cross on the hat, and a handkerchief
tied about the right arm.   The signal for beginning was to be

---

[1] The successive orders are given in the Archives curieuses, vii. 215-217.
[2] Discours du roy Henry III., 509.

given by the great bell of the " Palais de Justice " on the island of the old " cité." [1]

The preparations had not been so cautiously made but that they attracted the notice of some of the Huguenots living near Coligny. Going out to inquire the meaning of the clash of arms, and the unusual light in the streets, they received the answer that there was to be a mock combat in the Louvre—a pleasure castle was to be assaulted for the king's diversion.[2] But, as they went farther and approached the Louvre, their eyes were greeted by the sight of more torches and a great number of armed men. The guards, full of the contemplated plot, could not refrain from insults. It soon came to blows, and a Gascon soldier wounded a Protestant gentleman with his halberd. It may have been at this time that the shot was fired which Catharine and her sons heard from the open window of the Louvre. Declaring that the fury of the troops could no longer be restrained, the queen now gave orders to ring the bell of the neighboring church of St. Germain l'Auxerrois.[3]

Meantime Henry of Guise, Henry of Valois, the Bastard of Angoulême, and their attendants, had reached the admiral's Murder of Admiral Coligny. house. The wounded man was almost alone. Could there be any clearer proof of the rectitude of his purpose, of the utter falsity of the charges of conspiracy with which his enemies afterward attempted to blacken his memory?[4] Guerchy and other Protestant gentlemen had expressed the desire to spend the night with him ; but his son-in-law, Téligny, full of confidence in Charles's good intentions, had declined

---

[1] Tocsain contre les massacreurs, 121 ; Mém. de l'estat, *ubi sup.*, 116 ; Jean de Serres, iv. (1575), fol. 31.

[2] Jean de Serres, iv. (1575), fol. 30.

[3] Mém. de l'estat, *ubi sup.*, 117, 118 ; Jean de Serres (1575), iv. 32.

[4] The startling inconsistency evidently struck Capilupi very strongly, for he tries to reconcile it, but succeeds only poorly. According to him, it was either a ruse to throw Charles IX. off his guard by a pretence of confidence in his good faith, or an act of consummate folly. Any way, great thanks are due to Heaven ! "Et sia stato fatto questo da lui, ò con arte, per dimostrar di non dubitare della fede del Re, per tanto più assicurar sua Maestà, fin che fosse in termine d'effettuar i diabolici suoi pensieri ; ò vero scioccamente, non diffidando veramente di cosa alcuna ; in tutti modi si ha da riconoscer da gratia particolare di Dio," etc. Lo stratagema di Carlo IX., 1574, 80.

their offers, and had, indeed, himself gone to his own lodgings, not far off, in the Rue St. Honoré.[1] With Coligny were Merlin, his chaplain, Paré, the king's surgeon, his ensign Cornaton, La Bonne, Yolet, and four or five servants. In the court below there were five of Navarre's Swiss guards on duty.[2] Coligny, awakened by the growing noise in the streets, had at first felt no alarm, so implicitly did he rely upon the protestations of Charles, so confident was he that Cosseins and his guards would readily quell any rising of the Parisians.[3] But now some one knocks at the outer door, and demands an entrance in the king's name. Word is given to La Bonne, who at once descends and unlocks. It is Cosseins, followed by the soldiers whom he commands. No sooner does he pass the threshold than he stabs La Bonne with his dagger. Next he seeks the admiral's room, but it is not easy to reach it, for the brave Swiss, even at the risk of their own lives, defend first the door leading to the stairs, and then the stairs themselves. And now Coligny could no longer doubt the meaning of the uproar. He rose from his bed, and, wrapping his dressing-gown about him, asked his chaplain to pray; and while Merlin endeavored to fulfil his request, he himself in audible petitions invoked Jesus Christ as his God and Saviour, and committed to His hands again the soul he had received from Him. It was then that the person to whom we are indebted for this account—and he can scarcely have been another than Cornaton—rushed into the room. When Paré asked him what the disturbance imported, he turned to the admiral and said : "My lord, it is God that is calling us to Himself ! The house has been forced, and we have no means of resistance !" To whom the admiral, unmoved by fear, and even, as all who saw him testified, without the least change of countenance, replied : "For a long time have I kept myself in readiness for death. As for you, save yourselves, if you can.

---

[1] The topography of the massacre is made the subject of a paper, entitled : "Les victimes de la Saint-Barthélemy," Bulletin de la Soc. de l'hist. du prot. fr., ix. (1860) 34–44.

[2] G. Colinii Vita (1575), 127. Mém. de l'estat, *ubi sup.*, 114.

[3] Mém. de l'estat, 118, 119; Jean de Serres (1575), iv., fol. 32 ; Reveille-Matin, 180; Euseb. Philad. Dialogi (1574), 39, 40.

It were in vain for you to attempt to save my life. I commend my soul to the mercy of God." Obedient to his directions, all that were with him, save Nicholas Muss or de la Mouche, his faithful German interpreter, fled to the roof, and escaped under cover of the darkness.

One of Coligny's Swiss guards had been shot at the foot of the stairs. When Cosseins had removed the barricade of boxes that had been erected farther up, the Swiss in his own company, whose uniform of green, white, and black, showed them to belong to the Duke of Anjou, found their countrymen on the other side, but did them no harm. Cosseins following them, however, no sooner saw these armed men, than he ordered his arquebusiers to shoot, and one of them fell dead. It was a German follower of Guise, named Besme, who first reached and entered Coligny's chamber, and who for the exploit was subsequently rewarded with the hand of a natural daughter of the Cardinal of Lorraine. Cosseins, Attin, Sarlaboux, and others, were behind him. " Is not this the admiral?" said Besme of the wounded man, whom he found quietly seated and awaiting his coming. "I am he," Coligny calmly replied. "Young man, thou oughtest to have respect for my old age and my feebleness; but thou shalt not, nevertheless, shorten my life." [1] There were those who asserted that he added: "At least, would that some man, and not this blackguard, put me to death." But most of the murderers— and among them Attin, who confessed that never had he seen any one more assured in the presence of death—affirmed that Coligny said nothing beyond the words first mentioned. No sooner had Besme heard the admiral's reply, than, with a curse, he struck him with his sword, first in the breast, and then on the head. [2] The rest took part, and quickly despatched him.

---

[1] Joh. Wilh. von Botzheim, in his narrative, gives several versions of the words. According to one they were: " *Behem*—'N'est tu pas Admiral?' *Admiralius*—'Ouy, je le suis. Mais vous estes bien un jeune souldat pour parler ainsi avec un vieil capitaine, pour le moins au respect de ma vielesse.' *Behem* —'Je suis assez aage (agé) por te faire ta reste.'" Cyclopica illa atque inaudita hactenus detestanda atque execranda laniena, quæ facta est Lutetia, Aureliis, etc., published in F. W. Ebeling, Archivalische Beiträge zur Geschichte Frankreichs unter Carl IX. (Leipsic, 1872), 107, 108.

[2] Capilupi puts in Besme's mouth the words: "Now, traitor, restore to me

In the court below, Guise was impatiently waiting to hear that his mortal enemy was dead. "Besme," he cried out at last, "have you finished?" "It is done," the assassin replied. "Monsieur le Chevalier (the Bastard of Angoulême) will not believe it," again said Guise, "unless he sees him with his own eyes. Throw him out of the window!" Besme and Sarlaboux promptly obeyed the command. When the lifeless remains lay upon the pavement of the court, Henry of Guise stooped down and with his handkerchief wiped away the blood from the admiral's face. "I recognize him," he said; "it is he himself!" Then, after ignobly kicking the face of his fallen antagonist, he went out gayly encouraging his followers: "Come, soldiers, take courage; we have begun well. Let us go on to the others, for so the king commands!" And often through the day Guise repeated the words, "The king commands; it is the king's pleasure; it is his express command!" Just then a bell was heard, and the cry was raised that the Huguenots were in arms to kill the king.[1]

As for Admiral Coligny's body, after the head had been cut off by an Italian of the guard of the Duke de Nevers, the trunk was treated with every indignity. The hands were cut off, and it was otherwise mutilated in a shameless manner. Three days was it dragged about the streets by a band of inhuman boys.[2]

---

the blood of my master, which thou didst impiously take away from me!" It is not at all improbable that he used some such expression. Lo stratagema di Carlo IX., 34.

[1] Jean de Serres, De statu reipub. et rel. (1575), iv., fols. 32, 33; Mémoires de l'estat, *ubi supra*, 119–122; Vita Gasparis Colinii Castellonii, magni quondam Franciæ Amirallii (*sine loco*, 1575), pp. 127–131; 178–180. These latter accounts, which agree perfectly, are the best. Reveille-Matin, *ubi sup.*, 182, and Euseb. Philad. Dialogi (1574), i. 39, 40; Tocsain contre les massacreurs (Rheims, 1579), 121–123; Capilupi, Lo stratagema di Carlo IX. (1574), 33, etc. ; Journal d'un curé liguenr (Jehan de la Fosse), 148, 149; Relation of Olaegui, secretary of D. de Cuñiga, Spanish ambassador at Paris; Particularités inédites sur la St. Barthélemi, Gachard in Bulletins de l'Académie royale de Belgique, xvi. (1849), 252, 253; Alva's bulletin prepared for distribution, ibid., ix. (1842), 563. Both are very inaccurate. De Thou, iv. (liv. lii.) 584, 585; Agrippa d'Aubigné, ii. 16 (liv. i., c. 4).

[2] "Le lundy d'après, ayant la teste ostée et les parties honteuses coupées *par les petits enfans*, fut d'iceulx petits enfans qui estoient jusques au nombre de 2 ou 300, traîné, le ventre en haut, parmy les ruisseaux de la ville de Paris."

Meantime the head had been carried to the Louvre, where, after Catharine and Charles had sufficiently feasted their eyes on the spectacle, it was embalmed and sent to Rome, a grateful present to the Cardinal of Lorraine and Pope Gregory the Thirteenth.[1] It has been questioned whether the ghastly trophy ever reached its destination. Indeed, the French court seems to have become ashamed of its inhumanity, and to have regretted that so startling a token of its barbarous hatred had been allowed to go abroad. Accordingly, soon after the departure of the courier, a second courier was despatched in great haste to Mandelot, governor of Lyons, bidding him stop the first and take away from him the admiral's head. He arrived too late, however; four hours before Mandelot received the king's letter, "a squire of the Duke of Guise, named Pauli," had passed through the city, doubtless carrying the precious relic.[2] That it was actually placed in the hands of the Cardinal of Lorraine at Rome, need not be doubted.

Gaspard de Coligny was in his fifty-sixth year at the time of his death. For twelve years he had been the most prominent man in the Huguenot party, occupying a position secured to him not more by his resplendent abilities as a general than by the respect exacted by high moral principles. With the light and frivolous side of French character he had little in common. It was to a sterner and more severe class that he belonged—a class of which Michel de l'Hospital might be regarded as the type. Men who had little affinity with them, and bore them still less resemblance, but who could not fail to admire their excellence, were wont to liken both the great Huguenot warrior and the chancellor to that Cato whose grave demeanor and imposing dignity were a perpetual censure upon the flippancy and lax morality of his countrymen. Although not above the ordinary height of men, his appearance was dignified and commanding. In speech he was slow and deliberate.

Coligny's character and work.

Jehan de la Fosse, 149. See the long account in Von Botzheim's narration, *ubi supra*, 113.

[1] Mémoires de l'estat, *ubi supra*, 122.

[2] Letter of Mandelot to Charles IX., Sept. 5, 1572, Correspondance du roi Charles IX. et du sieur de Mandelot (Edited by P. Paris, Paris, 1830), 56–58.

His prudence, never carried to the extreme of over-caution, was signalized on many occasions.   Success did not elate him ; reverses did not dishearten him.   The siege of the city of St. Quentin, into which he threw himself with a handful of troops, and which he long defended against the best soldiers of Spain, displayed on a conspicuous stage his military sagacity, his indomitable determination, and the marvellous control he maintained over his followers.   It did much to prevent Philip from reaping more substantial fruits from the brilliant victory gained by Count Egmont on the feast-day of St. Lawrence.[1]   It was, however, above all in the civil wars that his abilities shone forth resplendent.   Equally averse to beginning war without absolute necessity, and to ending it without securing the objects for which it had been undertaken, he was the good genius whose wholesome advice was frequently disregarded, but never without subsequent regret on the part of those who had slighted it.   We have seen, in a former chapter,[2] the touching account given by Agrippa d'Aubigné of the appeal of the admiral's wife, which alone was successful in moving him to overcome his almost invincible repugnance to taking up arms, even in behalf of a cause which he knew to be most holy.   I find a striking confirmation of the accuracy of the report in a passage of his will, wherein he defends himself from the calumnies of his enemies.[3]   " And for-

---

[1] Of this memorable enterprise Coligny has left " Mémoires " which are contained in the collection of Petitot, etc.   It is the only military treatise we possess coming from the admiral's hand, and it enters into the subject with technical minuteness.   The destruction by his royal murderers of the admiral's papers (including diaries that would have thrown great light upon the transactions of the last two years of his life), see Vita Gasparis Colinii (1575), i. 138, was an irretrievable loss to history.   We are told also of a much more recent act of vandalism, not even palliated by the miserable excuse of political expediency :   " In 1810, an inhabitant of Châtillon having discovered in the solitary remaining tower of the old castle a walled chamber wherein were the archives of the Coligny family and of the family of Luxemburg, burned all the papers from motives of private interest.   Some fragments that escaped this conflagration, and which are preserved in the mairie, prove that a correspondence between Catharine de' Medici and Coligny had been laid away in this repository."   Bulletin de la Société de l'histoire du prot. français, iii. (1854) 351.

[2] *Ante*, chapter xiii.

[3] Testament olographe de l'amiral Coligny, Bulletin de la Soc. de l'hist. du

asmuch as I have learned that the attempt has been made to impute to me a purpose to attack the persons of the king, the queen, and the king's brothers, I protest before God that I never had any such will or desire, and that I never was present at any place where such plans were ever proposed or discussed. And as I have also been accused of ambition in taking up arms with those of the reformed religion, I make the same protestation, that only zeal for religion, together with fear for my own life, compelled me to assume them. And, indeed, I must confess my weakness, and that the greatest fault which I have always committed in this respect has been that I have not been sufficiently alive to the acts of injustice and the slaughter to which my brethren were subjected, and that the dangers and the traps that were laid for myself were necessary to move me to do what I have done. But I also declare before God, that I tried every means in my power, in order so long as possible to maintain peace, fearing nothing so much as civil disturbances and wars, and clearly foreseeing that these would bring after them the ruin of this kingdom, whose preservation I have always desired and labored for to the utmost of my ability."

To Coligny's strategy too much praise could scarcely be accorded. The Venetian ambassador, Contarini, in the report of his mission to the senate, in the early part of the year 1572, expressed his amazement that the admiral, a simple gentleman with slender resources, had waged war against his own powerful sovereign, who was assisted by the King of Spain and by a few German and several Italian princes ; and that, in spite of many battles lost, he preserved so great a reputation that the reiters and lansquenets never rebelled, although their wages were much in arrears, and their booty was often lost in adverse combats. He was, in fact, said the enthusiastic Italian, entitled to be held in higher esteem than Hannibal, inasmuch as the Carthaginian general retained the respect of foreign nations by

---

prot. français, i. (1852) 263, etc. The authenticity of this document, though called in question on historical grounds, has been conclusively established by M. Jules Bonnet, Bulletin, xxiv. (1875) 332–335.

being uniformly victorious; but the admiral retained it, although his cause was almost always unsuccessful.[1]

But all Coligny's military achievements pale in the light of his manly and unaffected piety. It is as a type of the best class among the Huguenot nobility that he deserves everlasting remembrance. From his youth he had been plunged in the engrossing pursuits of a soldier's life; but he was not ashamed, so soon as he embraced the views of the reformers, to acknowledge the superior claims of religion upon his time and his allegiance. He gloried in being a Christian. The influence of his faith was felt in every action of his life. In the busiest part of an active life, he yet found time for the recognition of God; and, whether in the camp or in his castle of Châtillon-sur-Loing, he consecrated no insignificant portion of the day to devotion. Of the ordinary life of Admiral Coligny, the anonymous author of his Life, who had himself been an inmate in his house, has left an interesting description, derived from what he himself saw and heard:

"As soon as he had risen from bed, which was always at an early hour, putting on his morning-gown, and kneeling, as did those who were with him, he himself prayed in the form which is customary with the churches of France. After this, while waiting for the commencement of the sermon, which was delivered on alternate days, accompanied with psalmody, he gave audience to the deputies of the churches who were sent to him, or devoted the time to public business. This he resumed for a while after the service was over, until the hour for dinner. When that was come, such of his domestic servants as were not prevented by necessary engagements elsewhere, met in the

---

[1] Albèri, Relazioni Venete, vol. iv., 1st series, *apud* Baschet, La diplomatie vénitienne, i. 536, 537. There is, however, the greatest improbability in the story that Coligny advanced such claims in his own behalf as his admirers made for him. We may reject as apocryphal—for they stand in palpable contradiction with the whole tenor of his utterances—the words ascribed by Lord Macaulay to the great Huguenot hero (History of England, New York, 1879, iv. 488): "'In one respect,' said the Admiral Coligni, 'I may claim superiority over Alexander, over Scipio, over Cæsar. They won great battles, it is true. I have lost four great battles; and yet I show to the enemy a more formidable front than ever.'" Cf. Davila, bk. v., p. 179.

hall where the table was spread, standing by which, with his wife at his side, if there had been no preaching service, he engaged with them in singing a psalm, and then the ordinary blessing was said.

" On the removal of the cloth, rising and standing with his wife and the rest of the company, he either returned thanks himself or called on his minister to do so.   Such, also, was his practice at supper, and, finding that the members of his household could not, without much discomfort, attend prayers so late as at bedtime—an hour, besides, which the diversity of his occupations prevented from being regularly fixed—his orders were that, so soon as supper was over, a psalm should be sung and prayer offered. It cannot be told how many of the French nobility began to establish this religious order in their own families, after the example of the admiral, who used often to exhort them to the practice of true piety, and to warn them that it was not enough for the father of a family to live a holy and religious life, if he did not by his example bring all his people to the same rule.

" On the approach of the time for the celebration of the Lord's Supper, calling together all the members of his household, he told them that he had to render an account to God, not only of his own life, but also of their behavior, and reconciled such of them as might have had differences.   . . . Moreover, he regarded the institution of colleges for youth, and of schools for the instruction of children, a singular benefit from God, and called the school a seminary of the church and an apprenticeship of piety ; holding that ignorance of letters had introduced into both church and state that thick darkness in which the tyranny of the Pope had had its birth and increase.   . . . This conviction led him to lay out a large sum in building a college at Châtillon, and there he maintained three very learned professors of Hebrew, Greek, and Latin, respectively, and a number of students.

" There could not be a stronger proof of his integrity, and of the moderation of his desires with respect to the possession of property, than that, notwithstanding the high offices he held, and the opportunities they afforded, as is usual with courtiers, of attending to his own interests and acquiring great wealth, he did not increase his patrimonial estates by a single acre; and, although he was an excellent economist, yet the number of persons of high rank, and, indeed, of all conditions, that came to consult him on public affairs from all parts of France, obliged him to draw largely on the savings effected by his good management; so that he left to his heirs not less than forty thousand livres of debts, besides six thousand livres of interest which he paid annually to his creditors."[1]

Such was the Christian hero whom his enemies represented as breathing out menaces upon the bed on which Maurevel's arquebuse had laid him, and as exclaiming: "If my arm is wounded, my head is not. If I have to lose my arm, I shall get the head of those who are the cause of it. They intended to kill me; I shall anticipate them." Such was the disinterested patriot whom, in the infatuation of their lying fabrications, the murderers of Paris, their hands still reeking with the blood of thousands of women and children incontestably innocent of any crime laid to the charge of their husbands or fathers, pictured as plotting the wholesale assassination of the royal family—even to the very Henry of Navarre whose wedding he had come to honor by his presence—that he might place upon the throne of France that stubborn heretic, the Prince of Condé![2]

While the murder of Coligny was in course of execution, or but shortly after, a tragedy not less atrocious was enacted in the royal palace itself. A number of Huguenot gentlemen of the highest distinction were lodged in the Louvre. Charles, after the admiral's wound, had suggested to the King of Navarre that he would do well to invite some of his friends to act as a guard against any attack that might be made upon him by the Duke of Guise, whom he characterized

Murder of Huguenot nobles in the Louvre.

---

[1] Vita Gasparis Colinii (1575), pp. 133–137, translated by D. D. Scott, under the title, "Memoirs of the Admiral de Coligny," 183–187. I have abridged the account by omitting some less important particulars.

[2] Discours sur les causes de l'exécution faicte és personnes de ceux qui avoient conjuré contre le Roy et son estat. A Paris, à l'olivier de P. l'Huillier, rue St. Jacques. 1572. *Avec privilège.* (Archives curieuses, vii. 231–249.) Capilupi, Lo stratagema di Carlo IX., 1574, p. 26.

as a "mauvois garçon." [1] Late on Saturday night, as Margaret of Valois informs us in her Memoirs, and long after she and her husband had retired, these Huguenot lords, gathered around Henry of Navarre's bed to the number of thirty, had discussed the occurrences of the last two eventful days, and declared their purpose to go to the king on the morrow and demand the punishment of the Guises. Margaret herself had been purposely kept in ignorance of the plan for the extirpation of the Protestants. For, if the Huguenots suspected her, because she was a Roman Catholic, the papists suspected her equally because she had married a Protestant. On parting with her mother for the night, her elder sister Claude, Duchess of Lorraine, who happened to be on a visit to the French court, had vainly attempted to detain Margaret, expressing with tears the apprehension that some evil would befall her. But Catharine had peremptorily sent her to bed, assuring her with words which, seen in the light of subsequent revelations, approach the climax of profanity : "That, if God pleased, she would receive no injury." [2] So deep was the impression of impending danger made upon Margaret's mind, that she remained awake, she tells us, until morning, when her husband arose, saying that he would go and divert himself with a game of tennis until Charles should awake. After his departure, the Queen of Navarre, relieved of her misgivings, as the night was now spent, ordered her maid to lock her door, and composed herself to sleep. [3]

Meantime the Protestant gentlemen who accompanied Navarre, and all the others who lodged in the Louvre, had been disarmed by Nançay, captain of the guard. In this defenceless condition ten or twelve of their number were conducted, one by one, to the gate of the building. Here soldiers stood in readiness, and despatched them with their halberds as they successively made their appearance. Such was the fate of the

---

[1] Memoirs de l'estat, *ubi supra*, 123 ; Jean de Serres (1575), iv., fol. 30 ; Reveille-Matin, 182 ; Eusebii Philadelphi Dialogi, i. 40.

[2] " La Royne ma mère respond, que s'il plaisoit à Dieu je n'auroit point de mal ; mais quoy que ce fust, il falloit que j'allasse, de peur de leur faire soupçonner quelque chose qui empeschast l'effect."

[3] Mémoires de Marguerite de Valois, 32, 33.

brave Pardaillan, of St. Martin, of Boursis, of Beauvais, former
tutor of Henry of Navarre, and of others; some of whom in a
loud voice called upon Charles, whom they saw at a window, an
approving spectator of the butchery, to remember the solemn
pledges he had given them. M. de Piles—that brave Huguenot captain, whose valor, if it did not save St. Jean d'Angely in
the third civil war, had at least detained the entire Roman
Catholic army for seven weeks before fortifications that were
none of the best, and rendered Moncontour a field barren of
substantial fruits [1]—was the object of special hatred, and his
conduct was particularly remarked for its magnanimity. Observing among the bystanders a Roman Catholic acquaintance in
whose honor he might perhaps confide, he stripped himself of
his cloak, and would have handed it to him, with the words:
"De Piles makes you a present of this; remember hereafter the
death of him who is now so unjustly put to death!" "Mon
capitaine," answered the other, fearful of incurring the enmity
of Catharine and Charles, "I am not of the company of these
persons. I thank you for your cloak; but I cannot take it upon
such conditions." The next moment M. de Piles fell, pierced
by the halberd of one of the archers of the guard. "These are
the men," cried the murderers at their bloody work, "who resorted to violence, in order to kill the king afterward." [2] One
of the victims marked out for the slaughter escaped the death
of his fellows. Margaret of Valois had not been long asleep,
when her slumbers were rudely disturbed by loud blows struck
upon the door, and shouts of "Navarre! Navarre!" Her
attendant, supposing it to be Henry himself, hastily opened the
door; when there rushed in instead, a Huguenot nobleman, the
Viscount de Léran, [3] wounded in the arm by sword and halberd,
and pursued by four archers. In his terror he threw himself on
Margaret's bed, and when she jumped up, in doubt of what
could be the meaning of this strange incident, he clung to her

---

[1] See *ante*, chapter xvi.

[2] Mémoires de l'estat, *ubi supra*, 123, 124; Jean de Serres (1575), iv., fol.
34; Reveille-Matin, 182; Eusebii Philadelphi Dialogi, i. 40; Tocsain contre
les massacreurs, 125, 126.

[3] Agrippa d'Aubigné, ii. 18 (liv. i., c. 4).

night-dress which was drenched with his blood. Nançay angrily reproved the indiscretion of his soldiers, and Margaret, leaving the Huguenot in her room to have his wounds dressed, suffered herself to be conducted to the chamber of her sister, the Duchess of Lorraine. It was but a few steps; but, on the way, a Huguenot was killed at three paces' distance from her, and two others—the first gentleman of the King of Navarre, and his first valet-de-chambre—ran to her imploring her to save their lives. She sought and obtained the favor on her knees before Catharine and Charles.[1] A few other Huguenots who were in the Louvre were ready to purchase their lives at any price, even to that of abjuring their faith. They obtained pardon on promising the king to comply with all his commands; and this, we are told, "the more easily, as Charles very well knew that they had little or no religion."[2]

The King of Navarre and the Prince of Condé were spared, although there were not wanting those who would gladly have
Navarre and Condé spared. seen the ruin of the family of Bourbon. Navarre was brother-in-law of Charles, and Condé of the Duke of Nevers; this may have guaranteed their safety. Both of the young princes, however, were summoned into the king's presence, where Charles, acknowledging the murder of Coligny, the great cause of disturbances, and the similar acts then perpetrated throughout the city, as sanctioned by his authority, sternly told the two youths that he intended no longer to tolerate two religions in his dominions. He desired them, therefore, to conform to that creed which had been professed by all his predecessors, and which he intended to uphold. They must renounce the profane doctrines they had embraced, and return to the Catholic and Roman religion. If they refused, they must expect to suffer the treatment which had just been experienced by so many others.[3]

---

[1] Mémoires de Marguerite de Valois, 345.

[2] Reveille-Matin, *ubi supra*, 183; Euseb. Philad. Dialogi, i. 40; Mém. de l'estat, *ubi supra*, 126. Charles was not generally so complaisant. Fervaques in vain interceded for his friend Captain Moneins. Tocsain, 126.

[3] Mém. de l'estat, *ubi sup.*, 124; Jean de Serres (1575), iv., fol. 35; Reveille-Matin, 182; Euseb. Philadelphi Dial., i. 40; De Thou, iv. (liv. lii.) 590.

The replies of the two princes were singularly unlike. Henry of Navarre, bold enough where only physical bravery was demanded, exhibited for the first time that lamentable absence of moral courage which was to render his life, in its highest relations, a splendid failure. His countenance betrayed agitation and faint-heartedness.[1] With great " humility "—almost whining, it would appear—he begged that his own life and the life of Condé might be spared, and reminded Charles of his promised protection. " He would act," he said, " so as to satisfy his Majesty; yet he besought him to remember that conscience was a great thing, and that it was hard to renounce the religion in which one had been brought up from infancy." On the other hand, Henry of Condé, in no way abashed,[2] declared " that he could not believe that his royal cousin intended to violate a promise confirmed by so solemn an oath. As to fealty, he had always been an obedient subject of the king, and would ever be. Touching his religion, if the king had given him the exercise of its worship, God had given him the knowledge of it; and to Him he must needs give up an account. So far as his body and his possessions were concerned, they were in the king's hands to dispose of as he might choose. Yet it was his own determination to remain constant in his religion, which he would always maintain to be the true religion, even should he be compelled to lay down his life for it." So stout an answer kindled the anger of Charles, who was in no mood to meet with opposition. He called Condé " a rebel," " a seditious man," and " the son of a seditious father," and warned him that he would lose his head, if, within three days, he should not think better of the matter.[3]

And now the great bell of the " Palais de Justice " pealed forth the tocsin. About the Louvre the work of blood had

[1] " Avec une contenance fort esmeue et abatue." Mém. de l'estat. " Humilissimo animo et consternato ore." Jean de Serres, *ubi supra*.

[2] Jean de Serres's " *consternatiori* tamen animo " is an evident misprint for " *constantiori* tamen animo."

[3] Mémoires de l'estat, 124, 125; Jean de Serres, iv., fol. 35 *verso;* Reveille-Matin, 183; Eusebii Philad. Dial. (1574), i. 40; De Thou, iv. (liv. lii) 590; Agrippa d'Aubigné, Hist. univ., ii. 19 (liv. i., c. 4).

begun when Catharine, impatient, and fearful lest Charles's resolution should again waver at the last moment, gave
orders to anticipate the appointed time by ringing
the bell of the neighboring church of St. Germain
l'Auxerrois. But now the loud and unusual clangor from the
tower of the parliament house carried the warning far and wide.
All Paris awoke. The conspirators everywhere recognized the
stipulated signal, and spread among the excited townsmen the
wildest and most extravagant reports. A foul plot, formed by
the Huguenots, against the king, his mother, and his brothers,
had come to light. They had killed more than fifteen of the
royal guards. The king, therefore, commanded that quarter
should not be given to a single Huguenot.[1]

The massacre becomes general.

Nothing more was needed to inflame the popular hatred of
the Huguenots, nor to prepare the rabble for an indiscriminate
slaughter of the Protestants.

Among the earliest victims of this day of carnage was Count
de la Rochefoucauld. This witty and lively young noble had
been in the Louvre until a late hour on Saturday
night, diverting himself with the king, with whom he
was a great favorite. Apparently in his anxiety to
save La Rochefoucauld's life, Charles invited, and even urged
him, to spend the night in the royal "garde-robe;" but the
count, suspecting no danger, insisted on returning to his lodgings,

La Rochefou-cauld and Téligny fall.

---

[1] Eusebii Phil. Dialogi, i. 40, 41; Reveille-Matin, *ubi sup.*, 183, copied
verbatim in Mém. de l'estat, 126. The Reveille-Matin removes the apparent
contradiction between the various accounts respecting the bell that gave the
signal for the massacre by showing that *both* bells were rung. So also
Agrippa d'Aubigné, ii. 16 (liv. i., c. 4), after mentioning how Catharine, for
the time being, removed Charles's hesitation by alleging the necessity of cutting off the corrupt members in order to save the Church, the Bride of Christ,
and citing the saying: "Che pietà lor ser crudele. Che crudeltà lor ser pie-
tosa," adds: "Le roi se resout, et elle avance le tocsain du Palais, en faisant
sonner *une heure et demie* devant celui de Sainct Germain de l'Auxerrois."
By neglecting the clue thus given, the chronological order of the events of
the day has been lost by a number of historians. It will be noticed that the
number of the royal guards reported to have been slain was, strangely enough,
derived from that of the Huguenot gentlemen butchered in the Louvre by
those very guards. The story may have been perpetuated by misapprehension
of the facts; it could have arisen only from wilful falsehood.

while the king reluctantly abandoned his boon companion to his fate, rather than betray his secret. Early awakened from his sleep at his lodgings by loud knocking at the door and by demands for admission in the king's name, and seeing a band of masked men enter, he recalled Charles's threat at parting, that he would come and administer to him a whipping. The practical joke would not have been unlike many of the mad antics of the royal jester, and La Rochefoucauld, addressing himself to the person whom he supposed to be his Majesty in disguise, begged him to treat him with humanity. His deception was not long continued; for the maskers, after rifling his trunks, drew him from his place of concealment and murdered him. His lifeless body was dragged through the streets of Paris.[1]

Téligny was, perhaps, even more unfortunate than the rest, because he awoke too late to the fact that his own blind confidance in the word of a faithless prince had been a chief instrument of involving his father-in-law and his friends in destruction. He was among the first to pay the penalty of his credulity. More than one of the parties sent to destroy him, it is said, overcome by compassion for his youth and manly beauty, or by respect for his graceful manners and extraordinary learning, left their commission unexecuted. To avoid further peril, he ascended to the roof, from which he made his way to an adjoining house; but he had not gone far before he was seen and shot with an arquebuse by one of the Duke of Anjou's guards.[2]

The Huguenots, attacked in the midst of their slumbers by Self-defence of the courtiers and the soldiers of the royal guard,[3] a few nobles. among whom were prominent the Swiss of Charles or his brother, or by the people of Paris, who every moment swelled

---

[1] Tocsain contre les massacreurs (Rheims, 1579), 124, 125; Reveille-Matin, 126; Eusebii Philadelphi Dialogi, i. 41; Agrippa d'Aubigné, ii. 18; De Thou, iv. (liv. lii.) 586.

[2] Tocsain contre les massacreurs, 125; Agrippa d'Aubigné, ii. 18; De Thou, iv. (liv. lii.) 586; Euseb. Philad. Dialogi, *ubi supra*.

[3] " The courtiers and the soldiers of the royal guard were the executioners of this commission on the (Huguenot) noblesse, terminating, they said, by the sword and general disorder, those processes which pens and paper and the order of justice had hitherto failed to bring to an issue." Reveille-Matin, *ubi supra*, 184; Eusebii Philad. Dialogi, i. 41; Mémoires de l'estat, 127.

the ranks of the assassins, were too much taken by surprise to offer even the slightest resistance. Guerchy, the same gentleman who had offered his services to Coligny the night before, is almost the only man reported to have fought for his life. With his sword in his right hand, and winding his cloak around his left arm, he defended himself for a long time, though the breastplates of his enemies were proof against his blows. At last, he fell, overborne by numbers.[1] The Lieutenant de la Mareschaussée, if not more determined, was better prepared for the combat. All day long, with a single soldier as his comrade, he defended his house against the assailants, expecting at every moment to be relieved from his perilous situation by the king. But, far from meriting such confidence on the part of his subjects, Charles was indignant at his prolonged resistance, and sent a powerful detachment of guards, with orders to bring him the lieutenant's head. The brave Huguenot, however, still maintained the unequal siege, and fought till his last breath. The soldiers had only the poor satisfaction of pillaging his house, of dragging his sick daughter naked through the streets until she died of maltreatment, and of wounding and imprisoning his wife.[2]

Personal hatred, jealousy, cupidity, mingled with religious and political zeal, and private ends were attained in fulfilling the king's murderous commands. Bussy d'Amboise, meeting his Protestant cousin, the Marquis de Renel (half-brother of the late Prince of Porcien), by a well-directed blow with his poniard rid himself of an unpleasant suit at law which Renel had come to Paris to prosecute.

Victims of personal hatred.

The case of Caumont de la Force was still more revolting. His daughter, Madame de la Châtaigneraie, in accordance with the shameless code of morals in vogue at the French court, had taken for her lover Archan, captain of the guard of Henry of Anjou; and it was to gratify her covetousness that Archan obtained from the Duke the order to despatch La Force and his two sons. The plan was successfully executed so far as the father and his elder son were concerned.

Adventure of young La Force.

---

[1] Agrippa d'Aubigné, ii. 18.
[2] Tocsain contre les massacreurs, 136, 137.

The second, a boy of twelve, escaped by his remarkable presence of mind and self-control. Certain that his youth would excite no pity in the breast of his inhuman assailants, when his father and his brother fell at his side and he perceived himself covered with their blood, he dropped down with the exclamation that he was dead. So perfectly did he counterfeit death, all that long day, that, although his body was examined by successive bands of plunderers, and deprived not only of every valuable, but even of its clothing, he did not by a motion betray that he was alive. Most of these persons applauded the crime. It was well, they said, to kill the little wolves with the greater. But, toward evening, a more humane person came, who, while engaged in drawing off a stocking which had been left on the boy's foot, gave expression to his abhorrence of the bloody deed. To his astonishment the boy raised his head, and whispered, " I am not dead." The compassionate man at once commanded him not to stir, and went home; but as soon as it was dark he returned with a cloak, which he threw about young La Force's shoulders, and bade him follow. It was no easy matter to thread the streets unmolested; but his guide dispelled the suspicions of those who questioned him respecting the boy by declaring that it was his nephew whom he had found drunk, and was going to whip soundly for it. In the end the young nobleman reached the arsenal, where his relative, Marshal Biron, was in command. Even there, however, the avarice of his unnatural sister pursued him. Vexed that, on account of his preservation, she must fail to secure the entire inheritance of the family, Madame de la Châtaigneraie tried to effect herself what she had not been able to do by means of another; she visited the marshal in the arsenal, and, after expressing great joy that her brother had been saved, begged to be permitted to see and care for him. Biron thought it necessary, in order to preserve the boy's life, to deny her request.[1]

---

[1] Reveille-Matin, *ubi supra*, 184, 185; Eusebii Philad. Dial., i. 42; Mém. de l'estat, 127; Jean de Serres (1575), iv. 38; De Thou, iv. (liv. lii.) 588; Agrippa d'Aubigné, ii. 18. The minor details of the story are given, with variations, by different authors. D'Aubigné gives us Biron's answer to the commands and menaces with which Madame de la Châtaigneraie sought to

The frenzy that had fallen upon Paris affected all classes alike. Every feeling of pity seemed to have been blotted out. Natural affection disappeared. A man's foes were those of his own household. On the plea of religious zeal the most barbarous acts were committed. Spire Niquet, a poor bookbinder, whose scanty earnings barely sufficed to support the wants of his seven children, was half-roasted in a bonfire made of his own books, and then dragged to the river and drowned.[1] The weaker sex was not spared in the universal carnage, and, as in a town taken by assault, suffered outrages that were worse than death. Matron and maiden alike welcomed as merciful the blow that liberated them from an existence now rendered insupportable. Women approaching maternity were selected for more excruciating torments, and savage delight was exhibited in destroying the unborn fruit of the womb. Nor was any rank respected. Madame d'Yverny, the niece of Cardinal Briçonnet, was recognized, as she fled, by the costly underclothing that appeared from beneath the shabby habit of a nun which she had assumed; and, after suffering every indignity, upon her refusal to go to mass, was thrown from a bridge into the Seine and drowned.[2] Occasionally the women rivalled the cruelty of the men. A poor carpenter, of advanced age, with whom the author of the "Tocsain contre les massacreurs" was personally acquainted, had been taken by night and cast into the river. He swam, however, to a bridge, and succeeded in climbing up by its timbers, and so fled naked to the house of a relative near the "Cousture Sainte Catherine,"

Pitiless butchery.

gain possession of young La Force: "I would certainly intrust him in the hands of his relative, in order to take care of him, but not in the hands of his next heir, who took too great care of him yesterday morning," ii. 21. It must be noted, however, that the "Mémoires authentiques de Jacques Nompar de Caumont, Duc de la Force. Maréchal de France, recueillis par le Marquis de la Grange" (Paris, 1843), i. 2–37, so far from accusing the sister of La Force, ascribe the persistent attempts to secure his death solely to Archan (or Larchant), who had *married* this sister; and they state that, at her death, she left her property, including what she had inherited from her husband, to her brother.

[1] Mémoires de l'estat, *ubi supra*, 146

[2] Mém. de l'estat, 146; Tocsain contre les massacreurs, 129, 130; De Thou, iv. (liv. lii.) 592; Claude Haton, ii. 678; Agrippa d'Aubigné, ii. 20.

where his wife had taken refuge. But, instead of welcoming him, his wife drove him away, and he was soon recaptured and killed.[1] It is related that the daughter of one Jean de Cologne, a mercer of the " Palais," betrayed her own mother to death, and subsequently married one of the murderers.[2] The very innocence of childhood furnished no sufficient protection —so literally did the pious Catholics of Paris interpret the oft-repeated exhortations of their holy father to exterminate not only the roots of heresy, but the very fibres of the roots.[3] Two infants, whose parents had just been murdered, were carried in a hod and cast into the Seine. A little girl was plunged naked in the blood of her father and mother, with horrible oaths and threats that, if she should become a Huguenot, the like fate would befall her. And a crowd of boys, between nine and ten years of age, was seen dragging through the streets the body of a babe yet in its swaddling-clothes, which they had fastened to a rope by means of a belt tied about its neck.[4]

The bodies of the more inconspicuous victims lay for hours in whatever spot they happened to be killed; but the court required ocular demonstration that the leaders of the Huguenots who had been most prominent in the late wars were really dead. Accordingly the naked corpses of Soubise, of Guerchy, of Beaudiné, d'Acier's brother, and of others, were dragged from all quarters to the square in front of the Louvre. There, as an indignant contemporary writes, extended in a long row, they lay exposed to the view of the varlets, of whom when alive they had

---

[1] Tocsain, 136.

[2] Mém. de l'estat, 146.

[3] " Radices, atque etiam radicum fibras, funditus evellas." Pii Quinti Epistolæ, 111. See *ante*, chapter xvi., p. 308.

[4] Mém. de l'estat, 147. The children of other cities emulated the example of those of Paris. In Provins, in the month of October, 1572, a Huguenot, Jean Crespin, after having been hung by the officers of justice, was taken down from the gallows by " les petis enfans de Provins, *de l'âge de douze ans et au dessoubz*," to the number of more than one hundred. By these mimic judges he was declared unworthy to be dragged save by his feet, and, his punishment by hanging being reckoned too light, he was roasted in a fire of straw, and presently thrown into the river. Numbers of older persons looked on, approving and encouraging the children; a few good Catholics were grieved to see such cruelty practised on a dead body. Mém. de Claude Haton, ii. 704–706.

been the terror.[1] Cruelty and lust are twin sisters: when the one is at hand, the other is generally not far distant. The court of Catharine de' Medici was noted for its impurity, as it was infamous for its recklessness of human life. It was not out of keeping with its general reputation that toward evening a bevy of ladies—among them the queen mother—tripped down the palace stairs to feast their eyes upon the sight of the uncovered dead.[2] Indeed, the king, the queen mother, and their intimate friends seemed to be in an ecstasy of joy. They indulged in boisterous laughter[3] as the successive reports of the municipal authorities, from hour to hour, brought in tidings of the extent of the massacre.[4] "The war is now ended in reality," they were heard to say, "and we shall henceforth live in peace."[5] The Duke of Anjou took a more active part. In the street and on the Pont de Notre Dame he was to be seen encouraging the assassins.[6] The Duke of Montpensier was surpassed by no one in his zealous advocacy of the murderous work. "Let every man exert himself to the utmost," he cried, as he rode through the streets, "if he wishes to prove himself a good servant to the king."[7] Tavannes, if we may believe Brantôme's account, endeavored to rival him, and, all day long, as he rode about amid the carnage, amused himself by facetiously crying to the people: "Bleed! Bleed! The doctors say that bleeding is as good in the month of August as in May."[8]

Shamelessness of the court ladies.

Anjou encourages the assassins.

Of the Duke of Alençon it was noticed that, alone of Catha-

---

[1] Mém. de l'estat, *ubi supra*, 128.

[2] "On en remarqua qui avoient les yeux attachés sur le corps du Baron du Pont, pour voir si elles y trouveroient quelque cause ou quelque marque de l'impuissance qu'on lui reprochoit." De Thou, iv. (liv. lii.) 587. See Euseb. Philadelphi Dial., i. 45, and Jean de Serres (1575) iv., fol. 39.

[3] "Le Roy, la Royne mère, et leurs courtisans, rioyent à gorge desployée." Mém. de l'estat, *ubi supra*, 132.

[4] The prévôt, échevins, etc., "du tout, auroient, d'heure en heure, rendu compte et tesmoignage à sadicte Majesté." Extrait des registres et croniques du bureau de la ville de Paris, Archives curieuses, vii. 215.

[5] Mém. de l'estat, *ubi supra*.

[6] Tocsain contre les massacreurs, Rheims, 1579, p. 140.

[7] Ibid., *ubi supra*.

[8] Brantôme, Hommes illustres français, M. de Thavannes.

rine's sons, he took no part in the massacre. The Protestants even regarded him as their friend, and the rumor was current that the pity he exhibited excited the indignation of his mother and brothers. Indeed, Catharine, it was said, openly told him that, if he ventured to meddle with her plans, she would put him in a sack and throw him into the river.[1]

Of the pastors of the Church of Paris, it was noticed as a remarkable circumstance that but two—Buirette and Desgorris —were killed; for it was certain that no lives were more eagerly sought than theirs.[2] But several Protestant pastors had wonderful escapes. The celebrated D'Espine —the converted monk who took part in the Colloquy of Poissy —was in company with Madame d'Yverny when her disguise was discovered, but he was not recognized.[3] In the case of Merlin, chaplain of Admiral Coligny, the divine interposition seemed almost as distinct as in that of the prophet Elijah. After reluctantly leaving Coligny, at his earnest request, and clambering over the roof of a neighboring house, he fell through an opening into a garret full of hay. Not daring to show himself, since he knew not whether he would encounter friends or foes, he remained for three days in this retreat, his sole food an egg which a hen daily laid within his reach.[4]

Wonderful escapes.

The future minister of Henry the Fourth, Maximilien de Béthune, Duke of Sully, at this time a boy of twelve and a student in the college of Burgundy in Paris, has left us in his "Economies royales" a thrilling account of his escape. Awakened, about three o'clock in the morning, by the uproar in the streets, his tutor and his valet-de-chambre went out to learn the

---

[1] " Declarant (Alençon) qu'il ne pouvoit approuver vn tel desordre, ny qu'on rompit si ouvertement la foy promise, qui fut cause que sa mere luy dit en termes clairs que s'il bougeoit elle le feroit ietter dans vn sac aual l'eau." Tocsain contre les massacreurs, 141.

[2] Id., 133.

[3] De Thou, iv. 592.

[4] His son, Jacques Merlin, at a later time pastor at La Rochelle, although he does not mention the particulars of his father's escape, in the journal published for the first time by M. Gaberel in an appendix to the second vol. of his Histoire de l'église de Genève, pp. 153–207, alludes to it—" fut deliuré par une grace de Dieu spéciale " (p. 155).

occasion of it, and never returned.   They were doubtless among the first victims.   Sully's trembling host—a Protestant who consented through fear to abjure his faith—now came in, and advised the youth to save his life by going to mass.   Sully was not prepared to take this counsel, and, so putting on his scholar's gown, he ventured upon the desperate step of trying to reach the college.   A horrible scene presented itself to view.   Everywhere men were breaking into houses, or slaughtering their captives in the public streets, while the cry of "Kill the Huguenots!" was heard on all sides.   Sully himself owed his preservation to two thick volumes of "Heures"—Romish books of devotion—which he had the presence of mind to take under his arm, and which effectually disarmed the suspicions of the three successive bands of soldiers that stopped him.   At the college, after with difficulty gaining admission, he incurred still greater danger.   Happily the principal, M. Du Faye, was a kind-hearted man.   In vain was he urged, by two priests who were his guests, to surrender the Huguenot boy to death, saying that the order was to massacre even the very babes at the breast.   Du Faye would not consent; and after having secretly kept Sully locked up for three days in a closet, he found means to restore him to his friends.[1]

No loss was more sensibly felt by the scientific world than that of the learned Pierre de la Ramée, or Ramus, a philosopher second to none of his day.   The professor might possibly have escaped if his only offence had been his Protestant views; but Ramus had had the temerity to attack Aristotle, and to attempt to reform the faulty pronunciation of the Latin language.   For these unpardonable sins he was tracked to the cellar in which he had hidden, by a band of robbers under the guidance of Jacques Charpentier, a jealous rival, with whom he had had acrimonious discussions.   After being compelled to give up a considerable sum of money, he was despatched with daggers, and thrown from an upper window into the court of his college.   Never was philosophic heterodoxy more thoroughly punished; for if the whipping, dragging

Death of the philosopher Ramus.

---

[1] Mémoires de Sully (London, 1748), i. pp. 29, 30.

through the filthy streets, and dismembering of a corpse by indignant students with the approval of their teachers, could atone for such grave errors, the anger of the illustrious Stagirite must have been fully appeased. If anything can clearly exhibit the depth of moral degradation to which Roman Catholic France had fallen, it is the fact that Charpentier unblushingly accepted the praise which was liberally showered upon him for his participation in this disgraceful affair.[1]

Scarcely less signal a misfortune to France was the murder of Pierre de la Place, president of the Cour d'Aides, whose excellent "Commentaries on the State of Religion and the Republic" constitute one of our best guides through the short reign of Francis the Second and the early part of the reign of Charles the Ninth. This eminent jurist, even more distinguished as a writer on Christian morals than as a historian, had first embraced the Reformation at a time when the recent martyrdom of Anne du Bourg served as a significant reminder of the perils attending a profession of Protestant views. President de la Place had been visited in his house early in the morning, on the first day of the massacre, by Captain Michel, an arquebusier of the king, who, entering boldly with his weapons and with the white napkin bound on his left arm, informed him of the death of Coligny, and the fate in reserve for the rest of the Huguenots. The soldier pretended that the king wished to exempt La Place from the general slaughter, and bade him accompany him to the Louvre. However, a gift of a thousand crowns induced the fellow instead to lead the president's daughter and her husband to a place of safety in the house of a Roman Catholic friend. But La Place himself, after having applied at three different houses belonging to persons of his acquaintance and been denied admission, was compelled to return to his home and there await his doom. A day passed, during which La Place and his wife were subjected to constant alarms. At length new orders came in the king's

(marginal note) President Pierre de la Place.

---

[1] Tocsain contre les massacreurs, 131; Mém. de l'estat, *ubi supra*, 142, etc. De Thou, iv. (liv. lii.) 592, 593. Strange to say, Von Botzheim was so far misinformed, that he makes Charpentier *weep* for the fate of Ramus! Archival. Beiträge, p. 117.

name, enjoining upon him without fail to repair instantly to
the palace. The meaning was unmistakable; it was the road
to death. But neither the Huguenot's piety nor his courage
failed him. He gently raised his wife, who had fallen on her
knees to beg the messenger to save her husband's life, and reminded her that she should have recourse to God alone, not to
an arm of flesh. And he sternly rebuked his eldest son, who,
in a moment of weakness, had placed a white cross on his hat,
in the hope of saving his life. " The true cross we must wear,"
he said, " is the trials and afflictions sent to us by God as sure
pledges of the bliss and eternal life He has prepared for His own
followers." It was with unruffled composure that he bade his
weeping friends farewell. His apprehensions were soon realized;
he was despatched by murderers who had been waiting for him,
and before long his body was floating down the Seine toward
the sea.[1]

From such instances of inhumanity it is a relief to turn to
one of a few incidents wherein the finer feelings triumphed
Regnier and over prejudice, difference of religious tenets, and
Vezins. even personal hatred. There were in Paris two gentlemen, named Vezins and Regnier, of good families in the
province of Quercy in southern France. Both were equally
distinguished for their valor; but their dispositions were singularly unlike, for while the Huguenot Regnier was noted for his
gentle manners, the Roman Catholic Vezins, who was lieutenant
of the governor, the Viscount of Villars, had acquired unenviable notoriety because of his ferocity. Between the two there
had for some time existed a mortal feud, which their common
friends had striven in vain to heal. While the massacre was at
its height, Regnier was visited by his enemy, Vezins. The
latter, after effecting an entrance into the house by breaking
down the door, fiercely ordered the Huguenot—who, well assured
that his last hour was come, had fallen upon his knees to im-

---

[1] De Thou, iv. (liv. lii.) 596; Mémoires de l'estat de France sous Charles
IX. (Cimber et Danjou, vii. 137–142, and in M. Buchon's biographical notice
prefixed to the " Commentaires "). An appreciative chapter on Pierre de la
Place and his works may be read in Victor Bujeaud, Chronique protestante de
l'Angoumois (Angoulême, 1860), 50–66.

plore the mercy of God—to rise and follow him. A horse stood saddled at the door, upon which Regnier was told to mount. In his enemy's train he rode unharmed through the streets of Paris, then through the gates of the city. Still Vezins, without vouchsafing a word of explanation, kept on his way toward Cahors, the capital of Quercy, whither he had been despatched by the government.[1] For many successive days the journey lasted. The prisoner was well guarded, but he was also well lodged and fed. At last the party reached the very castle of Regnier, and here his captor broke the long silence. "As you have seen," said he, "it would have depended only on myself to take advantage of the opportunity which I have long been seeking; but I should be ashamed to avenge myself in this way upon a man so brave as you. In settling our quarrel I desire that the danger shall be equal. Be well assured that you will find me as ready to decide our dispute in a manner becoming gentlemen, as I have been eager to save you from inevitable destruction." It need scarcely be said that the Huguenot could not find words sufficiently strong to express his gratitude; but Vezins merely replied: "I leave it to you to choose whether you wish me to be your friend or your enemy; I saved your life only to enable you to make your election." With these words he abruptly left him and rode away, nor would he ever consent even to take back the horse upon which he had brought Regnier in safety so many leagues.[2]

A number of the Huguenot noblemen were lodged on the southern side of the Seine, outside of the walls, in the Faubourg
Escape of Montgomery and Chartres.
Saint Germain. Count Montgomery, the Vidame of Chartres, Beauvoir la Nocle, and Frontenay, a member of the powerful Rohan family, were among the most distinguished. After the admiral, there were certainly no Huguenots whom Catharine was more anxious to destroy than Montgomery and Chartres. Accordingly the massacre, which began near the Louvre, was to have been executed simultaneously upon them, and the work was intrusted to M. de Maugi-

---

[1] Cahors is over 300 miles in a straight line from Paris, more than 400 miles—153 leagues—by the roads.

[2] De Thou, iv. (liv. lii.) 594, 595; Agrippa d'Aubigné, Hist. univ., ii. 23.

ron. But the delay of the Roman Catholics saved them. Marcel, the former prevôt des marchands, who had been instructed to furnish one thousand men, was not ready in time; and Dumas, who was to have acted as guide, overslept the appointed hour. About five o'clock in the morning a Huguenot succeeded in swimming across the river, and carried to Montgomery the first tidings of the events of the last two hours. The count at once notified his comrades, but, although there were among them those who had been most urgent to leave Paris immediately after Maurevel's attack upon Coligny, few of the nobles would harbor the thought that Charles was so lost to honor as to have plotted the assassination of his invited guests. They preferred to believe that the king was himself in danger through a sudden commotion occasioned by the Guises. Acting upon this theory, the Huguenots proceeded in a body toward the Seine, intending to cross and lend assistance to the royal cause; but, on reaching the river's bank, they were speedily undeceived. They saw a band of two hundred soldiers of the royal guard coming toward them in boats, and discharging their arquebuses, with cries of "*Tue! Tue!*"—"Kill! Kill!" Charles himself was descried at a window of the Louvre, looking with approval upon the scene. There is good authority also, for the story that, in his eagerness to exterminate the Huguenots, Charles snatched an arquebuse from the hand of an attendant, and fired at them, exclaiming, "Let us shoot, *mort Dieu,* they are fleeing!"[1]

Charles himself fires at them from the Louvre.

---

[1] The incident of Charles IX.'s firing upon the Huguenots has been of late the subject of much discussion. M. Fournier and M. Méry have denied the existence, in 1572, of the pavilion at which tradition makes the king to have stationed himself. See Bulletin de la Soc. de l'hist. du prot. français, v. (1857) 332, etc. It has, I think, been conclusively shown that they are mistaken. The pavilion *was* in existence. But, besides, there is no reason why an incident should be deemed apocryphal because of a popular mistake in assigning the spot of its occurrence. The "Reveille-Matin" and the Eusebii Philadelphi Dialogi, published in 1574, are the earliest documents that refer to it. They place Charles at the window of his own room. So does Brantôme, writing considerably later. Jean de Serres (in the fourth vol. of his Commentaria de statu, etc. (fol. 37), published in 1575) says: "Regem quoque ex hypæthrio (*i.e.*, from a covered gallery) aiunt, adhibitis, ut solebat, diris contenta voce conclamare, et tormento etiam ipsum ejaculari." Agrippa d'Aubigné alludes to it not only in

Montgomery and his companions had by this time recognized their mistake, and hesitated no longer to flee from the perfidious capital. They promptly took to horse, and rode hard to reach Normandy and the sea. This part of the prey was, however, too precious to be permitted to escape. Accordingly, Guise, Aumale, the Bastard of Angoulême, and a number of "gentilhommes tueurs," started in pursuit. But an accident prevented them from overtaking the Huguenots. When Guise and his party reached the Porte de Bussy [1]—the gate leading from the city into the faubourg in which the Protestants had been lodging—which was closed in accordance with the king's orders, they found that they had been provided by mistake with the wrong key, and the delay experienced in finding the right one afforded Montgomery an advantage in the race, of which he made good use. [2]

---

his Histoire universelle (ii. 19, 21), but in his Tragiques (Bulletin, vii. 185), a poem which he commenced as early as in 1577 (See Bulletin, x. 202). M. Henri Bordier has been so fortunate as to discover and has reprinted a contemporary engraving of the massacre, in which Charles is represented as excitedly looking on the slaughter from a window in the Louvre, while behind him stand two halberdiers and several noblemen (Bulletin, x. 106, 107). The question is discussed in an able and exhaustive manner by MM. Fournier, Ludovic Lalanne, Bernard, Berty, Bordier, and others, in the Bulletin, v. 332–340; vi. 118–126; vii. 182–187; x. 5–11, 105–107, 199–204.

[1] The Porte de Bussy, or Bucy, was the first gate toward the west on the southern side of the Seine. During the reign of Francis I. and his successors of the house of Valois, the walls of Paris were of small compass. In this quarter their general direction is well marked out by the Rue Mazarine. The circuit started from the Tour de Nesle, which was nearly opposite the eastern front of the Louvre—the short Rue de Bussy fixes the situation of the gate where Guise was delayed. A little west of this is the abbey church of St. Germain-des-Prés, which gave its name to the suburb opposite the Louvre and the Tuileries. This quaint pile—the oldest church, or, indeed, edifice of any kind in Paris—after being built in the sixth century, and injured by the Normans in the ninth, was rebuilt and dedicated in 1163 A.D., by Alexander III. in person. On that occasion the Bishop of Paris was not even permitted by the jealous monks to be present, on the ground that the abbey of St. Germain-des-Prés was exempt from his jurisdiction. The pontiff confirmed their position, and his sermon, instead of being an exposition of the Gospel, was devoted to setting forth the privileges accorded to the abbey by St. Germain, Bishop of Paris, in 886. Dulaure, Histoire de Paris, ii. 79-84.

[2] Tocsain contre les massacreurs, 138, 139; Reveille-Matin, 186–188; Mém. de l'estat, 129–131.

The carnival of blood, which had been so successfully ushered in on that ill-starred Sunday of August, was maintained on the succeeding days with little abatement of its frenzied excitement.   Paris soon resembled a vast charnel-house.   The dead or dying lay in the open streets and squares, they blocked the doors and carriage-ways, they were heaped in the courtyards.   When the utmost that impotent passion could do to these lifeless remains was accomplished, the Seine became the receptacle.   Besides those Huguenots whom their murderers dragged to the bridges or wharves to despatch by drowning, both by day and by night wagons laden with the corpses of men and women, and even of young children, were driven down to the river and emptied of their human freight.   But the current of the crooked Seine refused to carry away from the capital all these evidences of guilt.   The shores of its first curve, from Paris to the bridge of St. Cloud, were covered with putrefying remains, which the municipality were compelled to inter, through fear of their generating a pestilence.   And so we read, in the registers of the Hôtel-de-Ville, of a payment of fifteen livres tournois, on the ninth of September, for the burial of the dead bodies found near the Convent of Chaillot, and of a second payment of twenty livres on the twenty-third, for the burial of eleven hundred more, near Chaillot, Auteuil, and St. Cloud.[1]

The massacre continues.

The massacre was not in its origin a popular outbreak.   It sprang from the ambition and vindictive passions of the queen mother, and others, whom the ministers of a corrupt religion had long accustomed to the idea that the extermination of heretics is not a sin, but the highest type of piety.   The people were called in only as assistants.   Probably the first intention was only to hold the municipal forces in readiness to overcome any resistance which the Protestants might offer.   But the massacre succeeded beyond the most sanguine expectations of the conspirators.   Very few of the victims defended themselves or their property; scarcely one Roman Catholic was slain.   And now the populace, having had a taste of blood, could no longer be restrained.   Whether the plunder

Not a popular movement.

---

[1] See Henry White, Massacre of St. Bartholomew, p. 460.

of the Protestants entered into the original calculations of Catharine and her advisers, may perhaps be doubted. But there is no question as to the turn which the affair soon took in the minds of those engaged in it. Pillage was not always counte-
Plunder of the rich. nanced by church and state: as a violation of the second table of the Law, it was, under ordinary circumstances, atoned for by penance and ecclesiastical censures ; as a breach of the royal edicts, it was likely to be punished with hanging or still more painful modes of execution. Consequently, when by furnishing arms the civil power authorized the most severe measures against those whom it accused of foul conspiracy against the king, and when the professed minister of Christ and His gospel of peace blessed the work of exterminating God's enemies and the king's, there was no lack of men willing to profit by the rare and unexpected opportunity. Nor did the courtiers disdain dishonest gain. The Duke of Anjou was known to have enriched himself by the plunder of the shop of Baduère, the king's jeweller.[1] Noblemen, besides robbing their victims of money, extorted from them, in return for a promise to spare their lives, deeds of valuable lands, or papers resigning in their favor high offices in the government. It was frequently the case that, after giving such presents, the Huguenot was put out of the way at once, in order to prevent him from ever retracting. Thus, Martial de Loménie, a secretary of the king, was murdered in prison, after having resigned his office in favor of Marshal Retz, and sold to him his estate of Versailles, at such a price as the latter chose to name, in the

---

[1] Valued at from 100,000 to 200,000 crowns, Reveille-Matin, 190 ; Mém. de l'estat, 151. The interesting anonymous letter from Heidelberg, Dec. 22, 1573, published first by the Marquis de Noailles in his " Henri de Valois et la Pologne en 1572 " (Paris, 1867), iii. 533, from the MSS. of Prince Czartoryski, alludes to the costly jewels which Henry, now king-elect of Poland, made to the elector palatine, his host, and remarks : " Fortasse magna hæc fuisse videbitur liberalitas et rege digna, at parva certe vel nulla potius fuit, si vel sumptibus quos illustrissimus noster princeps in deducendo et excipiendo hoc hospite sustinuit conferamus, vel si unde hæc dona sint profecta expendamus. Ipse siquidem rex (Henry) ne teruncium pro iis solvisse, sed ex taberna cujusdam prædivitis aurifabri Parisiensis, quam scelerati sui ministri in strage illa nobilium ut alias multas diripuerunt, accepisse ea fertur."

vain hope that this would secure him liberty and life.[1] The
extent to which robbery was carried on the occasion of the
massacre is reluctantly conceded in the pamphlet, which was
published immediately after, as an apology of the court for the
hideous crime ; and an attempt is made to justify it, which is
worthy of the source from which it drew its inspiration : " Now
this good-will of the people to sustain and defend its prince, to
espouse his quarrel, and to hate those who are not of his religion, is very praiseworthy ; and if in this execution [the
massacre] some pillaging has taken place, we must excuse the
fury of a people impelled by a worthy zeal—a zeal hard to be
restrained and bridled when once excited." [2]

But, despite panegyrists, the massacre had not been in progress many hours before the very magistrates of the city appear
to have become apprehensive lest the movement might assume
dangerous dimensions. It was only about eleven o'clock on
Sunday morning, as the registers of the Hôtel de Ville inform
us, when Charles was waited upon by the prévôt des marchands
and the échevins. They came to inform him that "a number
of persons, partly belonging to the suite of his Majesty, partly
to that of the princes, princesses, and lords of the court—gentlemen, archers of the king's body-guard, soldiers of his suite, as
well as all sorts of people mingled with them and under their
authority—were plundering and pillaging many houses and killing many persons in the streets." This was certainly no news
to Charles ; but as he desired, now that the massacre had begun,
not to enrich the Roman Catholic inhabitants of Paris, but to
fill his own coffers, he deemed it best to prohibit any further

---

[1] Mémoires de l'estat, *ubi supra*, 150. Versailles, which thus passed into the
hands of the family of Marshal Retz—the Gondi family—was an old castle situated in the midst of an almost unbroken forest.   The Gondi family sold it to
Louis XIII., who built a hunting lodge, afterward transmuted by Louis XIV.
into the magnificent palace, which, for more than a century, was the favorite
residence of the most splendid court in Europe.   The mode in which the title
was acquired did not augur well for the justice or the morality which was to
reign there.   M. L. Lacour has contributed an animated sketch, " Versailles
et les protestants de France," to the Bulletin de la Soc. de l'hist. du prot. fr.,
viii. (1859) 352–367.

[2] Discours sur les causes de l'execution, *ubi supra*, 249.

action on their part, and to leave the rest of the work to his own commissioned servants. Accordingly the municipal authorities were directed to ride through the city with all the troops at their disposal, and to see to it, both by day and night, that the bloodshed and robbery should cease.

Orders issued to lay down arms.

"Sir William Guerrier"—thus runs one of the commissions to the "quarteniers" issued from the central bureau of the city, in pursuance of these directions—"give commandment to all burgesses and inhabitants of your quarter, who to-day have taken up arms *according to the king's order*, to lay them down, and to retire and remain quietly in their houses, . . . according to the king's command conveyed to us by my Lord of Nevers." And this document is accompanied with another, of the same date, applying to soldiers of the guard or others, who should pillage or maltreat Protestants, and threatening them with punishment. Such a proclamation, it is well known, was made by trumpet at about five o'clock that afternoon. The registers tell us that the instructions were so well carried out that all disorder "was at once appeased and ceased." They contain, however, a distinct refutation of this falsehood, in the frequent repetition of similar orders and the variety of forms in which the same statements are made on subsequent days. Again and again does the king direct that soldiers be placed at the head of every street to prevent robbery and murder ;[1] the guards either were never posted, or, as is more likely, became foremost in the work which they were sent to repress. Indeed, the instructions given on Monday to visit all the houses in the city and its suburbs where there were any Protestants, and obtain their names and surnames,[2] afforded an opportunity which was not permitted to slip by unimproved, for the exaction of heavy bribes, as well as for more open plunder and violence. So notorious was it, nearly a week after the butchery began, that the massacre had only abated in intensity, that, on the thirtieth of August, meas-

Little heed given to them.

---

[1] Royal orders of Aug. 25th, Aug. 27th, etc. Order of the Prévôt des marchands, Aug. 30th. Registres du bureau de la ville, Archives curieuses, vii. 222–230. Euseb. Philadelphi Dialog., i. 45.

[2] Registres du bureau de la ville, pp. 222, 223.

ures were adopted to prevent any wrong from being done to foreign merchants sojourning in Paris, and especially to the German, English, and Flemish students of the university.[1]

The smile of Heaven, it was said by the Roman Catholic clergy, rested upon the effort to extirpate heresy in France. *Miracle of the "Cimetière des Innocents."* They convinced the people of the truth of their assertion by pointing to an unusual phenomenon which they declared to be evidently miraculous. In the Cimetière des Innocents and before a small chapel of the Virgin Mary, there grew a white hawthorn, which, according to some accounts, had for several years been to all appearance dead. Great then was the surprise of those who, on the eventful St. Bartholomew's Day, beheld the tree covered with a great profusion of blossoms as fragrant as those flowers which the hawthorn usually puts forth in May. It was true that no good reason could be assigned why the wonder might not with greater propriety be explained, as the Protestants afterward suggested, rather as a mark of Heaven's sympathy with oppressed innocence. But no doubts entered the minds of the Parisian ecclesiastics. They spread abroad the fame of the prodigy. They rang the church-bells in token of joy, and invited the blood-stained populace to witness the sight, and gain new courage in their murderous work. It may well be doubted whether either the hawthorn or the virgin of the neighboring chapel wrought the wonderful cures recorded by the curate of Mériot.[2] But certainly the reported intervention of Heaven setting its seal upon treacherous assassination prolonged the slaughter of Huguenots. "It seemed," says Claude Haton, reflecting the popular belief, "that God, by this miracle, approved and accepted as well-pleasing to Him the Catholic uprising and the death of His great enemy the admiral and his followers, who for twelve years had been audaciously rending His seamless coat, which is

---

[1] Ibid., p. 227.

[2] "Aucuns malades languissans, ayant ouy ce miracle, se firent porter audit cymetière pour veoir laditte espine; lesquelz, estans là avec ferme foy, firent leur prière à Dieu en l'honneur de nostre dame la vierge Marie et devant son ymage qui est en laditte chapelle, pour recouvrer leur santé, et, après leur oraison faicte, s'en retournèrent en leurs maisons sains et guaris de leur maladie, chose très-véritable et bien approuvée." Mém. de Claude Haton, ii. 682.

His true Church and His Bride."[1]   And so, what with the encouragement afforded by the wonderful thorn-tree of the Cimetière des Innocents—what with the continuous fair weather, which was interpreted after the same manner, the task of extirpating the heretical Huguenots was prosecuted with a perseverance that never flagged.   It is true that the greater part of the work was done in the first three or four days; but it was not terminated for several weeks, and many a Huguenot, coming out of his place of concealment with the hope that time might have caused the passions of his enemies to become less violent, was murdered in cold blood by those who coveted his property.   Several thousand persons were butchered in Paris alone during the first few days, besides these later victims; precisely how many, it is useless and perhaps impossible to fix with certainty.[2]

Meantime it became necessary to explain to the world the extraordinary tragedy which had been enacted on so conspicuous a stage.   Each of the different parties to the nefarious compact, with that easy faith which characterizes great criminals, had expected to satisfy its own resentment at the sole expense of the honor and reputation of the others.   The king and his mother, while securing the death of Coligny and a few other personal enemies, were not unwilling to have the world believe

---

[1] Ibid., *ubi supra;* Tocsain contre les massacreurs, 146; Reveille-Matin, 193, 194; Mém. de l'estat, 155; Jean de Serres, iv., fol. 41; De Thou, iv. (liv. lii.) 596.

[2] Dr. White (Massacre of St. Bartholomew, 459) has tabulated the estimates, nine in number, afforded by twenty-one distinct authorities.   The lowest estimate—1,000 victims—is that of the Abbé Caveyrac, whose undisguised aim was to place the number as low as possible, so as to palliate the atrocity of the massacre.   Being based apparently upon the number of the *names* of victims that have been recorded, it may be dismissed as unworthy of consideration.   The highest estimate, of 10,000, though adopted by such writers as the authors of the Reveille-Matin and the Mémoires de l'estat de France, is vague or excessive.   The Tocsain and Agrippa d'Aubigné are, perhaps, too moderate in respectively stating the number as 2,000 and 3,000.   On the whole, it appears to me, the contribution of Paris to the massacre of the Huguenots may be set down with the greatest probability at between 4,000 and 5,000 persons of all ages and conditions.   Von Botzheim, who estimates the total at 8,000 (F. W. Ebeling, Archivalische Beiträge, p. 120), makes 500 of these to be women (Ibid., p. 119).

that the entire occurrence had been an outburst of the old animosity of the Guises against the Châtillons. In fact, this was distinctly stated in the circular letter of Charles IX., despatched on the very Sunday on which the massacre began, to the governors of the principal cities of the realm. " Mon-

The king's first letter to Mandelot.

sieur de Mandelot "—so runs one of these extraordinary epistles—" you have learned what I wrote to you, the day before yesterday, respecting the wounding of the admiral, and how that I was about to do my utmost in the investigation of the case and the punishment of the guilty, wherein nothing has been forgotten. Since then it has happened that the members of the house of Guise, and the other lords and gentlemen who are their adherents, and who have no small influence in this city, as everybody knows, having received certain information that the friends of the admiral intended to avenge this wound upon them—since they suspected them of being its cause and occasion—became so much excited that, between the one party and the other, there arose a great and lamentable commotion. The body of guards which had been posted around the admiral's house was overpowered, and he was killed with some other gentlemen, as there have also been others massacred in various parts of this city. This was done so furiously that it was impossible to apply such a remedy as could have been desired; for I had as much as I could do in employing my guards and other forces to retain my superiority in this castle of the Louvre,[1] so as afterward to take measures for allaying the commotion throughout the city. At the present hour it has, thank God, subsided! It occurred through the private quarrel which has long existed between these two houses. Always foreseeing that some bad consequences would result from it, I have heretofore done all that I could to appease it, as every one knows. There is in this nothing leading to the rupture of the Edict of

---

[1] In other letters Charles had even the effrontery to represent the King of Navarre as having been in like danger with his brothers and himself. See Eusebii Philadelphi Dialog. (1574), i. 45 : " se quidem metu propriæ salutis in arcem Luparam (the Louvre) compulsum illic se continuisse, una cum fratre charissimo Rege Navarræ, et dilectissimo Principe Condensi, ut in communi periculo eundem fortunæ exitum experirentur ! "

Pacification, which, on the contrary, I intend to be maintained as much as ever." [1]

In view of the undeniable fact that Charles affixed his signature to this letter in the midst of a horrible massacre for which he himself had given the signal, which he still directed, and concerning whose progress he received hourly bulletins from the municipal authorities, it must be admitted that the king showed himself no novice in the ignoble art of shameless misrepresentation.

Guise, on his part, was not less solicitous to relieve himself of responsibility, and to lay the burden upon the king's shoulders. We have seen that, at the very moment of Coligny's assassination, he began to repeat the words: "It is the king's pleasure; it is his express command!" as his warrant for the crime. As the massacre grew in extent he and his associates became more reluctant to be held accountable for it,[2] and at last they forced Charles to acknowledge himself its sole author. The queen mother and Anjou, it is said, were mainly instrumental in leading the monarch to take this unexpected step. His original intention had been to compel the Guises to leave the capital immediately after the death of Coligny—a movement which would have given color to the theory of their guilt. But it was not difficult for Catharine and Henry to convince him that by so doing he would only render more irreconcilable the enmity between the Guises and the Montmorencies, who plainly exhibited their intention to exact vengeance for the death of their illustrious kinsman, the admiral. In short, he would purchase brief respite from trouble at the price of a fresh civil war, more cruel than any which had preceded.[3]

Guise throws the responsibility on the king.

---

[1] Correspondance du roi Charles IX. et du sieur de Mandelot, 39–41. Letter to the Governor of Burgundy, *apud* Mém. de l'estat, *ubi sup.*, 133–135.

[2] It was undoubtedly with the object of showing that they were not the prime movers in the massacre, or, as the author of the Mém. de l'estat expresses himself, that they had no particular quarrel save with Admiral Coligny, that Henry of Guise and his uncle actually rescued a few Huguenots from the hands of those who were about to put them to death. Reveille-Matin, 188; Mémoires de l'estat, 150.

[3] Mém. de l'estat, *ubi supra*, 154, from Reveille-Matin, 192; De Thou, iv. (liv. lii.) 597, 598; Euseb. Philad. Dial., i. 47.

It was on Tuesday morning, the twenty-sixth of August, that the king formally and publicly assumed the weighty responsi-

The king ac-
cepts it.
bility. After hearing a solemn mass, to render thanks to Almighty God for his happy deliverance from his enemies, Charles, accompanied by his brothers, the Dukes of Anjou and Alençon, by the King of Navarre, and by a numerous body of his principal lords, proceeded to the parliament house, and there, in the presence of all the chambers,

The "Lit de
Justice."
held his "Lit de Justice." [1]   He opened this extraordinary meeting by an address, in which he dilated upon the intolerable insults he had, from his very childhood, experienced at the hands of Coligny, and many other culprits, who had made religion a pretext for rebellion. His attempts to secure peace by large concessions had emboldened Coligny so far that he had at last ventured to conspire to kill him, his mother, and his brothers, and even the King of Navarre, although a Huguenot like himself ; intending to place the Prince of Condé upon the throne, and subsequently to put him also out of the way, and appropriate the regal authority after the destruction of the entire royal family. In order to ward off so horrible a blow, he had, he said, been compelled to resort to extreme measures of rigor. He desired all men to know that the steps taken on the preceding Sunday for the punishment of the guilty had been in accordance with his orders. He is even reported to have gone farther, and to have invoked the aid of parliament in condemning the memory and confiscating the property of those against whom he had alleged such abominable crimes. [2]

---

[1] It was while Charles was on his way to the Palais de Justice that a gentleman in his train, and not far from him, was recognized as being a Protestant, and was killed. The king, hearing the disturbance, turned around ; but, on being informed that it was a Huguenot whom they were putting to death, lightly said : " Let us go on. Would to God that he were the last ! " Reveille-Matin, 194 (copied in Mém. de l'estat, 157) ; Euseb. Philad. Dial., i. 50.

[2] De Thou, whom I have chiefly followed, iv. (liv. lii.) 599 ; Tocsain contre les massacreurs, 142 ; Reveille-Matin, 193, 194 ; Euseb. Phil. Dial., i. 49 ; Mém. de l'estat, 156 ; Jean de Serres (1575), iv., fol. 43 ; Capilupi, 45 ; Relation of Olaegui, secretary of Don Diego de Cuñiga, Spanish ambassador at Paris, to be laid before Philip II., Simancas MSS., *apud* Bulletins de l'Acad. Roy. des Sciences, etc., de Belgique, vol. xvi. (1849) 254.

To this allocution the parliament replied with all servility. Christopher de Thou, the first president, lauded the prudence Servile reply of a monarch who had known how to bear patiently of parliament. repeated insults, and at last to crush a conspiracy so dangerous to the quiet of the realm. And he quoted with approval the infamous apothegm of Louis the Eleventh : " *Qui nescit dissimulare, nescit regnare.*" The solitary suggestion that breathed any manly spirit was that of Pibrac, the " avocat-général," to the effect that orders should be published to put an end to the work of murder and robbery—a request which Charles readily granted.[1] Never had the supreme tribunal of justice abased itself more ignobly than when it listened so complaisantly to the king, and approved without qualification an organized massacre perpetrated unblushingly under its very eyes. As for the distinguished man who lent himself to be the Christopher mouthpiece of adulation worse than slavish, we are de Thou. less inclined to commiserate the difficulty of his position than to pity the ingenuous historian who strives to touch leniently upon a fault of his father which he can neither conceal nor palliate.[2] We may credit his assertion that his father remonstrated with the king in private with respect to that for which he had praised him in public, and that Christopher de Thou marked his detestation of that ill-starred day by applying to it the lines of Statius :

> Excidat illa dies ævo, ne postera credant
> Sæcula : nos certe taceamus, et obruta multa
> Nocte tegi propriæ patiamur crimina gentis.

But we cannot forget that this was not the first time that Chris-

---

[1] De Thou, Tocsain, etc., *ubi supra.*

[2] Returning to the unpleasant theme in a subsequent book of his noble history (iv. (liv. liii.) 644), Jacques Auguste de Thou remarks, with an integrity which cannot swerve even out of consideration for filial respect : " Ce qu'il y avoit de déplorable, étoit de voir des personnes respectables par leur piété, leur science, et leur intégrité, revêtues des premières charges du Royaume, ennemies d'ailleurs de tout déguisement et de tout artifice, tels que Morvilliers, de Thou, Pibrac, Montluc et Bellièvre, louer contre leurs sentimens, ou excuser par complaisance une action qu'ils détestoient dans le cœur, sans y être engagés par aucun motif de crainte ou d'espérance ; mais dans la fausse persuasion où ils étoient que les circonstances présentes et le bien de l'État demandoient qu'ils tinssent ce langage."

topher de Thou " accommodated " his words or his actions to
the supposed " exigencies of the times." He was a member of
that commission that sentenced Louis of Condé to death, in
deference to the desires of another king and his uncles, the
Guises; and the prince would doubtless have lost his head in
consequence, but for the sudden death of Francis the Second.
Since that time he had repeatedly acquiesced in the bloody
sentences of the Parisian parliament. His voice was never
heard opposing the proscription instituted in the late civil wars,
even in the case of the atrocious sentence against Gaspard de
Coligny. If we concede to his son that no one was of a less
sanguinary or of a milder disposition than President De Thou,
we must also insist that few judges on the bench displayed less
magnanimity or conscientiousness.[1]

But it was not a simple congratulatory address that Charles,
or his mother, required of his parliament. Tyrannical power is
rarely satisfied with the mere acquiescence of servile judges ; it
demands, and ordinarily obtains from them, a positive indorsement of its schemes of successful villainy. It was necessary—
especially, as we shall see later, after the cry of horror was
heard that rose toward heaven from all parts of Europe on
receipt of the tidings of the massacre in Paris and elsewhere—
to palliate its atrocity by affixing to the slain Huguenots, and
above all to Coligny, a note of rebellious and murderous designs
against the king and the royal family. And here again the
Parliament of Paris was as pliant as its rulers could desire.

---

[1] The case stands much worse if we accept the statement of the author of
the Mémoires de l'estat de France sous Charles IX., who, after contrasting
the honorable conduct of President La Vaquerie, in the time of Louis XI.,
with that of Christopher de Thou, adds : " 'Mais cestui-ci n'avoit garde de
faire le semblable ; il prend trop de plaisir à toute sorte d'injustice pour s'y
vouloir opposer." (*Ubi supra*, pp. 156, 157.) So, also Euseb. Philad. Dial.,
i. 50: " Nam quomodo sese injustitiæ viriliter opponeret, qui ex ea tam
uberes fructus colligit? " The Mém. de l'estat accuse him of having instigated the murder of Rouillard—a counsellor of parliament and canon of
Notre Dame, and one of a very few Roman Catholics that were assassinated—
because the latter loved justice, and had prosecuted one of the first president's friends (p. 148). According to the historian De Thou, on the other
hand (iv. 593), Rouillard was " homme inquiet, querelleux, et ennemi des
officiers des compagnies de ville."

Coligny's papers, both in Paris and at Châtillon-sur-Loing, were
Ineffectual effort to inculpate Coligny. subjected to close scrutiny; but nothing could be discovered to warrant the suspicion that any seditious design had ever been entertained by him.   In default
of something better, therefore, the queen mother endeavored to
make capital out of two passages of these private manuscripts.
In one—it was, we are told, the will of the admiral, written
toward the end of the third civil war[1]—he dissuaded Charles
from assigning to his brothers appanages that might diminish
the authority of the crown.   Catharine triumphantly showed
it to Alençon.   "See!" said she; "this is your good friend
the admiral, whom you so greatly loved and respected!"   "I
know not," replied the young prince, "how much of a friend
he was to me; but certainly he showed by this advice how
much he loved the king."[2]   With Walsingham a similar attempt was made to deprive the murdered hero of Queen Elizabeth's sympathy, but with as little success.   "To the end you
may see how little your mistress was beholden to him," said
Catharine de' Medici one day to the English ambassador, "you
may see a discourse found with his testament, made at such
time as he was sick at Rochel, wherein, amongst other advices
that he gave to the king my son, this is one, that he willed
him in any case to keep the queen, your mistress, and the King
of Spain as low as he could, as a thing that tended much to
the safety and maintenance of this crown."   "To that I answered," says Walsingham, "that in this point, howsoever he
was affected towards the queen my mistress, he showed himself
a most true and faithful subject to the crown of France, and
the Queen's Majestie, my mistress, made the more account of
him, for that she knew him faithfully affected to the same."[3]
   The complete absence of proof of all designs save the most

---

[1] The passage is not in the will in the admiral's own handwriting, dated
Archiac, June 5, 1569, a fac-simile of which has been accurately lithographed
by the French Protestant Historical Society, and which has also been printed
in the Bulletin, i. (1852) 263–268.   See *ante*, p. 461, 462.

[2] Mémoires de l'estat, *ubi supra*, 153; Gasparis Coiinii Vita (1575), 131.

[3] "The said discourse was all written with his own hand."   Walsingham
to Smith, Sept. 14, 1572; Digges, 241, 242; Mém. de l'estat, *ubi supra*, 153;
Gasparis Colinii Vita, 131, 132.

patriotic, and, on the other hand, the clear evidence that Coligny
sought for the quiet and growth of the religious community to
which he belonged, only in connection with the honor and prosperity of his own country, did not deter the pliant parliament
from pursuing the course prescribed for it. A little more than
two months after the Massacre of St. Bartholomew's Day (Oc-

Coligny's   tober the twenty-seventh, 1572), the admiral's sentence
memory de-
clared infa- was formally pronounced. He was proclaimed a
mous.   traitor and the author of a conspiracy against the
king; his goods were confiscated, his memory declared infamous. His children were degraded from their rank as nobles,
and pronounced "ignoble, villains, *roturiers*, infamous, unworthy, and incapable of making a will, or of holding offices,
dignities or possessions in France." It was ordered that his

Petty indig- castle of Châtillon-sur-Loing should be razed to the
nities.   ground, never to be rebuilt, and that the site should
be sown with salt; that the trees of the park should be cut down
to half their height, and a monumental pillar be erected on the
spot, with a copy of this decree inscribed upon it. His portraits
and statues were to be destroyed; his arms, wherever found, to
be dragged at the horse's tail and publicly destroyed by the
hangman; his body—if any fragments could be obtained, or, if
not, his effigy—was to be dragged on a hurdle, and hung first on
the Grève and then on a loftier gibbet at Montfaucon. Finally,
public prayers and a solemn procession were ordered to take
place in Paris on every successive anniversary of the feast of
St. Bartholomew.[1]

Thus was the memory of one of the noblest characters that
illustrated the sixteenth century pursued with envenomed hatred,
after death had placed Coligny himself beyond the power of the
murderous queen mother to inflict more substantial injury upon
him. To his mortal remains all that malice could do had already
been done. What remained of a mutilated body had been taken
from the hands of those precocious criminals, the boys of Paris,

---

[1] Jean de Serres (1575), iv., fols. 57, 58 ; Eusebii Philadelphi Dial. (1574), i.
82, 83 ; Reveille-Matin, 203–205 ; De Thou, iv. (liv. liii.) 645, 646. For many
years the disgraceful commomorative procession was faithfully observed.

and hung up by the feet upon the gallows at Montfaucon.[1] A great part of the capital had gone out to look upon the grateful sight. Charles the Ninth was of the number of the visitors, and, when others showed signs of disgust at the stench arising from the putrefaction of a corpse long unburied, is said to have exclaimed "that the smell of a dead enemy is very sweet."[2] Great was the merriment of the low populace; copious were the effusions of wit. Jacques Copp de Vellay, in his poetical diatribe, published with privilege—"Le Déluge des Huguenotz"—sings with great delight of

> Mont-Faulcon, où les attend
> Ce grand Gaspar au curedent,
> Attaché par les piedz sans teste.[3]

At last, four or five days after Coligny's death, a body of thirty or forty horse, sent by Marshal Montmorency, took down the remains by night, and gave them decent burial.[4]

---

[1] The slight eminence of Montfaucon, the Tyburn of Paris, was between the Faubourg St. Martin and the Faubourg du Temple, near the site of the Hôpital St. Louis. See Dulaure, Atlas de Paris.

[2] "Il les en reprit et leur dist: 'Je ne bousche comme vous autres, car l'odeur de son ennemy est très-bonne'—odeur certes point bonne et la parolle aussi mauvaise." Brantôme, Le Roy Charles IX., edit. Lalanne, v. 258. The original authority for this odious remark is Papyrius Masson (1575) in his life of Charles IX., which Brantôme had under his eyes: "Servis fœtorem non ferentibus, hostis mortui odor bonus est inquit." Le Laboureur, iii. 16.

[3] Le deluge des Huguenots avec leur Tumbeau, 1572. Reprinted in Archives curieuses, vii. 251-259.

[4] Tocsain contre les massacreurs, Rheims, 1579, p. 143. It has been well remarked by a writer in the Bulletin de la Soc. de l'hist. du prot. français (iii. 346) as one of the paradoxes of history, that Coligny's mangled remains, "after being carefully subjected to the most ignominious treatment, were saved from the annihilation to which they appeared to be infallibly condemned, and have been transmitted from place to place, and from hand to hand, until our own days, and better preserved for three centuries than many other illustrious corpses carefully laid up in costly mausoleums!" Marshal Montmorency placed the admiral's body in a lead coffin in his castle of Chantilly, whence he sent it to Montauban. François de Coligny brought it back to Châtillon-sur-Loing, when, in 1599, the sentence of parliament was formally rescinded. In 1786 it was taken to Maupertuis and placed in a black marble sarcophagus. Since 1851 it has been resting in its new tomb under the ruins of that part of the castle of Châtillon where Coligny was probably born. Bulletin, iii. 346-351.

Not content with the public admission of his responsibility for the massacre which he had made before the parliament, Charles with his court participated two days later (Thursday, the twenty-eighth of August) in the celebration of a jubilee, and walked in a procession through the streets of Paris; at successive "stations" rendering thanks to Heaven, with fair show of devotion, for the preservation of his own life, and the lives of his brothers and of *the King of Navarre*. It would have served greatly to give a color of plausibility to the report of the conspiracy of the Huguenots, could Navarre and Condé have been prevailed upon to appear in the king's company on this occasion. But it must be mentioned to their honor, that they were proof against the persuasions as well as the threats of Charles.[1] The same day a royal declaration was published, reiterating the allegations made in the Palais de Justice, but protesting that the king was determined to maintain his edict of pacification. As, however, the Protestants were forbidden for the present from holding any public or private assemblies for worship, it must be admitted that they were not far wrong in regarding the declaration as only another part of the trap cunningly devised for their destruction.[2]

A jubilee procession.

Charles declares that he will maintain his edict.

Although the conversion of the young King of Navarre and his cousin, the Prince of Condé, did not occur until some weeks later, it may be appropriately mentioned here. No means were left untried to gain them over to the Roman Catholic religion. The sophistries of monks

Forced conversion of Navarre and Condé.

---

[1] Tocsain contre les Massacreurs, 146; Reveille-Matin, 195; Euseb. Philadelphi Dial., i. 51; Mém. de l'estat, 161; Jean de Serres, iv., fol. 44 *verso*.

[2] The text of the declaration is to be found in the Mémoires de Claude Haton, ii. 683–685, in the Recueil des anciennes lois françaises (Isambert), xiv. 257, etc., and in the Mémoires de l'estat, *ubi supra*, 162–164. See De Thou, iv. (liv. lii.) 600. The Reveille-Matin calls attention (p. 196) to the circumstance that in the first copies of the document the name of Navarre did not occur; but that in the next issue the admiral's unhappy and detestable conspiracy was represented as directed against "la personne dudit sieur roy et contre son estat, la royne sa mère, messieurs ses frères, *le roy de Navarre*, princes et seigneurs estans près d'eulx." The policy of introducing Navarre, and, by implication, Condé, among the proposed victims of the Huguenots, was certainly sufficiently bold and reckless. See *ante*, p. 490.

were supplemented by the more dangerous persuasions of a renegade Protestant minister, Hugues Sureau du Rosier, formerly
one of the pastors of the church of Orleans.[1] Whatever excuse
his arguments may have furnished by covering their renunciation of their faith with the decent cloak of conviction, *fear* was
certainly the chief instrument in effecting the desired change in
the Huguenot princes. There is no room for doubt that the
character of Charles underwent a marked change, as we shall
see later, from the time that he consented to the massacre. He
became more sullen, more violent, more impatient of contradiction or opposition. It is not at all unlikely that a mind never
fully under control of reason, and now assuredly thrown from its
poise by a desperation engendered of remorse for the fearful
crime he had reluctantly approved, at times formed the resolution to kill the obstinate King of Navarre and his cousin. On
one occasion Charles is said to have been deterred by the supplications of his young wife from going in person to destroy
them.[2] At length, when the alternative of death or the Bastile
was the only one presented, the courage of the Bourbons began
to falter. Navarre was the first to yield, and his sister, the
excellent Catharine de Bourbon, followed his example. On the
thirteenth of September the ambassador Walsingham wrote:
"They prepare Bastile for some persons of quality. It is
thought that it is for the Prince of Condé and his brethren." [3]
But three days later (the sixteenth of September) he wrote again:
"On Sunday last, which was the fourteenth of this month, the
young Princess of Condé was constrained to go to mass, being
threatened otherwise to go to prison, and so consequently to be
made away. The Prince of Condé hath also yielded to hear
mass upon Sunday next, being otherwise threatened to go to
the Bastile, where he is not like long to serve." [4] Such conversions did not promise to prove very sincere. They were accepted,
however, by the king and his mother; although both Navarre
and Condé were detained at court rather as prisoners than as

---

[1] See De Thou, iv. (liv. liii.), 630; Jean de Serres, iv., fols. 53, 54.
[2] Euseb. Philadelphi Dial., i. 52.
[3] Digges, 239, 240.
[4] Ibid., 245.

free princes. Pope Gregory the Thirteenth received the submission of both cousins to the authority of the See of Rome, recognized the validity of their marriages, and formally admitted them to his favor, by a special bull of the twenty-seventh of October, 1572.[1] In return for these concessions Henry of Navarre repealed the ordinances which his mother had made for the government of Béarn, and re-established the Roman Catholic worship.[2]

The reports of the Venetian Ambassadors, Michele and Cavalli, agree with the despatches of the Papal Nuncio, Salviati, in relieving the king of all complicity in the arquebusade of Maurevel. The plot to assassinate Coligny was the work of Catharine and Anjou alone. Cavalli declares that Charles not only was certainly ignorant of the existence of his mother's design, but exhibited great annoyance and apprehension at the prospect of new civil commotions. When the queen mother and her younger son, at a late hour on Saturday night, succeeded in overcoming the king's fears and scruples, it was only after arguing with him for more than an hour and a half, and finally threatening to withdraw from his court should he refuse to avail himself of "the glorious opportunity which God had given him of ridding himself of such a plague" as the Huguenots. Michele adds that the task of persuading Charles was facilitated by the tale of Bouchavannes. The traitor told not, indeed, of a conspiracy to murder the king, but of a projected assembly of the Huguenots, foot and horse, to take place at Melun on the fifth of September, with the view of compelling the defenceless monarch to avenge the injury done to the admiral. "This," says the Venetian, "is the conspiracy which the king subsequently alleged in Parliament that he had discovered against himself, his mother, and his brothers, adding, also, in order to make the matter more dishonorable, his kinsman, the King of Navarre." Michele believes that had the arquebuse shot taken effect, the slaughter would scarcely have stopped with Coligny; for the gates of Paris would have been closed under pretext of a search for the murderer, and the Huguenots universally slain on that day or on the succeeding night, provision having been made against the escape of even one of their number. On the other hand, Cavalli is positive in the opinion that so many mistakes were committed in the execution of the massacre, and such instability and contradiction were displayed, as to prove that the plan had been adopted suddenly, and not after long deliberation (risoluta all' improviso, et non di lunga mano). See the relations in Ranke, V. (Doc.), 75–87.

The Venetian relations.

---

[1] Documents historiques inédits, i. 713–715.

[2] Agrippa d'Aubigné, Hist. univ., ii. 30; Jean de Serres (1575), iv., fol. 55.

CHAPTER XIX.

THE MASSACRE IN THE PROVINCES, AND THE RECEPTION OF THE TIDINGS ABROAD.

THE massacre of St. Bartholomew's Day would have been terrible enough had it been confined to Paris, for its victims in that single city were to be reckoned by thousands.

The massacre in the provinces. Charles the Ninth himself, on the third day, admitted in a letter to Mondoucet, his envoy in the Netherlands, that " a very great number of the adherents of the new religion who were in this city had been massacred and cut to pieces." [1] But this was little in comparison with the multitudes that were yet to lose their lives in other parts of France. Here, however, the enterprise assumed a different character. Not only did it not commence on the same day as in the capital, but it began at different dates in different places. It is evident that there had been no well-concerted plan long entertained and freely communicated to the governors of the provinces and cities. On the contrary, the greatest variety of procedure prevailed—all tending, nevertheless, to the same end of the total destruction of the Protestants. And this was intended from the very moment the project of the Parisian butchery was hastily and inconsiderately adopted by the king. Charles meant to be as good as his word when he announced his determination that not a single Huguenot should survive to reproach him with what he had done. More frightful than his most passionate outburst of bloodthirsty frenzy is the cool calculation with which he, or the minister

---

[1] Charles IX. to Mondoucet, August 26th, Compte rendu de la com. roy. d'histoire, Brussels, 1852, iv. 344.

who wrote the words he subscribed, predicts the chain of successive murders in provincial France, scarcely one of which had as yet been attempted. "*It is probable*," he said, in the same letter of the twenty-sixth of August, that has just been cited, "*that the fire thus kindled will go coursing through all the cities of my kingdom*, which, following the example of what has been done in this city, will assure themselves of all the adherents of the said religion." [1]

No mere surmise, founded upon the probable effects of the exhibition of cruelty in Paris, led to the penning of this sentence. Charles had purposely fired the train which was to explode with the utmost violence at almost every point of his wide dominions. "As it has pleased God," he wrote to Mondoucet, "to bring matters to the state in which they now are, I do not intend to neglect the opportunity not only to re-establish, if I shall be able, lasting quietness in my kingdom, but also to serve Christendom." [2] Accordingly, secret orders, for the most part verbal, had already been sent in all directions, commanding the provinces to imitate the example set by Paris. The reality of these orders does not rest upon conjecture, but is attested by documentary evidence over the king's own hand. As we have seen in the last chapter, Charles published, on the twenty-eighth of August, a declaration of his motives and intentions. This was despatched to the governors of the provinces and to other high officers, in company with a circular letter, of which the final sentence deserves particular notice. "Moreover," says the king, "whatever verbal command I may have given to those whom I sent to you, as well as to my other governors and lieutenants-general, at a time when I had just reason to fear some inauspicious events, from having discovered the conspiracy which the admiral was making against

Verbal orders.

---

[1] "Estant croiable que ce feu ainsy allumé ira courant par toutes les villes de mon royaume, lesquelles, à l'exemple de ce qui s'est faict en ccstedite ville, s'assureront de tous ceulx de ladite religion." Charles to Mondoucet, Aug. 26th, *ubi supra*, iv. 345.

[2] "Car puisqu'il a pleu à Dieu conduire les choses ès termes où elles sont, je ne veulx négliger l'occasion, non seulement pour remectre, s'il m'est possible, ung perpétuel repos en mon royaume, mais aussy servir à la chrestienté."

me, I have revoked and revoke it completely, intending that nothing therein contained be put into execution by you or by others; for such is my pleasure." [1]

What was the import of these orders? The manuscripts in the archives of Angers seem to leave no room for doubt. This city was the capital of the Duchy of Anjou, given in appanage to Henry, the king's brother, and was, consequently, under his special government. On Tuesday, the twenty-sixth of August, the duke sent to the Governor of Saumur a short note running thus: "Monsieur de Montsoreau, I have instructed the sieur de Puigaillard to write to you respecting a matter that concerns the service of the king, my lord and brother, as well as my own. You will, therefore, not fail to believe and to do whatever he may tell you, just as if it were I myself." In the same package with these credentials Montsoreau [2] received a letter from Puigaillard, like himself a knight of the royal order of St. Michael, which reveals only too clearly the purpose of the king and his brother. "Monsieur mon compagnon, I will not fail to acquaint you with the fact that, on Sunday morning the king caused a very great execution to be made against the Huguenots; so much so that the admiral and all the Huguenots that were in this city were killed. And his Majesty's will is that the same be done wherever there are any to be found. Accordingly, if you desire ever to do a service that may be agreeable to the king and to Monsieur (the Duke of Anjou), you must go to Saumur with the greatest possible number of your friends, and put to death all that you can

(marginal note:) Instructions to Montsoreau at Saumur.

---

[1] "Au surplus, quelque commandement verbal que j'aye peu faire à ceulx que j'aye envoyé tant devers vous que autres gouverneurs. . . . . j'ay révocqué et révocque tout celà, ne voulant que par vous ne autres en soit aucune chose exécuté." Charles IX. to Mandelot, Governor of Lyons, Correspondance, etc. (Paris, 1830), 53, 54; the same to the Mayor of Bourges, Mém. de l'estat (Archives curieuses), vii. 313. The variations of language are trifling.

[2] He seems at this time to have been at his castle of Montsoreau, situated six or seven miles above Saumur, on the left bank of the Loire, and within a short distance of Candes. M. de Montsoreau himself is described as "gentilhomme de Poictou fort renommé pour beaucoup de pillages et violences, qui finalement luy ont fait perdre la vie, ayant esté tué depuis en qualité de meurtrier." Mém. de l'estat, vii. 349.

find there of the principal Huguenots. . . . Having made this execution at Saumur, I beg you to go to Angers and do the same, with the assistance of the captain of the castle. And you must not expect to receive any other command from the king, nor from Monseigneur, for they will send you none, inasmuch as they depend upon what I write you. You must use diligence in this affair, and lose as little time as possible. I am very sorry that I cannot be there to help you in putting this into execution." [1]

The statement of the author of the Mémoires de l'estat de France is, therefore, in full agreement with the ascertained Two kinds of facts of the case. He informs us that, soon after the letters. Parisian massacre commenced, the secret council by which the plan had been drawn up despatched two widely differing kinds of letters. The first were of a private character, and were addressed to governors of cities and to seditious Roman Catholics where there were many Protestants, by which they were instigated to murder and rapine; [2] the others were public, and were addressed to the same functionaries, their object being to amuse and entrap the professors of the reformed faith. And in addition to the double sets of written instructions, the same author says that messengers were sent to various points, to give orders for special executions. [3] We shall not find it very difficult to account for the rapidity with which the mas-

---

[1] These letters, and some others relating to the massacre at Angers, contained in the archives of the municipality, are printed in the Bulletin de la Soc. de l'hist. du prot. français, xi. (1862) 120–124.

[2] I know, however, of no letters of this kind signed by Charles IX. himself. They all seem to have been written by his inferior agents, such as Puigaillard in the case of Saumur, or Masso and Rubys in that of Lyons. The advantage of this course was apparent. The king could not be *proved* to have ordered any massacre; he could throw off the responsibility upon others. On the other hand, such politic governors as Mandelot were naturally reluctant to act upon instructions which could at any moment be disavowed. The verbal messages of Charles himself would seem, from the Mandelot correspondence, to have been less definite—perhaps going to no greater lengths than to order the arrest of the persons and the sequestration of the effects of the Huguenots. May we not naturally suppose that the king and his council counted upon such subsequent massacres of the imprisoned Protestants as occurred in many places ?

[3] Mémoires de l'estat, 132, 133. Compare De Thou, iv. (liv. lii.) 601.

sacre spread to the provincial towns—of which the secretary of
the Spanish ambassador, in his hurried journey from Paris to
Madrid, was an eye-witness [1]—if we bear in mind the previous
ripeness of the lowest classes of the Roman Catholic population
for the perpetration of any possible acts of insult and injury
toward their Protestant fellow-citizens. The time had come
for the seed sown broadcast by monk and priest in Lenten
and Advent discourses to bear its legitimate harvest in the pitiless murder of heretics.

Meaux was naturally one of the first of smaller cities to catch
the contagion from the capital. Not only was it the nearest
city that contained any considerable body of Huguenots, but, if we may credit the report current among
them, Catharine, in virtue of her rank as Countess of Meaux,
had placed it first upon the roll. It is not impossible that the
circumstance that this was the cradle of Protestantism in
France may have secured it this distinction. About the middle
of Sunday afternoon a courier reached Meaux, and at once made
his way to the residence of the procureur-du-roi, one Cosset.
The nature of the message he bore may be inferred from the
fact that secret orders were at once given to those persons upon
whom Cosset thought that he could rely, to be in readiness about
nightfall. So completely had every outlet from Paris been
sealed, that it had proved almost impossible for a Protestant to
find the means of escaping to carry the tidings abroad. Consequently the adherents of the reformed faith were yet in ignorance of the impending catastrophe. At the time appointed,
Cosset and his followers seized the gates of Meaux. It was the
hour when the peaceable and unsuspecting people were at
supper. The Protestants could now easily be found, and few
escaped arrest, either that evening or on the succeeding day.
Happily, however, a large number of Huguenots resided in a
quarter of Meaux known as the "Grand Marché," and separated
from the main part of the town by the river Marne. The inhabitants of the Grand Marché received timely warning of their

The massacre
at Meaux.

---

[1] Relation of Olaegui, Simancas MSS., Bulletins de l'académie royale de
Belgique, xvi. (1849) 254, 255.

danger ; and the men fled by night for temporary refuge to the neighboring villages. It was scarcely dawn on Monday morning when the work of plunder began. By eight o'clock little was left of the goods of the Huguenots on this side of the Marne, and the pillagers crossed the bridge to the Grand Marché. Finding only the women, who had remained in the vain hope of saving their family possessions, the papists wreaked their fury upon them. About twenty-five of these unhappy persons were murdered in cold blood ; [1] others were so severely beaten that they died within a few days ; a few were shamefully dishonored. In most cases, if not in all, outward acquiescence in the ceremonies of the Roman Catholic Church would have saved the lives of the victims, but the Huguenot women were constant and would yield no hypocritical consent. One poor woman, the wife of " Nicholas the cap-maker," was being dragged to mass, when her bold and impolitic expressions of detestation of the service so enraged her conductors, that, being at that moment upon the bridge which unites the two portions of the city, they stabbed her and threw her body into the river. In a short time the Grand Marché, which the precise chronicler tells us contained more than four hundred houses, was robbed of everything which could be removed, for not the most insignificant article escaped the cupidity of the Roman Catholic populace. [2]

These were but the preliminaries of the general massacre. The prisons were full of Huguenots, whom it was necessary to put out of the way. Late in the day, on Tuesday the twenty-sixth, Cosset and his band made their appearance. They were provided with a list of their destined victims, more than two hundred in number. Of a score or two the names have been preserved, with their respective avocations. They were merchants, judicial officers, industrious artisans—in short, the representatives of the better class of the population of Meaux. Not one escaped. The murderous band were stationed in the courtyard of the prison,

---

[1] The names of nine are given. Archives curieuses, vii. 264.

[2] The procureur Cosset did not neglect his own interests, if, as we are informed, his house and courtyard were so full of stolen furniture that it was scarcely possible to enter the premises.

while Cosset, armed with a pistol in either hand, mounted the steps, and by his roll summoned the Protestants to the slaughter awaiting them below. The bloody work was long and tedious. The assassins adjourned awhile for their supper, and, unable to complete the task before weariness blunted the edge of their ferocity, reserved a part of the Protestants for the next day. None the less was the task accomplished with thoroughness, and the exultant cutthroats now had leisure to pursue the fugitives of the Grand Marché to the villages in which they had taken refuge.[1]

The news of the Parisian massacre reached Troyes, the flourishing capital of Champagne, on Tuesday, the twenty-sixth of August, and spread great alarm among the Protestants, who, with the recent disturbances[2] still fresh in their memories, apprehended immediate death. But their enemies for the time confined themselves to closing the gates to prevent their escape. It was not until Saturday, the thirtieth, that the "bailli," Anne de Vaudrey, sieur de St. Phalle, sent throughout the city and brought all the Protestants to the prisons. Meantime one of the most turbulent of the Roman Catholics, named Pierre Belin, had been in Paris, having been deputed, some weeks before, to endeavor to procure the removal of the place of worship of the reformed from the castle of Isle-au-Mont, two or three leagues from the city, to some more distant and inconvenient spot. He remained in the capital until the Saturday after the massacre, and started that day for Troyes, with a copy of the declaration of Thursday forbidding injury to the persons and goods of unoffending Protestants, and ordering the release of any that might have been imprisoned. It was believed, indeed, that he was commissioned to give the declaration to the bailli for publication. On Wednesday, the third of September, he reached Troyes. As he rode through the streets, he inquired again and again whether the Huguenots at Troyes were all killed as they were elsewhere. When interrogated by peaceable Roman Catholics respecting a rumor

The massacre at Troyes.

---

[1] Mémoires de l'estat, *apud* Archives curieuses, vii. 261–270.
[2] See *ante*, chapter xviii., p. 432.

that the king had revoked his sanguinary orders, he boldly denied its truth, accompanying his words with oaths and imprecations. Finding the bailli, he had no difficulty in persuading him to suppress the royal order, and to convene a council, at which Belin was introduced as the bearer of verbal instructions, and a bishop was brought forward to confirm them. Belin and the bishop maintained that the royal pleasure was that the heretics of Troyes should all be murdered on the following Saturday night, without distinction of rank, sex, or age, and their bodies be exposed in the streets to the sight of those who should on the morrow join in a solemn procession to be held in honor of the achievement. A writing attached to the neck of each was to contain the words : " Seditious persons and rebels against the king, who have conspired against his Majesty."

The task of butchering the helpless Huguenots in the prison was first proposed to the public hangman. He refused to take any part in it : this, he said, was no duty of his office, and he would consent to perform it only when all the forms of law should have been observed. Other persons were found more pliable, and, under the leadership of one Perremet, the bloody scenes of the prison of Meaux were re-enacted, on Thursday, the fourth day of September, in that of Troyes. How many were the victims we know not ; we have, however, the names of over thirty, apparently the most prominent of the number. Others were assassinated in the streets. At last, when all had been done that malice could effect, the king's declaration, which promised protection to the Huguenots, was published on Friday, the fifth of September.[1]

In Orleans, a city once the headquarters of the Huguenots, where their iconoclastic assaults upon the churches during the first civil war had left permanent memorials of their former supremacy, the massacre assumed the largest proportions. One of the king's court preachers, Arnauld Sorbin, better known as M. de Sainte Foy, had written from Paris letters instigating the inhabitants of Orleans to imi-

The great bloodshed at Orleans.

---

[1] Recordon, le Protestantisme en Champagne (from the MSS. of N. Pithou, seigneur de Chamgobert), Paris, 1863, 174–192 ; Mém. de l'estat, Archives curieuses, vii. 271–292.

tate the example of the capital, and the letters came to hand with the earliest tidings of the Parisian massacre. The first murder took place on Monday. M. de Champeaux, a royal counsellor and a Protestant, who as yet was in ignorance of the events of St. Bartholomew's Day, received late on Monday the visit of Tessier, surnamed La Court, the leader of the assassins of Orleans, and some of his followers. Imagining it to be a friendly call — for they were acquaintances — Champeaux received them courteously, and invited them to sup with him. The meal over, his guests recounted the story of the tragic occurrence at Paris, and, before he was well over his surprise and horror, asked him for his purse. The unhappy host, still mistaking the character of those whom he had entertained, at first regarded the demand as a pleasantry; but when he had been convinced of his error and had complied, his treacherous visitors instantly stabbed him to death in his very dining-room.[1] The general butchery began on Tuesday night, in the neighborhood of the ramparts, where the Protestants were most numerous, and from Wednesday to Saturday there was no intermission in the slaughter. Here, more even than elsewhere, the murderers distinguished themselves by their profanity and their undisguised hatred of the Protestant faith and worship. "Where is your God?" "Where are your prayers and your psalms?" "Where is the God they invoke so much? Let Him save, if He can." Such were the expressions with which the blows of the assassin were interlarded. At times he thought to aggravate his victim's sufferings by singing snatches of favorite psalms from the Huguenot psalm-book. It might be the forty-third, so appropriate to the condition of oppressed innocence, in its quaint old French garb:

> Revenge-moi, pren la querelle
> De moi, Seigneur, de ta merci,
> Contre la gent fausse et cruelle :
> De l'homme rempli de cautelle,
> Et en sa malice endurci,
> Delivre moi aussi.

---

[1] Dr. Henry White, besides mistaking the Huguenot for the Papist, has incorrectly stated the circumstances. Massacre of St. Bartholomew, 450. See Mém. de l'estat, *ubi supra*, 295, and De Thou, iv. (liv. lii.) 601.

Or it might be the fifty-first—the words never more sincerely accepted, even when chanted to all the perfection of choral music, in the Sistine Chapel or in St. Peter's, than when, in the ears of constant sufferers for their Christian faith, ribald voices contemptuously sang or drawled the familiar lines :

> Misericorde au povre vicieux,
> Dieu tout-puissant, selon ta grand' clemence.[1]

" These execrable outrages," adds the chronicler who gives us this interesting information, " did not in the least unnerve the Protestants, who died with great constancy; and, if some were shaken (as were some, but in very small numbers), this in no wise lessened the patience and endurance of the rest."[2] The number of the killed was great. The murderers themselves boasted of the slaughter of more than twelve hundred men and of one hundred and fifty women, besides a large number of children of nine years old and under. And there was a dreary uniformity in the method of their death. They were shot with pistols, then stripped, and dragged to the river, or thrown into the city moat.[3] But it is, after all, not the numbers of name-less victims whose honorable deaths leave no distinct impression upon the mind, but the individual instances of Christian hero-ism, teaching lessons of imitable human virtues, that speak most directly to the sympathies of the reader of an age so long posterior. The records of French Protestantism are full of these, and one or two of the most striking that occurred in Orleans deserve mention. M. de Coudray—whom the Roman Catholics had in vain endeavored on previous occasions to shake—seeing his house beset and no prospect of deliverance, himself opened the door of his dwelling to the murderers, tell-ing them, with wonderful assurance of faith : " You do but hasten the coming of that blessedness which I have long been expecting."[4] Whereupon they killed him, in the midst of his

---

[1] Mémoires de l'estat, *ubi supra*, 295.   " Le mesme fut fait à Paris et en d'autres lieux aussi," writes the same historian.
[2] Ibid., *ubi supra*.
[3] Ibid., 296.
[4] Mémoires de l'estat de France, *ubi supra*, 297.

invocation of his God. Another Huguenot, De St. Thomas, a schoolmaster, died uttering words as courageous as ever fell from lips of early Christian martyrs : " Why ! do you think that you move me by your blasphemies and acts of cruelty ? It is not within your power to deprive me of the assurance of the grace of my God. Strike as much as you please ; I fear not your blows." [1] Sometimes the dying men were allowed a few moments to utter a final prayer; but, if their zeal led them too far, their impatient murderers cut short their devotions with oaths and curses, and exclaimed : " Here are people that take a great while to pray to their God ! " [2] Of resistance there was little, so far were the Huguenots from having collected arms and prepared for such a conspiracy as was imputed to them. If a Huguenot teacher of fencing killed one or two of his assailants, or if a few gentlemen at different places kept them at bay awhile with stones or other missiles, this, so far from proving their evil intentions, on the contrary, furnishes undeniable proof of the very different results that might have ensued had their means of defence been equal to their courage. For fifteen days after the principal massacre the work went on more quietly, the dead bodies being still thrown into the ditch— where wolves, which in the sixteenth century abounded in the valley of the Loire, were permitted to feed upon them undisturbed—or into the river, of whose fish, fattened upon this human carrion, the people feared to eat. [3]

At Bourges the news of the massacre was received late on Tuesday. Meantime, some of the more sagacious of the Huguenots (among others, the celebrated Francis Hotman, at this time a professor of law in the University of Bourges), alarmed by the wounding of Admiral Coligny, had fled from the city. Even after the news came, the massacre was but partial. Although the mayor, Jean Joupitre, had received sealed orders (lettres de cachet) instructing him as to the part he was to take, the municipal officers, knowing the ill-will

Massacre at Bourges.

---

[1] Mém. de l'estat, 298, 299.

[2] Ibid., 299, 300.

[3] A horrible story is told of the discovery of some human relics several weeks later. Ibid., 305.

the Guises had always borne to the Huguenots, were in doubt
how far the king countenanced the bloody work.   But the
royal letter of the thirtieth of August, accompanying the declaration of the twenty-eighth, to which reference was made above,[1]
so far from putting an end to the disorder, only rendered it
more general.   Bourges became the scene of another of those
butcheries of Huguenots first gathered in the public prisons, of
which there are so many similar instances that it seems impossible to avoid the conclusion that the orders to effect them
emanated from a single source at court.[2]

We have already been admitted to the secret of the instructions sent by the Duke of Anjou, through Puigaillard, to M. de
Montsoreau, for the destruction of the Huguenots of
At Angers.Saumur and Angers.   Certainly there was on his
part no lack of readiness to fulfil his sanguinary commission;
but the local officers were less zealous, and many of the Protestants were merely thrown into prison.   Montsoreau's first exploit at Angers deserves particular mention.   M. de la Rivière,
the first reformed pastor of Paris, of whom I have spoken in a
previous chapter, was at this time residing in Angers, and
Montsoreau seems to have been acquainted with him.   Going
straight to his house, the governor met the pastor's wife, whom,
according to the gallant custom prevailing, especially among the
French courtiers, he first kissed, and then inquired for her
husband.   He was told that he was walking in his garden, and
thither his hostess led him.   After courteously embracing him,
Montsoreau thus abruptly disclosed the object of his visit:
" Monsieur de la Rivière, do you know why I am come ?   The
king has ordered me to kill you, and that at once.   I have a
special commission to this effect, as you will know from these
letters."   While saying this he exhibited a pistol which he
held in his hand.   "I know of no crime that I have done,"
calmly replied De la Rivière ; and then, after obtaining permission to offer a brief prayer to God, he fearlessly presented
his breast to the cowardly assassin.   Montsoreau did not complete the extermination of the Huguenots of Angers, and Pui-

---

[1] See *ante*, p. 502.   [2] Mém. de l'estat, 309–315.

gaillard soon after arrived to prosecute it; but the Protestant prisoners whom he was to have murdered knew his venal disposition, and found little difficulty in purchasing their liberation.[1]

The important city of Lyons, inhabited by a population intensely hostile to the Reformation, had for its governor M. de Mandelot, a decided partisan of the Roman Catholic faction.

Butchery at Lyons.

The municipal authorities, however, either surpassed him in zeal, or, as is more probable, were less apprehensive of the dangers to be incurred by assuming the responsibility of a massacre; for of all the "échevins," only two opposed the violent measures of their associates. The written protest which they insisted upon entering on the official records is still extant.[2] The first tidings of the wounding of Coligny by Maurevel reached Lyons on Wednesday morning, the twenty-seventh of August, in a letter from Charles the Ninth to Governor Mandelot, similar in tenor to those which were despatched to every other part of France.[3] Although the king spoke only of displeasure at the outrage, and of his determination to avenge it, the populace interpreted the event according to their wishes, and instantly circulated reports of the murder of the admiral and all his adherents. The Roman Catholics, long discontented with the toleration extended to those who dissented from the creed of the dominant church, were jubilant and menacing; the Protestants were disheartened, but exhibited a self-control only to be accounted for by the long years of oppression which had wellnigh broken their spirit. The next

---

[1] Mém. de l'estat, *ubi supra*, 349–351. "Puigaillard . . . . homme au reste indigne de vivre pour l'acte détestable par luy commis en la personne de sa première femme tuée à sa sollicitation pour en espouser une autre qu'il entretenoit." (P. 351.)

[2] Registres consulaires, *apud* "La Saint-Barthélemy à Lyon et le gouverneur Mandelot," by M. Puyroche, p. 311. This monograph which I quote from the Bulletin de la Soc. de l'hist. du prot. français, in which it first appeared (vol. xviii., 1869, pp. 305–323, 353–367, and 401–420), is by far the most accurate and complete treatise on this subject, and contains a fund of fresh information based upon unpublished manuscripts, especially the local records.

[3] Charles IX. to Mandelot, Aug. 22, 1572, Correspondance du roi Charles IX. et du sieur de Mandelot, published by P. Paris, 1830 (pp. 36, 37). A portion of this letter has already been given.

day came the news of the events of Sunday, and, in the afternoon, letters from Masso and Rubys, prominent citizens of
Lyons then at Paris, who said that they had been instructed by
the king to order the authorities to copy the example of the
capital. The fanatical party was now clamorous ; but Mandelot,
cautious and politic, would act on no such instructions, although
he had taken the precaution of closing the gates, and of commanding the Protestants, on pain of imprisonment, to remain in their
houses. Friday morning came, and with it the arrival of Sieur
du Peyrat from court, bearing the royal letter written on the
day of the massacre, in which it was represented as the exclusive
work of the Guises, and the king strenuously enjoined the
maintenance of the Edict of Pacification.[1] These were the *public*
instructions sent to Mandelot; but they were not all. There is
a suspicious little postscript to the letter: " Monsieur de Mandelot, you will give credit to the bearer respecting the matter
which I have charged him to tell you." [2] What these verbal
orders were which the king, not venturing to commit to paper,
commissioned Du Peyrat to communicate, the reply of the
governor himself distinctly reveals ; it was the arrest of the
Protestants and the confiscation of their property.[3] Still more
perplexed as to what course to pursue, Mandelot held a long
private conference with the messenger, while the échevins impatiently awaited its conclusion. The governor now called in
the municipal officers for consultation, and with them agreed to
order the immediate imprisonment of the Huguenots. He was
not, however, even yet fully convinced of the propriety of this
step, for scarcely had he given the order when he recalled it.[4]
Fearing that the troops at his disposal might prove insufficient,

---

[1] Charles IX. to Mandelot, Aug. 24, 1572, Correspondance, etc., 39–42.

[2] " Monsieur de Mandelot, vous croirez le présent porteur de ce que je luy
ay donné charge de vous dire." Ibid., 42.

[3] " Suivant icelles (the king's letters of Aug. 22d and 24th) et *ce que le sieur du
Perat m'auroit dict de sa part,* je n'auroit failly pourveoir par toutz moyens à
la seureté de ceste ville : *sy bien, Sire, que et les cors* (corps) *et les biens de
ceulx de la relligion auroient esté saisiz et mis soubz votre main* sans aucun tu-
multe ny scandale." Mandelot to Charles IX., Sept. 2, 1572, Correspondance,
etc., 45.

[4] Puyroche, 319.

and dreading with good reason lest the employment of the city militia for this purpose might lead to scenes of disorder which he would find himself powerless to control, he preferred to send for such reinforcements as the neighboring noblemen of the province could furnish.[1] Meantime, the commotion throughout Lyons had rapidly increased. On Thursday and Friday nights many members of the Reformed Church had been dragged from their houses as if to prison, but most of them had been barbarously despatched by the way. Among others, one of the ministers, Monsieur Jacques l'Anglois, was stabbed and thrown into the river. On Saturday morning Mandelot, seeing the confusion hourly increasing, deemed it impolitic to wait any longer for the troops he was expecting, and resolved upon effecting his purpose by ruse. He therefore published a proclamation by sound of trumpet, bidding all the Huguenots to assemble at his house to hear the good pleasure of the king. The Huguenots, deceived by the professions of his Majesty, came in great numbers ; but no sooner had they all arrived, than they were seized by the soldiers and hurried away to prison. The common prison, " La Roanne," being too contracted to contain so large a multitude, three hundred or more were placed in that of the Archbishop's palace, and others in the cloisters of the Celestine Monks and the Gray Friars. At the same time an inventory was being made of all the goods belonging to Protestants throughout the city.

These measures, instead of allaying, only inflamed the passions of the populace the more. That night the murders surpassed those of the previous nights in number and atrocity, and when Sunday morning dawned the people were ready for still greater excesses. At about eight o'clock they entered unopposed the Gray Friars, and butchered every Huguenot they found. Two hours later, assuming the forms of law, a self-constituted commission, headed by André Mornieu, one of the échevins or aldermen, presenting themselves successively at the archiepiscopal prison and at the Roanne, summoned the inmates to abjure their faith and go to mass. Only thirty persons in the one, and

---

[1] " Il n'etait pas d'avis," dit-il, " que tout le peuple s'en mélat, craignant quelque désordre, mêmement un sac." Puyroche, 320.

about twenty in the other, consented. These were sent to the Celestine monastery and afterward released. Of the others a careful list was drawn up. Their fate was sealed; but an unexpected difficulty arose. The public hangman refused to execute the sentence of an unauthorized tribunal. So did the soldiers. At last assassins were obtained from the ranks of the turbulent inhabitants. About three o'clock that afternoon the archbishop's prison was visited. To describe with minuteness the scene of horror that ensued would scarcely be possible. Two hundred and sixty-three persons,[1] of the very best and most industrious part of the population of Lyons,[2] called by name according to the roll previously made, were murdered in rapid succession. Never was there an exhibition of more pitiless cruelty. Meanwhile, where was the governor? He had gone, in company with the commandant of the citadel, to suppress a threatened disturbance in the Faubourg de la Guillotière, on the left bank of the Rhône. He returned only in time to find the deed done, and to disperse those who had gone to the Roanne to repeat it there. His demonstrations of anger were loud, and a liberal reward was offered for the detection of any that had participated in the slaughter.[3] But this did not prevent the same body of cutthroats from visiting the Roanne, soon after nightfall, and despatching all the Protestants that were there, to the number of about seventy. Many of them, by an excess of barbarity, the assassins tied together by a single rope, and threw, while yet alive, into the water. On the follow-

---

[1] "Quelques deux cens," says Mandelot to Charles IX., Sept. 2d; but he was anxious to make the number as small as possible. Jean de Masso, "receveur général" (Sept. 1st), says, "sept à huit vingt," and sieur Talaize (Sept. 2d), "deux cent soixante et trois." So also Coste (Sept. 3d). Puyroche, 365, 366.

[2] Mandelot tells Charles IX. (Sept. 17th) that he had sent all the *poorer* Huguenots to other prisons; that he had left here only the rich and those who had borne arms for the Protestant cause. To exhibit his own incorruptibility, he added that there were among them, of his own certain knowledge, at least twenty who would have paid a ransom of thirty thousand or even forty thousand crowns, "qui estoit assez," he significantly adds, "pour tenter ung homme corruptible." Correspondance du roi Charles IX. et du Sieur de Mandelot, 71, 72.

[3] Correspondance, etc., p. 46, 47.

ing day the bodies which had not yet found a watery grave
were carried to the other side of the Saône, where, stripped and
mangled, they were about to be buried in the cemetery of the
Abbaye d'Esnay, when the monks refused them admission into
the consecrated ground, and pointed to the Rhône as a more
fitting destination. Even now they were not spared further
mutilation; for an apothecary of Lyons, having initiated the
murderers into the valuable properties of human fat as a medi-
cinal substance, the miserable remains were put to new use before being consigned to the river. Down to the Mediterranean
these ghastly witnesses of the ferocity of the passions of the
Lyonnese Roman Catholics carried fear and disgust, and for
weeks the inhabitants of Arles and other places carefully abstained from drinking the water of the polluted stream.[1]

The part which Mandelot took in this awful tragedy has been
very differently estimated, but I am inclined to think that the
Responsibility governor is not chargeable with any direct responsi-
of Mandelot. bility for the butchery in the prisons of Lyons. Certainly this seems to be established by his letter to the king,
written in the morning of the day on which it occurred; for he
would scarcely have expressed his great desire and hope to be

---

[1] Puyroche, La Saint-Barthélemy à Lyon et le gouverneur Mandelot, *ubi
supra;* Mém. de l'estat, *ubi supra*, 321–343; Crespin, Hist. des martyrs, 1582,
p. 725, etc., *apud* Époques de l'église de Lyon (Lyon, 1827), 173–185; De
Thou, iv. (liv. lii.) 602–604, etc.; Jean de Serres (1575), iv., fol. 45, etc. The
number of Huguenots killed is variously estimated, by some as high as from
twelve hundred to fifteen hundred (Crespin, *ubi supra*). It must have been
not less than seven hundred or eight hundred; for private letters written
immediately after the occurrence by prominent and well-informed Roman
Catholics state it at about seven hundred, and they would certainly not be
inclined to exaggerate. The rumor at Paris even then set it at twelve hundred. See the letters in Puyroche, 365–367. Among the one hundred and
twenty-three names that have been preserved, the most interesting is that of
Claude Goudimel, who set Marot's and Beza's psalms to music, and who was
killed by envious rivals. At the time of his death he was engaged in adapt-
ing the psalms to a more elaborate arrangement, according to a contemporary
writer: "Excellent musicien, et la mémoire duquel sera perpétuelle pour
avoir heureusement besogné les psaumes de David en français, la plupart des-
quels il a mis en musique en forme de motets à quatre, cinq, six et huit parties, et sans la mort eût tôt après rendu cette œuvre accomplie." Sommaire
et vrai discours de la Félonie, etc. Puyroche, 402.

able to prevent any outbreak, if he had planned, or even foreseen, the events of the evening.[1]   The story must therefore be
apocryphal, that Mandelot, in commissioning one of the chief
assassins to execute the bloody work, blasphemously said : " I
intrust the whole to you, and, as Jesus Christ said to Saint
Peter, whatsoever thou shalt bind on earth shall be bound in
heaven ; and whatsoever thou shalt loose on earth shall be
loosed in heaven." [2]   It was, however, no conscientious scruple
that deterred the governor from actively taking part.   Mandelot was scandalously anxious to obtain his part of the plunder,
and was not ashamed to appear as a suppliant for the confiscated property of the Huguenots almost before their bodies
were cold.[3]   But he was unwilling, without the express orders
of his sovereign, written with his own hand, to commit an act
which, the more successful it might be, was the more certain
to be disavowed and punished.   He was right : a subordinate
could not be too careful in dealing with so treacherous a court.

Few cities were so ripe for the massacre of the Protestants as
the capital of Normandy.   There the passions of the Roman

---

[1] " Faisant cependant contenir ce peuple par toutes les remontrances et
raisons que je puis leur persuader de ne s'émouvoir à aucune sédition ni tu-
multe, comme je m'aperçois qu'il y en peut avoir quelque danger auquel toutes
fois j'espère prévenir." Mandelot to Charles IX., Aug. 31, 1572, Puyroche, 356.
This letter is not contained in Paulin Paris, Correspondance de Charles IX.
et du sieur de Mandelot.

[2] Mém. de l'estat, 330 ; De Thou, iv. (liv. lii.) 603.

[3] " Je ne veulx estre le premier à en demander à votre Majesté ; m'asseu-
rant que si elle a commencé par quelques autres, elle me faict tant d'honneur
de ne m'oblier (oublier)." Mandelot to Charles IX., September 2, 1572, Correspondance, p. 49.   I find the clearest evidence both of Mandelot's having
had no hand in the massacres of August 31st, and of his utter want of principle, in the craven apology he makes, in his letter of September 17th, for not
having done more, on the ground that he only knew his Majesty's pleasure as
it were in a shadow, and very late, and that he had rather feared the king
would be angry at what the people had done, than that so little had been
done !   " La pouvant asseurer sur ma vie que si elle n'a esté satisfaitte en ce
faict icy, je n'en ay aucune coulpe, n'ayant sceu quelle estoit sa volunté que
par umbre, encores bien tard et à demy ; et ay craint, Sire, que votre Majesté
fust plustost courroucée de ce que le peuple auroit faict, que de trop peu,
d'aultant que par toutes les autres provinces circonvoysines il ne s'est rien
touché." Correspondance, etc., 72, 73.

Catholics, inflamed by the civil wars, had not been suffered to
cool. Even in the provincial parliament the papists
could hardly submit to receive into their deliberations again the five or six Huguenot counsellors who had been
expelled or had fled at the outbreak of hostilities, but whom the
Edict of Pacification restored to their ancient functions and dignity; and the secret registers, among other unfortunate scenes,
chronicle particularly a violent discussion, degenerating into
angry altercation between President Vialard and the Huguenot
member Maynet.[1] The bloody assault of the populace of Rouen
upon the reformed in March, 1571, mentioned in a previous
page,[2] had been but slightly punished. Few of the guilty failed
to escape from the city, and the sole penalty suffered had been
an execution in effigy. These turbulent men had ever since
that time been watching an opportunity to return. They were
now burning with a desire to signalize their advent by bloody
reprisals. Monsieur de Carouge, governor of the city, was,
however, a just and upright man,[3] and they could not hope for
countenance in their plans from him. In fact, the contemporary accounts inform us that he received from the king repeated
orders to exterminate the Huguenots of Rouen,[4] which he could
not bring himself to execute, and that he sent messengers to remonstrate with his Majesty who returned without succeeding in
shaking his determination; and hereupon the governor found
himself obliged to shut himself up in the castle, and permit the
work which had been intrusted to others also, to take its course.[5]
The secret records of parliament, however, reveal the fact that
Carouge received from Paris the order to leave Rouen and
visit other portions of Normandy, in order to restore the quiet
and peace which had been much disturbed of late. The real,

The massacre at Rouen.

---

[1] It is given word for word, from the MS. registers of the parliament, by
Floquet, Hist. du parlement de Normandie, iii. 81–85.

[2] *Ante*, chapter xvii., p. 374.

[3] "Encor qu'il se soit tousjours monstré fort peu amy de telles inhuma-
nitez." Mémoires de l'estat, 371.

[4] "Receut lettres du Roy qui luy mandoit et commandoit expressément
d'exterminer tous ceux qui faisoyent profession de la religion audit lieu, sans
en excepter aucun." Mém. de l'estat, Arch. cur., vii. 370.

[5] Ibid., 371.

though perhaps not the ostensible object of this commission was to rid the city of the presence of a magistrate whose well known integrity might render it futile to attempt a massacre of the innocent. The records also show that, contrary to the current report, both the municipal authorities and the parliament, greatly alarmed at the danger menacing Rouen in case of his departure, implored him to remain;[1] but that the king's peremptory commands left him no discretion, and he was obliged to leave the unhappy city to its fate. The able historian of the Norman Parliament has rightly observed that the governor, whether he left Rouen because he could not consent to execute the barbarous injunctions that were sent him, or because his character was so well known that the court was unwilling to intrust them to him, is equally deserving of praise; and not without reason does this writer claim similar respect for the judicial body which manifested its desire to save everything, by retaining him at Rouen.[2] Here, as elsewhere, a great part of the Protestants had been arrested and placed in the prisons, to shield them from popular violence. The governor believed this to be the safest place for them; and at least one instance is known of a father who was so convinced of it that he brought thither his Huguenot son, whom he might have sent out of the city.[3]

The storm, so long delayed, broke out at last on Wednesday, the seventeenth of September, and lasted four entire days. The gates were closed, and the organized bands of murderers, under the leadership of Laurent de Maromme, one of the most sanguinary of the turbulent men who had returned from banishment, and of a priest, Claude Montereul, curate of the church of St. Pierre, had undisputed possession of the city. First they slaughtered like sheep the prisoners in the spacious "conciergerie" of the parliament house and in the other prisons of the city. Next they burst into the houses, and nearly every atrocity

---

[1] "Il n'y a aultre que vous," said they, "qui puisse commander aux armes céans, contenir le peuple en l'obéissance au roy, et la ville en paix." Reg. secr. du parlement, 9 Septembre, 1572, *apud* Floquet, 120. See also Reg. de l'hôtel-de-ville de Rouen, 7 Septembre, *ibid.*

[2] Floquet, 122.

[3] Mém. de l'estat, *apud* Archives curieuses, vii. 373.

which history is compelled at any time reluctantly to chronicle, was perpetrated on unresisting men, on tender women, on unoffending children. Not less than five hundred persons, and perhaps even more, perished in a butchery, whose details I gladly pass over in silence.[1] Grim humor and charity were incongruously mingled with the most brutal inhumanity. The assassins jocularly denominated their work one of "accommodating" their victims;[2] and the clothes of the Protestants—whose bodies were buried in great ditches outside of the Porte Cauchoise—after having been carefully washed, were piously distributed among the poor.[3] The tragedy finished, the farce of an investigation was instituted by the officers of justice, but no punishment was ever inflicted upon any Roman Catholic, other than that which could be recognized in the retributive judgments befalling a few of the most notable, and especially the cruel Maromme, at the hand of God.[4]

The previous character of Toulouse, as among the most sanguinary cities of France, was already sufficiently well established.

At Toulouse. If behind some of the rest on this occasion in the number of victims, Toulouse was inferior only because its previous massacres had rendered it a suspicious place of sojourn in the eyes of the Huguenots. Here, too, notwithstanding deceitful proclamations guaranteeing safety and protection, the Protestants were gathered into the public prisons and jails attached to monasteries; and after having been reserved for several weeks, on receipt of orders from Paris were butchered

---

[1] Mémoires de l'estat, *apud* Arch. curieuses, vii. 372; Floquet, iii. 127. Floquet is incorrect in stating that the names of only about a hundred are known. We have (Mém. de l'estat, Archives curieuses, vii. 372–378) a partial list of 186 men, whose names and trades are generally given, and of 33 women —that is 219, besides a reference to many others whose names the writer did not obtain.

[2] "Les autres estoyent *accommodez* à coups de dague. Les massacreurs usoyent de ce mot *accommoder*, l'accommodans à leur bestiale et diabolique cruauté." Mém. de l'estat, *ubi sup.*, 372.

[3] Mém. de l'estat, *ubi sup.*, 378.

[4] Ibid., 379. The story of the massacre is well told in the Mém. de l'estat, and by M. Floquet, whose original sources of information throw a flood of light upon the transactions; also by De Thou, iv. (liv. lii.) 606; Agrippa d'Aubigné, ii. 27; Jean de Serres (1575), iv., fol. 50.

to the number of two or three hundred. Among others, some Protestant members of parliament were hung in their long red gowns to the branches of a great elm growing in the court of the parliament house.[1] The miscreants that voluntarily assumed the functions of executioners were in this case drawn in great part from the more unruly class of the law students of the university.[2] It is needless to add that here, as elsewhere, the opportunity for plunder was by no means neglected.

The procedure in Bordeaux was so extraordinary, and is so authentically related in a letter of a prominent judicial officer who was present, as well as in the records of the Parliament of Guyenne, that the story of its massacre must be added to the notices already given. At first the city was quiet, and the friends of order congratulated themselves that their efforts had been successful in removing the stigma which previous transactions had affixed to its escutcheon. Meantime this policy, united to the fear of a fate similar to that which had befallen their fellow-believers elsewhere, is said to have led to a great number of conversions to the Roman Catholic Church.[3] But there were those who were unwilling that their prey should so easily escape them. On the fifth of September, M. de Montferrand, Governor of Bordeaux, affecting to have information of a general plot on the part of the Huguenots of the city, had sought and obtained permission of the parliament to introduce three hundred soldiers from abroad. He had thereupon forbidden the celebration of Protestant worship, hitherto held at a distance of three leagues from Bordeaux, on the plain between

At Bordeaux.

---

[1] One of them, Jean Coras, had committed an unpardonable offence. When passing in 1562 with the Protestant army through Roquemadour, in the province of Quercy, he had taken advantage of the opportunity to examine the relics of St. Amadour, of whom the monks boasted that they possessed not only the bones, but also some of the flesh. He was never forgiven for having exhibited the close resemblance of the holy remains to a shoulder of mutton. De Thou, iv. 606, note.

[2] Mém. de l'estat, Archives curieuses, vii. 381–385 ; De Thou, *ubi supra ;* Agrippa d'Aubigné, ii. 27, 28 (liv. i., c. 5); Jean de Serres (1575), iv., fol. 50.

[3] President Lagebaston even says that, had this been suffered to go on a week longer—so rapidly were the Protestants flocking to the mass—there would not have been eight Huguenots in town.

the Garonne and the Jalle.[1] Meantime the churches resounded
with the violent denunciations of a famous preacher, Friar Ed-
mond Auger or Augier, "a great scourge for heresy," as his
partisans styled him. He exhorted his hearers to imitate the
example of Paris, and accused the royal officers of indolence and
pusillanimity. At this juncture the governor received a visit
from Monsieur de Montpézat, son-in-law of Villars, the newly
appointed admiral. What the latter told him is unknown. But,
on the third of October, Montferrand having given out that he
had received from the king a roll of names of forty of the chief
men of the place, whom he was commissioned to put to death
without judge or trial, set about his bloody work. Persistently
refusing to exhibit his warrant, for three days the governor
butchered the citizens at will.[2] One member of parliament,
against whom he bore a personal grudge, he stabbed with his
own hand. The murderers wore red bonnets supplied by one
of the "jurats" or aldermen of the city. They executed their
commission so thoroughly that the number of the slain was
reported as two hundred and sixty-four persons, all Protestants.
If any one be mercifully inclined to regard this statement as an
exaggeration, and to base upon this instance a general theory
that throughout France the number of the victims has been
grossly over-estimated, let him read the following entry made
in the records of the Parliament of Bordeaux, and recently
brought to light; he will learn from this not only the approxi-
mate number of the slain as given by the chief agent in the

---

[1] Registers of Parliament, in Boscheron des Portes, Hist. du parl. de Bordeaux (Bordeaux, 1877), i. 241.

[2] Letter of President Lagebaston to Charles IX., October 7, 1572, Mackintosh, Hist. of England, iii., App. E, 351–353. See also De Thou, iv. 651, 652,
and Agrippa d'Aubigné, ii. 27. Lagebaston was "first president" of the
Bordalese parliament, but, so far from being able to prevent the massacre,
received information that his own name was on Montferrand's list, and fled
to the castle of Ha, whence he wrote to the king. His remonstrances against
a butchery based upon a pretended order which was not exhibited, his delineation of the impolitic and disgraceful work, and his reasons why an execution, that might have been necessary to crush a secret conspiracy at Paris,
was altogether unnecessary in a city "six or seven score leagues distant,"
where there could be no thought of a conspiracy, render his letter very interesting.

bloody work, but the anxiety which the latter felt that he should receive due credit for his share in the great undertaking of the destruction of the French Protestants: "On the ninth of October, the Sieur de Montferrand, having been summoned to the court, among other things said, 'that he had been informed that there were some members of the court who had written to the Sieur Admiral de Villars, royal lieutenant in Guyenne, that the said De Montferrand had killed, on the day of the execution by him made, October the third, only ten or twelve men, a thing (under correction of the court) wholly false, inasmuch as there had been more than two hundred and fifty slain ; and he would show the list to any one who might desire to see it.'" [1]

The same hand that placed upon the parliamentary registers this shameless and atrocious boast, for the benefit of those that should come after, has briefly noted the assassination of two members of parliament itself, with an absence of comment in which we can read the evidence of fear. "From the talk of to-day it appears that Messieurs Jean de Guilloche and Pierre de Sevyn were killed as belonging to the new religion." [2] The tardy and flagrantly unnecessary effusion of blood at Bordeaux exercised no mean influence in emboldening the Huguenots of La Rochelle to persevere in their refusal to admit the emissaries of Charles the Ninth.

The massacre was, however, neither universal throughout France, nor equally destructive in all places where it occurred.

Why the massacre was not universal. The reason for this is to be found partly in the geographical distribution of the Huguenots, partly in the temper of the people, partly in the policy or the humanity of the governors of cities and provinces. Where the number of Protestants was small, and especially where they had never rendered themselves formidable, it was not easy for the clergy to excite the people to that frenzy of sectarian hatred under the influence of which they were willing to imbrue their hands in the blood of peaceable neighbors. In such places —in Provins, for instance—the Huguenots generally kept themselves as far as possible out of sight, while a few of the more

---

[1] Registres du Parlement, Boscheron des Portes, i. 246, 247.
[2] Boscheron des Portes, *ubi supra*.

timid consented to place a white cross on their hats, a convenient badge of Roman Catholicism which some were willing to
assume, when they would rather have died than go to mass.[1]

In the province of Champagne the Protestants were spared
any general massacre by the prudent foresight of the Guises, to
whom its government was confided. The duke, in order to
Policy of the free himself from the imputation of being the author
Guises. of the bloody plot, and to prove that his private resentment did not extend beyond Admiral Coligny and a few
other chiefs, had himself taken several Huguenots in Paris
under his special protection. With the same object in view, he
made his province an exception to the widespread slaughter.[2]

Others, however, were merciful from more honorable motives.
A number of instances of clemency are mentioned. It is not, in-
deed, always safe to accept the stories, some of which
Spurious
accounts of are suspicious from their very form, while others are
clemency. manifest inventions of an age when tolerance had
become more popular than persecution. To the category of
fable we are compelled to assign the famous response which
Le Hennuyer, Bishop of Lisieux, is reported, by au-
Bishop Le
Hennuyer, of thors writing long after the event, as having returned
Lisieux. to the lieutenant sent to him by Charles the Ninth.
History is occasionally capricious, but she has rarely indulged
in a more remarkable freak than when putting into the mouth
of an advocate of persecution, a courtier and the almoner of the
king, who was not even in his diocese, but undoubtedly in Paris
itself, at the time the incident is said to have occurred, this
declamatory speech: " No, no, sir; I oppose, and shall always
oppose, the execution of such an order. I am the shepherd of
the church of Lisieux, and the people I am commanded to
slaughter are my flock. Although at present wanderers, having
strayed from the fold intrusted to me by Jesus Christ the great
shepherd, they may, nevertheless, return. I do not read in the
Gospel that the shepherd should suffer the blood of his sheep

---

[1] Claude Haton waxes facetious when describing the sudden popularity
acquired by the sign of the cross, and the numbers of rosaries that could be
seen in the hands, or tied to the belt, of fugitive Huguenot ladies.

[2] Tocsain contre les massacreurs, 156. See *ante*, chapter xviii., p. 491.

to be shed; on the contrary, I find there that he is bound to pour out his own blood and give his own life for them. Take the order back, for it shall never be executed so long as I live." [1]

Fortunately, there are other instances on record which are not apocryphal. Monsieur de Matignon seems to have saved

Kind offices of Matignon at Caen and Alençon; Caen and Alençon from becoming the scenes of general massacres, and thus to have endeared himself to the Protestants of both places. [2] The Duke of Longueville prevented the massacre from extending to his province

of Longueville and Gordes; of Picardy. [3] Gordes, Governor of Dauphiny, who had obtained advancement by the assistance of the Montmorency influence, excused himself, when repeatedly urged to kill the Huguenots, on the plea that Montbrun and others of their leaders were alive and out of his reach, and that any attempt of the kind would only lead to still greater difficulties. He therefore waited for more direct instructions. When, in his letter of the fifth of September, in reference to a clause in the king's letter just come to hand, he stated that he had received no verbal orders, but merely his letters of the twenty-second, twenty-fourth, and twenty-eighth of August, Charles replied bidding him give himself no solicitude as to them, as they were addressed only to a few persons who hap-

---

[1] De Félice, Hist. of the Protestants of France (New York, 1859), 214, and Henry White, 455, from Maimbourg, Histoire du Calvinisme, 486. I refer the reader to Mr. L. D. Paumier's exhaustive discussion of the story in his paper, " La Saint-Barthélemy en Normandie," Bulletin de la Soc. de l'hist. du prot. français, vi. (1858), 466-470. Mr. Paumier has also completely demolished the scanty foundation on which rested the similar story told of Sigognes, Governor of Dieppe, pp. 470-474. See also M. C. Osmont de Courtisigny's monograph, " Jean Le Hennuyer et les Huguenots de Lisieux en 1572," in the Bulletin, xxvi. (1877) 145, etc.

[2] Tocsain contre les massacreurs, 156 ; Odolant Desnos, Mémoires historiques sur la ville d'Alençon, ii. 285, apud Bulletin de la Soc. de l'hist. du prot. français, viii. (1859), 68. The truth of the story as to Alençon seems to be proved by the circumstance that when, in February, 1575, Matignon marched against Alençon, in order to suppress the conspiracy which the duke, Charles's youngest brother, had entered into to prevent Henry of Anjou from succeeding peaceably to the throne of France, the grateful Protestants at once opened their gates to him. Ibid., 305, Bulletin, ubi supra.

[3] Tocsain, 156.

pened to be near him,[1] and enjoined upon him to enforce the royal " declaration," and cause all murder and rapine to cease in his government. Yet even here a number of Huguenots were imprisoned, and a few lost their lives at Romans.[2]

The manly boldness of the Comte de Tende is said in like manner to have saved the Protestants of Provence. Receiving *of Tende in* from the hands of La Mole, a gentleman of Arles and *Provence.* servant of the Duke of Alençon, a letter from the secret council ordering him to massacre all the Huguenots in his province, the governor replied : " I do not believe that such commands have emanated from the king's free will ; but some of the members of his council have usurped the royal authority in order to satisfy their own passions. I need no more conclusive testimony than the letters which his Majesty sent me a few days ago, by which he threw upon the Guises the blame for this massacre of Paris. I prefer to obey these first letters, as more befitting the royal dignity. Besides, this last order is so cruel and barbarous, that even were the king himself in person to command me to put it into execution, I would not do it." The magnanimity of the count spared Provence the horrors of a repetition of the massacres of Mérindol and Cabrières, but perhaps cost him his own life, for he soon after died at Avignon, and rumor ascribed his death to poison. The infamous Count de Retz, Catharine's favorite, succeeded him as governor.[3] Saint Héran, Governor of Auvergne, is said to have replied in very similar words ; but as he managed to induce a great part of the Protestants within his jurisdiction to apostatize, less notice was taken of his insubordination.[4]

---

[1] " Par lesquelles vous me mandez n'avoir receu aucun commandement verbal de moy, ains seulement mes lettres du 22, 24 et 28 du passé, dont ne vous mettrez en aucune peine, car elles s'adressoyent seulement à quelques-uns qui s'estoyent trouvez près de moy." Charles IX. to Gordes, Sept. 14, 1572, Archives curieuses, vii. 365, 366.

[2] Ibid., 367, 368.

[3] Mémoires de l'estat, Archives curieuses, vii. 366, 367 ; De Thou, iv. 605. The Tocsain contre les massacreurs, however, p. 156, gives credit instead to M. de Carces.

[4] Dr. White has shown some reasons for doubting the accuracy of the story. Among the Dulaure MSS. is preserved a full account of the manner in which a Protestant, fleeing from Paris, fell in with the messenger who was carrying

Perhaps the most striking instance of a magnanimous refusal to comply with the bloody mandate of the Parisian court, was that of Viscount D'Orthez,[1] Governor of Bayonne.

Viscount D'Orthez at Bayonne. This nobleman was not only of a violent and imperious temper, but on other occasions so severe in his treatment of the Protestants of the border city, that the king was obliged to write to him to moderate his rigor. When, however, the messenger from Paris (who on his way had caused an indiscriminate slaughter to be made of all the men, women and children who had taken refuge in the prisons of Dax) delivered his orders to the viscount, the latter returned the following laconic answer:

"Sire, I have communicated your Majesty's commands to your faithful inhabitants and warriors in the garrison. I have found among them only good citizens and brave soldiers, but not one hangman. For this reason they and I very humbly beg your Majesty to employ our arms and our lives in all things possible, however hazardous they may be, as we are, so long as our lives shall last, your very humble, etc."[2]

the order to St. Hérem or Héran, and robbed him of his instructions. The Protestant hastened on to warn his brethren of their danger, while the messenger could only relate to the governor the contents of the lost despatch. Notwithstanding this, eighty Huguenots were murdered in one city (Aurillac) of this province. Massacre of St. Bartholomew, 454, 455.

[1] Adiram d'Aspremont.

[2] Agrippa d'Aubigné, Hist. univ., ii. 28 (liv. i., c. 5). The authenticity of this letter has been much disputed, partly because of the Viscount's severe and cruel character (which, however, D'Aubigné himself notices when he tells the story), partly because it rests on the sole authority of D'Aubigné. It is to be observed, however, that although he alone relates it, he alludes to it in several of his works, as e. g., in his Tragiques. But the truth of the incident is apparently placed beyond all legitimate doubt by its intimate and necessary connection with an event which D'Aubigné narrates considerably later in his history, and from personal knowledge. Hist. univ., ii. 291, 292 (liv. iii., c. 13). In 1577, D'Aubigné, having lost much of Henry of Navarre's favor through his fidelity or his bluntness (see Mém. de d'Aubigné, éd. Panth., p. 486), retired from Nérac to the neighboring town of Castel-jaloux, of which he was in command. Making a foray at the head of a small detachment of Huguenot soldiers, he fell in with and easily routed a Roman Catholic troop, consisting of a score of light horsemen belonging to Viscount D'Orthez, and a number of men raised at Bayonne and Dax, who were conducting three young ladies condemned at Bordeaux to be beheaded. The vanquished Roman Catholics

Nor were the municipal authorities in some places behind the royal governors in their determination to have no part in the nefarious designs of the court. At Nantes, the mayor, échevins, and judges received from Paris, on the eighth of September, a letter of the Duke of Montpensier-Bourbon, Governor of Brittany, in which, after narrating the discovery of the pretended conspiracy of Coligny and his adherents, and their consequent assassination, he added: "By this his Majesty's intention respecting the treatment which the Huguenots are to receive in the other cities is sufficiently evident, as well as the means by which some assured rest may be expected in our poor Catholic Church." [1] But the municipal and judicial officers of Nantes, instead of following the bloody path thus marked out for them by the governor of their province, "held a meeting in the town hall, and swore to main-

The munici-
pality of
Nantes.

---

threw themselves on the ground and sued for mercy. On hearing who they were, D'Aubigné called to him all those who came from Bayonne and then cried out to his followers to treat the rest in memory of the massacre in the prisons of Dax. The Huguenots needed no further reminder. It was not long before they had cut to pieces the twenty-two men from Dax who had fallen into their hands. On the other hand they restored to the soldiers of Bayonne their horses and arms, and, after dressing their wounds in a neighboring village, sent them home to tell their governor, Viscount D'Orthez, "that they had seen the different treatment the Huguenots accorded to *soldiers* and to *hangmen*." A week later, a herald from Bayonne arrived at Castel-jaloux, with worked scarfs and handkerchiefs for the entire Huguenot band. Nor did the exchange of courtesies end here. The mad notion seized Henry of Navarre to accept an invitation to a feast extended to him by the Bayonnese. Six Huguenots accompanied him, of whom D'Aubigné was one. The table was sumptuous, the presents were rare and costly. D'Aubigné being recognized, was overwhelmed with thanks, "his courtesy being much more liberally repaid than he had deserved;" while the King of Navarre and his Huguenots, at the table, "at the expense of the rest of France, extolled to heaven the rare and unexampled act and glory of the men of Bayonne." It is certainly an easier supposition that D'Aubigné has faithfully reproduced D'Orthez's letter to Charles IX., than that he has manufactured so long and consistent a story. The discussion in the Bulletin de la Soc. de l'histoire du prot. franç. is full, xi. 13–15, 116, etc., xii. 240.

[1] Letter of Louis de Bourbon, Duke of Montpensier, Aug. 26th (it should evidently be the 25th; for the Duke speaks of Coligny as killed "ledit jour d'hier," and the mythical Huguenot plot was to have been executed "hier ou aujourd'hui"). Bulletin de la Soc. de l'hist. du prot. fr., i. (1852) 60, and Soldan, Geschichte des Prot. in Frankreich, ii., App., 599.

tain their previous oath not to violate the Edict of Pacification published in favor of the Calvinists, and forbade the inhabitants from indulging in any excess against them." [1]

Such are the general outlines and a few details of a massacre the full horrors of which it is outside of the province and beyond the ability of history to relate. Nor is it even possible to set down figures that may be relied upon as expressing the true number of those who were unjustly put to death. The difficulty experienced by a well informed contemporary, has not been removed; notwithstanding the careful investigations of those who earnestly desired "that posterity might not be deprived of what it needed to know, in order that it might become wiser at the expense of others." [2] We shall be safe in supposing that the number of Huguenot victims throughout France was somewhere between twenty thousand, as conjectured by De Thou and La Popelinière, and thirty thousand, as stated by Jean de Serres and the Mémoires de l'estat de France, rather than in adopting the extreme views of Sully and Perefixe, the latter of whom swells the count of the slain to one hundred thousand men, women, and children. [3] It can scarcely have been much less than the lower number I have suggested.

While the massacre begun on St. Bartholomew's Day was spreading with the speed of some foul contagion to the most distant parts of France, the tidings had been carried beyond its boundaries, and excited a thrill of delight, or a cry of execration, according to the character and sympathies of those to whom they came. Nowhere was the surprise greater, nor the joy more intense, than at Rome. Pope Gregory, like his predecessor, had been very sceptical respecting the pious intentions of the French court. Nuncios and legates brought them, it is true, a great profusion of brilliant assurances, on the part of Catharine and Charles, of devotion to the Roman

Uncertain number of the victims.

News of the massacre received at Rome.

---

[1] The words are those of an inscription of the seventeenth or the early part of the eighteenth century, in the Hôtel de Ville of Nantes. Bulletin, i. (1852) 61.

[2] Mém. de l'estat, Archives cur., vii. 385, 386.

[3] See a table in White, Massacre of St. Bartholomew, 461.

Church, and to the interests of the Pontifical See, but accompanied by lugubrious vaticinations of their own, based upon the tolerant course on which the king, under Coligny's guidance, had entered. The Cardinal of Alessandria had made little account of the ring offered him by Charles as a pledge of his sincerity, and preferred to wait for the proof which the sequel might exhibit. The last defiant act of the French monarch, in marrying his sister to a professed heretic, and within the degrees of consanguinity prohibited by the Church, without obtaining the Pope's dispensation, served to confirm all the sinister suspicions entertained at Rome. Under these circumstances the papal astonishment and rejoicing can well be imagined, when couriers sent by the Guises brought the intelligence of the massacre to the Cardinal of Lorraine, and when letters from the King of France and from the Nuncio Salviati in Paris to the Pope himself confirmed its accuracy. Salviati's letters having been read in the full consistory, on the sixth of September, the pontiff and the cardinals resolved to go at once in solemn procession to the church of San Marco, there to render thanks to God for the signal blessing conferred upon the Roman See and all Christendom. A solemn mass was appointed for the succeeding Monday, and a jubilee published for the whole Christian world. In the evening the cannon from the Castle of San Angelo, and firearms discharged here and there throughout the city, proclaimed to all the joy felt for so signal a victory over the enemies of the Church. For three successive nights there was a general illumination. Cardinal Orsini, who seems to have been on the point of starting for France as a special legate to urge the court to withdraw from the course of toleration, now received different instructions, and was commissioned to congratulate Charles, and to encourage him to pursue the path upon which he had entered. Charles of Lorraine, as was natural, distinguished himself for his demonstrations of joy. He made a present of one thousand crowns to the bearer of such glad tidings.[1] Under his auspices a brilliant celebration of the event

---

[1] Narrative appended to Capilupi, Stratagema di Carlo IX. (1574). The cardinal's adulatory letter to Charles IX., on receipt of the king's missive, is strongly corroborative of the view to which everything forces us, that the

took place in the church of San Luigi de' Francesi, which was

Public thanks-givings. magnificently decorated for the occasion.   Gregory himself, attended by his cardinals and bishops, by princes, foreign ambassadors, and large numbers of nobles and of the people, walked thither under the pontifical canopy, and high mass was said.   The Cardinal of Lorraine had affixed above the entrance a pompous declaration, in the form of a congratulatory notice from Charles the Ninth to Gregory and the "sacred college of cardinals," wherein the Very Christian King renders thanks to Heaven that, "inflamed by zeal for the Lord God of Hosts, like a smiting angel divinely sent, he had suddenly destroyed by a single slaughter almost all the heretics and enemies of his kingdom."   The latinity of the placard might not be above reproach; but it is certain that its sentiments received the cordial approval of the assembled prelates.[1] Set forth in golden characters, and decorated with festive leaves and ribbons,[2] it proclaimed that the hierarchy of the Roman Church had no qualms of conscience in indorsing the traitorous deed of Charles and Catharine.   But still more unequivocal proofs were not wanting.   A well known medal was struck in honor of the event, bearing on the one side the head of the Pope

---

massacre was not long definitely premeditated. "Sire," he said, "estant arrivé le sieur de Beauville avecques lettres de Vostre Majesté, qui confirmoyent les nouvelles des tres-crestiennes et héroicques délibération et exéquutions faictes non-seulement à Paris, mais aussi partout voz principales villes, je m'asseure qu'il vous plaira bien me tant honorer . . . . que de vous asseurer que entre tous voz très humbles subjects, je ne suis le dernier à an (en) louer Dieu et à me resjouir. Et véritablement, Sire, c'est tout le myeus (mieux) que j'eusse osé jamais désirer ni esperer.   Je me tienz asseuré que des ce commencement les actions de Vostre Majesté accroistront chacung jour à la gloire de Dieu et à l'immortalité de vostre nom," etc.   Card. Lorraine to the king, Rome, Sept. 10, 1572, MSS. Nat. Library, *apud* Lestoile, éd. Michaud et Poujoulat, 25, 26, note.

[1] Conjouissance de M^r. le Cardinal de Lorraine, au nom du Roy, faicte au Pape, le vij^e jour de sept. 1572, sur la mort de l'Admiral et ses complices. Correspondance diplom. de La Mothe Fénélon, vii. 341, 342.   Also Jean de Serres (1575) iv., fol. 56, and in a French translation appended to Capilupi, Lo stratagema di Carlo IX. (1574), 111–113, and reproduced in Mém. de l'estat, Arch. cur., vii. 360.

[2] "Literis romanis aureis majusculis descriptum, festa fronte velatum, ac lemniscatum, et supra limen aedis Sancti Ludovici Romæ affixum."

and the words "Gregorius XIII. Pont. Max. An. I.," and on the other an angel with cross and sword pursuing the heretics, and the superscription, " Ugonottorum strages, 1572." [1]

By the order of the Pope, the famous Vasari painted in the Sala Regia of the Vatican palace several pictures representing different scenes in the Parisian massacre. Upon one

Paintings by Vasari in the Vatican.

an inscription was placed which tersely expressed the true state of the case: " Pontifex Colinii necem probat." [2] The paintings may still be seen in the magnificent room which serves as antechamber to the Sistine Chapel. [3]

---

[1] The genuineness of this medal, in spite of the clumsy attempts made to discredit it, is established beyond all possible doubt. The Jesuit Bonanni, in his " Numismata Pontificum " (2 vols. fol., Rome, 1689), has figured and described it as No. 27 of the medals of Gregory XIII. A translation of his account and a facsimile of the medal may be seen in the Bulletin de la Société de l'hist. du prot. français, i. (1852) 240–242. It is also admirably représented in the Trésor de Numismatique (Delaroche, etc., Paris, 1839), Médailles des papes, plate 15, No. 8. The late Alexander Thomson, Esq., of Banchory, Aberdeenshire, purchased at the papal mint in the city of Rome, in 1828 or 1829, among other medals for which he applied, not less than seven copies of this medal, six of them struck off expressly for him from the original die still in possession of the mint. See his own account, given in his Memoir by Professor Smeaton, and reproduced in the *New York Evangelist* of October 17, 1872.

[2] Recueil des lettres missives de Henri IV., i. 36.

[3] See Pistolesi, Il Museo Vaticano descritto ed illustrato (Roma, 1838) vol. viii. 97. There are three paintings, of which the first represents " the King of France sitting in parliament, and approving and ordering that the death of Gaspard Coligny, Grand Admiral of France, and declared to be head of the Huguenots, be registered." " The mischance of Coligny is delineated in the following picture in a spacious square, among many heads of streets (capistrade) and façades of temples. The admiral, clothed in the French costume of that period, is carried in the arms of several military men ; although lifeless (estinto, read rather, *faint*), he still preserves in his countenance threatening and terrible looks." The third is the massacre of St. Bartholomew's day itself, in which the beholder scarcely knows which to admire most, the artistic skill of the painter, or his success in bringing into a narrow compass so many of the most revolting incidents of the tragedy—the murder of men in the streets, the butchery of helpless and unoffending women, the throwing of Coligny's remains from the window of his room, etc. Dr. Henry White gives a sketch of this painting, taken from De Potter's Lettres de Pie V. Of the fresco representing the wounding of Coligny there is an engraving in Pistolesi, *ubi supra*, vol. viii. plate 84. By an odd mistake, both the text and the index to the plates, make this belong to the reconciliation of Frederick

To the French ambassador, M. de Ferralz, Gregory expressed
in the most extravagant terms his satisfaction, and that of the
college of cardinals, not only with the events of Paris, but with
the news daily coming to Rome of similar massacres in progress
in different cities of France. He convinced Ferralz that no more
delightful tidings could have reached the pontifical court. The
battle of Lepanto could not compare with it. "Tell your master,"
said he to the envoy at the conclusion of his audience, "that
this event has given me a hundred times more pleasure than fifty
victories like that which the League obtained over the Turk last
year." In the excess of his joy he did not forget to enjoin on
every one he spoke to, especially all Frenchmen, to light bonfires
in honor of the massacre, hinting that whoever should fail to do
so must be unsound in the faith.[1] A few weeks later, the pontiff
shocked even some devout Roman Catholics by allowing Cardinal Lorraine and the French ambassador to present to him
Maurevel, the assassin who had fired the arquebuse shot at Admiral Coligny.[2]

"The pontiff," says his countryman, the historian Adriani,
"and all Italy universally rejoiced greatly, and forgave the king
and queen their previous dissimulation."[3] For the French at
Rome now pretended that the massacre had long been planned
by their monarch, and that every favor to the Huguenots for the
past two years had been shown to them merely for the purpose

Barbarossa and the pontificate of Alexander III.—on what grounds it is hard
to imagine. The character of the wound of the person borne in the arms of
his companions, indicated by *the loss of two fingers of his right hand*, from which
the blood is seen to be dropping, leaves no doubt that he is the Admiral
Coligny. Unfortunately, Pistolesi's splendid work is disfigured by other
blunders, or typographical errors, equally gross. In describing other paintings
of the same Sala Regia (pp. 95, 96), he assigns, or is made by the types to
assign, various events in the quarrel of Barbarossa and Adrian IV. and Alexander III., to the years 1554, 1555, 1577, etc.

[1] Ferralz to Charles IX., Rome, Sept. 11, 1572, *apud* North British Review,
Oct., 1869, p. 31.

[2] Prospero Count Arco to the emperor, Rome, Nov. 15, 1572, *ubi supra*.

[3] "Il pontefice, e universalmente tutta d'Italia grandemente se ne rallegrò,
facendo pardonare cotale effetto al Re e alla Reina, che molte cose avevano
sostenuto di fare in benefizio di quella parte." G. B. Adriani, Istoria de' suoi
tempi, ii. 378.

of lulling them into a false security. The Pope accepted the plea without troubling himself much whether it were true or not, satisfied as he was with the event. But not so the Spanish envoy at the Roman court, Don Juan de Cuñiga.

French boasts go for nothing. "The French wish to give the impression," he wrote to his master, "that the king meditated this blow from the time he made peace with the Huguenots; and, in order that it may be believed that he was capable of preparing it and concealing it until the proper time for the execution, they attribute to him stratagems which do not seem allowable even against heretics and rebels. I deem it certain that, if the shooting of the arquebuse at the admiral was a thing projected a few days beforehand, and authorized by the king, all the rest was inspired by circumstances." [1] Equally positive, though not at all doubtful respecting the morality of the transaction, and more jubilant, was the Nuncio Salviati, in Paris. While desiring that the cardinal secretary " should kiss the feet of his Holiness in his name," and " rejoicing with him in the bowels of his heart at the blessed and honorable commencement of his pontificate," [2] while declaring that, despite his previous belief that the court of France would not much longer tolerate the admiral's arrogance, he would never have imagined the tenth part of what he now saw with his own eyes, he also stated he could not bring himself to believe that, had the admiral been killed by Maurevel's shot, so much would have been done by a great deal. [3] Now, however, " the queen intended not only to revoke the Edict of Pacification, but by means of justice to restore the ancient observance of the Catholic faith."

There was another monarch whose joy was not less sincere than Gregory's. This was Philip of Spain. Catharine had

---

[1] Cuñiga to Philip, Sept. 8th, Simancas MSS. Gachard, Bull. de l'acad. de Bruxelles, xvi. 249, 250.

[2] " A. N. S. mi faccia gratia di basciar i piedi in nome mio, col quale mi rallegro con le viscere del cuore che sia piaciuto alla Dva. Msa. d'incaminar, nel principio del suo pontificato, si felicemente e honoratamente le cose di questo regno." Salviati to Card. sec. of State, Aug. 24, Mackintosh, iii., App. G., p. 355.

[3] " Non si risolvo a credere che si fusse fatto tanto a un pezzo." Ibid., ubi supra.

not delayed writing to her royal son-in-law. In her endeavor to make capital out of the massacre she betrayed great satisfac-

Catharine writes to Philip, her son-in-law.

tion at her supposed masterly stroke of policy. Her letter—a misspelled scrawl—furnishes a fresh illustration of the fact that singular shrewdness in planning and executing criminal projects is not incompatible with a trust, amounting almost to fatuity, in the unsuspecting credulity of others. Catharine actually imagined that she could, by her counterfeit piety, impose upon one who knew her character so well as Philip of Spain. Therefore she was lavish of the use of the name of the Deity to cover her own villainy. " Monsieur my son," she wrote, " I entertain no doubt that you will appreciate, as we do, the happiness God has conferred upon us in giving the king, my son, the means of ridding himself of his subjects, rebels against God and himself, and [rejoice] that it has pleased Him graciously to preserve him and us all from the cruelty of their hands. For this we are assured that you will praise God with us, as well on our account as for the advantage that will accrue to all Christendom, and to the service, and honor, and glory of God. This, we hope, will soon be made known, and the fruit thereof be perceived.[1] By this event we afford the testimony of our good and upright intentions, which have never tended but to His honor. And I rejoice still more that this occasion will confirm and augment the friendship between your Majesty and the king your brother— which is the thing I desire most of all in this world." [2]

Philip had good reason to be glad. To all human appear-

The delight of Philip the Second.

ance it had depended only upon the word of Charles to secure, at once and forever, the independence from the Spanish tyranny of the provinces on the lower Rhine,

---

[1] " De quoy nous aseurons que en leoures Dieu aveques nous, tant pour nostre particulier coment pour le bien qui en reviendré à toute la cretienté et au service et honeur et gloyre de Dieu," etc.

[2] " Et randons par cet ayfect le temognage de nos bonnes et droyctes yntantions, cor ne les avons jeamés eu aultre que tendant à son honneur," etc. Letter of Catharine de' Medici to Philip II., Aug. 28, 1572, in Musée des archives nationales ; documents originaux de l'hist. de France, exposés dans l'Hôtel Soubise (published by the Gen. Directory of the Archives, 1872), p. 392.

which, under William of Orange, were battling for religious and civil freedom. True, Genlis and his small forces had been captured or destroyed ; but what were they in comparison with the men whom the French king could have marshalled under the command of Coligny, La Noue, and other experienced leaders ? And now Charles, at a single stroke, had cut off all prospect of obtaining the sovereignty of the Netherlands or of any part, had assassinated his own generals in their beds, had butchered in cold blood those who would gladly have marched as soldiers to achieve his conquests, and had freed Philip from all fear of French interference in behalf of the Dutch patriots. No wonder then, that, when a courier, sent by the Spanish ambassador at Paris, with tidings of the events of St. Bartholomew's Day, reached Madrid, on the evening of Saturday, the seventh of September—so slowly did news travel in those days—Philip was almost beside himself with joy.[1] "He showed so much gayety, contrary to his native temperament and custom," the French envoy, St. Goard, wrote to his master, "that he was evidently more delighted than with all the pieces of good fortune that had ever befallen him ; and he called to him his familiars to tell them that he knew that your Majesty was his good brother, and that he saw that there was no one else in the world that deserved the title of 'Very Christian.'" Not content with gloating over the bloody bulletin with his cronies, he promptly sent his secretary, Cayas, to congratulate the French ambassador, and to inform him that "the king his master was

---

[1] Philip had evidently no intimation that a massacre was in contemplation. When Mr. Motley says (United Netherlands, i. 15): "It is as certain that Philip knew beforehand, and testified his approbation of the massacre of St. Bartholomew, as that he was the murderer of Orange," the statement must be interpreted in accordance with that other statement in the same author's earlier work (Rise of the Dutch Republic, ii. 388) : "The crime was not committed with the connivance of the Spanish government. On the contrary, the two courts were at the moment bitterly opposed to each other," etc. As the eminent historian can scarcely be supposed to contradict himself on so important a point, we must understand him to mean that Philip had, indeed, long since instigated Catharine and her son to rid themselves of the Huguenot leaders by some form of treachery or other, but was quite ignorant of, and unprepared for, the particular means adopted by them for compassing the end.

going that very hour to St. Jerome, to render all manner of thanks to God, and to pray that in matters of so great importance his Majesty might be sustained by His hand." When, the next morning, St. Goard had been very graciously admitted to an audience, he tells us that Philip—the man who rarely or never gave a hearty or manly expression to his feelings—" began to laugh, and, with demonstrations of extreme pleasure and satisfaction, praised your Majesty as having earned your title of ' Very Christian,' telling me there was no king that could claim to be your companion, either in valor or in prudence." It was natural that Philip should chiefly extol Charles's alleged dissimulation, and dwell on the happiness of Christendom saved from a frightful war. It was equally politic for St. Goard to chime in, and echo his master's praise. But there was sound truth in the concluding remark he made to Philip : " However this may be, *Sire, you must confess that you owe your Netherlands to his Majesty, the King of France.*" [1]

We have also more direct testimony to Philip's delight at the Parisian massacre, in the form of a letter from the monarch to the Duke of Alva. In this extraordinary communication, worthy of the depraved source from which it emanated, the bloodthirsty king does not attempt to conceal the satisfaction with which he has received the tidings of Charles's " honorable and Christian resolution to rid himself of the admiral and other important personages," both for religion's sake and because the King of France will now be a firmer friend to the Spanish crown—since neither the German Protestants nor Elizabeth will

---

[1] St. Goard to Charles, Sept. 12th, Bodel Nijenhuis, Supplement to Groen van Prinsterer, Archives de la maison d'Orange Nassau, 124–126. St. Goard was not deceived by Philip's pious congratulations. " Ce faict," he writes to Catharine, a week later (ibid., pp. 126, 127), " a esté aussi bien pris de se (ce) Roy comme on le peult penser, *pour luy estre tant profitable pour ses affaires ;* toutesfois, comme il est le prince du monde qui sçait et faict le plus profession de dissimuler toutes choses, si n'a il sçeu celler en ceste-cy le plaisir qu'il en a reçeu, et encores que je infère touts ses mouvements proceder du bien que en recepvoient ses affaires, lesquelles il voioit pour desplorer sans ce seul remedde, si a il faict croire à tout le monde par ces aparens (apparences) que c'estoit pour le respect du bon succez que voz Majestez avoient eu en si haultes entreprises, tantost louant le filz d'avoir une telle mère, l'aiant si bien gardé," etc.

trust him any longer—a circumstance which will have a decided influence upon the restoration of his authority in the Netherlands. Another matter upon which he touches, places in the clearest light the infamy to which Charles and his council had sunk, and the hypocrisy of Philip the Catholic himself. Until the very moment of the Massacre of St. Bartholomew's Day, Charles had been earnestly desirous of saving the lives of the French Huguenots who had been taken prisoners with Genlis near Mons; while, by the most barefaced assumptions of innocence, he endeavored to induce the Spaniard to believe that he was in no way responsible for Genlis's undertaking.[1] Now, however, it is Charles himself who, by his envoys at Madrid and Brussels, begs from Philip the murder of his own French subjects, lest they return to do mischief in France. Not only the soldiers taken with Genlis, but the garrison of Mons, if that city, as now seemed all but certain, should fall into Alva's hands, must be put to death.[2] " If Alva object," he wrote to Mondoucet, " that your request is the same thing as tacitly requiring him to kill the prisoners and cut to pieces the garrison of Mons, you will tell him that that is precisely what he ought to do, and that he will inflict a very great wrong upon himself and upon all Christendom if he shall do otherwise." [3] Drawing his inspiration from the same source, St. Goard said to Philip himself : " One of the greatest services that can be done for Christendom, will be to capture Mons and put everybody to the edge of the sword." [4] And, so Philip thought too ; for he not only wrote to Alva that the sooner the

Marginal note: Charles instigates the murder of French prisoners.

[1] See the Mondoucet correspondence, Compte rendu de la commission royale d'histoire, second series, iv. (Brux., 1852), 340–349, pub. by M. Émile Gachet, especially the letter of Charles IX. of Aug. 12th, 1572.

[2] " El dicho embaxador me propusó . . . . con grande instancia, que sin dilacion se devia executar la justicia en Janlis (Genlis) y en los otros sus complices que hay estan presos, y en los que se tomassen en Mons." Philip to Alva, Sept. 18th. Simancas MSS. Gachard, Particularités inédits sur la St. Barthélemy, Bulletin de l'académie royale de Belgique, xvi. (1849), 256.

[3] Charles IX. to Mondoucet, Aug. 31st, Mondoucet correspondence, p. 349 ; see also another letter of the same date, p. 348.

[4] " Estant l'un plus grands services que se puisse faire pour la Chrestienté, que de la prendre et passer tout au fil de l'espée." St. Goard to Charles IX., Sept. 19th, Supp. to Archives de la maison d'Orange Nassau, 127.

earth were freed of such bad plants, the less solicitude would be necessary in future, but he scribbled with his own hand on the draft of the letter : "I desire, if you have not already rid the world of them, you should do it at once and let me know, for I see no reason for delay." [1]   The more clear-headed Alva, however, saw reasons not only for delay, but for extending to some of the prisoners a counterfeit mercy ; for he soon replied to his master, that "he was not at all of opinion that it was best to cut off the heads of Genlis and

The Duke of Alva jubilant but wary.

the other French prisoners, as the King of France asked him to do.   He had resolved to do so before the admiral's death, but now things had changed.   Charles must know that Philip has in his power men capable of giving him great trouble." [2]   None the less, however, did Alva communicate the glad tidings to all parts of the Netherlands, and cause solemn Te Deums to be sung in the churches. [3]   "These occurrences," he wrote to Count Bossu, Governor of Holland, "come so marvellously apropos in this conjunction for the affairs of the king our master, that nothing could be more timely.   For this we cannot sufficiently render thanks to the Divine goodness." [4]   Philip promptly sent the Marquis d'Ayamonte to congratulate Charles and the queen mother. [5]   Alva had already a special envoy at the French court, who returned soon after the massacre to Brussels.   On asking Catharine what reply he should carry back, the Italian princess, intoxicated with her success, impiously said : "I do not know that I can make any other answer than that which Jesus Christ gave to St. John's disciples, 'Go and show again those things which ye have seen and heard—the blind receive their sight, and the lame walk, the lepers are cleansed, and the deaf hear, the dead are raised up, and the poor have the gospel preached to them.' "   "And do not forget," she added, "to say to the Duke of Alva, 'Blessed is he, whosoever shall not be offended in

---

[1] Philip to Alva, *ubi supra.*

[2] Alva to Philip, Oct. 13th, Gachard, Correspondance de Philippe II. (Brux., 1848), ii. 287.

[3] Mondoucet to Charles IX., Aug. 29th, Bull. de l'acad. roy. de Brux.

[4] Bulletin de l'acad. roy. de Bruxelles, ix. (1842), 561.

[5] Philip to Alva, *ubi supra.*

me.'"[1] Such was the new gospel of blood and rapine with which it was proposed to replace the Bible in the vernacular, and the Psalms of David translated by Marot and Beza!

But Spain and Rome were only exceptions. From almost every part of the civilized world there arose a loud and unanimous cry of execration. It was natural, however, that the feeling of horror should be deepest in the neighboring Protestant countries, whose religion and liberties seemed to be menaced England's with destruction by the treacherous blow. Above all, horror. in England with whose queen a matrimonial treaty had for months been pending, the abhorrence of the crime and its perpetrators was the more intense because of the violence of the revulsion. Resident Frenchmen were startled at the sudden change. The warmest friends of France became its open enemies, loudly reproaching the broken faith of the king, and pouring curses upon the people that had exercised such indignities upon unoffending citizens. If we may believe La Mothe Fénélon, the men who customarily wore arms indulged in much insulting bravado and in threats directed against any one that dared to gainsay them.[2] The French ambassador has himself left on record the description of a remarkable interview which he had with Queen Elizabeth. Rarely had a diplomatic agent Perplexity of been placed in a more embarrassing position. His the French ambassador letters and despatches from home were of the most at London. contradictory character. Scarcely had he, with protestations of sincerity and truthfulness, published the account of events in Paris which was sent him, when new instructions arrived recalling, modifying, or contradicting the former. First, with the startling news of the disturbance of the peace, by Admiral Coligny's wounding, came a letter from the king, expressing "infinite displeasure" at the "bad" and "unhappy" act, and a resolution to inflict "very exemplary justice." To which this postscript was appended: "Monsieur de la Mothe Fénélon, I will not forget to tell you that this wicked act proceeds from

---

[1] Bulletin of Alva from the report of his agent, the Seigneur de Gomicourt, published by M. Gachard, from MSS. of Mons, in Bull. de l'acad. de Bruxelles, ix. (1842), 560, etc.

[2] Despatch of Sept. 14, 1572, Correspondance diplomatique, v. 121.

the enmity between the admiral's house and the Guises, and that I have taken steps to prevent their involving my subjects in their quarrels, for I intend that my edict of pacification shall be observed in every point."[1]   Two days later Charles wrote again, communicating intelligence of the massacre, beginning with the murder of Coligny, in almost the identical words of the circular he was sending to Mandelot and other governors of provinces and important cities.[2]   Still it is the work of the Guises, and he himself has had enough to do in protecting his own person in the castle of the Louvre.   He wishes Queen Elizabeth to be assured that he has no part in the deed,[3] and, in fact, that all should know that he entertains great displeasure for what has so unfortunately happened, and that it is the thing which he detests more than anything else.[4]   And he adds in a tone of well counterfeited innocence: "I have near me my brother the King of Navarre, and my cousin the Prince of Condé, to share in the same fortune with me."[5]   After receiving and spreading abroad these explanations, what must have been the unfortunate ambassador's perplexity and annoyance, when he received, but too late, a brief letter written on Monday, the day after the massacre began, containing these words: "As we are beginning to discover the conspiracy which the adherents of the pretended reformed religion had entered into against me, my mother and my brothers, you will not speak of the particulars of the disturbance, nor of its occasion until you receive fuller and more certain intelligence from me; for, by to-night or to-morrow morning, I hope to have cleared up the whole matter."[6]   No wonder the courier to whom the last letter was intrusted was bidden ride with all speed to overtake the other; nor that La Mothe Fénélon hardly knew how to extricate himself from the dilemma in which the king his master had placed

---

[1] Charles IX. to La Mothe Fénélon, Aug. 22, 1572, Corresp. dipl., vii. 322, 323.

[2] See *ante*, chap. xviii., p. 490.

[3] " Ni que j'y aye aucune volonté."

[4] " C'est bien la chose que je déteste le plus."

[5] Despatch of Aug. 24th, Corresp. diplom., vii. 324, 325.

[6] Charles IX. to La Mothe Fénélon, Aug. 25, 1572, ibid., 325, 326.

him. Had not Charles, by throwing all the blame, in his first letter, upon the Guises and by positively denying any participation of his own, unambiguously proclaimed his ignorance up to that moment of any Huguenot conspiracy? How, then, could the French envoy go to the same Englishmen to whom he had made known the contents of this despatch, and tell them that the king was the author of the deed he had stigmatized as most detestable, and that the motive that had impelled him reluctantly to order the slaughter of the Huguenots was a conspiracy which he did not discover until a day or two after he gave the order? Yet this was the contradictory story which was sketched in the letter of the twenty-fifth of August, and more fully elaborated in subsequent despatches.[1]

The crestfallen ambassador is said—and the authority for the disputed statement is no less than that of the members of the queen's council, Burleigh, Leicester, Knowles, Thomas Smith, and Croft—to have exclaimed bitterly "that he was ashamed to be counted a Frenchman."[2] At first he believed that an audience would be denied him; and when the queen at last vouchsafed to see him at Woodstock, it was only after he had waited three days in Oxford, while Elizabeth and her council met frequently to deliberate upon the contents of Walsingham's His cold reception by Queen Elizabeth. despatches. He was admitted to the private apartments of the queen, where he found her Majesty surrounded by the lords of the council and the principal ladies of the court, awaiting his coming in profound silence. Elizabeth advanced to meet him, and greeted him with a countenance on which sorrow and severity were mingled with more kindly feelings. Drawing the ambassador aside to a window, she began the discourse with a dignity which few sovereigns have ever known better how to assume. She gave particular expression to the regret she felt in hearing such tidings from a prince in whom she had had more confidence than in any other

---

[1] Charles IX., Aug. 26th and 27th, Corresp. dipl., vii. 331, etc., and a justificatory "Instruction à M. de la Mothe Fénélon."

[2] Letter of Burleigh, etc., Sept. 9th, to Walsingham, Digges, 247. The truth of the statement is called in question by M. Cooper, editor of La Mothe Fénélon's Correspondance diplomatique.

living monarch. And when the ambassador had stammered out the lying excuse based upon " the horrible ingratitude and perverse intentions of the Huguenots " against his master, and had tragically recounted the sorrow of Charles at being constrained to cut off an arm to save the rest of the body, she replied that she hoped that if the informations against the admiral and his were confirmed by investigation, the king " might be excused in some part, both toward God and the world, in permitting the admiral's enemies by force to prevent his enterprises." But she would not admit that even then the cruelty of the mode of punishment was capable of defence, most of all in the case of Coligny, who, " being in his bed, lamed both on the right hand and left arm, lying in danger under the care of chyrurgions, being also guarded about his private house with a number of the king's guard, might have been, by a word of the king's mouth, brought to any place to have answered when and how the king should have thought meet." But she preferred to ascribe the fault, not to Charles, but to those around him whose age and knowledge " ought in such case to have foreseen how offenders ought to be justified with the sword of the prince, and not with the bloody swords of murderers, being also the mortal enemies of the party murdered." [1]

Elizabeth's council was even more outspoken. " Doubtless," said they, " the most heinous act that has occurred in the world, since the crucifixion of Jesus Christ, is that which has been recently committed by the French ; an act which the Italians and the Spaniards, ardent as they are, are far from applauding in their heart, since it was a deed too full of blood, for the greater part innocent, and too much suspected of fraud, which had violated the pledged security of a great king, and disturbed the serenity of the royal nuptials of his sister, insupportable to be heard by the ears of princes, and abominable to all classes of subjects, perpetrated contrary to all law, divine or human, and without a parallel among all acts ever undertaken in the pres-

---

[1] The interview is described both by La Mothe Fénélon (Corresp. diplom., v. 122-126), and by the English council, despatch of Sept. 9th to Walsingham (Digges, 247-249). Hume has a graphic account, History of England, chap. xl.

ence of any prince, and which has even rather involved the King of France in danger than rescued him from it." [1]

The success of the French ambassador, therefore, was not flattering. The most that he could do was to correct the impression that the massacre was only a part of a more general plan for the extirpation of Protestantism everywhere. But when the news came of the barbarous butchery of Huguenots in Lyons and elsewhere; when Villiers, Fuguerel, and other Protestant ministers escaping from France, brought to London the report that one hundred thousand victims to religious intolerance had fallen since St. Bartholomew's Day; [2] when English merchants who had witnessed the scenes of horror at Rouen returned, bringing a true account of what had occurred; when they overturned the audacious assertion that religion had nothing to do with the deed, by declaring that the Huguenots whose lives were spared were constrained to go to mass; that numbers had lost their lives who might have saved them by consenting to take part in services which they regarded as idolatrous; that there were instances of children taken from their parents, and forcibly rebaptized; when, in short, every assertion of La Mothe Fénélon was disproved, the irritation of the English grew deeper. And at last the French ambassador was forced to confess that they would believe neither him nor the despatches that he occasionally produced, saying that the event, which is wont to give the lie to words and letters, showed them what they had to fear. [3] The life of Mary, Queen of Scots, was in

---

[1] This striking, and, certainly, somewhat undiplomatic speech is reported by the ambassador himself in his despatches (Corresp. dipl., v. 127). It looks as if the honest Frenchman was not sorry to let the court know some of the severe criticisms that were uttered respecting a crime with which he had no sympathy. La Mothe Fénélon tells of the impression, proved erroneous by the king's letter, "qu'ilz avoient que ce fût ung acte projecté de longtemps, et que vous heussiez accordé avecques le Pape et le Roy d'Espaigne de faire servir les nopces de Madame, vostre seur, avec le Roy de Navarre, à une telle exécution pour y atraper, à la foys, toutz les principaulx de la dicte religion assemblés." La Mothe Fénélon to Charles, Sept. 2, 1572, *ubi supra*, v. 116.

[2] La Mothe Fénélon endeavored, he says, to persuade the English that there were not over five thousand, and that Catharine and Charles were sorry that one hundred could not have answered. Corr. diplom., v. 155.

[3] See the despondent despatch of October 2d, Corresp. diplom., v., 155-162.

danger. There were many who regarded it as a measure of self-defence to put to death so open a sympathizer with the work of persecution. La Mothe Fénélon, disheartened, promised Catharine de' Medici to do all that he could to promote the interests of France, but the chief influence must come from the king and herself. "Otherwise," he said, "your word will come to be of no authority, and I shall become ridiculous in everything that I tell them or promise them in your name."[1]

The ambassador disheartened.

About the same time one of the most acute statesmen, one of the most vigorous writers of the age, Sir Thomas Smith, himself a former ambassador at the French court, correctly and eloquently expressed the universal feeling of true Protestants in England, in a letter to Walsingham which has become deservedly famous. "What warrant can the French make, now seals and words of princes being traps to catch innocents and bring them to the butchery? If the admiral and all those murdered on that bloody Bartholomew day were guilty, why were they not apprehended, imprisoned, interrogated, and judged, but so much made of as might be, within two hours of the assumation? Is that the manner to handle men either culpable or suspected? So is the journeyer slain by the robber; so is the hen of the fox; so is the hind of the lion; so Abel of Cain; so the innocent of the wicked; so Abner of Joab. But grant they were guilty— they dreamt treason that night in their sleep; what did the innocent men, women, and children at Lyons? What did the sucking children and their mothers at Roan (Rouen) deserve? at Cane (Caen)? at Rochel? . . . Will God, think you, still sleep? Will not their blood ask vengeance; shall not the earth be accursed that hath sucked up the innocent blood poured out like water upon it? . . . I am glad you shall come home, and would wish you were at home, out of that country so contaminate with innocent blood, that the sun cannot look upon it but to prognosticate the wrath and vengeance of God. The ruin and desolation of Jerusalem could not

Letter of Sir Thomas Smith.

---

[1] La Mothe Fénélon to Catharine, ibid., v. 164.

come till all the Christians were either killed there or expelled thence." [1]

Neither Catharine nor Charles was insensible to the impression made upon the English court by the French atrocities. It became important to furnish, if possible, some more convincing proofs of the existence of a Huguenot plot, since the assurances of both monarch and ambassador had lost all weight. The papers of the admiral, both in Paris and in his castle of Châtillon-sur-Loing, had been searched in vain for anything which, even after the murder, might seem to justify the king in violating his pledged word and every principle of law and right. Not a scrap of a letter could be found inculpating him. Not the slightest approach to a hint that it would be well to make way with the king or any of the royal family. The most private manuscripts of the admiral, unlike those of many courtiers even in our own day, contained not a disrespectful expression, nothing that could be twisted into a mark of disaffection or treason. Catharine could lay her hand upon nothing that suited her purpose better than the paper, which, as stated in a former chapter,[2] she showed to Walsingham, wherein he advised Charles to keep Elizabeth and Philip " as low as he could, as a thing that tended much to the safety and maintenance of his crown." But the finesse of the queen mother failed of accomplishing its object; for neither Elizabeth nor Walsingham would think less of Coligny for proving himself faithful to his own sovereign's interests. Elizabeth's incredulity was, doubtless, enhanced by the hypocritical pretence of Catharine that her son intended to maintain his edict of pacification in full force.[3] " The king's meaning is," the queen

Catharine's unsuccessful representations.

---

[1] Letter of Sept. 26th, Digges, 262.

[2] See *ante*, chapter xviii., p. 495.

[3] As well as by the queen mother's assurances respecting the massacre in the provinces—too heavy a draft upon the credulity of her royal sister. " Pour ce qu'ilz disent que, voyant les meurtres qui ont esté faictz en plusieurs villes de ce royaume par les Catholiques contre les Huguenotz, ils ne se peuvent asseurer de l'intantion et volonté du Roy, qu'ilz n'en voyent quelque punission et justice et ses édictz mieux observés, *elle cognoistra bientost que ce qui est advenu ès autres lieux que en ceste ville, a esté entièrement contre la volonté du Roy*, mon dict sieur et filz, lequel a délibéré d'en faire faire telle

mother once said to the English envoy, "that the Huguenots shall enjoy the liberty of their conscience." "What, Madam," observed Walsingham, " and the exercise of their religion too ? " " No," Catharine replied, " my son will have exercise but of one religion in his realm." "Then, how can it agree, that the observation of the edict, whereof you willed me to advertise the queen my mistress, that the same should continue in his former strength ? " interposed Walsingham. To that Catharine answered " that they had discovered certain matters of late, that they saw it necessary to abolish all exercise of the same." "Why, Madam," said the puzzled and somewhat pertinacious diplomatist, " will you have them live without exercise of religion ? " " Even," quoth Catharine, who fancied that she had discovered a pertinent retort, " even as your mistress suffereth the Catholics of England." But the ambassador could not be so easily silenced. Parrying the home thrust, and trenching on an uncourtly bluntness of speech, he quietly called attention to a distinction which her Majesty had not perhaps observed. " My mistress did never promise them anything by edict; if she had, she would not fail to have performed it." After that, there was plainly nothing more to be said, and Catharine resorted to the usual refuge of worsted argument, and said : " The queen your mistress must direct the government of her own country, and the king my son his own." [1]

Some victims were needed to be immolated upon the altar of justice to atone for the alleged Huguenot conspiracy. They were found in Briquemault and Cavaignes, two distinguished Protestants. The former, a knight of the royal order, had, contrary to all rules of international law, been forcibly taken from the house of the English ambassador, whither he had fled for refuge.[2] It was not difficult for the court to obtain what was desired from the cowardly parliament over which Christopher de Thou presided.

Briquemault and Cavaignes hung for alleged conspiracy.

---

pugnition et y establir bientost ung si bon ordre que ung chascun cognoistra quelle a esté en cest endroit son intantion." Catharine to La Mothe Fénélon, Cor. dipl., vii. 377.

[1] Walsingham to Sir Thomas Smith, Sept. 14th, Digges, 242.

[2] Tocsain contre les massacreurs, 150.

Convicted by false testimony, and complaining that even their own words were falsified by their partial judges, the two Protestants were publicly hung on the Place de Grève. It was noticed that they both died exhibiting great fortitude,[1] and protesting to the last that they had neither taken part in, nor even heard of any plot against the king or the state. Charles, hardened by the sight of so much blood, wished to witness in person this new spectacle also, and not only looked on from a neighboring window, but, as it was too dark to see the sufferers distinctly, ordered torches to be lighted, and diverted himself with great laughter in observing their expiring agonies. The King of Navarre and the Prince of Condé were likewise forced to be present, in order to give color to the absurd story that one or both had been included among those whom Coligny and the Huguenots had intended to murder. An hour after, and the Parisian populace cut down the bodies, dragged them in contumely through the streets, and amused themselves by stabbing them, shooting at them, and maiming them. It was an additional aggravation of the judicial crime and the king's ill-timed merriment, that the execution took place on the evening of the day upon which the young Queen of France gave birth to Charles's only legitimate child—a daughter, whom the Salic law excluded from the succession to the throne. Still unconvinced of Coligny's guilt, even by the conviction and death of Brique-

---

[1] It is true that when their sentences were read to them, and particularly that portion which branded with infamy their innocent children, the courage of the old man of seventy, Briquemault, momentarily failed, and he condescended to offer to do great services to the king in retaking La Rochelle whose fortifications he had himself begun; and when this proposal was rejected, it is said that he made more humiliating advances. But the constancy and pious exhortations of his younger companion, who sustained his own courage by repeating many of the psalms in Latin, recalled Briquemault to himself, and from that moment " he had nothing but contempt for death." De Thou (iv. 646), a youth of nineteen, who was present in the chapel when the sentence was read, remembered the incident well. Cf. Agrippa d'Aubigné, ii. 32 (bk. i., c. 6). Walsingham, when he says in his letter of Nov. 1, 1572," that " Cavannes (Cavaignes) showed himself void of all magnanimity, etc.," has evidently confused the persons. Here is an instance where the later account of an eye-witness—De Thou—is entitled to far more credit than the contemporary statement of one whose means of obtaining information were not so good.

mault and Cavaignes, Queen Elizabeth very frankly expressed to La Mothe Fénélon her deep regret that her brother, the French king, had profaned the day of his daughter's birth by the sanguinary spectacle he had that evening gone to behold.[1]

In Scotland, when the news of the massacre arrived, the aged reformer, John Knox, summoned all his remaining energy to The news in preach a last time before the regent and the estates. Scotland; In the midst of his sermon, turning to Du Croc, the French ambassador, who was present, he sternly addressed to him these prophetic words: "Go tell your king that sentence has gone out against him, that God's vengeance shall never depart from him nor his house, that his name shall remain an execration to the posterities to come, and that none that shall come of his loins shall enjoy that kingdom unless he repent." The indignant ambassador called upon the regent "to check the tongue which was reviling an anointed king;" but the regent refused to silence the minister of God, and suffered Du Croc to leave Edinburgh in anger.[2]

Monsieur de Vulcob, the French ambassador at the court of the Emperor of Germany, was equally unsuccessful in con-
in Germany; vincing that monarch of the truth of the story con-
tained in his despatches from Paris. The emperor did not disguise his great disappointment and sorrow, nor his belief that the murderous project had been known for weeks before at Rome.[3] It need scarcely be said that the negotiations of Schomberg, who had been sent to procure an offensive and defensive alliance between the Protestant princes of Germany

---

[1] " N'ayant regret sinon que vous ayez voulu profaner le jour de sa nays-sence par ung si fascheus espectacle qu'allastes voir en grève." Corresp. diplom. de la Mothe Fénélon, v. 205 ; Tocsain contre les massacreurs, 151, 152 ; Reveille-Matin, Arch. cur., vii. 206 ; Walsingham to Smith, Nov. 1, 1572, Digges, 278, 279.

[2] Froude, x. 444, 445.

[3] " Entre autres choses, il me dist qu'on luy avoit escript de Rome, n'avoit que trois semaines ou environ, sur le propos des noces du Roy de Navarre en ces propres termes : ' que à ceste heure que tous les oyseaux estoient en cage, on les pouvoit prendre tous ensemble.' " M. de Vulcob to Charles IX., Pres-burg, Sept. 26th, apud De Noailles, Henri de Valois et la Pologne en 1572 (Paris, 1867), iii., Pièces just., 214.

and the crown of France, were rendered abortive by the advent
of tidings of the treacherous massacre at Paris.   Like the rest
of the diplomatists sent out from France, the able envoy to
Germany had been left in profound ignorance of the blow
that was to disturb all his calculations.   He had even been
empowered to promise that Charles would assume toward the
enterprise of William of Orange the same position that the
princes would take ; and he seemed likely to be successful in
inducing the princes to make common cause with his master.

To Schomberg, as to the rest, there had been despatched, on
the very day that Coligny was wounded, a narrative of that
event to be laid before the Protestant princes—a narrative
wherein the occurrence was deplored; wherein Charles stated
that he had taken just such measures for the apprehension of
the perpetrator of the crime as he would have taken had the
victim been one of his own brothers; wherein he promised to
spare neither diligence nor trouble, and to inflict condign punishment, "in order that all men might know that no greater
misdeed could have been committed in his kingdom, nor more
displeasing to himself ; " wherein he protested his unalterable
determination to maintain completely and sedulously his edict
of pacification.[1] But to Schomberg, as to the other French
ambassadors, there had come subsequent tidings and despatches
giving the lie to all these assurances.

And now, as he wrote home with some bitterness, "all his
negotiations had ended in smoke."[2]   Their Highnesses "could
not get it out of their heads" that the events of St. Bartholomew's Day were premeditated, with the view of enabling the
Duke of Alva to make way with the forces of the Prince of
Orange.   So high did feeling run, that the rumor prevailed
that Schomberg had been thrown into prison as an accomplice

---

[1] See in Kluckhohn, Briefe Friedrich des Frommen, ii. 482, a short letter
of Charles IX. to the elector palatine, Aug. 22, 1572, referring him for details
to the account which Schomberg would give him verbally; and, ibid., ii.
483, 484, the narrative signed by Charles IX. and Brulart, secretary of state,
in a translation evidently made at the time for the elector's use.

[2] " Toute ma negociation s'en estoit allée en fumée."   Schomberg to M.
de Limoges, Nov. 8th, De Noailles, iii. 300.

in the perfidy, and that Coligny's death was about to be avenged upon him.[1]

Instead of forming an alliance with Charles, the Landgrave of Hesse and the three Protestant electors began instantly to concert measures of defence against what they verily believed to be a general war of extermination, set on foot by the Pope and his followers, in pursuance of the resolutions of the Council of Trent. " The princes of the Augsburg Confession," wrote Landgrave William to the Electors of Saxony and Brandenburg, " can see in this inhuman incident, as in a mirror, how the papists are disposed toward all the professors of the pure doctrine. The Pope and his party follow even at this day the rule which they followed respecting John Huss in the Council of Constance. When it is their interest so to act, they do not deem themselves bound to keep any faith with heretics. . . . Last year the Pope and his followers obtained a glorious victory over the Turk. It is of the very nature of victories that they commonly make the victors more insolent." To Frederick the Pious, elector palatine, the landgrave wrote a day later: " There is nothing better for us Germans than to have nothing to do with them; for neither credit nor confidence can be reposed in them." " I marvel greatly," he added, " that the admiral and the other Huguenot gentlemen, although they, too, had doubtless studied Macchiavelli's ' Il Principe ' — *the Italian bible* [2]—should have been so trustful, and should not have been too much upon their guard to suffer themselves to be enticed unarmed into so suspicious a place." [3]

Montluc, Bishop of Valence, had just been sent to Poland to endeavor to secure the vacant throne for Henry of Anjou. His
In Poland.   ultimate success and its consequences will be seen in another place. But now the attempt seemed desperate. The bishop, who was the most wily and experienced negotiator

---

[1] A large number of Schomberg's despatches are inserted in De Noailles, iii. 286, etc.

[2] " Als die sonder zweifel *die welsche bibel* ' El principe Macchiavelli ' auch studirt."

[3] Landgrave William to the Electors of Saxony and Brandenburg, Cassel, Sept. 5, 1572 ; same to Frederick, elector palatine, Sept. 6th. A. Kluckhohn, Briefe Friedrich des Frommen, ii. 496–498.

the French court possessed, and was fully conscious of his rare qualifications, was vexed almost beyond endurance at the stupidity of the king and queen who had employed him. " By the despatch I send the king, and by what the Dean of Die will tell you," he wrote (on the twentieth of November) to one of the secretaries of state, " you will learn how this unfortunate blast from France has sunk the ship which we had already brought to the mouth of the harbor. You may imagine how well pleased the person who was in command of it has reason to be when he sees that by another's fault he loses the fruit of his labors. I say another's fault, for, since a desire was felt for this kingdom, the execution which has been made might and ought to have been deferred."[1] Again and again Montluc begged that there might be no repetition of such cruelties, suggesting that an edict, guaranteeing that no one's conscience should be constrained, might be made or fabricated. If the king had no intention of carrying it into effect, he could at least send it to the governors, with private orders to make such disposition of it as he pleased.[2] But, above all, there must be no fresh outrages done to the Protestants. " If between this and the day of the election there were to come the news of some cruelty," he wrote in midwinter, " we could do nothing, even had we here ten millions in gold with which to gain men over. The king and the Duke of Anjou will have to consider whether a purpose of revenge is of more moment to them than the acquisition of a kingdom."[3]

---

[1] Bp. of Valence to M. Brulart, Konin, Nov. 20th, Colbert MSS. *apud* De Noailles, iii. 218.

[2] Montluc to Charles IX., January 22, 1573, De Noailles, iii. 220. Does not the frank suggestion furnish a clue to the method which was sometimes practised in other cases ?

[3] Montluc to Brulart, Jan. 20, 1573, De Noailles, iii. 223. The worthy bishop, who was certainly at any time more at home in the cabinet than in the church, did not intermit his toil or yield to discouragement. If we may believe him, he " had not leisure so much as to say his prayers." The panegyrists of the massacre, and especially Charpentier, had done him good service by their writings, and at one time he greatly desired that the learned doctor might be sent to his assistance, particularly as (to use his own words) " all the suite of Monsieur de l'Isle and myself do not know enough of Latin to admit a deacon to orders, even at Puy in Auvergne." *Ubi supra.*

The ministers of Geneva, somewhat removed from the mists that prevented the greater part of the Huguenot leaders from Sympathy of descrying the perils environing them, had long fore-the Genevese. seen the coming catastrophe, and had in vain implored Admiral Coligny, in particular, to have a greater care for his safety. "How often have I predicted it to him! How often have I warned him!" exclaimed Theodore Beza, in the first paroxysm of grief at the assassination of his noble friend.[1] The city government, participating in the same apprehensions, early in the fatal month of August, 1572, instructed some of the reformed ministers who had occasion to revisit their native land on private business, to hasten out of a country where they were exposed to the treachery of a Florentine woman.[2] Their solicitude was only too well grounded. On Saturday, the thirtieth of August, some merchants arrived in Geneva from Lyons, with the appalling intelligence that their Protestant countrymen were everywhere the victims of unparalleled cruelty. From the inn they went on without delay to the city hall, and narrated to the magistrates the revolting atrocities of which they had been eye-witnesses. They besought the city to prepare hospitable shelter and food for the throng of refugees who would soon make their appearance, having scarce escaped the bloody snares in which their brethren in great numbers had lost their lives.[3] "The frightful news," writes the historian of the Genevan church, describing the scene, "courses through the city with the speed of lightning: the shops are closed, and the citizens assemble on the public squares. They know, by past experience, the burdens and sacrifices that await men of good-will. Within doors, the women get in readiness an abundance of clothing, of medicines, and of food. The magistrates send wagons and litters to the villages of the district of Gex; and the peasants with their pastors take their station upon the border, to obtain intelligence and to render assistance to the first that may arrive. They have not long to wait. On the first of September a few travellers

---

[1] Beza to Thomas Tilius, Sept. 10, 1572, Bulletin, vii. 16.

[2] Registres de la compagnie, 1er août, 1572, *apud* Gaberel, Histoire de l'église de Genève, ii. 320.

[3] Reg. du conseil, 30 août, 1572 ; Reg. de la compagnie, Gaberel, ii. 321.

make their appearance, pale, worn out with fatigue, scarcely answering the greeting they receive. They cannot credit the reality of their deliverance. For days death has been lying in wait for them at the threshold of every village. Soon their numbers increase. The wounded uncover the wounds they have carefully concealed, that they might not be taken for reformers. They declare that, since the twenty-sixth of August, the country and the cities have been deluged with the blood of their brethren." [1]

Nobly did the citizens of the little commonwealth welcome the scarred and bleeding confessors of their faith, contending with magnanimous rivalry for the most cruelly mangled, and carrying them in triumph into their homes and to their frugal boards. Not one refugee was suffered to find his way to the city hall ; and there was no need of any public distribution of alms. [2] Within a few days twenty-three hundred families of French Protestants were gathered in the hospitable inclosure of Geneva. Besides those that subsequently returned to France, on the arrival of more propitious times, more than two hundred of these families yet remain, comprising the most honorable citizens of the republic. [3]

A solemn fast was instituted. In the presence of the remarkable assembly gathered in the old cathedral of Saint Pierre, no word of threatening, no prayer for vengeance was uttered. But a firm conviction of the power and goodness of God seemed to dwell in every heart, and was uttered in impressive words by Theodore Beza—since Calvin's death, eight years before, the leading theologian of Geneva. "The hand of the Lord is not shortened," said the reformer. "He will not suffer a hair of our head to fall to the ground without His will. Let us not, therefore, be at all affrighted because of the plot of the men who have unjustly devised to put us all to death with our wives and our children. Let us rather be assured, that, if the Lord

---

[1] Gaberel, ii. 321, 322.

[2] Ibid., ii. 322.

[3] Ibid., ii. 307. See also in the Pièces justificatives, pp. 213–217 : " Liste des réfugiés de la St. Barthélemy dont les familles existent de nos jours à Genève."

has ordained to deliver all or any of us, none shall be able to resist Him.   If it shall please Him that we all die, let us not fear ; for it is our Father's good pleasure to give us another home, which is the heavenly kingdom, in which there is no change, no poverty, no want, no tear, no crying, no mourning, no sorrow, but, on the contrary, eternal joy and blessedness.   It is far better to be lodged with the beggar Lazarus in the bosom of Abraham, than with the rich man, with Cain, with Saul, with Herod, or with Judas, in hell.   Meanwhile, we must drink the cup which the Lord has prepared for us, each according to his portion.   We must not be ashamed of the Cross of Christ, nor be loth to drink the gall of which He has first drunk : knowing that our sorrow shall be turned into joy, and that we shall laugh in our turn, when the wicked shall weep and gnash their teeth." [1]

Twenty Huguenot pastors from France were among the refugees, and were kindly invited to take part in the honorable office of preaching in the churches.   They preferred, however, to sit among the hearers, and listen to the sermons of Beza and his venerated colleagues. [2]

Heaven smiled on the generous hospitality of the little republic.   The plague, which had been raging in Geneva, disappeared simultaneously with the arrival of the fugitives from

---

[1] Gaberel, ii. 325.   The author of the really able and learned article on the massacre, in the North British Review for October, 1869, conveys an altogether unfounded and cruel impression, not only with regard to Beza, but respecting his fellow Protestants, in these sentences : " The very men whose own brethren had perished in France were not hearty or unanimous in execrating the deed. There were Huguenots who thought that their party had brought ruin on itself, by provoking its enemies and following the rash counsels of ambitious men.   This was the opinion of their chief, Theodore Beza, himself," etc. The belief of Beza that the French Protestants had merited even so severe a chastisement as this at the hands of God, by reason of the ambition of some and the unbelief or lack of spirituality of others, was a very different thing from failing to execrate the deed with heartiness.   If the words of Bullinger to Hotman, quoted in support of the first sentence ("sunt tamen qui hoc factum et excusare et defendere tentant") really referred to Protestants at all, it can only have been to an insignificant number who took the position from a love of singularity, and who were below contempt.   The execration of the deed was pre-eminently unanimous and hearty.
[2] Gaberel, ii. 326.

France.[1]   Still the burden which their hosts had assumed was
by no means light.   They were not rich, and the
Their gener-
osity and   rigorous winter that followed would have reduced
danger.
them to great straits even without this additional
drain upon their resources.   Besides, they had incurred the
dangerous enmity of the King of France.   While professing
deep gratitude to the Genevese for the advice they had given
to the Protestants of Nismes to liberate the agents of the royal
court, who had been sent to procure their destruction, but had
been discovered and incarcerated, Charles the Ninth was in
secret plotting the ruin of the city which furnished an asylum
to so many of his persecuted subjects.   At one time the danger
was imminent.   The Duke of Savoy was reported to have collected an army of eighteen thousand men near Chambéry and
Annecy, while rumors of domestic treachery took so definite
a form, that it was said that two hundred papal soldiers in the
disguise of Protestant refugees were lurking in Geneva itself.
On the other hand, the Roman Catholic cantons of Fribourg
and Soleure, when on the point of joining Berne and Zurich in
sending assistance, undertook to stipulate for the reinstatement
of the mass within the walls of Geneva ; and the Genevese, who,
whatever other faults they might possess, were no cowards, declined an alliance upon such conditions.[2]   But the threatened
contest of arms never came.   By one of those strange turns of
affairs, which, from their frequent recurrence in the history of
Geneva, an impartial beholder can scarcely interpret otherwise
than as interpositions of providence in behalf of a city that was
destined for ages to be a safe refuge for the oppressed confessors of a purer faith, the storm was dissipated as rapidly as it had
gathered.   The bodily ailments of Charles the Ninth were,
humanly speaking, the salvation of Geneva.[3]
In other parts of Switzerland the King of France made great

---

[1] Beza to T. Tilius, Dec. 3, 1572, Bulletin de la Soc. de l'hist. du prot. fr.,
vii. 17.

[2] Gaberel, ii. 330–333.

[3] Nearly four years later, on the 8th of June, 1576, Monsieur de Chandieu
received the news of the publication of Henry III.'s edict of peace permitting
the refugees to return home.   All the Protestants who had not adopted
Switzerland as their future country congregated at Geneva.   A solemn re-

efforts to counteract the injurious influence upon his interests which the intelligence of the massacre could but exert. Almost immediately after the events of the last week of August, the royal ambassador, Monsieur de la Fontaine, and the treasurer whom the French monarch was accustomed to keep in Switzerland, were instructed to write out an account for the benefit of his Majesty's "best and perfect friends," "the magnificent seigniors," wherein among the numerous falsehoods with which they attempted to feed the unsophistical mountaineers, was at least a single truth: "This young and magnanimous prince, since his accession to the throne, has, so to speak, reaped only thorns in place of a sceptre." [1]

A little later M. de Bellièvre, his special envoy at the diet of Baden, was profuse in assurances to the effect that the deed was

Impression at Baden.

not premeditated, but had been rendered necessary by the machinations of the admiral—"a wretched man, or rather, not a man, but a furious and irreconcilable beast who had lost all fear of God and man." He particularly defended the king from all responsibility for the excesses that had been committed, insisting that it was the people that "had taken the bit in its teeth," while Charles, Anjou, and Alençon, did their best to check its mad impetuosity, and Catharine felt "unspeakable regret." [2] But the envoy had little reason to congratulate

---

ligious service was held in the church of Saint Pierre, where French and Genevese united in that favorite Huguenot psalm (the 118th)—

> La voici l'heureuse journée
> Que Dieu a faite à plein désir—

the same which the soldiers of Henry IV. set up on the field of Coutras (Agrippa d'Aubigné, iii. 53). M. de Chandieu then rendered thanks in tender and affectionate terms to all the departments of government, exclaiming : " We shall always regard the Church of Geneva as our benefactress and our mother ; and from all the French reformed churches will arise, every Sunday, words of blessing, in remembrance of your admirable benefits to us." The next day the refugees started for their homes, accompanied, as far as the border, by a great crowd of citizens. Gaberel, ii. 337, 338.

[1] Les ambassadeurs de Charles IX. aux cantons suisses protestants, Bulletin, iii. 274–276. A copy was sent by Beza to the consuls of Montauban, together with a letter, Oct. 3. 1572. Also Mém. de l'estat (Arch. cur., vii. 158–161.)

[2] Harangue de M. de Bellièvre aux Suisses à la diette tenue à Baden, Mackintosh, Hist. of England, iii., Appendix L.

himself upon his success. " Sire," he wrote with some disgust to his master, " it is all but impossible to get it out of the heads of the Protestants, that your Majesty's intention is to join the rest of the Catholic princes, in order by force to put (the decrees of) the Council of Trent into execution in their countries." They would not be satisfied entirely by Bellièvre's plausible explanations. " Simple and rude people are violently excited by such things, and are very difficult to be reassured." [1]

Charles the Ninth stood convicted in the eyes of the world of a great crime. No elaborate vindications, by their sophistry, or by barefaced misstatements of facts, could clear him, in the judgment of impartial men of either creed, from the guilt of such a butchery of his subjects as scarcely another monarch on record had ever perpetrated. Medals were early struck in honor of Medals and vindications. the event, upon which " valor and piety "—the king's motto—were represented as gloriously exhibited in the destruction of rebels and heretics.[2] But the wise regarded it as " a cruelty worse than Scythian," and deplored the realm where " *neither piety nor justice* restrained the malice and sword of the raging populace." [3] The Protestants of all countries—and they were his natural allies against Spanish ambition for world-empire—had forever lost confidence in the honor of Charles of Valois.

Multis minatur, qui uni facit, injuriam.

" If that king be author and doer of this act," wrote the Earl

---

[1] Bellièvre to Charles IX., Baden, Dec. 15, 1572, Mackintosh, App. L, p. 360. De Thou, iv. (liv. liii.) 642.

[2] As early as September 3d the superintendent of the mint submitted specimens of two kinds of commemorative medals: the one bearing the devices, "*Virtus in Rebelles*" and "*Pietas excitavit Justitiam ;*" and the other, "*Charles IX. dompteur des Rebelles, le 24 aoust* 1572." The Mém. de l'estat (Archives cur., vii. 355–357) contain the elaborate description furnished by the designer, accompanied with comments by the Protestant author. The Trésor de Numismatique, etc. (Paul Delaroche, etc.), Med. françaises, pt. 3d, plate 19, Nos. 3, 4, and 5, gives facsimiles of *three* medals, the first two mentioned above, and a third on which Charles figures as Hercules armed with sword and torch confronting the three-headed Hydra of heresy. The motto is, " Ne ferrum temnat, simul ignibus obsto."

[3] Smith to Walsingham, Digges, 252.

of Leicester, expressing the common judgment of the civilized world, " shame and confusion light upon him ; be he never so strong in the sight of men, the Lord hath not His power for naught. . . . If he continue in confirming the fact, and allowing the persons that did it, then must he be a prince detested of all honest men, what religion soever they have ; for as his fact was ugly, so was it inhumane. For whom should a man trust, if not his prince's word ; and these men he hath put to slaughter, not only had his word, but his writing, and not public, but private, with open proclamations and all other manner of declarations that could be devised for the safety, which now being violated and broken, who can believe and trust him ? " [1]

Upon the king himself the results of the fearful atrocities which he had been induced by his mother and brother to sanction, were equally lasting and disastrous. The change was startling even to those who were its chief cause : from a gentle boy he had become transformed into a morose and cruel man. " The king is grown now so bloody-minded," writes one who enjoyed good opportunities of observing him, " as they that advised him thereto do repent the same, and do fear that the old saying will prove true, *Malum consilium consultori pessimum.*" [2] The story of the frenzy of Charles who, on one occasion, seemed to be resolved to take the lives of Navarre and Condé, unless they should instantly recant, and was only prevented by the entreaties of his young wife, may be exaggerated.[3] But certain it is that the unhappy king was the victim of haunting memories of the past, which, while continually robbing him of peace of mind, sometimes drove him to the borders of madness. Agrippa d'Aubigné tells us, on the often repeated testimony of Henry of Navarre, that one night, a week after the massacre, Charles leaped up in affright from

Disastrous effects of the massacre on Charles himself.

---

[1] Leicester to Walsingham, Sept. 11th, Digges, 251.

[2] Walsingham to Smith, Nov. 1, Digges, 279. The politic Montluc, Bishop of Valence, seems to allude to the same alteration in his master : " Au diable soyt la cause qui de tant de maux est cause, et qui d'ung bon roy et humain, s'il en fust jamais, l'ont contrainct de mectre la main au sang, qui est un morceau si friant, que jamais prince n'en tasta qu'il n'y voulust revenir." De Noailles, iii. 223, 224.

[3] Agrippa d'Aubigné, ii. 29, 30.

his bed, and summoned his gentlemen of the bedcha[..]
well as his brother-in-law, to listen to a confused sound of cries
of distress and lamentations, similar to that which he had heard
on the eventful night of the butchery. So convinced was he
that his ears had not deceived him, that he gave orders that the
new attack which he fancied to be made upon the partisans of
Montmorency should at once be repressed by his guards. It was
not until the soldiers returned with the assurance that everything was quiet throughout the city, that he consented to retire
to his rest again. For an entire week the delusive cries seemed
to return at the self-same hour.[1] These fancies—the creations
of his fevered brain—may soon have left him, not to return
until the general closing in at the death-bed. But there were
marks of the violence of the passions of which he was the
victim in his altered mien and deportment. Even before the
event that has fixed upon him an infamous notoriety, he acted
at times like a madman in the indulgence of his whims and
coarse tastes. Sir Thomas Smith, five months before the fatal
St. Bartholomew's Day, wrote of "his inordinate hunting, so
early in the morning and so late at night, without sparing frost,
snow or rain, and in so desperate doings as makes her (his
mother) and them that love him to be often in great fear."[2]
But now the picture, as faithfully drawn by the friendly hand
of the Venetian ambassador, early in the year 1574, is still
more pitiful. His countenance had become sad and forbidding.
When obliged to give audience to the representatives of foreign
powers, as well as in his ordinary interviews, he avoided the
glance of those who addressed him. He bent his head toward
the ground and shut his eyes. At short intervals he would
open them with a start, and in a moment, as though the effort
caused him pain, he would close them again with no less sudden-
ness. "It is feared," adds the writer, "that the spirit of vengeance has taken possession of him; formerly he was only
severe, now his friends dread lest he will become cruel." He
must at all hazards find hard work to do. He was on horseback for twelve or fourteen consecutive hours, and pursued the

[1] Agrippa d'Aubigné, ii. 29 (liv. i., c. 6).
[2] Letter of May 22, 157½, Digges, 193.

same deer for two or three days, stopping only to take nourishment, or snatch a little rest at night.   His hands were scarred and callous.   When in the palace, his passion for violent exercise drove him to the forge, where for three or four hours he would work without intermission, with a ponderous hammer fashioning a cuirass or some other piece of armor, and exhibiting more pride in being able to tire out his gentle competitors, than in more royal accomplishments.[1]   We have no means of tracing accurately the influence of the massacre upon others. The Abbé Brantôme, however, early pointed out the remarkable fact that of those who took a principal part in the work of murder and rapine many soon after met with violent deaths, either at the siege of La Rochelle or in the ensuing wars, and that the riches they had so iniquitously accumulated profited them little.[2]

Before dismissing the consideration of the stupendous crime for which Divine vengeance — to use the words of Sully — "made France atone by twenty-six consecutive years of disaster, carnage, and horror,"[3] it is at once interesting and important to glance at a historical question which still agitates the world, and for a correct and impartial solution of which we are, perhaps, more favorably situated than were even the contemporaries of the event.   I allude to the inquiry respecting the extent to which the Roman Church, and the Pope in particular, must be held responsible for the Massacre of St. Bartholomew's Day.

How far was the Roman Church responsible?

---

[1] Relation of Sigismondo Cavalli.   I follow the résumé of Baschet, La diplomatie vénitienne, 556, 562.

[2] " Leurs butins et richesses ne leur proffitarent point, non plus qu'à plusieurs massacreurs, sacquemens, pillardz et paillards de la feste de Sainct-Barthélemy que j'ay cogneu, au moins des principaux, qui ne vesquirent guières longtemps qu'ils ne fussent tuez au siége de la Rochelle, et autres guerres qui vindrent emprès, et qui furent aussi pauvres que devant.   Aussi, comme disoient les Espagnolz pillards, ' *Que el diablo les avia dado, el diablo les avia llevado.*' " Œuvres, i. 277 (Ed. of Hist. Soc. of Fr., 1864).   I need only refer to the fate of the famous assassin who boasted of having killed four hundred men that day with his own arm, and who afterward, having embraced a hermit's life, was finally hung for the crime of murdering travellers (Agrippa d'Aubigné, ii. 20) ; and to that of Coconnas, put to death for the part he took in the conspiracy of which I shall shortly have to speak.

[3] Mémoires de Sully, i. 28, 29.

So far as Queen Catharine was concerned (and the same is true of some of her advisers), it is admitted by all that no zeal for religion controlled her conduct. A dissolute and ambitious woman, and, moreover, almost an avowed atheist, she could not have acted from a sincere but mistaken belief that it was her duty to exterminate heresy. But among the inferior agents it can scarcely be doubted that there were some who believed themselves to be doing God service in ridding the world of the enemies of His church. Had not the preachers in their sermons extolled the deed as the most meritorious that could be performed, and as furnishing an unquestionable passport to paradise? The number, however, of these *religious* assassins—if so we may style them—could be but small in comparison with the multitude of those to whom religion served merely as a pretext, while cupidity or partisan hatred was the true motive; men who, nevertheless, derived their incentive from the lessons of their spiritual guides, and who would never have dreamed of giving loose rein to their passions, but for the suggestions of these sanguinary teachers. At the bar of history the priesthood that countenanced assassination must be held no less accountable for the actions of this class than for the deeds of more sincere devotees.

It is immaterial to the question of the responsibility of the Papal Church, whether the queen mother and the king's ministers were honest, or were Roman Catholics, or, indeed, Christians only in name. If the Pope had for years, by letter and by his accredited agents, been insinuating that the life of a heretic was a thing of little value; if he systematically advocated a war of extermination, and opposed every negotiation for peace, every truce, every edict of pacification that did not look to the annihilation of the Huguenots; if he had familiarized the minds of king and queen with the thought of justifiable massacre, it is of little importance to ascertain whether his too ready pupils executed the injunction from a pure desire to further the interests of the Papal See, or with more selfish designs. Unfortunately for humanity and for religion, the course I have indicated was that which had been consistently and indefatigably pursued during the entire pontificate of Pius the Fifth, and during the few months that had elapsed since the election of his successor.

Contrary to the firm persuasion of the Protestants who wrote contemporary accounts of the massacre, we must in all probability, as we have already seen,[1] acquit Gregory the Thirteenth of any knowledge of the disaster impending over the admiral and the Huguenots. It was what he wished for and prayed for, but with little hope of seeing the accomplishment. In fact, he was brought to the verge of despair in respect to the hold of the papacy upon the kingdom of France. Nuncio Salviati, at Paris, had, indeed, conceived the hope that some disaster would befal the Huguenots in consequence of Coligny's imprudence and the desperation of the queen mother and of the Roman Catholic party at finding the authority slipping from their hands. But his astonishment and that of the pontiff at the general massacre of the Protestants was surpassed only by their common delight. The fragments of the despatches from Salviati to the Roman secretary of state, which have been suffered to find their way into print, seem to settle this point beyond all controversy.

Gregory probably not aware of the intended massacre.

We have in previous chapters seen the Pope assisting Charles with money and troops in the prosecution of the last two wars against the Huguenots. But this aid was accompanied with perpetual exhortations to do the work thoroughly, and not to repeat the mistakes committed by his predecessors. "That heresy cannot be tolerated in the same kingdom with the worship of the Catholic religion," writes Pius the Fifth to Sigismund Augustus of Poland, "is proved by that very example of the kingdom of France, which your Majesty brings up for the purpose of excusing yourself. If the former kings of France had not suffered this evil to grow by neglect and indulgence, they would easily have been able to extirpate heresy and secure the peace and quiet of their realm."[2] Of all the leaders of the day, the Duke of Alva alone earned, by his unrelenting

Pius the Fifth instigates the French court.

---

[1] See *ante*, p. 530–532.

[2] Apostolicarum Pii Quinti Epistolarum libri quinque. Letter of March 26, 1568, p. 73.

destruction of heretics, the unqualified approval of the pontiff.

When the tidings of the successes of the " Blood Council " reached Rome, Pius could not contain himself for
joy. He must congratulate the duke, and spur him on
in a course upon which the blessing of Heaven so manifestly
rested. " Nothing can occur to us," said he, " more glorious for the
dignity of the Church, or more delightful to the truly paternal
disposition of our mind to all men, than when we perceive that
warriors and very brave generals, such as we previously knew
you to be and now find you in this most perilous war, consult
not their own interest, nor their own glory alone, but war in behalf of that Almighty God who stands ready to crown His soldiers
contending for Him and His glory, not with a corruptible crown,
but with one that is eternal and fadeth not away." [1]

He indorses the cruelties of Alva.

With this express indorsement of Alva's merciless cruelty
before us, it is not difficult to understand what Pius demanded
of Charles of France. Early in 1569, while sending the Duke of
Sforza with auxiliaries, he wrote to the king: "When
God shall by His kindness have given to you and to
us, as we hope, the victory, it will be your duty to
punish the heretics and their leaders with all severity, and
thus justly to avenge not only your own wrongs, but those of
Almighty God : in order that, by your execution of the righteous
judgment of God, they may pay the penalty which they have
deserved by their crimes." [2]   After the battle of Jarnac and
Condé's death, we have seen that Pius wrote promptly, bidding
Charles " pursue and destroy the remnants of the enemy, and
wholly tear up not only the roots of an evil so great and which
had gathered to itself such strength, but even the very fibres of
the roots." He begged him not to spare those who had not
spared God nor their king. [3] To Catharine and to the Duke of
Anjou, to the Cardinal of Bourbon, and to the Cardinal of Lorraine, the same language was addressed. Again and again the
Pope held up the example of Saul, who disregarded the commands of the Lord through Samuel and spared the Amalekites,

He repeatedly counsels exter- minating the Huguenots.

---

[1] Pii Quinti Epistolæ, 111.   [2] Ibid., 150.
[3] Ibid., 152. See *ante*, chapter xvi., p. 308.

as a solemn warning against disobedience. To the queen mother he said: "Under no circumstances and from no considerations ought the enemies of God to be spared.[1] If your Majesty shall continue, as heretofore, to seek with right purpose of mind and a simple heart the honor of Almighty God, and shall assail the foes of the Catholic religion openly and freely even to extermination,[2] be well assured that the Divine assistance will never fail, and that still greater victories will be prepared by God for you and for the king your son, until, *when all shall have been destroyed,* the pristine worship of the Catholic religion shall be restored to that most illustrious realm."[3] The Duke of Anjou was urged to incite his brother to punish the rebels with great severity, and to be inexorable in refusing the prayers of all who would intercede for them.[4] Charles was given to understand that if, induced by any motives, he should defer the punishment of God's enemies, he would certainly tempt the Divine patience to change to anger.[5]

The victory of Moncontour furnished an occasion for fresh exhortations to the king not to neglect to inflict upon the enemies of Almighty God the punishments fixed by the laws. "For what else would this be," said Pius, "than to make of no effect the blessing of God, namely, victory itself, whose fruit indeed consists in this, that by just punishment the execrable heretics, common enemies, having been taken away, the former peace and tranquillity should be restored to the kingdom. And do not allow yourself, by the suggestion of the empty name of pity, to be deceived so far as to seek, by pardoning Divine injuries, to obtain false praise for compassion; for nothing is more cruel than that pity and compassion which is extended to the impious and those who deserve the worst of torments."[6] The

---

[1] "Nullo modo, nullisque de causis, hostibus Dei parcendum est."

[2] "Catholicæ religionis hostes aperte ac libere ad internecionem usque oppugnaverit." Ibid., 155.

[3] "Deletis omnibus," etc. Ibid., 155.   [4] Ibid., 160, 161.

[5] Ibid., 166.

[6] "Nec vero, vano pietatis nomine objecto, te eo usque decipi sinas, ut condonandis divinis injuriis falsam tibi misericordiæ laudem quæras: nihil est enim ea pietate misericordiaque crudelius, quæ in impios et ultima supplicia meritos confertur." Ibid., 242.

work begun by victories in the field was, therefore, to be completed by the institution of inquisitors of the faith in every city, and the adoption of such other measures as might, with God's help, at length create the kingdom anew and restore it to its former state.[1]

As often as rumors of negotiations for peace reached him, Pius was in anguish of soul, and wrote to Charles, to Catharine, to Anjou, to the French cardinals, in almost the same words. He protested that, as light has no communion with darkness, so no compact between Catholics and heretics could be other than feigned and full of treachery.[2]   As the prospect of peace grew more distinct, his prognostications of coming disaster grew darker, and sounded almost like threats.   Even if the heretics, in concluding the peace, had no intention of laying snares, God would put it into their minds as a punishment to the king.   " Now, how fearful a thing it is to fall into the hands of the living God, who is wont not only to chastise the corrupt manners of men by war, but, on account of the sins of kings and people, to dash kingdoms in pieces, and to transfer them from their ancient masters to new ones, is too evident to need to be proved by examples." [3]   When at last the peace of Saint Germain was definitely concluded, the Pope did not cease to lament over " a pacification in which the conquered heretics imposed upon the victorious king conditions so horrible and so pernicious that he could not speak of them without tears." And he expressed at the same time his paternal fears lest the young Charles and those who had consented to the unholy compact would be given over to a reprobate mind, that seeing they might not see, and hearing they might not hear.[4]

To his last breath Pius retained the same thirst for the blood of the heretics of France.   He violently opposed the marriage of the king's sister to Henry of Navarre, and instructed his envoy at the French court to bring up again that " matter of

---

[1] " Hæreticæ pravitatis inquisitores per singulas civitates constituere." Ibid., 242.

[2] Letter of Jan. 29, 1570, ibid., 267.

[3] Letter of April 23, 1570, ibid., 275.

[4] Letter to Cardinal Bourbon, Sept. 23, 1570, ibid., 282, 283.

conciliation so fatal to the Catholics." [1]   His last letters are as sanguinary as his first.   Meanwhile his acts corresponded with his words, and left the King of France and his mother in no doubt respecting the value which the pretended vicegerent of God upon earth, and the future saint, [2] set upon the life of a heretic; for, when the town of Mornas was on one occasion captured by the Roman Catholic forces, and a number of prisoners were taken, Pius—" such," his admiring biographer informs us, " was his burning zeal for religion "—ransomed them from the hands of their captors, that he might have the satisfaction of ordering their public execution in the pontifical city of Avignon ! [3]   And when the same holy father learned that Count Santa Fiore, the commander of the papal troops sent to Charles's assistance, had accepted the offer of a ransom for the life of a distinguished Huguenot nobleman, he wrote to him complaining bitterly that he had disobeyed his orders, which were that every heretic that fell into his hands should straightway be put to death. [4]   As, however, Pius wanted not Huguenot treasure, but Huguenot blood, with more consistency than

---

[1] Letter to Charles IX., January 25, 1572, ibid., 443.

[2] Saint Pius V. is, I believe, the only pope that has been canonized since Saint Celestine V., near the end of the thirteenth century.

[3] " Qui autem a militibus captivi ducebantur, eos Pius pretio redemptos, in jusque sibi vindicatos, atque Avenionem perductos, publico supplicio afficiendos *pro ardenti suo religionis studio* decrevit." Gabutius, Vita Pii Quinti, Acta Sanctorum Maii, § 97, p. 642.

[4] " Id Pius ubi cognovit, de Comite Sanctæ Floræ conquestus est, quod jussa non fecisset, dudum imperantis, *necandos protinus esse hæreticos omnes quoscumque ille capere potuisset.*" Ibid., § 125. It must not be forgotten that, in holding these sentiments, Pius V. did not stand alone; his predecessors on the pontifical throne were of the same mind. We have seen the anger of Paul IV., in 1558, upon learning that Henry II. had spared D'Andelot (see *ante*, chapter viii., vol. i., p. 320). Paul was for instantaneous execution, and *did not believe a heretic could ever be converted.* He told the French ambassador " que c'estoit abus d'estimer que un hérétique revint jamais; que ce n'estoit que toute dissimulation, et que c'estoit un mal où il ne falloit que le feu, et soubdain ! " The last expression is a clue to the attitude of the Roman See to heresy under every successive occupant of the papal throne. Letter of La Bourdaisière to the constable, Rome, Feb. 25, 1559, MS. Nat. Lib. Paris, Bulletin, xxvii. (1878) 105.

at first appears, he ordered the captive nobleman whose head had been spared to be released without ransom.[1]

With such continual papal exhortations to bloodshed, before us, with such suggestive examples of the treatment which heretics ought, according to the pontiff, to receive, and in the light of the extravagant joy displayed at Rome over the consummation of the massacre, we can scarcely hesitate to find the head of the Roman Catholic Church guilty—if not, by a happy accident, of having known or devised the precise mode of its execution, at least of having long instigated and paved the way for the commission of the crime. Without the teachings of Pius the Fifth, the conspiracy of Catharine and Anjou would have been almost impossible. Without the preaching of priests and friars at Lent and Advent, the passions of the low populace could not have been inflamed to such a pitch as to render it capable of perpetrating atrocities which will forever render the reign of Charles the Ninth infamous in the French annals.

One of the most vivid accounts of the massacre in any city outside of Paris is the contemporary narrative of Johann Wilhelm von Botzheim, a young German, who was at the time pursuing his studies in Orleans. It forms the sequel to the description of the Parisian massacre, to which reference has already been made several times, and was first published by Dr. F. W. Ebeling, in his "Archivalische Beiträge zur Geschichte Frankreichs unter Carl IX." (Leipsic, 1872), 129–189. It was also translated into French by M. Charles Read, for the number of the Bulletin de la Société de l'histoire du protestantisme français issued on the occasion of the tercentenary of the Massacre of St. Bartholomew's Day. The chief interest of the narration centres in the anxieties and dangers of the little community of Germans in attendance upon the famous law school. Besides this, however, much light is thrown upon the general features of the bloody transactions. The first intimation of Coligny's wounding reached the Protestants as they were returning from the prêche, but created less excitement because of the statement accompanying it, that Charles was greatly displeased at the occurrence. That night a messenger arrived with letters addressed to the provost of the city, announcing the death of the admiral and the Huguenots of Paris, and enjoining the like execution at Orleans. Although the letters bore the royal seal, the information they contained appeared so

[margin note: A German account of the massacre at Orleans.]

---

[1] Gabutius, *ubi supra.*

incredible that the provost commanded the messenger to be imprisoned until two captains, whom he at once despatched to Paris, returned bringing full confirmation of the story.   The provost, a man averse to bloodshed, issued, early on Monday morning, as a precautionary measure, an order to guard the city gates.   But the control of affairs rapidly passed out of his hands ; and, threatened with death because of his moderate counsels, the provost was himself forced to take refuge for safety in the citadel.   Ten captains, at the head of as many bands of soldiers, ruled the city, and were foremost in the work of murder and rapine that now ensued.   But there were other bands engaged in the same occupation, not to speak of single persons acting strictly on their own account.   Moreover, four hundred ruffians came in from the country, intent upon making up for losses which they pretended to have sustained during the late civil wars. They showed no mercy to the Huguenots that fell into their hands. Of the Protestants scarcely one made resistance, so hopeless was their situation.   Pierre Pillier, a bell-founder, had indeed barred his door with iron ; but, finding that his assailants were on the point of forcing the entrance, he first threw his money from a window, and then, seizing his opportunity when the miscreants were scrambling for their prize, deluged them with molten lead ; after which he set fire to his house, and perished, with his wife and children, in the flames.

There is, happily, no need of repeating here the shocking details of the butchery told by the student. As a German, and not generally known to be a Protestant, he managed to escape the fate of his Huguenot friends, but he witnessed, and was forced to appear to applaud, the most revolting exhibitions both of cruelty and of selfishness. His favorite professor, the venerable François Taillebois, after having been twice plundered by bands of marauders, was treacherously conducted by the second band to the Loire, despatched with the dagger, and thrown into the river. " The last lecture, which he gave on Monday at nine o'clock," says his pupil, " was on the *Lex Cornelia* [de sicariis] of which he made the demonstration by the sacrifice of his own life."   It is pitiful to read that even professors in the university were not ashamed to enrich their libraries by the plunder of the law-books of their colleagues, or of their scholars. The writer traced his own copies of Alciat, of Mynsinger and " Speculator," to the shelves of Laurent Godefroid, Professor of the Pandects, and the entire library of his brother Bernhard to those of his neighbor, Dr. Beaupied, Professor of Canon Law.

In the midst of the almost universal unchaining of the worst passions of human or demoniacal nature, it is pleasant to note a few exceptions.   Some Roman Catholics were found not only unwilling to imbrue their hands in the blood of their Huguenot neighbors and friends, but actually ready to incur personal peril in rescuing them from assassination. Such magnanimity, however, was very rare.   All respect for authority human or divine, all sense of shame or pity, all fear of hell and hope of heaven, seemed to have been obliterated from the breasts of the murderers. The blasphemous words of the furious Captain Gaillard, when opposed in his plan to destroy Botzheim and his fellow Germans, truly expressed the sentiments which others might possibly have hesitated to utter so distinctly : " Par la mort Dieu ! il faut qu'il

soit. . . . Il n'y a ny Dieu, ny diable, ny juge qui me puisse commander. Vostre vie est en ma puissance, il fault mourir. . . . Baillez-
moy mon espée, je tuerai l'ung après l'autre, je ne saurois tuer trestous à la fois
avec la pistolle." Men, with blood-stained hands and clothes, boasted over
their cups of having plundered and murdered thirty, forty, fifty men each.
At last, on Saturday afternoon, after the Huguenots had been almost all
killed, an edict was published prohibiting murder and pillage on pain of death.
Gallows, too, were erected in nearly every street, to hang the disobedient; but
not a man was hung, and the murders still continued. Soon after a second
edict directed the restoration of stolen property to its rightful owners; it was
a mere trick to entice any remaining Huguenot from his refuge and secure
his apprehension and death. The Huguenots were not even able to recover,
at a later time, the property they had intrusted to their Roman Catholic
friends in time of danger, and did not dare to bring the latter before courts of
justice. The Huguenots killed at Orleans, in this writer's opinion, were at
least fifteen hundred, perhaps even two thousand, in number.

The Pope's anxiety that Charles should pursue his work of extermination
to the bitter end is but too clearly attested. In the bull proclaiming a jubilee, Gregory recites his visit, in company with his venerable
brethren the cardinals, to the church of San Marco, and declares
his object to have been not merely to render thanks to God
Almighty, but to beseech Him "of His immense goodness to
deign to preserve and guard the king in the prosecution of so
pious and salutary a design," and to minister to his majesty "strength to
purge his heretofore very religious kingdom of most pestilential heresies, and
restore it to the pristine worship of the Catholic religion." In the same document the faithful are enjoined to supplicate Heaven that what the most
Christian king "has by Divine suggestion (Deo auctore) resolved to do, he
may have the power, with God's assistance (ipso operante), to fulfil." (See
the text in Lord Acton's letter to the London *Times*, of Nov. 24, 1874). By
his nuncio, and subsequently by his special legate, Orsini, the pontiff, while
expressing his delight at "the glorious and truly incomparable achievement"
of Charles, repeatedly reminded his majesty of the promise which he had given
Salviati, that soon (infra pochi giorni) not a single Huguenot should remain
in all his dominions. (Despatch of Orsini, *apud Acton, ubi supra.*) Meanwhile there is, unfortunately, no room for doubt that the Pope was fully
aware of the true character of the massacre. He knew that it was justified
by no discovery of a conspiracy to kill the king and his brothers. The first
despatch of Salviati, dated Aug. 24th, read in the consistory of Sept. 6th (see
the letter from Rome appended to Capilupi, ed. of 1574, p. 84), contains no
allusion to such a discovery (see the despatch in Mackintosh, iii. App. G).
The despatch of Sept. 2d referred, indeed, to the pretended discovery of a
Protestant plot, but denounced it as not only false but absurd in the extreme.
"Cela n'en demeurera pas moins faux en tous points, et ce serait une honte
pour quiconque est à même de connaitre quelque chose aux affaires de ce
monde de le croire." (Chateaubriand's trans. *apud* Acton *ubi supra.*)

Anxiety of the Pope that the massacre should con- tinue.

CHAPTER XX.

THE SEQUEL OF THE MASSACRE, TO THE DEATH OF CHARLES THE NINTH.

THE blow had been struck by which the Huguenots were to be exterminated. If a single adherent of the reformed faith Wide-spread still lived in Paris, he dared not show his face. France terror. had, as usual, copied the example of the capital, and there were few districts to which the fratricidal plot had not extended. Enough blood had been shed, it would seem, to satisfy the most sanguinary appetite. After the massacre in which the admiral and all the most noted leaders had perished— after the defection of Henry of Navarre and his more courageous cousin, it was confidently expected that the feeble remnants of the Huguenots, deprived of their head, could easily be reduced to submission. The stipulation of Charles the Ninth, when yielding a reluctant consent to the infamous project, would be fulfilled : not one of the hated sect would remain to reproach him with his crime. And, in point of fact, throughout the greater number of the cities of France, even where there had been no actual massacre, so wide-spread was the terror, that every Protestant had either fled from the country or sought safety in concealment, if he had not actually apostatized from the faith.[1]

---

[1] Jean de Serres, Commentaria de statu rel. et reipublicæ, iv., fol. 60 verso. I have made use, up to 1570, of the first edition of this work, published in three volumes in 1571, my copy being one formerly belonging to the library of Ludovico Manini, the last doge of Venice. From 1570 on I refer to the edition of 1575, which comprises a fourth and rarer volume, bringing down the history to the close of the reign of Charles. A comparison between this edition and the later edition of 1577 brings out the interesting circumstance

But when the storm had spent its first fury, and it became once more possible to look around and measure its frightful *La Rochelle and other cities in Protestant hands.* effects, it was found that the devastation was not universal. A few cities held for the Huguenots. La Rochelle and Sancerre—the former on the western coast, the latter in the centre of France—with Montauban, Nismes, Milhau, Aubenas, Privas, and certain other places of minor importance in the south, closed their gates, and refused to receive the royal governors sent them from Paris.[1] Not that there were wanting those, even among the Protestants, who interposed conscientious scruples, and denied the right of resistance to the authority of the king;[2] but with the vast majority the dictates of self-preservation prevailed over the slavish doctrine of unquestioning submission. The right to worship God as He commands cannot, they argued, be abridged even by the legitimate sovereign; and in this case there is even the greatest probability that he acts under constraint, or that wily courtiers forge his name, since the most contradictory orders emanate ostensibly from him.

Such was the attitude assumed by the brave inhabitants of Nismes. Here the Roman Catholics had displayed a more *Nismes.* charitable disposition than in many other places. The "juge mage," on receipt of secret orders to massacre the Protestants, instead of complying, gave directions for assembling the extraordinary council, consisting of the magistrates and most notable citizens. By this council, upon his recommendation, it was unanimously resolved to close all the gates of Nismes, with the exception of one. This was to be guarded in turn by the Roman Catholics and the Protestants. All the citizens were directed to take a common oath that they would assist each other without distinction of creed, and main-

---

that many Huguenots of little courage, who at first apostatized, afterward returned to their old faith. Thus, the edition of 1575 reads (iv. 51 *v.*): "Vix enim dici possit, quam multi ad primum illum impetum a Religione resiluerint, mortis amittendarumque facultatum metu, *quorum plerique etiamnum hærent in luto.*" The words I have italicized are omitted in the edition of 1577, as quoted by Soldan, ii. 473.

[1] Jean de Serres, iv., fol. 61.   [2] Ib., *ubi supra.*

tain order and security, in obedience to the king's authority, and according to the provisions of his edict of pacification.   It was a solemn scene when all those present in the great municipal meeting, the vicar-general of the diocese among the number, with uplifted hands called upon God to witness their engagement.[1]   The oath was well observed.   The Viscount of Joyeuse, acting as lieutenant-governor of Charles in Languedoc, at first approved the compact; for the king's early letters, as we have seen, expressed indignation at Coligny's murder, and ascribed it to the personal enmity of the Guises.   But the viscount took a different view of the matter when the monarch, throwing off the mask, himself accepted the responsibility. Joyeuse now called on the citizens of Nismes to lay down their arms, to expel all the refugees, and to receive a garrison.   But the Nismois firmly declined the summons, grounding their refusal partly on their duty to themselves, partly on the manifest inhumanity of surrendering their fellow-citizens to certain butchery.   As was true in more than one instance, it was the. *people* that, by their decision, saved the rich from the inevitable results of their own timid counsels.   Most of the judges of the royal court of justice, and most of the opulent citizens, advocated a surrender of Nismes to Joyeuse, which must have been the prelude to a fresh and perhaps indiscriminate massacre.[2]

Scarcely less important to the Protestants of southern France was the refuge they found in Montauban.   Regnier, the same Huguenot gentleman who had himself been rescued from slaughter at Paris by the magnanimity of Vezins,[3] was the instrument of its deliverance.   On finding himself safe, his first impulse was to hasten to Montauban and urge his brethren to adopt instant measures for self-defence. But despair had taken possession of the inhabitants.   They had heard that the dreaded black cavalry of the ferocious Montluc,

Montauban.

---

[1] Borrel, Histoire de l'église réformée de Nîmes (Toulouse, 1856), pp. 77, 78, from Archives of the Hôtel-de-ville.

[2] J. de Serres, iv., fols. 68–70; Borrel, Hist. de l'égl. réf. de Nîmes, 78, 79 ; De Thou, iv. 663.

[3] See *ante*, chapter xviii., p. 480.

the men-at-arms of Fontenille, and other troops, were on the march against them. Their enemies were already reported to be so near the city as Castel-Sarrasin. Not a gate, therefore, would the panic-stricken citizens close; not a sword would they draw. Nothing was left but for Regnier, with the little band of less than forty followers he had gathered, to abandon the devoted place. As he was wandering about the country, uncertain whither to betake himself, he unexpectedly fell in with the very enemy before whom Montauban was quailing. Neither Regnier nor his handful of followers hesitated. It was a glorious opportunity for the display of heroism in a good cause, for there were ten Roman Catholics to one Protestant. Happily the ground was favorable to the display of individual prowess; a river and a tributary brook rendered the field so contracted that only a few men could fight abreast. "Brethren and comrades," cried Regnier, "whether for life or for combat, there is no other road than this." Then putting forward a detachment of ten horsemen headed by an experienced leader, when he saw the enemy pause to put on their helmets, he seized the opportunity in true Huguenot fashion to act as the minister of his followers, and uttered a brief prayer, devout and courageous. Next came the charge, such as those men of iron determination knew well how to make. The van of the enemy made no attempt to resist them; the cavalry in the centre was driven back in confusion upon the mounted arquebusiers of the rear. The fight became in a few minutes a disgraceful rout, and for a whole league the handful of Huguenots continued the pursuit. Of nearly four hundred royalists, eighty were killed and fifty captured. When Regnier, returning to Montauban, brought the flags of the enemy and a body of prisoners outnumbering his own band, the citizens renounced their fears, accepted the omen as a pledge of Divine assistance, and cast in their lot with their brethren of La Rochelle.[1]

---

[1] Agrippa d'Aubigné, Hist. univ., ii. 38 (liv. i., c. 8). Neither De Thou, iv. (liv. liii.) 659, nor J. de Serres (either in his Commentaria de statu rel. et reip., iv. 68, or in his Inventaire général de l'histoire de France, Genève, 1619), makes any allusion to Regnier's combat, while the former expressly, and the latter by implication, refer to his agency in persuading the inhabitants of

For La Rochelle had now become the centre of interest, and Montauban, Nismes, and even Sancerre, whose brave and obstinate siege will soon occupy us, were for the time almost wholly dismissed from consideration. The strongly fortified Protestant town, the only point upon the shores of the ocean which during the former civil wars had defied every assault of the papal leaders, was now the safe and favorite refuge of the Huguenots, and the coveted prey of the enemy. Within a very short time after the massacre, a stream of fugitives set in toward La Rochelle. It was not long before her hospitable walls sheltered fifty of the Protestant nobles of the neighboring provinces, fifty-five ministers, and fifteen hundred soldiers, chiefly from Saintonge, Aunis, and Poitou. Among the new-comers were not a few who had with difficulty escaped from the bloody scenes at Paris.[1] All were inspired with the same courage, all possessed by the same determination to sell their lives as dear as possible; for the successive accounts of the cruelties perpetrated in all parts of France left no doubt respecting the fate of the Rochellois should they too succumb.

And there were not wanting circumstances of an alarming nature. At Brouage, then a flourishing port some twenty-five miles south of La Rochelle, a considerable body of troops had been gathered under Philip Strozzi, the chief officer of the French infantry, while a fleet was in course of preparation under the well-known Baron de la Garde. This occurred previously to the massacre. The force, it was given out, was intended for a secret expedition against the Spaniards. While the Huguenots of Coligny, forming a junction with the troops of William of Orange, should attack Alva in Flanders, Strozzi and La Garde were to make a diversion upon the coasts of Spain itself. But the inhabitants of La Rochelle gave little credit to this explanation, and even the personal assurances of the admiral had not entirely removed their fears that their own destruction was in-

La Rochelle the centre of interest.

Montauban to espouse the Protestant cause in arms. I incline to think, nevertheless, that D'Aubigné has neither misplaced nor exaggerated a brilliant little affair which was certainly to his taste.

[1] J. de Serres, De statu, etc., iv., fol. 63; De Thou, iv. (liv. liii.) 647.

tended. It is not strange, therefore, that they accepted the Massacre of St. Bartholomew's Day as a complete demonstration of the correctness of their suspicions, and at once took measures for protecting their city against surprise or open assault. Nor is it altogether easy to ascertain how far their apprehensions were unfounded. There were intelligent and well-informed contemporary writers, who felt no doubt that Strozzi was waiting with sealed orders for the coming of the fatal twenty-fourth of August. Two months before, they say, there had been sent him by Catharine de' Medici a packet which he was strictly forbidden to open until that day. It proved to be a letter of instruction couched in these words: "Strozzi, I notify you that this day, the twenty-fourth of August, the admiral and all the Huguenots who were with him here have been slain. Consequently, take diligent measures to make yourself master of La Rochelle, and do to the Huguenots who shall fall into your hands the same that we have done to those who were here. Take good heed that you fail not, insomuch as you fear to displease the king my son, and myself. CATHARINE."[1]

A spurious letter of Catharine de' Medici.

If, as I can but believe, this letter be spurious, none the less may it serve to indicate how firmly the persuasion was fixed in the minds of the Protestants that insidious designs were cherished against La Rochelle.

It was not long before those designs began to develop. Strozzi, to whom the inhabitants had sent a deputation, avowedly to obtain explanations respecting the circumstances of the massacre, but in reality to discover the plans of the government, graciously offered some companies of his soldiers for their protection. But the Rochellois with equal politeness declined to accept such help. Meanwhile, they set themselves vigorously at work, and not only organized the inhabitants and refugees into companies for military defence, but repaired and manned the fortifications, and introduced a great abundance of provisions and munitions of war into the city.[2] A

Designs upon the city.

---

[1] Reveille-Matin, 200; Eusebii Philadelphi Dialogi (1574), i. 57.

[2] Arcère, Histoire de la Rochelle, i. 405. The records of the customs showed that 30,000 casks of wine were brought in. An ample supply of pow-

few days later, letters were received from Charles himself, which, while endeavoring to calm the minds of the inhabitants respecting recent occurrences, promised them full protection in their religious rights, proclaimed the king's unaltered determination to maintain his edict, and called upon them to receive with due submission M. de Biron, whom he sent them to be their governor. No better choice could have been made among the Roman Catholics; for Biron, it was currently reported, so far from approving of severity, had himself narrowly escaped being involved in the massacre, and had owed his safety mainly to the fact that he was in command at the arsenal.

The shrewd Rochellois, however, while they greeted the king's assurances with all outward show of credit, were not willing to be duped. They listened respectfully to the king's envoys, and professed themselves his most devoted subjects; but they begged to be excused from receiving Marshal Biron as their governor until the troops of Strozzi should have been removed from their dangerous proximity to the city, and until the fleet should have set sail from Brouage. Nor, indeed, could Biron himself obtain better conditions, when, having sought an interview with the deputies of La Rochelle outside of the walls, he entreated them, with sincere or well-feigned emotion, to forestall the ruin impending over them.[1] In vain did he humor their claim, dating from regal concessions and long prescription, that La Rochelle need receive no garrison but of her own municipal militia.[2] In vain did he offer to make his entry with but one or two followers, and promise that, when they had duly submitted, he would secure them from injury at the hands of the royal troops, and would relieve them of the presence of a fleet. The citizens were inflexible. The experience of Castres, where lately the credulous inhabitants had in-

---

der was also secured by offering a bonus of ten per cent. to all that imported it from abroad.

[1] Jean de Serres, iv., fol. 65; De Thou, iv. 649.

[2] "Affirmabant vero haudquaquam se facere contra officium et antiqua sua privilegia, per quæ illis tribueretur exemptio ab omni præterquam ex sua civitate delecto ab ipsis præsidio, et facultas sese suis armis custodiendi." Such was the claim of the Rochellois in answer to Strozzi's summons. Jean de Serres, iv. 63.

considerately admitted a governor sent them by the king, and
had paid for their folly with their lives, confirmed them in the
resolution rather to die with sword in hand than to be slaughtered like sheep.[1]

Two months (September and October) passed in fruitless
negotiations—precious time, which the citizens put to good
service in preparing for the inevitable struggle. It was not
until the eighth of November that the first skirmish took place,
in which one of two royal galleys sent to reconnoitre the situation of La Rochelle was captured and brought into harbor by
some Huguenot boats that had sailed out intending to secure
the neighboring Île de Ré for the Protestant cause.[2]

Meantime the court, reluctant to undertake an enterprise so
formidable as the regular siege of La Rochelle seemed likely to
prove, resorted to pacific measures, and resolved to
employ for the purpose a person the most unlikely to
be selected by Roman Catholics. This was none other than the
famous François de la Noue, a Protestant leader not less remarkable for generalship than for literary ability, of whose
"Political and Military Discourses," written during a later
captivity, it has been said with justice that, in perspicuity,
force, and good judgment, they are not inferior to the most
celebrated commentaries of antiquity.[3] La Noue was with
Louis of Nassau in the city of Mons when the news of Admiral
Coligny's murder, and of the consequent failure of the promised
support of France, reached him. Mons soon after surrendered
to the Duke of Alva, and La Noue scarcely knew whither to
turn for refuge, when he received from his old friend, the Duke
of Longueville, Governor of Picardy, a cordial invitation to
return to France. Not without many misgivings, he visited
Paris, where, contrary to his expectations, Charles greeted him
very graciously, and even restored to him the confiscated property of his wife's murdered brother, Téligny. Taking advan-

Mission of La Noue.

---

[1] Arcère, i. 412.

[2] Ibid., i. 422; De Thou, iv. (liv. liii.) 654 ; J. de Serres, iv., fols. 75, 76.

[3] Delmas, Église réf. de la Rochelle, 105, 106. The same author cites
Henry IV.'s eulogy : " Il était grand homme de guerre, et plus grand homme
de bien." See also De Thou's strong expressions, viii. (liv. cii.) 8.

tage of the moment, the king now requested La Noue to undertake the task of mediating between the government and La
Rochelle, and thus preventing the outbreak of a new civil war
and the effusion of more blood. At first La Noue positively
declined the appointment; but the king was urgent, and the
arguments which he adduced coincided with the Huguenot's
own impressions of the hopelessness of a struggle undertaken
by a single city against the united forces of the most powerful
kingdom of Christendom. It was only after the most solemn
protestations of Charles, that he would not make use of him as
an instrument to deceive and ruin his Protestant brethren, that
La Noue reluctantly consented to accept a commission from
which he was more likely to reap embarrassment than glory.

And certainly his first reception by the Rochellois was far
from flattering. In a conference with the deputies of the city,
He is badly received by the Rochellois. in the suburban village of Tadon [1]—for La Noue was
not permitted to enter the walls—the burghers clearly
revealed the suspicion with which they viewed him.
They bluntly told him, after listening to the propositions he
brought from the king, "that they had come to confer with M.
de la Noue, but that they did not recognize him in the person
before them. The brave warrior so closely bound to them in
former years, and who had lost an arm in their defence, had a
different heart, never came to them with vain hopes, nor, under
the guise of friendship, invited them to conferences destined
only to betray them." [2]   But, in spite of this somewhat uncour-
teous reception, the well-known and trusted integrity of the
great Huguenot captain soon broke through the thin crust of
coolness, which, after all, was rather assumed than really felt.
La Noue was suffered to enter the city, and at the échevinage,
or city hall, was permitted to lay before the general assembly,
or municipal government, as well as the other citizens, the full
extent of the king's concessions. Amnesty for the past, con-

---

[1] See the detailed " Carte du Pays d'Aulnis, avec les Isles de Ré, d'Oléron,
et Provinces voisines, dressée en 1756," prefixed to the first volume of Arcère,
Histoire de la Rochelle.
[2] Agrippa d'Aubigné, ii. 34, 35 (liv. i., c. 6); De Thou, iv. (liv. liii.) 655-
656; Jean de Serres, iv., fol. 75; Arcère, i. 427-429.

firmation of the city's privileges, passports for any who might wish to remove to England or Germany, safe return for those whom fear had banished, free exercise of the Protestant religion in two quarters of the city, with three ministers to be chosen by the people and approved by the governor—all this he offered. On the other hand, a new church must be built for the Roman Catholics, the strangers who had lately come must remove elsewhere, and, of course, the governor must be admitted, although the king kindly consented to let them designate any other sufficiently distinguished and capable person, if they preferred to do so.[1]

Neither the exposition of the terms of the royal clemency, nor the dark picture drawn of the ruin overhanging the city, shook the constancy of its brave advocates. They replied that they would consent to receive neither garrison nor royal governor, and they exhibited to La Noue

The royal proposals rejected.

their charters granted by Charles the Fifth, and ratified both by Louis the Eleventh and by the reigning monarch. They added, "that, with God's help, they hoped not to be caught in their beds as their brethren had been at the Parisian matins."[2] Yet, even after this conference, the Rochellois were so far from losing their respect for La Noue, that they made him three propositions: either he might remain in La Rochelle as a private citizen; or he might assume the military command, as their commander-in-chief; or, if he should prefer so to do, he might pass over into England in one of their vessels. La Noue went to consult with Marshal Biron and others, and shortly returned. With their full concurrence he accepted the military command—the unparalleled anomaly being thus exhibited of a general of great experience and high reputation voluntarily given by the besiegers to the besieged, because of the confidence they entertained that by his moderation and pacific inclination he would restrain the excesses of the mob and hasten the return of peace.[3]

---

[1] Arcère, i. 429, partly on MS. authority.

[2] Ibid., i. 430.

[3] The attitude of the Huguenot general had been and yet was one of the strangest. That he was able in the end to extricate himself without a stain

And now the siege, which the court had long hesitated to undertake, began in earnest. On the fourth of December, Marshal Biron approached La Rochelle with seven ensigns of horse and eighteen companies of foot, and two larger cannon.[1] Meantime the most strenuous efforts were put forth to collect an adequate besieging force. When milder measures failed to secure prompt obedience, recourse was had to threats, and the nobles were summoned on pain, in case of disobedience, of losing their privileges, and being reduced to the rank of "roturiers." The menace had its effect, and in the month of January, 1573, the force under Biron had swollen to sixty companies of foot, with not less than thirty-seven large cannon—a considerable provision of artillery for that period.[2]

The city of La Rochelle occupies the head of a deep bay, stretching in a north-easterly direction from the ocean, and serving at present as the large and convenient harbor for its extensive commerce. The old town, whose origin is lost in the mists of antiquity, covered only a small part of the area since inclosed by walls. A narrow peninsula, protected on the one side by a sheet of water and on the other by marshes, offered a tempting site, and was first occupied. The larger inlet on the west was the old, and probably for a long time the only haven; but long before the middle of the sixteenth century the action of the tide, which washes in great quantities of sand, combining with the gradual deposit of alluvium made by the neighboring springs, had converted this inlet into a marsh— "les Marais Salans"—intersected by ditches and used only in the manufacture of salt. The marsh itself has since been entirely reclaimed. The "new" harbor, as the smaller inlet was still called, at the period of which I am speaking, was of much

Marshal Biron appears before La Rochelle.

Beginning of the fourth religious war.

Description of La Rochelle.

---

attaching to his honor is still more remarkable. Both king and Protestants understood full well that he would counsel nothing which was not for the interest of both; and it was, therefore, no violation of his duty as envoy of Charles, if, as Jean de Serres informs us, when urging an amicable arrangement, he privately advised the Rochellois to admit no one into the city in the king's name, before receiving ample provisions for their security. Commentarii de statu religionis et reipublicæ, iv., fol. 75.

[1] Jean de Serres, iv., fol. 76.   [2] Ibid., iv., fol. 81.

inferior capacity, and was included within the circuit of the walls.[1] A chain, extended between the two towers guarding its narrow entrance, effectually precluded the passage of hostile vessels.

For considerably more than one-half of their circuit, the walls of La Rochelle were inaccessible to the land forces; and the deep foss skirting them was full of water, except on the north and north-east. The fortifications, everywhere formidable, had, therefore, been constructed with extraordinary care in these directions; for it was here that the brunt of the attack must be borne. With Puritan simplicity and faith, the reformed inhabitants of La Rochelle had named the strong work at the north-western angle of the circuit the "Bastion de l'Évangile," or the "Bastion of the Gospel." It was appropriately supported on the right by the "Cavalier de l'Épître." Other forts, such as that of Cognes at the north-eastern angle, were but little inferior in importance; it was evident, however, that upon the ability of the Rochellois to defend the Bastion de l'Évangile must depend the salvation of the city.[2]

But the chief strength of the city was to be found in the manly resolution of the inhabitants to secure for themselves and their children the right to worship God according to the purer faith, or perish in the attempt. An incident occurring about this time served to illustrate and to confirm their courage. A short distance in advance of the Bastion de l'Évangile there stood a solitary windmill, which, on account of its advantageous position, the Rochellois were anxious to retain. The captain to whose guard it was intrusted, recognizing the ease with which he might be surprised and cut off, took the precaution to draw off at dusk the small detachment which he had placed there by day, leaving but a single soldier to act as sentry. Meantime, Strozzi had determined to capture the mill. This he attempted to do, taking advantage of

Resoluteness of the Rochellois.

---

[1] See the very clear account in the "Description chorographique de l'Aulnis," by Arcère, prefixed to his history of La Rochelle, i. 97, etc.

[2] Compare Arcère, i. 418, etc., and, especially, his plan of the city in 1573. See also Jean de Serres, iv., fol. 83; De Thou, iv. (liv. lv.) 759-761; D'Aubigné, ii. 36, 37 (liv. i., c. 7).

a moonlight night. To the two culverines brought to play upon him, the solitary defender could answer only with his arquebuse; but so briskly did he fire, and so well did he counterfeit the voices of others, that the assailants believed an entire company to be present. At last, when he no longer could hold out, the soldier only surrendered after stipulating for the life of himself and his entire band. Notwithstanding his promise, Strozzi, when once his astonishment at the appearance of the single actor who had played so many parts had given place to anger at the deceit practised upon him, was in favor of hanging the Huguenot for his audacity. But Biron would only consent to have him sent to the galleys, a punishment which he escaped by finding means to slip away from the hands of the royalists.[1]

The entire military force of the besieged comprised about thirteen hundred regular troops, besides two thousand citizens, Their military well armed and drilled, and under competent cap-strength. tains. There was an abundance of powder, of wine, biscuit, and other provisions, although of wheat there was but little.[2] Meantime assistance was anxiously expected from England, and the courage of the common people, incited by the exhortations of the ministers, did not flag, notwithstanding the feebler spirit of the rich and the actual desertion of a few leaders.[3]

The besiegers were not idle. Besides occupying positions north, east, and south of the city, which effectually cut off communication from the land side, they built forts on opposite sides of the outer harbor, and stranded at the entrance a large carack, which was made firm in its position with stones and sand. The work, when provided with guns and troops, commanded the passage, and was christened "le Fort de l'Aiguille." In vain did the Rochellois attempt to destroy or capture it; the carack, while it proved unavailing to prevent the entrance of an occasional vessel laden with grain or ammunition, remained the most formidable point in the possession of the enemy.

In order to give her favorite son a new opportunity to acquire

---

[1] De Thou, iv. (liv. lv.) 765 ; Arcère, i. 436.
[2] De Thou, iv. 761 ; Jean de Serres, iv., fol. 68.
[3] *E. g.*, of Virolet, Jean de Serres, iv., fol. 76.

military distinction, the queen mother now persuaded Charles
to permit the Duke of Anjou to conduct the siege.
He arrived before La Rochelle about the middle of
February,[1] with a brilliant train of princes and nobles,
among whom were Alençon, Guise, Aumale, and
Montluc, besides Henry of Navarre and his cousin Condé, who,
as they had to sustain the rôle of good Roman Catholics, could
scarcely avoid taking part in the campaign against their former
brethren.   In the ordinances soon after published by Anjou, he
seems to have hoped to weaken the Huguenots by copying their
own strictness of moral discipline.   The very Catholic practice
of profane swearing, in which his Majesty was so proficient,
was prohibited on pain of severe punishment; and it was prescribed that a sermon should daily be preached in the camp.[2]   A
good round oath none the less continued to be received by the
soldiers, in all doubtful cases, as a sufficient proof of loyalty to
Mother Church, nor did they cease because of the ordinance
from ridiculing the idea that such good Christians as they
needed preaching, which was well enough for unevangelized
pagans.[3]

Henry, Duke of Anjou, appointed to conduct the siege.

In view of the impending peril, the Protestants had recourse,
as their custom was, to prayer and fasting.   The sixteenth and
eighteenth of February were days of public humiliation.   From their knees the Huguenots went with
redoubled courage to the ramparts.   The crisis had at length
arrived.   A series of furious assaults were given, directed prin-
pally against the northern wall and the Bastion de l'Évangile.
It was in one of these attacks, on the third of March, that the
Duke of Aumale was killed.   By the besieged the death of so
eminent a member of the house of Lorraine was interpreted as
a signal judgment of God upon the most cruel member of a
persecuting family — another presage that the sword should
never depart from the princely stock which had begun the war,

The besieged pray and fight.

---

[1] Feb. 15th, according to J. de Serres, iv., fol. 83. Arcère (i. 452) says
Feb. 12th.

[2] Arcère, i. 458.

[3] So, at least, Brantôme expressed himself. He was with the army before
La Rochelle.

until it should be altogether destroyed. The royalists, on the other hand, found in it a great source of regret; while Catharine, terrified at the danger to which her son might be exposed, wrote one of her ill-spelt letters to Montpensier, entreating him and the other veterans not to suffer any of the princes to go imprudently near the walls.[1]

It does not enter into the plan of this history to detail the progress of the siege. Let it suffice to say that the enemy was met at every point and repulsed. Not content with simply defending their walls, the Huguenots made sorties, in which many of Anjou's followers were slain. Sometimes dressing in the uniform of those they had killed or taken prisoners, they returned and penetrated into the hostile camp, learned the plans of the assailants, and cut off more than one man of note. The Bravery of the women. presence of women among them became an element of strength; for these, surmounting the weakness of their sex, did good service in the mines, or, donning armor, defended the breach and drove the enemy into the ditch.[2] It was remarked that, as the supply of fresh provisions diminished, the lack was in some degree compensated by such an abundance of cockles on the sands as had never before been known. If the Protestants regarded this incident as a providential interposition in their behalf,[3] the Roman Catholics sought to account for it by supposing that the operations of the siege had permitted the fish to multiply undisturbed.[4] However this might be, the women of La Rochelle sallied forth to hus-

---

[1] Letter of Catharine, March 17th, Arcère, i. 466.

[2] De Thou, iv. (liv. lvi.) 789; Arcère, i. 489, 490; Jean de Serres, iv., fol. 99, etc.

[3] The poor, according to Jean de Serres, came to use the shell-fish in lieu of bread. If, as he assures us on the authority of men deserving credit, the supply ceased almost on that precise day upon which the royal army left the neighborhood, after the conclusion of peace, the reformed may be pardoned for regarding the fact as a miracle little inferior to that of the manna which never failed the ancient Israelites until they set foot in Canaan. Commentarii de statu religionis et reipublicæ, iv. 104 *verso*. "Dont lez reformez ont encores les tableaux en leurs maisons pour mémoire comme d'un miracle," writes Agrippa d'Aubigné, about forty years later (Hist. universelle, 1616, ii. 53).

[4] Arcère, i. 504, 505.

band this new resource; but their imprudence in straying beyond the range of the guns was rewarded with insolent outrage on the part of such of the enemy as were in the vicinity. Even this circumstance the Huguenots knew how to turn to advantage. Disguising themselves in feminine attire, a troop of Huguenot soldiers, a day or two later, issued from the city when the tide was out, apparently bent on the same errand. It was not long before the royalists undertook to repeat a diversion which seemed to offer little danger to them. Scarcely, however, had they approached when the clumsy costume was hastily thrown aside, and the assailants discovered too late the trap into which they had fallen. Many a hot-headed soldier of Anjou atoned for his temerity with his life.[1]

The ordinary wiles of Catharine were not left untried; but she effected little or nothing by negotiation. The people were not so easily cajoled and duped as their leaders had often been, and would accept no terms except such as the court utterly refused to offer—the restoration of the privileges conferred by the edict, its confirmation by oath, and the interchange of hostages, to be kept in some neutral state in Germany, with entire liberty of worship and exemption from royal garrison in and around La Rochelle, Montauban, Nismes, and Sancerre.[2] Even François de la Noue became impatient at the excessive caution which the Huguenots seemed to him to display, and, redeeming the promise he had given the king before he took command, retired from the city (on the eleventh of March) when all hope of reconciliation had apparently disappeared. With wonderful prudence he had managed to forfeit the confidence of neither party. Yet on some occasions, it must be admitted, his self-control was sorely tried. For example, at one time a minister—not long after deposed from the sacred office—so far forgot himself in the heat of angry discussion as to give La Noue a sound box upon the ear. Even then the great captain refused to order the offender's punishment, and confined himself to sending him,

La Noue retires. Failure of diplomacy.

---

[1] Arcère, *ubi supra*.   [2] Arcère, i. 477, 480.

under guard, to his wife, with directions to keep him carefully until he should recover his reason.[1]

The assistance which La Rochelle had counted upon receiving from England never came. Count Montgomery was a skilful *English aid miscarries.* negotiator. If he was unable to prevail upon Elizabeth to give open countenance to the Huguenots, on account of the league recently entered into, which Retz had been specially sent by Charles to confirm, he at least succeeded in obtaining a sum of forty thousand francs from various English, French, and Flemish sympathizers, with which he was permitted, notwithstanding protests from Paris, to fit out a fleet. Elizabeth, indeed, so far overcame her scruples as to allow a large vessel of her own to follow. But when Montgomery's squadron reached the roads of La Rochelle, the fifty-three ships of which it was composed, and which carried eighteen hundred or two thousand men, were so small and badly-appointed—in short, so inferior in strength to the fewer vessels of the king standing off the entrance—that they avoided coming to close quarters, stood off to Belle Isle, and finally returned to England. Queen Elizabeth, at all times very doubtful respecting the propriety of assisting subjects against their monarch, had meantime disowned the enterprise as piratical, and expressed the hope the culprits might be destroyed. It was not, in this case, merely her customary dissimulation. The plundering by some French and Netherland sailors of the vessel on which the Earl of Worcester was proceeding, in the queen's name, to stand as sponsor at the baptism of Charles's infant daughter, had greatly incensed her.[2] Not, however, that Elizabeth lost any of that remarkable interest which she had always taken in Count Montgomery, or felt at all inclined to give him up to the French government for his breach of the peace. For when, a little later, a demand was made for the culprit, she assured the ambassador of Charles that she could swear she was ignorant that the count was in her dominions. "But," she added, "were he

---

[1] De Thou, iv. (liv. lvi.) 780; Arcère, i. 477; D'Aubigné, ii. 45 (liv. i., c. 9).

[2] Jean de Serres, iv., fol. 102 ; Agrippa d'Aubigné, ii. 48 (liv. i., c. 9) ; De Thou, iv. 767, 786, 787, etc.

to come, I would answer your master as his father answered my sister, Queen Mary, when he said, ' I will not consent to be the hangman of the Queen of England.' So his Majesty, the King of France, must excuse me if I can no more act as executioner of those of my religion than King Henry would discharge a similar office in the case of those that were not of his religion." [1]

In other parts of France it had fared no better with the attempt to crush the Huguenots. Montauban and Nismes still held out. Various places in the south-east fell into Huguenot hands. The siege of Sommières, near Nismes, by the Roman Catholics, was so obstinate, and the garrison capitulated on such favorable terms, that the Protestants were rather elated than discouraged. Marshal Damville had assailed it only in order to save his credit, and the little town detained him nearly two months, —from the eleventh of February to the ninth of April. Every device was employed to retard his success. Streams of boiling oil were poured upon the heads of the assailants, and red-hot hoops of iron were dexterously tossed over their shoulders. In the end the garrison marched out with all the honors of war. [2] The Huguenots surprised Villeneuve, near the Rhône, by effecting an entrance, much as they had entered Nismes in 1569, through the grated opening by which the waters of a sewer issued from the walls. [3]

Huguenot successes in the south.

Sommières.

Villeneuve.

But it was Sancerre which, next to La Rochelle, occasioned the court the greatest annoyance, both because of its central position [4] and because of its comparative proximity to Paris. Here the Protestants of Berry and the adjacent provinces had found a welcome refuge. Citizens and refugees refused to admit a royal garrison, and foiled the attempt to capture the place by escalade. Treachery was at

Beginning of the siege of Sancerre.

---

[1] La Mothe Fénélon to Charles IX., June 3, 1573. Corresp. diplom., v. 339.

[2] Jean de Serres (iv., fol. 87) states the length of the siege of Sommières as *four* months, and the loss of men as five thousand killed. The Recueil des choses mémorables, 1598 (p. 485), ascribed to the same author, reduces the loss one-half. Cf. De Thou, iv. 746–748.

[3] Jean de Serres, iv., fols. 88, 89 ; De Thou, iv. (liv. lvi.) 749, 750.

[4] " In ipso regni umbilico." Jean de Serres, iv., fol. 92.

work, and, as usual, it was most rife among the richer class. By their connivance the citadel or castle was surprised by the troops sent by the governor of the province, M. de la Chastre; but it was retaken on the same day.[1] Notwithstanding this warning, the people of Sancerre took none of the precautions which their situation demanded, apparently unable to believe that, when such a city as La Rochelle was in revolt, the king would undertake to subdue so small a place as Sancerre. There were no stores of provisions, and the buildings in proximity to the walls, from which an enemy could incommode the city, had not been torn down, when, between the third and ninth of January, 1573, a force of five thousand foot and five hundred horse, under La Chastre, besides many nobles and gentlemen of the vicinage, made its appearance before the walls. The inhabitants now discovered their capital mistakes, but it was too late to remedy them. Hunger began almost immediately to make itself felt, while the places they had neglected to destroy or preoccupy proved very convenient to the royalists for the next two or three months, during which it was attempted to take Sancerre by assault. Yet the direct attack proved a failure, and, on the twentieth of March, the siege was changed to a blockade. Forts were erected in the most advantageous spots, and a wide trench was dug around the entire city.[2] Sancerre was to be tried by the severe ordeal of hunger; and certainly the most frightful among ancient sieges can scarcely be said to have surpassed in horror that of this small city.[3]

Did not the sufferings of the heroic inhabitants claim our sympathy, we might read with entertainment the singular The incipient devices they resorted to in grappling with a terrible famine. foe whose insidious advances were more difficult to oppose than the open assaults of the enemy. For the famine of Sancerre boasts of a historian more copious and minute than Josephus or Livy. In reading the narrative of the famous Jean

---

[1] Ibid., iv., fols. 72, 77, 79; Ag. d'Aubigné, ii. 40, 41; De Thou, iv. (liv. liv.) 660–663.

[2] Jean de Serres, iv., fol. 93, 94.

[3] "Ut Ierosolymitanæ, Samaritanæ, Saguntinæ famis memoriam exæquare, nisi et exsuperare videatur." Ibid., iv., fol. 92.

de Léry [1]—the same writer to whom we are indebted for an authentic account of Villegagnon's unfortunate scheme of American colonization—we seem to be perusing a great pathological treatise. Never was physician more watchful of his patient's symptoms than Léry with his hand upon the pulse of famishing Sancerre. It would almost seem that the restless Huguenot, who united in his own person the opposite qualifications of clergyman and soldier, desired to make his little work a useful guide in similar circumstances, for a portion of it, at least, has been appropriately styled " a cookery book for the besieged." [2]

Early in the siege, not without some qualms, the inhabitants made trial of the flesh of a horse accidentally killed. Next an ass, and then the mules, of which there was a considerable number, were brought to the shambles. The butchers were now ordered to sell this new kind of meat, and a maximum price was fixed. For a fortnight the supply of cats held out, after which rats and mice became the chief staple of food. Dog-flesh was next reluctantly tasted, and found, as our conscientious chronicler observes, to be somewhat sweet and insipid. [3] And so the spring of 1573 passed away, and summer came; but no succor arrived for the beleaguered city. On the contrary, there came the disheartening tidings from the west that a peace had been concluded by the Huguenots of La Rochelle, in which no mention was made of Sancerre.

So successful had been the defence of the citadel of Protestantism on the shores of the ocean, so unexpectedly large the

Losses of the royal army before La Rochelle.

royal losses, that the court was only waiting for a decent pretext to abandon the unfortunate siege. Pestilence added its victims to those of the sword, and it was currently reported that forty thousand of the be-

---

[1] " Discours de l'extreme famine, cherté de vivre, chairs, et autres choses non acoustumées pour la nourriture de l'homme, dont les assiégez dans la ville de Sancerre ont été affligez." 1574. Reprinted in Archives curieuses, viii. 19–82.

[2] Edward Smedley, History of the Reformed Religion in France (London, 1834), ii. 88.

[3] " Fade et douceastre," p. 24.

siegers were swept away by their combined assaults.[1]   A more careful enumeration, however, shows that, while the Rochellois, out of thirty-one hundred soldiers, lost thirteen hundred, including twenty-eight "pairs," the king, out of a little more than forty thousand troops, had lost twenty-two thousand, ten thousand of whom died in the breach or in engagements elsewhere.   Nor was the loss of officers trifling ; two hundred had died, including fifty of great distinction, and five "maîtres de camp."[2]   And, with all this expenditure of life, and with the heavy drafts upon the public treasure, little or nothing had been accomplished.   Meanwhile, in other parts of France there

Roman Catholic processions.   existed a scarcity of food amounting almost to a famine ; nor had the solemn processions to the shrines of the saints—processions for the most part rendered contemptible by the irreverent conduct both of the clergymen and the laity that took part in them[3]—averted the wrath of heaven.   The poor suffered extremely.   Selfishness gained such ascendancy in some towns, that cruel ruses were adopted to remove the destitute that had taken refuge within their walls.   It was not strange that the extraordinary mortality which soon fell upon the well-to-do burghers was viewed by many as a direct punishment sent by the Almighty.[4]

The event which came just in time to free the court from its embarrassment was the election of Henry of Anjou to the vacant throne of Poland.   We have already witnessed the perplexity of Bishop Montluc when the tidings of the massacre

---

[1] De Thou, iv. (liv. lvi.) 796.   As early as on the twelfth of April, such was the discouragement felt in Paris, that orders were published to make "Paradises" in each parish, and to institute processions, to supplicate the favor of heaven, in view of the repulses experienced by the Roman Catholics before La Rochelle.   Journal d'un curé ligueur (Jehan de la Fosse), p. 158.

[2] Histoire du siége de La Rochelle par le duc d'Anjou en 1573, par A. Genet, capitaine du génie ; *apud* Bulletin de la Société de l'histoire du prot. français, ii. (1854) 96, 190.

[3] Mémoires de Claude Haton, ii. 722.

[4] At Troyes, for instance, where the poor who had flocked to the city were invited to meet at one of the gates, to receive each a loaf of bread and a piece of money.   This done, they saw the gates closed upon them, and were informed from the ramparts that they must go elsewhere to find their living until the next harvest.   Claude Haton, ii. 729.

first reached him.[1] If he could have denied its reality, he would
have done so. This being impossible, he was forced
to content himself with misrepresenting the origin of
the slaughter, slandering the admiral and the other
victims, and circulating the calumnies of Charpentier
and others who prated about a Huguenot conspiracy. A judicious distribution of French gold assisted his own eloquent
sophistry ; and the Duke of Anjou, portrayed as a chivalric
prince and one who was not ill-affected to religious liberty, was
chosen king over his formidable rivals. Charles and Catharine
were alike delighted. The former could scarcely find words to
express his joy[2] at the prospect of being freed from the presence of a brother whom he feared, and perhaps hated ; while
the queen mother's gratification was even more intense at the
peaceful solution of the prophecy of Nostradamus, than at the
elevation of her favorite son.

Election of Henry of Anjou to the crown of Poland.

The peace between the king and the Rochellois was concluded in June, and was formally promulgated in July, 1573,
in a royal edict from Boulogne. The chief provision
was that the Protestants in the cities of La Rochelle,
Montauban, and Nismes should enjoy entire freedom
of public worship, while their brethren throughout the kingdom
should have liberty of conscience and the right to sell their property and remove wherever they might choose, whether within
or without the realm. Only gentlemen and others enjoying
high jurisdiction, who had remained constant in their faith,
and had taken up arms with the three cities, were to be allowed
to collect their friends to the number of ten to witness their
marriages and baptisms, according to the custom of the Reformed Church. Even this privilege could not be exercised
within the distance of two leagues from the royal court or from

Edict of Pacification, Boulogne, July, 1573.

---

[1] *Ante*, chapter xix., p. 552.

[2] Here is his letter to Henry : " Mon frère, Dieu nous a fait la grasse
que vous estes ellu roy de Poulogne. J'en suis si ayse que je ne sçay que
vous mander. Je loue Dieu de bon cœur ; pardonnés moy, l'ayse me garde
d'escrire. Je ne sceay que dire. Mon frère, je avons receu vostre lestre.
Je suis vostre bien bon frère et amy, CHARLES." MS. Bibliothèque nationale,
apud Haton, ii. 733.

the city of Paris; nor did the edict confer the right to preach or celebrate the Lord's Supper.[1] La Rochelle, Nismes, and Montauban gained their point, and were to be exempted from receiving garrisons or having citadels built, with the condition that they should for two years constantly keep four of their principal citizens at court as pledges of their fidelity. All promises of abjuration were declared null and void. Amnesty was proclaimed, and, to cap the climax of absurdity, the brave Huguenots who had defended their homes for months against Charles were solemnly declared to be held the king's "good, loyal, and faithful subjects and servants."

The results of the war on the king's side were certainly very meagre. To have fought for the greater part of a year with the miserable Huguenots that had escaped the massacre of St. Bartholomew's Day, and then to conclude the war by such a peace, was certainly ignominious enough for Charles and his mother. For the Huguenot party was now, more than ever, a recognized power in the state, with three strongholds—one in the west and two in the south. Into no one of these could a royal garrison be introduced. La Rochelle, in particular, having repulsed every assault of the best army that could be brought against it, was acknowledged invincible by the exemptions accorded to it in common with Nismes and Montauban. It was hardly by such expectations that Charles had been prevailed upon to throw down the gage of war to his subjects of the reformed faith.

Meagre results of the war.

Meanwhile, the inhabitants of Sancerre, not even named in the edict,[2] had been sustained under appalling difficulties by the

---

[1] The edict says expressly (Art. 5th): "Et y faire seulement les baptesmes et mariages à leur façon accoustumée sans plus grande assemblée, outre les parens, parrins et marrines, jusques au nombre de dix." Text in Agrippa d'Aubigné, ii. 98, etc., and Haag, France protestante, x. (Documents) 110–114. Jean de Serres (iv., fol. 107, etc.) and Von Polenz (Gesch. des Franz. Calvinismus, ii. 632) give a correct synopsis; but Soldan is wrong in including among the concessions "den Hausgottesdienst" (ii. 536), and De Thou still more incorrect when he speaks of "les prêches et la Cène" (iv., liv. lvi. 796).

[2] According to Davila, Sancerre was *not comprehended* in the terms made with the Rochellois, "because it was not a free town under the king's abso-

confident hope of assistance from the south.   But the hope
was long deferred, and they grew sick at heart.   The
prospect was already dark enough, when, on the
second of June, a Protestant soldier, who had made
his way into the city through the enemy's lines, brought the de-
pressing announcement that no aid must be expected from Languedoc for six weeks.   As but little wheat remained in Sancerre,
the immediate effect of the intelligence was that liberty was
given to some seventy of the poor to leave the city walls.   At
the same time the daily ration was limited to half a pound of
grain.   A week later it was reduced to one-quarter of a pound.
Not long after only a single pound was doled out once a week,
and by the end of the month the supply entirely gave out.   The
beginning of July reduced the besieged to the necessity of task-
ing their ingenuity to make palatable food of the hides of cattle,
next of the skins of horses, dogs, and asses.   The stock of even
this unsavory material soon became exhausted ; whereupon, not
very unnaturally, parchment was turned to good account.   Manuscripts a good century old were eaten with relish.   Soaked for
a couple of days in water, and afterward boiled as much longer,
when they became glutinous they were fried, like tripe, or prepared with herbs and spices, after the manner of a hodge-podge.
The writer who is our authority for these culinary details, informs us that he had seen the dish devoured with eagerness
while the original letters written upon the parchment were still
legible.[1]   But the urgent necessities of their situation did not
suffer the half-famished inhabitants to stop here.   With the
proverbial ingenuity of their nation, they turned their attention
to the parchment on old drums, and subjected to the skilful
hands of cooks the discarded hoofs, horns, and bones of animals,
the harness of horses, and even refuse scraps of leather.   There
seemed to be nothing they could not lay under contribution to
furnish at least a little nutriment.

And yet ghastly hunger little by little tightened her relentless
embrace.   Almost all the children under twelve years of age

---

lute dominion as the rest, but under the seigniory of the Counts of Sancerre."
London trans. of 1678, 193.

[1] Jean de Léry, Discours de l'extreme famine, etc., 25–27.

died. In the universal reign of famine there were at last found those who were ready to repeat the horrible crime of feeding upon the flesh of their own kindred. It was discovered that a husband and wife, with a neighboring crone, had endeavored to satisfy the gnawings of hunger by eating a newly dead child. Their guilt came speedily to light, and was punished according to the severe code of the sixteenth century. The father was sentenced by the council to be burned alive; his wife to be strangled and her body consigned to the flames; while the corpse of the old woman who had instigated the foul deed but had meanwhile died, was ordered to be dug up and burned. But the feeling of the great majority of the besieged was far removed from that despair which prompts to an inhuman disregard of natural decency and affection. Near the close of July a boy of barely ten years, as he lay on his death-bed, said to his weeping parents: "Why do you weep thus at seeing me die of hunger? I do not ask bread, mother; I know you have none. But since God wills that I die thus, we must accept it cheerfully. Was not that holy man Lazarus hungry? Have I not so read in the Bible?"[1]

The catastrophe could not much longer be deferred. Within the city speedy death stared every man in the face. Permission had, we have seen, been accorded to the poor, early in June, to go forth from the city walls; but the besieging force had mercilessly driven them back when they attempted to gain the open country. Numbers, unwilling to accept a second time the fatal hospitality of the city, preferred to remain in their exposed situation, miserably dragging out a precarious existence by subsisting upon snails, buds of trees and shrubs—even to the very grass of the field.

Happily for Sancerre, the political exigencies of the royal court insured for the besieged Protestants, in the inevitable capitulation, more favorable terms than they might otherwise have obtained. As early as the eighteenth of July, Léry had been informed at a parley, by a former acquaintance on the Roman Catholic side, that a general peace had been concluded,

---

[1] Jean de Léry, 38.

and that Henry of Anjou had been elected. to the throne of Poland. This first intimation was discredited by the cautious Protestants, not unused to the wiles of the enemy. But when, some twenty days later (on the sixth of August), the statement Sancerre was confirmed, and the Sancerrois received the addi- capitulates. tional assurance that they would be mildly treated, their surprise knew no bounds. The terms of surrender were easily arranged. A ransom of forty thousand livres was to be exacted from the city. On the thirty-first of August, M. de la Chastre made his solemn entry into Sancerre, accompanied by a band of Roman Catholic priests chanting a *Te Deum* over his success. As was too frequently the case, the promise of immu- nity to the inhabitants was but poorly kept. Scarcely had two weeks passed before the " bailli " Johanneau,[1] summoned from his house by the archers of the prévôt, on the plea that M. de la Chastre desired his presence, was treacherously murdered on the way to the governor's house. Besides assassination, other infractions of the capitulation were committed ; the gates of the city were burned, the walls dismantled, many of the houses torn down. In fact, so unmercifully was Sancerre harried, partly by the troops, partly by the peasantry of the neighborhood, and by the " bailli " of Berry, that the reformed church of this place seems to have been, for the time, completely dispersed.[2]

Thus ended a siege which had lasted some eight months. The besieged had lost only eighty-four men by the direct effects

---

[1] Styled also, in the articles of capitulation, " *le gouverneur par élection* de ladite ville." He was an able and influential magistrate, who had been elected to the governorship of his native city at the time of the former trou- bles. Léry, 78–80.

[2] Agrippa d'Aubigné (Hist. univ., ii. 104) distinctly represents La Chastre as desirous of destroying the entire city ; while Léry (p. 77) and Davila (p. 193) are in doubt whether Johanneau's murder was not effected by his orders. Yet Léry himself records a conversation he held about this time with La Chastre (p. 67), in which the latter protested that he was not, as commonly reported, of a sanguinary disposition, and appealed for corroboration to his merciful treat- ment of some Huguenot prisoners that fell into his hands in the third civil war, whom he refused to surrender to the Parisian parliament when formally summoned to do so. Claude de la Chastre's noble letter to Charles IX., of January 21, 1570 (Bulletin, iv. 28), seems to be a sufficient voucher for his veracity. See *ante*, chapter xvi., p. 345.

of warfare; but more than five hundred persons perished during the last six weeks of sheer starvation.[1]

Sancerre owed its release from the horrors of the siege in great part to the same causes that had powerfully contributed to the conclusion of the peace. The Polish ambassadors, coming to proffer the crown to the king's brother, Henry of Anjou, were about to reach the French court. They were already not a little surprised at the discovery that the statements and promises made in the king's name by that not over-scrupulous negotiator, Montluc, Bishop of Valence, were impudent impostures, fabricated for no other purpose than to secure at all hazards the success of the French candidate for the Polish throne. To exhibit to them at this critical juncture the edifying spectacle of a royal governor of the province of Berry engaged in the reduction of a city the only crime of which was its desire to enjoy religious liberty—this would have been a dangerous venture. Consequently it was no fortuitous coincidence that Sancerre capitulated the very day the Polish ambassadors made their appearance.

We shall not dwell upon the pomp attending their reception. The banquet held in the new palace of the Tuileries was brilliant. In the pageant succeeding it was displayed a massive rock of silver, with sixteen nymphs in as many niches, personating the provinces of the French kingdom. When, after some verses well sung but indifferently composed, these nymphs descended from their elevation, and took part in an intricate maze of dance, the Polish spectators remarked, in the excess of their admiration, that the French ballet was something that could be imitated by none of the kings of the earth. "I would rather," dryly adds a contemporary historian, "that they had said as much respecting our *armies.*"[2]

Reception of the Polish ambassadors.

---

[1] Jean de Léry, 42.

[2] Agrippa d'Aubigné, i. 104. It would be a great relief could we believe that inordinate fondness for the dance was the chief vice of the French court. Unfortunately the moral turpitude of the king and his favorites rests upon less suspicious grounds than the revolting stories told on hearsay by the unfriendly writer of the Eusebii Philadelphi Dialogi (Edinburgi, 1574), ii. 117, 118. The "Affair of Nantouillet," occurring just about the time of the

The Protestants of Southern France had been included in the Edict of Pacification.   In fact, Nismes and Montauban were as *Discontent of* distinctly referred to by name as La Rochelle.[1]   But *the south with the terms of* the terms of peace were not to the taste of the enter- *peace.* prising and self-reliant Huguenots of Languedoc and Guyenne.   They had learned, during the last ten years, to distrust all assurances emanating from the court, even when claiming the authority of the king's name.   Experience had taught them that previous edicts were framed simply to secure the destruction of those whom open warfare had failed to destroy.[2] Without, therefore, either definitely accepting or rejecting the terms offered them, the Protestants of Nismes applied to Marshal Damville, who, at the conclusion of the peace, found himself with the royal troops at the hamlet of Milhaud, a league or

---

Polish ambassadors' arrival in Paris, is only too authentic.   The "Prévôt de Paris," M. de Nantouillet (Cf. *ante,* chapter xv., page 258, note), grandson of Cardinal du Prat, Chancellor of France under Francis I., offended Anjou by somewhat contemptuously declining the hand of the duke's discarded mistress, Mademoiselle de Châteauneuf.   The lady easily induced her princely lover to avenge her wounded vanity.   One evening Charles IX., the new king of Poland, the King of Navarre, the Grand Prior of France, and their attendants, presented themselves at the stately mansion of Nantouillet, on the southern bank of the Seine, opposite the Louvre, and demanded that a banquet be prepared for them.   Though the royal party was masked, the unwilling host knew his guests but too well, and dared not deny their peremptory command.   In the midst of the carousal, at a preconcerted signal, the king's followers began to ransack the house, maltreating the occupants, wantonly destroying the costly furniture, appropriating the silver plate, and breaking open doors and coffers in search of money.   The next day even Paris itself was indignant at the base conduct of its king.   To the first president of parliament, who that day visited the palace and informed Charles of the current rumors respecting his having been present and conniving at the pillage, the despicable monarch denied their truth with his customary horrible imprecation.   But when the president expressed his great satisfaction, and said that parliament would at once institute proceedings to discover and punish the guilty, Charles promptly responded : " By no means.   You will lose your trouble ; " and he added a significant threat for Nantouillet, that, should he pursue his attempt to obtain satisfaction, he would find that he had to do with an opponent infinitely his superior.   Euseb. Phil. Dialogi, ii. 117, 118 ; Jean de Serres, iv., fol. 114, *verso ;* D'Aubigné, ii. 104 ; De Thou, iv. (liv. lvi.) 821.

[1] Article 4th.   Text in Agrippa d'Aubigné, ii. 98.

[2] J. de Serres, iv., fol. 112.

two from their gates,[1] for a fortnight's suspension of hostilities. The request being granted, a truce was established which was extended by successive prolongations beyond the beginning of the next year.[2]

Meantime the Protestants, notified by the Duke of Anjou of the conclusion of the peace, sent messengers to his camp requesting that as the matter was one vitally affecting the entire Protestant population, they might receive permission to meet, under protection of the royal authority, and deliberate respecting it. The king's consent having been obtained, Protestant depu-

Assembly of Milhau and Montauban.

ties from almost all parts of the kingdom came together, late in the month of August, 1573, in the city of Milhau-en-Rouergue, from which they shortly transferred their sessions to Montauban.

This important assembly resolved to accept no peace unless based upon equitable terms and secured by ample guarantees. In view of the possibility of the recurrence of war, provision

Military organization of the Huguenots.

was made for a complete military organization of the Huguenot resources in the south of France. For this purpose Languedoc was divided into two "généralités" or governments—the government of Nismes, or Lower Languedoc, placed under command of M. de Saint Romain, and that of Upper Languedoc, with Montauban for its chief city, to which the Viscount de Paulin was assigned as military chief. Both governments were in turn subdivided into dioceses or particular governments, each furnished with a governor and a deliberative assembly. It was provided that in Nismes and Montauban respectively a council should be convened consisting of deputies from all the dioceses of the government, and that to this council, together with the governor, should be intrusted the administration of the finances, with authority to impose taxes alike upon Protestants and Roman Catholics. The organization, it was estimated, could readily place twenty thousand men in the field.[3]

---

[1] This hamlet must not be confounded with the important town of Milhaud, or Milhau-en-Rouergue, mentioned below, nearly seventy miles farther west.

[2] Histoire du Languedoc, v. 321.

[3] Jean de Serres, iv., fols. 113, 114; De Thou, v. (liv. lvii.) 12, 13;

Such were the first attempts to perfect a system of warfare forced upon the Huguenots by the treacherous assaults of their enemies—a fatal necessity of instituting a state within a state, foreboding nothing but ruin to France.

One of the chief results of the deliberations at Montauban was the preparation of a petition to be laid before the king. Petition to the king. This paper, which has come down to us with the signatures of the viscounts, barons, and other adherents of the Huguenot party, was intended to be an expression not only of their own individual views, but also of the sentiments of the churches they represented.[1] The language is sharp and incisive, the demands are unmistakably bold. For a sufficient justification of their recent words and actions, the Huguenots of Guyenne point the monarch to his own letter of the twenty-fourth of August, 1572, by which constraint was laid upon them to assume arms. They call upon Charles, in accordance with the promise contained in that letter, to follow up the traces there alleged to have been found regarding the murder of Gaspard de Coligny, to appoint impartial judges for this purpose, and to execute exemplary justice upon the guilty. Not satisfied with claiming the annulling of all judicial proceedings, the destruction of all monuments erected to perpetuate the memory of the Massacre of St. Bartholomew's Day, and the abolition of processions instituted by the parliaments of Paris and Toulouse with the same end in view, they call on Charles to make a dec-

---

Agrippa d'Aubigné, ii. 107; Histoire du Languedoc, v. 322. It ought to be noted that the Montauban assembly in reality did little more than confirm the regulations drawn up by previous and less conspicuous political assemblies of the Huguenots held at Anduze in February, and at Réalmont, in May, 1573. This clearly appears from references to that earlier legislation contained in the more complete "organization" adopted four months later at Milhau. See the document in Haag, France Protestante, x. (Pièces justificatives) 124, 125. M. Jean Loutchitzki has published in the Bulletin, xxii. (1873) 507–511, a list of the political assemblies much fuller than given by any previous writer.

[1] As it is of interest to fix the geographical distribution of the provinces represented, I give the list contained in the preamble : "Guyenne, Vivaretz, Gevaudan, Séneschaussée de Toloze, Auvergne, haute et basse Marche, Quercy, Périgord, Limosin, Agenois, Armignac, Cominges, Coustraux, Bigorre, Albret, Foix, Lauraguay, Albigeois, païs de Castres et Villelargue, Mirepoix, Carcassonne, et autres païs et provinces adjacentes."

laration "that justly and for good reasons have 'those of the religion' taken arms, resisting and warring in these last troubles, as constrained thereto by the violent acts with which they have been assailed and driven to distraction." They next demand those concessions which alone can make the position of the Protestants in France secure and endurable—freedom of worship and church discipline established by perpetual provision, irrespective of place or time; the right of honorable burial; immunity from taxation for the support of Roman Catholic ceremonies; admission to schools and colleges; just regulations as to marriage; amnesty; the power to hold civil office, etc. They request permission to levy a sum of one hundred and twenty thousand livres among themselves to pay off the indebtedness incurred by them in past wars. And they go so far as not only to stipulate that the King of France shall renounce all leagues he may have contracted with the enemies of his Protestant subjects for their destruction, but even to propose that he shall conclude a defensive alliance with the Protestant states of Germany, Switzerland, England, and Scotland. Meanwhile, in order to prevent the recurrence of "a conspiracy and Sicilian Vespers," of which the Huguenots would be the victims, they ask to be permitted to hold forever the guard of those cities which they now have in their possession, and in addition some other cities in each of the provinces of the realm. The Protestant cities, it is stipulated, shall retain their walls and munitions, and the royal governors shall enter them accompanied only by a small retinue. The observance of these articles the Huguenots insist shall be solemnly sworn in privy and public council, and by the inhabitants of all places, the oath to be renewed every five years.[1]

Such stout demands did the Protestants of the south and south-west address to Charles the Ninth on the first anniversary of the fatal matins of Paris. They were, it must be admitted, somewhat different from what might have been expected, a brief year before, from the fugitives who made their escape

---

[1] Requéte de l'assemblée de Montauban, in Haag, La France Protestante, x. (Pièces just.) 114–121.

from the bloody sword of their enemies. Moreover, the terms laid down by the Huguenots of Lower Languedoc and Nismes were conceived in the same brave language, and their demands were virtually identical. Huguenot troops, paid by the king, to garrison both the cities now in the hands of the Protestants, and two cities in each of the sixteen provinces required for additional protection ; free worship irrespective of place ; new parliaments in all the provinces, with Protestant judges to administer justice to Protestants ; liberty to levy tithes for the support of reformed churches ; punishment of the instigators and perpetrators of the atrocities of the Massacre of St. Bartholomew's Day, as robbers and disturbers of the public peace.[1] The Tiers État of Provence and Dauphiny added to the demands of Languedoc and Guyenne an urgent petition in favor of the reduction of the onerous imposts under which the country was groaning.[2]

The bearers of these demands were well able to give them forcible and fearless enunciation—Yolet, Philippi, Chavagnac, and others of the men known by the expressive designation of " Les fronts d'airain." [3] Assuredly a brow of brass was not out of place, when the Protestant deputies, after a delay of some weeks, were reluctantly admitted to an audience. Charles the Ninth and his court were at this time at Villers-Cotterets, on their way to the eastern frontiers of France, accompanying the newly elected King of Poland as he slowly and unwillingly journeyed toward the capital of a kingdom regarded by him in the light of a detestable place of exile. Contemporary writers inform us that Yolet and his companions were in no degree overawed by the splendor of the scene, and made no weak abatement in the terms they had been instructed to propose. Charles heard them through with patient attention. He was not a little astonished at the extent of their demands, we may be certain ; but he made no comment upon the courageous assertion of Protestant rights. Not so with the queen mother. When the deputies had at length finished their

" Les fronts d'airain."

---

[1] Jean de Serres, iv., fols. 113, 114 ; De Thou, v. (liv. lvii.) 12, 13 ; Agrippa d'Aubigné, ii. 106.

[2] Histoire du Languedoc, v. 322.   [3] Agrippa d'Aubigné, *ubi supra.*

harangue, Catharine could no longer contain her indignation.
Catharine's bitter reply. "Why," she exclaimed with marked bitterness of tone, "if your Condé himself were alive and in the heart of the kingdom with twenty thousand horse and fifty thousand foot, and held the chief cities in his power, he would not make half so great demands!"[1]

Despite the unwelcome character of the claims of the Huguenot deputies, some answer must be given. It was found impossible to induce the envoys to modify them. They **The Huguenots firm.** denied that they had the power, even if they had the inclination, to alter the action of those who had sent them. They were therefore dismissed with expressions of good-will and the assurance that two royal commissioners, the Duc d'Uzès and the Chevalier de Caylus, would be sent to treat with the delegates whom the Huguenots might choose. Marshal Damville, governor of the province, was to participate in the negotiations and to appoint some city in the vicinity of Montauban where they might be held. Charles was to hear the result of their conference on his return from the German borders. Meanwhile he promised to instruct Damville to put an end to all hostilities, provided the Huguenots should desist from everything tending to provoke retaliation.[2] The Tiers État received the answer to their petition more promptly. It was naturally to the effect that a return to the meagre scale of imposts under Louis XI. was utterly impracticable, in view of the burdens of the treasury arising from recent wars and the pensions yearly payable to various members of the royal family.[3]

It would be out of place to describe here at any length the

---

[1] Jean de Serres, iv. (lib. xii.) fol. 114 ; D'Aubigné and De Thou, *ubi supra*. See also Languet (Epistolæ secretæ, i. 216), who, writing November 14, 1573, considers the Huguenots to be virtually demanding the re-enactment of the edict of January, 1562.

[2] De Thou and D'Aubigné, *ubi supra*. Hist. du Languedoc, v. 322 : "pourvû que lesdits de la religion donnent ordre de leur part, qu'il ne soit entrepris aucune chose au contraire, comme il est avenu ces jours passés, ce que je leur défens très-expressement." Charles IX. to Damville, Oct. 18, 1573. Unfortunately, neither the promise nor the condition was observed over scrupulously.

[3] The king's aunt, the Duchess of Savoy, his mother, and his brothers of Anjou and Alençon.

slow progress of the French court as it escorted the King

Progress of
the court to
the borders of
France.
of Poland to the borders of the realm. To none of the principal personages taking part was it the occasion of much satisfaction. Catharine was as reluctant to part from Henry, her favorite son, as he was himself averse to exchange the pleasures of the Louvre and Saint Germain for the crown of an unruly and half-civilized kingdom. As for Charles, the gratification he could not conceal at the

Decline of
the health of
Charles IX.
prospect of being soon freed from the presence of a brother whom he both disliked and feared was more than counterbalanced by the rapid decline of his own health. The boy of eleven, whom the Venetian ambassador had described about the time of his accession to the throne as handsome, amiable, and graceful in appearance, quick, vivacious, and humane—in short, as possessing every quality from which a great prince and a great king might be expected,[1] was now a man of twenty-three. But his constitution, never robust, had gained nothing. The violent exercises to which he had been addicted even as a child, and which, though princely, had been pronounced dangerous by the ambassador, had been incessantly practised—the ball, horsemanship, arms—and bodily feebleness, not strength, had been the result. Other excesses had contributed to hasten the catastrophe. More than all, if we may believe the testimony of those who were familiar with the young monarch's later life, the mental and moral experience of the last eighteen months left their impress on his physical system. Charles, with the Massacre of St. Bartholomew's Day, had lost all the elasticity of youth. Remorse for complicity in the crime then perpetrated co-operated with the persuasion of the uselessness and complete failure of the attempt to exterminate the Huguenots, and the consciousness of having incurred the indelible mark of hatred and detestation of an impartial posterity. Even in his sleeping hours the curse of the murdered victims pursued him and disturbed his rest. Neither by day nor by night could he banish the remembrance of the time when blood ran so freely in the streets of Paris.

---

[1] Relazione di Giov. Michiel, 1561, Tommaseo, i. 418–420.

No attentive observer could doubt that the end was drawing near. The court had gone no farther on its way to Lorraine than the little town of Vitry-le-Français, on the river Marne, when Charles fell so seriously ill as to be unable to prosecute his journey. As was usual in such cases, while the physicians alleged as a sufficient explanation of the attack the king's immoderate exercise in the chase and in blowing the trumpet, the more suspicious frequenters of the court and the credulous people did not hesitate to invent the story that he had been poisoned. But by whom the crime had been committed was not settled. Some ascribed it to Catharine, others to Henry of Anjou, while others still laid the guilt at the door of a person of less note, whose honor the licentious king had offended.[1]

Meanwhile, neither the monarch's feeble health, nor the journeying of the court, interrupted the prosecution of those diplomatic intrigues from which Catharine still looked for valuable results. The election of Henry to the Polish crown left but one of her sons upon whom the regal dignity had not been conferred. The prophecy of Nostradamus might have its complete fulfilment if only a kingdom could be found for Alençon.[2] Otherwise the superstitious queen mother did not doubt that she was fated to see not only Charles, but Henry also die, to make place for her youngest child on the throne of France. La Mothe Fénélon was therefore instructed to put forth every exertion to bring Queen Elizabeth to the point of consenting definitely to wed a prince her junior by about a score of years. Nor did the negotiations appear altogether hopeless. The suitor was, indeed, we have seen, as insignificant in body as he was contemptible in intellectual ability. Moreover, the deep traces left on his face by the small-pox rendered him sufficiently ungainly. The blemish was said to be increasing, instead of diminishing, with his years.[3] But the French courtiers might perhaps have overcome this impediment had Elizabeth been able to see it to be her interest

Project of an English match renewed.

---

[1] De Thou, v. (liv. lvii.) 18.

[2] Of this Queen Elizabeth reminded La Mothe Fénélon in a conversation reported by him June 3, 1573, Corr. dipl., v. 345, 346.

[3] La Mothe Fénélon to Charles IX., July 26, 1573, Corr. dipl., v. 382.

to contract such close relations with her neighbors across the channel. As it was, an agreement was actually made that Alençon should visit England and press his suit in person; but when the time arrived for him to cross to Dover, Catharine justified the despatch of Marshal de Retz in his place, on the plea of her son's illness. The excuse may have contained some truth,[1] for, albeit Francis of Alençon had received the baptismal name of Hercules, he was a puny weakling, from whom no labors could ever be expected, but rather a dull existence of sloth and imbecility. It was, however, a stretch even of diplomatic assurance, for La Mothe Fénélon to suggest to the virgin queen of England, as he deliberately reports that he did, that Alençon's malady was probably due to his disappointment at Elizabeth's failure to reciprocate his honest affection![2] Possibly his mother and his brother the king may about this time have begun to realize how impolitic it would be to strengthen overmuch the personal consideration of the young prince. Disgusted with the subordinate position assigned him at court, and especially with the failure of his efforts to obtain the appointment of lieutenant-general of the kingdom, lately held by Henry of Anjou, Alençon was even now drifting into an association with the political and religious malcontents whose existence could not altogether be ignored. The French ambassador at the English court was, however, instructed by no means to let the projected marriage drop.[3]

With the patriots in the Low Countries and with the Protestant princes of Germany, the French agents were in even more active conference. In the Netherlands there was a possibility of securing some high position for Anjou or Alençon, in Germany

---

[1] The story was certainly not invented by his mother, " comme il estoit sorty de sa dernière maladye *aussy jaune que cuyvre, tout bouffy, deffiguré, bien fort petit et mince.*" No wonder that Leicester, while expressing the hope that the account might be false, hinted that it operated against the proposed marriage. La Mothe Fénélon to Charles IX., November 11, 1573, Correspondance diplomatique, v. 443.

[2] Despatch of Aug. 20, ibid., v. 394.

[3] The correspondence of La Mothe Fénélon, as preserved, is not destitute of interest. See volumes v. and vi., *passim ;* as also Le Laboureur, Additions à Castelnau, vol. iii., pp. 350, *seq.*

a chance to divert the imperial crown from the Hapsburg to the Valois family. It may reasonably be doubted whether the project was ever distinctly entertained, as the historian De Thou asserts,[1] of conferring upon Anjou the command in chief of the confederates in Flanders, where it was expected that he would have a well equipped fleet at his disposition; for the correspondence of Gaspard de Schomberg, the French agent, contains no allusion to the proposal. Certainly, however, France was, at least, anxious that England should gain no advantage over her in this part of Europe. In fact, nothing but the natural fear entertained of the great power and apparently limitless resources of Spain deterred both Elizabeth and Charles from attempting to secure the sovereignty of the revolted Netherlands.

In Germany the field for intrigue was more open. The imperial dignity had not yet become purely hereditary. In choosing a new King of the Romans, the presumptive heir of the German Empire, the three Protestant Electors, if they could but secure the concurrence of one of the four Roman Catholic Electors, might have it in their power to correct the mistake committed by Frederick the Wise of Saxony, a half-century earlier, in declining the crown in favor of Charles of Spain. Schomberg was therefore instructed to recommend to the Protestants of Germany and the Low Countries, that one of their own number should be placed in the line of succession to the Empire, or, if they could find no German Protestant prince sufficiently powerful to oppose the Hapsburgs, that the dignity should be offered to the King of France. This was a somewhat startling suggestion to emanate from a king who, but a brief twelvemonth before had been butchering his Protestant subjects by tens of thousands. But the sixteenth century furnishes not a few paradoxes equally remarkable. Both Protestants and Roman Catholics often found it convenient to have very short memories. In this case, however, the proposal to set aside the son of the tolerant Maximilian the Second in behalf of a son of Catharine de' Medici met with

Intrigues with the German princes.

---

[1] De Thou, v. 12.

little favor at the hands of one at least of the Protestant leaders. The Landgrave of Hesse declared he would have nothing to do with a project intended solely to sow divisions in the empire. The French, since the successful issue of their intrigues in Poland, he said, had become so arrogant that they thought they must be nothing less than masters of the whole world.[1] As for himself, he was quite satisfied with the present emperor, whom he prayed that God might long preserve, and then graciously provide them in his place with a pious Christian leader who should rule the empire well and faithfully.[2]

At Blamont, in the duchy of Lorraine, Catharine took leave of the King of Poland. Here the old ally of the Huguenots, Louis of Nassau, accompanied by Duke Christopher, younger son of the elector palatine, met them. Louis had been unremitting in his efforts to obtain French assistance in the desperate struggle in which he and his brother were engaged. If words and assurances could be of any worth, he was successful. Catharine promised in Charles's name that France would not be behind the German Protestant princes in rendering assistance to the Dutch patriots. Louis was so cordially received by the queen mother, and especially by Alençon, that he departed greatly encouraged with the prospect. Alençon had pressed the Dutch patriot's hand, and whispered in his ear: "I now have the government, as my brother, the King of Poland formerly had it, and I shall devote myself wholly to seconding the efforts of the Prince of Orange."[3] The promised succor from France Nassau never received. Four months later (on the four-

---

[1] "Achten's dafür dieweil es den Franzosen gelungen das sie das Königreich Polen ann sich practicirt, das sie darvon so hochmüthig wordenn das sie müssen nun Hern der ganze weltt werdenn."

[2] Letters of Landgrave William, Sept. 8th, Oct. 17th and Nov. 6th, 1573, Groen van Prinsterer, iv. 116*, 118*, 123*. See also Soldan, ii. 552–556, who, as usual, is very full and satisfactory in everything bearing upon the relations of France to Germany. Rudolph, Maximilian's son, who succeeded his father three years later, was unfortunately far from embodying the excellences desired by the landgrave. It may be questioned whether the Protestants of Germany would have fared worse even under a Valois than under this degenerate Hapsburger.

[3] Louis of Nassau to William of Orange, December, 1573. Groen van Prinsterer, iv. 278–281.

teenth of April, 1574) the brave young count, in company with
his friend and comrade, Duke Christopher, lost his
life in the fatal battle of Mook, on the banks of the
Meuse.[1]   Not the Prince of Orange nor Holland
alone, but the entire Protestant world deplored the untimely
death of one of the boldest and most unselfish of the champions
of religion and liberty.

Death of Count Louis of Nassau.

With the details of the journey of Henry of Anjou to take
possession of his new kingdom, we cannot here concern ourselves.   One incident, however, naturally connects itself with
the fortunes of the French Huguenots.

After traversing Alsace, Henry and his suite presented themselves, unwelcome guests, at Heidelberg, capital of the palatinate.   The Elector, Frederick the Third, and his subjects were, perhaps, equally displeased at the arrival
of the prime mover in the Massacre of St. Bartholomew's Day.   But, while the people felt some freedom in the
expression of their disgust, motives of state policy prevented
their prince from openly displaying his antipathy.   However,
he neither could nor would conceal the lively remembrance in
which the events of August, 1572, were still held by him.   It
was on Friday, the eleventh of December, that the French
party, under the escort of a large body of soldiers sent out to
do them honor, ascended to the castle, then as now occupying a
commanding site overlooking the valley of the Neckar.[2]   The
King of Poland was somewhat surprised when, on entering the
portal, instead of the elector, the rhinegrave, with two French
refugees escaped from the massacre, came to escort him to the

Anjou's re-ception at Heidelberg.

---

[1] Motley, Rise of the Dutch Republic, ii. 534–538.   J. de Serres, iv., fol.
134, gives the date as April 17th.   This volume of Serres was published in the
succeeding year, 1575.

[2] The writer of an anonymous letter (now in the library of Prince Czartoryski), who saw Henry as he rode into Heidelberg, with Louis of Nassau
on his right hand, and Duke Christopher, the elector's son, on his left, thus
describes his personal appearance : "Homo procera statura, corpore gracili,
facie oblonga pallida, oculis paululum prominentibus, vultu subtruculento,
indutus pallio holoserico rubri coloris."   Heidelberg letter "de transitu Hen-
rici," etc., Dec. 22, 1573, *apud* Marquis de Noailles, Henri de Valois et la
Pologne (Paris, 1867), iii. (Pièces justif.), 532.

rooms prepared for his reception. Frederick had directed the
rhinegrave to request Henry to excuse this apparent discourtesy
on the ground of his feeble health. It is more probable that
the true motive was the elector's desire to avoid incurring, by
too great complaisance, the displeasure of the emperor, who
was naturally much irritated at the success of the French intrigues in Poland. When, later, Frederick made his tardy
appearance, it was only to greet Anjou in a brief address, reserving for the morrow their more extended conference. On
Saturday the elector politely conducted his guest through his
extensive picture gallery. Pausing before one painting the
face of which was protected from sight, he ordered an attendant
to draw aside the curtain. To his astonishment, Henry found
himself confronted with a life-like portrait of Gaspard de Coligny. To the question, " Does your Royal Highness recognize
the subject ? " Henry replied with sufficient composure : " I do ;
it is the late Admiral of France." " Yes," rejoined Frederick,
" it is the admiral—a man whom I have found, of all the
French nobles, the most zealous for the glory of the French
name ; and I am not afraid to assert that in him the king and
all France have sustained an irreparable loss." Elsewhere
Henry's attention was directed to a large painting representing
the very scenes of the massacre, and he was asked whether he
could distinguish any of the victims. Nor did Frederick confine himself to these casual references. In pointed
terms he exposed to the young Valois both the sin
and the mistaken policy of the events of a twelvemonth since. The slaughter of the admiral and of so many
other innocent men and women had not only provoked the
Divine retribution, but had diminished not a little the reputation and influence of the French with all orders of persons in
Germany.[1] Henry listened with commendable patience to the

Frankness of
the elector
palatine.

---

[1] Germany seems to have been full of blind rumors of treacherous designs
on the part of its French neighbors. I have before me a pamphlet of little
historical value, and evidently intended for popular circulation, entitled
" Entdeckung etlicher heimlichen Practicken, so jetzund vorhanden wider
unser geliebtes Vatterland, die Teutsche Nation, was man gäntzlich willens
und ins werck zubringen, gegen den Evangelischen fürgenommen habe, durch

old elector's denunciations, alleging by way of excuse that the French court had been under the influence of the passions then running high, and readily promised great caution and tolerance in future.¹ He did, indeed, strike on his breast and begged Frederick to believe him that things had occurred otherwise than had been reported. But his auditor dryly remarked that he was fully informed of what had taken place in France.² As the elector also took occasion to remind Anjou of sundry miserable deaths of notorious persecutors, such as Herod the Great, Herod Agrippa, and Maxentius; as he openly ridiculed the absurd suggestion that Coligny, a wounded man, with both arms disabled in consequence of Maurevel's shot, planned on his bed an attack on the king; and as, furthermore, he plainly denounced the shocking immorality of Catharine de' Medici's court ladies—it must be confessed that Frederick the Pious, on the present occasion, made more of a virtue of frankness than of diplomacy.³

On Sunday the French left Heidelberg, with little regret on their own part or on that of their hosts. Not to speak of their treatment by the elector, which even the historian De Thou regarded as scarcely comporting with the dignity with which Henry was invested,⁴ the followers of the Polish king met with frequent insults, both in coming and in going. One of them relates how he heard cries of "Those dogs from Lorraine! Those Italian traitors!" And a German eye-witness of the scenes

---

einen guthertzigen und getrewen Christen unserm Vatterland zu gütem an tag geben. M.D.LXXIII."

¹ De Thou, v. (liv. lvii.), 22; Mém. de Pierre de Lestoile (éd. Michaud et Poujoulat), i. 27.

² " Was sich in Franckreich zugetragen, weiss man auch."

³ The minute of the conversation drawn up by the elector palatine with his own hand, and printed by Lalanne in the appendix to the fourth volume of his edition of Brantôme's Works (411–418), is by far the most trustworthy source of information we possess. On the last count of the elector's indictment, Anjou's defence was certainly very lame: " Dass ich selbst an seines Altvatters Hof gesehen *que ç'a été une Cour fort dissolue*, aber seines Brudern und Frau Mutter Hof demselbigen bey weitem nicht zu vergleichen." Ibid., 414.

⁴ " C'est ce qui fit croire à bien des gens, que l'Electeur n'avoit pas reçu un hôte comme Henri aussi poliment qu'il le devoit." De Thou, v. (liv. lvii.) 22.

expresses it as his opinion that the French nobles would not have been safe had they not been escorted by the palatine troops. The sight of "that notable cut-throat, the Duke of Nevers," of the Marshal de Retz, of Captain Du Gast, and "very many others of that band of villains who so cruelly butchered the admiral and other nobles in Paris," provoked the populace almost beyond endurance. The very diamonds and jewels presented by Henry on his departure, to the elector and to the ladies of his court, aroused the popular indignation; for they were known, as we have already seen, to have constituted a part of the plunder of a certain rich Huguenot jeweller, whose shop had been robbed at the time of the Parisian matins.[1] There were not wanting those who would even have counselled the worthy elector to follow the course indicated by the Spanish grandee, who informed Charles the Fifth that he intended to burn his castle to the ground so soon as the traitorous Constable de Bourbon had relieved it of his polluting presence.[2]

Meantime, within the borders of France all was ferment and disquiet. The Roman Catholic element, comprising the overwhelming majority of the people, had become split into two factions, both animated by inextinguishable hatred, and each resolved to compass the destruction of the other. Of conciliatory measures there was a dearth. Among the men of wide influence there was no one to take the place of the virtuous Michel de l'Hospital. That truly great statesman had

Last days of Chancellor de l'Hospital.

died nine months before (on the thirteenth of March, 1573). The storm of war at that moment raging about La Rochelle was a fit expression of the utter failure of the aged chancellor's policy. For a dozen years there had not been a candid and sincere effort made to restore tranquillity to France which had not either originated with him or received his cordial support. But of the sanguine hopes of ultimate success entertained in the earlier stages of his political career, he retained little toward its close. The last years of his presence at court witnessed an uninterrupted struggle between the chan-

---

[1] Heidelberg letter of Dec. 22, 1573, Czartoryski MSS., De Noailles, Pièces justif., iii. 533. See ante, p. 485.

[2] Heidelberg letter, ubi supra, iii. 534.

cellor and that family of Guise which he had come to regard as the prime cause of the misery afflicting the kingdom. More than once the latent personal hostility had broken out in an open quarrel between L'Hospital and the Cardinal of Lorraine. Two or three exciting scenes of recrimination, which the tact of Catharine de' Medici was scarcely able to allay, have met us in this history. At length, when the third civil war burst forth, L'Hospital, seeing himself altogether powerless to resist the more violent counsels then in the ascendant, had received permission to retire from the royal court to his estate in the vicinity of Étampes.[1] It was none the less an exile that it wore the appearance of a voluntary withdrawal. Birague discharged the real functions of the chancellor's office. Finally, after barely escaping a violent death in the Massacre of St. Bartholomew's Day, the chancellor received, in January, 1573, the formal order to give up the guardianship of the seals, which for more than four years had been only nominally under his control. His touching reply to the royal summons is the last production of the chancellor's pen that has come down to us. Interposing no obstacle to the execution of the king's will, the writer invoked the testimony of the queen mother that, in all things pertaining to the royal interests, "he had been forgetful rather of his own advantage than of the king's service, and had always followed *the great royal road*, turning neither to the right hand nor to the left, and giving himself to no private faction." "And now," he added, "that my maladies and my age have rendered me useless to do you service, just as you have seen the old galleys in the port of Marseilles, which, though dismantled, are yet regarded with pleasure, so I very humbly beg you to view me both in my present state and my past, which shall be an instruction and an example to all your subjects to do you good service. God give you grace to choose servants and counsellors more com-

---

[1] Jean de Serres (edit. 1571), iii. 284; A. d'Aubigné, i. 264, "Pource que le Chancelier de l'Hospital ne pouvoit travailler de cœur en mesme temps aux violentes depesches de Thavanes, de Montluc et autres, et aux douceurs du Mareschal de Cossé, il ne fallut qu'un souspir de probité pour lui faire oster les sceaux; ce que fit la Roine en le relegant en sa maison près Estampes jusques à la fin de ses jours." See also Languet's letter of September 20, 1568.

petent than I have been, and as affectionate and devoted to your service as I am." The closing words were characteristic of the life-long advocate of toleration : a recommendation of gentleness and clemency, in imitation of a long-suffering and pardoning God.[1] Two months later Michel de l'Hospital ended his eventful life. France could ill afford to lose at this juncture a magistrate[2] so upright—a statesman who "had the lilies of France in his heart."[3]

Since the siege of La Rochelle, or more properly since the day of the massacre, a new party had been forming, of those who could not bring themselves to approve the cruel acts of the court, or who, for any reason, were jealous of the faction now in power. As opposed to the Italian counsellors by whom the queen mother had surrounded the throne, it was pre-eminently a French or patriotic party. It demanded the expulsion of Florentines and of Lorrainers from the kingdom, or at least from the management of public affairs. The " Malcontents," or " Politiques," as they now began to be called,[4] demanded a return to the former usages of the kingdom, in accordance with which the most important decisions were never made without consulting the States General. Two books appearing about this time made a deep impression. In an erudite treatise entitled " Franco-Gallia," from the pen of Francis Hotman, an acute scholar and a civilian of great reputation, attention was drawn to the original constitution of the kingdom ; and the writer showed by irrefragable proofs that the regal dignity was not hereditary like a private possession, but was a gift of the people, which they could as lawfully transfer from one to another, as originally confer. The participation of women in the administration of the

The party of the " Politiques."

Hotman's Franco-Gallia.

---

[1] Chancellor de l'Hospital to Charles IX., January 12, 1573, copy discovered in the MSS. of the National Library, Paris, by Prof. Soldan, and printed in Appendix XI. of his history.

[2] *Ante*, chapter xv., p. 264, note.

[3] " M. le chancelier de l'Hospital qui avoit les fleurs de lys dans le cœur." Journal de Lestoile, p. 16.

[4] " Politici (novum enim hoc nomen ex novo negotio sub hoc tempus natum)." Jean de Serres, iv., fol. 132.

government was declared to be abhorrent to the ideas of the founders of the French monarchy.[1] In another work appearing not long after, the principle was enunciated that an unbounded obedience is due to the Almighty alone, while obedience to human magistrates is in its very nature subject to limitations and exceptions. The supreme authority of kings and other high magistrates was explained to be of such a nature "that if they violate the laws, to the observance of which they have bound themselves by oath, and become manifest tyrants, giving no room for better counsels, then it is lawful for the inferior magistrates to make provision both for themselves and for those committed to their charge, and oppose the tyrant."[2] The circumstance is not without significance that in a Huguenot work, published early in the succeeding year, the guilty king who authorized the butchery of his innocent subjects on St. Bartholomew's Day, is for the first time distinctly designated as the "tyrant."[3]

The lesson that no trust could be reposed in Charles and his court was one which the world had learned pretty thoroughly before this; and the events at La Rochelle during the month of December, 1573, were well calculated to prevent it from being forgotten. The definite peace, made five months before, guaranteed the safety of the Protestants, and secured to them the free exercise of their religious rights. None the less was a project set on foot to introduce a royal garrison into the city by treachery. M. de Biron and other captains had been unable to conceal their disgust at the abandonment of the siege of La Rochelle, when, as they pretended, it must very shortly have fallen into the king's hands, and Biron had been soundly berated by Anjou for his pains. He had not, however,

Treacherous attempt on La Rochelle.

---

[1] The title in my copy is "Franc. Hotomani Jurisconsulti Francogallia." S. l. [Genevæ] 1573. The dedication to the elector palatine is dated Aug. 21.

[2] Jean de Serres, iv., fol. 122. Serres gives an extended summary of the work, whose author is unknown to him, fols. 119–128.

[3] Eusebii Philadelphi Dialog., ii. 117, *et passim.* See also the Tocsain contre les massacreurs, which, although published as late as 1579, was written before the death of Charles the Ninth (see the address of the printer, dated June 25, 1577), where the king is directly compared to the Emperor Nero. Archives curieuses, vii. 162.

given up the notion of making himself master of the Huguenot stronghold, and there were others in the royal army intent upon the same end.   A scheme to smuggle soldiers through the gates, in wagons covered with branches of trees, was so freely talked of that it reached the citizens' ears, and only augmented their suspicions.   A more serious plot was set on foot, in accordance with which one Jacques du Lyon, Seigneur de Grandfief, prominent in the late defence of La Rochelle, was to gain possession of one of the city gates, and admit Puigaillard, who, for this purpose, had massed considerable numbers of royal soldiers at Nuaillé, on the east, and at Saint-Vivien, on the south of La Rochelle.   Happily the treacherous design was itself betrayed by an accomplice.   Grandfief was killed while defending himself against those who had been sent to arrest him.   Several of the supposed leaders[1] were condemned to be broken on the wheel, and the barbarous sentence was executed. The papers discovered in the house of Grandfief clearly proved that the plot had received the full approval not only of Biron, but of the queen mother herself.   After inflicting summary vengeance on the miserable instruments of perfidy, the Rochellois, therefore, addressed their complaints to the French court. It need not surprise us, however, to learn that they received in reply letters from Charles not only disowning the conspiracy, but assuring them that he heartily detested it, and approved the rigorous measures adopted.[2]

Shortly before the discovery of the conspiracy at La Rochelle, the Huguenots had again assembled at Milhau-en-Rouergue.

The Hugue- nots reassem- ble at Milhau.
The delegates, about one hundred in number, represented very fully the gentry and tiers état of the south and south-west of France, while a few names from the central and northern provinces indicated the weaker hold gained by Protestantism in that portion of the kingdom.[3]

---

[1] They had, however, generally retracted their admissions of complicity made on the rack.

[2] Jean de Serres, iv., fol. 118 ; De Thou, v. (liv. lvii.) 19, 20; Arcère, Histoire de la ville de la Rochelle, i. 533–540; Languet, Letter of Feb. 8, 1574, i. 229.

[3] See the list of members in the protocol of the proceedings first published in the Bulletin de la Société de l'hist. du prot. français, x. (1862) 351–353.

Ostensibly meeting, with the royal permission, to receive the report of the commissioners sent to the king, and to entertain the terms proposed by Marshal Damville, the Huguenots availed themselves of the opportunity to perfect the organiza-

They complete their organiza- tion of their party which had been sketched in pre- tion. vious political assemblies. Accepting it as notorious that, whether in time of peace, or of open war, or of truce, the Protestants were in peril from the daily intrigues and assaults of their enemies, all tending to their complete ruin, the Hugue- not assembly renewed and swore to maintain a permanent union comprising all their brethren of the same faith not only in France proper, but in the papal Comtât Venaissin, the princi- pality of Orange, and other districts less closely united to the crown. To this end they determined that the "States General," composed of a delegate from the nobility, the tiers état, and the magistracy of each "généralité" or government, should meet every six months; while the particular assemblies of the gov- ernments should be convened at least as often as once in three months. The functions of the generals and their councils were expressly limited to the military and financial concerns of the Huguenots, with other matters of public interest. They were strictly forbidden from intermeddling, under any pretext, with the discharge of civil or criminal justice. This last function was to be referred to the royal courts, save that, instead of ap- pealing to the parliaments, known to be too hostile to Protestant- ism to afford hope of obtaining justice, arbitrators were to be chosen by the Protestants among themselves.[1] Not forgetting their common religious bond, the Huguenots at Milhau declared it to be the duty of the ministers of God's word and of the consistories to keep watch over criminal and dissolute behavior, and denounce it for punishment to the civil magistrate. At the same time, in order that the ministers might be the better able to devote themselves to their sacred functions, it was directed that

---

[1] In this, as in other particulars, the political assembly of Milhau merely re-enacted the provisions of the assembly of Réalmont. For the dates of the early political assemblies of the Huguenots, which must of course be carefully distinguished from their synods or ecclesiastical assemblies, see the list in the Bulletin, etc., xxii. (1873) 508.

they be regularly paid from the common funds "without making any further use of notices (billettes) or other unworthy and illusory methods, as has been done heretofore, to the great scandal of all good people." The levy of imposts and the creation of loans were made the exclusive right of the particular states, while the administration of the funds arising from the royal revenues was to be intrusted to the provincial councils.[1]

Such were the chief features in a plan for organization evidently looking to the speedy renewal of the warfare temporarily suspended by virtue of the truce.

While the revelation of the treacherous attempt of the royal party upon La Rochelle proved to the Politiques, or Malcontents, the impossibility of relying upon the assurances given in the name of Charles the Ninth, the resolutions of the Huguenots in Milhau encouraged them in their project to remove the present advisers of the king. In the absence of any better leader, The Duke of they looked to the Duke of Alençon as their head. Alençon. He alone of the royal family was guiltless of the Massacre of St. Bartholomew's Day. His antagonism to Anjou and to his mother was well known. It was even reported that he had himself been exposed to serious danger by reason of his avowed sympathy with the imprisoned King of Navarre and his cousin of Condé. In fact, he was himself little better than a captive at the court of Charles—eyed with suspicion, unable to obtain favors for his friends, and vainly suing to be appointed to the office of lieutenant-general of the kingdom. It was perhaps not strange that, in looking about for a nominal head, the Politiques should have settled upon Alençon, who received their overtures with undisguised satisfaction and large promises of support. And yet there could scarcely have been a more unhappy selection. Of the feeble children of Catharine de' Medici, he was undoubtedly the feeblest. He possessed neither the courage to undertake nor the fortitude to prosecute any

---

[1] Text of the document embodying the resolutions of the political assembly of Milhau, in Haag, La France protestante (vol. x.), Pièces justificatives, 121–126. The correct date seems to be Dec. 17th, instead of 16th; Bulletin, as above, x. 351. Cf. also Léonce Anquez, Histoire des assemblées politiques des réformés de France (1573–1622), Paris, 1859, 7–11.

really bold enterprise. All who had the misfortune at any time
to credit his plighted word discovered in their own cases a fresh
and pointed application of the warning against putting trust
in princes. Of him Busbec, the emperor's ambassador, gave
a life-like delineation when he characterized him as "a prince
who allowed himself to be ensnared by the bad counsels of unskilful ministers, who could not distinguish friends from flat-
terers, nor a great from a good reputation ; ready to undertake,
still more ready to desist; always inconstant, restless, and
frivolous ; always prepared to disturb the best established tranquillity." [1]

Circumstances almost beyond their control seemed now to be
forcing the Huguenots to make common cause with the Malcontents. Yet there were not wanting those who looked upon the
alliance as more likely to retard than to advance their true interests, and who pointed with convincing force to the disastrous
results of a similar union in the time of the tumult of Amboise,
fourteen years before. The cloak of the reformed name, they
argued, would certainly be assumed by men having no desire
for a reformation of manners or morals—men whose lives would
only dishonor the cause with which they were supposed to be
identified. Nor was the fear an idle one, as was shown by an
incident that occurred about this very time. The truce which
had been made for Languedoc did not extend to the Comtât
Venaissin. Naturally enough, there were many in the Huguenot ranks who, remembering past injuries received at the hands
of the troops of the Pope, were not unwilling to turn their
arms in this direction. But their leader was no Huguenot.

M. de Glandage, a gentleman of Dauphiny, was a soldier of fortune, and would doubtless have fought with
as little reluctance against the Protestants as for them,
had it been to his advantage to enlist under the papal standard.
As it was otherwise, he made himself master of the city of
Orange, with the assistance of a party of citizens, and expelled
Berchon, who, in the name of William the Silent, had strictly
abstained from acts of hostility against the neighboring pontifi-

Glandage
plunders the
city of Orange.

[1] Lettres d'Auger Gislen, seigneur de Busbec, amb. de l'emp. Rodolphe II.
auprès de Henri III. Cimber et Danjou, Archives curieuses, x. 115.

cal towns. Not so with the new governor of Orange. The city became the starting-point for a continuous series of incursions. It was not war, but open rapine. The very traders were plundered of their wares when they fell into his hands. One might have fancied that a mediæval robber-baron had reappeared on the banks of the Rhône. It was true that Glandage, making a virtue of bluntness, was wont to say that "there was nothing Huguenot about him but the point of his sword." None the less did his violent acts bring discredit upon the Huguenots.[1]

Although war had not yet been formally resumed, there were parts of France in which it already raged, or rather where peace had never been restored. This was the case in particular on both banks of the Rhône, in Dauphiny and in Vivarez and the adjoining districts. So rapid had been the movements of the veteran Huguenot chief Montbrun, and so successful every blow he struck, that terror spread far and wide. Important towns fell into his hands ; a rich abbey but a few miles from Grenoble was plundered, and the silent monks of St. Bruno, in the secluded retreat of the Grande Chartreuse—the mother house of their order—were glad to summon troops to defend their rich fields from a similar fate.[2] From Lyons to Avignon the Huguenots were stronger than the king's forces.[3]

Montbrun's exploits in Dauphiny.

But the time for hollow truce and a desultory and irregular warfare was rapidly passing away. It was but little more than a month after the beginning of the new year before the conflagration again burst forth. The Protestants of all parts of the kingdom were at length of one mind ; there was no

---

[1] "Dictitabat se Religionem reformatam minime probare ; ensis tantum sui mucronem esse Religiosum : id est, se non Religionis doctrinam, sed Religiosorum causam sequi. Hujusmodi exemplis magnæ offensiones adversus Religiosos conflabantur." Jean de Serres, iv., fol. 118. The reader needs perhaps to be reminded that *Religiosi* here stands as the equivalent for the French designation of the Huguenots as "ceux de la Religion."

[2] Agrippa d'Aubigné, ii. 113, 114 (liv. ii., c. 4); Jean de Serres, iv., fol. 117. Of "La Grande Chartreuse," which lies ten miles north of Grenoble, see a good account in R. Töpffer, Voyages en Zigzag, seconde série.

[3] Languet, Epistolæ secretæ, i. 214, etc.

room for doubt that any hopes offered them had as their sole
object to sow discord among the adherents of the reformed
faith. If anything had been wanting to prove this, it was made
clear by the refusal of the court to extend the benefits of the
Edict of Pacification of July, 1573, to the whole of France.
The limitation of the liberty of worship by the provisions of
that edict to La Rochelle, Montauban, and Nismes, was evidently
intended to render the inhabitants of the three strongest Huguenot cities selfishly indifferent to the injustice done to their
brethren in other parts of France. In fact, this result was partially effected in the first of the cities named. The Rochellois
were at first very reluctant to resume hostilities, and began to
plead conscientious scruples forbidding them to break the compact made with the king. Happily their hesitation was removed
by François de la Noue, who, returning in a capacity entirely
different from that in which he had last appeared, used all the
arts of persuasion to induce the Huguenot stronghold by the
sea to become again the rallying-point for the Protestants of
the west. It was not difficult to show the citizens, when once
they would listen to reason, that the starving of Sancerre and numberless murders of adherents of the
reformed doctrine throughout France were violations
of the peace quite sufficient to justify its formal abrogation by the injured party. The fears dictated by apparent
weakness were dispelled by pointing to the signal success that
had crowned the arms of Montbrun in Dauphiny,[1] while the
reluctance of loyal subjects to rise in arms against their lawful
sovereign, even in order to redress great wrongs, unless authorized by the leadership of a prince of the blood, was answered
by the assurance that they would have a head of much higher
rank than any under whose protection the Huguenots had heretofore taken the field.[2] It was clear that the personage thus
hinted at could be no other than the king's brother. No wonder
that the Rochellois yielded to La Noue's arguments, for almost

La Rochelle
resumes arms.
Beginning of
the fifth reli-
gious war.

---

[1] E. Arnaud, Histoire des protestants du Dauphiné aux xvie, xviie et xviii^e
siècles, Paris, 1875, i. 277–281 ; Ch. Charronet, Les guerres de religion et la
société protestante dans les Hautes-Alpes (1560–1789), Gap., 1861, p. 75, etc.
[2] Agrippa d'Aubigné, ii. 113 ; De Thou, v. (liv. lvii.), 30.

every Roman Catholic whose hands were clean of the blood shed in the massacre applauded the justice of the new uprising.[1]

The city of La Rochelle began again to repair its shattered walls, and La Noue was unanimously appointed to the chief command of the Huguenots in Saintonge and the adjacent regions. In the effort next made to prevent the great Protestant leader from espousing the side of his brethren, and to persuade the city of La Rochelle to rest content with the guarantees offered by the edict of 1573, and remain neutral in the coming conflict, Catharine and her advisers signally failed. The royal envoys —Biron, Strozzi and Pinart—were, indeed, courteously treated by La Noue, Frontenay, and Mirambeau, who repeatedly came out to meet them at the village of Ernandes. But the Huguenots, in

Diplomacy tried in vain. reply to their reiterated request, declined absolutely to abate a single important point in their demands. They would not hear the suggestion that by the Edict of Boulogne, in 1573, previous ordinances had been repealed, but persisted in assuming that Charles had always intended that the edict of 1570 should remain in force, and, in proof of this, they alleged one of the king's own declarations after the massacre. They insisted that the privileges accorded to the three privileged cities of La Rochelle, Montauban, and Nismes, should be extended to the Protestant nobility throughout the kingdom ; and when Biron and his companions reluctantly consented that the right to have baptism and marriage celebrated in their houses be conceded to all Protestant noblemen who enjoyed the right of "haute justice," and who had always remained constant in their religious opinions, La Noue protested against the restriction to baptism and marriage. "We desire to worship God freely," he said, "and you give only a part of what we need for the exercise of our religion. What you offer is a snare to catch us again and expose us to greater peril than we were ever in before. But we would much rather die with arms in our hands than be involved again in such disasters."

---

[1] " Fere omnes qui non fuerunt participes cædis Amiralii et aliorum, dicunt, Huguenotos merito corripere arma ad tutandam suam salutem, cum nihil observetur eorum quæ hactenus fuerunt ipsis promissa." Languet, letter of April 14, 1574, Epistolæ secretæ, i. 239.

In vain did the royalists assure them that the king was ready to grant the Protestants complete liberty of conscience and protection against their enemies, but could not give them what they demanded.   In vain did they repeat in substance the famous exclamation of Catharine de' Medici, and say, among other arguments : " You could make no greater demands if the king had nothing ready, and you had a large and powerful army, with all the advantages you could desire ; whereas, we know full well that you are feeble in every direction, and that the king has great forces, as you yourselves must be aware." The Huguenots had the Massacre of St. Bartholomew's Day on their tongues continually,[1] and could not be fed with fair prom- ises.   They required securities.   First, Charles must give them a city in each province of the kingdom, as a refuge in case they were assailed.   Next, the maintenance of the promises made to them must be guaranteed by the signatures of the princes of the blood and all the chief nobles, by governors, by lieutenants- general, and by the gentry of the provinces, as well as by the chief inhabitants of the towns.   Hostages must be interchanged. While the last and most remarkable proposal of all was, " that his Majesty, on his part, and the Huguenots, on theirs, should place a large sum of money in the hands of some German prince, who should promise to employ it in levying and paying a body of reiters to be used against that party which should violate the peace."   All this was to be registered in the various parliaments and in the inferior courts of the bailiwicks and sénéchaussées.   The king was further requested to call the States General within three months, to give the royal edict of pacification their formal sanction.[2]

We need not be surprised that a conference to which the two parties brought views so diametrically opposed, should have proved utterly abortive.

---

[1] " Et parmy leurs discours se representoient a chacun coup la journée de St. Barthélemy."

[2] The interesting particulars of the conference we obtain from two long and very important despatches of Biron to Charles IX., dated, the one, Ernan- des, April 24th, the other, April 26th and 27th, 1574, MSS. Imperial Lib. of St. Petersburg, communicated to the Bulletin de la Soc. de l'hist. du prot. fr., xxii. (1873) 401–413, by M. Jean Loutchitzki.

It scarcely falls within the province of this history to narrate in detail the unsuccessful attempt of the Malcontents, made some weeks before the negotiations just described, to overthrow The "Poli- the government, whose bad counsels were believed to tiques" make be the cause of the misery under which France was an unsuccess-ful rising. groaning; for the alliance between the Malcontents and the Huguenots was only fortuitous and partial. A few words of explanation, however, seem to be necessary. The plan contemplated a simultaneous uprising on the tenth of March. The day had been selected by La Noue himself, who rightly judged that the license and uproar indulged in by the populace up to a late hour in the night of "Mardi Gras" (Shrove Tuesday) would greatly facilitate the military under-taking.[1] Alençon and the King of Navarre, who, since the massacre immediately succeeding his nuptials, had found him-self less a guest than a captive at court, were to flee secretly to Sedan, where they would find safety under the protection of the Duc de Bouillon. For the influence of this great nobleman, together with the still more powerful support of the Montmo-rency family, was given to the projected movement. But the timidity and vacillation of Alençon frustrated the well-con-ceived design. Ten days or a fortnight before the set time for the escape of the princes from court, Navarre, who, under pre-text of hunting, had been allowed to leave the royal palace of Saint Germain, received a secret visit from M. de Guitry, a gen-tleman who had succeeded in bringing into the vicinity an armed body of the confederates. The meeting took place by night, in Navarre's bedchamber, in the little hamlet of St. Prix.[2] On the morrow Guitry found means to confer with M. de Thoré, Tu-renne, and La Nocle, "all in despair by reason of Alençon's variable moods."[3] This feeble prince, it would seem, was not even yet decided, and trembled at the peril he might run in at-

---

[1] Agrippa d'Aubigné, ii. 117. Shrove Tuesday fell, in 1574, on March 9th.

[2] Ten miles from the château de St. Germain, and about the same dis-tance from the palace of the Louvre. A part of the old forest yet remains.

[3] I follow Agrippa d'Aubigné, who here must be regarded as excellent au-thority, for not only was he present, but it was by his means (" par ma con-duitte.") that Guitry was introduced into Navarre's chamber. Hist. univ., ii. 119.

tempting to reach Sedan. Under these circumstances the plan of
flight was modified. Guitry was instructed to bring his force
nearer to St. Germain, and wait for Alençon and Navarre, who,
under his escort, were to gain Mantes, a little farther down the
Seine, and perhaps ultimately join the confederates near La Rochelle. Guitry waited in vain: Alençon and Navarre never came.

Either Alençon himself, or La Mole, his favorite, in his
name, betrayed the project to the queen mother. The discovery
of a body of armed men in the vicinity, albeit they gave assurance that they meant no injury to the king, threw the entire
court into consternation. Catharine, reminding Charles that
her soothsayers had long since warned her of Saint Germain as
a place that boded no good to her or hers, was among the first
to flee, leaving the king, who was ill with quartan fever, to
follow the next day.[1] The court partook of Cath-

Flight of the
court from
St. Germain.
arine's terror, and imitated her example. Layman
and churchman vied in haste to gain Paris, whence
in a few days they retreated in a more leisurely manner to the
safer refuge of the castle of Vincennes. While some hurried
by the main road, or picked their way along the banks of the
Seine, others took to boats as a less dangerous means of con-
veyance. But, among those who joined in the disorderly flight,
there were some who retained their composure sufficiently to
note the ludicrous features of the scene. Long after they recalled with undisguised amusement the terror-stricken counte-
nances of the new chancellor and of three French cardinals, as,
mounted on fiery Italian or Spanish steeds, they clung with
both hands to the saddle-bow, evidently fearing their horses
even more than the dreaded Huguenot.[2] It was a very pretty
farce; but the tragedy was yet to come.

---

[1] Jean de Serres (iv., fol. 138) and the Mémoires de l'estat (Archives curieuses, "Discours de l'entreprise de St. Germain," viii. 107–118) give the
last of February for the date of the discovery of the undertaking of Alençon; but, from a comparison of letters, Prof. Soldan has shown (ii. 580) that
it really was March 1st.

[2] It is Agrippa d'Aubigné (Hist. univ., ii. 119) who depicts the scene. As
he seems to have been present on the occasion, we may rely upon the truthfulness of the groundwork of his sketch, while ascribing a little of the coloring to the free hand of the artist.

A second attempt at flight made by Alençon and Navarre also failed, through the treachery of one of those to whom the secret had been confided. Alençon and Navarre were now placed under close guard, and subjected to long and repeated examinations before a royal commission. Alençon was sufficiently craven in his bearing, and did not hesitate by his admissions to involve in ruin the minor instruments in the execution of the plan. Navarre, in his answers to the interrogatories, displayed a courageous frankness. He was not, in truth, content with a simple denial of the evil designs attributed to him. On the contrary, he availed himself of the opportunity to rehearse the grievances under which he had been suffering for nearly two years. Detained at court only to find himself an object of suspicion, his ears had been filled with successive rumors of an approaching massacre, a second St. Bartholomew's Day, when he would not be spared in the general destruction. These rumors had, indeed, been declared false by the Duke of Anjou, before the walls of La Rochelle ; but that prince had failed to keep the promises made before his departure for Poland—to commend Navarre to the royal favor. Consequently he had been subjected to the indignity of frequently being refused admission to the presence of Charles, while seeing La Chastre, and others of those who had figured most prominently among the actors in the Parisian matins, freely received at the king's rising. He had at length resolved to leave the court in company with his cousin of Alençon, partly in order to consult his own safety, partly that he might restore order in his estates of Béarn and Navarre, now suffering from his protracted absence. When his design had come to the queen mother's knowledge, he had explained the motives of his action to her, and obtained the promise of her protection. Subsequently there had reached him the intelligence that he was to be imprisoned with Alençon in the castle of Vincennes ; whereupon he had renewed the attempt to escape the impending peril. In his second examination, in the presence of Catharine de' Medici and his uncle, Cardinal Bourbon, Henry reiterated his statements respecting the alarming reports that continually reached him. At one time

Margin notes: A second failure. Alençon and Navarre examined.

he learned that it was decided that, should Margaret of Navarre
bear a son, the luckless father would be put out of the way, in
order that the child might inherit his dignities. At another time,
in the very chamber of King Charles, the opinion had been
boldly uttered, that, so long as a single member of the house of
Bourbon should survive, there would always be war in France.
Nor had the young prince dared to complain of these menaces.[1]

It was no part of Catharine de' Medici's plan, at this juncture,
to wreak her vengeance for the blow that had been aimed at her
authority, either upon her son or upon her son-in-law. The
Montmorencies, also, though suspected and long since the objects
of jealousy, ultimately escaped with little difficulty. It is true
that the eldest brother, Marshal François de Montmorency, was
enticed to the court, as was also another marshal, M. de Cossé,
and that both were thrown into the Bastile. But the younger
Montmorencies, Thoré and Méru, had escaped, while their more
energetic brother Marshal Damville, was too firmly fixed in the
governorship of Languedoc, to be removed without a struggle.
It was hardly prudent to drive so influential a family to extremities. Moreover, Catharine was too wise to desire the utter destruction of a clan whose authority might on occasion be employed, as it had often been in the past, as a counterpoise to the
formidable power of the Guises.

Some victims of inferior rank were needed. They were found
in the persons of Joseph Boniface de la Mole and Hannibal,
Count de Coconnas, who, with one M. de Tourtray, expiated
their error and that of their superiors, on the Place
de Grève. The cruel procedure known as the administration of justice in the sixteenth century has no
more striking illustration than in the barbarous torture, including the terrible trial by water, inflicted upon these wretched
men. By such means it was not difficult to extort admissions
which the prisoner was likely to retract at a subsequent time.
Consequently it is not quite clear, even with the full record
before us, how far La Mole and Coconnas were really impli-

Execution of La Mole and Coconnas.

---

[1] The testimony of Navarre and others is preserved, and has been published, together with the interrogatories, in the Archives curieuses, viii. 127-
221.

cated. As for the sufferers themselves, there was little about them to call forth our special sympathy. La Mole, of handsome appearance, but of cowardly disposition, was a firm believer in the magic that passed current in his day, and was questioned on the rack respecting the object of a waxen figure found among his effects. He admitted he had employed it for sorcery, to advance his suit with a lady whose love he sought. Coconnas, an Italian, instead of inviting contempt for his poltroonery, inspires aversion for his crimes. No assassin had distinguished himself more at the Massacre of St. Bartholomew's Day. We are inclined to believe the contemporary chronicler, who states that Charles the Ninth himself averred that he had never liked Coconnas since hearing the latter's sanguinary boast that he had redeemed as many as thirty Huguenots from the hands of the populace, only that he might induce them to abjure their religion, under promise of life, and afterward enjoy the satisfaction of murdering them by inches under his dagger.[1]

Had Coconnas and La Mole been persons more entitled to our respect, we might have pitied their misfortune in falling into the hands of a royal commission with whom the evidence of the guilt of the prisoners was apparently of less weight than the desire to gratify the court by their condemnation. The first president of parliament, Christopher de Thou, again headed the commission. The same pliant tool of despotism who had signed the death-warrant of Prince Louis of Condé, just before the sudden close of the brief reign of Francis the Second, and had congratulated Charles the Ninth, twelve years later, in the name of the judiciary of the kingdom, on the "piety" he had displayed in butchering his unoffending subjects, again obeyed with docility the instructions of his superiors, and suppressed those more generous sentiments, which, if we may credit his son's account, he secretly entertained.

Meantime the arrests and judicial proceedings at the capital
Condé retires
to Germany. did not delay the military enterprise in which the Huguenots and Malcontents were alike embarked. More fortunate than his cousin of Navarre, the Prince of Condé,

[1] Pierre de Lestoile, Mémoires (éd. Michaud et Poujoulat), 30. Languet, letter of May 11, 1574, ii. 7, 8.

chancing to be in Picardy at the outbreak of the pretended conspiracy of St. Germain, took Thoré's advice and fled out of the kingdom to Strasbourg.[1] Himself free from the dangers encompassing his confederates in France, he was able to assist them materially by addressing personal solicitations to the German princes, and by superintending the levy of auxiliary troops.

The Huguenots were entering in good earnest upon the fifth religious war, and used their successes with such moderation as Reasons for to conciliate even hostile populations. Their enemies, the success of the Hugue- judging only from superficial indications, might nots in face wonder at their strange recuperative energies. Cath- of great diffi- culties. arine might exclaim, in amazement at their progress and presumption, that "the Huguenots were like cats, for, in falling, they always alighted on their feet."[2] But those who looked into the matter more closely saw that this was no mere accident. A contemporary writer, who is also a declared antagonist, praises their prudence and good conduct at the present juncture. "We must not be astonished," he remarks, "if in a short time the Protestants carry through such great repairs and so difficult to be believed. No sooner have they set foot in a place than they consider its position and deliberate as to what can be done to render it strong, or at least tenable. In all diligence they execute their decisions and enterprises, however great and difficult they may be, by the good order they practise and by a prompt obedience to the commands given them. So that I confess that they surpass us in prudence and conduct. Moreover, so soon as they are in a place, they appoint persons in whom they have the greatest confidence, to collect the king's revenues, as well as the income of the ecclesiastics and of those bearing arms against them, without regard for any save the gentilhommes. Their receipts are faithfully applied to the benefit of their cause, and they know how to employ these sums so well, that with little money they carry on great enterprises. So far as possible they relieve the poor husbandmen. In this

---

[1] Jean de Serres, iv. 136; Languet, letter of May 11, 1574, ii. 8.

[2] "Je sçais bien que ce sont des chats que vos huguenots, qui se retrouvent tousjours sur leurs pieds." Mém. de Pierre de Lestoile (éd. Michaud et Poujoulat), 53.

they conform to the fashion of the Indians, who, in time of war, do not injure the laborers, their families, their beasts of burden, and the implements used in cultivating the earth, but abstain from burning their houses and villages, and leave them in peace, deeming the tillers of the ground to be ministers of the common weal and the nursing fathers of the other estates.[1] . . . If necessity constrain them to make use of the husbandmen, they bring them to it as freely and graciously as possible, more by fair words than by force, employing caresses, and meantime protecting their cattle, their harvests, and all their property. When marching through the country, without indulging in insolence, abusive language, or plunder, they eat what they find in the houses, and keep their soldiers under good control. They instantly establish in the places they hold a council of the most capable and experienced persons. . . . This they convene daily and for so long a time as their affairs demand, and here they listen to the complaints made to them, whether by word of mouth or by written petition, and answer as well as they can to the satisfaction of the plaintiffs."[2]

About the same time that Condé was leaving France for Germany, another Huguenot leader was entering it from the opposite quarter. Count Montgomery, who from England had come to the island of Jersey, suddenly made his appearance in western Normandy. In this province the Huguenots had lately made themselves masters of the important town of Saint Lô, as well as of Domfront on the borders of the province of Maine.[3] To these gains Montgomery soon added Carentan, an important point on the north, which he took care to provision. He seemed likely, indeed, to bring all this extensive territory under the power of the Protestants. His brilliant career was, however, destined to be very brief. The royal forces sent against him under Matignon were strong, his

Montgomery lands in Normandy.

---

[1] "Ains les laissant en paix comme ministres de l'utilité commune, et pères nourriciers des autres estats."

[2] P. Brisson, Hist. et vray discours des guerres civiles ès pays de Poictou, *apud* Histoire des protestants et des églises réf. du Poitou, par Auguste Lièvre (Poitiers, 1856), i. 189, 190.

[3] De Thou, v. (liv. lvii.) 33.

own troops were few. From Saint Lô, where he was besieged, he succeeded by a bold dash in escaping with a small company of horse; but at Domfront, whither he betook himself in hope of receiving reinforcements from the south, his manly defence availed nothing. Against an army of four thousand foot and one thousand horse, besides a large number of Roman Catholic gentlemen serving at their own charges, the little band of not over ninety arquebusiers and fifty horse could offer no protracted resistance. Domfront, strong in itself, was commanded by neighboring heights, and the walls, through long neglect, had become so weak that they crumbled and fell at the very first cannonade. Montgomery, deserted by some of his soldiers and

He is forced to surrender and is taken prisoner.

enfeebled by the loss of others, was compelled to surrender to the besieging army. The story was current that he had received a pledge of life and liberty at the hands of Matignon.[1] But Agrippa d'Aubigné is undoubtedly correct in declaring that the report was a mistaken one, and that Montgomery barely received the assurance that he would be placed in the hands of the king alone. "There have been only too many acts of perfidy in France, without the invention of others," says this historian. "If there were any infractions of the capitulation, they were in the case of some other gentlemen and soldiers, who were maltreated or slain."[2]

There was one person to whom the capture of Count Montgomery was peculiarly gratifying. Catharine de' Medici had

Delight of Catharine de' Medici.

never forgotten the murderous wound Montgomery's lance had inflicted upon her husband in the rough tournament held in honor of Isabella's nuptials. True, the count had entered the lists with Henry only by the

---

[1] De Thou, v. 44; Olhagaray, Hist. de Foix, etc., 638. Miss Freer ("Henry III., King of France, His Court and Times," i. 366) accepts the statement without question, while Prof. Soldan, ii. 587, rejects it, basing his action upon a passage in another treatise of D'Aubigné than that referred to below, viz.: "Choses notables et qui semblent dignes de l'histoire," in Archives curieuses, viii. 411.

[2] Hist. univ., ii. 126. See a contemporary account: "La Prinse du Comte de Montgommery dedans le Chasteau de Donfron . . . . le Jeudy xxvii. de May, mil cinq cens soixante et quatorze. A Paris, 1574. Avec Privilege." Archives curieuses, viii. 223–238.

king's express command, and the fatal effects of the blow that shattered Henry's visor and drove the splintered stock into his eye, were due to no malicious intent. Nevertheless, Montgomery was never sincerely forgiven; and when the slayer of the father was captured fighting against the son, Catharine resolved that no considerations of pity should prevent his expiating his unintended crime. Nor was the Roman Catholic party loth to see summary punishment inflicted upon Montgomery in revenge for the blow he had struck the "noblesse" of Béarn and the frightful slaughter of their partisans he had authorized, five years before, during the third civil war, at the storming of Orthez.[1] On the other hand, the Parisian populace was excited by the revival of the false rumor already referred to, that Count Montgomery, glorying in the mischance whereby France was robbed of her king, had substituted for his ancestral coat of arms a novel escutcheon of his own device, whereon was figured a broken lance.[2] It need not surprise us, therefore, that though guiltless of any crime of which the law of even that cruel age ordinarily took cognizance, the Huguenot leader, after being placed on the rack in the vain attempt to obtain from him admissions criminating his associates, was condemned, as a traitor found in arms against his king, to be beheaded and quartered, on the Place de Grève, on the twenty-sixth of June, 1574.

Both enemies and friends unite in testifying to the fortitude with which Count Montgomery underwent the execution of his severe sentence. Roman Catholic writers, indeed, hint that he may have received profit from the ministrations of five or six theological doctors, to whom they represent him as gladly listening.[3] But Protestant historians

Execution of Montgomery on the Place de Grève.

---

[1] Aug. 13, 1569; see Olhagaray, Histoire de Foix, Béarn, et Navarre (Paris, 1609), pp. 616, 617. According to this author, "le voyage de Béarn, et le coup de Navarreux sur la noblesse du païs luy cousta cela," *i. e.*, his execution. Ib., p. 639.

[2] Mémoires d'un curé ligueur (Jehan de la Fosse), pp. 168, 169. See *ante*, chapter xiii., p. 78. Chantonnay (despatch of May 6, 1562) speaks of Montgomery as "se ventant que la plus belle et digne œuvre que se soit jamais faicte en France, fut le coup de lance dont il tua le roy Henry. Je m'esbayhis comme la royne le peult dissimuler." Mém. de Condé, ii. 37.

[3] "Discours de la Mort et Exécution de Gabriel Comte de Montgommery,

give us a circumstantial account that seems better entitled to credit, and leaves no room for doubt that Gabriel de Montgomery died constant to the faith which he had embraced in his retirement, after the death of Henry the Second. He refused to confess to the famous Vigor, Archbishop of Narbonne, and would neither kiss the crucifix offered to him by the priest who rode with him in the tumbrel, nor listen to his words, nor even look at him. To a Gray Friar, who attempted to convince him that he was in error and had been deceived, he replied : " How deceived ? If I have been deceived, it was by members of your own order ; for the first person that ever gave me a Bible in French, and bade me read it, was a Franciscan like yourself. And therein I learned the religion that I now hold, which is the only true religion. Having lived in it ever since, I wish, by the grace of God, to die in it to-day." On the scaffold, after a touching address to the spectators, he recited in a loud voice the Apostles' Creed, in the confession of which he protested that he died, and then, " having made his prayer to God after the manner of those of the (reformed) religion," [1] manfully offered his neck to the executioner's sword. [2]

par Arrest de la Court, pour les conspirations et menees par luy commises, contre le Roy et son estat. Qui fut à Paris, le vingtsixiesme de Iuing, 1574. A Paris, 1574. Avec priv." (Archives cur., viii. 239–253.)

[1] Doubtless repeating the words of the Confession of Sins, beginning : " Seigneur Dieu, Père Eternel et Tout-puissant," etc., a form loved by the Huguenots, and often on the lips of martyrs for the faith.

[2] Mémoires de Lestoile, i. 38. Agrippa d'Aubigné gives us (ii. 131) a full account of Montgomery's address, which he himself heard, mounted, as he informs us, " en croupe " behind M. de Fervaques, to whom Montgomery bade farewell just before his death. The Huguenot captain made but two requests of the bystanders : " the first, that they would tell his children, whom the judges had declared to be degraded to the rank of ' roturiers,' that, if they had not virtue of nobility enough to reassert their position, their father consented to the act; as for the other request, he conjured them, by the respect due to the words of a dying man, not to represent him to others as beheaded for any of the reasons assigned in his judicial condemnation—his wars, expeditions, and ensigns won—subjects of frivolous praise to vain men— but to make him the companion in cause and in death of so many simple persons according to the world—old men, young men, and poor women—who in that same place (the Place de Grève) had endured fire and knife." D'Aubigné's narrative, as usual, is vivid, and mentions somewhat trivial details, which, however, are additional pledges of its accuracy ; e. g., he alludes to

But the scene just described belongs strictly to the reign of the next French monarch. The capture of Montgomery at Domfront had been followed, within three days, by the death of the young king against whom the count had been fighting.

It is difficult to determine the exact proportions in which physical weakness and remorse for the past entered as ingre-

Last days of Charles IX.

dients of the malady that cut short the life of Charles the Ninth. It may not be prudent to accept implicitly all the stories told by contemporaries respecting the wretched fancies to which the king became a victim. But it would be carrying historical scepticism to the very verge of absurdity to reject the whole series of reports that come down to us respecting the strange hallucinations of Charles during the last months of his life. De Thou, perhaps the most candid and dispassionate historian of the period, has left the statement on record that, ever since St. Bartholomew's Day, Charles, who at no time slept well, used frequently to have his rest broken by the sudden recollection of its dreadful scenes. To lull him to repose, his attendants had no resource but singing, the king being passionately fond of music and of poetry.[1] Agrippa d'Aubigné corroborates the statement, adding, on the authority of high noblemen who had been present, that the king would awake trembling and groaning, and that his agitation was sure to find expression in frightful imprecations and words expressive of utter despair.[2]

With the growing certainty of his approaching death, the mental distress of Charles proportionately increased. His old Huguenot nurse, to whom he talked without reserve, was the witness of the startling conflict through which he was passing in his last hours. While sitting near his bedside on one occasion, she was suddenly recalled from a revery by the sound of the sighs and sobs of the royal patient. To her solicitous questions as to the cause of his distress, she received the most piteous

---

the fact that, having spoken as above to those who stood on the side toward the river, he repeated his remarks to those on the other side of the Place de Grève, beginning with the words, " I was saying to the men yonder," etc.

[1] De Thou, v. (liv. lvii.) 48.

[2] Hist. univ., ii. (liv. ii.) 129.

exclamations, interrupted by weeping: "Ah, my nurse, my friend, how much blood! how many murders! Ah, what wicked counsels have I had! My God, have pity upon me and pardon me! I know not where I am; so perplexed and agitated have they made me. What will become of me? What shall I do? I am lost; I know it full well." The pious attendant's earnest exhortations and consoling words had little effect in dispelling the gloom that had settled on the termination of a life so auspiciously begun. She might pray, in his hearing, that the blood of the murdered Huguenots might be on the heads of those who gave the young king such treacherous advice. She might encourage and urge him to rest in the confidence that, in view of his penitence, God would not impute to him his crime, but cover him with the mantle of Christ's righteousness.[1] Her words had little power to dissipate his extreme despondency.

For months the life of Charles had been despaired of. Now he was visibly dying. The news of the capture of Montgomery, which his mother came to announce to him with a delight she neither was able nor anxious to hide, brought him no pleasure. He had, he said, ceased to care for these things. Meanwhile, Catharine, if not altogether devoid of natural affection—if not experiencing unmingled satisfaction at the prospect that the sceptre was likely to pass into the hands of her favorite son, the King of Poland—at least took care to provide for the contingency of Charles's speedy death, by obtaining, on the twenty-ninth of May, letters to the governors of provinces, and the next day the more authoritative letters patent conferring upon her the regency until the return of Henry from Poland.[2] More sincere in her sorrow, the young Queen Elizabeth, Charles's Distress of his wife, endeavored to ward off the stroke of Heaven by young queen. solemn processions. For nine successive days, laying aside all tokens of her royal rank, simply clad, and with uncovered face, she walked barefooted, and accompanied by a large number of poor boys and girls, from the wood of Vincennes, where the court still lingered, to the city of Paris.   After

---

[1] Mémoires de Pierre de Lestoile (éd. Michaud et Poujoulat), i. 31.

[2] De Thou, v. 48; text in Isambert, Recueil des anc. lois fr., xiv. 262.

1574. THE DEATH OF CHARLES IX.

devoutly praying for the king's recovery at the Sainte-Chapelle and at the shrine of Notre Dame, she returned from her pilgrimage in the same painful and humble manner, her ladies and the officers of her court following at a respectful distance.[1]

Upon Sorbin, the king's confessor, devolved the duty of administering to Charles the last rites of religion—Sorbin, who was accustomed to speak of the perfidy and cruelty of the massacre as true magnanimity and gentleness. It has been well remarked that, in all the dark drama of guilt and retribution upon which the curtain was about to fall, no part is more tragic than the scene in which the last words preparing the soul for judgment were spoken by such a confessor as Sorbin to such a penitent as Charles.[2] Under such spiritual guidance the un-happy boy-king may possibly have expressed the sentiment which the priest ascribes to him at the hour of death: that his greatest regret was that he had not seen the Reformation wholly crushed.[3]

On Sunday, May the thirtieth, 1574, the festival of Pentecost, Charles died, late in the afternoon.[4] Almost his last words had been of congratulation that he left no son to inherit the throne, since he knew very well that France had need of a man, and that under a child both king and kingdom were wretched.[5]

The general usage was not violated in the present instance. Charles, like a host of prominent princes and statesmen of the sixteenth century, was currently reported to have fallen a victim to the poisoner's art, then in its prime. Nor did the examina-

---

[1] Mémoires de Claude Haton, ii. 764.

[2] North British Review, Oct., 1869, p. 27.

[3] Or, as Sorbin expressed it, "qu'il voyoit l'idole Calvinesque n'estre encores du tout chassée." Le vray resveille-matin des Calvinistes, 88, ibid., *ubi supra*. The expression, it will be noticed, contains a distinct reference to the anagram upon the name of "Charles de Valois"—"va chasser l'idole," upon which the Huguenots had founded brilliant hopes. See *ante*, chapter xiii., p. 123. On the other hand, since the massacre, some Huguenot had discovered that from the same name could be obtained the appropriate words "*chasseur déloyal.*" Recueil des choses mémorables (1598), 506.

[4] Languet, ii. 16.

[5] Agrippa D'Aubigné, ii. 129; De Thou, v. (liv. lvii.) 50. Charles left but one legitimate child, a daughter, born Oct. 27, 1572, who died in her sixth year.

tion made after his death, though clearly proving that the event had a natural cause, suffice to clear away the unhappy impression.[1] The Huguenots had, perhaps, more reason than others to regard the circumstances attending it as strange, if not miraculous. That the king, whose guilty acquiescence in the murderous scheme of Catharine, Anjou, and Guise, had deluged his realm in blood, should himself have perished of a malady that caused blood to exude from every pore in his body,[2] was certainly sufficiently singular to arrest the attention of the world.

Death of Charles.

The phenomenon has been shown beyond all question to have many parallels in the annals of medicine.[3] But the coincidence was so remarkable that we scarcely wonder that, in the eyes of many, it partook of a supernatural character.

Thus perished, in the twenty-fourth year of his age, a prince whom fair natural endowments seemed to have destined to play a creditable, if not a resplendent part in the history of his period ; but whom the evil counsels and examples of his mother, and the corrupt education which, designedly or through an unfortunate accident, she had given him, had so depraved, that his morals were regarded with disgust and reprobation by an age by no means scrupulously pure.[4]

The forty days' funeral rites were performed in honor of the deceased king with all the detail of pomp customary on such

The funeral rites.

occasions. For forty days, on a bed of cloth of gold, lay in state the life-like effigy of Charles of Valois, dressed in crimson and blue satin, and in ermine, with a jewelled

---

[1] Claude Haton, never more himself than when recounting the circumstances of a case of murder, whether by sword or by poison, fully credits the story ; but the letter of Catharine to M. de Matignon, written on the 31st of May, gives an intelligible account of the results of the medical examination establishing the pulmonary nature of the king's disease.

[2] Jean de Serres, Comment de statu, etc., iv., fol. 137.

[3] See examples given by White (Massacre of St. Bartholomew, 480) and others.

[4] De Thou and others ascribe to Albert de Gondy, Count of Retz, one of Charles's early instructors and a creature of Catharine de' Medici, the unenviable credit of having taught the young monarch never to tell the truth, and to use those horrible imprecations which startled even the profane when coming from the lips of a dying man. De Thou, v. 47, etc. See also Jean de Serres, iv., fol. 137, and Brantôme, Le roy Charles IXᵉ.

crown upon its head, and with sceptre and other emblems of royalty at its side. For forty days the service of the king's table remained unchanged, and the pleasing fiction was maintained that the monarch was yet alive. The gentlemen in waiting, the cupbearer, the pantler, the carver, and all the retinue of servants who, as in feudal times, appeared at the royal meals, discharged each his appointed office with punctilious precision. Courses of viands were brought on in regular succession, and as regularly removed from the board. A cardinal or prelate blessed the table before the empty show of a meal, and rendered thanks at its conclusion. Only at the close, by the sad repetition of the De profundis, and other psalms appropriate to funeral occasions, did the pageant differ materially from many a scene of convivial entertainment in which Charles had taken part. When the prescribed term of waiting was at length over, the miserable show ended, the effigy was replaced by the bier, funeral decorations took the place of festive emblems, and the body of the late king was laid in its last resting-place.[1]

The courtiers had already turned their eyes from the dead monarch to the successor whose speedy return from Poland all eagerly awaited. Henry the Third had already precipitately fled from Cracow, and was on his way to assume his ancestral throne. He was to find the kingdom plunged in disquiet, a

Had persecution, war, and treachery succeeded? prey to internal discord fostered by foreign princes. Neither Huguenot nor Roman Catholic was satisfied. A full half-century from the first promulgation of the reformed doctrines by Lefèvre d'Étaples found the friends of the purer faith more resolute than ever in its assertion, despite fire, massacre, and open warfare. No candid beholder could deny that the system of persecution had thus far proved an utter failure. It remained to be seen whether the new king would choose to repeat a dangerous experiment.

---

[1] See the contemporary pamphlet, " Le Trespas et Obsèques du très-chrestien roy de France, Charles IXe. de ce Nom ; " reprinted in Cimber et Danjou, Archives curieuses.

INDEX.

INDEX.

THE HUGUENOTS AND THE REVOCATION OF THE EDICT OF NANTES

In Two Volumes. Octavo. $7.50.

Uniform with the "Rise of the Huguenots" and the "Huguenots and Henry of Navarre"

In this history, which concludes the historical series of which the two works heretofore published form a part, the author treats a theme different but not inferior in interest to the story told in those works. The scene opens with the Edict of Nantes, the Magna Charta of Huguenot rights, in full force, at the death of its author, Henry IV. of France. Before long the attempt to abridge the privileges guaranteed to the Huguenots is made. The immediate consequence is seen in three successive wars, in which the interest centers about the person of the brave and chivalrous Henry of Rohan and the gallant defense of the city of La Rochelle. With the fall of La Rochelle the Huguenots as a political party disappear from history; but under the tolerant régime of the two cardinal ministers, Richelieu and Mazarin, they become as noted for their advance in the arts of peace as they had previously been distinguished in war. Their prosperity is rudely interrupted when Louis XIV., reaching his majority, begins his personal reign; and with that reign is inaugurated a petty, but unrelenting, persecution which culminates in the formal recall of the Edict. The Dragonnades that preceded and accompanied the recall, and the great emigration which was one of its direct fruits, have attained a world-wide fame. Professor Baird has depicted this period in its tragic detail. His work contains in particular an account, fuller, perhaps, than has elsewhere been given in English, of that romantic episode, the War of the Camisards—a struggle in itself worthy of the treatment here accorded to it as a distinct and complete transaction. It was not, however, by force of arms that the Huguenot cause was to be resuscitated. That honor belongs to the more quiet but not less heroic virtues of the preachers of the so-called "Desert"—Antoine Court, Paul Rabant, and their associates. Their work receives, consequently, full recognition at the hands of the author. It constitutes, in some regards, the most fascinating part of the subject of the book. The reign of proscription ends with the Edict of Toleration issued by Louis XVI., and the Declaration of the Rights of Man at the beginning of the French Revolution. In the formal acknowledgment of Protestantism as the religion of a considerable part of the French nation, made by Napoleon Bonaparte as First Consul, in the second year of the nineteenth century, the history reaches its natural conclusion.

HISTORY

OF THE

RISE OF THE HUGUENOTS OF FRANCE

By HENRY M. BAIRD

PROFESSOR IN THE UNIVERSITY OF THE CITY OF NEW YORK

With Map. *Two Volumes.* *Octavo.* *$5.00*

The rise of the Protestants of France was one of the most important, as it was one of the most brilliant and heroic, of those great struggles for civil and religious liberty that followed the Reformation. But it has hitherto wanted a historian who could bring to its treatment the peculiar talent which makes such a period fairly *living* to the reader's mind. The intense action and striking scenes included in the half-century which these volumes cover, are hardly surpassed in modern history. Professor Baird has told the story with a vigor and force which make it stir the reader with the true spirit and feeling of the time. The high praise may be given to his history, that, accurate and judicial as it is, it cannot be read coldly.

CRITICAL NOTICES.

"A harmonious and symmetrical history of one of the most stirring and desperate struggles for freedom of thought and liberty of opinion which the world has witnessed."—*Boston Advertiser.*

"Prof. Baird's 'History of the Rise of the Huguenots of France' is the most important and original work of its class that has appeared in this country for several years."—*Philadelphia Press.*

"To the vital merit of fidelity—making no sacrifice of truth for dramatic effect—the book adds the charm of an animated and lucid recital of the thrilling events of the period under consideration."—*New York Observer.*

"With an accurate, clear, and calm judgment, the author has expressed himself in a style most suitable for such a history—simple and attractive from its plain and unimpaired, and therefore most trustworthy statements."—*Episcopal Register.*

"Prof. Baird's narrative is founded on thorough researches, and is an accurate and impartial, and at the same time vivid description of the progress of the Reformation in France, from its beginning to the close of the reign of Charles IX."—PROF. FISHER in the *New Englander.*

"This book is written in a style clear and vigorous, spirited and very attractive ; the narrative never flags in interest, and is all along enlivened by the most interesting personal details. Not less noteworthy is the excellent balance of judgment in the estimate of character and events."—*Hartford Courant.*

"Prof. Baird's work is so finely constructed and so perfectly put together that no hint as to the nature of this or that part can present any fair idea of the whole. We regard it as, in some respects, the best example of historical writing on foreign subjects which this country has yet produced."—*The Churchman.*

"The two solid volumes of Prof. Henry Baird's 'Rise of the Huguenots of France' seem to us likely to take a classical position among American historical writings. . . . Looking for a word with which to characterize Professor Baird's work, we are tempted to use *neatness.* . . . To find the results of clean, scholar-like investigation, expressed in a lucid, consecutive, and sober narrative, gives a sense of positive satisfaction to the critical reader which the finest of fine writing is powerless to bestow."—*Nation.*

"The fruits of the author's studious labors, as presented in these volumes, attest his diligence, his fidelity, his equipoise of judgment, his fairness of mind, his clearness of perception, and his accuracy of statement. . . . While the research and well-digested erudition exhibited in this work are eminently creditable to the learning and scholarship of the author, its literary execution amply attests the excellence of his taste, and his judgment and skill in the art of composition. . . . The mort conspicuous features of his writing are purity and force of diction, with felicity of arrangement ; but there are not infrequent passages in the narrative equally striking for their simple beauty and quiet strength. His work is one of the most important recent contributions to American literature, and is entitled to a sincere greeting for its manifold learning and scholarly spirit."—*New York Tribune.*

The Huguenots and Henry of Navarre

By HENRY M. BAIRD

PROFESSOR IN THE UNIVERSITY OF THE CITY OF NEW YORK; AUTHOR OF "THE HISTORY OF THE RISE OF THE HUGUENOTS OF FRANCE."

With Maps. Two Volumes. 8vo. $5.00.

Professor Baird gives an account of the persistent struggle of the Huguenots of France to secure a fair degree of religious liberty, such as they finally attained in the Edict of Nantes; fifteen years of the struggle (1574-1589) falling in the reign of their deadly enemy, Henry III., and nine more (1589-1598) in the reign of the friendly Henry of Navarre, now known in history as Henry IV., of France. The book narrates the story of the heroic and unflinching determination which finally secured the Edict of Nantes, the last chapter giving a sketch of the halcyon days of Protestantism in France under the Edict, and down to the death of Henry IV. The work, while distinct in itself, is supplementary to the author's "The Rise of the Huguenots of France."

CRITICAL NOTICES.

" Professor Baird, of New York, is the only living American author worthy to compare with Irving, Prescott and Motley, as writers of the history of foreign countries."
— *Philadelphia Evening Bulletin.*

"The narrative is written with a grace and finish which remind one of Motley, there is the same ease of manner and the air of understanding the subject perfectly, the writer having studied it diligently from many sides."—*Brooklyn Union.*

"Professor Baird has established for himself a high and secure position among American historians. . . . . His style is very clear and correct, his preparation is conscientious and thorough ; he possesses great skill in the selection and arrangement of his material, and he has given us a thoroughly interesting and valuable work."—*Nation.*

" The professor belongs to the advanced wing of the modern school of historians. His mind is as free from prejudice as possible. His researches are minute and patient, omitting no details which shed even the faintest light upon his great subject. His narrative style is animated, comparing favorably with that of Motley while differing from it. . . . Qualifications such as these would make almost any history interesting. When the theme is the varying fortunes of the Huguenots during the most critical epoch of their struggles for religious liberty, gifts like those of Professor Baird shine to extraordinary advantage."—*N. Y. Journal of Commerce.*

" Professor Baird's ' History of the Rise of the Huguenots of France ' published some years ago, was so well received on all hands, that to the writer was assigned a place by the side of the best American historians. . . . The present volumes are a continuation of the story so well told and so full of interest to the lovers of freedom in religion as well as in the State."—*New York Times.*

" It was indeed a stirring drama which was enacted in these two reigns, and the rapid succession of incidents and sudden development of unexpected situations offer a tempting subject for the historical writer. Professor Baird has already made so distinguished a reputation by the closeness of his researches into Huguenot records, his patient study of original and not very accessible authorities, and the strength of his sympathies, that it is almost superfluous to call attention to the fresh display of these qualities in the present volumes. He is entitled to a prominent place among the American scholars who have treated history not as a mere literary exercise but as an exact science."—*New York Tribune.*

PROF. BAIRD AND HIS WORK

"Several years ago Professor Baird published a 'History of the Rise of the Huguenots in France,' which was characterized by judicial moderation of tone, and by a rare faculty of seizing and emphasizing outstanding points in the history of the time. . . . It was only natural that the author, whose success in depicting the period of reverse had been acknowledged, should be encouraged by that success to continue his labors in the same field. The result is seen in the work on 'The Huguenots and Henry of Navarre.' It puts on the stage the second act in a great drama. . . . Professor Baird indicates in the preface to the work a desire, if not an intention, to complete his labors by writing the history of the Catholic reaction in France. There is every reason to hope that he may be induced to fulfill this purpose. He has shown capacity for historical investigation and he has alighted on an interesting period of European history. It is an interesting, but not an unaccountable, fact that the struggle for freedom of conscience both in the Netherlands and in France should have strong attractions for American writers. The aim of Professor Baird is the same as that of Mr. Motley, though in a different part of the field."—*Scotsman*, Edinburgh.

"Professor Baird is entitled to a place among the distinguished Americans who take high rank among modern historians. Some of them, like Prescott, Motley, and Bancroft, are become at least as popular abroad as with their countrymen. . . . Much must depend, no doubt, on the choice of a subject, and so far as the selection of his subject goes, Mr. Baird has had everything in his favor. The story of the rise and struggles of the Huguenots must enlist the sympathies not merely of earnest Protestants, but of all the admirers of freedom and progress. Mr. Baird has undertaken to elucidate the history of an epoch that is rich in the many materials of romance. He has to dilate on the serene constancy of martyrs and the chivalrous courage of soldiers and gentlemen. He has succeeded in throwing new and original lights upon characters who have been flattered or abused in the hottest spirit of partisanship, and whose wayward changes of conduct and policy have made them standing enigmas to students of the times. He has studied his subject conscientiously. . . . Mr. Baird has done justice to a theme which deserved a sympathetic and eloquent historian. His arrangement is admirably lucid ; his style is clear, terse, and vigorous ; his facts are carefully marshalled in chronological order, while they are made to converge towards the common center of interest at the Parisian Court ; the lights and shades of his characters are dashed in with an assured hand, on a comparison of the most reliable contemporary evidence ; and the manners and the stirring scenes of the times are depicted with a picturesqueness which leaves little to desire."—*The London Times*.

"Mr. Baird has proved himself an able and earnest champion of the French Huguenots. . . . We thoroughly endorse his interesting narrative of their vicissitudes and persecutions, their loyalty and courage, and their steadfast determination to uphold and practice the tenets of their religion. The various stirring events that culminated in the Edict of Nantes have been skillfully handled, and they either succeed or are fitted into one another in a masterly manner."—*Spectator*, London.

CHARLES SCRIBNER'S SONS
153-157 Fifth Avenue, New York